THE BOOK OF
HUMOROUS VERSE

CAROLYN WELLS

THE BOOK OF
Humorous Verse

Compiled by
CAROLYN WELLS, d.1942, com

REVISED AND AMPLIFIED EDITION

Granger Index Reprint Series

BOOKS FOR LIBRARIES PRESS
FREEPORT, NEW YORK

PR
1195
.H8
W4

STANDARD BOOK NUMBER:
8369-6162-5

LIBRARY OF CONGRESS CATALOG CARD NUMBER:
73-116419

MANUFACTURED
BY
HALLMARK LITHOGRAPHERS, INC.
IN THE U.S.A.

TO

ROBERT CHAPMAN SPRAGUE

INTRODUCTION

A HOPE of immortality and a sense of humor distinguish man from the beasts of the field.

A single exception may be made, perhaps, of the Laughing Hyena, and, on the other hand, not every one of the human race possesses the power of laughter. For those who do, this volume is intended.

And since there can be nothing humorous about an introduction, there can be small need of a lengthy one.

Merely a few explanations of conditions which may be censured by captious critics.

First, the limitations of space had to be recognized. Hence, the book is a compilation, not a collection. It is representative, but not exhaustive. My ambition was toward a volume to which everyone could go, with a surety of finding any one of his favorite humorous poems between these covers. But no covers of one book could insure that, so I reluctantly gave up the dream for a reality which I trust will make it possible for a majority of seekers to find their favorites here.

The compiler's course is a difficult one. The Scylla of Popularity lures him on the one hand, while the Charybdis of the Classical charms him on the other. He has nothing to steer by but his own good taste, and good taste, alack, is greatly a matter of opinion.

And no opinion seemeth good unto an honest compiler, save his own. Wherefore, the choice of these selections, like kissing, went by favor. As to the arrangement of them, every compiler will tell you that Classification is Vexation. And why not? When many a poem may be both Parody and Satire,—both Romance and Cynicism. Wherefore, the compiler sorted with loving care the selections here presented striving to do justice to the verses themselves, and taking a chance on the tolerant good nature of the reader.

Introduction

For,

> " A jest's prosperity lies in the ear
> Of him that hears it.
> Never in the tongue
> Of him that makes it."

Which made me all the more careful to do my authors justice, leaving the prosperity of the jests to the hearers.

CAROLYN WELLS.

ACKNOWLEDGMENTS

THE compiler is indebted to the publisher or author, as noted below, for the use of copyright material included in this volume. Special arrangements have been made with the authorized publishers of those American poets, whose works in whole or in part have lapsed copyright. All rights of these poems have been reserved by the authorized publisher, author or holder of the copyright as indicated in the following:

Little, Brown & Company: For selections from the Poems and Limericks of Edward Lear.

The Macmillan Company: For selections from the Poems of Lewis Carroll and Verses from "Alice's Adventures in Wonderland" and "Through the Looking Glass."

Harr Wagner Publishing Company: For permission to reprint from "The Complete Poems" of Joaquin Miller "That Gentle Man From Boston Town," "That Texan Cattle Man," "William Brown of Oregon."

Frederick A. Stokes Company: "Bessie Brown, M.D." and "A Kiss in the Rain," by Samuel Minturn Peck.

Lothrop, Lee & Shepard Company: For the inclusion of the following Poems by Sam Walter Foss: "The Meeting of the Clabberhuses," "A Philosopher" and "The Prayer of Cyrus Brown" from "Dreams in Homespun," copyright, 1897. "Then Agin—" and "Husband and Heathen," from "Back Country Poems," copyright, 1894. "The Ideal Husband to His Wife," from "Whiffs from Wild Meadows," copyright, 1895.

Forbes & Company: "How Often?" "If I Should Die To-night," and "The Pessimist," by Ben King.

The Century Company: For permission to reprint from *St. Nicholas Magazine* the following poems by Ruth McEnery Stuart: "The Endless Song" and "The Hen-Roost Man"; and by Tudor Jenks: "An Old Bachelor"; and by Mary

Acknowledgments

Mapes Dodge: "Home and Mother," "Life in Laconics," "Over the Way" and "The Zealless Xylographer."

Thomas L. Masson: For permission to reprint "The Kiss" from "Life."

E. P. Dutton & Company: "The Converted Cannibals" and "The Retired Pork-Butcher and the Spook," by G. E. Farrow.

Houghton Mifflin Company: With their permission and by special arrangement, as authorized publishers of the following authors' works, are used: Selections from Nora Perry, John Townsend Trowbridge, Charles E. Carryl, Oliver Wendell Holmes, John Greenleaf Whittier, Ralph Waldo Emerson, Bret Harte, James Thomas Fields, John G. Saxe, James Russell Lowell and Bayard Taylor.

A. P. Watt & Son and Doubleday, Page & Company: For their permission to use "Divided Destinies," "Study of an Elevation, in Indian Ink," and "Commonplaces," by Rudyard Kipling.

G. P. Putnam's Sons: Selections from the Poems of Eugene Fitch Ware and "The Wreck of the 'Julie Plante,'" by William Henry Drummond.

Henry Holt & Company: Two Parodies from "———— and Other Poets," by Louis Untermeyer.

Dodd, Mead & Company: "The Constant Cannibal Maiden," "Blow Me Eyes" and "A Grain of Salt," by Wallace Irwin.

John Lane Company: For Poems by Owen Seaman, Anthony C. Deane and G. K. Chesterton.

The Smart Set: "Dighton is Engaged," and "Kitty Wants to Write," by Gelett Burgess.

Small, Maynard & Company: For selections from Holman F. Day, Richard Hovey and Clinton Scollard.

The Bobbs-Merrill Company: For special permission to reprint from the Biographical Edition of the Complete Works of James Whitcomb Riley (copyright, 1913) the following Poems: "Little Orphant Annie," "The Lugubrious Whing-Whang," "The Man in the Moon," "The Old Man and Jim," "Prior to Miss Belle's Appearance," "Spirk Throll-Derisive," "When the Frost is on the Punkin."

The Bobbs-Merrill Company: For permission to use the

Acknowledgments

following Poems by Robert J. Burdette, from "Smiles Yoked with Sighs" (copyright, 1900), "Orphan Born," "The Romance of the Carpet," "Soldier, Rest!", "Songs without Words," "What Will We Do?".

Charles Scribner's Sons: For permission to use "The Dinkey-Bird," "Dutch Lullaby," "The Little Peach," "The Truth About Horace," by Eugene Field.

In the section devoted to recent verse debt is acknowledged to the following publishers for the use of copyright material:

Harper & Brothers: For permission to use "Commuters" and "Nugatory" by E. B. White.

Alfred A. Knopf: For permission to use "Thais" and "Rain" by Newman Levy and "Our Friend the Egg" by Clarence Day.

E. P. Dutton & Company: For two poems by Margaret Fishback.

Harcourt Brace & Company: For permission to use "Between Two Loves" by T. A. Daly.

T. Werner Laurie, Ltd.: For permission to use three stanzas by E. C. Bentley from "Biography for Beginners."

Chas. Scribner's Sons: For permission to use "If I Ever Have Time for the Things That Matter" by Vilda Sauvage Owens and "Backstairs Ballad" by David McCord.

The "New Yorker": For the poem "To the Crocus—With My Love" by Marion Sturges-Jones.

Simon and Schuster: For two poems by Ogden Nash.

The Viking Press: For permission to use "Ballade of Unfortunate Mammals," "On Being a Woman," and "Theory" by Dorothy Parker.

The Liveright Publishing Corp.: For permission to use Miss Parker's "Social Note" and "Coda" and for extracts from "Poems in Praise of Practically Nothing" by Samuel Hoffenstein.

Doubleday, Doran & Company: For permission to use verses by Roland Young and Christopher Morley.

Edna St. Vincent Millay: For permission to use her "The Penitent" from "A Few Figs from Thistles."

CONTENTS

I: BANTER

Contents

II: THE ETERNAL FEMININE

Contents

III: LOVE AND COURTSHIP

Contents

Contents

V: CYNICISM

Contents

VI: EPIGRAMS

VII: BURLESQUE

Contents

VIII: BATHOS

Contents

IX: PARODY

Contents

X : NARRATIVE

Contents

XI: TRIBUTE

XII: WHIMSEY

Contents

Contents

XIII: NONSENSE

Contents

XIV: NATURAL HISTORY

XV: JUNIORS

Contents

XVI: IMMORTAL STANZAS

XVII: CONTEMPORARY VERSE

Contents

THE BOOK OF
HUMOROUS VERSE

I

BANTER

THE PLAYED-OUT HUMOURIST

Quixotic is his enterprise and hopeless his adventure is,
　　Who seeks for jocularities that haven't yet been said;
The world has joked incessantly for over fifty centuries,
　　And every joke that's possible has long ago been made.
I started as a humourist with lots of mental fizziness,
　　But humour is a drug which it's the fashion to abuse;
For my stock-in-trade, my fixtures and the good-will of the
　　　business
　　No reasonable offer I am likely to refuse.
　　　　　And if anybody choose
　　　　　He may circulate the news
　　That no reasonable offer I am likely to refuse.

Oh, happy was that humourist—the first that made a pun at
　　　all—
　　Who when a joke occurred to him, however poor and mean,
Was absolutely certain that it never had been done at all—
　　How popular at dinners must that humourist have been!
Oh, the days when some step-father for a query held a handle
　　　out,—
　　The door-mat from the scraper, is it distant very far?
And when no one knew where Moses was when Aaron put the
　　　candle out,
　　And no one had discovered that a door could be a-jar!
　　　　　But your modern hearers are
　　　　　In their tastes particular,
　　And they sneer if you inform them that a door can be a jar!

In search of quip and quiddity I've sat all day alone, apart—
　　And all that I could hit on as a problem was—to find
Analogy between a scrag of mutton and a Bony-part,
　　Which offers slight employment to the speculative mind.

For you cannot call it very good, however great your
    charity—
  It's not the sort of humour that is greeted with a shout—
And I've come to the conclusion that my mine of jocularity,
  In present Anno Domini is worked completely out!
              Though the notion you may scout,
              I can prove beyond a doubt
    That my mine of jocularity is worked completely out!

W. S. Gilbert.

THE PRACTICAL JOKER

  OH, what a fund of joy jocund lies hid in harmless
    hoaxes!
              What keen enjoyment springs
              From cheap and simple things!
  What deep delight from sources trite inventive
    humour coaxes,
              That pain and trouble brew
              For every one but you!

  Gunpowder placed inside its waist improves a mild
    Havana,
              Its unexpected flash
              Burns eyebrows and moustache.
  When people dine no kind of wine beats ipecacuanha,
              But common sense suggests
              You keep it for your guests—

  Then naught annoys the organ boys like throwing
    red hot coppers.
              And much amusement bides
              In common butter slides;
  And stringy snares across the stairs cause unexpected
    croppers.

              Coal scuttles, recollect,
              Produce the same effect.

              A man possessed
              Of common sense
              Need not invest
              At great expense—

It does not call
For pocket deep,
These jokes are all
Extremely cheap.

If you commence with eighteenpence—it's all you'll
have to pay;
You may command a pleasant and a most instructive
day.

A good spring gun breeds endless fun, and makes
men jump like rockets—

And turnip heads on posts
Make very decent ghosts.

Then hornets sting like anything, when placed in
waistcoat pockets—

Burnt cork and walnut juice
Are not without their use.

No fun compares with easy chairs whose seats are
stuffed with needles—

Live shrimps their patience tax
When put down people's backs.

Surprising, too, what one can do with a pint of fat
black beetles—

And treacle on a chair
Will make a Quaker swear!

Then sharp tin tacks
And pocket squirts—
And cobbler's wax
For ladies' skirts—

And slimy slugs
On bedroom floors—
And water jugs
On open doors—

Prepared with these cheap properties, amusing
tricks to play
Upon a friend a man may spend a most delightful
day.   *W. S. Gilbert.*

TO PHŒBE

"Gentle, modest little flower,
　　Sweet epitome of May,
Love me but for half an hour,
　　Love me, love me, little fay."
Sentences so fiercely flaming
　　In your tiny, shell-like ear,
I should always be exclaiming
　　If I loved you, Phœbe dear.

"Smiles that thrill from any distance
　　Shed upon me while I sing!
Please ecstaticize existence,
　　Love me, oh, thou fairy thing!"
Words like these, outpouring sadly,
　　You'd perpetually hear,
If I loved you fondly, madly;—
　　But I do not, Phœbe dear.

W. S. Gilbert.

MALBROUCK

Malbrouck, the prince of commanders,
Is gone to the war in Flanders;
His fame is like Alexander's;
　　But when will he come home?

Perhaps at Trinity Feast, or
Perhaps he may come at Easter.
Egad! he had better make haste, or
　　We fear he may never come.

For Trinity Feast is over,
And has brought no news from Dover;
And Easter is past, moreover,
　　And Malbrouck still delays.

Milady in her watch-tower
Spends many a pensive hour,
Not well knowing why or how her
   Dear lord from England stays.

While sitting quite forlorn in
That tower, she spies returning
A page clad in deep mourning,
   With fainting steps and slow.

" O page, prithee, come faster!
What news do you bring of your master?
I fear there is some disaster,
   Your looks are so full of woe."

" The news I bring, fair lady,"
With sorrowful accent said he,
" Is one you are not ready
   So soon, alas! to hear.

" But since to speak I'm hurried,"
Added this page, quite flurried,
" Malbrouck is dead and buried!"
   (And here he shed a tear.)

" He's dead! he's dead as a herring!
For I beheld his ' berring,'
And four officers transferring
   His corpse away from the field.

" One officer carried his sabre,
And he carried it not without labour,
Much envying his next neighbour,
   Who only bore a shield.

" The third was helmet-bearer—
That helmet which on its wearer
Filled all who saw with terror,
   And covered a hero's brains.

" Now, having got so far, I
Find that (by the Lord Harry!)
The fourth is left nothing to carry;
    So there the thing remains."

Translated by *Father Prout*

MARK TWAIN: A PIPE DREAM

WELL I recall how first I met
    Mark Twain—an infant barely three
Rolling a tiny cigarette
    While cooing on his nurse's knee.

Since then in every sort of place
    I've met with Mark and heard him joke,
Yet how can I describe his face?
    I never saw it for the smoke.

At school he won a *smokership,*
    At Harvard College (Cambridge, Mass.)
His name was soon on every lip,
    They made him " smoker " of his class.

Who will forget his smoking bout
    With Mount Vesuvius—our cheers—
When Mount Vesuvius went out
    And didn't smoke again for years?

The news was flashed to England's King,
    Who begged Mark Twain to come and stay,
Offered him dukedoms—anything
    To smoke the London fog away.

But Mark was firm. " I bow," said he,
    " To no imperial command,
No ducal coronet for me,
    My smoke is for my native land! "

For Mark there waits a brighter crown!
When Peter comes his card to read—
He'll take the sign " No Smoking" down,
Then Heaven will be Heaven indeed.
Oliver Herford.

FROM A FULL HEART

In days of peace my fellow-men
  Rightly regarded me as more like
A Bishop than a Major-Gen.,
  And nothing since has made me warlike;
But when this age-long struggle ends
  And I have seen the Allies dish up
The goose of Hindenburg—oh, friends!
  I shall out-bish the mildest Bishop.

When the War is over and the Kaiser's out of print
I'm going to buy some tortoises and watch the beggars sprint;
When the War is over and the sword at last we sheathe
I'm going to keep a jelly-fish and listen to it breathe.

I never really longed for gore,
  And any taste for red corpuscles
That lingered with me left before
  The German troops had entered Brussels.
In early days the Colonel's " 'Shun!"
  Froze me; and as the war grew older
The noise of some one else's gun
  Left me considerably colder.

When the War is over and the battle has been won
I'm going to buy a barnacle and take it for a run;
When the War is over and the German fleet we sink
I'm going to keep a silkworm's egg and listen to it think.

The Captains and the Kings depart—
  It may be so, but not lieutenants;
Dawn after weary dawn I start
  The never ending round of penance;

One rock amid the welter stands
  On which my gaze is fixed intently:
An after-life in quiet lands
  Lived very lazily and gently.

When the War is over and we've done the Belgians proud
I'm going to keep a chrysalis and read to it aloud;
When the War is over and we've finished up the show
I'm going to plant a lemon pip and listen to it grow.

Oh, I'm tired of the noise and turmoil of battle,
And I'm even upset by the lowing of cattle,
And the clang of the bluebells is death to my liver,
And the roar of the dandelion gives me a shiver,
And a glacier, in movement, is much too exciting,
And I'm nervous, when standing on one, of alighting—
Give me Peace; that is all, that is all that I seek. . . .
    Say, starting on Saturday week.

                              A. A. Milne.

THE ULTIMATE JOY

I HAVE felt the thrill of passion in the poet's mystic book
And I've lingered in delight to catch the rhythm of the brook;
I've felt the ecstasy that comes when prima donnas reach
For upper C and hold it in a long, melodious screech.
And yet the charm of all these blissful memories fades away
As I think upon the fortune that befell the other day,
As I bring to recollection, with a joyous, wistful sigh,
That I woke and felt the need of extra covers in July.

Oh, eerie hour of drowsiness—'twas like a fairy spell,
That respite from the terrors we have known, alas, so well,
The malevolent mosquito, with a limp and idle bill,
Hung supinely from the ceiling, all exhausted by his chill.
And the early morning sunbeam lost his customary leer
And brought a gracious greeting and a prophecy of cheer;
A generous affability reached up from earth to sky,
When I woke and felt the need of extra covers in July.

In every life there comes a time of happiness supreme,
When joy becomes reality and not a glittering dream.
'Tis less appreciated, but it's worth a great deal more
Than tides which taken at their flood lead on to fortune's
    shore.
How vain is Art's illusion, and how potent Nature's sway
When once in kindly mood she deigns to waft our woes
    away!
And the memory will cheer me, though all other pleasures
    fly,
Of how I woke and needed extra covers in July.

Unknown.

OLD FASHIONED FUN

WHEN that old joke was new,
    It was not hard to joke,
And puns we now pooh-pooh,
    Great laughter would provoke.

True wit was seldom heard,
    And humor shown by few,
When reign'd King George the Third,
    And that old joke was new.

It passed indeed for wit,
    Did this achievement rare,
When down your friend would sit,
    To steal away his chair.

You brought him to the floor,
    You bruised him black and blue,
And this would cause a roar,
    When your old joke was new.

W. M. Thackeray.

WHEN MOONLIKE ORE THE HAZURE SEAS

When moonlike ore the hazure seas
In soft effulgence swells,
When silver jews and balmy breaze
Bend down the Lily's bells;
When calm and deap, the rosy sleap
Has lapt your soal in dreems,
R Hangeline! R lady mine!
Dost thou remember Jeames?

I mark thee in the Marble all,
Where England's loveliest shine—
I say the fairest of them hall
Is Lady Hangeline.
My soul, in desolate eclipse,
With recollection teems—
And then I hask, with weeping lips,
Dost thou remember Jeames?

Away! I may not tell thee hall
This soughring heart endures—
There is a lonely sperrit-call
That Sorrow never cures;
There is a little, little Star,
That still above me beams;
It is the Star of Hope—but ar!
Dost thou remember Jeames?

                                        W. M. Thackeray.

WHEN THE FROST IS ON THE PUNKIN

When the frost is on the punkin and the fodder's in the shock,
And you hear the kyouck and gobble of the struttin' turkey-
    cock,
And the clackin' of the guineys, and the cluckin' of the hens,
And the rooster's hallylooyer as he tiptoes on the fence;
O it's then's the times a feller is a-feelin' at his best,
With the risin' sun to greet him from a night of peaceful rest,

As he leaves the house, bare-headed, and goes out to feed the
  stock,
When the frost is on the punkin and the fodder's in the shock.

They's something kindo' hearty-like about the atmosphere,
When the heat of summer's over and the coolin' fall is here—
Of course we miss the flowers, and the blossoms on the trees,
And the mumble of the hummin'-birds and buzzin' of the
  bees;
But the air's so appetisin'; and the landscape through the
  haze
Of a crisp and sunny morning of the airly autumn days
Is a pictur that no painter has the colorin' to mock—
When the frost is on the punkin and the fodder's in the shock.

The husky, rusty rustle of the tossels of the corn,
And the raspin' of the tangled leaves, as golden as the morn;
The stubble in the furries—kindo' lonesome-like, but still
A-preachin' sermons to us of the barns they growed to fill;
The strawstack in the medder, and the reaper in the shed;
The hosses in theyr stalls below—the clover overhead!—
O, it sets my heart a-clickin' like the tickin' of a clock,
When the frost is on the punkin and the fodder's in the shock!

James Whitcomb Riley.

TWO MEN

There be two men of all mankind
  That I should like to know about;
But search and question where I will,
  I cannot ever find them out.

Melchizedek he praised the Lord,
  And gave some wine to Abraham;
But who can tell what else he did
  Must be more learned than I am.

Ucalegon he lost his house
  When Agamemnon came to Troy;
But who can tell me who he was—
  I'll pray the gods to give him joy.

There be two men of all mankind
That I'm forever thinking on;
They chase me everywhere I go,—
Melchizedek, Ucalegon.

Edwin Arlington Robinson.

A FAMILIAR LETTER TO SEVERAL CORRESPONDENTS

YES, write if you want to—there's nothing like trying;
  Who knows what a treasure your casket may hold?
I'll show you that rhyming's as easy as lying,
  If you'll listen to me while the art I unfold.

Here's a book full of words: one can choose as he fancies,
  As a painter his tint, as a workman his tool;
Just think! all the poems and plays and romances
  Were drawn out of this, like the fish from a pool!

You can wander at will through its syllabled mazes,
  And take all you want—not a copper they cost;
What is there to hinder your picking out phrases
  For an epic as clever as "Paradise Lost"?

Don't mind if the index of sense is at zero;
  Use words that run smoothly, whatever they mean;
Leander and Lillian and Lillibullero
  Are much the same thing in the rhyming machine.

There are words so delicious their sweetness will smother
  That boarding-school flavour of which we're afraid;
There is "lush" is a good one and "swirl" is another;
  Put both in one stanza, its fortune is made.

With musical murmurs and rhythmical closes
  You can cheat us of smiles when you've nothing to tell;
You hand us a nosegay of milliner's roses,
  And we cry with delight, "Oh, how sweet they do smell!"

Perhaps you will answer all needful conditions
  For winning the laurels to which you aspire,
By docking the tails of the two prepositions
  I' the style o' the bards you so greatly admire.

As for subjects of verse, they are only too plenty
  For ringing the changes on metrical chimes;
A maiden, a moonbeam, a lover of twenty,
  Have filled that great basket with bushels of rhymes.

Let me show you a picture—'tis far from irrelevant—
  By a famous old hand in the arts of design;
'Tis only a photographed sketch of an elephant;
  The name of the draughtsman was Rembrandt of Rhine.

How easy! no troublesome colours to lay on;
  It can't have fatigued him, no, not in the least;
A dash here and there with a haphazard crayon,
  And there stands the wrinkled-skinned, baggy-limbed beast.

Just so with your verse—'tis as easy as sketching;
  You can reel off a song without knitting your brow,
As lightly as Rembrandt a drawing or etching;
  It is nothing at all, if you only know how.

Well, imagine you've printed your volume of verses;
  Your forehead is wreathed with the garland of fame;
Your poem the eloquent school-boy rehearses;
  Her album the school-girl presents for your name.

Each morning the post brings you autograph letters;
  You'll answer them promptly—an hour isn't much
For the honour of sharing a page with your betters,
  With magistrates, members of Congress, and such.

Of course you're delighted to serve the committees
  That come with requests from the country all round;
You would grace the occasion with poems and ditties
  When they've got a new school-house, or poor-house, or
    pound.

With a hymn for the saints, and a song for the sinners,
 You go and are welcome wherever you please;
You're a privileged guest at all manner of dinners;
 You've a seat on the platform among the grandees.

At length your mere presence becomes a sensation;
 Your cup of enjoyment is filled to its brim
With the pleasure Horatian of digitmonstration,
 As the whisper runs round of " That's he! " or " That's
   him! "

But, remember, O dealer in phrases sonorous,
 So daintily chosen, so tunefully matched,
Though you soar with the wings of the cherubim o'er us,
 The ovum was human from which you were hatched.

No will of your own, with its puny compulsion,
 Can summon the spirit that quickens the lyre;
It comes, if at all, like the sibyl's convulsion,
 And touches the brain with a finger of fire.

So, perhaps, after all, it's as well to be quiet,
 If you've nothing you think is worth saying in prose,
As to furnish a meal of their cannibal diet
 To the critics, by publishing, as you propose.

But it's all of no use, and I'm sorry I've written;
 I shall see your thin volume some day on my shelf;
For the rhyming tarantula surely has bitten,
 And music must cure you, so pipe it yourself.

                              Oliver Wendell Holmes.

THE HEIGHT OF THE RIDICULOUS

I WROTE some lines once on a time
   In wondrous merry mood,
And thought, as usual, men would say
   They were exceeding good.

They were so queer, so very queer,
  I laughed as I would die;
Albeit, in the general way,
  A sober man am I.

I called my servant, and he came;
  How kind it was of him,
To mind a slender man like me,
  He of the mighty limb!

" These to the printer," I exclaimed,
  And, in my humorous way,
I added (as a trifling jest),
  " There'll be the devil to pay."

He took the paper, and I watched,
  And saw him peep within;
At the first line he read, his face
  Was all upon a grin.

He read the next, the grin grew broad,
  And shot from ear to ear;
He read the third, a chuckling noise
  I now began to hear.

The fourth, he broke into a roar;
  The fifth, his waistband split;
The sixth, he burst five buttons off,
  And tumbled in a fit.

Ten days and nights, with sleepless eye,
  I watched that wretched man,
And since, I never dare to write
  As funny as I can.

                  Oliver Wendell Holmes.

SHAKE, MULLEARY AND GO-ETHE

I

I HAVE a bookcase, which is what
Many much better men have not.
There are no books inside, for books,
I am afraid, might spoil its looks.
But I've three busts, all second-hand,
Upon the top. You understand
I could not put them underneath—
Shake, Mulleary and Go-ethe.

II

Shake was a dramatist of note;
He lived by writing things to quote,
He long ago put on his shroud:
Some of his works are rather loud.
His bald-spot's dusty, I suppose.
I know there's dust upon his nose.
I'll have to give each nose a sheath—
Shake, Mulleary and Go-ethe.

III

Mulleary's line was quite the same;
He has more hair, but far less fame.
I would not from that fame retrench—
But he is foreign, being French.
Yet high his haughty head he heaves,
The only one done up in leaves,
They're rather limited on wreath—
Shake, Mulleary and Go-ethe.

IV

Go-ethe wrote in the German tongue:
He must have learned it very young.
His nose is quite a butt for scoff,
Although an inch of it is off.

A Rondelay

He did quite nicely for the Dutch;
But here he doesn't count for much.
They all are off their native heath—
Shake, Mulleary and Go-ethe.

V

They sit there, on their chests, as bland
As if they were not second-hand.
I do not know of what they think,
Nor why they never frown or wink.
But why from smiling they refrain
I think I clearly can explain:
They none of them could show much teeth—
Shake, Mulleary and Go-ethe.

H. C. Bunner.

A RONDELAY

Man is for woman made,
  And woman made for man:
As the spur is for the jade,
As the scabbard for the blade,
  As for liquor is the can,
So man's for woman made,
  And woman made for man.

As the sceptre to be sway'd,
As to night the serenade,
  As for pudding is the pan,
  As to cool us is the fan,
So man's for woman made,
  And woman made for man.

Be she widow, wife, or maid,
Be she wanton, be she staid,
Be she well or ill array'd,
So man's for woman made,
  And woman made for man.

Peter A. Motteux.

WINTER DUSK

THE prospect is bare and white,
  And the air is crisp and chill;
While the ebon wings of night
  Are spread on the distant hill.

The roar of the stormy sea
  Seem the dirges shrill and sharp
That winter plays on the tree—
  His wild Æolian harp.

In the pool that darkly creeps
  In ripples before the gale,
A star like a lily sleeps
  And wiggles its silver tail.

                              R. K. Munkittrick.

COMIC MISERIES

MY dear young friend, whose shining wit
  Sets all the room a-blaze,
Don't think yourself a " happy dog,"
  For all your merry ways;
But learn to wear a sober phiz,
  Be stupid, if you can,
It's such a very serious thing
  To be a funny man!

You're at an evening party, with
  A group of pleasant folks,—
You venture quietly to crack
  The least of little jokes,—
A lady doesn't catch the point,
  And begs you to explain—
Alas for one that drops a jest
  And takes it up again!

You're talking deep philosophy
   With very special force,
To edify a clergyman
   With suitable discourse,—
You think you've got him—when he calls
   A friend across the way,
And begs you'll say that funny thing
   You said the other day!

You drop a pretty *jeu-de-mot*
   Into a neighbor's ears,
Who likes to give you credit for
   The clever thing he hears,
And so he hawks your jest about,
   The old authentic one,
Just breaking off the point of it,
   And leaving out the pun!

By sudden change in politics,
   Or sadder change in Polly,
You, lose your love, or loaves, and fall
   A prey to melancholy,
While everybody marvels why
   Your mirth is under ban,—
They think your very grief " a joke,"
   You're such a funny man!

You follow up a stylish card
   That bids you come and dine,
And bring along your freshest wit
   (To pay for musty wine),
You're looking very dismal, when
   My lady bounces in,
And wonders what you're thinking of
   And why you don't begin!

You're telling to a knot of friends
   A fancy-tale of woes
That cloud your matrimonial sky,
   And banish all repose—

A solemn lady overhears
   The story of your strife,
And tells the town the pleasant news:
   You quarrel with your wife!

My dear young friend, whose shining wit
   Sets all the room a-blaze,
Don't think yourself "a happy dog,"
   For all your merry ways;
But learn to wear a sober phiz,
   Be stupid, if you can,
It's such a very serious thing
   To be a funny man!

John G. Saxe.

EARLY RISING

"God bless the man who first invented sleep!"
   So Sancho Panza said, and so say I:
And bless him, also, that he didn't keep
   His great discovery to himself; nor try
To make it—as the lucky fellow might—
A close monopoly by patent-right!

Yes—bless the man who first invented sleep,
   (I really can't avoid the iteration;)
But blast the man, with curses loud and deep,
   Whate'er the rascal's name, or age, or station,
Who first invented, and went round advising,
That artificial cut-off—Early Rising!

"Rise with the lark, and with the lark to bed,"
   Observes some solemn, sentimental owl;
Maxims like these are very cheaply said;
   But, ere you make yourself a fool or fowl,
Pray just inquire about his rise and fall,
And whether larks have any beds at all!

The time for honest folks to be a-bed
　　Is in the morning, if I reason right;
And he who cannot keep his precious head
　　Upon his pillow till it's fairly light,
And so enjoy his forty morning winks,
Is up to knavery; or else—he drinks!

Thompson, who sung about the "Seasons," said
　　It was a glorious thing to *rise* in season;
But then he said it—lying—in his bed,
　　At ten o'clock A.M.,—the very reason
He wrote so charmingly. The simple fact is
His preaching wasn't sanctioned by his practice.

'Tis, doubtless, well to be sometimes awake,—
　　Awake to duty, and awake to truth,—
But when, alas! a nice review we take
　　Of our best deeds and days, we find, in sooth,
The hours that leave the slightest cause to weep
Are those we passed in childhood or asleep!

'Tis beautiful to leave the world awhile
　　For the soft visions of the gentle night;
And free, at last, from mortal care or guile,
　　To live as only in the angel's sight,
In sleep's sweet realm so cosily shut in,
Where, at the worst, we only *dream* of sin!

So let us sleep, and give the Maker praise.
　　I like the lad who, when his father thought
To clip his morning nap by hackneyed phrase
　　Of vagrant worm by early songster caught,
Cried, "Served him right!—it's not at all surprising;
The worm was punished, sir, for early rising!"

John G. Saxe.

TO THE PLIOCENE SKULL

" Speak, O man less recent!
          Fragmentary fossil!
  Primal pioneer of pliocene formation,
  Hid in lowest drifts below the earliest stratum
          Of volcanic tufa!

" Older than the beasts, the oldest Palæotherium;
  Older than the trees, the oldest Cryptogami;
  Older than the hills, those infantile eruptions
          Of earth's epidermis!

" Eo—Mio—Plio—whatsoe'er the ' cene ' was
  That those vacant sockets filled with awe and wonder,—
  Whether shores Devonian or Silurian beaches,—
          Tell us thy strange story!

" Or has the professor slightly antedated
  By some thousand years thy advent on this planet,
  Giving thee an air that's somewhat better fitted
          For cold-blooded creatures?

" Wert thou true spectator of that mighty forest
  When above thy head the stately Sigillaria
  Reared its columned trunks in that remote and distant
          Carboniferous epoch?

" Tell us of that scene—the dim and watery woodland,
  Songless, silent, hushed, with never bird or insect,
  Veiled with spreading fronds and screened with tall club-
          mosses,
          Lycopodiacea,—

" When beside thee walked the solemn Plesiosaurus,
  And all around thee crept the festive Ichthyosaurus,
  While from time to time above thee flew and circled
          Cheerful Pterodactyls;—

" Tell us of thy food,—those half-marine refections,
   Crinoids on the shell, and Brachipods *au naturel*,—
Cuttle-fish to which the *pieuvre* of Victor Hugo
    Seems a periwinkle.

" Speak, thou awful vestige of the Earth's creation—
   Solitary fragment of remains organic!
Tell the wondrous secret of thy past existence—
    Speak! thou oldest primate!"

Even as I gazed, a thrill of the maxilla,
   And a lateral movement of the condyloid process,
With post-pliocene sounds of healthy mastication,
    Ground the teeth together.

And, from that imperfect dental exhibition,
   Stained with expressed juices of the weed Nicotian,
Came these hollow accents, blent with softer murmurs
    Of expectoration:

" Which my name is Bowers, and my crust was busted
   Falling down a shaft in Calaveras county,
But I'd take it kindly if you'd send the pieces
    Home to old Missouri!"

                    Bret Harte.

ODE TO WORK IN SPRINGTIME

Oh, would that working I might shun,
   From labour my connection sever,
That I might do a bit—or none
    Whatever!

That I might wander over hills,
   Establish friendship with a daisy,
O'er pretty things like daffodils
    Go crazy!

That I might at the heavens gaze,
   Concern myself with nothing weighty,
Loaf, at a stretch, for seven days—
   Or eighty.

Why can't I cease a slave to be,
   And taste existence beatific
On some fair island, hid in the
   Pacific?

Instead of sitting at a desk
   'Mid undone labours, grimly lurking—
Oh, say, what is there picturesque
   In working?

But no!—to loaf were misery!—
   I love to work! Hang isles of coral!
(To end this otherwise would be
   Immoral!)

                Thomas R. Ybarra.

OLD STUFF

IF I go to see the play,
   Of the story I am certain;
Promptly it gets under way
   With the lifting of the curtain.
Builded all that's said and done
   On the ancient recipe—
'Tis the same old Two and One:
   A and B in love with C.

If I read the latest book,
   There's the mossy situation;
One may confidently look
   For the trite triangulation.
Old as time, but ever new,
   Seemingly, this tale of Three—
Same old yarn of One and Two:
   A and C in love with B.

If I cast my eyes around,
   Far and near and middle distance,
Still the formula is found
   In our everyday existence.
Everywhere I look I see—
   Fact or fiction, life or play—
Still the little game of Three:
   B and C in love with A.

While the ancient law fulfills,
   Myriad moons shall wane and wax.
Jack must have his pair of Jills,
   Jill must have her pair of Jacks.

Bert Leston Taylor.

TO MINERVA

My temples throb, my pulses boil,
   I'm sick of Song and Ode and Ballad—
So Thyrsis, take the midnight oil,
   And pour it on a lobster salad.

My brain is dull, my sight is foul,
   I cannot write a verse, or read—
Then Pallas, take away thine Owl,
   And let us have a Lark instead.

Thomas Hood.

THE LEGEND OF HEINZ VON STEIN

Out rode from his wild, dark castle
   The terrible Heinz von Stein;
He came to the door of a tavern
   And gazed on its swinging sign.

He sat himself down at a table,
   And growled for a bottle of wine;
Up came with a flask and a corkscrew
   A maiden of beauty divine.

Then, seized with a deep love-longing,
  He uttered, " O damosel mine,
Suppose you just give a few kisses
  To the valorous Ritter von Stein! "

But she answered, " The kissing business
  Is entirely out of my line;
And I certainly will not begin it
  On a countenance ugly as thine! "

Oh, then the bold knight was angry,
  And cursed both coarse and fine;
And asked, " How much is the swindle
  For your sour and nasty wine? "

And fiercely he rode to the castle
  And sat himself down to dine;
And this is the dreadful legend
  Of the terrible Heinz von Stein.

            Charles Godfrey Leland.

THE TRUTH ABOUT HORACE

It is very aggravating
To hear the solemn prating
Of the fossils who are stating
  That old Horace was a prude;
When we know that with the ladies
He was always raising Hades.
And with many an escapade his
  Best productions are imbued.

There's really not much harm in a
Large number of his carmina,
But these people find alarm in a
  Few records of his acts;

Propinquity Needed

So they'd squelch the muse caloric,
And to students sophomoric
They'd present as metaphoric
    What old Horace meant for facts.

We have always thought 'em lazy;
Now we adjudge 'em crazy!
Why, Horace was a daisy
    That was very much alive!
And the wisest of us know him
As his Lydia verses show him,—
Go, read that virile poem,—
    It is No. 25.

He was a very owl, sir,
And starting out to prowl, sir,
You bet he made Rome howl, sir,
    Until he filled his date;
With a massic-laden ditty
And a classic maiden pretty,
He painted up the city,
    And Mæcenas paid the freight!

Eugene Field.

PROPINQUITY NEEDED

CELESTINE Silvousplait Justine de Mouton Rosalie,
A coryphée who lived and danced in naughty, gay Paree,
Was every bit as pretty as a French girl e'er can be
        (Which isn't saying much).

Maurice Boulanger (there's a name that would adorn a king),
But Morris Baker was the name they called the man I sing.
He lived in New York City in the Street that's labeled Spring
        (Chosen because it rhymed).

Now Baker was a lonesome youth and wanted to be wed,
And for a wife, all over town he hunted, it is said;
And up and down Fifth Avenue he ofttimes wanderéd
        (He was a peripatetic Baker, he was).

And had he met Celestine, not a doubt but Cupid's darts
Would in a trice have wounded both of their fond, loving
          hearts;
But he has never left New York to stray in foreign parts
          (Because he hasn't the price).

And she has never left Paree and so, of course, you see
There's not the slightest chance at all she'll marry Morris B.
For love to get well started, really needs propinquity
          (Hence my title).

Charles Battell Loomis.

IN THE CATACOMBS

SAM BROWN was a fellow from way down East,
Who never was "staggered" in the least.
No tale of marvellous beast or bird
Could match the stories he had heard;
No curious place or wondrous view
"Was ekil to Podunk, I tell yu."

If they told him of Italy's sunny clime,
"Maine kin beat it, every time!"
If they marvelled at Ætna's fount of fire,
They roused his ire:
With an injured air
He'd reply, "I swear
I don't think much of a smokin' hill;
We've got a moderate little rill
Kin make yer old volcaner still;
Jes' pour old Kennebec down the crater,
'N' I guess it'll cool her fiery nater!"

They showed him a room where a queen had slept;
"'Twan't up to the tavern daddy kept."
They showed him Lucerne; but he had drunk
From the beautiful Molechunkamunk.
They took him at last to ancient Rome,
And inveigled him into a catacomb:

Here they plied him with draughts of wine,
Though he vowed old cider was twice as fine,
Till the fumes of Falernian filled his head,
And he slept as sound as the silent dead;
They removed a mummy to make him room,
And laid him at length in the rocky tomb.

They piled old skeletons round the stone,
Set a " dip " in a candlestick of bone,
And left him to slumber there alone;
Then watched from a distance the taper's gleam,
Waiting to jeer at his frightened scream,
When he should wake from his drunken dream.

After a time the Yankee woke,
But instantly saw through the flimsy joke;
So never a cry or shout he uttered,
But solemnly rose, and slowly muttered:
" I see how it is. It's the judgment day,
We've all been dead and stowed away;
All these stone furreners sleepin' yet,
An' I'm the fust one up, you bet!
Can't none o' you Romans start, I wonder?
United States ahead, by thunder! "

Harlan Hoge Ballard.

OUR NATIVE BIRDS

Alone I sit at eventide;
  The twilight glory pales,
And o'er the meadows far and wide
  I hear the bobolinks—
  (We have no nightingales!)

Song-sparrows warble on the tree,
  I hear the purling brook,
And from the old manse on the lea
  Flies slow the cawing crow—
  (In England 'twere a rook!)

The last faint golden beams of day
  Still glow on cottage panes,
And on their lingering homeward way
  Walk weary laboring men—
    (Alas! we have no swains!)

From farmyards, down fair rural glades
  Come sounds of tinkling bells,
And songs of merry brown milkmaids
  Sweeter than catbird's strains—
    (I should say Philomel's!)

I could sit here till morning came,
  All through the night hours dark,
Until I saw the sun's bright flame
  And heard the oriole—
    (Alas! we have no lark!)

We have no leas, no larks, no rooks,
  No swains, no nightingales,
No singing milkmaids (save in books)
  The poet does his best:—
    It is the rhyme that fails.

Nathan Haskell Dole.

THE PRAYER OF CYRUS BROWN

" The proper way for a man to pray,"
  Said Deacon Lemuel Keyes,
" And the only proper attitude
  Is down upon his knees."

" No, I should say the way to pray,"
  Said Rev. Doctor Wise,
" Is standing straight with outstretched arms
  And rapt and upturned eyes."

" Oh, no; no, no," said Elder Slow,
  " Such posture is too proud:
A man should pray with eyes fast closed
  And head contritely bowed."

"It seems to me his hands should be
    Austerely clasped in front,
With both thumbs pointing toward the ground,"
    Said Rev. Doctor Blunt.

"Las' year I fell in Hodgkin's well
    Head first," said Cyrus Brown,
"With both my heels a-stickin' up,
    My head a-pinting down;

"An' I made a prayer right then an' there—
    Best prayer I ever said,
The prayingest prayer I ever prayed,
    A-standing on my head."

Sam Walter Foss.

ERRING IN COMPANY

"If I have erred, I err in company with Abraham Lincoln."—
Theodore Roosevelt.

IF e'er my rhyming be at fault,
    If e'er I chance to scribble dope,
If that my metre ever halt,
    I err in company with Pope.

An that my grammar go awry,
    An that my English be askew,
Sooth, I can prove an alibi—
    The Bard of Avon did it too.

If often toward the bottled grape
    My errant fancy fondly turns,
Remember, leering jackanape,
    I err in company with Burns.

If now and then I sigh "Mine own!"
    Unto another's wedded wife,
Remember, I am not alone—
    Hast ever read Lord Byron's Life?

If frequently I fret and fume,
    And absolutely will not smile,
I err in company with Hume,
    Old Socrates and T. Carlyle.

If e'er I fail in etiquette,
    And foozle on The Proper Stuff
Regarding manners, don't forget
    A. Tennyson's were pretty tough.

Eke if I err upon the side
    Of talking overmuch of Me,
I err, it cannot be denied,
    In most illustrious company.

Franklin P. Adams.

CUPID

WHY was Cupid a boy,
    And why a boy was he?
He should have been a girl,
    For aught that I can see.

For he shoots with his bow,
    And the girl shoots with her eye;
And they both are merry and glad,
    And laugh when we do cry.

Then to make Cupid a boy
    Was surely a woman's plan,
For a boy never learns so much
    Till he has become a man.

And then he's so pierced with cares,
    And wounded with arrowy smarts,
That the whole business of his life
    Is to pick out the heads of the darts.

William Blake.

IF WE DIDN'T HAVE TO EAT

LIFE would be an easy matter
  If we didn't have to eat.
    If we never had to utter,
    " Won't you pass the bread and butter,
Likewise push along that platter
  Full of meat?"
  Yes, if food were obsolete
  Life would be a jolly treat,
If we didn't—shine or shower,
Old or young, 'bout every hour—
  Have to eat, eat, eat, eat, eat—
  'Twould be jolly if we didn't have to eat.

We could save a lot of money
  If we didn't have to eat.
    Could we cease our busy buying,
    Baking, broiling, brewing, frying,
Life would then be oh, so sunny
  And complete;
  And we wouldn't fear to greet
  Every grocer in the street
If we didn't—man and woman,
Every hungry, helpless human—
  Have to eat, eat, eat, eat, eat—
  We'd save money if we didn't have to eat.

All our worry would be over
  If we didn't have to eat.
    Would the butcher, baker, grocer
    Get our hard-earned dollars? No, Sir!
We would then be right in clover
  Cool and sweet.
  Want and hunger we could cheat,
  And we'd get there with both feet,
If we didn't—poor or wealthy,
Halt or nimble, sick or healthy—
  Have to eat, eat, eat, eat, eat,
  We could get there if we didn't have to eat.
                              Nixon Waterman.

TO MY EMPTY PURSE

To you, my purse, and to none other wight,
Complain I, for ye be my lady dere;
I am sorry now that ye be light,
For, certes, ye now make me heavy chere;
Me were as lefe be laid upon a bere,
For which unto your mercy thus I crie,
Be heavy againe, or els mote I die.

Now vouchsafe this day or it be night,
That I of you the blissful sowne may here,
Or see your color like the sunne bright,
That of yellowness had never pere;
Ye are my life, ye be my hertes stere,
Queen of comfort and of good companie,
Be heavy againe, or els mote I die.

Now purse, thou art to me my lives light,
And saviour, as downe in this world here,
Out of this towne helpe me by your might,
Sith that you will not be my treasure,
For I am slave as nere as any frere,
But I pray unto your curtesie,
Be heavy againe, or els mote I die.

Geoffrey Chaucer.

THE BIRTH OF SAINT PATRICK

On the eighth day of March it was, some people say,
That Saint Pathrick at midnight he first saw the day;
While others declare 'twas the ninth he was born,
And 'twas all a mistake between midnight and morn;
For mistakes *will* occur in a hurry and shock,
And some blam'd the baby—and some blam'd the clock—
Till with all their cross-questions sure no one could know,
If the child was too fast—or the clock was too slow.

Now the first faction fight in ould Ireland, they say,
Was all on account of Saint Pathrick's birthday,
Some fought for the eighth—for the ninth more would
    die.
And who wouldn't see right, sure they blacken'd his eye!
At last, both the factions so positive grew,
That *each* kept a birthday, so Pat then had *two,*
Till Father Mulcahy, who showed them their sins,
Said, " No one could have two birthdays but a *twins.*"

Says he, " Boys, don't be fightin' for eight or for nine,
Don't be always dividin'—but sometimes combine;
Combine eight with nine, and seventeen is the mark,
So let that be his birthday."—" Amen," says the clerk.
" If he wasn't a *twins,* sure our hist'ry will show—
That, at least, he's worth any *two* saints that we know! "
Then they all got blind dhrunk—which complated their
    bliss,
And we keep up the practice from that day to this.

                                        Samuel Lover.

HER LITTLE FEET

Her little feet! . . . Beneath us ranged the sea,
    She sat, from sun and wind umbrella-shaded,
One shoe above the other danglingly,
    And lo! a Something exquisitely graded,
Brown rings and white, distracting—to the knee!

The band was loud. A wild waltz melody
    Flowed rhythmic forth. The nobodies paraded.
And thro' my dream went pulsing fast and free:
        Her little feet.

Till she made room for some one. It was He!
    A port-wine flavored He, a He who traded,
Rich, rosy, round, obese to a degree!
A sense of injury overmastered me.
    Quite bulbously his ample boots upbraided
        Her little feet.

                                William Ernest Henley.

SCHOOL

If there is a vile, pernicious,
   Wicked and degraded rule,
Tending to debase the vicious,
   And corrupt the harmless fool;
If there is a hateful habit
   Making man a senseless tool,
With the feelings of a rabbit
   And the wisdom of a mule;
It's the rule which inculcates,
It's the habit which dictates
The wrong and sinful practice of
   going into school.

If there's anything improving
   To an erring sinner's state,
Which is useful in removing
   All the ills of human fate;
If there's any glorious custom
   Which our faults can dissipate,
And can casually thrust 'em
   Out of sight and make us great;
It's the plan by which we shirk
Half our matu-ti-nal work,
The glorious institution of always
   being late.

                   James Kenneth Stephen.

THE MILLENNIUM

TO R. K.

*As long I dwell on some stupendous
And tremendous (Heaven defend us!)*

Monstr'-inform'-ingens-horrendous
Demoniaco-seraphic
Penman's latest piece of graphic.

—ROBERT BROWNING.

WILL there never come a season
  Which shall rid us from the curse
Of a prose which knows no reason
  And an unmelodious verse:
When the world shall cease to wonder
  At the genius of an Ass,
And a boy's eccentric blunder
  Shall not bring success to pass:

When mankind shall be delivered
  From the clash of magazines,
And the inkstand shall be shivered
  Into countless smithereens:
When there stands a muzzled stripling,
  Mute, beside a muzzled bore:
When the Rudyards cease from Kipling
  And the Haggards Ride no more?

James Kenneth Stephen.

" EXACTLY SO "

A SPEECH, both pithy and concise,
Marks a mind acute and wise;
What speech, my friend, say, do you know,
Can stand before " Exactly so? "

I have a dear and witty friend
Who turns this phrase to every end;
None can deny that " Yes " or " No "
Is meant in this " Exactly so."

Or when a bore his ear assails,
Good-humour in his bosom fails,
No response from his lips will flow,
Save, now and then, " Exactly so."

Is there remark on matters grave
That he may wish perchance to waive,
Or thinks perhaps is rather slow,
He stops it by " Exactly so."

It saves the trouble of a thought—
No sour dispute can thence be sought;
It leaves the thing in *statu quo,*
This beautiful "Exactly so."

It has another charm, this phrase,
For it implies the speaker's praise
Of what has just been said—*ergo*—
It pleases, this " Exactly so."

Nor need the conscience feel distress,
By answ'ring wrongly " No " or " Yes; "
It 'scapes a falsehood, which is low,
And substitutes " Exactly so."

Each mortal loves to think he's right,
That his opinion, too, is bright;
Then, Christian, you may soothe your foe
By chiming in " Exactly so."

Whoe'er these lines may chance peruse,
Of this famed word will see the use,
And mention where'er he may go,
The praises of " Exactly so."

Of this more could my muse relate,
But you, kind reader, I'll not sate;
For if I did you'd cry " Hallo!
I've heard enough "—" Exactly so."

Lady T. Hastings.

COMPANIONS

A TALE OF A GRANDFATHER

I KNOW not of what we ponder'd
  Or made pretty pretence to talk,
As, her hand within mine, we wander'd
  Tow'rd the pool by the lime-tree walk,
While the dew fell in showers from the passion flowers
  And the blush-rose bent on her stalk.

I cannot recall her figure:
  Was it regal as Juno's own?
Or only a trifle bigger
  Than the elves who surround the throne
Of the Faëry Queen, and are seen, I ween,
  By mortals in dreams alone?

What her eyes were like, I know not:
  Perhaps they were blurr'd with tears;
And perhaps in your skies there glow not
  (On the contrary) clearer spheres.
No! as to her eyes I am just as wise
  As you or the cat, my dears.

Her teeth, I presume, were " pearly " :
  But which was she, brunette or blonde?
Her hair, was it quaintly curly,
  Or as straight as a beadle's wand?
That I fail'd to remark;—it was rather dark
  And shadowy round the pond.

Then the hand that reposed so snugly
  In mine,—was it plump or spare?
Was the countenance fair or ugly?
  Nay, children, you have me there!
My eyes were p'r'aps blurr'd; and besides I'd heard
  That it's horribly rude to stare.

And I—was I brusque and surly?
  Or oppressively bland and fond?
Was I partial to rising early?
  Or why did we twain abscond,
All breakfastless, too, from the public view,
  To prowl by a misty pond?

What pass'd, what was felt or spoken—
  Whether anything pass'd at all—
And whether the heart was broken
  That beat under that shelt'ring shawl—
(If shawl she had on, which I doubt)—has gone,
  Yes, gone from me past recall.

Was I haply the lady's suitor?
  Or her uncle? I can't make out—
Ask your governess, dears, or tutor.
  For myself, I'm in hopeless doubt
As to why we were there, who on earth we were,
  And what this is all about.

Charles Stuart Calverley.

THE SCHOOLMASTER

ABROAD WITH HIS SON

O WHAT harper could worthily harp it,
  Mine Edward! this wide-stretching wold
(Look out *wold*) with its wonderful carpet
  Of emerald, purple and gold!
Look well at it—also look sharp, it
    Is getting so cold.

The purple is heather (*erica*);
  The yellow, gorse—call'd sometimes " whin."
Cruel boys on its prickles might spike a
  Green beetle as if on a pin.
You may roll in it, if you would like a
    Few holes in your skin.

You wouldn't? Then think of how kind you
  Should be to the insects who crave
Your compassion—and then, look behind you
  At yon barley-ears! Don't they look brave
As they undulate—(*undulate,* mind you,
      From *unda, a wave*).

The noise of those sheep-bells, how faint it
  Sounds here—(on account of our height)!
And this hillock itself—who could paint it,
  With its changes of shadow and light?
Is it not—(never, Eddy, say "ain't it")—
  A marvelous sight?

Then yon desolate eerie morasses,
  The haunts of the snipe and the hern—
(I shall question the two upper classes
  On *aquatiles,* when we return)—
Why, I see on them absolute masses
  Of *filix* or fern.

How it interests e'en a beginner
  (Or *tiro*) like dear little Ned!
Is he listening? As I am a sinner
  He's asleep—he is wagging his head.
Wake up! I'll go home to my dinner,
  And you to your bed.

The boundless ineffable prairie;
  The splendor of mountain and lake
With their hues that seem ever to vary;
  The mighty pine forests which shake
In the wind, and in which the unwary
  May tread on a snake;

And this wold with its heathery garment—
  Are themes undeniably great.
But—although there is not any harm in't—
  It's perhaps little good to dilate
On their charms to a dull little varmint
  Of seven or eight.

                              Charles Stuart Calverley.

A APPEAL FOR ARE TO THE SEXTANT OF THE OLD BRICK MEETINOUSE

BY A GASPER

The sextant of the meetinouse, which sweeps
And dusts, or is supposed too! and makes fiers,
And lites the gas and sometimes leaves a screw loose,
in which case it smells orful—worse than lampile;
And wrings the Bel and toles it when men dyes
to the grief of survivin pardners, and sweeps pathes;
And for the servases gits $100 per annum,
Which them that thinks deer, let em try it;
Getting up be foar star-lite in all weathers and
Kindlin-fires when the wether it is cold
As zero, and like as not green wood for kindlers;
I wouldn't be hired to do it for no some—
But o sextant! there are 1 kermoddity
Which's more than gold, wich doant cost nothin,
Worth more than anything exsep the Sole of Man.
i mean pewer Are, sextent, i mean pewer are!
O it is plenty out o dores, so plenty it doant no
What on airth to dew with itself, but flys about
Scaterin levs and bloin of men's hatts;
in short, jest "fre as are" out dores.
But o sextant, in our church its scarce as piety,
scarce as bank bills wen agints beg for mischuns,
Wich some say purty often (taint nothin to me,
Wat I give aint nothin to nobody), but o sextant,
u shut 500 mens wimmen and children,
Speshally the latter, up in a tite place,
Some has bad breths, none aint 2 swete,
some is fevery, some is scrofilus, some has bad teeth,
And some haint none, and some aint over clean;
But every 1 on em breethes in and out and out and in,
Say 50 times a minit, or 1 million and a half breths an our,
Now how long will a church ful of are last at that rate,
I ask you, say 15 minutes, and then wats to be did?
Why then they must brethe it all over agin.

And then agin, and so on, till each has took it down,
At least ten times, and let it up again, and wats more
The same individible don't have the privilege
of brethen his own are, and no one's else;
Each one mus take whatever comes to him.
O sextant, don't you know our lungs is bellusses,
To blo the fier of life, and keep it from
goin out; and how can bellusses blow without wind,
And aint wind *are?* i put it to your conscens.
Are is the same to us as milk to babes,
Or water to fish, or pendlums to clox—
Or roots and airbs unto an injun Doctor,
Or little pils to an omepath,
Or boys to gurls. Are is for us to brethe,
Wat signifies who preeches if i cant brethe?
Wats Pol? Wats Pollus? to sinners who are ded?
Ded for want of breth? why sextant, when we die
Its only coz we cant brethe no more—that's all.
And now, O sextant, let me beg of you
2 let a little are into our church.
(Pewer are is sertin proper for the pews)
And do it weak days and Sundays tew—
It aint much trouble—only make a hole
And the are will come in itself;
(It luvs to come in whare it can git warm):
And o how it will rouse the people up
And sperrit up the preacher, and stop garbs,
And yawns and figgits as effectooal
As wind on the dry Boans the Profit tells of.

                                        'rabella Willson.

CUPID'S DARTS

WHICH ARE A GROWING MENACE TO THE PUBLIC

Do not worry if I scurry from the grill room in a hurry,
  Dropping hastily my curry and retiring into balk;
Do not let it cause you wonder if, by some mischance or
    blunder,
  We encounter on the Underground and I get out and
    walk.

If I double as a cub'll when you meet him in the stubble,
  Do not think I am in trouble or attempt to make a fuss;
Do not judge me melancholy or attribute it to folly
  If I leave the Metropolitan and travel 'n a bus.

Do not quiet your anxiety by giving me a diet,
  Or by base resort to *vi et armis* fold me to your arms,
And let no suspicious tremor violate your wonted phlegm or
  Any fear that Harold's memory is faithless to your
    charms.

For my passion as I dash on in that disconcerting fashion
  Is as ardently irrational as when we forged the link
When you gave your little hand away to me, my own
    Amanda
  As we sat 'n the veranda till the stars began to wink.

And I am in such a famine when your beauty I examine
  That it lures me as the jam invites a hungry little brat;
But I fancy that, at any rate, I'd rather waste a penny
  Then be spitted by the many pins that bristle from your
    hat.

                                        Unknown.

A PLEA FOR TRIGAMY

I'VE been trying to fashion a wifely ideal,
  And find that my tastes are so far from concise
That, to marry completely, no fewer than three'll
      Suffice

I've subjected my views to severe atmospheric
  Compression, but still, in defiance of force,
They distinctly fall under three heads, like a cleric
      Discourse.

My *first* must be fashion's own fancy-bred daughter,
  Proud, peerless, and perfect—in fact, *comme il faut;*
A waltzer and wit of the very first water—
      For *show.*

But these beauties that serve to make all the men jealous,
Once face them alone in the family cot,
Heaven's angels incarnate (the novelists tell us)
They're *not*.

But so much for appearances. Now for my *second*,
My lover, the wife of my home and my heart:
Of all fortune and fate of my life to be reckon'd
A part.

She must know all the needs of a rational being,
Be skilled to keep counsel, to comfort, to coax;
And, above all things else, be accomplished at seeing
My jokes.

I complete the ménage by including the other
With all the domestic prestige of a hen:
As my housekeeper, nurse, or it may be, a mother
Of men.

Total *three!* and the virtues all well represented;
With fewer than this such a thing can't be done;
Though I've known married men who declare they're con-
tented
With one.

Would you hunt during harvest, or hay-make in winter?
And how can one woman expect to combine
Certain qualifications essentially inter-
necine?

You may say that my prospects are (legally) sunless;
I state that I find them as clear as can be:—
I will marry *no* wife, since I can't do with one less
Than three.

Owen Seaman.

THE POPE

THE Pope he leads a happy life,
He fears not married care nor strife.
He drinks the best of Rhenish wine,—
I would the Pope's gay lot were mine.

But yet all happy's not his life,
He has no maid, nor blooming wife;
No child has he to raise his hope,—
I would not wish to be the Pope.

The Sultan better pleases me,
His is a life of jollity;
He's wives as many as he will,—
I would the Sultan's throne then fill.

But even he's a wretched man,
He must obey the Alcoran;
He dare not drink one drop of wine—
I would not change his lot for mine.

So here I'll take my lowly stand,
I'll drink my own, my native land;
I'll kiss my maiden fair and fine,
And drink the best of Rhenish wine.

And when my maiden kisses me
I'll think that I the Sultan be;
And when my cheery glass I tope,
I'll fancy then I am the Pope.

Charles Lever.

ALL AT SEA

THE VOYAGE OF A CERTAIN UNCERTAIN SAILORMAN

I SAW a certain sailorman who sat beside the sea,
And in the manner of his tribe he yawned this yarn
    to me:

" 'Twere back in eighteen-fifty-three, or mebbe fifty-four,
I skipped the farm,—no, 't were the shop,—an' went to
    Baltimore.
I shipped aboard the *Lizzie*—or she might ha' bin the
    Jane;
Them wimmin names are mixey, so I don't remember
    plain;
But anyhow, she were a craft that carried schooner rig,
(Although Sam Swab, the bo'sun, allus swore she were
    a brig);
We sailed away from Salem Town,—no, lemme think;—
    't were *Lynn,*—
An' steered a course for Africa (or Greece, it might ha'
    bin);
But anyway, we tacked an' backed an' weathered many a
    storm—
Oh, no,—as I recall it now, that week was fine an' warm!
Who did I say the cap'n was? I *didn't* say at all?
Wa-a-ll now, his name were 'Lijah Bell—or was it Eli
    Ball?
I kinder guess 't were Eli. He'd a big, red, bushy beard—
No-o-o, come to think, he allus kept *his* whiskers nicely
    sheared.

But anyhow, that voyage was the first I'd ever took,
An' all I had to do was cut up cabbage for the cook;
But come to talk o' cabbage just reminds me,—that there
    trip
Would prob'ly be my *third* one, on a Hong Kong clipper-
    ship.

The crew they were a jolly lot, an' used to sing ' *Avast,*'
I think it were, or else ' *Ahoy,*' while bailing out the mast.
And as I recollect it now,—"
                But here I cut him short,
And said: " It's time to tack again, and bring your wits
    to port;
I came to get a story both adventurous and *true,*
And here is how I started out to write the interview:
' I saw a *certain* sailorman,' but you turn out to be
The most *un*-certain sailorman that ever sailed the sea!"

He puffed his pipe, and answered, "Wa-a-ll, I *thought*
  'twere mine, but still,
I must ha' told the one belongs to my twin brother Bill!"
                                  Frederick Moxon.

BALLAD OF THE PRIMITIVE JEST

I AM an ancient Jest!
Paleolithic man
In his arboreal nest
The sparks of fun would fan;
My outline did he plan,
And laughed like one possessed,
'Twas thus my course began,
I am a Merry Jest.

I am an early Jest!
Man delved and built and span;
Then wandered South and West
The peoples Aryan,
I journeyed in their van;
The Semites, too, confessed,—
From Beersheba to Dan,—
I am a Merry Jest.

I am an ancient Jest,
Through all the human clan,
Red, black, white, free, oppressed,
Hilarious I ran!
I'm found in Lucian,
In Poggio, and the rest,
I'm dear to Moll and Nan!
I am a Merry Jest!

ENVOY:

Prince, you may storm and ban—
Joe Millers *are* a pest,
Suppress me if you can!
I am a Merry Jest!
                                  Andrew Lang.

VILLANELLE OF THINGS AMUSING

These are the things that make me laugh—
  Life's a preposterous farce, say I!
And I've missed of too many jokes by half.

The high-heeled antics of colt and calf,
  The men who think they can act, and try—
These are the things that make me laugh.

The hard-boiled poses in photograph,
  The groom still wearing his wedding tie—
And I've missed of too many jokes by half!

These are the bubbles I gayly quaff
  With the rank conceit of the new-born fly—
These are the things that make me laugh!

For, Heaven help me! I needs must chaff,
  And people will tickle me till I die—
And I've missed of too many jokes by half!

So write me down in my epitaph
  As one too fond of his health to cry—
These are the things that make me laugh,
And I've missed of too many jokes by half!

                                    Gelett Burgess.

HOW TO EAT WATERMELONS

When you slice a Georgy melon you mus' know what you
      is at
An' look out .how de knife is gwine in.
Put one-half on dis side er you—de yuther half on dat,
  En' den you gits betwixt 'em, en begin!
        Oh, melons!
          Honey good ter see;
        But we'en it comes ter sweetness,
          De melon make fer me!

En den you puts yo' knife up, en you sorter licks de blade,
  En never stop fer sayin' any grace;
But eat ontell you satisfy—roll over in de shade,
  En sleep ontell de sun shine in yo' face!
        Oh, melons!
          Honey good ter see;
        But we'en it comes ter sweetness,
          De melon make fer me!

Frank Libby Stanton.

A VAGUE STORY

PERCHANCE it was her eyes of blue,
  Her cheeks that might the rose have shamed,
Her figure in proportion true
  To all the rules by artists framed;
Perhaps it was her mental worth
  That made her lover love her so,
Perhaps her name, or wealth, or birth—
  I cannot tell—I do not know.

He may have had a rival, who
  Did fiercely gage him to a duel,
And, being luckier of the two,
  Defeated him with triumph cruel;
Then *she* may have proved false, and turned
  To welcome to her arms his foe,
Left *him* despairing, conquered, spurned—
  I cannot tell—I do not know.

So oft such woes will counteract
  The thousand ecstacies of love,
That you may fix on base of fact
  The story hinted at above;
But all on earth so doubtful is,
  Man *knows* so little here below,
That, if you ask for proof of this,
  I cannot tell—I do not know.

Walter Parke.

HIS MOTHER-IN-LAW

He stood on his head by the wild seashore,
  And danced on his hands a jig;
In all his emotions, as never before,
  A wildly hilarious grig.

And why? In that ship just crossing the bay
  His mother-in-law had sailed
For a tropical country far away,
  Where tigers and fever prevailed.

Oh, now he might hope for a peaceful life
  And even be happy yet,
Though owning no end of neuralgic wife,
  And up to his collar in debt.

He had borne the old lady through thick and thin,
  And she lectured him out of breath;
And now as he looked at the ship she was in
  He howled for her violent death.

He watched as the good ship cut the sea,
  And bumpishly up-and-downed,
And thought if already she qualmish might be,
  He'd consider his happiness crowned.

He watched till beneath the horizon's edge
  The ship was passing from view;
And he sprang to the top of a rocky ledge
  And pranced like a kangaroo.

He watched till the vessel became a speck
  That was lost in the wandering sea;
And then, at the risk of breaking his neck,
  Turned somersaults home to tea.

                                    Walter Parke.

ON A DEAF HOUSEKEEPER

Of all life's plagues I recommend to no man
To hire as a domestic a deaf woman.
I've got one who my orders does not hear,
Mishears them rather, and keeps blundering near.
Thirsty and hot, I asked her for a *drink;*
She bustled out, and brought me back some *ink.*
Eating a good rump-steak, I called for *mustard;*
Away she went, and whipped me up a *custard.*
I wanted with my chicken to have *ham;*
Blundering once more, she brought a pot of *jam.*
I wished in season for a cut of *salmon;*
And what she brought me was a huge fat *gammon.*
I can't my voice raise higher and still higher,
As if I were a herald or town-crier.
'T would better be if she were deaf outright;
But anyhow she quits my house this night.

Unknown.

HOMŒOPATHIC SOUP

Take a robin's leg
(Mind, the drumstick merely);
Put it in a tub
Filled with water nearly;
Set it out of doors,
In a place that's shady;
Let it stand a week
(Three days if for a lady);
Drop a spoonful of it
In a five-pail kettle,
Which may be made of tin
Or any baser metal;
Fill the kettle up,
Set it on a boiling,
Strain the liquor well,
To prevent its oiling;
One atom add of salt;
For the thickening one rice kernel.

And use to light the fire
"The Homœopathic Journal."
Let the liquor boil
Half an hour, no longer,
(If 'tis for a man
Of course you'll make it stronger).
Should you now desire
That the soup be flavoury,
Stir it once around,
With a stalk of savoury.
When the broth is made,
Nothing can excell it:
Then three times a day
Let the patient *smell* it.
If he chance to die,
Say 'twas Nature did it:
If he chance to live,
Give the soup the credit.

Unknown.

SOME LITTLE BUG

In these days of indigestion
It is oftentimes a question
    As to what to eat and what to leave alone;
For each microbe and bacillus
Has a different way to kill us,
    And in time they always claim us for their own.
There are germs of every kind
In any food that you can find
    In the market or upon the bill of fare.
Drinking water's just as risky
As the so-called deadly whiskey,
    And it's often a mistake to breathe the air.

Some little bug is going to find you some day,
Some little bug will creep behind you some day,
    Then he'll send for his bug friends
    And all your earthly trouble ends;
Some little bug is going to find you some day.

The inviting green cucumber
Gets most everybody's number,
    While the green corn has a system of its own;
Though a radish seems nutritious
Its behaviour is quite vicious,
    And a doctor will be coming to your home.
Eating lobster cooked or plain
Is only flirting with ptomaine,
    While an oyster sometimes has a lot to say,
But the clams we eat in chowder
Make the angels chant the louder,
    For they know that we'll be with them right away.

Take a slice of nice fried onion
And you're fit for Dr. Munyon,
    Apple dumplings kill you quicker than a train.
Chew a cheesy midnight " rabbit "
And a grave you'll soon inhabit—
    Ah, to eat at all is such a foolish game.
Eating huckleberry pie
Is a pleasing way to die,
    While sauerkraut brings on softening of the brain.
When you eat banana fritters
Every undertaker titters,
    And the casket makers nearly go insane.

Some little bug is going to find you some day,
Some little bug will creep behind you some day,
    With a nervous little quiver
    He'll give cirrhosis of the liver;
Some little bug is going to find you some day.

When cold storage vaults I visit
I can only say what is it
    Makes poor mortals fill their systems with such
        stuff?
Now, for breakfast, prunes are dandy
If a stomach pump is handy
    And your doctor can be found quite soon enough.
Eat a plate of fine pigs' knuckles
And the headstone cutter chuckles,

While the grave digger makes a note upon his cuff.
Eat that lovely red bologna
And you'll wear a wooden kimona,
    As your relatives start scrappin 'bout your stuff.

Some little bug is going to find you some day,
Some little bug will creep behind you some day,
    Eating juicy sliced pineapple
    Makes the sexton dust the chapel;
Some little bug is going to find you some day.

All those crazy foods they mix
Will float us 'cross the River Styx,
    Or they'll start us climbing up the milky way.
And the meals we eat in courses
Mean a hearse and two black horses
    So before a meal some people always pray.
Luscious grapes breed 'pendicitis,
And the juice leads to gastritis,
    So there's only death to greet us either way;
And fried liver's nice, but, mind you,
Friends will soon ride slow behind you
    And the papers then will have nice things to say.

Some little bug is going to find you some day,
Some little bug will creep behind you some day
    Eat some sauce, they call it chili,
    On your breast they'll place a lily;
Some little bug is going to find you some day.

                                        Roy Atwell.

ON THE DOWNTOWN SIDE OF AN UPTOWN STREET

On the downtown side of an uptown street
Is the home of a girl that I'd like to meet,
    But I'm on the uptown,
    And she's on the downtown,
On the downtown side of an uptown street.

On the uptown side of the crowded old " L,"
I see her so often I know her quite well,
    But I'm on the downtown
    When she's on the uptown,
On the uptown side of the crowded old " L."

On the uptown side of a downtown street
This girl is employed that I'd like to meet,
    But I work on the downtown
    And she on the uptown,
The uptown side of a downtown street.

On a downtown car of the Broadway line
Often I see her for whom I repine,
    But when I'm on a uptown
    She's on a downtown,
On a downtown car of the Broadway line.

Oh, to be downtown when I am uptown,
Oh, to be uptown when I am downtown,
    I work at night time,
    She in the daytime,
Never the right time for us to meet,
Uptown or downtown, in " L," car or street.

William Johnston.

WRITTEN AFTER SWIMMING FROM SESTOS TO ABYDOS

If, in the month of dark December,
    Leander, who was nightly wont
(What maid will not the tale remember?)
    To cross thy stream broad Hellespont.

If, when the wint'ry tempest roar'd,
    He sped to Hero nothing loth,
And thus of old thy current pour'd,
    Fair Venus! how I pity both!

For *me*, degenerate, modern wretch,
  Though in the genial month of May,
My dripping limbs I faintly stretch,
  And think I've done a feat to-day.

But since he crossed the rapid tide,
  According to the doubtful story,
To woo—and—Lord knows what beside,
  And swam for Love, as I for Glory;

'T were hard to say who fared the best:
  Sad mortals! thus the gods still plague you!
He lost his labor, I my jest;
  For he was drowned, and I've the ague.

                          Lord Byron.

THE FISHERMAN'S CHANT

Oh, the fisherman is a happy wight!
He dibbles by day, and he sniggles by night.
He trolls for fish, and he trolls his lay—
He sniggles by night, and he dibbles by day.
    Oh, who so merry as he!
    On the river or the sea!
        Sniggling,
        Wriggling
        Eels, and higgling
        Over the price
        Of a nice
        Slice
        Of fish, twice
        As much as it ought to be.

Oh, the fisherman is a happy man!
He dibbles, and sniggles, and fills his can!
With a sharpened hook, and a sharper eye,
He sniggles and dibbles for what comes by,
    Oh, who so merry as he!
    On the river or the sea!

Dibbling
Nibbling
Chub, and quibbling
Over the price
Of a nice
Slice
Of fish, twice
As much as it ought to be.

F. C. Burnand.

REPORT OF AN ADJUDGED CASE

NOT TO BE FOUND IN ANY OF THE BOOKS

BETWEEN Nose and Eyes a strange contest arose,
  The spectacles set them unhappily wrong;
The point in dispute was, as all the world knows,
  To which the said spectacles ought to belong.

So Tongue was the lawyer, and argued the cause
  With a great deal of skill, and a wig full of learning;
While chief baron Ear sat to balance the laws,
  So famed for his talent in nicely discerning.

In behalf of the Nose it will quickly appear,
  And your lordship, he said, will undoubtedly find,
That the Nose has had spectacles always to wear,
  Which amounts to possession time out of mind.

Then holding the spectacles up to the court—
  Your lordship observes they are made with a straddle
As wide as the ridge of the Nose is; in short,
  Designed to sit close to it, just like a saddle.

Again, would your lordship a moment suppose
  ('Tis a case that has happened, and may be again)
That the visage or countenance had not a nose,
  Pray who would, or who could, wear spectacles then!

On the whole it appears, and my argument shows
   With a reasoning the court will never condemn,
That the spectacles plainly were made for the Nose,
   And the Nose was as plainly intended for them.

Then shifting his side (as a lawyer knows how),
   He pleaded again in behalf of the Eyes;
But what were his arguments few people know,
   For the court did not think they were equally wise.

So his lordship decreed with a grave solemn tone,
   Decisive and clear, without one *if* or *but*—
That, whenever the Nose put his spectacles on,
   By daylight or candlelight—Eyes should be shut!

William Cowper.

PREHISTORIC SMITH

QUATERNARY EPOCH—POST-PLIOCENE PERIOD

A MAN sat on a rock and sought
   Refreshment from his thumb;
A dinotherium wandered by
   And scared him some.

His name was Smith. The kind of rock
   He sat upon was shale.
One feature quite distinguished him—
   He had a tail.

The danger past, he fell into
   A revery austere;
While with his tail he whisked a fly
   From off his ear.

" Mankind deteriorates," he said,
   " Grows weak and incomplete;
And each new generation seems
   Yet more effete.

" Nature abhors imperfect work,
　　And on it lays her ban;
And all creation must despise
　　A tailless man.

" But fashion's dictates rule supreme,
　　Ignoring common sense;
And fashion says, to dock your tail
　　Is just immense.

" And children now come in the world
　　With half a tail or less;
Too stumpy to convey a thought,
　　And meaningless.

" It kills expression. How can one
　　Set forth, in words that drag,
The best emotions of the soul,
　　Without a wag? "

Sadly he mused upon the world,
　　Its follies and its woes;
Then wiped the moisture from his eyes,
　　And blew his nose.

But clothed in earrings, Mrs. Smith
　　Came wandering down the dale;
And, smiling, Mr. Smith arose,
　　And wagged his tail.

David Law Proudfit.

SONG

OF ONE ELEVEN YEARS IN PRISON

I

WHENE'ER with haggard eyes I view
This dungeon that I'm rotting in,
I think of those companions true

Who studied with me at the U
    niversity of Gottingen,
    niversity of Gottingen.

[Weeps, and pulls out a blue kerchief, with which he
wipes his eyes; gazing tenderly at it, he proceeds—

II

Sweet kerchief, check'd with heavenly blue,
  Which once my love sat knotting in!—
Alas! Matilda *then* was true!
  At least I thought so at the U
    niversity of Gottingen,
    niversity of Gottingen.

[At the repetition of this line he clanks his chains
in cadence.

III

Barbs! Barbs! alas! how swift you flew,
  Her neat post-wagon trotting in!
Ye bore Matilda from my view;
  Forlorn I languish'd at the U
    niversity of Gottingen,
    niversity of Gottingen.

IV

This faded form! this pallid hue!
  This blood my veins is clotting in,
My years are many—they were few
  When first I entered at the U
    niversity of Gottingen,
    niversity of Gottingen.

V

There first for thee my passion grew,
  Sweet, sweet Matilda Pottengen!
Thou wast the daughter of my tu
  tor, law professor at the U
    niversity of Gottingen,
    niversity of Gottingen.

VI

Sun, moon and thou, vain world, adieu,
  That kings and priests are plotting in;
Here doom'd to starve on water gru
  el, never shall I see the U
    niversity of Gottingen,
    niversity of Gottingen.

[During the last stanza he dashes his head repeatedly against the
  walls of his prison; and, finally, so hard as to produce a visible
  contusion; he then throws himself on the floor in an agony.
  The curtain drops; the music still continuing to play till it is
  wholly fallen.

George Canning.

LYING

I DO confess, in many a sigh,
My lips have breath'd you many a lie,
And who, with such delights in view,
Would lose them for a lie or two?

Nay—look not thus, with brow reproving:
Lies are, my dear, the soul of loving!
If half we tell the girls were true,
If half we swear to think and do,
Were aught but lying's bright illusion,
The world would be in strange confusion!
If ladies' eyes were, every one,
As lovers swear, a radiant sun,
Astronomy should leave the skies,
To learn her lore in ladies' eyes!
Oh no!—believe me, lovely girl,
When nature turns your teeth to pearl,
Your neck to snow, your eyes to fire,
Your yellow locks to golden wire,
Then, only then, can heaven decree,
That you should live for only me,
Or I for you, as night and morn,
We've swearing kiss'd, and kissing sworn.

And now, my gentle hints to clear,
For once, I'll tell you truth, my dear!
Whenever you may chance to meet
A loving youth, whose love is sweet,
Long as you're false and he believes you,
Long as you trust and he deceives you,
So long the blissful bond endures;
And while he lies, his heart is yours:
But, oh! you've wholly lost the youth
The instant that he tells you truth!

Thomas Moore.

STRICTLY GERM-PROOF

THE Antiseptic Baby and the Prophylactic Pup
Were playing in the garden when the Bunny gamboled up;
They looked upon the Creature with a loathing undis-
    guised;—
It wasn't Disinfected and it wasn't Sterilized.

They said it was a Microbe and a Hotbed of Disease;
They steamed it in a vapor of a thousand-odd degrees;
They froze it in a freezer that was cold as Banished Hope
And washed it in permanganate with carbolated soap.

In sulphureted hydrogen they steeped its wiggly ears;
They trimmed its frisky whiskers with a pair of hard-boiled
    shears;
They donned their rubber mittens and they took it by the
    hand
And 'lected it a member of the Fumigated Band.

There's not a Micrococcus in the garden where they play;
They bathe in pure iodoform a dozen times a day;
And each imbibes his rations from a Hygienic Cup—
The Bunny and the Baby and the Prophylactic Pup.

Arthur Guiterman.

THE LAY OF THE LOVER'S FRIEND

Air—"*The days we went a-gipsying.*"

I would all womankind were dead,
  Or banished o'er the sea;
For they have been a bitter plague
  These last six weeks to me:
It is not that I'm touched myself,
  For that I do not fear;
No female face hath shown me grace
  For many a bygone year.
    But 'tis the most infernal bore,
      Of all the bores I know,
    To have a friend who's lost his heart
      A short time ago.

Whene'er we steam it to Blackwall,
  Or down to Greenwich run,
To quaff the pleasant cider cup,
  And feed on fish and fun;
Or climb the slopes of Richmond Hill,
  To catch a breath of air:
Then, for my sins, he straight begins
  To rave about his fair.
    Oh, 'tis the most tremendous bore,
      Of all the bores I know,
    To have a friend who's lost his heart
      A short time ago.

In vain you pour into his ear
  Your own confiding grief;
In vain you claim his sympathy,
  In vain you ask relief;
In vain you try to rouse him by
  Joke, repartee, or quiz;
His sole reply's a burning sigh,
  And "What a mind it is!"
    O Lord! it is the greatest bore,
      Of all the bores I know,
    To have a friend who's lost his heart
      A short time ago.

I've heard her thoroughly described
A hundred times, I'm sure;
And all the while I've tried to smile,
And patiently endure;
He waxes strong upon his pangs,
And potters o'er his grog;
And still I say, in a playful way—
"Why you're a lucky dog!"
But oh! it is the heaviest bore,
Of all the bores I know,
To have a friend who's lost his heart
A short time ago.

I really wish he'd do like me
When I was young and strong;
I formed a passion every week,
But never kept it long.
But he has not the sportive mood
That always rescued me,
And so I would all women could
Be banished o'er the sea.
For 'tis the most egregious bore,
Of all the bores I know,
To have a friend who's lost his heart
A short time ago.

William E. Aytoun.

MAN'S PLACE IN NATURE

DEDICATED TO DARWIN AND HUXLEY

They told him gently he was made
Of nicely tempered mud,
That man no lengthened part had played
Anterior to the Flood.
'Twas all in vain; he heeded not,
Referring plant and worm,
Fish, reptile, ape, and Hottentot,
To one primordial germ.

They asked him whether he could bear
To think his kind allied
To all those brutal forms which were
In structure Pithecoid;
Whether he thought the apes and us
Homologous in form;
He said, " Homo and Pithecus
Came from one common germ."

They called him " atheistical,"
" Sceptic," and " infidel."
They swore his doctrines without fail
Would plunge him into hell.
But he with proofs in no way lame,
Made this deduction firm,
That all organic beings came
From one primordial germ.

That as for the Noachian flood,
'Twas long ago disproved,
That as for man being made of mud,
All by whom truth is loved
Accept as fact what, *malgré* strife,
Research tends to confirm—
That man, and everything with life,
Came from one common germ.

Unknown.

THE NEW VERSION

A SOLDIER of the Russians
Lay japanned at Tschrtzvkjskivitch,
There was lack of woman's nursing
And other comforts which
Might add to his last moments
And smooth the final way;—
But a comrade stood beside him
To hear what he might say.
The japanned Russian faltered
As he took that comrade's hand,

And he said: " I never more shall see
   My own, my native land;
Take a message and a token
   To some distant friends of mine,
For I was born at Smnlxzrskgqrxzski,
   Fair Smnlxzrskgqrxzski on the Irkztrvzkimnov."

W. J. Lampton.

AMAZING FACTS ABOUT FOOD

   The Food Scientist tells us: " A deficiency of iron, phosphorus, potassium, calcium and the other mineral salts, colloids and vitamines of vegetable origin leads to numerous forms of physical disorder."

   I YEARN to bite on a Colloid
      With phosphorus, iron and Beans;
   I want to be filled with Calcium, grilled,
      And Veg'table Vitamines!

   I yearn to bite on a Colloid
      (Though I don't know what it means)
   To line my inside with Potassium, fried,
      And Veg'table Vitamines.

   I would sate my soul with spinach
      And dandelion greens.
   No eggs, nor ham, nor hard-boiled clam,
      But Veg'table Vitamines.

   Hi, Waiter! Coddle the Colloids
      With phosphorus, iron and Beans;
   Though Mineral Salts may have some faults,
      Bring on the Vitamines.

Unknown.

TRANSCENDENTALISM

It is told, in Buddhi-theosophic schools,
        There are rules,
By observing which, when mundane labor irks
One can simulate quiescence
By a timely evanescence
From his Active Mortal Essence,
        (Or his Works.)

The particular procedure leaves research
        In the lurch,
But, apparently, this matter-moulded form
        Is a kind of outer plaster,
        Which a well-instructed Master
        Can remove without disaster
            When he's warm.

And to such as mourn an Indian Solar Clime
        At its prime
'Twere a thesis most immeasurably fit,
        So expansively elastic,
        And so plausibly fantastic,
        That one gets enthusiastic
            For a bit.

                                                Unknown.

A "CAUDAL" LECTURE

Philosophy shows us 'twixt monkey and man
    One simious line in unbroken extendage;
Development only since first it began—
    And chiefly in losing the caudal appendage.

Our ancestors' holding was wholly *in tail,*
    And the loss of this feature we claim as a merit;
But though often at tale-bearing people we rail,
    'Tis rather a loss than a gain we inherit.

The tail was a rudder—a capital thing
    To a man who was half—or a quarter—seas over;
And as for a sailor, by that he could cling,
    And use for his hands and his feet both discover.

In the Arts it would quickly have found out a place;
    The painter would use it to steady his pencil;
In music, how handy to pound at the bass!
    And then one could write by its coilings prehensile.

The Army had gained had the fashion endured—
    'Twould carry a sword, or be good in saluting;
If the foe should turn tail, they'd be quickly secured;
    Or, used as a lasso, 'twould help in recruiting.

To the Force 'twould add force—they could " run 'em in " so
    That one to three culprits would find himself equal;
He could collar the two, have the other in tow—
    A very good form of the Tale and its Sequel.

In life many uses 'twould serve we should see—
    A man with no bed could hang cosily snoozing;
'Twould hold an umbrella, hand cups round at tea,
    Or a candle support while our novel perusing.

In fact, when one thinks of our loss from of old,
    It makes us regret that we can't go in for it, or
Wish, like the Dane, we a *tail* could unfold,
    Instead of remaining each one a *stump* orator.

                        William Sawyer.

SALAD

To make this condiment, your poet begs
The pounded yellow of two hard-boiled eggs;
Two boiled potatoes, passed through kitchen-sieve,
Smoothness and softness to the salad give;
Let onion atoms lurk within the bowl,
And, half-suspected, animate the whole.
Of mordant mustard add a single spoon,
Distrust the condiment that bites so soon;

But deem it not, thou man of herbs, a fault,
To add a double quantity of salt.
And, lastly, o'er the flavored compound toss
A magic soup-spoon of anchovy sauce.
Oh, green and glorious! Oh, herbaceous treat!
'Twould tempt the dying anchorite to eat;
Back to the world he'd turn his fleeting soul,
And plunge his fingers in the salad bowl!
Serenely full, the epicure would say,
Fate can not harm me, I have dined to-day!

Sydney Smith.

NEMESIS

THE man who invented the women's waists that button down
　　behind,
And the man who invented the cans with keys and the strips
　　that will never wind,
Were put to sea in a leaky boat and with never a bite to eat
But a couple of dozen of patent cans in which was their only
　　meat.

And they sailed and sailed o'er the ocean wide and never
　　they had a taste
Of aught to eat, for the cans stayed shut, and a peek-a-boo
　　shirtwaist
Was all they had to bale the brine that came in the leaky
　　boat;
And their tongues were thick and their throats were dry,
　　and they barely kept afloat.

They came at last to an island fair, and a man stood on the
　　shore,
So they flew a signal of distress and their hopes rose high
　　once more,
And they called to him to fetch a boat, for their craft was
　　sinking fast,
And a couple of hours at best they knew was all their boat
　　would last.

So he called to them a cheery call and he said he would make
    haste,
But first he must go back to his wife and button up her
    waist,
Which would only take him an hour or so and then he would
    fetch a boat.
And the man who invented the backstairs waist, he groaned
    in his swollen throat.

The hours passed by on leaden wings and they saw another
    man
In the window of a bungalow, and he held a tin meat can
In his bleeding hands, and they called to him, not once but
    twice and thrice,
And he said: "Just wait till I open this and I'll be there
    in a trice!"

And the man who invented the patent cans he knew what
    the promise meant,
So he leaped in air with a horrid cry and into the sea he went,
And the bubbles rose where he sank and sank and a groan
    choked in the throat
Of the man who invented the backstairs waist and he sank
    with the leaky boat!

J. W. Foley.

"MONA LISA"

Mona Lisa, Mona Lisa!
Have you gone? Great Julius Cæsar!
Who's the Chap so bold and pinchey
Thus to swipe the great da Vinci,
Taking France's first Chef d'oeuvre
Squarely from old Mr. Louvre,
Easy as some pocket-picker
Would remove our handkerchicker
As we ride in careless folly
On some gaily bounding trolley?

Mona Lisa, Mona Lisa,
Who's your Captor?   Doubtless he's a
Crafty sort of treasure-seeker—
Ne'er a Turpin e'er was sleeker—
But, alas, if he can win you
Easily as I could chin you,
What is safe in all the nations
From his dreadful depredations?
He's the style of Chap, I'm thinkin',
Who will drive us all to drinkin'!

Mona Lisa, Mona Lisa,
Next he'll swipe the Tower of Pisa,
Pulling it from out its socket
For to hide it in his pocket;
Or perhaps he'll up and steal, O,
Madame Venus, late of Milo;
Or maybe while on the grab he
Will annex Westminster Abbey,
And elope with that distinguished
Heap of Ashes long extinguished.

Maybe too, O Mona Lisa,
He will come across the seas a—
Searching for the style of treasure
That we have in richest measure.
Sunset Cox's brazen statue,
Have a care lest he shall catch you!
Or maybe he'll set his eye on
Hammerstein's, or the Flatiron,
Or some bit of White Wash done
By those lads at Washington—

Truly he's a crafty geezer,
Is your Captor, Mona Lisa!
                                        John Kendrick Bangs.

THE SIEGE OF DJKLXPRWBZ

BEFORE a Turkish town
    The Russians came,
And with huge cannon
    Did bombard the same.

They got up close
  And rained fat bombshells down,
And blew out every
  Vowel in the town.

And then the Turks,
  Becoming somewhat sad,
Surrendered every
  Consonant they had.

Eugene Fitch Ware.

RURAL BLISS

THE poet is, or ought to be, a hater of the city,
  And so, when happiness is mine, and Maud becomes my
    wife,
We'll look on town inhabitants with sympathetic pity,
  For we shall lead a peaceful and serene Arcadian life.

Then shall I sing in eloquent and most effective phrases,
  The grandeur of geraniums and the beauty of the rose;
Immortalise in deathless strains the buttercups and daisies—
  For even I can hardly be mistaken as to those.

The music of the nightingale will ring from leafy hollow,
  And fill us with a rapture indescribable in words;
And we shall also listen to the robin and the swallow
  (I wonder if a swallow sings?) and . . . well, the other
    birds.

Too long I dwelt in ignorance of all the countless treasures
  Which dwellers in the country have in such abundant
    store;
To give a single instance of the multitude of pleasures—
  The music of the nighting—oh, I mentioned that before.

And shall I prune potato-trees and artichokes, I wonder,
  And cultivate the silo-plant, which springs (I hope it
    springs?)
In graceful foliage overhead?—Excuse me if I blunder,
  It's really inconvenient not to know the name of things!

No matter; in the future, when I celebrate the beauty
　　Of country life in glowing terms, and "build the lofty
　　　　rhyme"
Aware that every Englishman is bound to do his duty,
　　I'll learn to give the stupid things their proper names in
　　　　time!

Meanwhile, you needn't wonder at the view I've indicated,
　　The country life appears to me indubitably blest,
For, even if its other charms are somewhat overstated,
　　As long as Maud is there, you see,—what matters all the
　　　　rest?

Anthony C. Deane.

AN OLD BACHELOR

'Twas raw, and chill, and cold outside,
　　With a boisterous wind untamed,
But I was sitting snug within,
　　Where my good log-fire flamed.
　　　　As my clock ticked,
　　　　My cat purred,
　　　　And my kettle sang.

I read me a tale of war and love,
　　Brave knights and their ladies fair;
And I brewed a brew of stiff hot-scotch
　　To drive away dull care.
　　　　As my clock ticked,
　　　　My cat purred,
　　　　And my kettle sang.

At last the candles sputtered out,
　　But the embers still were bright,
When I turned my tumbler upside down,
　　An' bade m'self g' night!
　　　　As th' ket'l t-hic-ked,
　　　　The clock purred,
　　　　And the cat (hic) sang!

Tudor Jenks.

SONG

THREE score and ten by common calculation
   The years of man amount to; but we'll say
He turns four-score, yet, in my estimation,
   In all those years he has not lived a day.

Out of the eighty you must first remember
   The hours of night you pass asleep in bed;
And, counting from December to December,
   Just half your life you'll find you have been dead.

To forty years at once by this reduction
   We come; and sure, the first five from your birth,
While cutting teeth and living upon suction,
   You're not alive to what this life is worth.

From thirty-five next take for education
   Fifteen at least at college and at school;
When, notwithstanding all your application,
   The chances are you may turn out a fool.

Still twenty we have left us to dispose of,
   But during them your fortune you've to make;
And granting, with the luck of some one knows of,
   'Tis made in ten—that's ten from life to take.

Out of the ten yet left you must allow for
   The time for shaving, tooth and other aches,
Say four—and that leaves, six, too short, I vow, for
   Regretting past and making fresh mistakes.

Meanwhile each hour dispels some fond illusion;
   Until at length, *sans* eyes, *sans* teeth, you may
Have scarcely sense to come to this conclusion—
   You've reached four-score, but haven't lived a day!

J. R. Planché.

THE QUEST OF THE PURPLE COW

HE girded on his shining sword,
    He clad him in his suit of mail,
He gave his friends the parting word,
    With high resolve his face was pale.
They said, "You've kissed the Papal Toe,
    To great Moguls you've made your bow,
Why will you thus world-wandering go?"
    "I never saw a purple cow!"

"I never saw a purple cow!
    Oh, hinder not my wild emprise—
Let me depart! For even now
    Perhaps, before some yokel's eyes
The purpling creature dashes by,
    Bending its noble, hornèd brow.
They see its glowing charms, but I—
    I never saw a purple cow!"

"But other cows there be," they said,
    "Both cows of high and low degree,
Suffolk and Devon, brown, black, red,
    The Ayrshire and the Alderney.
Content yourself with these." "No, no,"
    He cried, "Not these! Not these! For how
Can common kine bring comfort? Oh!
    I never saw a purple cow!"

He flung him to his charger's back,
    He left his kindred limp and weak,
They cried: "He goes, alack! alack!
    The unattainable to seek."
But westward still he rode—pardee!
    The West! Where such freaks be; I vow,
I'd not be much surprised if he
    Should some day see
                A
            Purple
                Cow!

Hilda Johnson.

ST. PATRICK OF IRELAND, MY DEAR!

A FIG for St. Denis of France—
    He's a trumpery fellow to brag on;
A fig for St. George and his lance,
    Which spitted a heathenish dragon;
And the saints of the Welshman or Scot
    Are a couple of pitiful pipers,
Both of whom may just travel to pot,
    Compared with that patron of swipers—
        St. Patrick of Ireland, my dear!

He came to the Emerald Isle
    On a lump of a paving-stone mounted;
The steamboat he beat by a mile,
    Which mighty good sailing was counted.
Says he, " The salt water, I think,
    Has made me most bloodily thirsty;
So bring me a flagon of drink
    To keep down the mulligrubs, burst ye!
        Of drink that is fit for a saint! "

He preached, then, with wonderful force,
    The ignorant natives a-teaching;
With a pint he washed down his discourse,
    " For," says he, " I detest your dry preaching."
The people, with wonderment struck
    At a pastor so pious and civil,
Exclaimed—" We're for you, my old buck!
    And we pitch our blind gods to the devil,
        Who dwells in hot water below! "

This ended, our worshipful spoon
    Went to visit an elegant fellow,
Whose practice, each cool afternoon,
    Was to get most delightfully mellow.
That day with a black-jack of beer,
    It chanced he was treating a party;
Says the saint—" This good day, do you hear,
    I drank nothing to speak of, my hearty!
        So give me a pull at the pot! "

The pewter he lifted in sport
  (Believe me, I tell you no fable);
A gallon he drank from the quart,
  And then placed it full on the table.
" A miracle!" every one said—
  And they all took a haul at the stingo;
They were capital hands at the trade,
  And drank till they fell; yet, by jingo,
    The pot still frothed over the brim.

Next day, quoth his host, " 'Tis a fast,
  And I've nought in my larder but mutton;
And on Fridays who'd made such repast,
  Except an unchristian-like glutton?"
Says Pat, " Cease your nonsense, I beg—
  What you tell me is nothing but gammon;
Take my compliments down to the leg,
  And bid it come hither a salmon!"
    And the leg most politely complied.

You've heard, I suppose, long ago,
  How the snakes, in a manner most antic,
He marched to the county Mayo,
  And trundled them into th' Atlantic.
Hence, not to use water for drink,
  The people of Ireland determine—
With mighty good reason, I think,
  Since St. Patrick has filled it with vermin
    And vipers, and other such stuff!

Oh, he was an elegant blade
  As you'd meet from Fairhead to Kilcrumper;
And though under the sod he is laid,
  Yet here goes his health in a bumper!
I wish he was here, that my glass
  He might by art magic replenish;
But since he is not—why, alas!
  My ditty must come to a finish,—
    Because all the liquor is out!

William Maginn.

THE IRISH SCHOOLMASTER

" Come here, my boy; hould up your head,
  And look like a jintlemàn, Sir;
Jist tell me who King David was—
  Now tell me if you can, Sir."
" King David was a mighty man,
  And he was King of Spain, Sir;
His eldest daughter ' Jessie ' was
  The ' Flower of Dunblane,' Sir."

" You're right, my boy; hould up your head,
  And look like a jintlemàn, Sir;
Sir Isaac Newton—who was he?
  Now tell me if you can, Sir."
" Sir Isaac Newton was the boy
  That climbed the apple-tree, Sir;
He then fell down and broke his crown,
  And lost his gravity, Sir."

" You're right, my boy; hould up your head,
  And look like a jintlemàn, Sir;
Jist tell me who ould Marmion was—
  Now tell me if you can, Sir."
" Ould Marmion was a soldier bold,
  But he went all to pot, Sir;
He was hanged upon the gallows tree,
  For killing Sir Walter Scott, Sir."

" You're right, my boy; hould up your head,
  And look like a jintlemàn, Sir;
Jist tell me who Sir Rob Roy was;
  Now tell me if you can, Sir."
" Sir Rob Roy was a tailor to
  The King of the Cannibal Islands;
He spoiled a pair of breeches, and
  Was banished to the Highlands."

" You're right, my boy; hould up your head,
    And look like a jintlemàn, Sir;
Then, Bonaparte—say, who was he?
    Now tell me if you can, Sir."
" Ould Bonaparte was King of France
    Before the Revolution;
But he was kilt at Waterloo,
    Which ruined his constitution."

" You're right, my boy; hould up your head,
    And look like a jintlemàn, Sir;
Jist tell me who King Jonah was;
    Now tell me if you can, Sir."
" King Jonah was the strangest man
    That ever wore a crown, Sir;
For though the whale did swallow him,
    It couldn't keep him down, Sir."

" You're right, my boy; hould up your head,
    And look like a jintlemàn, Sir;
Jist tell me who that Moses was;
    Now tell me if you can, Sir."
" Shure Moses was the Christian name
    Of good King Pharaoh's daughter;
She was a milkmaid, and she took
    A *profit* from the water."

" You're right, my boy; hould up your head,
    And look like a jintlemàn, Sir;
Jist tell me now where Dublin is;
    Now tell me if you can, Sir."
" Och, Dublin is a town in Cork,
    And built on the equator;
It's close to Mount Vesuvius,
    And watered by the ' craythur.' "

" You're right, my boy; hould up your head,
    And look like a jintlemàn, Sir;
Jist tell me now where London is;
    Now tell me if you can, Sir."

" Och, London is a town in Spain;
    'Twas lost in the earthquake, Sir;
The cockneys murther English there,
    Whenever they do spake, Sir."

" You're right, my boy; hould up your head,
    Ye're now a jintlemàn, Sir;
For in history and geography
    I've taught you all I can, Sir.
And if any one should ask you now,
    Where you got all your knowledge,
Jist tell them 'twas from Paddy Blake,
    Of Bally Blarney College."

                 James A. Sidey.

REFLECTIONS ON CLEOPATHERA'S NEEDLE

So that's Cleopathera's Needle, bedad,
    An' a quare lookin' needle it is, I'll be bound;
What a powerful muscle the queen must have had
    That could grasp such a weapon an' wind it around!

Imagine her sittin' there stitchin' like mad
    Wid a needle like that in her hand! I declare
It's as big as the Round Tower of Slane, an', bedad,
    It would pass for a round tower, only it's square!

The taste of her, ordherin' a needle of granite!
    Begorra, the sight of it sthrikes me quite dumb!
An' look at the quare sort of figures upon it;
    I wondher can these be the thracks of her thumb!

I once was astonished to hear of the faste
    Cleopathera made upon pearls; but now
I declare, I would not be surprised in the laste
    If ye told me the woman had swallowed a cow!

It's aisy to see why bould Cæsar should quail
    In her presence, an' meekly submit to her rule;

Wid a weapon like that in her fist I'll go bail
   She could frighten the sowl out of big Finn MacCool!

But, Lord, what poor pigmies the women are now,
   Compared with the monsthers they must have been then!
Whin the darlin's in those days would kick up a row,
   Holy smoke, but it must have been hot for the men!

Just think how a chap that goes courtin' would start
   If his girl was to prod him wid that in the shins!
I have often seen needles, but bouldly assart
   That the needle in front of me there takes the pins!

O, sweet Cleopathera! I'm sorry you're dead;
   An' whin lavin' this wondherful needle behind
Had ye thought of bequathin' a spool of your thread
   An' yer thimble an' scissors, it would have been kind.

But pace to your ashes, ye plague of great men,
   Yer strength is departed, yer glory is past;
Ye'll never wield sceptre or needle again,
   An' a poor little asp did yer bizzness at last!

                    Cormac O'Leary.

THE ORIGIN OF IRELAND

With due condescension, I'd call your attention
   To what I shall mention of Erin so green,
And without hesitation I will show how that nation
   Became of creation the gem and the queen.

'Twas early one morning, without any warning,
   That Vanus was born in the beautiful say,
And by the same token, and sure 'twas provoking,
   Her pinions were soaking and wouldn't give play.

Old Neptune, who knew her, began to pursue her,
   In order to woo her—the wicked old Jew—
And almost had caught her atop of the water—
   Great Jupiter's daughter!—which never would do.

But Jove, the great janius, looked down and saw Vanus,
And Neptune so heinous pursuing her wild,
And he spoke out in thunder, he'd rend him asunder—
And sure 'twas no wonder—for tazing his child.

A star that was flying hard by him espying,
He caught with small trying, and down let it snap;
It fell quick as winking, on Neptune a-sinking,
And gave him, I'm thinking, a bit of a rap.

That star it was dry land, both low land and high land,
And formed a sweet island, the land of my birth;
Thus plain is the story, that sent down from glory,
Old Erin asthore as the gem of the earth!

Upon Erin nately jumped Vanus so stately,
But fainted, kase lately so hard she was pressed—
Which much did bewilder, but ere it had killed her
Her father distilled her a drop of the best.

That sup was victorious, it made her feel glorious—
A little uproarious, I fear it might prove—
So how can you blame us that Ireland's so famous
For drinking and beauty, for fighting and love?

Unknown.

AS TO THE WEATHER

I remember, I remember,
　　Ere my childhood flitted by,
It was cold then in December,
　　And was warmer in July.
In the winter there were freezings—
　　In the summer there were thaws;
But the weather isn't now at all
　　Like what it used to was!

Unknown.

THE TWINS

In form and feature, face and limb,
   I grew so like my brother,
That folks got taking me for him,
   And each for one another.
It puzzled all our kith and kin,
   It reach'd an awful pitch;
For one of us was born a twin,
   Yet not a soul knew which.

One day (to make the matter worse),
   Before our names were fix'd,
As we were being wash'd by nurse
   We got completely mix'd;
And thus, you see, by Fate's decree,
   (Or rather nurse's whim),
My brother John got christen'd *me,*
   And I got christen'd *him.*

This fatal likeness even dogg'd
   My footsteps when at school,
And I was always getting flogg'd,
   For John turned out a fool.
I put this question hopelessly
   To every one I knew—
What *would* you do, if you were me,
   To prove that you were *you?*

Our close resemblance turn'd the tide
   Of my domestic life;
For somehow my intended bride
   Became my brother's wife.
In short, year after year the same
   Absurd mistakes went on;
And when I died—the neighbors came
   And buried brother John!

Henry S. Leigh.

II

THE ETERNAL FEMININE

HE AND SHE

WHEN I am dead you'll find it hard,
  Said he,
To ever find another man
  Like me.

What makes you think, as I suppose
  You do,
I'd ever want another man
  Like you?

Eugene Fitch Ware.

THE KISS

" WHAT other men have dared, I dare,"
  He said. " I'm daring, too:
And tho' they told me to beware,
  One kiss I'll take from you.

" Did I say one? Forgive me, dear;
  That was a grave mistake,
For when I've taken one, I fear,
  One hundred more I'll take.

" 'Tis sweet one kiss from you to win,
  But to stop there? Oh, no!
One kiss is only to begin;
  There is no end, you know."

The maiden rose from where she sat
And gently raised her head:
" No man has ever talked like that—
You may begin," she said.

Tom Masson

THE COURTIN'

GOD makes sech nights, all white an' still
Fur 'z you can look or listen,
Moonshine an' snow on field an' hill,
All silence an' all glisten.

Zekle crep' up quite unbeknown
An' peeked in thru' the winder,
An' there sot Huldy all alone,
'Ith no one nigh to hender.

A fireplace filled the room's one side
With half a cord o' wood in—
There warn't no stoves (tell comfort died)
To bake ye to a puddin'.

The wa'nut logs shot sparkles out
Towards the pootiest, bless her,
An' leetle flames danced all about
The chiny on the dresser.

Agin the chimbley crook-necks hung,
An' in amongst 'em rusted
The ole queen's-arm that Gran'ther Young
Fetched back f'om Concord busted.

The very room, coz she was in,
Seemed warm f'om floor to ceilin',
An' she looked full ez rosy agin
Ez the apples she was peelin'.

'Twas kin' o' kingdom-come to look
　　On sech a blessed cretur;
A dogrose blushin' to a brook
　　Ain't modester nor sweeter.

He was six foot o' man, A 1,
　　Clear grit an' human natur';
None couldn't quicker pitch a ton
　　Nor dror a furrer straighter.

He'd sparked it with full twenty gals,
　　He'd squired 'em, danced 'em, druv 'em,
Fust this one, an' then thet, by spells—
　　All is, he couldn't love 'em.

But long o' her his veins 'ould run
　　All crinkly like curled maple;
The side she breshed felt full o' sun
　　Ez a south slope in Ap'il.

She thought no v'ice hed sech a swing
　　Ez hisn in the choir;
My! when he made Ole Hunderd ring,
　　She *knowed* the Lord was nigher.

An' she'd blush scarlit, right in prayer,
　　When her new meetin'-bunnet
Felt somehow thru its crown a pair
　　O' blue eyes sot upun it.

Thet night, I tell ye, she looked *some!*
　　She seemed to 've gut a new soul,
For she felt sartin-sure he'd come,
　　Down to her very shoe-sole.

She heered a foot, an' knowed it tu,
　　A-raspin' on the scraper—
All ways to once her feelins flew
　　Like sparks in burnt-up paper.

He kin' o' l'itered on the mat,
    Some doubtfle o' the sekle;
His heart kep' goin' pity-pat,
    But hern went pity Zekle.

An' yit she gin her cheer a jerk
    Ez though she wished him furder,
An' on her apples kep' to work,
    Parin' away like murder.

" You want to see my Pa, I s'pose ? "
    " Wal . . . no . . . I come dasignin'—"
" To see my Ma ? She's sprinklin' clo'es
    Agin to-morrer's i'nin'."

To say why gals act so or so,
    Or don't, 'ould be presumin';
Mebbe to mean *yes* an' say *no*
    Comes nateral to women.

He stood a spell on one foot fust,
    Then stood a spell on t'other,
An' on which one he felt the wust
    He couldn't ha' told ye nuther.

Says he, " I'd better call agin ";
    Says she, " Think likely, Mister ";
Thet last word pricked him like a pin,
    An' . . . Wal, he up an' kist her.

When Ma bimeby upon 'em slips,
    Huldy sot pale ez ashes,
All kin' o' smily roun' the lips
    An' teary roun' the lashes.

For she was jes' the quiet kind
    Whose naturs never vary,
Like streams that keep a summer mind
    Snowhid in Jenooary.

The blood clost roun' her heart felt glued
　　Too tight for all expressin',
Tell mother see how metters stood,
　　An' gin 'em both her blessin'.

Then her red come back like the tide
　　Down to the Bay o' Fundy,
An' all I know is they was cried
　　In meetin' come nex' Sunday.

James Russell Lowell.

HIRAM HOVER

A BALLAD OF NEW ENGLAND LIFE

WHERE the Moosatockmaguntic
Pours its waters in the Skuntic,
　　Met, along the forest side
　　Hiram Hover, Huldah Hyde.

She, a maiden fair and dapper,
He, a red-haired, stalwart trapper,
　　Hunting beaver, mink, and skunk
　　In the woodlands of Squeedunk.

She, Pentucket's pensive daughter,
Walked beside the Skuntic water
　　Gathering, in her apron wet,
　　Snake-root, mint, and bouncing-bet.

" Why," he murmured, loth to leave her,
" Gather yarbs for chills and fever,
　　When a lovyer bold and true,
　　Only waits to gather you? "

" Go," she answered, " I'm not hasty,
I prefer a man more tasty;
　　Leastways, one to please me well
　　Should not have a beasty smell."

" Haughty Huldah ! " Hiram answered,
" Mind and heart alike are cancered;
    Jest look here! these peltries give
    Cash, wherefrom a pair may live.

" I, you think, am but a vagrant,
Trapping beasts by no means fragrant;
    Yet, I'm sure it's worth a thank—
    I've a handsome sum in bank."

Turned and vanished Hiram Hover,
And, before the year was over,
    Huldah, with the yarbs she sold,
    Bought a cape, against the cold.

Black and thick the furry cape was,
Of a stylish cut the shape was;
    And the girls, in all the town,
    Envied Huldah up and down.

Then at last, one winter morning,
Hiram came without a warning.
    " Either," said he, " you are blind,
    Huldah, or you've changed your mind.

" Me you snub for trapping varmints,
Yet you take the skins for garments;
    Since you wear the skunk and mink,
    There's no harm in me, I think."

" Well," said she, " we will not quarrel,
Hiram; I accept the moral,
    Now the fashion's so I guess
    I can't hardly do no less."

Thus the trouble all was over
Of the love of Hiram Hover.
    Thus he made sweet Huldah Hyde
    Huldah Hover as his bride.

Love employs, with equal favor,
Things of good and evil savor;
  That which first appeared to part,
  Warmed, at last, the maiden's heart.

Under one impartial banner,
Life, the hunter, Love the tanner,
  Draw, from every beast they snare,
  Comfort for a wedded pair!

                  Bayard Taylor.

BLOW ME EYES!

WHEN I was young and full o' pride,
  A-standin' on the grass
And gazin' o'er the water-side,
  I seen a fisher lass.
" O, fisher lass, be kind awhile,"
  I asks 'er quite unbid.
" Please look into me face and smile "–
  And, blow me eyes, she did!

O, blow me light and blow me blow,
I didn't think she'd charm me so—
  But, blow me eyes, she did!

She seemed so young and beautiful
  I *had* to speak perlite,
(The afternoon was long and dull,
  But she was short and bright).
" This ain't no place," I says, " to stand—
  Let's take a walk instid,
Each holdin' of the other's hand "—
  And, blow me eyes, she did!

O, blow me light and blow me blow,
I sort o' thunk she wouldn't go—
  But, blow me eyes, she did!

And as we walked along a lane
  With no one else to see,
Me heart was filled with sudden pain,
  And so I says to she:
" If you would have me actions speak
  The words what can't be hid,
You'd sort o' let me kiss yer cheek "—
  And, blow me eyes, she did!

O, blow me light and blow me blow,
How sweet she was I didn't know—
  But, blow me eyes, *she* did!

But pretty soon me shipmate Jim
  Came strollin' down the beach,
And she began a-oglin' him
  As pretty as a peach.
" O, fickle maid o' false intent,"
  Impulsively I chid,
" Why don't you go and wed that gent? "
  And, blow me eyes, she did!

O, blow me light and blow me blow,
I didn't think she'd treat me so—
  But, blow me eyes, she did!

Wallace Irwin.

FIRST LOVE

O MY earliest love, who, ere I number'd
  Ten sweet summers, made my bosom thrill!
Will a swallow—or a swift, or some bird—
  Fly to her and say, I love her still?

Say my life's a desert drear and arid,
  To its one green spot I aye recur:
Never, never—although three times married—
  Have I cared a jot for aught but her.

No, mine own! though early forced to leave you,
    Still my heart was there where first we met;
In those " Lodgings with an ample sea-view,"
    Which were, forty years ago, " To Let."

There I saw her first, our landlord's oldest
    Little daughter. On a thing so fair
Thou, O Sun,—who (so they say) beholdest
    Everything,—hast gazed, I tell thee, ne'er.

There she sat—so near me, yet remoter
    Than a star—a blue-eyed, bashful imp:
On her lap she held a happy bloater,
    'Twixt her lips a yet more happy shrimp.

And I loved her, and our troth we plighted
    On the morrow by the shingly shore:
In a fortnight to be disunited
    By a bitter fate forevermore.

O my own, my beautiful, my blue-eyed!
    To be young once more, and bite my thumb
At the world and all its cares with you, I'd
    Give no inconsiderable sum.

Hand in hand we tramp'd the golden seaweed,
    Soon as o'er the gray cliff peep'd the dawn:
Side by side, when came the hour for tea, we'd
    Crunch the mottled shrimp and hairy prawn:—

Has she wedded some gigantic shrimper,
    That sweet mite with whom I loved to play?
Is she girt with babes that whine and whimper,
    That bright being who was always gay?

Yes—she has at least a dozen wee things!
    Yes—I see her darning corduroys,
Scouring floors, and setting out the tea-things,
    For a howling herd of hungry boys,

In a home that reeks of tar and sperm-oil!
But at intervals she thinks, I know,
Of those days which we, afar from turmoil,
Spent together forty years ago.

O my earliest love, still unforgotten,
With your downcast eyes of dreamy blue!
Never, somehow, could I seem to cotton
To another as I did to you!

Charles Stuart Calverley.

WHAT IS A WOMAN LIKE?

A WOMAN is like to—but stay—
What a woman is like, who can say?
There is no living with or without one.
Love bites like a fly,
Now an ear, now an eye,
Buzz, buzz, always buzzing about one.
When she's tender and kind
She is like to my mind,
(And Fanny was so, I remember).
She's like to—Oh, dear!
She's as good, very near,
As a ripe, melting peach in September.
If she laugh, and she chat,
Play, joke, and all that,
And with smiles and good humor she meet me,
She's like a rich dish
Of venison or fish,
That cries from the table, Come eat me!
But she'll plague you and vex you,
Distract and perplex you;
False-hearted and ranging,
Unsettled and changing,
What then do you think, she is like?
Like sand? Like a rock?
Like a wheel? Like a clock?
Ay, a clock that is always at strike.

Her head's like the island folks tell on,
Which nothing but monkeys can dwell on;
Her heart's like a lemon—so nice
She carves for each lover a slice;
  In truth she's to me,
  Like the wind, like the sea,
Whose raging will hearken to no man;
  Like a mill, like a pill,
  Like a flail, like a whale,
  Like an ass, like a glass
Whose image is constant to no man;
  Like a shower, like a flower,
  Like a fly, like a pie,
  Like a pea, like a flea,
  Like a thief, like—in brief,
She's like nothing on earth—but a woman!

Unknown.

MIS' SMITH

All day she hurried to get through,
The same as lots of wimmin do;
Sometimes at night her husban' said,
" Ma, ain't you goin' to come to bed?"
And then she'd kinder give a hitch,
And pause half way between a stitch,
And sorter sigh, and say that she
    Was ready as she'd ever be,
    She reckoned.

And so the years went one by one,
An' somehow she was never done;
An' when the angel said, as how
" Mis' Smith, it's time you rested now,"
She sorter raised her eyes to look
A second, as a stitch she took;
" All right, I'm comin' now," says she,
" I'm ready as I'll ever be,
    I reckon."

Albert Bigelow Paine.

TRIOLET

"I LOVE you, my lord!"
    Was all that she said—
What a dissonant chord,
    "I love you, my lord!"
Ah! how I abhorrèd
    That sarcastic maid!—
"*I* love you? My *Lord!*"
    Was all that she said.

Paul T. Gilbert.

BESSIE BROWN, M.D.

'TWAS April when she came to town;
    The birds had come; the bees were swarming.
Her name, she said, was Doctor Brown;
    I saw at once that she was charming.
She took a cottage tinted green,
    Where dewy roses loved to mingle;
And on the door, next day, was seen
    A dainty little shingle.

Her hair was like an amber wreath;
    Her hat was darker, to enhance it.
The violet eyes that glowed beneath
    Were brighter than her keenest lancet,
The beauties of her glove and gown
    The sweetest rhyme would fail to utter.
Ere she had been a day in town
    The town was in a flutter.

The gallants viewed her feet and hands,
    And swore they never saw such wee things;
The gossips met in purring bands,
    And tore her piecemeal o'er the tea-things.
The former drank the Doctor's health
    With clinking cups, the gay carousers;
The latter watched her door by stealth,
    Just like so many mousers.

But Doctor Bessie went her way,
　　Unmindful of the spiteful cronies,
And drove her buggy every day
　　Behind a dashing pair of ponies.
Her flower-like face so bright she bore
　　I hoped that time might never wilt her.
The way she tripped across the floor
　　　　Was better than a philter.

Her patients thronged the village street;
　　Her snowy slate was always quite full.
Some said her bitters tasted sweet,
　　And some pronounced her pills delightful.
'Twas strange—I knew not what it meant—
　　She seemed a nymph from Eldorado;
Where'er she came, where'er she went,
　　　　Grief lost its gloomy shadow.

Like all the rest I, too, grew ill;
　　My aching heart there was no quelling.
I tremble at my doctor's bill—
　　And lo! the items still are swelling.
The drugs I've drunk you'd weep to hear!
　　They've quite enriched the fair concocter,
And I'm a ruined man, I fear,
　　　　Unless—I wed the Doctor!

　　　　　　　　　　Samuel Minturn Peck.

A SKETCH FROM THE LIFE

Its eyes are gray;
　　　　Its hair is either brown
　　　　　　Or black;
And, strange to say,
　　　　Its dresses button down
　　　　　　The back!

It wears a plume
　　　　That loves to frisk around
　　　　　　My ear.

It crowds the room
　　With cushions in a mound
　　　And queer

Old rugs and lamps
　　In corners à la Turque
　　　And things.
It steals my stamps,
　　And when I want to work
　　　It sings!

It rides and skates—
　　But then it comes and fills
　　　My walls
With plaques and plates
　　And keeps me paying bills
　　　And calls.

It's firm; and if
　　I should my many woes
　　　Deplore,
'Twould only sniff
　　And perk its little nose
　　　Some more.

It's bright, though small;
　　Its name, you may have guessed,
　　　Is " Wife."
But, after all,
　　It gives a wondrous zest
　　　To life!

Arthur Guiterman.

MINGUILLO'S KISS

SINCE for kissing thee, Minguillo,
　　Mother's ever scolding me,
Give me swiftly back, thou dear one,
　　Give the kiss I gave to thee.
Give me back the kiss—that one, now;

Let my mother scold no more;
Let us tell her all is o'er:
What was done is all undone now.
Yes, it will be wise, Minguillo,
My fond kiss to give to me;
Give me swiftly back, thou dear one,
Give the kiss I gave to thee.
Give me back the kiss, for mother
Is impatient—prithee, do!
For that one thou shalt have two:
Give me that, and take another.
Yes, then will they be contented,
Then can't they complain of me;
Give me swiftly back, thou dear one,
Give the kiss I gave to thee.

Unknown.

A KISS IN THE RAIN

ONE stormy morn I chanced to meet
A lassie in the town;
Her locks were like the ripened wheat,
Her laughing eyes were brown.
I watched her as she tripped along
Till madness filled my brain,
And then—and then—I know 'twas wrong—
I kissed her in the rain!

With rain-drops shining on her cheek,
Like dew-drops on a rose,
The little lassie strove to speak
My boldness to oppose;
She strove in vain, and quivering
Her fingers stole in mine;
And then the birds began to sing,
The sun began to shine.

Oh, let the clouds grow dark above,
My heart is light below;
'Tis always summer when we love,
However winds may blow;

And I'm as proud as any prince,
  All honors I disdain:
She says I am her *rain beau* since
  I kissed her in the rain.

Samuel Minturn Peck.

THE LOVE-KNOT

Tying her bonnet under her chin,
She tied her raven ringlets in;
But, not alone in the silken snare
Did she catch her lovely floating hair,
For, tying her bonnet under her chin,
She tied a young man's heart within.

They were strolling together up the hill,
Where the wind comes blowing merry and chill;
And it blew the curls, a frolicsome race,
All over the happy peach-coloured face,
Till, scolding and laughing, she tied them in,
Under her beautiful dimpled chin.

And it blew a colour bright as the bloom
Of the pinkest fuchsia's tossing plume,
All over the cheeks of the prettiest girl
That ever imprisoned a romping curl,
Or, in tying her bonnet under her chin,
Tied a young man's heart within.

Steeper and steeper grew the hill—
Madder, merrier, chillier still—
The western wind blew down and played
The wildest tricks with the little maid,
As, tying her bonnet under her chin,
She tied a young man's heart within.

Oh, western wind, do you think it was fair
To play such tricks with her floating hair?—
To gladly, gleefully do your best
To blow her against the young man's breast,

Where he as gladly folded her in,
And kissed her mouth and dimpled chin?

Oh, Ellery Vane! you little thought
An hour ago, when you besought
This country lass to walk with you,
After the sun had dried the dew,
What perilous danger you'd be in
As she tied her bonnet under her chin.

Nora Perry.

OVER THE WAY

Over the way, over the way,
I've seen a head that's fair and gray;
I've seen kind eyes not new to tears,
A form of grace, though full of years—
    Her fifty summers have left no flaw—
And I, a youth of twenty-three,
So love this lady, fair to see,
    I want her for my mother-in-law!

Over the way, over the way,
I've seen her with the children play;
I've seen her with a royal grace
Before the mirror adjust her lace;
    A kinder woman none ever saw;
God bless and cheer her onward path,
And bless all treasures that she hath,
    And let her be my mother-in-law!

Over the way, over the way,
I think I'll venture, dear, some day
(If you will lend a helping hand,
And sanctify the scheme I've planned);
    I'll kneel in loving, reverent awe
Down at the lady's feet, and say:
"I've loved your daughter many a day—
    Please won't you be my mother-in-law?"

Mary Mapes Dodge.

CHORUS OF WOMEN

FROM THE " THESMOPHORIAZUSÆ."

They're always abusing the women,
    As a terrible plague to men;
They say we're the root of all evil,
    And repeat it again and again—
Of war, and quarrels, and bloodshed,
    All mischief, be what it may.
And pray, then, why do you marry us,
    If we're all the plagues you say?
And why do you take such care of us,
    And keep us so safe at home,
And are never easy a moment
    If ever we chance to roam?
When you ought to be thanking Heaven
    That your plague is out of the way,
You all keep fussing and fretting—
    "Where is my Plague to-day?"
If a Plague peeps out of the window,
    Up go the eyes of men;
If she hides, then they all keep staring
    Until she looks out again.

Aristophanes.

THE WIDOW MALONE

Did you hear of the Widow Malone
                O hone!
Who lived in the town of Athlone
                Alone?
O, she melted the hearts
Of the swains in them parts;
So lovely the Widow Malone,
                O hone!
So lovely the Widow Malone.

Of lovers she had a full score
                    Or more;
And fortunes they all had galore
                    In store;
From the minister down
To the clerk of the Crown,
All were courting the Widow Malone
                    O hone!
All were courting the Widow Malone.

But so modest was Mrs. Malone,
                    'Twas known,
That no one could see her alone,
                    O hone!
Let them ogle and sigh,
They could ne'er catch her eye;
So bashful the Widow Malone,
                    O hone!
So bashful the Widow Malone.

Till one Mister O'Brien from Clare,
                    How quare!
'Tis little for blushing they care
                    Down there;
Put his arm round her waist,
Gave ten kisses at laste,
And says he, " You're my Molly Malone,
                    My own."
Says he, " You're my Molly Malone."

And the widow they all thought so shy—
                    My eye!
Never thought of a simper or sigh;
                    For why?
" O Lucius," said she,
" Since you've now made so free,
You may marry your Mary Malone,
                    Your own;
You may marry your Mary Malone."

There's a moral contained in my song,
        Not wrong;
And one comfort it's not very long,
        But strong:—
If for widows you die,
Learn to kiss—not to sigh,
For they're all like sweet Mistress Malone!
        O hone!
O they're all like sweet Mistress Malone!

Charles Lever.

THE SMACK IN SCHOOL

A DISTRICT school, not far away,
Mid Berkshire's hills, one winter's day,
Was humming with its wonted noise
Of threescore mingled girls and boys;
Some few upon their tasks intent,
But more on furtive mischief bent.
The while the master's downward look
Was fastened on a copy-book;
When suddenly, behind his back,
Rose sharp and clear a rousing smack!
As 'twere a battery of bliss
Let off in one tremendous kiss!
" What's that? " the startled master cries;
" That, thir," a little imp replies,
" Wath William Willith, if you pleathe,—
I thaw him kith Thuthanna Peathe! "
With frown to make a statue thrill,
The master thundered, " Hither, Will! "
Like wretch o'ertaken in his track,
With stolen chattels on his back,
Will hung his head in fear and shame,
And to the awful presence came,—
A great, green, bashful simpleton,
The butt of all good-natured fun.
With smile suppressed, and birch upraised,
The thunderer faltered,—" I'm amazed
That you, my biggest pupil, should

Be guilty of an act so rude!
Before the whole set school to boot—
What evil genius put you to't?"
" 'Twas she herself, sir," sobbed the lad,
" I did not mean to be so bad;
But when Susannah shook her curls,
And whispered, I was 'fraid of girls
And dursn't kiss a baby's doll,
I couldn't stand it, sir, at all,
But up and kissed her on the spot!
I know—boo—hoo—I ought to not,
But, somehow, from her looks—boo—hoo—
I thought she kind o' wished me to!"

William Pitt Palmer.

'SPÄCIALLY JIM

I wus mighty good-lookin' when I wus young—
   Peert an' black-eyed an' slim,
With fellers a-courtin' me Sunday nights,
      'Späcially Jim.

The likeliest one of 'em all wus he,
   Chipper an' han'som' an' trim;
But I toss'd up my head, an' made fun o' the crowd,
      'Späcially Jim.

I said I hadn't no 'pinion o' men
   An' I wouldn't take stock in him!
But they kep' up a-comin' in spite o' my talk,
      'Späcially Jim.

I got so tired o' havin' 'em roun'
   ('Späcially Jim!),
I made up my mind I'd settle down
   An' take up with him;

So we was married one Sunday in church,
   'Twas crowded full to the brim,
'Twas the only way to get rid of 'em all,
      'Späcially Jim.

Bessie Morgan.

KITTY OF COLERAINE

As beautiful Kitty one morning was tripping,
  With a pitcher of milk from the fair of Coleraine,
When she saw me she stumbled, the pitcher it tumbled,
  And all the sweet buttermilk water'd the plain.

" O, what shall I do now, 'twas looking at you now,
  Sure, sure, such a pitcher I'll ne'er meet again!
'Twas the pride of my dairy: O Barney M'Cleary!
  You're sent as a plague to the girls of Coleraine."

1 sat down beside her,—and gently did chide her,
  That such a misfortune should give her such pain;
A kiss then I gave her,—and ere I did leave her,
  She vow'd for such pleasure she'd break it again.

'Twas hay-making season, I can't tell the reason,
  Misfortunes will never come single,—that's plain,
For, very soon after poor Kitty's disaster,
  The devil a pitcher was whole in Coleraine.

Edward Lysaght.

WHY DON'T THE MEN PROPOSE?

WHY don't the men propose, mamma?
  Why don't the men propose?
Each seems just coming to the point,
  And then away he goes;
It is no fault of yours, mamma,
  That everybody knows;
You *fête* the finest men in town,
  Yet, oh! they won't propose.

I'm sure I've done my best, mamma,
  To make a proper match;
For coronets and eldest sons,
  I'm ever on the watch;

I've hopes when some *distingué* beau
  A glance upon me throws;
But though he'll dance and smile and flirt,
  Alas! he won't propose.

I've tried to win by languishing,
  And dressing like a blue;
I've bought big books and talked of them
  As if I'd read them through!
With hair cropp'd like a man I've felt
  The heads of all the beaux;
But Spurzheim could not touch their hearts,
  And oh! they won't propose.

I threw aside the books, and thought
  That ignorance was bliss;
I felt convinced that men preferred
  A simple sort of Miss;
And so I lisped out nought beyond
  Plain "yesses" or plain "noes,"
And wore a sweet unmeaning smile;
  Yet, oh! they won't propose.

Last night at Lady Ramble's rout
  I heard Sir Henry Gale
Exclaim, "Now I *propose* again——"
  I started, turning pale;
I really thought my time was come,
  I blushed like any rose;
But oh! I found 'twas only at
  Ecarté he'd propose.

And what is to be done, mamma?
  Oh, what is to be done?
I really have no time to lose,
  For I am thirty-one;
At balls I am too often left
  Where spinsters sit in rows;
Why don't the men propose, mamma?
  Why *won't* the men propose?

                    Thomas Haynes Bayly.

A PIN

OH, I know a certain woman who is reckoned with the
good,
But she fills me with more terror than a raging lion
would.
The little chills run up and down my spine when'er we
meet,
Though she seems a gentle creature and she's very trim
and neat.

And she has a thousand virtues and not one acknowledged
sin,
But she is the sort of person you could liken to a pin,
And she pricks you, and she sticks you, in a way that
can't be said—
When you seek for what has hurt you, why, you cannot
find the head.

But she fills you with discomfort and exasperating pain—
If anybody asks you why, you really can't explain.
A pin is such a tiny thing,—of that there is no doubt,—
Yet when it's sticking in your flesh, you're wretched till
it's out!

She is wonderfully observing—when she meets a pretty girl
She is always sure to tell her if her " bang " is out of curl.
And she is so sympathetic: to a friend, who's much admired,
She is often heard remarking, " Dear, you look so worn and
tired! "

And she is a careful critic; for on yesterday she eyed
The new dress I was airing with a woman's natural pride,
And she said, " Oh, how becoming! " and then softly added,
" It
Is really a misfortune that the basque is such a fit."

Then she said, " If you had heard me yestereve, I'm sure,
my friend,
You would say I am a champion who knows how to defend."

And she left me with the feeling—most unpleasant, I aver—
That the whole world would despise me if it had not been for
　　her.

Whenever I encounter her, in such a nameless way
She gives me the impression I am at my worst that day,
And the hat that was imported (and that cost me half a
　　sonnet)
With just one glance from her round eyes becomes a Bowery
　　bonnet.

She is always bright and smiling, sharp and shining for
　　a thrust—
Use does not seem to blunt her point, not does she gather
　　rust—
Oh! I wish some hapless specimen of mankind would be-
　　gin
To tidy up the world for me, by picking up this pin.

Ella Wheeler Wilcox.

THE WHISTLER

" You have heard," said a youth to his sweetheart, who
　　stood
　　While he sat on a corn-sheaf, at daylight's decline—
" You have heard of the Danish boy's whistle of wood;
　　I wish that the Danish boy's whistle were mine ! "

" And what would you do with it?—tell me," she said,
　　While an arch smile play'd over her beautiful face.
" I would blow it," he answered, " and then my fair maid
　　Would fly to my side, and would there take her place."

" Is that all you wish for? Why, that may be yours
　　Without any magic," the fair maiden cried;
" A favour so slight one's good-nature secures; "
　　And she playfully seated herself by his side.

" I would blow it again," said the youth; " and the charm
　　Would work so, that not even modesty's check
　　Would be able to keep from my neck your white arm."
　　She smiled, and she laid her white arm round his
　　neck.

"Yet once more I would blow, and the music divine
    Would bring me a third time an exquisite bliss
You would lay your fair cheek to this brown one of mine
    And your lips, stealing past it, would give me a kiss."

The maiden laughed out in her innocent glee—
    "What a fool of yourself with the whistle you'd make!
For only consider how silly 'twould be
    To sit there and whistle for what you might take."

                                        Unknown.

THE CLOUD

AN IDYLL OF THE WESTERN FRONT

I

SCENE: *A wayside shrine in France.*
PERSONS: Celeste, Pierre, a Cloud.

CELESTE (*gazing at the solitary white Cloud*):
    I wonder what your thoughts are, little Cloud,
    Up in the sky, so lonely and so proud!
CLOUD: Not proud, dear maiden; lonely, if you will.
    Long have I watched you, sitting there so still
    Before that little shrine beside the way,
    And wondered where your thoughts might be astray;
    Your knitting lying idle on your knees,
    And worse than idle—like Penelope's,
    Working its own undoing!
CELESTE (*picks up her knitting*): Who was she?
    Saints! What a knot!—Who was Penelope?
    What happened to *her* knitting? Tell me, Cloud!
CLOUD: She was a Queen; she wove her husband's shroud.
CELESTE (*drops the knitting*).
    His shroud!
CLOUD: There, there! 'Twas only an excuse
    To put her lovers off, a wifely ruse,
    Bidding them bide till it was finished, she
    Each night the web unravelled secretly.
CELESTE: He came home safe?

CLOUD: If I remember right,
    It was the lovers needed shrouds that night!
    It is an old, old tale. I heard it through
    A Wind whose ancestor it was that blew
    Ulysses' ship across the purple sea
    Back to his people and Penelope.
    We Clouds pick up strange tales, as far and wide
    And to and fro above the world we ride,
    Across uncharted seas, upon the swell
    Of viewless waves and tides invisible,
    Freighted with friendly flood or forkèd flame,
    Knowing not whither bound nor whence we came;
    Now drifting lonely, now a company
    Of pond'rous galleons—

CELESTE: Oft-times I see
    A Cloud, as by some playful fancy stirred,
    Take likeness of a monstrous beast or bird
    Or some fantastic fish, as though 'twere clay
    Moulded by unseen hands.

CLOUD: Then tell me, pray,
    What I resemble now!

CELESTE: I scarcely know.
    But had you asked a little while ago,
    I should have said a camel; then your hump
    Dissolved, and you became a gosling plump,
    Downy and white and warm—

CLOUD: What! *Warm,* up here?
    Ten thousand feet above the earth!

CELESTE: Oh dear!
    What am I thinking of! Of course I know
    How cold it is. Pierre has told me so
    A thousand times.

CLOUD: And who is this Pierre
    That tells you all the secrets of the air?
    How came he to such frigid heights to soar?

CELESTE: Pierre's my—He is in the Flying Corps.

CLOUD: Ah, now I understand! And he's away?

CELESTE: He left at dawn, where for he would not say,
    Telling me only 'twas a bombing raid
    Somewhere—My God! What's that?

CLOUD: What, little maid?

CELESTE (*pointing*): That—over there—beyond the wooded
crest!

CLOUD: Only a skylark dropping to her nest;
Her mate is hov'ring somewhere near. I heard
His tremulous song of love—

CELESTE: That was no bird!
(*Drops upon her knees.*)
O Mary! Blessed Mother! Hear my prayer!
That one that fell—grant it was not Pierre!
Here is the cross my mother gave me—I
Will burn the longest candle it will buy!

CLOUD Courage, my child! Your prayer will not be
vain!
Who guards the lark, will guide your lover's plane.
The West Wind's calling. I must go!—Hark! There
He sings again! *Le bon Dieu garde, ma chère!*

II

PIERRE: I made a perfect landing over there
Behind the church—

CELESTE: The Virgin heard my prayer!
Now I must burn the candle that I vowed—

PIERRE: Then 'twas our Blessed Lady sent that Cloud
That saved me when the Boche came up behind.
I made a lightning turn, only to find
The Boche on top of me. It seemed a kind
Of miracle to see that Cloud—I swear
A moment past the sky was everywhere
As clear as clear; there was no Cloud in sight.
It looked to me, floating there calm and white.
Like a great mother hen, and I a chick.
She seemed to call me, and I scurried quick
Behind her wing. That spoiled the Boche's game,
And gave me time to turn and take good aim.
I emptied my last drum, and saw him drop
Ten thousand feet in flames—

CELESTE (*shuddering*):   Stop! Pierre, stop!
Maybe a girl is waiting for him too—

PIERRE: 'Twas either him or me—

CELESTE: Thank God, not you!

PIERRE (*pointing to the church*): Come, let us burn the
candle that you vowed.

CELESTE: Two candles!

PIERRE: Who's the other for?

CELESTE: The Cloud!

Oliver Herford.

CONSTANCY

"You gave me the key of your heart, my love;
    Then why do you make me knock?"
"Oh, that was yesterday, Saints above!
    And last night—I changed the lock!"

John Boyle O'Reilly.

AIN'T IT AWFUL, MABEL?

It worries me to beat the band
To hear folks say our lives is grand;
Wish they'd try some one-night stand.
    Ain't it awful, Mabel?

Nothin' ever seems to suit—
The manager's an awful brute;
Spend our lives jest lookin' cute.
    Ain't it awful, Mabel?

Met a boy last Tuesday night,
Was spendin' money left and right—
Me, gee! I couldn't eat a bite!
    Ain't it awful, Mabel?

Then I met another guy—
Hungry! well, I thought I'd die!
But I couldn't make him buy.
    Ain't it awful, Mabel?

Lots of men has called me dear,
Said without me life was drear,
But men is all so unsincere!
    Ain't it awful, Mabel?

I tell you, life is mighty hard,
I've had proposals by the yard—
Some of 'em would 'a had me starred.
    Ain't it awful, Mabel?

Remember that sealskin sacque of mine?
When I got it, look'd awful fine—
I found out it was a shine.
    Ain't it awful, Mabel?

Prima donna's sore on me;
My roses had her up a tree—
I jest told her to " twenty-three."
    Ain't it awful, Mabel?

My dear, she went right out and wired
The New York office to have me " fired ";
But say! 'twas the author had me hired.
    Ain't it awful, Mabel?

I think hotels is awful mean,
Jim and me put out of room sixteen—
An' we was only readin' Laura Jean.
    Ain't it awful, Mabel?

The way folks talk about us too;
For the smallest thing we do—
'Nuff to make a girl feel blue.
    Ain't it awful, Mabel?

My Gawd! is that the overture?
I never will be on, I'm sure—
The things us actresses endure,
    Ain't it awful, Mabel?

John Edward Hazzard.

WING TEE WEE

Oh, Wing Tee Wee
Was a sweet Chinee,
And she lived in the town of Tac.
Her eyes were blue,
And her curling queue
Hung dangling down her back;
And she fell in love with gay Win Sil
When he wrote his name on a laundry bill.

And, oh, Tim Told
Was a pirate bold,
And he sailed in a Chinese junk;
And he loved, ah me!
Sweet Wing Tee Wee,
But his valiant heart had sunk;
So he drowned his blues in fickle fizz,
And vowed the maid would yet be his.

So bold Tim Told
Showed all his gold
To the maid in the town of Tac;
And sweet Wing Wee
Eloped to sea,
And nevermore came back;
For in far Chinee the maids are fair,
And the maids are false,—as everywhere.

J. P. Denison.

PHYLLIS LEE

Beside a Primrose 'broider'd Rill
Sat Phyllis Lee in Silken Dress
Whilst Lucius limn'd with loving skill
Her likeness, as a Shepherdess.
Yet tho' he strove with loving skill
His Brush refused to work his Will.

"Dear Maid, unless you close your Eyes
    I cannot paint to-day," he said;
"Their Brightness shames the very Skies
    And turns their Turquoise into Lead."
Quoth Phyllis, then, "To save the Skies
And speed your Brush, I'll shut my Eyes."

Now when her Eyes were closed, the Dear,
    Not dreaming of such Treachery,
Felt a Soft Whisper in her Ear,
    "Without the Light, how can one See?"
"If you are *sure* that none can see
I'll keep them shut," said Phyllis Lee.

Oliver Herford.

THE SORROWS OF WERTHER

WERTHER had a love for Charlotte
    Such as words could never utter;
Would you know how first he met her?
    She was cutting bread and butter.

Charlotte was a married lady,
    And a moral man was Werther,
And for all the wealth of Indies,
    Would do nothing for to hurt her.

So he sigh'd and pined and ogled,
    And his passion boil'd and bubbled,
Till he blew his silly brains out,
    And no more was by it troubled.

Charlotte, having seen his body
    Borne before her on a shutter,
Like a well-conducted person,
    Went on cutting bread and butter.

W. M. Thackeray.

THE UNATTAINABLE

Tom's album was filled with the pictures of belles
   Who had captured his manly heart,
From the fairy who danced for the front-row swells
   To the maiden who tooled her cart;
But one face as fair as a cloudless dawn
   Caught my eye, and I said, " Who's this? "
" Oh, that," he replied, with a skilful yawn,
   " Is the girl I couldn't kiss."

Her face was the best in the book, no doubt,
   But I hastily turned the leaf,
For my friend had let his cigar go out,
   And I knew I had bared his grief:
For caresses we win and smiles we gain
   Yield only a transient bliss,
And we're all of us prone to sigh in vain
   For " the girl we couldn't kiss."

Harry Romaine.

RORY O'MORE; OR, GOOD OMENS

Young Rory O'More, courted Kathleen Bawn,
He was bold as a hawk,—she as soft as the dawn;
He wish'd in his heart pretty Kathleen to please,
And he thought the best way to do that was to tease.

" Now, Rory, be aisy," sweet Kathleen would cry,
(Reproof on her lip, but a smile in her eye),
" With your tricks I don't know, in troth, what I'm about,
Faith you've teased till I've put on my cloak inside out."
" Oh, jewel," says Rory, " that same is the way
You've thrated my heart for this many a day;
And 'tis plaz'd that I am, and why not to be sure?
For 'tis all for good luck," says bold Rory O'More.

" Indeed, then," says Kathleen, " don't think of the like,
For I half gave a promise to soothering Mike;
The ground that I walk on he loves, I'll be bound."
" Faith," says Rory, " I'd rather love you than the ground."

"Now, Rory, I'll cry if you don't let me go;
Sure I drame ev'ry night that I'm hating you so!"
"Oh," says Rory, "that same I'm delighted to hear,
For drames always go by conthraries, my dear;
Oh! jewel, keep draming that same till you die,
And bright morning will give dirty night the black lie!
And 'tis plaz'd that I am, and why not, to be sure?
Since 'tis all for good luck," says bold Rory O'More.

"Arrah, Kathleen, my darlint, you've teas'd me enough,
Sure I've thrash'd for your sake Dinny Grimes and Jim
     Duff;
And I've made myself, drinking your health, quite a baste,
So I think, after that, I may talk to the praste."
Then Rory, the rogue, stole his arm around her neck,
So soft and so white, without freckle or speck,
And he look'd in her eyes that were beaming with light,
And he kiss'd her sweet lips;—don't you think he was
     right?
"Now, Rory, leave off, sir; you'll hug me no more,
That's eight times to-day you have kiss'd me before."
"Then here goes another," says he, "to make sure,
For there's luck in odd numbers," says Rory O'More.

                                        Samuel Lover.

A DIALOGUE FROM PLATO

"Le temps le mieux employé est celui qu' on perd."
                              —CLAUDE TILLIER.

I'D read three hours. Both notes and text
     Were fast a mist becoming;
In bounced a vagrant bee, perplexed,
     And filled the room with humming.

Then out. The casement's leafage sways,
     And, parted light, discloses
Miss Di., with hat and book,—a maze
     Of muslin mixed with roses.

" You're reading Greek ? "   " I am—and you ? "
   " O, mine's a mere romancer ! "
" So Plato is."   " Then read him—do;
   And I'll read mine in answer."

I read.   " My Plato (Plato, too,—
   That wisdom thus should harden !)
Declares 'blue eyes look doubly blue
   Beneath a Dolly Varden.' "

She smiled.   " My book in turn avers
   (No author's name is stated)
That sometimes those Philosophers
   Are sadly mis-translated."

" But hear,—the next's in stronger style :
   The Cynic School asserted
That two red lips which part and smile
   May not be controverted ! "

She smiled once more—" My book, I find,
   Observes some modern doctors
Would make the Cynics out a kind
   Of album-verse concoctors."

Then I—" Why not ? ' Ephesian law,
   No less than time's tradition,
Enjoined fair speech on all who saw
   Diana's apparition.' "

She blushed—this time.   " If Plato's page
   No wiser precept teaches,
Then I'd renounce that doubtful sage,
   And walk to Burnham-beeches."

" Agreed," I said.   " For Socrates
   (I find he too is talking)
Thinks Learning can't remain at ease
   While Beauty goes a-walking."

She read no more. I leapt the sill:
    The sequel's scarce essential—
Nay, more than this, I hold it still
    Profoundly confidential.

Austin Dobson.

DORA VERSUS ROSE

" The case is proceeding."

FROM the tragic-est novels at Mudie's—
    At least, on a practical plan—
To the tales of mere Hodges and Judys,
    One love is enough for a man.
But no case that I ever yet met is
    Like mine: I am equally fond
Of Rose, who a charming brunette is,
                And Dora, a blonde.

Each rivals the other in powers—
    Each waltzes, each warbles, each paints—
Miss Rose, chiefly tumble-down towers;
    Miss Do., perpendicular saints.
In short, to distinguish is folly;
    'Twixt the pair I am come to the pass
Of Macheath, between Lucy and Polly,—
                Or Buridan's ass.

If it happens that Rosa I've singled
    For a soft celebration in rhyme,
Then the ringlets of Dora get mingled
    Somehow with the tune and the time;
Or I painfully pen me a sonnet
    To an eyebrow intended for Do.'s,
And behold I am writing upon it
                The legend, " To Rose."

Or I try to draw Dora (my blotter
    Is all overscrawled with her head),
If I fancy at last that I've got her,
    It turns to her rival instead;

Or I find myself placidly adding
  To the rapturous tresses of Rose
Miss Dora's bud-mouth, and her madding
         Ineffable nose.

Was there ever so sad a dilemma?
  For Rose I would perish (pro tem.);
For Dora I'd willingly stem a—
  (Whatever might offer to stem);
But to make the invidious election,—
  To declare that on either one's side
I've a scruple,—a grain, more affection,
        I *cannot* decide.

And, as either so hopelessly nice is,
  My sole and my final resource
Is to wait some indefinite crisis,—
  Some feat of molecular force,
To solve me this riddle conducive
  By no means to peace or repose,
Since the issue can scarce be inclusive
        Of Dora *and* Rose.

(Afterthought)

But, perhaps, if a third (say a Nora),
  Not quite so delightful as Rose,—
Not wholly so charming as Dora,—
  Should appear, is it wrong to suppose,—
As the claims of the others are equal,—
  And flight—in the main—is the best,—
That I might . . . But no matter,—the sequel
        Is easily guessed.

                Austin Dobson.

TU QUOQUE

AN IDYLL IN THE CONSERVATORY

NELLIE

If I were you, when ladies at the play, Sir,
Beckon and nod, a melodrama through,
I would not turn abstractedly away, Sir,
If I were you!

FRANK

If I were you, when persons I affected,
Wait for three hours to take me down to Kew,
I would at least pretend I recollected,
If I were you!

NELLIE

If I were you, when ladies are so lavish,
Sir, as to keep me every waltz but two,
I would not dance with *odious* Miss M'Tavish,
If I were you!

FRANK

If I were you, who vow you cannot suffer
Whiff of the best,—the mildest " honey dew,"
I would not dance with smoke-consuming Puffer,
If I were you!

NELLIE

If I were you, I would not, Sir, be bitter,
Even to write the " Cynical Review ";—

FRANK

No, I should doubtless find flirtation fitter,
If I were you!

NELLIE

Really! You would? Why, Frank, you're quite delightful,—
Hot as Othello, and as black of hue;
Borrow my fan. I would not look so *frightful*,
If I were you!

FRANK

"It is the cause." I mean your chaperon is
Bringing some well-curled juvenile. Adieu!
I shall retire. I'd spare that poor Adonis,
    If I were you!

NELLIE

Go, if you will. At once! And by express, Sir!
Where shall it be? To China—or Peru?
Go. I should leave inquirers my address, Sir,
    If I were you!

FRANK

No—I remain. To stay and fight a duel
Seems, on the whole, the proper thing to do—
Ah, you are strong,—I would not then be cruel,
    If I were you!

NELLIE

One does not like one's feelings to be doubted,—

FRANK

One does not like one's friends to misconstrue,—

NELLIE

If I confess that I a wee-bit pouted?

FRANK

I should admit that I was *piqué,* too.

NELLIE

Ask me to dance. I'd say no more about it,
    If I were you!

[Waltz—*Exeunt.*]

Austin Dobson.

NOTHING TO WEAR

Miss Flora McFlimsey, of Madison Square,
Has made three separate journeys to Paris;
And her father assures me, each time she was there,
That she and her friend Mrs. Harris
(Not the lady whose name is so famous in history,
But plain Mrs. H., without romance or mystery)
Spent six consecutive weeks without stopping,
In one continuous round of shopping;—
Shopping alone, and shopping together,
At all hours of the day, and in all sorts of weather:
For all manner of things that a woman can put
On the crown of her head or the sole of her foot,
Or wrap round her shoulders, or fit round her waist,
Or that can be sewed on, or pinned on, or laced,
Or tied on with a string, or stitched on with a bow,
In front or behind, above or below;
For bonnets, mantillas, capes, collars, and shawls;
Dresses for breakfasts, and dinners, and balls;
Dresses to sit in, and stand in, and walk in,
Dresses to dance in, and flirt in, and talk in;
Dresses in which to do nothing at all;
Dresses for winter, spring, summer, and fall,—
All of them different in color and pattern,
Silk, muslin, and lace, crape, velvet, and satin,
Brocade, and broadcloth, and other material
Quite as expensive and much more ethereal:
In short, for all things that could ever be thought of,
Or milliner, modiste, or tradesman be bought of,
From ten-thousand-francs robes to twenty-sous frills;
    In all quarters of Paris, and to every store:
    While McFlimsey in vain stormed, scolded, and swore.
They footed the streets, and he footed the bills.

The last trip, their goods shipped by the steamer *Argo*
Formed, McFlimsey declares, the bulk of her cargo,
Not to mention a quantity kept from the rest,
Sufficient to fill the largest-sized chest,
Which did not appear on the ship's manifest,

But for which the ladies themselves manifested
Such particular interest that they invested
Their own proper persons in layers and rows
Of muslins, embroideries, worked underclothes,
Gloves, handkerchiefs, scarfs, and such trifles as those;
Then, wrapped in great shawls, like Circassian beauties,
Gave *good-by* to the ship, and *go-by* to the duties.
Her relations at home all marvelled, no doubt,
Miss Flora had grown so enormously stout
    For an actual belle and a possible bride;
But the miracle ceased when she turned inside out,
    And the truth came to light, and the dry-goods beside,
Which, in spite of collector and custom-house sentry,
Had entered the port without any entry.
And yet, though scarce three months have passed since the
    day
The merchandise went, on twelve carts, up Broadway,
This same Miss McFlimsey, of Madison Square,
The last time we met, was in utter despair,
Because she had nothing whatever to wear!

NOTHING TO WEAR! Now, as this is a true ditty,
    I do not assert—this you know is between us—
That she's in a state of absolute nudity,
    Like Powers's Greek Slave, or the Medici Venus;
But I do mean to say I have heard her declare,
    When at the same moment she had on a dress
    Which cost five hundred dollars, and not a cent less,
    And jewelry worth ten times more, I should guess,
That she had not a thing in the wide world to wear!
I should mention just here, that out of Miss Flora's
Two hundred and fifty or sixty adorers,
I had just been selected as he who should throw all
The rest in the shade, by the gracious bestowal
On myself, after twenty or thirty rejections
Of those fossil remains which she called her " affections,"
And that rather decayed but well-known work of art,
Which Miss Flora persisted in styling " her heart."
So we were engaged. Our troth had been plighted
    Not by moonbeam or starbeam, by fountain or grove;
But in a front parlor, most brilliantly lighted,

Beneath the gas-fixtures we whispered our love—
Without any romance, or raptures, or sighs,
Without any tears in Miss Flora's blue eyes,
Or blushes, or transports, or such silly actions;
It was one of the quietest business transactions,
With a very small sprinkling of sentiment, if any,
And a very large diamond imported by Tiffany.
On her virginal lips while I printed a kiss,
She exclaimed, as a sort of parenthesis,
And by way of putting me quite at my ease,
" You know, I'm to polka as much as I please,
And flirt when I like,—now stop,—don't you speak,—
And you must not come here more than twice in the week,
Or talk to me either at party or ball;
But always be ready to come when I call:
So don't prose to me about duty and stuff,—
If we don't break this off, there will be time enough
For that sort of thing; but the bargain must be,
That as long as I choose I am perfectly free:
For this is a sort of engagement, you see,
Which is binding on you, but not binding on me."

Well, having thus wooed Miss McFlimsey, and gained her,
With the silks, crinolines, and hoops that contained her,
I had, as I thought, a contingent remainder
At least in the property, and the best right
To appear as its escort by day and by night;
And it being the week of the Stuckups' grand ball,—
Their cards had been out for a fortnight or so,
And set all the Avenue on the tiptoe,—
I considered it only my duty to call
And see if Miss Flora intended to go.
I found her—as ladies are apt to be found
When the time intervening between the first sound
Of the bell and the visitor's entry is shorter
Than usual—I found—I won't say I caught—her
Intent on the pier-glass, undoubtedly meaning
To see if perhaps it didn't need cleaning.
She turned as I entered—" Why, Harry, you sinner,
I thought that you went to the Flashers' to dinner!"
" So I did," I replied; " but the dinner is swallowed,

And digested, I trust; for 'tis now nine or more:
So being relieved from that duty, I followed
   Inclination, which led me, you see, to your door.
And now will your Ladyship so condescend
As just to inform me if you intend
Your beauty and graces and presence to lend
(All of which, when I own, I hope no one will borrow)
To the Stuckups, whose party, you know, is to-morrow?"
The fair Flora looked up with a pitiful air,
And answered quite promptly, " Why, Harry, *mon cher,*
I should like above all things to go with you there;
But really and truly—I've nothing to wear."

" Nothing to wear? Go just as you are:
Wear the dress you have on, and you'll be by far,
I engage, the most bright and particular star
   On the Stuckup horizon—" I stopped, for her eye,
Notwithstanding this delicate onset of flattery,
Opened on me at once a most terrible battery
   Of scorn and amazement. She made no reply,
But gave a slight turn to the end of her nose
   (That pure Grecian feature), as much as to say,
" How absurd that any sane man should suppose
That a lady would go to a ball in the clothes,
   No matter how fine, that she wears every day ! "
So I ventured again—" Wear your crimson brocade."
(Second turn-up of nose)—"That's too dark by a
   shade."—
" Your blue silk—" " That's too heavy."—" Your pink—"
   " That's too light."—
" Wear tulle over satin." " I can't endure white."—
" Your rose-colored, then, the best of the batch—"
" I haven't a thread of point lace to match."—
" Your brown moire-antique—" " Yes, and look like a
   Quaker."—
" The pearl-colored—" " I would, but that plaguy dress-
   maker
Has had it a week."—" Then that exquisite lilac,
In which you would melt the heart of a Shylock."
(Here the nose took again the same elevation)—
" I wouldn't wear that for the whole of creation."—

"Why not? It's my fancy, there's nothing could strike it
As more *comme il faut*"—"Yes, but, dear me, that lean
   Sophronia Stuckup has got one just like it,
And I won't appear dressed like a chit of sixteen."—
"Then that splendid purple, that sweet mazarine,
That superb *point d'aiguille,* that imperial green,
That zephyr-like tarlatan, that rich grenadine—"
   "Not one of all which is fit to be seen,"
Said the lady, becoming excited and flushed.
"Then wear," I exclaimed, in a tone which quite crushed
Opposition, "that gorgeous toilette which you sported
   In Paris last spring, at the grand presentation,
   When you quite turned the head of the head of the nation;
And by all the grand court were so very much courted."
The end of the nose was portentously tipped up,
   And both the bright eyes shot forth indignation,
   As she burst upon me with the fierce exclamation,
   "I have worn it three times at the least calculation,
And that and most of my dresses are ripped up!"
Here I *ripped out* something, perhaps rather rash—
   Quite innocent, though; but to use an expression
More striking than classic, it "settled my hash,"
   And proved very soon the last act of our session.
"Fiddlesticks, is it, sir? I wonder the ceiling
Doesn't fall down and crush you!—oh, you men have no
   feeling.
You selfish, unnatural, illiberal creatures,
Who set yourselves up as patterns and preachers,
Your silly pretence—why, what a mere guess it is!
Pray, what do you know of a woman's necessities?
I have told you and shown you I've nothing to wear,
And it's perfectly plain you not only don't care,
But you do not believe me" (here the nose went still higher):
"I suppose if you dared you would call me a liar.
Our engagement is ended, sir—yes, on the spot;
You're a brute, and a monster, and—I don't know what."
I mildly suggested the words Hottentot,
Pickpocket, and cannibal, Tartar, and thief,
As gentle expletives which might give relief:
But this only proved as a spark to the powder,
And the storm I had raised came faster and louder;

It blew, and it rained, thundered, lightened, and hailed
Interjections, verbs, pronouns, till language quite failed
To express the abusive, and then its arrears
Were brought up all at once by a torrent of tears;
And my last faint, despairing attempt at an obs-
Ervation was lost in a tempest of sobs.

Well, I felt for the lady, and felt for my hat too,
Improvised on the crown of the latter a tattoo,
In lieu of expressing the feelings which lay
Quite too deep for words, as Wordsworth would say:
Then, without going through the form of a bow,
Found myself in the entry,—I hardly knew how,—
On doorstep and sidewalk, past lamp-post and square,
At home and up-stairs, in my own easy-chair;
 Poked my feet into slippers, my fire into blaze,
And said to myself, as I lit my cigar,—
Supposing a man had the wealth of the Czar
 Of the Russias to boot, for the rest of his days,
On the whole do you think he would have much time to spare
If he married a woman with nothing to wear?

William Allen Butler.

MY MISTRESS'S BOOTS

THEY nearly strike me dumb,
And I tremble when they come
 Pit-a-pat:
This palpitation means
These boots are Geraldine's—
 Think of that!

Oh, where did hunter win
So delectable a skin
 For her feet?
You lucky little kid,
You perished, so you did,
 For my sweet!

The faëry stitching gleams
On the sides, and in the seams,
   And it shows
The Pixies were the wags
Who tipt those funny tags
   And these toes.

What soles to charm an elf!
Had Crusoe, sick of self,
   Chanced to view
One printed near the tide,
Oh, how hard he would have tried
   For the two!

For Gerry's debonair
And innocent, and fair
   As a rose;
She's an angel in a frock,
With a fascinating cock
   To her nose.

The simpletons who squeeze
Their extremities to please
   Mandarins,
Would positively flinch
From venturing to pinch
   Geraldine's.

Cinderella's *lefts and rights,*
To Geraldine's were frights;
   And I trow,
The damsel, deftly shod,
Has dutifully trod
   Until now.

Come, Gerry, since it suits
Such a pretty Puss (in Boots)
   These to don;
Set this dainty hand awhile
On my shoulder, dear, and I'll
   Put them on.

Frederick Locker-Lampson.

MRS. SMITH

Last year I trod these fields with Di,
Fields fresh with clover and with rye;
    They now seem arid!
Then Di was fair and single; how
Unfair it seems on me, for now
    Di's fair—and married!

A blissful swain—I scorn'd the song
Which says that though young Love is strong,
    The Fates are stronger;
Breezes then blew a boon to men,
The buttercups were bright, and then
    This grass was longer.

That day I saw and much esteem'd
Di's ankles, which the clover seem'd
    Inclined to smother;
It twitch'd, and soon untied (for fun)
The ribbon of her shoes, first one,
    And then the other.

I'm told that virgins augur some
Misfortune if their shoe-strings come
    To grief on Friday:
And so did Di, and then her pride
Decreed that shoe-strings so untied
    Are " so untidy! "

Of course I knelt; with fingers deft
I tied the right, and then the left;
    Says Di, " The stubble
Is very stupid!—as I live,
I'm quite ashamed!—I'm shock'd to give
    You so much trouble! "

For answer I was fain to sink
To what we all would say and think
          Were Beauty present:
"Don't mention such a simple act—
A trouble? not the least! in fact
          It's rather pleasant!"

I trust that Love will never tease
Poor little Di, or prove that he's
          A graceless rover.
She's happy now as *Mrs. Smith*—
And less polite when walking with
          Her chosen lover!

Heigh-ho! Although no moral clings
To Di's blue eyes, and sandal strings,
          We've had our quarrels!—
I think that Smith is thought an ass;
I know that when they walk in grass
          She wears *balmorals*.

                    Frederick Locker-Lampson.

A TERRIBLE INFANT

I RECOLLECT a nurse call'd Ann,
          Who carried me about the grass,
And one fine day a fine young man
          Came up, and kiss'd the pretty lass.
She did not make the least objection!
          Thinks I, "*Aha!*
     When I can talk I'll tell Mamma"
—And that's my earliest recollection."

                    Frederick Locker-Lampson.

SUSAN

A KIND PROVIDENCE

He dropt a tear on Susan's bier,
  He seem'd a most despairing swain;
But bluer sky brought newer tie,
  And—would he wish her back again?

The moments fly, and when we die,
  Will Philly Thistletop complain?
She'll cry and sigh, and—dry her eye,
  And let herself be woo'd again.

Frederick Locker-Lampson.

" I DIDN'T LIKE HIM "

Perhaps you may a-noticed I been soht o' solemn lately,
  Haven't been a-lookin' quite so pleasant.
Mabbe I have been a little bit too proud and stately;
  Dat's because I'se lonesome jes' at present.
I an' him agreed to quit a week or so ago,
  Fo' now dat I am in de social swim
I'se 'rived to de opinion dat he ain't my style o' beau,
  So I tole him dat my watch was fas' fo' him.

REFRAIN

Oh, I didn't like his clo'es,
  An' I didn't like his eyes,
Nor his walk, nor his talk,
  Nor his ready-made neckties.
I didn't like his name a bit,
  Jes' 'spise the name o' Jim;
If dem ere reasons ain't enough,
  I didn't like *Him*.

Dimon' ring he give to me, an' said it was a fine stone.
  Guess it's only alum mixed wif camphor.
Took it roun' to Eisenstein; he said it was a rhinestone,
  Kind, he said, he didn't give a dam fur.

Sealskin sack he give to me it got me in a row.
P'liceman called an' asked to see dat sack;
Said another lady lost it. Course *I* don't know how;
But I had to go to jail or give it back.

REFRAIN

Oh, I didn't like his trade;
Trade dat kep' him out all night.
He'd de look ob a crook,
An' he owned a bull's-eye light.
So when policemen come to ask
What *I* know 'bout dat Jim,
I come to de confusion dat
I didn't like *Him*.

Harry B. Smith.

MY ANGELINE

She kept her secret well, oh, yes,
Her hideous secret well.
We together were cast, I knew not her past;
For how was I to tell?
I married her, guileless lamb I was;
I'd have died for her sweet sake.
How could I have known that my Angeline
Had been a Human Snake?
Ah, we had been wed but a week or two
When I found her quite a wreck:
Her limbs were tied in a double bow-knot
At the back of her swan-like neck.
No curse there sprang to my pallid lips,
Nor did I reproach her then;
I calmly untied my bonny bride
And straightened her out again.

Refrain

My Angeline! My Angeline!
Why didst disturb my mind serene?
My well-belovèd circus queen,
My Human Snake, my Angeline!

At night I'd wake at the midnight hour,
　　With a weird and haunted feeling,
And there she'd be, in her *robe de nuit,*
　　A-walking upon the ceiling.
She said she was being " the human fly,"
　　And she'd lift me up from beneath
By a section slight of my garb of night,
　　Which she held in her pearly teeth.
For the sweet, sweet sake of the Human Snake
　　I'd have stood this conduct shady;
But she skipped in the end with an old, old friend,
　　An eminent bearded lady.
But, oh, at night, when my slumber's light,
　　Regret comes o'er me stealing;
For I miss the sound of those little feet,
　　As they pattered along the ceiling.

Refrain

My Angeline! My Angeline!
Why didst disturb my mind serene?
My well-belovèd circus queen,
My Human Snake, my Angeline!

　　　　　　　　　　　Harry B. Smith

NORA'S VOW

HEAR what Highland Nora said,—
" The Earlie's son I will not wed,
Should all the race of nature die,
And none be left but he and I.
For all the gold, for all the gear,
And all the lands both far and near,
That ever valour lost or won,
I would not wed the Earlie's son."

" A maiden's vows," old Callum spoke,
" Are lightly made and lightly broke,
The heather on the mountain's height
Begins to bloom in purple light;

The frost-wind soon shall sweep away
That lustre deep from glen and brae;
Yet Nora, ere its bloom be gone,
May blithely wed the Earlie's son."

" The swan," she said, " the lake's clear breast
May barter for the eagle's nest;
The Awe's fierce stream may backward turn,
Ben-Cruaichan fall, and crush Kilchurn;
Our kilted clans, when blood is high,
Before their foes may turn and fly;
But I, were all these marvels done,
Would never wed the Earlie's son."

Still in the water-lily's shade
Her wonted nest the wild swan made;
Ben-Cruaichan stands as fast as ever,
Still downward foams the Awe's fierce river;
To shun the clash of foeman's steel,
No Highland brogue has turn'd the heel;
But Nora's heart is lost and won,
—She's wedded to the Earlie's son!

Sir Walter Scott.

HUSBAND AND HEATHEN

O'er the men of Ethiopia she would pour her cornucopia,
And shower wealth and plenty on the people of Japan,
Send down jelly cake and candies to the Indians of the Andes,
And a cargo of plum pudding to the men of Hindoostan;
          And she said she loved 'em so,
          Bushman, Finn, and Eskimo.
If she had the wings of eagles to their succour she would fly
          Loaded down with jam and jelly,
          Succotash and vermicelli,
Prunes, pomegranates, plums and pudding, peaches, pine-
apples, and pie.

She would fly with speedy succour to the natives of Molucca
With whole loads of quail and salmon, and with tons of
fricassee

And give cake in fullest measure
To the men of Australasia
And all the Archipelagoes that dot the southern sea;
And the Anthropophagi,
All their lives deprived of pie,
She would satiate and satisfy with custards, cream, and
mince;
And those miserable Australians
And the Borrioboolighalians,
She would gorge with choicest jelly, raspberry, currant, grape,
and quince.

But like old war-time hardtackers, her poor husband lived on
crackers,
Bought at wholesale from a baker, eaten from the mantel-
shelf;
If the men of Madagascar,
And the natives of Alaska,
Had enough to sate their hunger, let him look out for himself.
And his coat had but one tail
And he used a shingle nail
To fasten up his galluses when he went out to his work;
And she used to spend his money
To buy sugar-plums and honey
For the Terra del Fuegian and the Turcoman and Turk.

Sam Walter Foss.

THE LOST PLEIAD

'Twas a pretty little maiden
In a garden gray and old,
Where the apple trees were laden
With the magic fruit of gold;
But she strayed beyond the portal
Of the garden of the Sun,
And she flirted with a mortal,
Which she oughtn't to have done!

For a giant was her father and a goddess was her mother,
She was Merope or Sterope—the one or else the other;
And the man was not the equal, though presentable and rich,
Of Merope or Sterope—I don't remember which!

Now the giant's daughters seven,
    She among them, if you please,
Were translated to the heaven
    As the starry Pleiades!
But amid their constellation
    One alone was always dark,
For she shrank from observation
    Or censorious remark.

She had yielded to a mortal when he came to flirt and flatter.
She was Merope or Sterope—the former or the latter;
So the planets all ignored her, and the comets wouldn't call
On Merope or Sterope—I am not sure at all!

But the Dog-star, brightly shining
    In the hottest of July,
Saw the pretty Pleiad pining
    In the shadow of the sky,
And he courted her and kissed her
    Till she kindled into light;
And the Pleiads' erring sister
    Was the lady of the night!

So her former indiscretion as a fault was never reckoned,
To Merope or Sterope—the first or else the second,
And you'll never see so rigidly respectable a dame
As Merope or Sterope—I can't recall her name!

Arthur Reed Ropes.

THE NEW CHURCH ORGAN

They've got a brand-new organ, Sue,
    For all their fuss and search;
They've done just as they said they'd do,
    And fetched it into church.

They're bound the critter shall be seen,
   And on the preacher's right
They've hoisted up their new machine
   In everybody's sight.
They've got a chorister and choir,
   Ag'in' *my* voice and vote;
For it was never *my* desire
   To praise the Lord by note.

I've been a sister good an' true
   For five-an'-thirty year;
I've done what seemed my part to do,
   An' prayed my duty clear;
I've sung the hymns both slow and quick,
   Just as the preacher read,
And twice, when Deacon Tubbs was sick,
   I took the fork an' led;
And now, their bold, new-fangled ways
   Is comin' all about;
And I, right in my latter days,
   Am fairly crowded out!

To-day the preacher, good old dear,
   With tears all in his eyes,
Read, " I can read my title clear
   To mansions in the skies."
I al'ays liked that blessed hymn—
   I s'pose I al'ays will—
It somehow gratifies *my* whim,
   In good old Ortonville;
But when that choir got up to sing,
   I couldn't catch a word;
They sung the most dog-gondest thing
   A body ever heard!

Some worldly chaps was standin' near;
   An' when I see them grin,
I bid farewell to every fear,
   And boldly waded in.
I thought I'd chase their tune along,
   An' tried with all my might;

But though my voice was good an' strong,
  I couldn't steer it right.
When they was high, then I was low,
  An' also contrawise;
An' I too fast, or they too slow,
  To " mansions in the skies."

An' after every verse, you know
  They play a little tune;
I didn't understand, and so
  I started in too soon.
I pitched it pretty middlin' high,
  I fetched a lusty tone,
But oh, alas! I found that I
  Was singin' there alone!
They laughed a little, I am told;
  But I had done my best;
And not a wave of trouble rolled
  Across my peaceful breast.

And Sister Brown—I could but look—
  She sits right front of me;
She never was no singin'-book,
  An' never went to be;
But then she al'ays tried to do
  The best she could, she said;
She understood the time right through,
  An' kep' it with her head;
But when she tried this mornin', oh,
  I had to laugh, or cough!
It kep' her head a-bobbin' so,
  It e'en a'most came off.

An' Deacon Tubbs—he all broke down,
  As one might well suppose;
He took one look at Sister Brown,
  And meekly scratched his nose.
He looked his hymn-book through and through,
  And laid it on the seat,
And then a pensive sigh he drew,
  And looked completely beat.

And when they took another bout,
    He didn't even rise;
But drawed his red bandanner out,
    An' wiped his weepin' eyes.

I've been a sister, good an' true,
    For five-an'-thirty year;
I've done what seemed my part to do,
    An' prayed my duty clear;
But Death will stop my voice, I know,
    For he is on my track;
And some day I to church will go,
    And nevermore come back;
And when the folks gets up to sing—
    Whene'er that time shall be—
I do not want no *patent* thing
    A-squealin' over me!

                                    Will Carleton.

LARRIE O'DEE

Now the Widow McGee,
    And Larrie O'Dee,
Had two little cottages out on the green,
With just room enough for two pig-pens between.
The widow was young and the widow was fair,
With the brightest of eyes and the brownest of hair,
And it frequently chanced, when she came in the morn,
With the swill for her pig, Larrie came with the corn,
And some of the ears that he tossed from his hand
In the pen of the widow were certain to land.

One morning said he:
    " Och! Misthress McGee,
It's a waste of good lumber, this runnin' two rigs,
Wid a fancy purtition betwane our two pigs! "
" Indade, sur, it is! " answered Widow McGee,
With the sweetest of smiles upon Larrie O'Dee.
" And thin, it looks kind o' hard-hearted and mane,
Kapin' two friendly pigs so exsaidenly near
That whiniver one grunts the other can hear,
And yit kape a cruel purtition betwane."

"Shwate Widow McGee,"
Answered Larrie O'Dee,
"If ye fale in your heart we are mane to the pigs,
Ain't we mane to ourselves to be runnin' two rigs?
Och! it made me heart ache when I paped through the cracks
Of me shanty, lasht March, at yez shwingin' yer axe;
An' a-bobbin' yer head an' a-shtompin' yer fate,
Wid yer purty white hands jisht as red as a bate,
A-shplittin' yer kindlin'-wood out in the shtorm,
When one little shtove it would kape us both warm!"

"Now, piggy," says she,
"Larrie's courtin' o' me,
Wid his dilicate tinder allusions to you;
So now yez must tell me jisht what I must do:
For, if I'm to say yes, shtir the swill wid yer snout;
But if I'm to say no, ye must kape yer nose out.
Now Larrie, for shame! to be bribin' a pig
By a-tossin' a handful of corn in its shwig!"
"Me darlint, the piggy says yes," answered he.
And that was the courtship of Larrie O'Dee.

William W. Fink.

NO FAULT IN WOMEN

No fault in women, to refuse
The offer which they most would choose.
No fault in women to confess
How tedious they are in their dress;
No fault in women, to lay on
The tincture of vermilion,
And there to give the cheek a dye
Of white, where Nature doth deny.
No fault in women, to make show
Of largeness, when they've nothing so;
When, true it is, the outside swells
With inward buckram, little else.
No fault in women, though they be
But seldom from suspicion free;
No fault in womankind at all,
If they but slip, and never fall.

Robert Herrick.

A COSMOPOLITAN WOMAN

She went round and asked subscriptions
For the heathen black Egyptians
And the Terra del Fuegians,
    She did;
For the tribes round Athabasca,
And the men of Madagascar,
And the poor souls of Alaska,
    So she did;
She longed, she said, to buy
Jelly, cake, and jam, and pie,
For the Anthropophagi,
    So she did.

Her heart ached for the Australians
And the Borriobooli-Ghalians,
And the poor dear Amahagger,
    Yes, it did;
And she loved the black Numidian,
And the ebon Abyssinian,
And the charcoal-coloured Guinean,
    Oh, she did!
And she said she'd cross the seas
With a ship of bread and cheese
For those starving Chimpanzees,
    So she did.

How she loved the cold Norwegian
And the poor half-melted Feejeean,
And the dear Molucca Islander,
    She did:
She sent tins of red tomato
To the tribes beyond the Equator,
But her husband ate potato,
    So he did;
The poor helpless, homeless thing
(My voice falters as I sing)
Tied his clothes up with a string,
    Yes, he did.

                                    Unknown.

COURTING IN KENTUCKY

WHEN Mary Ann Dollinger got the skule daown thar on
    Injun Bay,
I was glad, fer I like ter see a gal makin' her honest way.
I heerd some talk in the village abaout her flyin' high,
Tew high fer busy farmer folks with chores ter do ter fly;
But I paid no sorter attention ter all the talk ontell
She come in her reg'lar boardin' raound ter visit with us a
    spell.
My Jake an' her had been cronies ever since they could walk,
An' it tuk me aback to hear her kerrectin' him in his talk.

Jake ain't no hand at grammar, though he hain't his beat
    for work;
But I sez ter myself, " Look out, my gal, yer a-foolin' with
    a Turk ! "
Jake bore it wonderful patient, an' said in a mournful way,
He p'sumed he was behindhand with the doin's at Injun Bay.
I remember once he was askin' for some o' my Injun buns,
An' she said he should allus say, " them air," stid o' " them
    is " the ones.
Wal, Mary Ann kep' at him stiddy mornin' an' evenin' long,
Tell he dassent open his mouth for fear o' talkin' wrong.

One day I was pickin' currants daown by the old quince-tree,
When I heerd Jake's voice a-saying', " Be yer willin' ter
    marry me ? "
An' Mary Ann kerrectin', ' Air ye willin' yeou sh'd say ";
Our Jake he put his foot daown in a plum, decided way,
" No wimmen-folks is a-goin' ter be rearrangin' me,
Hereafter I says ' craps,' ' them is,' ' I calk'late,' an' ' I be.'
Ef folks don't like my talk they needn't hark ter what I say:
But I ain't a-goin' to take no sass from folks from Injun Bay.
I ask you free an' final, ' Be ye goin' ter marry me ? ' "
An' Mary Ann says, tremblin, yet anxious-like, " I be."

Florence E. Pratt.

ANY ONE WILL DO

A MAIDEN once, of certain age,
To catch a husband did engage;
But, having passed the prime of life
In striving to become a wife
Without success, she thought it time
To mend the follies of her prime.

Departing from the usual course
Of paint and such like for resource,
With all her might this ancient maid
Beneath an oak-tree knelt and prayed;
Unconscious that a grave old owl
Was perched above—the mousing fowl!

" Oh, give! a husband give! " she cried,
" While yet I may become a bride;
Soon will my day of grace be o'er,
And then, like many maids before,
I'll die without an early love,
And none to meet me there above!

" Oh, 'tis a fate too hard to bear!
Then answer this my humble prayer,
And oh, a husband give to me! "
Just then the owl from out the tree,
In deep bass tones cried, " Who—who—who! "
" Who, Lord? And dost Thou ask me who?
Why, any one, good Lord, will do."

Unknown.

A BIRD IN THE HAND

THERE were three young maids of Lee;
They were fair as fair can be,
And they had lovers three times three,
For they were fair as fair can be,
These three young maids of Lee.
But these young maids they cannot find
A lover each to suit her mind;
The plain-spoke lad is far too rough,
The rich young lord is not rich enough,
The one is too poor, and one is too tall,
And one just an inch too short for them all.
" Others pick and choose, and why not we?
We can very well wait," said the maids of Lee.
There were three young maids of Lee;
They were fair as fair can be,
And they had lovers three times three
For they were fair as fair can be,
These three young maids of Lee.

There are three old maids of Lee,
And they are old as old can be,
And one is deaf, and one cannot see,
And they are all as cross as a gallows-tree,
These three old maids of Lee.
Now, if any one chanced—'tis a chance remote—
One single charm in these maids to note,
He need not a poet nor handsome be,
For one is deaf and one cannot see;
He need not woo on his bended knee,
For they all are willing as willing can be.
He may take the one, or the two, or the three,
If he'll only take them away from Lee.
There are three old maids at Lee;
They are cross as cross can be;
And there they are, and there they'll be
To the end of the chapter, one, two, three,
These three old maids of Lee.

Frederic E. Weatherly.

THE BELLE OF THE BALL

YEARS—years ago,—ere yet my dreams
    Had been of being wise and witty,—
Ere I had done with writing themes,
    Or yawn'd o'er this infernal Chitty;—
Years, years ago, while all my joy
    Was in my fowling-piece and filly:
In short, while I was yet a boy,
    I fell in love with Laura Lily.

I saw her at the county ball;
    There, when the sounds of flute and fiddle
Gave signal sweet in that old hall
    Of hands across and down the middle,
Hers was the subtlest spell by far
    Of all that set young hearts romancing:
She was our queen, our rose, our star;
    And when she danced—O Heaven, her dancing!

Dark was her hair, her hand was white;
    Her voice was exquisitely tender,
Her eyes were full of liquid light;
    I never saw a waist so slender;
Her every look, her every smile,
    Shot right and left a score of arrows;
I thought 'twas Venus from her isle,
    And wonder'd where she'd left her sparrows.

She talk'd,—of politics or prayers;
    Of Southey's prose, or Wordsworth's sonnets;
Of daggers or of dancing bears,
    Of battles, or the last new bonnets;
By candle-light, at twelve o'clock,
    To me it matter'd not a tittle,
If those bright lips had quoted Locke,
    I might have thought they murmur'd Little.

Through sunny May, through sultry June,
    I loved her with a love eternal;
I spoke her praises to the moon,
    I wrote them for the *Sunday Journal.*
My mother laugh'd; I soon found out
    That ancient ladies have no feeling;
My father frown'd; but how should gout
    See any happiness in kneeling?

She was the daughter of a Dean,
    Rich, fat, and rather apoplectic;
She had one brother, just thirteen,
    Whose color was extremely hectic;
Her grandmother for many a year
    Had fed the parish with her bounty;
Her second cousin was a peer,
    And lord lieutenant of the county.

But titles and the three per cents,
    And mortgages, and great relations,
And India bonds, and tithes and rents,
    Oh! what are they to love's sensations?
Black eyes, fair forehead, clustering locks,
    Such wealth, such honors, Cupid chooses;
He cares as little for the stocks,
    As Baron Rothschild for the Muses.

She sketch'd; the vale, the wood, the beach,
    Grew lovelier from her pencil's shading;
She botanized; I envied each
    Young blossom in her boudoir fading;
She warbled Handel; it was grand—
    She made the Catalani jealous;
She touch'd the organ; I could stand
    For hours and hours to blow the bellows.

She kept an album, too, at home,
    Well fill'd with all an album's glories;
Paintings of butterflies, and Rome,
    Patterns for trimming, Persian stories;

Soft songs to Julia's cockatoo,
  Fierce odes to Famine and to Slaughter;
And autographs of Prince Leboo,
  And recipes for elder water.

And she was flatter'd, worshipp'd, bored;
  Her steps were watch'd, her dress was noted;
Her poodle dog was quite adored,
  Her sayings were extremely quoted.
She laugh'd, and every heart was glad,
  As if the taxes were abolish'd;
She frown'd, and every look was sad,
  As if the Opera were demolished.

She smil'd on many just for fun—
  I knew that there was nothing in it;
I was the first—the only one
  Her heart had thought of for a minute;
I knew it, for she told me so,
  In phrase which was divinely moulded;
She wrote a charming hand,—and oh!
  How sweetly all her notes were folded!

Our love was like most other loves—
  A little glow, a little shiver;
A rosebud and a pair of gloves,
  And " Fly Not Yet," upon the river;
Some jealousy of some one's heir,
  Some hopes of dying broken-hearted,
A miniature, a lock of hair,
  The usual vows—and then we parted.

We parted;—months and years roll'd by;
  We met again four summers after;
Our parting was all sob and sigh—
  Our meeting was all mirth and laughter;
For in my heart's most secret cell,
  There had been many other lodgers;
And she was not the ballroom belle,
  But only—Mrs. Something Rogers.

                    Winthrop· Mackworth Praed.

THE RETORT

OLD Nick, who taught the village school,
　　Wedded a maid of homespun habit;
He was as stubborn as a mule,
　　She was as playful as a rabbit.

Poor Jane had scarce become a wife,
　　Before her husband sought to make her
The pink of country-polished life,
　　And prim and formal as a Quaker.

One day the tutor went abroad,
　　And simple Jenny sadly missed him;
When he returned, behind her lord
　　She slyly stole, and fondly kissed him!

The husband's anger rose!—and red
　　And white his face alternate grew!
"Less freedom, ma'am!" Jane sighed and said,
　　"*Oh, dear! I didn't know 'twas you!*"

　　　　　　　　　　　George Pope Morris.

BEHAVE YOURSEL' BEFORE FOLK

BEHAVE yoursel' before folk,
Behave yoursel' before folk,
And dinna be sae rude to me,
　　As kiss me sae before folk.

It wadna gi'e me meikle pain,
Gin we were seen and heard by nane,
To tak' a kiss, or grant you ane;
　　But guidsake! no before folk.
　　Behave yoursel' before folk,
　　Behave yoursel' before folk;
Whate'er ye do, when out o' view,
　　Be cautious aye before folk.

Consider, lad, how folk will crack,
And what a great affair they'll mak'
O' naething but a simple smack,
   That's gi'en or ta'en before folk.
     Behave yoursel' before folk,
     Behave yoursel' before folk;
    Nor gi'e the tongue o' auld or young
     Occasion to come o'er folk.

It's no through hatred o' a kiss,
That I sae plainly tell you this;
But, losh! I tak' it sair amiss
   To be sae teazed before folk.
     Behave yoursel' before folk,
     Behave yoursel' before folk;
    When we're our lane ye may tak' ane,
     But fient a ane before folk.

I'm sure wi' you I've been as free
As ony modest lass should be;
But yet it doesna do to see
   Sic freedom used before folk.
     Behave yoursel' before folk,
     Behave yoursel' before folk;
    I'll ne'er submit again to it—
     So mind you that—before folk.

Ye tell me that my face is fair;
It may be sae—I dinna care—
But ne'er again gar't blush sae sair
   As ye ha'e done before folk.
     Behave yoursel' before folk,
     Behave yoursel' before folk;
    Nor heat my cheeks wi' your mad freaks,
     But aye de douce before folk.

Ye tell me that my lips are sweet,
Sic tales, I doubt, are a' deceit;
At ony rate, it's hardly meet
   To pree their sweets before folk.

Behave yoursel' before folk,
Behave yoursel' before folk;
Gin that's the case, there's time, and place,
But surely no before folk.

But, gin you really do insist
That I should suffer to be kiss'd,
Gae, get a license frae the priest,
    And mak' me yours before folk.
        Behave yoursel' before folk,
        Behave yoursel' before folk;
    And when we're ane, baith flesh and bane,
        Ye may tak' ten—before folk.

Alexander Rodger.

THE CHRONICLE: A BALLAD

MARGARITA first possess'd,
If I remember well, my breast,
    Margarita, first of all;
But when a while the wanton maid
With my restless heart had play'd,
    Martha took the flying ball.

Martha soon did it resign
To the beauteous Catharine.
    Beauteous Catharine gave place
(Though loth and angry she to part
With the possession of my heart)
    To Eliza's conquering face.

Eliza till this hour might reign,
Had she not evil counsel ta'en:
    Fundamental laws she broke,
And still new favourites she chose,
Till up in arms my passions rose,
    And cast away her yoke.

Mary then and gentle Anne,
Both to reign at once began,
    Alternately they swayed:
And sometimes Mary was the fair,
And sometimes Anne the crown did wear,
    And sometimes both I obey'd.

Another Mary then arose,
And did rigorous laws impose;
    A mighty tyrant she!
Long, alas, should I have been
Under that iron-scepter'd queen,
    Had not Rebecca set me free.

When fair Rebecca set me free,
'Twas then a golden time with me,
    But soon those pleasures fled;
For the gracious princess died
In her youth and beauty's pride,
    And Judith reigned in her stead.

One month, three days, and half an hour,
Judith held the sovereign power,
    Wondrous beautiful her face;
But so weak and small her wit,
That she to govern was unfit,
    And so Susanna took her place.

But when Isabella came,
Arm'd with a resistless flame,
    And th' artillery of her eye;
Whilst she proudly march'd about
Greater conquests to find out:
    She beat out Susan by the bye.

But in her place I then obey'd
Black-ey'd Bess, her viceroy maid,
    To whom ensued a vacancy:
Thousand worse passions then possess'd
The interregnum of my breast;
    Bless me from such an anarchy.

Gentle Henrietta then,
And a third Mary next began;
    Then Joan, and Jane, and Andria:
And then a pretty Thomasine,
And then another Catharine,
    And then a long et cætera.

But should I now to you relate
The strength and riches of their state,
    The powder, patches, and the pins,
The ribbons, jewels, and the rings,
The lace, the paint, and warlike things,
    That make up all their magazines:

If I should tell the politic arts
To take and keep men's hearts;
    The letters, embassies, and spies,
The frowns, and smiles, and flatteries,
The quarrels, tears, and perjuries,
    Numberless, nameless, mysteries!

And all the little lime-twigs laid
By Machiavel, the waiting maid;
    I more voluminous should grow
(Chiefly if I, like them, should tell
All change of weather that befel)
    Than Holinshed or Stow.

But I will briefer with them be,
Since few of them were long with me:
    An higher and a nobler strain
My present empress does claim,
Eleonora, first o' th' name,
    Whom God grant long to reign.

                        Abraham Cowley.

BUXOM JOAN

A SOLDIER and a sailor,
A tinker and a tailor,
Had once a doubtful strife, sir,
To make a maid a wife, sir,
    Whose name was Buxom Joan.
For now the time was ended,
When she no more intended
To lick her lips at men, sir,
And gnaw the sheets in vain, sir,
    And lie o' nights alone.

The soldier swore like thunder,
He loved her more than plunder;
And showed her many a scar, sir,
That he had brought from far, sir,
    With fighting for her sake.
The tailor thought to please her,
With offering her his measure.
The tinker too with mettle,
Said he could mend her kettle,
    And stop up every leak.

But while these three were prating,
The sailor slily waiting,
Thought if it came about, sir,
That they should all fall out, sir,
    He then might play his part.
And just e'en as he meant, sir,
To loggerheads they went, sir,
And then he let fly at her
A shot 'twixt wind and water,
    That won this fair maid's heart.

William Congreve.

OH, MY GERALDINE

Oh, my Geraldine,
No flow'r was ever seen so toodle um.
You are my lum ti toodle lay,
        Pretty, pretty queen,
Is rum ti Geraldine and something teen,
More sweet than tiddle lum in May.
        Like the star so bright
        That somethings all the night,
            My Geraldine!
You're fair as the rum ti lum ti sheen,
    Hark! there is what—ho!
    From something—um, you know,
        Dear, what I mean.
Oh! rum! tum!! tum!!! my Geraldine.

F. C. Burnand.

THE PARTERRE

I DON'T know any greatest treat
    As sit him in a gay parterre,
And sniff one up the perfume sweet
    Of every roses buttoning there.

It only want my charming miss
    Who make to blush the self red rose;
Oh! I have envy of to kiss
    The end's tip of her splendid nose.

Oh! I have envy of to be
    What grass 'neath her pantoffle push,
And too much happy seemeth me
    The margaret which her vestige crush.

But I will meet her nose at nose,
    And take occasion for her hairs,
And indicate her all my woes,
    That she in fine agree my prayers.

THE ENVOY

I don't know any greatest treat
    As sit him in a gay parterre,
With Madame who is too more sweet
    Than every roses buttoning there.

E. H. Palmer.

HOW TO ASK AND HAVE

" OH, 'tis time I should talk to your mother,
    Sweet Mary," says I;
" Oh, don't talk to my mother," says Mary,
    Beginning to cry:
" For my mother says men are decaivers,
    And never, I know, will consent;
She says girls in a hurry to marry,
    At leisure repent."

" Then, suppose I should talk to your father,
    Sweet Mary," says I;
" Oh, don't talk to my father," says Mary,
    Beginning to cry:
" For my father he loves me so dearly,
    He'll never consent I should go;—
If you talk to my father," says Mary,
    " He'll surely say ' No.' "

" Then how shall I get you, my jewel,
    Sweet Mary?" says I;
" If your father and mother's so cruel,
    Most surely I'll die! "
" Oh, never say die, dear," says Mary;
    " A way now to save you I see:
Since my parents are both so conthrairy,
    You'd better ask *me*."

Samuel Lover.

SALLY IN OUR ALLEY

Of all the girls that are so smart,
  There's none like Pretty Sally;
She is the darling of my heart,
  And lives in our alley.
There's ne'er a lady in the land
  That's half so sweet as Sally;
She is the darling of my heart,
  And lives in our alley.

Her father he makes cabbage-nets,
  And through the streets does cry them;
Her mother she sells laces long
  To such as please to buy them:
But sure such folk can have no part
  In such a girl as Sally;
She is the darling of my heart,
  And lives in our alley.

When she is by, I leave my work,
  I love her so sincerely;
My master comes, like any Turk,
  And bangs me most severely:
But let him bang, long as he will,
  I'll bear it all for Sally;
She is the darling of my heart,
  And lives in our alley.

Of all the days are in the week,
  I dearly love but one day,
And that's the day that comes betwixt
  A Saturday and Monday;
For then I'm dressed, all in my best,
  To walk abroad with Sally;
She is the darling of my heart,
  And lives in our alley.

My master carries me to church,
  And often am I blamed,
Because I leave him in the lurch,
  Soon as the text is named:
I leave the church in sermon time,
  And slink away to Sally;
She is the darling of my heart,
  And lives in our alley.

When Christmas comes about again,
  Oh, then I shall have money;
I'll hoard it up and, box and all,
  I'll give it to my honey;
Oh, would it were ten thousand pounds,
  I'd give it all to Sally;
For she's the darling of my heart,
  And lives in our alley.

My master, and the neighbors all,
  Make game of me and Sally,
And but for her I'd better be
  A slave, and row a galley:
But when my seven long years are out,
  Oh, then I'll marry Sally,
And then how happily we'll live—
  But not in our alley.

Henry Carey.

FALSE LOVE AND TRUE LOGIC

THE DISCONSOLATE

My heart will break—I'm sure it will:
  My lover, yes, my favorite—he
Who seemed my own through good and ill—
  Has basely turned his back on me.

THE COMFORTER

Ah! silly sorrower, weep no more;
  Your lover's turned his back, we see;
But you had turned his head before,
  And now he's as he ought to be.

Laman Blanchard.

PET'S PUNISHMENT

O, IF my love offended me,
   And we had words together,
To show her I would master be,
   I'd whip her with a feather!

If then she, like a naughty girl,
   Would tyranny declare it,
I'd give my pet a cross of pearl,
   And make her always bear it.

If still she tried to sulk and sigh,
   And threw away my posies,
I'd catch my darling on the sly,
   And smother her with roses.

But should she clench her dimpled fists,
   Or contradict her betters,
I'd manacle her tiny wrists
   With dainty jewelled fetters.

And if she dared her lips to pout,
   Like many pert young misses,
I'd wind my arm her waist about,
   And punish her—with kisses!

J. Ashby-Sterry.

AD CHLOEN, M.A.

FRESH FROM HER CAMBRIDGE EXAMINATION

LADY, very fair are you,
And your eyes are very blue,
   And your hose;
And your brow is like the snow,
And the various things you know,
   Goodness knows.

And the rose-flush on your cheek,
And your Algebra and Greek
  Perfect are;
And that loving lustrous eye
Recognizes in the sky
  Every star.

You have pouting piquant lips,
You can doubtless an eclipse
  Calculate;
But for your cerulean hue,
I had certainly from you
  Met my fate.

If by some arrangement dual
I were Adams mixed with Whewell,
  Then some day
I, as wooer, perhaps might come
To so sweet an Artium
  Magistra.

                                    Mortimer Collins.

CHLOE, M.A.

AD AMANTEM SUAM

Careless rhymer, it is true,
That my favourite colour's blue:
    But am I
To be made a victim, sir,
If to puddings I prefer
    Cambridge π?

If with giddier girls I play
Croquet through the summer day
  On the turf,
Then at night ('tis no great boon)
Let me study how the moon
    Sways the surf.

Tennyson's idyllic verse
Surely suits me none the worse
    If I seek
Old Sicilian birds and bees—
Music of sweet Sophocles—
    Golden Greek.

You have said my eyes are blue;
There may be a fairer hue,
    Perhaps—and yet
It is surely not a sin
If I keep my secrets in
    Violet.

Mortimer Collins.

THE FAIR MILLINGER

By the Watertown Horse-Car Conductor

It was a millinger most gay,
    As sat within her shop;
A student came along that way,
    And in he straight did pop.
Clean shaven he, of massive mould,
    He thought his looks was killing her;
So lots of stuff to him she sold:
    "Thanks!" says the millinger.

He loafed around and seemed to try
    On all things to converse;
The millinger did mind her eye,
    But also mound his purse.
He tried, then, with his flattering tongue,
    With nonsense to be filling her;
But she was sharp, though she was young:
    "Thanks," said the millinger.

He asked her to the theatre,
   They got into my car;
Our steeds were tired, could hardly stir,
   He thought the way not far.
A pretty pict-i-ure she made,
   No doctors had been pilling her;
Fairly the fair one's fare he paid:
   " Thanks! " said the millinger.

When we arrived in Bowdoin Square,
   A female to them ran;
Then says that millinger so fair:
   " O, thank you, Mary Ann!
She's going with us, she is," says she,
   " She only is fulfilling her
Duty in looking after me:
   Thanks! " said that millinger.

" Why," says that student chap to her,
   " I've but two seats to hand."
" Too bad," replied that millinger,
   " Then you will have to stand."
" I won't stand this," says he, " I own
   The joke which you've been drilling her;
Here, take the seats and go alone! "
   " Thanks! " says the millinger.

That ere much-taken-down young man
   Stepped back into my car.
We got fresh horses, off they ran;
   He thought the distance far.
And now she is my better half,
   And oft, when coo-and-billing her,
I think about that chap and laugh:
   " Thanks! " says my millinger.

                  Fred W. Loring.

TWO FISHERS

One morning when Spring was in her teens—
  A morn to a poet's wishing,
All tinted in delicate pinks and greens—
  Miss Bessie and I went fishing.

I in my rough and easy clothes,
  With my face at the sun-tan's mercy;
She with her hat tipped down to her nose,
  And her nose tipped—*vice versa.*

I with my rod, my reel, and my hooks,
  And a hamper for lunching recesses;
She with the bait of her comely looks,
  And the seine of her golden tresses.

So we sat us down on the sunny dike,
  Where the white pond-lilies teeter,
And I went to fishing like quaint old Ike,
  And she like Simon Peter.

All the noon I lay in the light of her eyes,
  And dreamily watched and waited,
But the fish were cunning and would not rise,
  And the baiter alone was baited.

And when the time of departure came,
  My bag hung flat as a flounder;
But Bessie had neatly hooked her game—
  A hundred-and-fifty-pounder.

                             Unknown.

MAUD

Nay, I cannot come into the garden just now,
  Tho' it vexes me much to refuse:
But I *must* have the next set of waltzes, I vow,
  With Lieutenant de Boots of the Blues.

I am sure you'll be heartily pleas'd when you hear
  That our ball has been quite a success.
As for *me*—I've been looking a monster, my dear,
  In that old-fashion'd guy of a dress.

You had better at once hurry home, dear, to bed;
  It is getting so dreadfully late.
You may catch the bronchitis or cold in the head
  If you linger so long at our gate.

Don't be obstinate, Alfy; come, take my advice—
  For I know you're in want of repose:
Take a basin of gruel (you'll find it *so* nice),
  And remember to tallow your nose.

No, I tell you I can't and I shan't get away,
  For De Boots has implor'd me to sing.
As to *you*—if you like it, of course you can stay,
  You were always an obstinate thing.

If you feel it a pleasure to talk to the flow'rs
  About "babble and revel and wine,"
When you might have been snoring for two or
    three hours,
    Why, it's not the least business of mine.

Henry S. Leigh.

ARE WOMEN FAIR?

" ARE women fair? " Ay, wondrous fair to see, too.
" Are women sweet? " Yea, passing sweet they be, too.
Most fair and sweet to them that only love them;
Chaste and discreet to all save them that prove them.

" Are women wise? " Not wise, but they be witty;
" Are women witty? " Yea, the more the pity;
They are so witty, and in wit so wily,
Though ye be ne'er so wise, they will beguile ye.

"Are women fools?" Not fools, but fondlings many;
"Can women fond be faithful unto any?"
When snow-white swans do turn to colour sable,
Then women fond will be both firm and stable.

"Are women saints?" No saints, nor yet no devils;
"Are women good?" Not good, but needful evils.
So Angel-like, that devils I do not doubt them,
So needful evils that few can live without them.

"Are women proud?" Ay! passing proud, an praise them.
"Are women kind?" Ay! wondrous kind, an please them.
Or so imperious, no man can endure them,
Or so kind-hearted, any may procure them.

Francis Davison.

THE PLAIDIE

Upon ane stormy Sunday,
   Coming adoon the lane,
Were a score of bonnie lassies—
   And the sweetest I maintain
     Was Caddie,
That I took unneath my plaidie,
   To shield her from the rain.

She said that the daisies blushed
   For the kiss that I had ta'en;
I wadna hae thought the lassie
   Wad sae of a kiss complain:
     "Now, laddie!
I winna stay under your plaidie,
   If I gang hame in the rain!"

But, on an after Sunday,
   When cloud there was not ane,
This selfsame winsome lassie
   (We chanced to meet in the lane),
     Said, "Laddie,
Why dinna ye wear your plaidie?
   Wha kens but it may rain?"

Charles Sibley

FEMININE ARITHMETIC

LAURA

On me he shall ne'er put a ring,
  So, mamma, 'tis in vain to take trouble—
For I was but eighteen in spring
  While his age exactly is double.

MAMMA

He's but in his thirty-sixth year,
  Tall, handsome, good-natured and witty,
And should you refuse him, my dear,
  May you die an old maid without pity!

LAURA

His figure, I grant you, will pass,
  And at present he's young enough plenty;
But when I am sixty, alas!
  Will not he be a hundred and twenty?

Charles Graham Halpine.

LORD GUY

When swallows Northward flew
  Forth from his home did fare
  Guy, Lord of Lanturlaire
    And Lanturlu.

Swore he to cross the brine,
  Pausing not, night nor day,
  That he might Paynims slay
    In Palestine.

Half a league on his way
  Met he a shepherdess
  Beaming with loveliness—
    Fair as Young Day.

Gazed he in eyes of blue—
Saw love in hiding there
Guy, Lord of Lanturlaire
And Lanturlu.

"Let the foul Paynim wait!"
Plead Love, "and stay with me.
Cruel and cold the sea—
Here's brighter fate."

When swallows Southward flew
Back to his home did fare
Guy, Lord of Lanturlaire
And Lanturlu.

Led he his charger gay
Bearing a shepherdess
Beaming with happiness—
Fair as Young Day.

White lambs, be-ribboned blue—
Tends now with anxious care,
Guy, Lord of Lanturlaire
And Lanturlu.

George F. Warren.

SARY "FIXES UP" THINGS

Oh, yes, we've be'n fixin' up some sence we sold that piece
o' groun'
Fer a place to put a golf-lynx to them crazy dudes from
town.
(Anyway, they laughed like crazy when I had it specified,
Ef they put a golf-lynx on it, thet they'd haf to keep him
tied.)
But they paid the price all reg'lar, an' then Sary says
to me,
"Now we're goin' to fix the parlor up, an' settin'-room,"
says she.

Fer she 'lowed she'd been a-scrimpin' an' a-scrapin' all
    her life,
An' she meant fer once to have things good as Cousin
    Ed'ard's wife.

Well, we went down to the city, an' she bought the
    blamedest mess;
An' them clerks there must 'a' took her fer a' Astoroid,
    I guess;
Fer they showed her fancy bureaus which they said was
    shiffoneers,
An' some more they said was dressers, an' some curtains
    called porteers.
An' she looked at that there furnicher, an' felt them cur-
    tains' heft;
Then she sailed in like a cyclone an' she bought 'em right
    an' left;
An' she picked a Bress'ls carpet thet was flowered like
    Cousin Ed's,
But she drawed the line com-pletely when we got to
    foldin'-beds.

Course, she said, 't 'u'd make the parlor lots more roomier,
    she s'posed;
But she 'lowed she'd have a bedstid thet was shore to stay
    un-closed;
An' she stopped right there an' told us sev'ral tales of
    folks she'd read
Bein' overtook in slumber by the "fatal foldin'-bed."
"Not ef it wuz set in di'mon's! Nary foldin'-bed fer me!
I ain't goin' to start fer glory in a rabbit-trap!" says she.
"When the time comes I'll be ready an' a-waitin'; but ez
    yet,
I shan't go to sleep a-thinkin' that I've got the triggers
    set."

Well, sir, shore as yo' 're a-livin', after all thet Sary said,
'Fore we started home that evenin' she hed bought a
    foldin'-bed;
An' she's put it in the parlor, where it adds a heap o' style;
An' we're sleepin' in the settin'-room at present fer a
    while.

Sary still maintains it's han'some, " an' them city folks
'll see
That we're posted on the fashions when they visit us,"
says she;
But it plagues her some to tell her, ef it ain't no other
use,
We can set it fer the golf-lynx ef he ever sh'u'd get loose.

Albert Bigelow Paine.

THE CONSTANT CANNIBAL MAIDEN

FAR, oh, far is the Mango island,
    Far, oh, far is the tropical sea—
Palms a-slant and the hills a-smile, and
    A cannibal maiden a-waiting for me.

I've been deceived by a damsel Spanish,
    And Indian maidens both red and brown,
A black-eyed Turk and a blue-eyed Danish,
    And a Puritan lassie of Salem town.

For the Puritan Prue she sets in the offing,
    A-castin' 'er eyes at a tall marine,
And the Spanish minx is the wust at scoffing
    Of all of the wimming I ever seen.

But the cannibal maid is a simple creetur,
    With a habit of gazin' over the sea,
A-hopin' in vain for the day I'll meet 'er,
    And constant and faithful a-yearnin' for me.

Me Turkish sweetheart she played me double—
    Eloped with the Sultan Harum In-Deed,
And the Danish damsel she made me trouble
    When she ups and married an oblong Swede.

But there's truth in the heart of the maid o'
  Mango,
Though her cheeks is black like the kiln-
  baked cork,
As she sets in the shade o' the whingo-whango,
A-waitin' for me—with a knife and fork.

Wallace Irwin.

WIDOW BEDOTT TO ELDER SNIFFLES

O REVEREND sir, I do declare
  It drives me most to frenzy,
To think of you a-lying there
  Down sick with influenzy.

A body'd thought it was enough
  To mourn your wife's departer,
Without sich trouble as this ere
  To come a-follerin' arter.

But sickness and affliction
  Are sent by a wise creation,
And always ought to be underwent
  By patience and resignation.

O, I could to your bedside fly,
  And wipe your weeping eyes,
And do my best to cure you up,
  If 'twouldn't create surprise.

It's a world of trouble we tarry in,
  But, Elder, don't despair;
That you may soon be movin' again
  Is constantly my prayer.

Both sick and well, you may depend
  You'll never be forgot
By your faithful and affectionate friend,
      PRISCILLA POOL BEDOTT.

Frances Miriam Whitcher.

UNDER THE MISTLETOE

She stood beneath the mistletoe
That hung above the door,
Quite conscious of the sprig above,
Revered by maids of yore.
A timid longing filled her heart;
Her pulses throbbed with heat;
He sprang to where the fair girl stood.
"May I—just one—my sweet?"
He asked his love, who tossed her head,
"Just do it—if—you dare!" she said.

He sat before the fireplace
Down at the club that night.
"She loves me not," he hotly said,
"Therefore she did but right!"
She sat alone within her room,
And with her finger-tips
She held his picture to her heart,
Then pressed it to her lips.
"My loved one!" sobbed she, "if you—cared
You surely would have—would have—dared."

George Francis Shults.

THE BROKEN PITCHER

It was a Moorish maiden was sitting by a well,
And what the maiden thought of I cannot, cannot tell,
When by there rode a valiant knight from the town of
Oviedo—
Alphonso Guzman was he hight, the Count of Desparedo.

"Oh, maiden, Moorish maiden! why sitt'st thou by the
spring?
Say, dost thou seek a lover, or any other thing?
Why gazest thou upon me, with eyes so large and wide,
And wherefore doth the pitcher lie broken by thy side?"

" I do not seek a lover, thou Christian knight so gay,
Because an article like that hath never come my way;
And why I gaze upon you, I cannot, cannot tell,
Except that in your iron hose you look uncommon swell.

" My pitcher it is broken, and this the reason is,—
A shepherd came behind me, and tried to snatch a kiss;
I would not stand his nonsense, so ne'er a word I spoke,
But scored him on the costard, and so the jug was broke.

" My uncle, the Alcaydè, he waits for me at home,
And will not take his tumbler until Zorayda come.
I cannot bring him water—the pitcher is in pieces—
And so I'm sure to catch it, 'cos he wallops all his nieces."

" Oh, maiden, Moorish maiden! wilt thou be ruled by me!
So wipe thine eyes and rosy lips, and give me kisses three;
And I'll give thee my helmet, thou kind and courteous
        lady,
To carry home the water to thy uncle, the Alcaydè."

He lighted down from off his steed—he tied him to a
        tree—
He bowed him to the maiden, and took his kisses three:
" To wrong thee, sweet Zorayda, I swear would be a sin!"
He knelt him at the fountain, and he dipped his hel-
        met in.

Up rose the Moorish maiden—behind the knight she steals,
And caught Alphonso Guzman up tightly by the heels;
She tipped him in, and held him down beneath the bub-
        bling water,—
" Now, take thou that for venturing to kiss Al Hamet's
        daughter!"

A Christian maid is weeping in the town of Oviedo;
She waits the coming of her love, the Count of Desparedo.
I pray you all in charity, that you will never tell,
How he met the Moorish maiden beside the lonely well.

                                        William E. Aytoun.

GIFTS RETURNED

"You must give back," her mother said,
  To a poor sobbing little maid,
"All the young man has given you,
  Hard as it now may seem to do."
"'Tis done already, mother dear!"
  Said the sweet girl, "So never fear."
    Mother. Are you quite certain? Come, recount
  (There was not much) the whole amount.
    Girl. The locket; the kid gloves.
    Mother.   Go on.
    Girl. Of the kid gloves I found but one.
    Mother. Never mind that. What else? Proceed.
  You gave back all his trash?
    Girl.   Indeed.
    Mother. And was there nothing you would save?
    Girl. Everything I could give I gave.
    Mother. To the last tittle?
    Girl.   Even to that.
    Mother. Freely?
    Girl.   My heart went pit-a-pat
  At giving up . . . ah me! ah me!
  I cry so I can hardly see . . .
  All the fond looks and words that past,
  And all the kisses, to the last.

Walter Savage Landor.

III

LOVE AND COURTSHIP

NOUREDDIN, THE SON OF THE SHAH

THERE once was a Shah had a second son
Who was very unlike his elder one,
For he went about on his own affairs,
And scorned the mosque and the daily prayers;
When his sire frowned fierce, then he cried, " Ha, ha! "
    Noureddin, the son of the Shah.

But worst of all of the pranks he played
Was to fall in love with a Christian maid,—
An Armenian maid who wore no veil,
Nor behind a lattice grew thin and pale;
At his sire's dark threats laughed the youth, " Ha, ha! "
    Noureddin, the son of the Shah.

"I will shut him close in an iron cage,"
The monarch said, in a fuming rage;
But the prince slipped out by a postern door,
And away to the mountains his loved one bore;
Loud his glee rang back on the winds, " Ha, ha! "
    Noureddin, the son of the Shah.

And still in the town of Teheran,
When a youth and a maid adopt this plan,—
All frowns and threats with a laugh defy,
And away from the mosques to the mountains fly,—
Folk meet and greet with a gay *"Ha, ha!"*
    Noureddin, the son of the Shah.

Clinton Scollard.

THE USUAL WAY

There was once a little man, and his rod and line he took,
For he said, "I'll go a-fishing in the neighboring brook."
And it chanced a little maiden was walking out that day,
    And they met—in the usual way.

Then he sat him down beside her, and an hour or two
    went by,
But still upon the grassy brink his rod and line did lie;
"I thought," she shyly whispered, "you'd be fishing all
    the day!"
    And he was—in the usual way.

So he gravely took his rod in hand, and threw the line
    about,
But the fish perceived distinctly that he was not looking
    out;
And he said, "Sweetheart, I love you!" but she said she
    could not stay:
    But she did—in the usual way.

Then the stars came out above them, and she gave a
    little sigh,
As they watched the silver ripples, like the moments, run-
    ning by;
"We must say good-by," she whispered, by the alders old
    and gray,
    And they did—in the usual way.

And day by day beside the stream they wandered to and
    fro,
And day by day the fishes swam securely down below;
Till this little story ended, as such little stories may,
    Very much—in the usual way.

And now that they are married, do they always bill and
    coo?
Do they never fret and quarrel as other couples do?
Does he cherish her and love her? Does she honor and
    obey?
       Well—they do—in the usual way.
              Frederic E. Weatherly.

THE WAY TO ARCADY

Oh, what's the way to Arcady,
  To Arcady, to Arcady;
Oh, what's the way to Arcady,
  Where all the leaves are merry?

Oh, what's the way to Arcady?
The spring is rustling in the tree—
The tree the wind is blowing through—
  It sets the blossoms flickering white.
I knew not skies could burn so blue
  Nor any breezes blow so light.
They blow an old-time way for me,
Across the world to Arcady.

Oh, what's the way to Arcady?
Sir Poet, with the rusty coat,
Quit mocking of the song-bird's note.
How have you heart for any tune,
You with the wayworn russet shoon?
Your scrip, a-swinging by your side,
Gapes with a gaunt mouth hungry-wide.
I'll brim it well with pieces red,
If you will tell the way to tread.

Oh, I am bound for Arcady,
And if you but keep pace with me
You tread the way to Arcady.

And where away lies Arcady,
And how long yet may the journey be?

Ah, that (quoth he) *I do not know—*
Across the clover and the snow—
Across the frost, across the flowers—
Through summer seconds and winter hours
I've trod the way my whole life long,
   And know not now where it may be;
My guide is but the stir to song,
That tells me I cannot go wrong,
   Or clear or dark the pathway be
   Upon the road to Arcady.

But how shall I do who cannot sing?
   I was wont to sing, once on a time—
There is never an echo now to ring
   Remembrance back to the trick of rhyme.

'Tis strange you cannot sing (quoth he),
The folk all sing in Arcady.

But how may he find Arcady
Who hath not youth nor melody?

What, know you not, old man (quoth he)—
   Your hair is white, your face is wise—
   That Love must kiss that Mortal's eyes
Who hopes to see fair Arcady?
No gold can buy you entrance there;
But beggared Love may go all bare—
No wisdom won with weariness;
But Love goes in with Folly's dress—
No fame that wit could ever win;
But only Love may lead Love in
   To Arcady, to Arcady.

Ah, woe is me, through all my days
   Wisdom and wealth I both have got,
And fame and name, and great men's praise;
   But Love, ah, Love! I have it not.

There was a time, when life was new—
  But far away, and half forgot—
I only know her eyes were blue;
  But Love—I fear I knew it not.
We did not wed, for lack of gold,
And she is dead, and I am old.
All things have come since then to me,
Save Love, ah, Love! and Arcady.
Ah, then I fear we part (quoth he),
My way's for Love and Arcady.

But you, you fare alone, like me;
  The gray is likewise in your hair.
  What love have you to lead you there,
To Arcady, to Arcady?

Ah, no, not lonely do I fare;
  My true companion's Memory.
With Love he fills the Spring-time air;
  With Love he clothes the Winter tree.
Oh, past this poor horizon's bound
  My song goes straight to one who stands—
Her face all gladdening at the sound—
  To lead me to the Spring-green lands,
  To wander with enlacing hands.
The songs within my breast that stir
Are all of her, are all of her.
My maid is dead long years (quoth he),
She waits for me in Arcady.

Oh, yon's the way to Arcady,
  To Arcady, to Arcady;
Oh, yon's the way to Arcady,
  Where all the leaves are merry.

                              H. C. Bunner.

MY LOVE AND MY HEART

Oh, the days were ever shiny
  When I ran to meet my love;
When I press'd her hand so tiny
  Through her tiny tiny glove.
Was I very deeply smitten?
  Oh, I loved like *anything!*
But my love she is a kitten,
  And my heart's a ball of string.

She was pleasingly poetic,
  And she loved my little rhymes;
For our tastes were sympathetic,
  In the old and happy times.
Oh, the ballads I have written,
  And have taught my love to sing!
But my love she is a kitten,
  And my heart's a ball of string.

Would she listen to my offer,
  On my knees I would impart
A sincere and ready proffer
  Of my hand and of my heart.
And below her dainty mitten
  I would fix a wedding ring—
But my love she is a kitten,
  And my heart's a ball of string.

Take a warning, happy lover,
  From the moral that I show;
Or too late you may discover
  What I learn'd a month ago.
We are scratch'd or we are bitten
  By the pets to whom we cling.
Oh, my love she is a kitten,
  And my heart's a ball of string.

Henry S. Leigh.

QUITE BY CHANCE

She flung the parlour window wide
  One eve of mid-July,
And he, as fate would have it tide,
  That moment sauntered by.
His eyes were blue and hers were brown,
  With drooping fringe of jet;
And he looked up as she looked down,
  And so their glances met.
    Things as strange, I dare to say,
    Happen somewhere every day.

A mile beyond the straggling street,
  A quiet pathway goes;
And lovers here are wont to meet,
  As all the country knows.
Now she one night at half-past eight
  Had sought that lonely lane,
When *he* came up, by will of fate,
  And so they met again.
    Things as strange, I dare to say,
    Happen somewhere every day.

The parish church, so old and gray,
  Is quite a sight to see;
And he was there at ten one day,
  And so, it chanced, was she.
And while they stood, with cheeks aflame,
  And neighbours liked the fun,
In stole and hood the parson came,
  And made the couple one.
    Things as strange, I dare to say,
    Happen somewhere every day.
              Frederick Langbridge.

THE NUN

SUGGESTED BY PART OF THE ITALIAN SONG, BEGINNING "SE MONECA TI FAI."

I

If you become a nun, dear,
    A friar I will be;
In any cell you run, dear,
    Pray look behind for me.
The roses all turn pale, too;
The doves all take the veil, too;
    The blind will see the show:
What! you become a nun, my dear!
    I'll not believe it, no.

II

If you become a nun, dear,
    The bishop Love will be;
The Cupids every one, dear,
    Will chaunt "We trust in thee";
The incense will go sighing,
The candles fall a dying,
    The water turn to wine:
What! you go take the vows, my dear!
    You may—but they'll be mine.

Leigh Hunt.

THE CHEMIST TO HIS LOVE

I love thee, Mary, and thou lovest me—
Our mutual flame is like th' affinity
That doth exist between two simple bodies:
I am Potassium to thine Oxygen.
'Tis little that the holy marriage vow
Shall shortly make us one. That unity
Is, after all, but metaphysical.
Oh, would that I, my Mary, were an acid,

A living acid; thou an alkali
Endow'd with human sense, that, brought together,
We both might coalesce into one salt,
One homogeneous crystal. Oh, that thou
Wert Carbon, and myself were Hydrogen;
We would unite to form olefiant gas,
Or common coal, or naphtha—would to heaven
That I were Phosphorus, and thou wert Lime!
And we of Lime composed a Phosphuret.
I'd be content to be Sulphuric Acid,
So that thou might be Soda. In that case
We should be Glauber's Salt. Wert thou Magnesia
Instead we'd form the salt that's named from Epsom.
Couldst thou Potassa be, I Aqua-fortis,
Our happy union should that compound form,
Nitrate of Potash—otherwise Saltpetre.
And thus our several natures sweetly blent,
We'd live and love together, until death
Should decompose the fleshly *tertium quid,*
Leaving our souls to all eternity
Amalgamated. Sweet, thy name is Briggs
And mine is Johnson. Wherefore should not we
Agree to form a Johnsonate of Briggs?

Unknown.

CATEGORICAL COURTSHIP

I SAT one night beside a blue-eyed girl—
   The fire was out, and so, too, was her mother;
A feeble flame around the lamp did curl,
   Making faint shadows, blending in each other:
'Twas nearly twelve o'clock, too, in November;
She had a shawl on, also, I remember.

Well, I had been to see her every night
   For thirteen days, and had a sneaking notion
To pop the question, thinking all was right,
   And once or twice had make an awkward motion
To take her hand, and stammer'd, cough'd, and stutter'd,
But, somehow, nothing to the point had utter'd.

I thought this chance too good now to be lost;
　I hitched my chair up pretty close beside her,
Drew a long breath, and then my legs I cross'd,
　Bent over, sighed, and for five minutes eyed her:
She looked as if she knew what next was coming,
And with her feet upon the floor was drumming.

I didn't know how to begin, or where—
　I couldn't speak—the words were always choking;
I scarce could move—I seem'd tied to the chair—
　I hardly breathed—'twas awfully provoking!
The perspiration from each pore came oozing,
My heart, and brain, and limbs their power seem'd losing.

At length I saw a brindle tabby cat
　Walk purring up, inviting me to pat her;
An idea came, electric-like at that—
　My doubts, like summer clouds, began to scatter,
I seized on tabby, though a scratch she gave me,
And said, " Come, Puss, ask Mary if she'll have me."

'Twas done at once—the murder now was out;
　The thing was all explain'd in half a minute.
She blush'd, and, turning pussy-cat about,
　Said, " Pussy, tell him ' yes ' "; her foot was in it!
The cat had thus saved me my category,
And here's the catastrophe of my story.

Unknown.

LANTY LEARY

Lanty was in love, you see,
　With lovely, lively Rosie Carey;
But her father can't agree
　To give the girl to Lanty Leary.
Up to fun, " Away we'll run,"
　Says she, " my father's so contrary.
Won't you follow me? Won't you follow me?"
　" Faith, I will!" says Lanty Leary.

But her father died one day
 (I hear 'twas not by dhrinkin' wather);
House and land and cash, they say,
 He left, by will, to Rose, his daughter;
House and land and cash to seize,
 Away she cut so light and airy.
" Won't you follow me? Won't you follow me?"
 " Faith, I will!" says Lanty Leary.

Rose, herself, was taken bad;
 The fayver worse each day was growin';
" Lanty, dear," says she, " 'tis sad,
 To th' other world I'm surely goin'.
You can't survive my loss, I know,
 Nor long remain in Tipperary.
Won't you follow me? Won't you follow me?"
 " Faith, I won't!" says Lanty Leary.

Samuel Lover.

THE SECRET COMBINATION

Her heart she locked fast in her breast,
 Away from molestation;
The lock was warranted the best—
 A patent combination.
She knew no simple lock and key
Would serve to keep out Love and me.

But Love a clever cracksman is,
 And cannot be resisted;
He likes such stubborn jobs as this,
 Complex and hard and twisted,
And though we worked a many day,
At last we bore her heart away.

For Love has learned full many tricks
 In his strange avocation;
He knew the figures were but six
 In this, her combination;
Nor did we for a minute rest
Until we had unlocked her breast.

First, then, we turned the knob to " Sighs,"
Then back to " Words Sincerest,"
Then " Gazing Fondly in Her Eyes,"
Then " Softly Murmured ' Dearest; '"
Then, next, " A Warm Embrace " we tried,
And at " A Kiss " the door flew wide.

Ellis Parker Butler.

FORTY YEARS AFTER

WE climbed to the top of Goat Point hill,
Sweet Kitty, my sweetheart, and I;
And watched the moon make stars on the waves,
And the dim white ships go by,
While a throne we made on a rough stone wall,
And the king and the queen were we;
And I sat with my arm about Kitty,
And she with her arm about me.

The water was mad in the moonlight,
And the sand like gold where it shone,
And our hearts kept time to its music,
As we sat in the splendour alone.
And Kitty's dear eyes twinkled brightly,
And Kitty's brown hair blew so free,
While I sat with my arm about Kitty,
And she with her arm about me.

Last night we drove in our carriage,
To the wall at the top of the hill;
And though we're forty years older,
We're children and sweethearts still.
And we talked again of that moonlight
That danced so mad on the sea,
When I sat with my arm about Kitty,
And she with her arm about me.

The throne on the wall was still standing,
　But we sat in the carriage last night,
For a wall is too high for old people
　Whose foreheads have linings of white.
And Kitty's waist measure is forty,
　While mine is full fifty and three,
So I can't get my arm about Kitty,
　Nor can she get both hers around me.

H. H. Porter.

CUPID

BEAUTIES, have ye seen this toy,
Calléd love, a little boy
Almost naked, wanton, blind,
Cruel now, and then as kind?
If he be amongst ye, say!
He is Venus' runaway.

He hath of marks about him plenty;
Ye shall know him among twenty;
All his body is a fire,
And his breath a flame entire,
That, being shot like lightning in,
Wounds the heart, but not the skin.

He doth bear a golden bow,
And a quiver, hanging low,
Full of arrows, that outbrave
Dian's shafts, where, if he have
Any head more sharp than other,
With that first he strikes his mother.

Trust him not: his words, though sweet,
Seldom with his heart do meet;
All his practice is deceit,
Every gift is but a bait;
Not a kiss but poison bears,
And most treason in his tears.

If by these ye please to know him,
Beauties, be not nice, but show him,
Though ye had a will to hide him.
Now, we hope, ye'll not abide him,
Since ye hear his falser play,
And that he's Venus' runaway.

Ben Jonson.

PARING-TIME ANTICIPATED

I SHALL not ask Jean Jacques Rousseau
If birds confabulate or no;
'Tis clear that they were always able
To hold discourse, at least in fable;
And e'en the child who knows no better
Than to interpret, by the letter,
A story of a cock and bull,
Must have a most uncommon skull.
It chanced, then, on a winter's day,
But warm, and bright, and calm as May,
The birds, conceiving a design
To forestall sweet St. Valentine,
In many an orchard, copse, and grove,
Assembled on affairs of love,
And, with much twitter and much chatter,
Began to agitate the matter.
At length a bullfinch, who could boast
More years and wisdom than the most,
Entreated, opening wide his beak,
A moment's liberty to speak;
And, silence publicly enjoin'd,
Deliver'd briefly thus his mind:
" My friends, be cautious how ye treat
The subject upon which we meet;
I fear we shall have winter yet."
A finch, whose tongue knew no control,
With golden wing and satin poll,
A last year's bird, who ne'er had tried
What marriage means, thus pert replied:

" Methinks the gentleman," quoth she,
" Opposite in the apple-tree,
By his good-will would keep us single
Till yonder heaven and earth shall mingle,
Or—which is likelier to befall—
'Til death exterminate us all.
I marry without more ado.
My dear Dick Redcap, what say you?"
Dick heard, and tweedling, ogling, bridling,
Turned short 'round, strutting, and sidling,
Attested, glad, his approbation
Of an immediate conjugation.
Their sentiments, so well express'd,
Influenced mightily the rest;
All pair'd, and each pair built a nest.
But, though the birds were thus in haste,
The leaves came on not quite so fast,
And destiny, that sometimes bears
An aspect stern on man's affairs,
Not altogether smiled on theirs.
The wind, of late breathed gently forth,
Now shifted east, and east by north;
Bare trees and shrubs but ill, you know,
Could shelter them from rain or snow.
Stepping into their nests, they paddled,
Themselves were chill'd, their eggs were addled.
Soon every father bird and mother
Grew quarrelsome, and peck'd each other,
Parted without the least regret,
Except that they had ever met,
And learn'd in future to be wiser
Than to neglect a good adviser.

MORAL

Misses, the tale that I relate
    This lesson seems to carry:
Choose not alone a proper mate,
    But proper time to marry.

William Cowper.

WHY

Do you know why the rabbits are caught in the snare
　　Or the tabby cat's shot on the tiles?
Why the tigers and lions creep out of their lair?
　　Why an ostrich will travel for miles?
Do you know why a sane man will whimper and cry
　　And weep o'er a ribbon or glove?
Why a cook will put sugar for salt in a pie?
　　Do you know?　Well, I'll tell you—it's Love.

H. P. Stevens.

THE SABINE FARMER'S SERENADE

I

'Twas on a windy night,
　　At two o'clock in the morning,
An Irish lad so tight,
　　All wind and weather scorning,
At Judy Callaghan's door.
　　Sitting upon the palings,
His love-tale he did pour,
　　And this was part of his wailings:—
　　　Only say
　You'll be Mrs. Brallaghan;
　　Don't say nay,
　Charming Judy Callaghan.

II

Oh! list to what I say,
　　Charms you've got like Venus;
Own your love you may,
　　There's but the wall between us.
You lie fast asleep
　　Snug in bed and snoring;
Round the house I creep,
　　Your hard heart imploring.

Only say
You'll have Mr. Brallaghan;
  Don't say nay,
Charming Judy Callaghan.

III

I've got a pig and a sow,
  I've got a sty to sleep 'em
A calf and a brindled cow,
  And a cabin too, to keep 'em;
Sunday hat and coat,
  An old grey mare to ride on,
Saddle and bridle to boot,
  Which you may ride astride on.
  Only say
You'll be Mrs. Brallaghan;
  Don't say nay,
Charming Judy Callaghan.

IV

I've got an acre of ground,
  I've got it set with praties;
I've got of 'baccy a pound,
  I've got some tea for the ladies;
I've got the ring to wed,
  Some whisky to make us gaily;
I've got a feather bed
  And a handsome new shillelagh.
  Only say
You'll have Mr. Brallaghan;
  Don't say nay,
Charming Judy Callaghan.

V

You've got a charming eye,
  You've got some spelling and reading
You've got, and so have I,
  A taste for genteel breeding
You're rich, and fair, and young,
  As everybody's knowing;

You've got a decent tongue
  Whene'er 'tis set a-going.
  Only say
You'll be Mrs. Brallaghan;
  Don't say nay,
Charming Judy Callaghan.

VI

For a wife till death
  I am willing to take ye;
But, och! I waste my breath,
  The devil himself can't wake ye.
'Tis just beginning to rain,
  So I'll get under cover;
To-morrow I'll come again,
  And be your constant lover.
  Only say
You'll be Mrs. Brallaghan;
  Don't say nay,
Charming Judy Callaghan.

Father Prout.

I HAE LAID A HERRING IN SAUT

I HAE laid a herring in saut—
  Lass, gin ye lo'e me, tell me now;
I hae brew'd a forpit o' maut,
  And I canna come ilka day to woo:

I hae a calf that will soon be a cow—
  Lass, gin ye lo'e me, tell me now;
I hae a stook, and I'll soon hae a mowe,
  And I canna come ilka day to woo:

I hae a house upon yon moor—
  Lass, gin ye lo'e me, tell me now;
Three sparrows may dance upon the floor,
  And I canna come ilka day to woo:
I hae a but, and I hae a ben—
  Lass, gin ye lo'e me, tell me now;

A penny to keep, and a penny to spen',
    And I canna come ilka day to woo:

I hae a hen wi' a happitie leg—
    Lass, gin ye lo'e me, tell me now;
That ilka day lays me an egg,
    And I canna come ilka day to woo:
I hae a cheese upon my skelf—
    Lass, gin ye lo'e me, tell me now;
And soon wi' mites 'twill rin itself,
    And I canna come ilka day to woo.

James Tytler.

THE CLOWN'S COURTSHIP

Quoth John to Joan, will thou have me;
I prithee now, wilt? and I'll marry thee,
My cow, my calf, my house, my rents,
And all my lands and tenements:
    Oh, say, my Joan, will not that do?
    I cannot come every day to woo.

I've corn and hay in the barn hardby,
And three fat hogs pent up in the sty,
I have a mare and she is coal black,
I ride on her tail to save my back.
           Then say, etc.

I have a cheese upon the shelf,
And I cannot eat it all myself;
I've three good marks that lie in a rag,
In a nook of the chimney, instead of a bag.
           Then say, etc.

To marry I would have thy consent,
But faith I never could compliment;
I can say nought but " Hoy, gee ho! "
Words that belong to the cart and the plough.
    So say, my Joan, will not that do,
    I cannot come every day to woo.

Unknown.

OUT UPON IT

Out upon it, I have loved
    Three whole days together;
And am like to love three more,
    If it prove fair weather.

Time shall moult away his wings,
    Ere he shall discover
In the whole wide world again
    Such a constant Lover.

But the spite on't is, no praise
    Is due at all to me:
Love with me had made no stays,
    Had it any been but she.

Had it any been but she,
    And that very face,
There had been at least ere this
    A dozen dozen in her place.

                Sir John Suckling.

LOVE IS LIKE A DIZZINESS

I lately lived in quiet case,
    An' ne'er wish'd to marry, O!
But when I saw my Peggy's face,
    I felt a sad quandary, O!
Though wild as ony Athol deer,
    She has trepann'd me fairly, O!
Her cherry cheeks an' een sae clear
    Torment me late an' early O!
    O, love, love, love!
        Love is like a dizziness;
    It winna let a poor body
        Gang about his biziness!

Love is Like a Dizziness

To tell my feats this single week
  Wad mak a daft-like diary, O!
I drave my cart out ow'r a dike,
  My horses in a miry, O!
I wear my stockings white an' blue,
  My love's sae fierce an' fiery, O!
I drill the land that I should pleugh,
  An' pleugh the drills entirely, O!
    O, love, love, love! etc.

Ae morning, by the dawn o' day,
  I rase to theek the stable, O!
I keust my coat, and plied away
  As fast as I was able, O!
I wrought that morning out an' out,
  As I'd been redding fire, O!
When I had done an look'd about,
  Gudefaith, it was the byre, O!
    O, love, love, love! etc.

Her wily glance I'll ne'er forget,
  The dear, the lovely blinkin o't
Has pierced me through an' through the heart,
  An' plagues me wi' the prinking o't.
I tried to sing, I tried to pray,
  I tried to drown't wi' drinkin' o't,
I tried with sport to drive't away,
  But ne'er can sleep for thinkin' o't.
    O, love, love, love! etc.

Nae man can tell what pains I prove,
  Or how severe my pliskie, O!
I swear I'm sairer drunk wi' love
  Than ever I was wi' whiskey, O!
For love has raked me fore an' aft,
  I scarce can lift a leggie, O!
I first grew dizzy, then gaed daft,
  An' soon I'll dee for Peggy, O!
    O, love, love, love!
      Love is like a dizziness;
      It winna let a poor body
      Gang about his biziness!

James Hogg.

THE KITCHEN CLOCK

KNITTING is the maid o' the kitchen, Milly,
Doing nothing sits the chore boy, Billy:
" Seconds reckoned,
Seconds reckoned;
Every minute,
Sixty in it.
Milly, Billy,
Billy, Milly,
Tick-tock, tock-tick,
Nick-knock, knock-nick,
Knockety-nick, nickety-knock,"—
　　Goes the kitchen clock.

Closer to the fire is rosy Milly,
Every whit as close and cosy, Billy:
" Time's a-flying,
Worth your trying;
Pretty Milly—
Kiss her, Billy!
Milly, Billy
Billy, Milly,
Tick-tock, tock-tick,
Now—now, quick—quick!
Knockety-nick, nickety-knock,"—
　　Goes the kitchen clock.

Something's happened, very red is Milly,
Billy boy is looking very silly;
" Pretty misses,
Plenty kisses;
Make it twenty,
Take a plenty.
Billy, Milly,
Milly, Billy,
Right—left, left—right,
That's right, all right,
Knockety-nick, nickety-knock,"—
　　Goes the kitchen clock.

Weeks gone, still they're sitting, Milly, Billy;
O, the winter winds are wondrous chilly!
" Winter weather,
Close together;
Wouldn't tarry,
Better marry.
Milly, Billy,
Billy, Milly,
Two—one, one—two,
Don't wait, 'twon't do,
Knockety-nick, nickety-knock,"—
    Goes the kitchen clock.

Winters two have gone, and where is Milly?
Spring has come again, and where is Billy?
" Give me credit,
For I did it;
Treat me kindly,
Mind you wind me.
Mister Billy,
Mistress Milly,
My—O, O—my,
By-by, by-by,
Nickety-knock, cradle rock,"—
    Goes the kitchen clock.

John Vance Cheney.

LADY MINE

LADY mine, most fair thou art
  With youth's gold and white and red;
'Tis a pity that thy heart
  Is so much harder than thy head.

This has stayed my kisses oft,
  This from all thy charms debarr'd,
That thy head is strangely soft,
  While thy heart is strangely hard.

Nothing had kept us apart—
    I had loved thee, I had wed—
Hadst thou had a softer heart
    Or a harder head.

But I think I'll bear Love's smart
    Till the wound has healed and fled,
Or thy head is like thy heart,
    Or thy heart is like thy head.

H. E. Clarke.

BALLADE OF THE GOLFER IN LOVE

In the "foursome" some would fain
    Find nepenthe for their woe;
Following through shine or rain
    Where the "greens" like satin show;
    But I vote such sport as "slow"—
Find it rather glum and gruesome;
    With a little maid I know
I would play a quiet "twosome"!

In the "threesome," some maintain,
    Lies excitement's gayest glow—
Strife that mounts unto the brain
    Like the sparkling *Veuve Clicquot;*
    My opinion? Nay, not so!
Noon or eve or morning dewsome
    With a little maid I know
I would play a quiet "twosome"!

Bays of glory some would gain
    With grim "Bogey" for their foe;
(He's a bogey who's not slain
    Save one smite with canny blow!)
    Yet I hold this tame, and though
My refrain seems trite, 'tis truesome;
    With a little maid I know
I would play a quiet "twosome"!

Comrades all who golfing go,
Happiness—if you would view some—
With a little maid *you* know,
Haste and play a quiet " twosome " !

Clinton Scollard.

BALLADE OF FORGOTTEN LOVES

SOME poets sing of sweethearts dead,
Some sing of true loves far away;
Some sing of those that others wed,
And some of idols turned to clay.
I sing a pensive roundelay
To sweethearts of a doubtful lot,
The passions vanished in a day—
The little loves that I've forgot.

For, as the happy years have sped,
And golden dreams have changed to gray,
How oft the flame of love was fed
By glance, or smile, from Maud or May,
When wayward Cupid was at play;
Mere fancies, formed of who knows what,
But still my debt I ne'er can pay—
The little loves that I've forgot.

O joyous hours forever fled!
O sudden hopes that would not stay!
Held only by the slender thread
Of memory that's all astray.
Their very names I cannot say.
Time's will is done, I know them not;
But blessings on them all, I pray—
The little loves that I've forgot.

ENVOI

Sweetheart, why foolish fears betray?
Ours is the one true lovers' knot;
Note well the burden of my lay—
The little loves that I've forgot.

Arthur Grissom.

IV

SATIRE

A BALLADE OF SUICIDE

The gallows in my garden, people say,
Is new and neat and adequately tall.
I tie the noose on in a knowing way
As one that knots his necktie for a ball;
But just as all the neighbours—on the wall—
Are drawing a long breath to shout "Hurray!"
The strangest whim has seized me. . . . After all
I think I will not hang myself to-day.

To-morrow is the time I get my pay—
My uncle's sword is hanging in the hall—
I see a little cloud all pink and grey—
Perhaps the rector's mother will *not* call—
I fancy that I heard from Mr. Gall
That mushrooms could be cooked another way—
I never read the works of Juvenal—
I think I will not hang myself to-day.

The world will have another washing day;
The decadents decay; the pedants pall;
And H. G. Wells has found that children play,
And Bernard Shaw discovered that they squall;
Rationalists are growing rational—
And through thick woods one finds a stream astray,
So secret that the very sky seems small—
I think I will not hang myself to-day.

Prince, I can hear the trump of Germinal,
The tumbrils toiling up the terrible way;
Even to-day your royal head may fall—
I think I will not hang myself to-day.

G. K. Chesterton.

FINNIGIN TO FLANNIGAN

SUPERINTENDENT wuz Flannigan;
Boss av the siction wuz Finnigin;
Whiniver the kyars got offen the thrack,
An' muddled up things t' th' divil an' back,
Finnigin writ it to Flannigan,
Afther the wrick wuz all on ag'in;
   That is, this Finnigin
   Repoorted to Flannigan.

Whin Finnigin furst writ to Flannigan,
He writed tin pages—did Finnigin,
An' he tould jist how the smash occurred;
Full minny a tajus, blunderin' wurrd
Did Finnigin write to Flannigan
Afther the cars had gone on ag'in.
   That wuz how Finnigin
   Repoorted to Flannigan.

Now Flannigan knowed more than Finnigin—
He'd more idjucation, had Flannigan;
An' it wore'm clane an' complately out
To tell what Finnigin writ about
In his writin' to Muster Flannigan.
So he writed back to Finnigin:
"Don't do sich a sin ag'in;
Make 'em brief, Finnigin!"

Whin Finnigin got this from Flannigan,
He blushed rosy rid, did Finnigin;
An' he said: " I'll gamble a whole month's pa-ay
That it will be minny an' minny a da-ay
Befoore Sup'rintindint—that's Flannigan—
Gits a whack at this very same sin ag'in.
From Finnigin to Flannigan
Repoorts won't be long ag'in."

.   .   .   .

Wan da-ay, on the siction av Finnigin,
On the road sup'rintinded by Flannigan,
A rail give way on a bit av a curve,
An' some kyars went off as they made the swerve.
" There's nobody hurted," sez Finnigin,
" But repoorts must be made to Flannigan."
An' he winked at McGorrigan,
As married a Finnigin.

He wuz shantyin' thin, wuz Finnigin,
As minny a railroader's been ag'in,
An' the shmoky ol' lamp wuz burnin' bright
In Finnigin's shanty all that night—
Bilin' down his repoort, was Finnigin!
An' he writed this here: " Muster Flannigan:
Off ag'in, on ag'in,
Gone ag'in—Finnigin."

S. W. Gillinan.

STUDY OF AN ELEVATION, IN INDIAN INK

POTIPHAR GUBBINS, C. E.,
Stands at the top of the tree;
And I muse in my bed on the reasons that led
To the hoisting of Potiphar G.

Potiphar Gubbins, C. E.,
Is seven years junior to Me;
Each bridge that he makes either buckles or breaks,
And his work is as rough as he.

Potiphar Gubbins, C. E.,
  Is coarse as a chimpanzee;
And I can't understand why you gave him your hand,
  Lovely Mehitabel Lee.

Potiphar Gubbins, C. E.,
  Is dear to the Powers that Be;
For they bow and They smile in an affable style
  Which is seldom accorded to Me.

Potiphar Gubbins, C. E.,
  Is certain as certain can be
Of a highly paid post which is claimed by a host
  Of seniors—including Me.

Careless and lazy is he,
  Greatly inferior to Me.
What is the spell that you manage so well,
  Commonplace Potiphar G.?

Lovely Mehitabel Lee,
  Let me inquire of thee,
Should I have riz to what Potiphar is,
  Hadst thou been mated to Me?

                              Rudyard Kipling.

THE V-A-S-E

From the madding crowd they stand apart,
The maidens four and the Work of Art;

And none might tell from sight alone
In which had culture ripest grown,—

The Gotham Million fair to see,
The Philadelphia Pedigree,

The Boston Mind of azure hue,
Or the soulful Soul from Kalamazoo,—

For all loved Art in a seemly way,
With an earnest soul and a capital A.

　·　·　·　·　·　·　·

Long they worshiped; but no one broke
The sacred stillness, until up spoke

The Western one from the nameless place,
Who blushing said, "What a lovely vace!"

Over three faces a sad smile flew,
And they edged away from Kalamazoo.

But Gotham's haughty soul was stirred
To crush the stranger with one small word.

Deftly hiding reproof in praise,
She cries, "'Tis, indeed, a lovely vaze!"

But brief her unworthy triumph when
The lofty one from the house of Penn,

With the consciousness of two grandpapas,
Exclaims, "It is quite a lovely vahs!"

And glances round with an anxious thrill,
Awaiting the word of Beacon Hill.

But the Boston maid smiles courteouslee,
And gently murmurs, "Oh, pardon me!

"I did not catch your remark, because
I was so entranced with that lovely vaws!"

> *Dies erit praegelida*
> *Sinistra quum Bostonia.*

                    James Jeffrey Roche.

MINIVER CHEEVY

Miniver Cheevy, child of scorn,
  Grew lean while he assailed the seasons;
He wept that he was ever born,
  And he had reasons.

Miniver loved the days of old
  When swords were bright and steeds were prancing;
The vision of a warrior bold
  Would set him dancing.

Miniver sighed for what was not,
  And dreamed and rested from his labors;
He dreamed of Thebes and Camelot
  And Priam's neighbors.

Miniver mourned the ripe renown
  That made so many a name so fragrant;
He mourned Romance, now on the town,
  And Art, a vagrant.

Miniver loved the Medici,
  Albeit he had never seen one;
He would have sinned incessantly
  Could he have been one.

Miniver cursed the commonplace,
  And eyed a khaki suit with loathing;
He missed the mediæval grace
  Of iron clothing.

Miniver scorned the gold he sought,
  But sore annoyed he was without it;
Miniver thought and thought and thought
  And thought about it.

Miniver Cheevy, born too late,
  Scratched his head and kept on thinking;
Miniver coughed, and called it fate,
  And kept on drinking.

Edwin Arlington Robinson.

THE RECRUIT

Sez Corporal Madden to Private McFadden:
    "Bedad, yer a bad un!
    Now turn out yer toes!
    Yer belt is unhookit,
    Yer cap is on crookit,
    Ye may not be dhrunk,
    But, be jabers, ye look it!
      Wan—two!
      Wan—two!
Ye monkey-faced divil, I'll jolly ye through!
      Wan—two!—
      Time! Mark!
Ye march like the aigle in Cintheral Parrk!"

Sez Corporal Madden to Private McFadden:
    "A saint it ud sadden
    To dhrill such a mug!
    Eyes front!—ye baboon, ye!—
    Chin up!—ye gossoon, ye!
    Ye've jaws like a goat—
    Halt! ye leather-lipped loon, ye!
      Wan—two!
      Wan—two!
Ye whiskered orang-outang, I'll fix you!
      Wan—two!—
      Time! Mark!
Ye've eyes like a bat!—can ye see in the dark?"

Sez Corporal Madden to Private McFadden:
    "Yer figger wants padd'n'—
    Sure, man, ye've no shape!
    Behind ye yer shoulders
    Stick out like two boulders;

Yer shins is as thin
As a pair of pen-holders!
    Wan—two!
    Wan—two!
Yer belly belongs on yer back, ye Jew!
    Wan—two!—
    Time! Mark!
I'm dhry as a dog—I can't shpake but I bark!"

Sez Corporal Madden to Private McFadden:
    " Me heart it ud gladden
    To blacken your eye.
    Ye're gettin' too bold, ye
    Compel me to scold ye,—
    'Tis halt! that I say,—
    Will ye heed what I told ye?
    Wan—two!
    Wan—two!
Be jabers, I'm dhryer than Brian Boru!
    Wan—two!—
    Time! Mark!
What's wur-ruk for chickens is sport for the lark!"

Sez Corporal Madden to Private McFadden:
    " I'll not stay a gaddin',
    Wid dagoes like you!
    I'll travel no farther,
    I'm dyin' for—wather;—
    Come on, if ye like,—
    Can ye loan me a quather?
    Ya-as, you—
    What,—two?
And ye'll pay the potheen? Ye're a daisy! Whurroo!
    You'll do!
    Whist! Mark!
The Rigiment's flattered to own ye, me spark!"

Robert W. Chambers.

OFFICER BRADY

THE MODERN RECRUIT

I

Sez Alderman Grady
To Officer Brady:
"G'wan! Ye're no lady!
  Luk here what ye've done:
Ye've run in Red Hogan,
Ye've pulled Paddy Grogan,
Ye've fanned Misther Brogan
  An' called him a 'gun'!

"Way up in Tammany Hall
They's a gintleman layin' f'r ou!
'An' what,' sez he, 't' 'ell,' sez he,
'Does the villyun mane to do?
Lock up the ass in his shtall!
He'll rue the day I rue,
F'r he's pulled the dive that kapes me alive,
An' he'll go to the goats! Whurroo!'"

II

Sez Alderman Grady
To Officer Brady:
"Ye pinched young Mullady
  F'r crackin' a safe!
An' Sinitor Moran
An' Alderman Doran
Is inside, a-roarin'
  F'r justice, ye thafe!

"'Way up in Tammany Hall
They's a gintleman layin' f'r you!
'What's this,' sez he, 'I hear?' sez he—
An' the air, bedad, grew blue!

'Well, I nivver did hear av such gall!
But if phwat ye say is thrue,
He's pulled a fri'nd av a fri'nd av me fri'nd,
An' he'll go to the goats! Whurroo!'"

III

Sez Alderman Grady
To Officer Brady:
"Here's Sullivan's lady
    Cavoortin' an' riled;
She lifted a locket
From Casey's coat pocket,
An' it goes to the docket,
    An' Sullivan's wild!

"'Way up in Tammany Hall
  They's a gintleman layin' f'r you!
'Tis a shame,' sez he, 'f'r to blame,' sez he,
'A lady so fair an' thrue,
  An' so divinely tall'—
'Tis po'ms he talked, ye Jew!
An' ye've cooked yer goose, an' now ye're loose
F'r to folly the goats! Whurroo!'"

IV

Sez Alderman Grady
To Officer Brady:
"Where's Katie Macready,
    The Confidence Queen?
She's niece to O'Lafferty's
Cousins, the Caffertys—
Sinitor Rafferty's
    Steady colleen!

"'Way up in Tammany Hall
  They's a gintleman layin' f'r you!
'He's pinched,' sez he, 'an' cinched,' sez he,
'A lady tray comme eel foo!

Go dangle th' tillyphone call,
An' gimme La Mulberry Roo,
F'r the town is too warrm f'r this gendarme,
An' he'll go to the goats, mon Dieu!'"

v

Sez Alderman Grady
To Officer Brady:
"McCabe is afraid he
Can't open to-night,
F'r throuble's a-brewin',
An' mischief's a-stewin',
Wid nothin' a-doin'
An' everything tight!
There's Register Ronnell,
Commissioner Donnell,
An' Congressman Connell
Preparin' f'r flight;
The Dhistrict Attorney
Told Magistrate Kearny
That Captain McBurney
Was dyin' o' fright!

"Oh!
'Way up in Tammany Hall
They's a gintleman lookin' f'r you!
' Bedad,' sez he, ' he's mad,' sez he.
' So turrn on the screw f'r Bellevue,
An' chain 'im ag'in' the wall,
An' lather 'im wan or two,
An' tether 'im out on the Bloomin'dale route
Like a loonytick goat! Whurroo!'"

Robert W. Chambers.

POST-IMPRESSIONISM

I CANNOT tell you how I love
The canvases of Mr. Dove,
Which Saturday I went to see
In Mr. Thurber's gallery.

At first you fancy they are built
As patterns for a crazy quilt,
But soon you see that they express
An ambient simultaneousness.

This thing which you would almost bet
Portrays a Spanish omelette,
Depicts instead, with wondrous skill,
A horse and cart upon a hill.

Now, Mr. Dove has too much art
To show the horse or show the cart;
Instead, he paints the *creak* and *strain,*
Get it? No pike is half as plain.

This thing which would appear to show
A fancy vest scenario,
Is really quite another thing,
A flock of pigeons on the wing.

But Mr. Dove is much too keen
To let a single bird be seen;
To show the pigeons would not do
And so he simply paints the *coo.*

It's all as simple as can be;
He paints the things you cannot see,
Just as composers please the ear
With " programme " things you cannot hear.

Dove is the cleverest of chaps;
And, gazing at his rhythmic maps,
I wondered (and I'm wondering yet)
Whether he did them on a bet.

Bert Leston Taylor.

TO THE PORTRAIT OF "A GENTLEMAN,"

IN THE ATHENÆUM GALLERY

It may be so—perhaps thou hast
　　A warm and loving heart;
I will not blame thee for thy face,
　　Poor devil as thou art.

That thing, thou fondly deem'st a nose,
　　Unsightly though it be,—
In spite of all the cold world's scorn,
　　It may be much to thee.

Those eyes,—among thine elder friends
　　Perhaps they pass for blue;—
No matter,—if a man can see,
　　What more have eyes to do?

Thy mouth—that fissure in thy face
　　By something like a chin,—
May be a very useful place
　　To put thy victual in.

I know thou hast a wife at home,
　　I know thou hast a child,
By that subdued, domestic smile
　　Upon thy features mild.

That wife sits fearless by thy side,
　　That cherub on thy knee;
They do not shudder at thy looks,
　　They do not shrink from thee.

Above thy mantel is a hook,—
　　A portrait once was there;
It was thine only ornament,—
　　Alas! that hook is bare.

She begged thee not to let it go,
    She begged thee all in vain:
She wept,—and breathed a trembling prayer
    To meet it safe again.

It was a bitter sight to see
    That picture torn away;
It was a solemn thought to think
    What all her friends would say!

And often in her calmer hours,
    And in her happy dreams,
Upon its long-deserted hook
    The absent portrait seems.

Thy wretched infant turns his head
    In melancholy wise,
And looks to meet the placid stare
    Of those unbending eyes.

I never saw thee, lovely one,—
    Perchance I never may;
It is not often that we cross
    Such people in our way;

But if we meet in distant years,
    Or on some foreign shore,
Sure I can take my Bible oath
    I've seen that face before.

                    Oliver Wendell Holmes.

CACOËTHES SCRIBENDI

If all the trees in all the woods were men,
And each and every blade of grass a pen;
If every leaf on every shrub and tree
Turned to a sheet of foolscap; every sea
Were changed to ink, and all earth's living tribes
Had nothing else to do but act as scribes,
And for ten thousand ages, day and night,
The human race should write, and write, and write,
Till all the pens and paper were used up,
And the huge inkstand was an empty cup,
Still would the scribblers clustered round its brink
Call for more pens, more paper, and more ink.

Oliver Wendell Holmes.

CONTENTMENT

" MAN WANTS BUT LITTLE HERE BELOW "

Little I ask; my wants are few;
    I only wish a hut of stone
(A very plain brone stone will do)
    That I may call my own;
And close at hand is such a one,
In yonder street that fronts the sun.

Plain food is quite enough for me;
    Three courses are as good as ten;
If Nature can subsist on three,
    Thank Heaven for three—Amen!
I always thought cold victual nice—
My choice would be vanilla-ice.

I care not much for gold or land;
    Give me a mortgage here and there,
Some good bank-stock, some note of hand,
    Or trifling railroad share.
I only ask that Fortune send
A little more than I shall spend.

Jewels are baubles; 'tis a sin
  To care for such unfruitful things;
One good-sized diamond in a pin,
  Some, *not so large,* in rings.
A ruby, and a pearl, or so,
Will do for me—I laugh at show.

My dame should dress in cheap attire
  (Good, heavy silks are never dear);
I own perhaps I *might* desire
  Some shawls of true Cashmere—
Some marrowy crapes of China silk,
Like wrinkled skins on scalded milk.

I would not have the horse I drive
  So fast that folks must stop and stare;
An easy gait—two, forty-five—
  Suits me; I do not care;
Perhaps, for just a *single spurt,*
Some seconds less would do no hurt.

Of pictures, I should like to own
  Titians and Raphaels three or four—
I love so much their style and tone—
  One Turner, and no more.
(A landscape, foreground golden dirt,
The sunshine painted with a squirt).

Of books but few—some fifty score
  For daily use, and bound for wear;
The rest upon an upper floor;
  Some *little* luxury *there*
Of red morocco's gilded gleam,
And vellum rich as country cream.

Busts, cameos, gems—such things as these,
  Which others often show for pride,
I value for their power to please,
  And selfish churls deride;
One Stradivarius, I confess,
Two Meerschaums, I would fain possess.

Wealth's wasteful tricks I will not learn,
   Nor ape the glittering upstart fool;
Shall not carved tables serve my turn,
   But *all* must be of buhl?
Give grasping pomp its double share—
I ask but *one* recumbent chair.

Thus humble let me live and die,
   Nor long for Midas' golden touch;
If Heaven more generous gifts deny,
   I shall not miss them *much*—
Too grateful for the blessing lent
Of simple tastes and mind content!

Oliver Wendell Holmes.

A BOSTON LULLABY

Baby's brain is tired of thinking
   On the Wherefore and the Whence;
Baby's precious eyes are blinking
   With incipient somnolence.

Little hands are weary turning
   Heavy leaves of lexicon;
Little nose is fretted learning
   How to keep its glasses on.

Baby knows the laws of nature
   Are beneficent and wise;
His medulla oblongata
   Bids my darling close his eyes.

And his pneumogastrics tell him
   Quietude is always best
When his little cerebellum
   Needs recuperative rest.

Baby must have relaxation,
   Let the world go wrong or right.
Sleep, my darling—leave Creation
   To its chances for the night.

James Jeffrey Roche.

A GRAIN OF SALT

Of all the wimming doubly blest
The sailor's wife's the happiest,
For all she does is stay to home
And knit and darn—and let 'im roam.

Of all the husbands on the earth
The sailor has the finest berth,
For in 'is cabin he can sit
And sail and sail—and let 'er knit.

Wallace Irwin.

SONG

Why should you swear I am forsworn,
    Since thine I vowed to be?
Lady, it is already morn,
    And 'twas last night I swore to thee
    That fond impossibility.

Have I not loved thee much and long,
    A tedious twelve hours' space?
I must all other beauties wrong,
    And rob thee of a new embrace,
    Could I still dote upon thy face.

Not but all joy in thy brown hair
    By others may be found;
But I must search the black and fair,
    Like skilful mineralists that sound
    For treasure in unploughed-up ground.

Then, if when I have loved my round,
    Thou prov'st the pleasant she;
With spoils of meaner beauties crowned
    I laden will return to thee,
    Even sated with variety.

Richard Lovelace.

A PHILOSOPHER

ZACK BUMSTEAD useter flosserfize
About the ocean an' the skies;
An' gab an' gas f'um morn till noon
About the other side the moon;
An' 'bout the natur of the place
Ten miles beyend the end of space.
An' if his wife she'd ask the crank
Ef he wouldn't kinder try to yank
Hisself out-doors an' git some wood
To make her kitchen fire good,
So she c'd bake her beans an' pies,
He'd say, " I've gotter flosserfize."

An' then he'd set an' flosserfize
About the natur an' the size
Of angels' wings, an' think, and gawp,
An' wonder how they make 'em flop.
He'd calkerlate how long a skid
'Twould take to move the sun, he did;
An' if the skid was strong an' prime,
It couldn't be moved to supper-time.
An' w'en his wife 'd ask the lout
Ef he wouldn't kinder waltz about
An' take a rag an' shoo the flies,
He'd say, " I've gotter flosserfize."

An' then he'd set an' flosserfize
'Bout schemes for fencing in the skies,
Then lettin' out the lots to rent,
So's he could make an honest cent.
An' if he'd find it pooty tough
To borry cash fer fencin'-stuff;
An' if 'twere best to take his wealth
An' go to Europe for his health,
Or save his cash till he'd enough
To buy some more of fencin'-stuff;
Then, ef his wife she'd ask the gump
Ef he wouldn't kinder try to hump

Hisself to t'other side the door,
So she c'd come an' sweep the floor,
He'd look at her with mournful eyes,
An' say, " I've gotter flosserfize."

An' so he'd set an' flosserfize
'Bout what it wuz held up the skies,
An' how God made this earthly ball
Jest simply out er nawthin' 'tall,
An' 'bout the natur, shape, an' form
Of nawthin' that he made it from.
Then, ef his wife sh'd ask the freak
Ef he wouldn't kinder try to sneak
Out to the barn an' find some aigs,
He'd never move, nor lift his laigs;
He'd never stir, nor try to rise,
But say, " I've gotter flosserfize."

An' so he'd set an' flosserfize
About the earth, an' sea, an' skies,
An' scratch his head, an' ask the cause
Of w'at there wuz before time wuz,
An' w'at the universe 'd do
Bimeby w'en time hed all got through;
An' jest how fur we'd have to climb
Ef we sh'd travel out er time;
An' ef we'd need, w'en we got there,
To keep our watches in repair.
Then, ef his wife she'd ask the gawk
Ef he wouldn't kinder try to walk
To where she had the table spread,
An' kinder git his stomach fed,
He'd leap for that ar kitchen door,
An' say, " W'y didn't you speak afore?"
An' when he'd got his supper et,
He'd set, an' set, an' set, an' set,
An' fold his arms, an' shet his eyes,
An' set, an' set, an' flosserfize.

Sam Walter Foss.

THE MEETING OF THE CLABBERHUSES

I

He was the Chairman of the Guild
Of Early Pleiocene Patriarchs;
He was chief Mentor of the Lodge
Of the Oracular Oligarchs;
He was the Lord High Autocrat
And Vizier of the Sons of Light,
And Sultan and Grand Mandarin
Of the Millennial Men of Might.

He was Grand Totem and High Priest
Of the Independent Potentates;
Grand Mogul of the Galaxy
Of the Illustrious Stay-out-lates;
The President of the Dandydudes,
The Treasurer of the Sons of Glee;
The Leader of the Clubtown Band
And Architects of Melody.

II

She was Grand Worthy Prophetess
Of the Illustrious Maids of Mark;
Of Vestals of the Third Degree
She was Most Potent Matriarch;
She was High Priestess of the Shrine
Of Clubtown's Culture Coterie,
And First Vice-President of the League
Of the illustrious G. A. B.

She was the First Dame of the Club
For teaching Patagonians Greek;
She was Chief Clerk and Auditor
Of Clubtown's Anti-Bachelor Clique;
She was High Treasurer of the Fund
For Borrioboolighalians,
And the Fund for Sending Browning's Poems
To Native-born Australians.

III

Once to a crowded social fête
  Both these much-titled people came,
And each perceived, when introduced,
  They had the selfsame name.
Their hostess said, when first they met:
  " Permit me now to introduce
My good friend Mr. Clabberhuse
  To Mrs. Clabberhuse."

" 'Tis very strange," said she to him,
  " Such an unusual name!—
A name so very seldom heard,
  That we should bear the same."
" Indeed, 'tis wonderful," said he,
  " And I'm surprised the more,
Because I never heard the name
  Outside my home before.

" But now I come to look at you,"
  Said he, " upon my life,
If I am not indeed deceived,
  You are—you are—my wife."
She gazed into his searching face
  And seemed to look him through;
" Indeed," said she, " it seems to me
  You are my husband, too.

" I've been so busy with my clubs
  And in my various spheres
I have not seen you now," she said,
  " For over fourteen years."
" That's just the way it's been with me,
  These clubs demand a sight "—
And then they both politely bowed,
  And sweetly said " Good night."

                        Sam Walter Foss.

THE IDEAL HUSBAND TO HIS WIFE

We've lived for forty years, dear wife,
    And walked together side by side,
And you to-day are just as dear
    As when you were my bride.
I've tried to make life glad for you,
    One long, sweet honeymoon of joy,
A dream of marital content,
    Without the least alloy.
I've smoothed all boulders from our path,
    That we in peace might toil along,
By always hastening to admit
    That I was right and you were wrong.

No mad diversity of creed
    Has ever sundered me from thee;
For I permit you evermore
    To borrow your ideas of me.
And thus it is, through weal or woe,
    Our love forevermore endures;
For I permit that you should take
    My views and creeds, and make them yours.
And thus I let you have my way,
    And thus in peace we toil along,
For I am willing to admit
    That I am right and you are wrong.

And when our matrimonial skiff
    Strikes snags in love's meandering stream,
I lift our shallop from the rocks,
    And float as in a placid dream.
And well I know our marriage bliss
    While life shall last will never cease;
For I shall always let thee do,
    In generous love, just what I please.
Peace comes, and discord flies away,
    Love's bright day follows hatred's night;
For I am ready to admit
    That you are wrong and I am right.

Sam Walter Foss.

DISTICHS

ISELY a woman prefers to a lover a man who neglects her.
his one may love her some day; some day the lover will not.

here are three species of creatures who when they seem
     coming are going,
hen they seem going they come: Diplomats, women, and
     crabs.

s the meek beasts in the Garden came flocking for Adam
     to name them,
en for a title to-day crawl to the feet of a king.

hat is a first love worth except to prepare for a secon
hat does the second love bring? Only regret for the first.

John Hay.

THE HEN-ROOST MAN

De Hen-roost Man he'll preach about Paul,
An' James an' John, an' Herod, an' all,
But nuver a word about Peter, oh, no!
He's afeard he'll hear dat rooster crow.
    An' he ain't by 'isself in dat, in dat—
    An' he ain't by 'isself in dat.

Ruth McEnery Stuart.

IF THEY MEANT ALL THEY SAID

Charm is a woman's strongest arm;
My charwoman is full of charm;
I chose her, not for strength of arm
But for her strange, elusive charm.

And how tears heighten woman's powers!
My typist weeps for hours and hours:
I took her for her weeping powers—
They so delight my business hours.

A woman lives by intuition.
Though my accountant shuns addition
She has the rarest intuition.
(And I myself can do addition.)

Timidity in girls is nice.
My cook is so afraid of mice.
Now you'll admit it's very nice
To feel your cook's afraid of mice.

Alice Duer Miller.

THE MAN

A MAN said to the universe,
" Sir, I exist! "
" However," replied the universe,
" The fact has not created in me
A sense of obligation."

Stephen Crane.

A THOUGHT

IF all the harm that women have done
Were put in a bundle and rolled into one,
    Earth would not hold it,
    The sky could not enfold it,
It could not be lighted nor warmed by the sun;
    Such masses of evil
    Would puzzle the devil,
And keep him in fuel while Time's wheels run.

But if all the harm that's been done by men
Were doubled, and doubled, and doubled again,
And melted and fused into vapour, and then
Were squared and raised to the power of ten,
There wouldn't be nearly enough, not near,
To keep a small girl for the tenth of a year.

James Kenneth Stephen.

THE MUSICAL ASS

The fable which I now present,
Occurred to me by accident:
And whether bad or excellent,
Is merely so by accident.

A stupid ass this morning went
Into a field by accident:
And cropped his food, and was content,
Until he spied by accident
A flute, which some oblivious gent
Had left behind by accident;
When, sniffling it with eager scent,
He breathed on it by accident,
And made the hollow instrument
Emit a sound by accident.
"Hurrah, hurrah!" exclaimed the brute,
"How cleverly I play the flute!"

A fool, in spite of nature's bent,
May shine for once,—by accident.

Tomaso de Yriarte.

THE KNIFE-GRINDER

Friend of Humanity

" Needy Knife-grinder! whither are you going?
Rough is the road—your wheel is out of order—
Bleak blows the blast; your hat has got a hole in't,
        So have your breeches!

" Weary Knife-grinder! little think the proud ones,
Who in their coaches roll along the turnpike-
Road, what hard work 'tis crying all day ' Knives and
        Scissors to grind O!'

" Tell me, Knife-grinder, how you came to grind knives?
Did some rich man tyrannically use you?
Was it the squire? or parson of the parish?
        Or the attorney?

" Was it the squire, for killing of his game? or
Covetous parson, for his tithes distraining?
Or roguish lawyer, made you lose your little
                All in a law-suit?

" (Have you not read the Rights of Man, by Tom Paine?)
Drops of compassion tremble on my eyelids,
Ready to fall, as soon as you have told your
                Pitiful story."

Knife-grinder

" Story! God bless you! I have none to tell, sir,
Only last night, a-drinking at the Chequers,
This poor old hat and breeches, as you see, were
                Torn in a scuffle.

" Constables came up for to take me into
Custody; they took me before the justice;
Justice Oldmixon put me in the parish-
                Stocks for a vagrant.

" I should be glad to drink your Honour's health in
A pot of beer, if you will give me sixpence;
But for my part, I never love to meddle
                With politics, sir."

Friend of Humanity

" *I* give thee sixpence! I will see thee damn'd first—
Wretch! whom no sense of wrongs can rouse to vengeance—
Sordid, unfeeling, reprobate, degraded,
                Spiritless outcast!"

[*Kicks the Knife-grinder, overturns his wheel, and exit in
a transport of Republican enthusiasm and universal philan-
thropy.*]

                         George Canning.

ST. ANTHONY'S SERMON TO THE FISHES

Saint Antohny at church
Was left in the lurch,
So he went to the ditches
And preached to the fishes.
  They wriggled their tails,
  In the sun glanced their scales.

The carps, with their spawn,
Are all thither drawn;
Have opened their jaws,
Eager for each clause.
  No sermon beside
  Had the carps so edified.

Sharp-snouted pikes,
Who keep fighting like tikes,
Now swam up harmonious
To hear Saint Antonius.
  No sermon beside
  Had the pikes so edified.

And that very odd fish,
Who loves fast-days, the cod-fish—
The stock-fish, I mean—
At the sermon was seen.
  No sermon beside
  Had the cods so edified.

Good eels and sturgeon,
Which aldermen gorge on,
Went out of their way
To hear preaching that day.
  No sermon beside
  Had the eels so edified.

Crabs and turtles also,
Who always move low,
Made haste from the bottom
As if the devil had got 'em.
    No sermon beside
    The crabs so edified.

Fish great and fish small,
Lords, lackeys, and all,
Each looked at the preacher
Like a reasonable creature.
    At God's word,
    They Anthony heard.

The sermon now ended,
Each turned and descended;
The pikes went on stealing,
The eels went on eeling.
    Much delighted were they,
    But preferred the old way.

The crabs are backsliders,
The stock-fish thick-siders,
The carps are sharp-set—
All the sermon forget.
    Much delighted were they,
    But preferred the old way.

                    Abraham á Sancta-Clara.

THE BATTLE OF BLENHEIM

It was a summer's evening;
    Old Casper's work was done,
And he before his cottage-door
    Was sitting in the sun;
And by him sported on the green
His little grandchild Wilhelmine.

She saw her brother Peterkin
   Roll something large and round,
That he beside the rivulet
   In playing there had found.
He came to ask what he had found,
That was so large, and smooth, and round.

Old Casper took it from the boy,
   Who stood expectant by;
And then the old man shook his head,
   And with a natural sigh,
" 'Tis some poor fellow's skull," said he,
" Who fell in the great victory.

" I find them in the garden, for
   There's many here about;
And often, when I go to plough,
   The ploughshare turns them out;
For many thousand men," said he,
" Were slain in the great victory."

" Now tell us what 'twas all about,"
   Young Peterkin he cries;
And little Wilhelmine looks up,
   With wonder-waiting eyes:
" Now tell us all about the war,
And what they kill'd each other for."

" It was the English," Casper cried,
   " That put the French to rout;
But what they kill'd each other for,
   I could not well make out;
But everybody said," quoth he,
" That 'twas a famous victory.

" My father lived at Blenheim then,
   Yon little stream hard by;
They burnt his dwelling to the ground,
   And he was forced to fly;
So with his wife and child he fled,
Nor had he where to rest his head.

"With fire and sword the country round
  Was wasted far and wide,
And many a childing mother then
  And new-born infant died.
But things like that, you know, must be
At every famous victory.

"They say it was a shocking sight,
  After the field was won,
For many a thousand bodies here
  Lay rotting in the sun.
But things like that, you know, must be
After a famous victory.

"Great praise the Duke of Marlbro' won,
  And our good Prince Eugene."
"Why, 'twas a very wicked thing!"
  Said little Wilhelmine.
"Nay, nay, my little girl," quoth he,
"It was a famous victory;

"And everybody praised the duke,
  Who such a fight did win."
"But what good came of it at last?"
  Quoth little Peterkin.
"Why, that I cannot tell," said he;
"But 'twas a famous victory."

Robert Southey.

THE THREE BLACK CROWS

Two honest tradesmen meeting in the Strand,
One took the other briskly by the hand;
"Hark-ye," said he, "'tis an odd story, this,
About the crows!" "I don't know what it is,"
Replied his friend. "No! I'm surprised at that;
Where I came from it is the common chat;
But you shall hear—an odd affair indeed!
And that it happened, they are all agreed.

Not to detain you from a thing so strange,
A gentleman, that lives not far from 'Change,
This week, in short, as all the alley knows,
Taking a puke, has thrown up three black crows."
" Impossible! " " Nay, but it's really true;
I have it from good hands, and so may you."
" From whose, I pray? " So, having named the man,
Straight to inquire his curious comrade ran.
" Sir, did you tell "—relating the affair.
" Yes, sir, I did; and, if it's worth your care,
Ask Mr. Such-a-one, he told it me.
But, by the bye, 'twas two black crows—not three."
Resolved to trace so wondrous an event,
Whip, to the third, the virtuoso went;
" Sir "—and so forth. " Why, yes; the thing is fact,
Though, in regard to number, not exact;
It was not two black crows—'twas only one;
The truth of that you may depend upon;
The gentleman himself told me the case."
" Where may I find him? " " Why, in such a place."
Away goes he, and, having found him out,
" Sir, be so good as to resolve a doubt."
Then to his last informant he referred,
And begged to know if true what he had heard.
" Did you, sir, throw up a black crow? " " Not I."
" Bless me! how people propagate a lie!
Black crows have been thrown up, three, two, and one;
And here, I find, all comes, at last, to none.
Did you say nothing of a crow at all? "
" Crow—crow—perhaps I might, now I recall
The matter over." " And pray, sir, what was't? "
" Why, I was horrid sick, and, at the last,
I did throw up, and told my neighbor so,
Something that was—as black, sir, as a crow."

John Byrom.

TO THE TERRESTRIAL GLOBE

BY A MISERABLE WRETCH

Roll on, thou ball, roll on!
Through pathless realms of space
Roll on!
What though I'm in a sorry case?
What though I cannot meet my bills?
What though I suffer toothache's ills?
What though I swallow countless pills?
Never *you* mind!
Roll on!

Roll on, thou ball, roll on!
Through seas of inky air
Roll on!
It's true I've got no shirts to wear;
It's true my butcher's bill is due;
It's true my prospects all look blue;
But don't let that unsettle you.
Never *you* mind!
Roll on!
(*It rolls on.*)

W. S. Gilbert.

ETIQUETTE

The *Ballyshannon* foundered off the coast of Cariboo,
And down in fathoms many went the captain and the crew;
Down went the owners—greedy men whom hope of gain
allured:
Oh, dry the starting tear, for they were heavily insured.

Besides the captain and the mate, the owners and the crew,
The passengers were also drowned excepting only two:
Young Peter Gray, who tasted teas for Baker, Croop, and Co.,
And Somers, who from Eastern shores imported indigo.

These passengers, by reason of their clinging to a mast,
Upon a desert island were eventually cast.
They hunted for their meals, as Alexander Selkirk used,
But they couldn't chat together—they had not been intro-
duced.

For Peter Gray, and Somers, too, though certainly in trade,
Were properly particular about the friends they made;
And somehow thus they settled it, without a word of mouth,
That Gray should take the northern half, while Somers took
the south.

On Peter's portion oysters grew—a delicacy rare,
But oysters were a delicacy Peter couldn't bear.
On Somer's side was turtle, on the shingle lying thick,
Which Somers couldn't eat, because it always made him sick.

Gray gnashed his teeth with envy as he saw a mighty store
Of turtle unmolested on his fellow-creature's shore.
The oysters at his feet aside impatiently he shoved,
For turtle and his mother were the only things he loved.

And Somers sighed in sorrow as he settled in the south,
For the thought of Peter's oysters brought the water to his
mouth.
He longed to lay him down upon the shelly bed, and stuff:
He had often eaten oysters, but had never had enough.

How they wished an introduction to each other they had had
When on board the *Ballyshannon!* And it drove them nearly
mad
To think how very friendly with each other they might get,
If it wasn't for the arbitrary rule of etiquette!

One day, when out a-hunting for the *mus ridiculus,*
Gray overheard his fellow-man soliloquising thus:
" I wonder how the playmates of my youth are getting on,
M'Connell, S. B. Walters, Paddy Byles, and Robinson?"

These simple words made Peter as delighted as could be;
Old chummies at the Charterhouse were Robinson and he.
He walked straight up to Somers, then he turned extremely
　　red,
Hesitated, hummed and hawed a bit, then cleared his throat,
　　and said:

" I beg your pardon—pray forgive me if I seem too bold,
But you have breathed a name I knew familiarly of old.
You spoke aloud of Robinson—I happened to be by.
You know him?" " Yes, extremely well." " Allow me, so
　　do I."

It was enough: they felt they could more pleasantly get on,
For (ah, the magic of the fact!) they each knew Robinson!
And Mr. Somers' turtle was at Peter's service quite,
And Mr. Somers punished Peter's oyster-beds all night.

They soon became like brothers from community of wrongs;
They wrote each other little odes and sang each other songs;
They told each other anecdotes disparaging their wives;
On several occasions, too, they saved each other's lives.

They felt quite melancholy when they parted for the night,
And got up in the morning soon as ever it was light;
Each other's pleasant company they reckoned so upon,
And all because it happened that they both knew Robinson!

They lived for many years on that inhospitable shore,
And day by day they learned to love each other more and
　　more.
At last, to their astonishment, on getting up one day,
They saw a frigate anchored in the offing of the bay.

To Peter an idea occurred. " Suppose we cross the main?
So good an opportunity may not be found again."
And Somers thought a minute, then ejaculated, " Done!
I wonder how my business in the City's getting on?"

" But stay," said Mr. Peter; " when in England, as you know,
I earned a living tasting teas for Baker, Croop, and Co.,
I may be superseded—my employers think me dead! "
" Then come with me," said Somers, " and taste indigo
    instead."

But all their plans were scattered in a moment when they
    found
The vessel was a convict ship from Portland outward bound;
When a boat came off to fetch them, though they felt it very
    kind,
To go on board they firmly but respectfully declined.

As both the happy settlers roared with laughter at the joke,
They recognized a gentlemanly fellow pulling stroke:
'Twas Robinson—a convict, in an unbecoming frock!
Condemned to seven years for misappropriating stock!!!

They laughed no more, for Somers thought he had been
    rather rash
In knowing one whose friend had misappropriated cash;
And Peter thought a foolish tack he must have gone upon
In making the acquaintance of a friend of Robinson.

At first they didn't quarrel very openly, I've heard;
They nodded when they met, and now and then exchanged a
    word:
The word grew rare, and rarer still the nodding of the head.
And when they meet each other now, they cut each other
    dead.

To allocate the island they agreed by word of mouth,
And Peter takes the north again, and Somers takes the south;
And Peter has the oysters, which he hates, in layers thick,
And Somers has the turtle—turtle always makes him sick.

                                        W. S. Gilbert.

A MODEST WIT

A SUPERCILIOUS nabob of the East—
  Haughty, being great—purse-proud, being rich—
A governor, or general, at the least,
  I have forgotten which—
Had in his family a humble youth,
  Who went from England in his patron's suite,
An unassuming boy, in truth
  A lad of decent parts, and good repute.

This youth had sense and spirit;
  But yet with all his sense,
  Excessive diffidence
Obscured his merit.

One day, at table, flushed with pride and wine,
  His honor, proudly free, severely merry,
Conceived it would be vastly fine
  To crack a joke upon his secretary.

" Young man," he said, " by what art, craft, or trade
  Did your good father gain a livelihood? "
" He was a saddler, sir," Modestus said,
  " And in his time was reckoned good."

" A saddler, eh? and taught you Greek,
  Instead of teaching you to sew!
Pray, why did not your father make
  A saddler, sir, of you? "

Each parasite, then, as in duty bound,
The joke applauded, and the laugh went round.
  At length Modestus, bowing low,
Said (craving pardon, if too free he made),
  " Sir, by your leave, I fain would know
Your father's trade! "

" My father's trade! by Heaven, that's too bad!
My father's trade? Why, blockhead, are you mad?
My father, sir, did never stoop so low—
He was a gentleman, I'd have you know."

" Excuse the liberty I take,"
  Modestus said, with archness on his brow,
" Pray, why did not your father make
  A gentleman of you? "

Selleck Osborn.

THE LATEST DECALOGUE

Thou shalt have one God only, who
Would be at the expense of two?
No graven images may be
Worshipped, except the currency:
Swear not at all; for, for thy curse
Thine enemy is none the worse:
At Church on Sunday to attend
Will serve to keep the world thy friend:
Honour thy parents; that is, all
From whom advancement may befall:
Thou shalt not kill; but need'st not strive
Officiously to keep alive:
Do not adultery commit;
Advantage rarely comes of it:
Thou shalt not steal; an empty feat,
When it's so lucrative to cheat:
Bear not false witness; let the lie
Have time on its own wings to fly:
Thou shalt not covet, but tradition
Approves all forms of competition.

Arthur Hugh Clough.

A SIMILE

DEAR Thomas, didst thou never pop
Thy head into a tin-man's shop?
There, Thomas, didst thou never see
('Tis but by way of simile)
A squirrel spend his little rage,
In jumping round a rolling cage?
The cage, as either side turn'd up,
Striking a ring of bells a-top?—
Mov'd in the orb, pleas'd with the chimes,
The foolish creature thinks he climbs:
But here or there, turn wood or wire,
He never gets two inches higher.
So fares it with those merry blades,
That frisk it under Pindus' shades.
In noble songs, and lofty odes,
They tread on stars, and talk with gods;
Still dancing in an airy round,
Still pleas'd with their own verses' sound;
Brought back, how fast soe'er they go,
Always aspiring, always low.

Matthew Prior.

BY PARCELS POST

A DOMESTIC IDYLL

I SENT my love a parcel
    In the days when we were young,
Or e'er by care and trouble
    Our heart-strings had been wrung.
By parcels post I sent it—
    What 'twas I do not know—
In the days when we were courting,
    A long time ago.

The spring-time waxed to summer,
    Then autumn leaves grew red,
And in the sweet September
    My love and I were wed.

But though the Church had blessed us,
  My little wife looked glum;
I'd posted her a parcel,
  And the parcel hadn't come.

Ah, many moons came after,
  And then there was a voice,
A little voice whose music
  Would make our hearts rejoice.
And, singing to her baby,
  My dear one oft would say,
" I wonder, baby darling,
  Will that parcel come to-day ? "

The gold had changed to silver
  Upon her matron brow;
The years were eight-and-twenty
  Since we breathed our marriage vow,
And our grandchildren were playing
  Hunt-the-slipper on the floor,
When they saw the postman standing
  By our open cottage door.

Then they ran with joy to greet him,
  For they knew he'd come at last;
They had heard me tell the story
  Very often in the past.
He handed them a parcel,
  And they brought it in to show—
'Twas the parcel I had posted
  Eight-and-twenty years ago.

George R. Sims.

ALL'S WELL THAT ENDS WELL

A FRIEND of mine was married to a scold,
To me he came, and all his troubles told.
Said he, " She's like a woman raving mad."
" Alas! my friend," said I, " that's very bad! "
" No, not so bad," said he; " for, with her, true
I had both house and land, and money too."
  " That was well," said I;
   " No, not so well," said he;
   " For I and her own brother
   Went to law with one another;
   I was cast, the suit was lost,
And every penny went to pay the cost."
   " That was bad," said I;
   " No, not so bad," said he:
" For we agreed that he the house should keep,
And give to me four score of Yorkshire sheep
All fat, and fair, and fine, they were to be."
" Well, then," said I, " sure that was well for thee? "
   " No, not so well," said he;
   " For, when the sheep I got,
   They every one died of the rot."
   " That was bad," said I;
   " No, not so bad," said he;
   " For I had thought to scrape the fat
   And keep it in an oaken vat;
Then into tallow melt for winter store."
" Well, then," said I, " that's better than before? "
   " 'Twas not so well," said he;
   " For having got a clumsy fellow
   To scrape the fat and melt the tallow;
Into the melting fat the fire catches,
   And, like brimstone matches,
   Burnt my house to ashes."
   " That *was* bad," said I;
" No! not so bad," said he; " for, what is best,
My scolding wife has gone among the rest."

Unknown.

THE CONTRAST

In London I never know what I'd be at,
Enraptured with this, and enchanted with that;
I'm wild with the sweets of variety's plan,
And life seems a blessing too happy for man.

But the country, Lord help me! sets all matters right,
So calm and composing from morning to night;
Oh, it settles the spirits when nothing is seen
But an ass on a common, a goose on a green!

In town, if it rain, why it damps not our hope,
The eye has her choice, and the fancy her scope;
What harm though it pour whole nights or whole days?
It spoils not our prospects, or stops not our ways.

In the country, what bliss, when it rains in the fields,
To live on the transports that shuttlecock yields;
Or go crawling from window to window, to see
A pig on a dunghill or crow on a tree.

In town, we've no use for the skies overhead,
For when the sun rises then we go to bed;
And as to that old-fashioned virgin the moon,
She shines out of season, like satin in June.

In the country, these planets delightfully glare,
Just to show us the object we want isn't there;
Oh, how cheering and gay, when their beauties arise,
To sit and gaze round with the tears in one's eyes!

But 'tis in the country alone we can find
That happy resource, the relief of the mind,
When, drove to despair, our last efforts we make,
And drag the old fish-pond, for novelty's sake:

Indeed I must own, 'tis a pleasure complete
To see ladies well-draggled and wet in their feet;
But what is all that to the transport we feel
When we capture, in triumph, two toads and an eel?

I have heard though, that love in a cottage is sweet,
When two hearts in one link of soft sympathy meet;
That's to come—for as yet I, alas! am a swain,
Who require, I own it, more links to my chain.

In the country, if Cupid should find a man out,
The poor tortured victim mopes hopeless about;
But in London, thank Heaven! our peace is secure,
Where for one eye to kill, there's a thousand to cure.

In town let me live then, in town let me die,
For in truth I can't relish the country, not I.
If one must have a villa in summer to dwell,
Oh, give me the sweet shady side of Pall Mall!

Captain C. Morris.

THE DEVONSHIRE LANE

In a Devonshire lane as I trotted along
T'other day, much in want of a subject for song;
Thinks I to myself, I have hit on a strain—
Sure marriage is much like a Devonshire lane.

In the first place, 'tis long, and when once you are in it,
It holds you as fast as the cage holds a linnet;
For howe'er rough and dirty the road may be found,
Drive forward you must, since there's no turning round.

But though 'tis so long, it is not very wide,
For two are the most that together can ride;
And e'en there 'tis a chance but they get in a pother,
And jostle and cross, and run foul of each other.

Old Poverty greets them with mendicant looks,
And Care pushes by them o'erladen with crooks,
And Strife's grating wheels try between them to pass,
Or Stubbornness blocks up the way on her ass.

Then the banks are so high, both to left hand and right,
That they shut up the beauties around from the sight;
And hence, you'll allow, 'tis an inference plain
That marriage is just like a Devonshire lane.

But, thinks I, too, these banks within which we are pent,
With bud, blossom, and berry are richly besprent;
And the conjugal fence which forbids us to roam
Looks lovely when deck'd with the comforts of home.

In the rock's gloomy crevice the bright holly grows,
The ivy waves fresh o'er the withering rose;
And the evergreen love of a virtuous wife
Smooths the roughness of care—cheers the winter of life.

Then long be the journey and narrow the way;
I'll rejoice that I've seldom a turnpike to pay;
And, whate'er others think, be the last to complain,
Though marriage is just like a Devonshire lane.

John Marriott.

A SPLENDID FELLOW

Delmonico's is where he dines
On quail on toast, washed down with wines;
Then lights a twenty-cent cigar
With quite a flourish at the bar.

He throws his money down so proud,
And " sets 'em up " for all the crowd;
A dozen games of billiards, too,
He gaily loses ere he's through.

Oh, he's a splendid fellow, quite;
He pays his debts with such delight,
And often boasts of—to his clan—
His honour as a gentleman.

But when this splendid fellow's wife,
Who leads at home a frugal life
Begs for a little change to buy
A dress, he looks at her so wry,

That she, alarmed at his distress,
Gives him a kiss and sweet caress,
And says, " Don't worry so, my dear,
" I'll turn the dress I made last year."

H. C. Dodge.

IF

If a man could live a thousand years,
    When half his life had passed,
He might, by strict economy,
    A fortune have amassed.

Then having gained some common-sense,,
    And knowledge, too, of life,
He could select the woman who
    Would make him a true wife.

But as it is, man hasn't time
    To even pay his debts,
And weds to be acquainted with
    The woman whom he gets.

H. C. Dodge.

ACCEPTED AND WILL APPEAR

One evening while reclining
    In my easy-chair, repining
O'er the lack of true religion, and the dearth of common
    sense,
    A solemn visaged lady,
    Who was surely on the shady
Side of thirty, entered proudly, and to crush me did com-
    mence:

" I sent a poem here, sir,"
Said the lady, growing fiercer,
And the subject which I'd chosen, you remember, sir, was
'Spring';
But, although I've scanned your paper,
Sir, by sunlight, gas, and taper,
've discovered of that poem not a solitary thing."

She was muscular and wiry,
And her temper sure was fiery,
And I knew to pacify her I would have to—fib like fun.
So I told her ere her verses,
Which were great, had come to—bless us,
We'd received just sixty-one on " Spring," of which we'd
printed one.

And I added, " We've decided
That they'd better be divided
Among the years that follow—one to each succeeding Spring.
So your work, I'm pleased to mention,
Will receive our best attention
In the year of nineteen-forty, when the birds begin to sing."

Parmenas Mix.

THE LITTLE VAGABOND

DEAR mother, dear mother, the Church is cold;
But the Alehouse is healthy, and pleasant, and warm.
Besides, I can tell where I am used well;
The poor parsons with wind like a blown bladder swell.

But, if at the Church they would give us some ale,
And a pleasant fire our souls to regale,
We'd sing and we'd pray all the livelong day,
Nor ever once wish from the Church to stray.

Then the Parson might preach, and drink, and sing,
And we'd be as happy as birds in the spring;

And modest Dame Lurch, who is always at Church,
Would not have bandy children, nor fasting, nor birch.

And God, like a father, rejoicing to see
His children as pleasant and happy as He,
Would have no more quarrel with the Devil or the barrel,
But kiss him, and give him both drink and apparel.

William Blake.

SYMPATHY

A KNIGHT and a lady once met in a grove
While each was in quest of a fugitive love;
A river ran mournfully murmuring by,
And they wept in its waters for sympathy.

"Oh, never was knight such a sorrow that bore!"
"Oh, never was maid so deserted before!"
"From life and its woes let us instantly fly,
And jump in together for company!"

They searched for an eddy that suited the deed,
But here was a bramble and there was a weed;
"How tiresome it is!" said the fair, with a sigh;
So they sat down to rest them in company.

They gazed at each other, the maid and the knight;
How fair was her form, and how goodly his height!
"One mournful embrace," sobbed the youth, "ere we die!"
So kissing and crying kept company.

"Oh, had I but loved such an angel as you!"
"Oh, had but my swain been a quarter as true!"
"To miss such perfection how blinded was I!"
Sure now they were excellent company!

At length spoke the lass, 'twixt a smile and a tear,
"The weather is cold for a watery bier;
When summer returns we may easily die,
Till then let us sorrow in company."

Reginald Heber.

THE RELIGION OF HUDIBRAS

For his religion it was fit
To match his learning and his wit:
'Twas Presbyterian true blue;
For he was of that stubborn crew
Of errant saints, whom all men grant
To be the true church militant;
Such as do build their faith upon
The holy text of pike and gun;
Decide all controversies by
Infallible artillery;
And prove their doctrine orthodox,
By apostolic blows and knocks;
Call fire, and sword, and desolation,
A godly, thorough reformation,
Which always must be carried on,
And still be doing, never done;
As if religion were intended
For nothing else but to be mended:
A sect whose chief devotion lies
In odd perverse antipathies;
In falling out with that or this,
And finding somewhat still amiss;
More peevish, cross, and splenetic,
Than dog distract, or monkey sick;
That with more care keep holy-day
The wrong, than others the right way,
Compound for sins they are inclin'd to,
By damning those they have no mind to:
Still so perverse and opposite,
As if they worshipped God for spite:
The self-same thing they will abhor
One way, and long another for:
Free-will they one way disavow,
Another, nothing else allow:
All piety consists therein
In them, in other men all sin:
Rather than fail, they will defy
That which they love most tenderly;

Quarrel with minc'd pies and disparage
Their best and dearest friend, plum porridge,
Fat pig and goose itself oppose,
And blaspheme custard through the nose.

Samuel Butler.

HOLY WILLIE'S PRAYER

O THOU wha in the heavens dost dwell,
Wha, as it pleases best Thysel,
Sends ane to Heaven, an' ten to Hell,
     A' for Thy glory,
And no for onie guid or ill
       They've done before Thee!

I bless and praise Thy matchless might,
When thousands Thou hast left in night,
That I am here, before Thy sight,
     For gifts an' grace,
A burnin' an' a shinin' light
     To a' this place.

What was I, or my generation,
That I should get sic exaltation!
I, wha deserv'd most just damnation,
     For broken laws
Sax thousand years ere my creation,
     Thro' Adam's cause.

When frae my mither's womb I fell,
Thou might hae plung'd me deep in Hell,
To gnash my gooms, to weep and wail
     In burnin' lakes,
Whare damnèd devils roar and yell,
     Chain'd to their stakes.

Yet I am here, a chosen sample,
To show Thy grace is great and ample;
I'm here a pillar o' Thy temple,
     Strong as a rock,
A guide, a buckler, an example
     To a' Thy flock!

But yet, O Lord! confess I must,
At times I'm fash'd wi' fleshly lust;
An' sometimes, too, in warldly trust,
          Vile self gets in;
But Thou remembers we are dust,
          Defil'd wi' sin.

May be Thou lets this fleshly thorn
Beset Thy servant e'en and morn,
Lest he owre proud and high should turn
          That he's sae gifted:
If sae, Thy han' maun e'en be borne
          Until Thou lift it.

Lord, bless Thy chosen in this place,
For here Thou has a chosen race:
But God confound their stubborn face,
          An' blast their name,
Wha bring Thy elders to disgrace
          An' open shame!

Lord, mind Gawn Hamilton's deserts,
He drinks, an' swears, an' plays at cartes,
Yet has sae monie takin' arts,
          Wi' great and sma',
Frae God's ain priest the people's hearts
          He steals awa.

An' when we chasten'd him therefore,
Thou kens how he bred sic a splore,
As set the warld in a roar
          O' laughin' at us;—
Curse Thou his basket and his store,
          Kail an' potatoes!

Lord, hear my earnest cry and pray'r
Against the Presbyt'ry of Ayr!
Thy strong right hand, Lord, mak it bare
          Upo' their heads!
Lord, visit them, an' dinna spare,
          For their misdeeds!

O Lord, my God! that glib-tongu'd Aiken,
My vera heart and saul are quakin'
To think how we stood sweatin', shakin',
          An' pish'd wi' dread,
While he wi' hingin' lip an' snakin',
          Held up his head.

Lord, in Thy day o' vengeance try him!
Lord, visit them wha did employ him,
And pass not in Thy mercy by them,
          Nor hear their pray'r;
But for Thy people's sake destroy them,
          An' dinna spare!

But, Lord, remember me and mine,
Wi' mercies temp'ral and divine,
That I for grace and gear may shine,
          Excell'd by nane,
An' a' the glory shall be Thine,
          Amen, Amen!

                                    Robert Burns.

THE LEARNED NEGRO

THERE was a negro preacher, I have heard,
In Southern parts before rebellion stirred,
Who did not spend his strength in empty sound;
His was a mind deep-reaching and profound.
Others might beat the air, and make a noise,
And help to amuse the silly girls and boys;
But as for him, he was a man of thought,
Deep in theology, although untaught.
He could not read or write, but he was wise,
And knew right smart how to extemporize.
One Sunday morn, when hymns and prayers were said,
The preacher rose and rubbing up his head,
" Bredren and sisterin, and companions dear,
Our preachment for to-day, as you shall hear,
Will be ob de creation,—ob de plan
On which God fashioned Adam, de fust man.

When God made Adam, in de ancient day,
He made his body out ob earth and clay,
He shape him all out right, den by and by,
He set him up again de fence to dry."
" Stop," said a voice; and straightway there arose
An ancient negro in his master's clothes.
" Tell me," said he, " before you farder go,
One little thing which I should like to know.
It does not quite get through dis niggar's har,
How came dat fence so nice and handy dar? "
Like one who in the mud is tightly stuck,
Or one nonplussed, astonished, thunderstruck,
The preacher looked severely on the pews,
And rubbed his hair to know what words to use:
" Bredren," said he, " dis word I hab to say;
De preacher can't be bothered in dis way;
For, if he is, it's jest as like as not,
Our whole theology will be upsot."

Unknown.

TRUE TO POLL

I'LL sing you a song, not very long,
But the story somewhat new,
Of William Kidd, who, whatever he did,
To his Poll was always true.
He sailed away in a galliant ship
From the port of old Bris*tol*,
And the last words he uttered,
As his hankercher he fluttered,
Were, " My heart is true to Poll."

His heart was true to Poll,
His heart was true to Poll,
It's no matter what you do
If your heart be only true:
And his heart *was* true to Poll.

'Twas a wreck. William, on shore he swam,
And looked about for an inn;
When a noble savage lady, of a color rather shady,
Came up with a kind of grin:
"Oh, marry *me*, and a king you'll be,
And in a palace loll;
    Or we'll eat you willy-nilly."
    So he gave his *hand*, did Billy,
But his *heart* was true to Poll.

Away a twelvemonth sped, and a happy life he led
As the King of the Kikeryboos;
His paint was red and yellar, and he used a big umbrella,
And he wore a pair of over-*shoes;*
He'd corals and knives, and twenty-six wives,
Whose beauties I cannot here extol;
    One day they all revolted,
    So he back to Bristol bolted,
For his *heart* was true to Poll.

His heart was true to Poll,
His heart was true to Poll,
    It's no matter what you do
    If your heart be only true:
And his heart *was* true to Poll.

F. C. Burnand.

TRUST IN WOMEN

When these things following be done to our intent,
Then put women in trust and confident.

WHEN nettles in winter bring forth roses red,
And all manner of thorn trees bear figs naturally,
And geese bear pearls in every mead,
And laurel bear cherries abundantly,
And oaks bear dates very plenteously,
And kisks give of honey superfluence,
Then put women in trust and confidence.

When box bear paper in every land and town,
　　And thistles bear berries in every place,
And pikes have naturally feathers in their crown,
　　And bulls of the sea sing a good bass,
　　And men be the ships fishes trace,
And in women be found no insipience,
Then put them in trust and confidence.

When whitings do walk forests to chase harts,
　　And herrings their horns in forests boldly blow,
And marmsets mourn in moors and lakes,
　　And gurnards shoot rooks out of a crossbow,
　　And goslings hunt the wolf to overthrow,
And sprats bear spears in armès of defence,
Then put women in trust and confidence.

When swine be cunning in all points of music,
　　And asses be doctors of every science,
And cats do heal men by practising of physic,
　　And buzzards to scripture give any credence,
　　And merchants buy with horn, instead of groats and pence,
And pyes be made poets for their eloquence,
Then put women in trust and confidence.

When sparrows build churches on a height,
　　And wrens carry sacks unto the mill,
And curlews carry timber houses to dight,
　　And fomalls bear butter to market to sell,
　　And woodcocks bear woodknives cranes to kill,
And greenfinches to goslings do obedience,
Then put women in trust and confidence.

When crows take salmon in woods and parks,
　　And be take with swifts and snails,
And camels in the air take swallows and larks,
　　And mice move mountains by wagging of their tails,
　　And shipmen take a ride instead of sails.
And when wives to their husbands do no offence,
Then put women in trust and confidence.

When antelopes surmount eagles in flight,
  And swans be swifter than hawks of the tower,
And wrens set gos-hawks by force and might,
  And muskets make verjuice of crabbes sour,
  And ships sail on dry land, silt give flower,
And apes in Westminster give judgment and sentence,
Then put women in trust and confidence.

Unknown.

THE LITERARY LADY

What motley cares Corilla's mind perplex,
Whom maids and metaphors conspire to vex!
In studious dishabille behold her sit,
A lettered gossip and a household wit;
At once invoking, though for different views,
Her gods, her cook, her milliner and muse.
Round her strewed room a frippery chaos lies,
A checkered wreck of notable and wise,
Bills, books, caps, couplets, combs, a varied mass,
Oppress the toilet and obscure the glass;
Unfinished here an epigram is laid,
And there a mantua-maker's bill unpaid.
There new-born plays foretaste the town's applause,
There dormant patterns pine for future gauze.
A moral essay now is all her care,
A satire next, and then a bill of fare.
A scene she now projects, and now a dish;
Here Act the First, and here, Remove with Fish.
Now, while this eye in a fine frenzy rolls,
That soberly casts up a bill for coals;
Black pins and daggers in one leaf she sticks,
And tears, and threads, and bowls, and thimbles mix.

Richard Brinsley Sheridan.

TWELVE ARTICLES

I

Lest it may more quarrels breed,
I will never hear you read.

II

By disputing, I will never,
To convince you once endeavor.

III

When a paradox you stick to.
I will never contradict you.

IV

When I talk and you are heedless,
I will show no anger needless.

V

When your speeches are absurd,
I will ne'er object a word.

VI

When you furious argue wrong,
I will grieve and hold my tongue.

VII

Not a jest or humorous story
Will I ever tell before ye:
To be chidden for explaining,
When you quite mistake the meaning.

VIII

Never more will I suppose,
You can taste my verse or prose.

IX

You no more at me shall fret,
While I teach and you forget.

X

You shall never hear me thunder,
When you blunder on, and blunder.

XI

Show your poverty of spirit,
And in dress place all your merit;
Give yourself ten thousand airs:
That with me shall break no squares.

XII

Never will I give advice,
Till you please to ask me thrice:
Which if you in scorn reject,
'T will be just as I expect.

Thus we both shall have our ends
And continue special friends.

Dean Swift.

ALL-SAINTS

In a church which is furnish'd with mullion and gable,
　With altar and reredos, with gargoyle and groin,
The penitents' dresses are sealskin and sable,
　The odour of sanctity's eau-de-Cologne.

But only could Lucifer, flying from Hades,
　Gaze down on this crowd with its panniers and paints,
He would say, as he look'd at the lords and the ladies,
　" Oh, where is All-Sinners', if this is All-Saints'? "

Edmund Yates.

HOW TO MAKE A MAN OF CONSEQUENCE

A brow austere, a circumspective eye.
A frequent shrug of the *os humeri;*
A nod significant, a stately gait,
A blustering manner, and a tone of weight,
A smile sarcastic, an expressive stare:
Adopt all these, as time and place will bear;
Then rest assur'd that those of little sense
Will deem you sure a man of consequence.

Mark Lemon.

ON A MAGAZINE SONNET

"Scorn not the sonnet," though its strength be sapped,
  Nor say malignant its inventor blundered;
The corpse that here in fourteen lines is wrapped
  Had otherwise been covered with a hundred.

Russell Hilliard Loines.

PARADISE

A HINDOO LEGEND

A Hindoo died—a happy thing to do
When twenty years united to a shrew.
Released, he hopefully for entrance cries
Before the gates of Brahma's Paradise.
" Hast been through Purgatory? " Brahma said.
" I have been married," and he hung his head.
" Come in, come in, and welcome, too, my son!
Marriage and Purgatory are as one."
In bliss extreme he entered heaven's door,
And knew the peace he ne'er had known before.

He scarce had entered in the Garden fair,
Another Hindoo asked admission there.
The self-same question Brahma asked again:
" Hast been through Purgatory? " " No; what then? "
" Thou canst not enter! " did the god reply.
" He that went in was no more there than I."
" Yes, that is true, but he has married been,
And so on earth has suffered for all sin."
" Married? 'Tis well; for I've been married twice! "
" Begone! We'll have no fools in Paradise! "

George Birdseye.

THE FRIAR OF ORDERS GRAY

I AM a friar of orders gray,
And down in the valleys I take my way;
I pull not blackberry, haw, or hip;
Good store of venison fills my scrip;
My long bead-roll I merrily chant;
Where'er I walk no money I want;
And why I'm so plump the reason I tell:
Who leads a good life is sure to live well.
    What baron or squire,
        Or knight of the shire,
    Lives half so well as a holy friar?

After supper, of heaven I dream,
But that is a pullet and clouted cream;
Myself by denial I mortify—
With a dainty bit of a warden-pie;
I'm clothed in sackcloth for my sin—
With old sack wine I'm lined within;
A chirping cup is my matin song,
And the vesper's bell is my bowl, ding-dong.
    What baron or squire,
        Or knight of the shire,
    Lives half so well as a holy friar?

John O'Keefe.

OF A CERTAIN MAN

THERE was (not certain when) a certain preacher
That never learned, and yet became a teacher,
Who, having read in Latin thus a text
Of *erat quidam homo,* much perplexed,
He seemed the same with study great to scan,
In English thus, *There was a certain man.*
" But now," quoth he, " good people, note you this,
He said there was: he doth not say there is;
For in these days of ours it is most plain
Of promise, oath, word, deed, no man's certain;
Yet by my text you see it comes to pass
That surely once a certain man there was;
But yet, I think, in all your Bible no man
Can find this text, *There was a certain woman.*"

Sir John Harrington.

CLEAN CLARA

WHAT! not know our Clean Clara?
Why, the hot folks in Sahara,
And the cold Esquimaux,
Our little Clara knows!
Clean Clara, the Poet sings,
Cleaned a hundred thousand things!

She cleaned the keys of the harpsichord,
She cleaned the hilt of the family sword,
She cleaned my lady, she cleaned my lord,
All the pictures in their frames,
Knights with daggers and stomachered dames—
Cecils, Godfreys, Montforts, Graemes,
Winifreds—all those nice old names!

She cleaned the works of the eight-day clock,
She cleaned the spring of a secret lock,
She cleaned the mirror, she cleaned the cupboard,
All the books she India-rubbered!
She cleaned the Dutch tiles in the place,
She cleaned some very old-fashioned lace;
The Countess of Miniver came to her,
"Pray, my dear, will you clean my fur?"
All her cleanings are admirable,
To count your teeth you will be able,
If you look in the walnut table.

She cleaned the tent-stitch and the sampler,
She cleaned the tapestry, which was ampler;
Joseph going down into the pit,
And the Shunammite woman with the boy in a fit.

You saw the reapers, *not* in the distance,
And Elisha, coming to the child's assistance,
With the house on the wall that was built for the prophet,
The chair, the bed and the bolster of it.
The eyebrows all had a twirl reflective,
Just like an eel: to spare invective
There was plenty of color but no perspective.

However, Clara cleaned it all,
With a curious lamp, that hangs in the hall;
She cleaned the drops of the chandeliers,
Madam, in mittens, was moved to tears.

She cleaned the cage of the cockatoo,
The oldest bird that ever grew;
I should say a thousand years old would do.
I'm sure he looked it, but nobody knew;
She cleaned the china, she cleaned the delf,
She cleaned the baby, she cleaned herself!

Tomorrow morning, she means to try
To clean the cobwebs from the sky;
Some people say the girl will rue it,
But my belief is she will do it.

So I've made up my mind to be there to see
There's a beautiful place in the walnut tree;
The bough is as firm as a solid rock;
She brings out her broom at six o'clock.

W. B. Rands.

CHRISTMAS CHIMES

LITTLE Penelope Socrates,
    A Boston maid of four,
Wide opened her eyes on Christmas morn,
    And looked the landscape o'er.
" What is it inflates my *bas de bleu?* "
    She asked with dignity;
" 'Tis Ibsen in the original!
    Oh, joy beyond degree! "

Miss Mary Cadwallader Rittenhouse
    Of Philadelphia town,
Awoke as much as they ever do there
    And watched the snow come down.
" I'm glad that it is Christmas,"
    You might have heard her say,
" For my family is one year older now
    Than it was last Christmas day."

'Twas Christmas in giddy Gotham,
  And Miss Irene de Jones
Awoke at noon and yawned and yawned,
  And stretched her languid bones.
" I'm sorry it is Christmas,
  Papa at home will stay,
For 'Change is closed and he won't make
  A single cent to-day."

Windily dawned the Christmas
  On the city by the lake,
And Miss Arabel Wabash Breezy
  Was instantly awake.
" What's that thing in my stocking?
  Well, in two jiffs I'll know!"
And she drew a grand piano forth
  From 'way down in the toe.

Unknown.

THE RULING PASSION

From " Moral Essays," Epistle I

THE frugal crone, whom praying priests attend,
Still tries to save the hallowed taper's end,
Collects her breath, as ebbing life retires,
For one puff more, and in that puff expires.
" Odious! in woollen! 'twould a saint provoke,"
Were the last words that poor Narcissa spoke;
" No, let a charming chintz and Brussels lace
Wrap my cold limbs, and shade my lifeless face:
One would not, sure, be frightful when one's dead,—
And—Betty—give this cheek a little red."
  The courtier smooth, who forty years had shined
An humble servant to all humankind,
Just brought out this, when scarce his tongue could stir,
" If—where I'm going—I could serve you, sir?"
  " I give and I devise" (old Euclio said,
And sighed) " my lands and tenements to Ned."

Your money, sir? "My money, sir! What, all?
Why—if I must" (then wept)—"I give it Paul."
The manor, sir? "The manor, hold!" he cried,
"Not that,—I cannot part with that,"—and died.

Alexander Pope.

THE POPE AND THE NET

WHAT, he on whom our voices unanimously ran,
Made Pope at our last Conclave? Full low his life began:
His father earned the daily bread as just a fisherman.

So much the more his boy minds book, gives proof of
mother-wit,
Becomes first Deacon, and then Priest, then Bishop: see
him sit
No less than Cardinal ere long, while no one cries "Unfit!"

But some one smirks, some other smiles, jogs elbow and
nods head;
Each wings at each: "I' faith, a rise! Saint Peter's net,
instead
Of sword and keys, is come in vogue!" You think he
blushes red?

Not he, of humble holy heart! "Unworthy me!" he sighs:
"From fisher's drudge to Church's prince—it is indeed a
rise:
So, here's my way to keep the fact forever in my eyes!"

And straightway in his palace-hall, where commonly is set
Some coat-of-arms, some portraiture ancestral, lo, we met
His mean estate's reminder in his fisher-father's net!

Which step conciliates all and some, stops cavil in a trice:
"The humble holy heart that holds of new-born pride no
spice!
He's just the saint to choose for Pope!" Each adds, "'Tis
my advice."

So Pope he was: and when we flocked—its sacred slipper
    on—
To kiss his foot, we lifted eyes, alack, the thing was gone—
That guarantee of lowlihead,—eclipsed that star which
    shone!

Each eyed his fellow, one and all kept silence. I cried
    "Pish!
I'll make me spokesman for the rest, express the common
    wish.
Why, Father, is the net removed?" "Son, it hath caught
    the fish."

Robert Browning.

AN ACTOR

A shabby fellow chanced one day to meet
The British Roscius in the street,
    Garrick, of whom our nation justly brags;
    The fellow hugged him with a kind embrace;—
"Good sir, I do not recollect your face,"
    Quoth Garrick. "No?" replied the man of rags;
"The boards of Drury you and I have trod
    Full many a time together, I am sure."
"When?" with an oath, cried Garrick, "for, by G—d,
I never saw that face of yours before!
    What characters, I pray,
    Did you and I together play?"
"Lord!" quoth the fellow, "think not that I mock—
When you played Hamlet, sir, I played the cock!"

John Wolcot.

THE LOST SPECTACLES

A country curate, visiting his flock,
At old Rebecca's cottage gave a knock.
"Good morrow, dame, I mean not any libel,
But in your dwelling have you got a Bible?"

"A Bible, sir?" exclaimed she in a rage,
"D'ye think I've turned a Pagan in my age?
Here, Judith, and run upstairs, my dear,
'Tis in the drawer, be quick and bring it here."
The girl return'd with Bible in a minute,
Not dreaming for a moment what was in it;
When lo! on opening it at parlor door,
Down fell her spectacles upon the floor.
Amaz'd she stared, was for a moment dumb,
But quick exclaim'd, "Dear sir, I'm glad you're come.
'Tis six years since these glasses first were lost,
And I have miss'd 'em to my poor eyes' cost!"
Then as the glasses to her nose she raised,
She closed the Bible—saying, "God be praised!"

Unknown.

THAT TEXAN CATTLE MAN

WE rode the tawny Texan hills,
  A bearded cattle man and I;
Below us laughed the blossomed rills,
  Above the dappled clouds blew by.
We talked. The topic? Guess. Why, sir,
  Three-fourths of man's whole time he keeps
To talk, to think, to *be* of HER;
  The other fourth he sleeps.

To learn what he might know of love,
  I laughed all constancy to scorn.
"Behold yon happy, changeful dove!
  Behold this day, all storm at morn,
Yet now 't is changed to cloud and sun.
  Yea, all things change—the heart, the head,
Behold on earth there is not one
  That changeth not," I said.

He drew a glass as if to scan
  The plain for steers; raised it and sighed.
He craned his neck, this cattle man,
  Then drove the cork home and replied:

" For twenty years (forgive these tears)—
    For twenty years no word of strife—
I have not known for twenty years
    One folly from my wife."

I looked that Texan in the face—
    That dark-browed, bearded cattle man,
He pulled his beard, then dropped in place
    A broad right hand, all scarred and tan,
And toyed with something shining there
    From out his holster, keen and small.
I was convinced. I did not care
    To argue it at all.

But rest I could not. Know I must
    The story of my Texan guide;
His dauntless love, enduring trust;
    His blessed, immortal bride.
I wondered, marvelled, marvelled much.
    Was she of Texan growth? Was she
Of Saxon blood, that boasted such
    Eternal constancy?

I could not rest until I knew—
    " Now twenty years, my man," said I,
" Is a long time." He turned and drew
    A pistol forth, also a sigh.
" 'Tis twenty years or more," said he,
    " Nay, nay, my honest man, I vow
I do not doubt that this may be;
    But tell, oh! tell me how.

" 'Twould make a poem true and grand;
    All time should note it near and far;
And thy fair, virgin Texan land
    Should stand out like a Winter star.

America should heed. And then
The doubtful French beyond the sea—
'T would make them truer, nobler men
To know how this may be."

" It's twenty years or more," urged he,
" Nay, that I know, good guide of mine;
But lead me where this wife may be,
And I a pilgrim at a shrine.
And kneeling, as a pilgrim true "—
He, scowling, shouted in my ear;
" I cannot show my wife to you;
She's dead this twenty year."

Joaquin Miller.

FABLE

THE mountain and the squirrel
Had a quarrel,
And the former called the latter " Little Prig ";
Bun replied,
" You are doubtless very big;
But all sorts of things and weather
Must be taken in together,
To make up a year
And a sphere,
And I think it no disgrace
To occupy my place.
If I'm not so large as you,
You are not so small as I,
And not half so spry.
I'll not deny you make
A very pretty squirrel track;
Talents differ; all is well and wisely put;
If I cannot carry forests on my back,
Neither can you crack a nut."

Ralph Waldo Emerson.

HOCH! DER KAISER

Der Kaiser of dis Faterland
Und Gott on high all dings command,
Ve two—ach! Don't you understand?
    Myself—und Gott.

Vile some men sing der power divine,
Mine soldiers sing, "Der Wacht am Rhine,"
Und drink der health in Rhenish wine
    Of Me—und Gott.

Dere's France, she swaggers all aroundt;
She's ausgespield, of no account,
To much we think she don't amount;
    Myself—und Gott.

She vill not dare to fight again,
But if she shouldt, I'll show her blain
Dot Elsass und (in French) Lorraine
    Are mein—by Gott!

Dere's grandma dinks she's nicht small beer,
Mit Boers und such she interfere;
She'll learn none owns dis hemisphere
    But me—und Gott!

She dinks, good frau, fine ships she's got
Und soldiers mit der scarlet goat.
Ach! We could knock them! Pouf! Like dot,
    Myself—mit Gott!

In dimes of peace, brebare for wars,
I bear the spear and helm of Mars,
Und care not for a thousand Czars,
    Myself—mit Gott!

In fact, I humor efery whim,
With aspect dark and visage grim;
Gott pulls mit Me, and I mit him,
    Myself—und Gott!

                        Rodney Blake.

WHAT MR. ROBINSON THINKS

GINERAL B. is a sensible man;
  He stays to his home an' looks arter his folks;
He draws his furrer ez straight ez he can,
  An' into nobody's tater-patch pokes;
          But John P.
          Robinson, he
    Sez he wunt vote for Gineral B.

My! ain't it terrible? Wut shall we do?
  We can't never choose him, o' course—that's flat:
Guess we shall hev to come round (don't you?),
  An' go in for thunder an' guns, an' all that;
          Fer John P.
          Robinson, he
          Sez he wunt vote for Gineral B.

Gineral C. is a dreffle smart man:
  He's been on all sides that give places or pelf;
But consistency still was a part of his plan—
  He's been true to *one* party, and that is himself;
          So John P.
          Robinson, he
          Sez he shall vote fer Gineral C.

Gineral C. goes in for the war;
  He don't vally principle mor'n an old cud;
What did God make us raytional creeturs fer,
  But glory an' gunpowder, plunder an' blood?
          So John P.
          Robinson, he
    Sez he shall vote fer Gineral C.

We're gettin' on nicely up here to our village,
  With good old idees o' wut's right an' wut ain't;
We kind o' thought Christ went against war and pillage,

An' that eppyletts worn't the best mark of a saint;
        But John P.
        Robinson, he
    Sez this kind o' thing's an exploded idee.

The side of our country must ollers be took,
    An' President Pulk, you know, *he* is our country;
An' the angel that writes all our sins in a book,
    Puts the *debit* to him, an' to us the *per contry;*
        An' John P.
        Robinson, he
    Sez this is his view o' the thing to a T.

Parson Wilbur he calls all these arguments lies;
    Sez they're nothin' on airth but jest *fee, faw, fum;*
An' that all this big talk of our destinies
    Is half on it ignorance, an' t'other half rum;
        But John P.
        Robinson, he
    Sez it ain't no such thing; an', of course, so must we.

Parson Wilbur sez *he* never heered in his life
    Thet the Apostles rigg'd out in their swallow-tail coats,
An' marched round in front of a drum an' a fife,
    To git some on 'em office, an' some on 'em votes;
        But John P.
        Robinson, he
    Sez they didn't know everythin' down in Judee.

Wal, it's a marcy we've gut folks to tell us
    The rights an' the wrongs o' these matters, I vow—
God sends country lawyers an' other wise fellers
    To drive the world's team wen it gits in a slough;
        For John P.
        Robinson, he
    Sez the world'll go right, ef he hollers out Gee!

                                James Russell Lowell.

THE CANDIDATE'S CREED

BIGLOW PAPERS

I DU believe in Freedom's cause,
   Ez fur away ez Paris is;
I love to see her stick her claws
   In them infarnal Pharisees;
It's wal enough agin a king
   To dror resolves and triggers,—
But libbaty's a kind o' thing
   Thet don't agree with niggers.

I du believe the people want
   A tax on teas and coffees,
Thet nothin' ain't extravygunt,—
   Purvidin' I'm in office;
For I hev loved my country sence
   My eye-teeth filled their sockets,
An' Uncle Sam I reverence,
   Partic'larly his pockets.

I du believe in *any* plan
   O' levyin' the taxes,
Ez long ez, like a lumberman,
   I git jest wut I axes:
I go free-trade thru thick an' thin,
   Because it kind o' rouses
The folks to vote—and keep us in
   Our quiet custom-houses.

I du believe it's wise an' good
   To sen' out furrin missions,
Thet is, on sartin understood
   An' orthydox conditions;—
I mean nine thousan' dolls. per ann.,
   Nine thousan' more fer outfit,
An' me to recommend a man
   The place 'ould jest about fit.

I du believe in special ways
    O' prayin' an' convartin';
The bread comes back in many days,
    An' buttered, tu, fer sartin;—
I mean in preyin' till one busts
    On wut the party chooses,
An' in convartin' public trusts
    To very privit uses.

I do believe hard coin the stuff
    Fer 'lectioneers to spout on;
The people's ollers soft enough
    To make hard money out on;
Dear Uncle Sam pervides fer his,
    An' gives a good-sized junk to all—
I don't care *how* hard money is,
    Ez long ez mine's paid punctooal.

I du believe with all my soul
    In the gret Press's freedom,
To pint the people to the goal
    An' in the traces lead 'em:
Palsied the arm thet forges yokes
    At my fat contracts squintin',
An' withered be the nose thet pokes
    Inter the gov'ment printin'!

I du believe thet I should give
    Wut's his'n unto Cæsar,
Fer it's by him I move an' live,
    From him my bread an' cheese air.
I du believe thet all o' me
    Doth bear his souperscription,—
Will, conscience, honor, honesty,
    An' things o' thet description.

I du believe in prayer an' praise
    To him thet hez the grantin'
O' jobs—in every thin' thet pays,
    But most of all in CANTIN';

This doth my cup with marcies fill,
　This lays all thought o' sin to rest—
I *don't* believe in princerple,
　But, O, I *du* in interest.

I du believe in bein' this
　Or thet, ez it may happen
One way, or t' other hendiest is
　To ketch the people nappin';
It ain't by princerples nor men
　My preudent course is steadied—
I scent wich pays the best, an' then
　Go into it baldheaded.

I du believe thet holdin' slaves
　Comes nat'ral tu a President,
Let 'lone the rowdedow it saves
　To have a wal-broke precedunt;
Fer any office, small or gret,
　I couldn't ax with no face,
Without I'd been, thru dry an' wet,
　The unrizziest kind o' doughface.

I du believe wutever trash
　'll keep the people in blindness,—
Thet we the Mexicans can thrash
　Right inter brotherly kindness—
Thet bombshells, grape, an' powder 'n' ball
　Air good-will's strongest magnets—
Thet peace, to make it stick at all,
　Must be druv in with bagnets.

In short, I firmly du believe
　In Humbug generally,
Fer it's a thing thet I perceive
　To hev a solid vally;
This heth my faithful shepherd ben,
　In pastures sweet heth led me,
An' this'll keep the people green
　To feed ez they have fed me.

James Russell Lowell.

THE RAZOR SELLER

A FELLOW in a market town,
Most musical, cried razors up and down,
  And offered twelve for eighteen-pence;
Which certainly seemed wondrous cheap,
And for the money quite a heap,
  As every man would buy, with cash and sense.

A country bumpkin the great offer heard:
Poor Hodge, who suffered by a broad black beard,
  That seemed a shoe-brush stuck beneath his nose
With cheerfulness the eighteen-pence he paid,
And proudly to himself, in whispers, said,
  "This rascal stole the razors, I suppose.

"No matter if the fellow *be* a knave,
Provided that the razors *shave;*
  It certainly will be a monstrous prize."
So home the clown, with his good fortune, went,
Smiling in heart and soul, content,
  And quickly soaped himself to ears and eyes.

Being well lathered from a dish or tub,
Hodge now began with grinning pain to grub,
  Just like a hedger cutting furze:
'Twas a vile razor!—then the rest he tried—
All were imposters—" Ah," Hodge sighed!
  "I wish my eighteen-pence within my purse."

In vain to chase his beard, and bring the graces,
  He cut, and dug, and winced, and stamped, and swore,
Brought blood, and danced, blasphemed, and made wry
    faces,
  And cursed each razor's body o'er and o'er:

His muzzle, formed of *opposition* stuff,
Firm as a Foxite, would not lose its ruff!
  So kept it—laughing at the steel and suds:
Hodge, in a passion, stretched his angry jaws,

Vowing the direst vengeance, with clenched claws,
  On the vile cheat that sold the goods.
" Razors; a damned, confounded dog,
Not fit to scrape a hog! "

Hodge sought the fellow—found him—and begun:
" P'rhaps, Master Razor rogue, to you 'tis fun,
  That people flay themselves out of their lives:
You rascal! for an hour have I been grubbing,
Giving my crying whiskers here a scrubbing,
  With razors just like oyster knives.
Sirrah! I tell you, you're a knave,
To cry up razors that can't *shave.*"
" Friend," quoth the razor-man, " I'm not a knave.
  As for the razors you have bought,
  Upon my soul I never thought
That they would *shave.*"
" Not think they'd *shave!* " quoth Hodge, with wond'ring
  eyes,
  And voice not much unlike an Indian yell;
" What were they made for then, you dog? " he cries:
  " Made! " quoth the fellow, with a smile—" to *sell.*"

John Wolcot.

THE DEVIL'S WALK ON EARTH

FROM his brimstone bed at break of day
  A walking the Devil is gone,
To look at his snug little farm of the World,
  And see how his stock went on.

Over the hill and over the dale,
  And he went over the plain;
And backward and forward he swish'd his tail
  As a gentleman swishes a cane.

How then was the Devil drest?
  Oh, he was in his Sunday's best
His coat was red and his breeches were blue,
And there was a hole where his tail came through.

A lady drove by in her pride,
In whose face an expression he spied
  For which he could have kiss'd her;
Such a flourishing, fine, clever woman was she,
With an eye as wicked as wicked can be,
I should take her for my Aunt, thought he,
  If my dam had had a sister.

  He met a lord of high degree,
    No matter what was his name;
Whose face with his own when he came to compare
  The expression, the look, and the air,
  And the character, too, as it seem'd to a hair—
  Such a twin-likeness there was in the pair
  That it made the Devil start and stare
For he thought there was surely a looking-glass there,
  But he could not see the frame.

He saw a Lawyer killing a viper,
  On a dung-hill beside his stable;
Ha! quoth he, thou put'st me in mind
  Of the story of Cain and Abel.

An Apothecary on a white horse
  Rode by on his vocation;
And the Devil thought of his old friend
  Death in the Revelation.

He pass'd a cottage with a double coach-house,
  A cottage of gentility,
And he own'd with a grin
That his favorite sin,
  Is pride that apes humility.

He saw a pig rapidly
  Down a river float;
The pig swam well, but every stroke
  Was cutting his own throat;

And Satan gave thereat his tail
   A twirl of admiration;
For he thought of his daughter War,
   And her suckling babe Taxation.

Well enough, in sooth, he liked that truth
   And nothing the worse for the jest;
But this was only a first thought
   And in this he did not rest:
Another came presently into his head,
And here it proved, as has often been said
   That second thoughts are best.

For as Piggy plied with wind and tide,
   His way with such celerity,
And at every stroke the water dyed
With his own red blood, the Devil cried,
Behold a swinish nation's pride
   In cotton-spun prosperity.

He walk'd into London leisurely,
   The streets were dirty and dim:
But there he saw Brothers the Prophet,
   And Brothers the Prophet saw him.

He entered a thriving bookseller's shop;
   Quoth he, we are both of one college,
For I myself sate like a Cormorant once
   Upon the Tree of Knowledge.

As he passed through Cold-Bath Fields he look'd
   At a solitary cell;
And he was well-pleased, for it gave him a hint
   For improving the prisons of Hell.

He saw a turnkey tie a thief's hands
   With a cordial tug and jerk;
Nimbly, quoth he, a man's fingers move
   When his heart is in his work.

He saw the same turnkey unfettering a man
    With little expedition;
And he chuckled to think of his dear slave-trade,
And the long debates and delays that were made,
    Concerning its abolition.

He met one of his favorite daughters
    By an Evangelical Meeting:
And forgetting himself for joy at her sight,
He would have accosted her outright,
    And given her a fatherly greeting.

But she tipt him the wink, drew back, and cried,
    Avaunt! my name's Religion!
And then she turn'd to the preacher
And leer'd like a love-sick pigeon.

A fine man and a famous Professor was he,
As the great Alexander now may be,
    Whose fame not yet o'erpast is:
Or that new Scotch performer
Who is fiercer and warmer,
    The great Sir Arch-Bombastes.

With throbs and throes, and ah's and oh's.
    Far famed his flock for frightning;
And thundering with his voice, the while
    His eyes zigzag like lightning.

This Scotch phenomenon, I trow,
    Beats Alexander hollow;
Even when most tame
He breathes more flame
    Then ten Fire-Kings could swallow.

Another daughter he presently met;
    With music of fife and drum,
    And a consecrated flag,
    And shout of tag and rag,
    And march of rank and file,
Which had fill'd the crowded aisle
Of the venerable pile,
    From church he saw her come.

He call'd her aside, and began to chide,
  For what dost thou here? said he,
My city of Rome is thy proper home,
  And there's work enough there for thee.

Thou hast confessions to listen,
  And, bells to christen,
And altars and dolls to dress;
  And fools to coax,
  And sinners to hoax,
And beads and bones to bless;
  And great pardons to sell
  For those who pay well,
And small ones for those who pay less.

Nay, Father, I boast, that this is my post,
  She answered; and thou wilt allow,
  That the great Harlot,
  Who is clothed in scarlet,
Can very well spare me now.

Upon her business I am come here,
  That we may extend our powers:
Whatever lets down this church that we hate,
  Is something in favor of ours.

You will not think, great Cosmocrat!
  That I spend my time in fooling;
Many irons, my sire, have we in the fire,
  And I must leave none of them cooling;
For you must know state-councils here,
  Are held which I bear rule in.
  When my liberal notions,
  Produce mischievous motions,
  There's many a man of good intent,
  In either house of Parliament,
  Whom I shall find a tool in;
  And I have hopeful pupils too
  Who all this while are schooling.

Fine progress they make in our liberal opinions,
   My Utilitarians,
   My all sorts of—inians
    And all sorts of—arians;
    My all sorts of—ists,
  And my Prigs and my Whigs
   Who have all sorts of twists
Train'd in the very way, I know,
Father, you would have them go;
   High and low,
  Wise and foolish, great and small,
  March-of-Intellect-Boys all.

Well pleased wilt thou be at no very far day
  When the caldron of mischief boils,
And I bring them forth in battle array
  And bid them suspend their broils,
That they may unite and fall on the prey,
  For which we are spreading our toils.
How the nice boys all will give mouth at the call,
  Hark away! hark away to the spoils!
My Macs and my Quacks and my lawless-Jacks,
My Shiels and O'Connells, my pious Mac-Donnells,
  My joke-smith Sydney, and all of his kidney,
   My Humes and my Broughams,
    My merry old Jerry,
  My Lord Kings, and my Doctor Doyles!

  At this good news, so great
   The Devil's pleasure grew,
That with a joyful swish he rent
  The hole where his tail came through.

His countenance fell for a moment
  When he felt the stitches go;
Ah! thought he, there's a job now
  That I've made for my tailor below.

Great news! bloody news! cried a newsman;
  The Devil said, Stop, let me see!
Great news? bloody news? thought the Devil,
  The bloodier the better for me.

So he bought the newspaper, and no news
  At all for his money he had.
Lying varlet, thought he, thus to take in old Nick!
  But it's some satisfaction, my lad,
To know thou art paid beforehand for the trick,
  For the sixpence I gave thee is bad.

And then it came into his head
  By oracular inspiration,
That what he had seen and what he had said
  In the course of this visitation,
Would be published in the Morning Post
  For all this reading nation.

Therewith in second sight he saw
  The place and the manner and time,
In which this mortal story
  Would be put in immortal rhyme.

That it would happen when two poets
  Should on a time be met,
In the town of Nether Stowey,
  In the shire of Somerset.

There while the one was shaving
  Would he the song begin;
And the other when he heard it at breakfast,
  In ready accord join in.

So each would help the other,
  Two heads being better than one;
    And the phrase and conceit
    Would in unison meet,
And so with glee the verse flow free,
  In ding-dong chime of sing-song rhyme,
    Till the whole were merrily done.

And because it was set to the razor,
  Not to the lute or harp,
Therefore it was that the fancy
Should be bright, and the wit be sharp.

But, then, said Satan to himself,
    As for that said beginner,
Against my infernal Majesty,
    There is no greater sinner.

He hath put me in ugly ballads
    With libelous pictures for sale;
He hath scoff'd at my hoofs and my horns,
    And has made very free with my tail.

But this Mister Poet shall find
    I am not a safe subject for whim;
For I'll set up a School of my own,
    And my Poets shall set upon him.

He went to a coffee-house to dine,
    And there he had soy in his dish;
Having ordered some soles for his dinner,
    Because he was fond of flat fish.

They are much to my palate, thought he,
    And now guess the reason who can,
Why no bait should be better than place,
    When I fish for a Parliament-man.

But the soles in the bill were ten shillings;
    Tell your master, quoth he, what I say;
If he charges at this rate for all things,
    He must be in a pretty good way.

But mark ye, said he to the waiter,
    I'm a dealer myself in this line,
And his business, between you and me,
    Nothing like so extensive as mine.

Now soles are exceedingly cheap,
    Which he will not attempt to deny,
When I see him at my fish-market,
    I warrant him, by-and-by.

As he went along the Strand
  Between three in the morning and four
He observed a queer-looking person
  Who staggered from Perry's door.

And he thought that all the world over
  In vain for a man you might seek,
Who could drink more like a Trojan
  Or talk more like a Greek.

The Devil then he prophesied
  It would one day be matter of talk,
    That with wine when smitten,
And with wit moreover being happily bitten,
The erudite bibber was he who had written
  The story of this walk.

A pretty mistake, quoth the Devil;
  A pretty mistake I opine!
I have put many ill thoughts in his mouth,
  He will never put good ones in mine.

And whoever shall say that to Porson
  These best of all verses belong,
He is an untruth-telling whore-son,
  And so shall be call'd in the song.

And if seeking an illicit connection with fame,
  Any one else should put in a claim,
    In this comical competition;
  That excellent poem will prove
    A man-trap for such foolish ambition,
Where the silly rogue shall be caught by the leg,
  And exposed in a second edition.

Now the morning air was cold for him
  Who was used to a warm abode;
And yet he did not immediately wish,
  To set out on his homeward road.

For he had some morning calls to make
  Before he went back to Hell;
So thought he I'll step into a gaming-house,
  And that will do as well;
But just before he could get to the door
  A wonderful chance befell.

For all on a sudden, in a dark place,
He came upon General ————'s burning face;
  And it struck him with such consternation,
That home in a hurry his way did he take,
Because he thought, by a slight mistake
  'Twas the general conflagration.

Robert Southey.

FATHER MOLLOY

OR, THE CONFESSION

Paddy McCabe was dying one day,
  And Father Molloy he came to confess him;
Paddy pray'd hard he would make no delay,
  But forgive him his sins and make haste for to bless
    him.
First tell me your sins," says Father Molloy,
For I'm thinking you've not been a very good boy."
Oh," says Paddy, " so late in the evenin', I fear,
'Twould throuble you such a long story to hear,
For you've ten long miles o'er the mountains to go,
While the road *I've* to travel's much longer, you know.
So give us your blessin' and get in the saddle,
To tell all my sins my poor brain it would addle;
And the docther gave ordhers to keep me so quiet—
'Twould disturb me to tell all my sins, if I'd thry it,
And your Reverence has towld us, unless we tell *all*,
'Tis worse than not makin' confession at all.
So I'll say in a word I'm no very good boy—
And, therefore, your blessin', sweet Father Molloy."

"Well, I'll read from a book," says Father Molloy,
 "The manifold sins that humanity's heir to;
And when you hear those that your conscience annoy,
 You'll just squeeze my hand, as acknowledging theret❮
Then the father began the dark roll of iniquity,
And Paddy, thereat, felt his conscience grow rickety,
And he gave such a squeeze that the priest gave a roar
"Oh, murdher," says Paddy, "don't read any more,
For, if you keep readin', by all that is thrüe,
Your Reverence's fist will be soon black and blue;
Besides, to be throubled my conscience begins,
That your Reverence should have any hand in my sins,
So you'd betther suppose I committed them all,
For whether they're great ones, or whether they're sma❮
Or if they're a dozen, or if they're fourscore,
'Tis your Reverence knows how to absolve them, asthore
So I'll say in a word, I'm no very good boy—
And, therefore, your blessin', sweet Father Molloy."

"Well," says Father Molloy, "if your sins I forgive,
 So you must forgive all your enemies truly;
And promise me also that, if you should live,
 You'll leave off your old tricks, and begin to live newly
"I forgive ev'rybody," says Pat, with a groan,
 "Except that big vagabone Micky Malone;
And him I will murdher if ever I can—"
 "Tut, tut," says the priest, "you're a very bad man;
For without your forgiveness, and also repentance,
You'll ne'er go to Heaven, and that is my sentence."
 "Poo!" says Paddy McCabe, "that's a very hard case—
With your Reverence and Heaven I'm content to mak❮
 pace;
But with Heaven and your Reverence I wondher—*Oc❮
 hone*—
You would think of comparin' that blackguard Malone—
But since I'm hard press'd and that I *must* forgive,
I forgive—if I die—but as sure as I live
That ugly blackguard I will surely desthroy!—
So, *now* for your blessin', sweet Father Molloy!"

Samuel Lover.

THE OWL-CRITIC

"Who stuffed that white owl?" No one spoke in the
    shop,
The barber was busy, and he couldn't stop;
The customers, waiting their turns, were all reading
The "Daily," the "Herald," the "Post," little heeding
The young man who blurted out such a blunt question;
Not one raised a head, or even made a suggestion;
      And the barber kept on shaving.

"Don't you see, Mr. Brown,"
Cried the youth, with a *frown,
"How wrong the whole thing is,
How preposterous each wing is
How flattened the head is, how jammed down the neck is—
In short, the whole owl, what an ignorant wreck 't is!
I make no apology;
I've learned owl-eology.

I've passed days and nights in a hundred collections,
And cannot be blinded to any deflections
Arising from unskilful fingers that fail
To stuff a bird right, from his beak to his tail.
Mister Brown! Mister Brown!
Do take that bird down,
Or you'll soon be the laughing-stock all over town!"
      And the barber kept on shaving.

"I've *studied* owls,
And other night-fowls,
And I tell you
What I know to be true;
An owl cannot roost
With his limbs so unloosed;
No owl in this world
Ever had his claws curled,
Ever had his legs slanted,
Ever had his bill canted,
Ever had his neck screwed
Into that attitude.
He can't *do* it, because
'Tis against all bird-laws.

Anatomy teaches,
Ornithology preaches,
An owl has a toe
That *can't* turn out so!
I've made the white owl my study for years,
And to see such a job almost moves me to tears!
Mr. Brown, I'm amazed
You should be so gone crazed
As to put up a bird
In that posture absurd!
To *look* at that owl really brings on a dizziness;
The man who stuffed *him* don't half know his business
       And the barber kept on shaving.

"Examine those eyes.
I'm filled with surprise
Taxidermists should pass
Off on you such poor glass;
So unnatural they seem
They'd make Audubon scream,
And John Burroughs laugh
To encounter such chaff.
Do take that bird down;
Have him stuffed again, Brown!"
       And the barber kept on shaving.

"With some sawdust and bark
I could stuff in the dark
An owl better than that.
I could make an old hat
Look more like an owl
Than that horrid fowl,
Stuck up there so stiff like a side of coarse leather.
In fact, about *him* there's not one natural feather."

Just then, with a wink and a sly normal lurch,
The owl, very gravely, got down from his perch,
Walked round, and regarded his fault-finding critic
(Who thought he was stuffed) with a glance analytic,
And then fairly hooted, as if he should say:
"Your learning's at fault *this* time, anyway;

Don't waste it again on a live bird, I pray.
I'm an owl; you're another. Sir Critic, good day!"
And the barber kept on shaving.

James Thomas Fields.

WHAT WILL WE DO?

WHAT will we do when the good days come—
When the prima donna's lips are dumb,
And the man who reads us his "little things"
Has lost his voice like the girl who sings;
When stilled is the breath of the cornet-man,
And the shrilling chords of the quartette clan;
When our neighbours' children have lost their drums—
Oh, what will we do when the good time comes?
Oh, what will we do in that good, blithe time,
When the tramp will work—oh, thing sublime!
And the scornful dame who stands on your feet
Will "Thank you, sir," for the proffered seat;
And the man you hire to work by the day,
Will allow you to do his work your way;
And the cook who trieth your appetite
Will steal no more than she thinks is right;
When the boy you hire will call you "Sir,"
Instead of "Say" and "Guverner";
When the funny man is humorsome—
How can we stand the millennium?

Robert J. Burdette.

LIFE IN LACONICS

GIVEN a roof, and a taste for rations,
And you have the key to the "wealth of nations."

Given a boy, a tree, and a hatchet,
And virtue strives in vain to match it.

Given a pair, a snake, and an apple,
You make the whole world need a chapel.

Given " no cards," broad views, and a hovel,
You have a realistic novel.

Given symptoms and doctors with potion and pill,
And your heirs will ere long be contesting your will.

That good leads to evil there's no denying:
If it were not for *truth* there would be no *lying*.

" I'm nobody! " should have a hearse;
But then, " I'm somebody! " is worse.

" Folks say," *et cetera!* Well, they shouldn't,
And if they knew you well, they wouldn't.

When you coddle your life, all its vigor and grace
Shrink away with the whisper, " We're in the wrong plac

Mary Mapes Dodge

ON KNOWING WHEN TO STOP

THE woodchuck told it all about.
" I'm going to build a dwelling
Six stories high, up to the sky! "
He never tired of telling.

He dug the cellar smooth and well
But made no more advances;
That lovely hole so pleased his soul
And satisfied his fancies.

L. J. Bridgman

REV. GABE TUCKER'S REMARKS

You may notch it on de palin's as a mighty resky plan
To make your judgment by de clo'es dat kivers up a man;
For I hardly needs to tell you how you often come across
A fifty-dollar saddle on a twenty-dollar hoss;
An', wukin' jn de low-groun's, you diskiver, as you go,
Dat de fines' shuck may hide de meanes' nubbin in a row.

think a man has got a mighty slender chance for heben
at holds on to his piety but one day out o' seben;
at talks about de sinners wid a heap o' solemn chat,
nd nebber draps a nickel in de missionary hat;
at's foremost in de meetin'-house for raisin' all de chunes,
ut lays aside his 'ligion wid his Sunday pantaloons.

nebber judge o' people dat I meets along de way
y de places whar dey come fum an' de houses whar dey stay;
or de bantam chicken's awful fond o' roostin' pretty high,
n' de turkey buzzard sails above de eagle in de sky;
ey ketches little minners in de middle ob de sea,
n' you finds de smalles' possum up de bigges' kind o' tree!

Unknown.

THURSDAY

THE sun was setting, and vespers done;
From chapel the monks came one by one,
And down they went thro' the garden trim,
In cassock and cowl, to the river's brim.
Ev'ry brother his rod he took;
Ev'ry rod had a line and a hook;
Ev'ry hook had a bait so fine,
And thus they sang in the even shine:
Oh, to-morrow will be Friday, so we'll fish the stream
     to-day!
h, to-morrow will be Friday, so we'll fish the stream to-day!
     Benedicite!"

So down they sate by the river's brim,
And fish'd till the light was growing dim;
They fish'd the stream till the moon was high,
But never a fish came wand'ring by.
They fish'd the stream in the bright moonshine,
But not one fish would he come to dine.
And the Abbot said, "It seems to me
These rascally fish are all gone to sea.

And to-morrow will be Friday, but we've caught no fish
    to-day;
Oh, to-morrow will be Friday, but we've caught no fish
    to-day!
        Maledicite!"

So back they went to the convent gate,
  Abbot and monks disconsolate;
For they thought of the morrow with faces white,
  Saying, "Oh, we must curb our appetite!
But down in the depths of the vault below
  There's Malvoisie for a world of woe!"
So they quaff their wine, and all declare
  That fish, after all, is but gruesome fare.
"Oh, to-morrow will be Friday, so we'll warm our souls
    to-day!
Oh, to-morrow will be Friday, so we'll warm our souls to-day!
    Benedicite!"

Frederick E. Weatherly.

SKY-MAKING

TO PROFESSOR TYNDALL

Just take a trifling handful, O philosopher,
Of magic matter, give it a slight toss over
  The ambient ether, and I don't see why
    You shouldn't make a sky.

O hours Utopian which we may anticipate!
Thick London fog how easy 'tis to dissipate,
  And make the most pea-soupy day as clear
    As Bass's brightest beer!

Poet-professor! now my brain thou kindlest;
I am become a most determined Tyndallist.
  If it is known a fellow can make skies,
    Why not make bright blue eyes?

This to deny, the folly of a dunce it is;
Surely a girl as easy as a sunset is.
  If you can make a halo or eclipse,
    Why not two laughing lips?

The creed of Archimedes, erst of Sicily,
And of D'Israeli . . . *forti nil difficile,*
 Is likewise mine. Pygmalion was a fool
 Who should have gone to school.

Why should an author scribble rhymes or articles?
Bring me a dozen tiny Tyndall particles;
 Therefrom I'll coin a dinner, Nash's wine,
 And a nice girl to dine.

Mortimer Collins.

THE POSITIVISTS

LIFE and the Universe show spontaneity:
Down with ridiculous notions of Deity!
 Churches and creeds are all lost in the mists;
 Truth must be sought with the Positivists.

Wise are their teachers beyond all comparison,
Comte, Huxley, Tyndall, Mill, Morley, and Harrison;
 Who will adventure to enter the lists
 With such a squadron of Positivists?

Social arrangements are awful miscarriages;
Cause of all crime is our system of marriages.
 Poets with sonnets, and lovers with trysts,
 Kindle the ire of the Positivists.

Husbands and wives should be all one community,
Exquisite freedom with absolute unity.
 Wedding-rings worse are than manacled wrists—
 Such is the creed of the Positivists.

There was an ape in the days that were earlier;
Centuries passed, and his hair became curlier;
 Centuries more gave a thumb to his wrist—
 Then he was Man, and a Positivist.

If you are pious (mild form of insanity)
Bow down and worship the mass of humanity.
Other religions are buried in mists;
We're our own Gods, say the Positivists.

Mortimer Collins.

MARTIAL IN LONDON

EXQUISITE wines and comestibles,
    From Slater, and Fortnum and Mason;
Billiard, écarté, and chess tables;
    Water in vast marble basin;
Luminous books (not voluminous)
To read under beech-trees cacuminous;
One friend, who is fond of a distich,
And doesn't get too syllogistic;
A valet, who knows the complete art
Of service—a maiden, his sweetheart:
Give me these, in some rural pavilion,
And I'll envy no Rothschild his million.

Mortimer Collins.

THE SPLENDID SHILLING

" . . . . Sing, heavenly Muse!
    Things unattempted yet, in prose or rhyme,"
A shilling, breeches, and chimeras dire.

HAPPY the man, who, void of cares and strife,
In silken or in leather purse retains
A Splendid Shilling: he nor hears with pain
New oysters cried, nor sighs for cheerful ale;
But with his friends, when nightly mists arise,
To Juniper's Magpie, or Town-hall repairs:
Where, mindful of the nymph, whose wanton eye
Transfix'd his soul, and kindled amorous flames,
Chloe, or Phillis, he each circling glass
Wisheth her health, and joy, and equal love.
Meanwhile, he smokes, and laughs at merry tale,

Or pun ambiguous, or conundrum quaint.
But I, whom griping penury surrounds,
And Hunger, sure attendant upon Want,
With scanty offals, and small acid tiff,
(Wretched repast!) my meagre corpse sustain:
Then solitary walk, or doze at home
In garret vile, and with a warming puff
Regale chill'd fingers: or from tube as black
As winter-chimney, or well-polish'd jet,
Exhale mundungus, ill-perfuming scent:
Not blacker tube, nor of a shorter size,
Smokes Cambro-Briton (vers'd in pedigree,
Sprung from Cadwallador and Arthur, kings
Full famous in romantic tale) when he,
O'er many a craggy hill and barren cliff,
Upon a cargo of fam'd Cestrian cheese,
High over-shadowing rides, with a design
To vend his wares, or at th' Avonian mart,
Or Maridunum, or the ancient town
Yclep'd Brechinia, or where Vaga's stream
Encircles Ariconium, fruitful soil!
Whence flow nectareous wines, that well may vie
With Massic, Setin, or renown'd Falern.

Thus while my joyless minutes tedious flow,
With looks demure, and silent pace, a Dun,
Horrible monster! hated by gods and men,
To my aërial citadel ascends,
With vocal heel thrice thundering at my gate,
With hideous accent thrice he calls; I know
The voice ill-boding, and the solemn sound.
What should I do? or whither turn? Amaz'd,
Confounded, to the dark recess I fly
Of wood-hole; straight my bristling hairs erect
Through sudden fear; a chilly sweat bedews
My shuddering limbs, and (wonderful to tell!)
My tongue forgets her faculty of speech;
So horrible he seems! His faded brow,
Intrench'd with many a frown, and conic beard,
And spreading band, admir'd by modern saints,
Disastrous acts forbode; in his right hand
Long scrolls of paper solemnly he waves,

With characters and figures dire inscrib'd,
Grievous to mortal eyes; (ye gods, avert
Such plagues from righteous men!) Behind him stalks
Another monster, not unlike himself,
Sullen of aspect, by the vulgar call'd
A catchpole, whose polluted hands the gods,
With force incredible, and magic charms,
First have endued: if he his ample palm
Should haply on ill-fated shoulder lay
Of debtor, straight his body, to the touch
Obsequious (as whilom knights were wont,)
To some enchanted castle is convey'd,
Where gates impregnable, and coercive chains,
In durance strict detain him, till, in form
Of money, Pallas sets the captive free.

Beware, ye debtors! when ye walk, beware,
Be circumspect; oft with insidious ken
The caitiff eyes your steps aloof, and oft
Lies perdu in a nook or gloomy cave,
Prompt to enchant some inadvertent wretch
With his unhallowed touch. So, (poets sing)
Grimalkin, to domestic vermin sworn
An everlasting foe, with watchful eye
Lies nightly brooding o'er a chinky gap,
Portending her fell claws, to thoughtless mice
Sure ruin. So her disembowell'd web
Arachne, in a hall or kitchen, spreads
Obvious to vagrant flies: she secret stands
Within her woven cell: the humming prey,
Regardless of their fate, rush on the toils
Inextricable, nor will aught avail
Their arts, or arms, or shapes of lovely hue;
The wasp insidious, and the buzzing drone,
And butterfly, proud of expanded wings
Distinct with gold, entangled in her snares,
Useless resistance make; with eager strides,
She towering flies to her expected spoils;
Then, with envenomed jaws, the vital blood
Drinks of reluctant foes, and to her cave
Their bulky carcasses triumphant drags.

So pass my days. But when nocturnal shades

This world envelop, and th' inclement air
Persuades men to repel benumbing frosts
With pleasant wines, and crackling blaze of wood;
Me, lonely sitting, nor the glimmering light
Of make-weight candle, nor the joyous talk
Of loving friend, delights: distress'd, forlorn,
Amidst the horrors of the tedious night,
Darkling I sigh, and feed with dismal thoughts
My anxious mind: or sometimes mournful verse
Indite, and sing of groves and myrtle shades,
Or desperate lady near a purling stream,
Or lover pendent on a willow tree.
Meanwhile I labor with eternal drought,
And restless wish, and rave; my parched throat
Finds no relief, nor heavy eyes repose:
But if a slumber haply does invade
My weary limbs, my fancy's still awake,
Thoughtful of drink, and eager, in a dream,
Tipples imaginary pots of ale,
In vain; awake I find the settled thirst
Still gnawing, and the pleasant phantom curse.

Thus do I live, from pleasure quite debarred,
Nor taste the fruits that the sun's genial rays
Mature, john-apple, nor the downy peach,
Nor walnut in rough-furrow'd coat secure,
Nor medlar, fruit delicious in decay;
Afflictions great! yet greater still remain:
My galligaskins, that have long withstood
The winter's fury, and encroaching frosts,
By time subdued (what will not time subdue!)
An horrid chasm disclos'd with orifice
Wide, discontinuous; at which the winds
Eurus and Auster, and the dreadful force
Of Boreas, that congeals the Cronian waves,
Tumultuous enter with dire chilling blasts,
Portending agues. Thus a well-fraught ship,
Long sail'd secure, or through th' Ægean deep,
Or the Ionian, till cruising near
The Lilybean shore, with hideous crush
On Scylla, or Charybdis (dangerous rocks!)
She strikes rebounding; whence the shatter'd oak,

So fierce a shock unable to withstand,
Admits the sea: in at the gaping side
The crowding waves gush with impetuous rage
Resistless, overwhelming; horrors seize
The mariners; Death in their eyes appears,
They stare, they lave, they pump, they swear, they pray
(Vain efforts!) still the battering waves rush in,
Implacable, till, delug'd by the foam,
The ship sinks foundering in the vast abyss.

John Philips.

AFTER HORACE

WHAT asks the Bard? He prays for nought
    But what the truly virtuous crave:
That is, the things he plainly ought
      To have.

'Tis not for wealth, with all the shocks
    That vex distracted millionaires,
Plagued by their fluctuating stocks
      And shares:

While plutocrats their millions new
    Expend upon each costly whim,
A great deal less than theirs will do
      For him:

The simple incomes of the poor
    His meek poetic soul content:
Say, £30,000 at four
      Per cent.!

His taste in residence is plain:
    No palaces his heart rejoice:
A cottage in a lane (Park Lane
      For choice)—

Here be his days in quiet spent:
　　Here let him meditate the Muse:
Baronial Halls were only meant
　　　　For Jews,

And lands that stretch with endless span
　　From east to west, from south to north,
Are often much more trouble than
　　　　They're worth!

Let epicures who eat too much
　　Become uncomfortably stout:
Let gourmets feel th' approaching touch
　　　　Of gout,—

The Bard subsists on simpler food:
　　A dinner, not severely plain,
A pint or so of really good
　　　　Champagne—

Grant him but these, no care he'll take
　　Though Laureates bask in Fortune's smile,
Though Kiplings and Corellis make
　　　　Their pile:

Contented with a scantier dole
　　His humble Muse serenely jogs,
Remote from scenes where authors roll
　　　　Their logs:

Far from the madding crowd she lurks,
　　And really cares no single jot
Whether the public read her works
　　　　Or not!

A. D. Godley.

OF A PRECISE TAILOR

A TAILOR, a man of an upright dealing,
True but for lying, honest but for stealing,
Did fall one day extremely sick by chance,
And on the sudden was in wondrous trance.
The Fiends of hell, mustering in fearful manner,
Of sundry-coloured silks displayed a banner,
Which he had stol'n; and wished, as they did tell,
That one day he might find it all in hell.
The man, affrighted at this apparition,
Upon recovery grew a great precisian.
He bought a Bible of the new translation,
And in his life he showed great reformation.
He walkèd mannerly and talkèd meekly;
He heard three lectures and two sermons weekly;
He vowed to shun all companies unruly,
And in his speech he used no oath but " truly ":
And, zealously to keep the Sabbath's rest,
His meat for that day on the even was dressed.
And, lest the custom that he had to steal
Might cause him sometime to forget his zeal,
He gives his journeyman a special charge
That, if the stuff allowed fell out too large,
And that to filch his fingers were inclined,
He then should put the Banner in his mind.
This done, I scant the rest can tell for laughter.
A Captain of a ship came three days after,
And bought three yards of velvet and three quarters,
To make Venetians down below the garters.
He, that precisely knew what was enough,
Soon slipped away three quarters of the stuff.
His man, espying it, said in derision,
" Remember, Master, how you saw the vision ! "
" Peace, knave," quoth he; " I did not see one rag
Of such-a-coloured silk in all the flag."

Sir John Harrington.

MONEY

Who money has, well wages the campaign;
Who money has, becomes of gentle strain;
Who money has, to honor all accord:
> He is my lord.
Who money has, the ladies ne'er disdain;
Who money has, loud praises will attain;
Who money has, in the world's heart is stored,
> The flower adored.
O'er all mankind he holds his conquering track—
They only are condemned who money lack.

Who money has, will wisdom's credit gain;
Who money has, all earth is his domain;
Who money has, praise is his sure reward,
> Which all afford.
Who money has, from nothing need refrain;
Who money has, on him is favor poured;
> And, in a word,
Who money has, need never fear attack—
They only are condemned who money lack.

Who money has, in every heart does reign;
Who money has, all to approach are fain;
Who money has, of him no fault is told,
> Nor harm can hold.
Who money has, none does his right restrain;
Who money has, can whom he will maintain;
Who money has, clerk, prior, by his gold,
> Is straight enrolled.
Who money has, all raise, none hold him back—
They only are condemned who money lack.

Jehan du Pontalais.

BOSTON NURSERY RHYMES

RHYME FOR A GEOLOGICAL BABY

Trilobite, Grapholite, Nautilus pie;
Seas were calcareous, oceans were dry.
Eocene, miocene, pliocene Tuff,
Lias and Trias and that is enough.

RHYME FOR ASTRONOMICAL BABY

Bye Baby Bunting,
Father's gone star-hunting;
Mother's at the telescope
Casting baby's horoscope.
Bye Baby Buntoid,
Father's found an asteroid;
Mother takes by calculation
The angle of its inclination.

RHYME FOR BOTANICAL BABY

Little bo-peepals
Has lost her sepals,
And can't tell where to find them;
In the involucre
By hook or by crook or
She'll make up her mind not to mind them.

RHYME FOR A CHEMICAL BABY

Oh, sing a song of phosphates,
    Fibrine in a line,
Four-and-twenty follicles
    In the van of time.

When the phosphorescence
    Evoluted brain,
Superstition ended,
    Men began to reign.

Rev. Joseph Cook.

KENTUCKY PHILOSOPHY

You Wi'yum, cum 'ere, suh, dis minute. Wut dat you got
    under dat box?
I don't want no foolin'—you hear me? Wut you say? Ain't
    nu'h'n but *rocks?*
'Peahs ter me you's owdashus perticler. S'posin' dey's uv a
    new kine.
I'll des take a look at dem rocks. Hi yi! der you think dat
    I's bline?

I calls dat a plain water-million, you scamp, en I knows whah
    it growed;
It come fum de Jimmerson cawn fiel', dah on ter side er de
    road.
You stole it, you rascal—you stole it! I watched you fum
    down in de lot.
En time I gits th'ough wid you, nigger, you won't eb'n be a
    grease spot!

I'll fix you. Mirandy! *Mira*ndy! go cut me a hick'ry—make
    'ase!
En cut me de toughes' en keenes' you c'n fine anywhah on de
    place.
I'll larn you, Mr. Wi'yum Joe Vetters, ter steal en ter lie, you
    young sinner,
Disgracin' yo' ole Christian mammy, en makin' her leave
    cookin' dinner!

Now ain't you ashamed er yo'se'f, suh? I is. I's 'shamed
    you's my son!
En de holy accorjun angel he's 'shamed er wut you has done;
En he's tuk it down up yander in coal-black, blood-red
    letters—
"One water-million stoled by Wi'yum Josephus Vetters."

En wut you s'posin' Brer Bascom, yo' teacher at Sunday
    school,
'Ud say ef he knowed how you's broke de good Lawd's Gol'n
    Rule?

Boy, whah's de raisin' I give you? Is you boun' fuh ter be
  a black villiun?
I's s'prised dat a chile er yo' mammy 'ud steal any man's
  water-million.

En I's now gwiner cut it right open, en you shain't have
  narry bite,
Fuh a boy who'll steal water-millions—en dat in de day's
  broad light—
Ain't—*Lawdy!* it's GREEN! Mirandy; Mi-ran-dy! come on
  wi' dat switch!
Well, stealin' a g-r-e-e-n water-million! who ever heered tell
  er des sich?

Cain't tell w'en dey's ripe? W'y, you thump 'um, en w'en dey
  go pank dey is green;
But when dey go *punk,* now you mine me, dey's ripe—en
  dat's des wut I mean.
En nex' time you hook water-millions—*you* heered me, you
  ign'ant young hunk,
Ef you don't want a lickin' all over, be sho dat dey allers go
  " punk "!

Harrison Robertson.

JOHN GRUMLIE

JOHN GRUMLIE swore by the light o' the moon
  And the green leaves on the tree,
That he could do more work in a day
  Than his wife could do in three.
His wife rose up in the morning
  Wi' cares and troubles enow—
John Grumlie bide at hame, John,
  And I'll go haud the plow.

First ye maun dress your children fair,
  And put them a' in their gear;
And ye maun turn the malt, John,
  Or else ye'll spoil the beer;

And ye maun reel the tweel, John,
  That I span yesterday;
And ye maun ca' in the hens, John,
  Else they'll all lay away.

O he did dress his children fair,
  And put them a' in their gear;
But he forgot to turn the malt,
  And so he spoil'd the beer:
And he sang loud as he reeled the tweel
  That his wife span yesterday;
But he forgot to put up the hens,
  And the hens all layed away.

The hawket crummie loot down nae milk;
  He kirned, nor butter gat;
And a' gade wrang, and nought gade right;
  He danced with rage, and grat;
Then up he ran to the head o' the knowe
  Wi' mony a wave and shout—
She heard him as she heard him not,
  And steered the stots about.

John Grumlie's wife cam hame at e'en,
  A weary wife and sad,
And burst into a laughter loud,
  And laughed as she'd been mad:
While John Grumlie swore by the light o' the moon
  And the green leaves on the tree,
If my wife should na win a penny a day
  She's aye have her will for me.

               Allan Cunningham.

A SONG OF IMPOSSIBILITIES

LADY, I loved you all last year,
  How honestly and well—
Alas! would weary you to hear,
  And torture me to tell;
I raved beneath the midnight sky,
  I sang beneath the limes—

Orlando in my lunacy,
    And Petrarch in my rhymes.
But all is over! When the sun
    Dries up the boundless main,
When black is white, false-hearted one,
    I may be yours again!

When passion's early hopes and fears
    Are not derided things;
When truth is found in falling tears,
    Or faith in golden rings;
When the dark Fates that rule our way
    Instruct me where they hide
One woman that would ne'er betray,
    One friend that never lied;
When summer shines without a cloud,
    And bliss without a pain;
When worth is noticed in a crowd,
    I may be yours again!

When science pours the light of day
    Upon the lords of lands;
When Huskisson is heard to say
    That Lethbridge understands;
When wrinkles work their way in youth,
    Or Eldon's in a hurry;
When lawyers represent the truth,
    Or Mr. Sumner Surrey;
When aldermen taste eloquence
    Or bricklayers champagne;
When common law is common sense,
    I may be yours again!

When learned judges play the beau,
    Or learned pigs the tabor;
When traveller Bankes beats Cicero,
    Or Mr. Bishop Weber;
When sinking funds discharge a debt,
    Or female hands a bomb;
When bankrupts study the *Gazette,*
    Or colleges *Tom Thumb;*

When little fishes learn to speak,
  Or poets not to feign;
When Dr. Geldart construes Greek,
  I may be yours again!

When Pole and Thornton honour cheques,
  Or Mr. Const a rogue;
When Jericho's in Middlesex,
  Or minuets in vogue;
When Highgate goes to Devonport,
  Or fashion to Guildhall;
When argument is heard at Court,
  Or Mr. Wynn at all;
When Sydney Smith forgets to jest,
  Or farmers to complain;
When kings that are are not the best,
  I may be yours again!

When peers from telling money shrink,
  Or monks from telling lies;
When hydrogen begins to sink,
  Or Grecian scrip to rise;
When German poets cease to dream,
  Americans to guess;
When Freedom sheds her holy beam
  On Negroes, and the Press;
When there is any fear of Rome,
  Or any hope of Spain;
When Ireland is a happy home,
  I may be yours again!

When you can cancel what has been,
  Or alter what must be,
Or bring once more that vanished scene,
  Those withered joys to me;
When you can tune the broken lute,
  Or deck the blighted wreath,
Or rear the garden's richest fruit,
  Upon a blasted heath;
When you can lure the wolf at bay
  Back to his shattered chain,
To-day may then be yesterday—
  I may be yours again!

               Winthrop Mackworth Praed.

SONG

Go and catch a falling star,
   Get with child a mandrake root;
Tell me where all past years are,
   Or who cleft the Devil's foot;
Teach me to hear Mermaids singing,—
Or to keep off envy's stinging,
         And find
         What wind
Serves to advance an honest mind.

If thou beest born to strange sights,
   Things invisible to see,
Ride ten thousand days and nights,
   Till age snow white hairs on thee;
Thou, when thou return'st, wilt tell me
All strange wonders that befell thee,
         And swear
         Nowhere
Lives a woman true and fair.

If thou find'st one, let me know;
   Such a pilgrimage were sweet.
Yet do not; I would not go,
   Though at next door we might meet.
Though she were true when you met her,
And last till you write your letter,
         Yet she
         Will be
False, ere I come, to two or three.

                                   John Donne.

THE OUBIT

It was an hairy oubit, sae proud he crept alang;
A feckless hairy oubit, and merrily he sang:
"My Minnie bade me bide at home until I won my wings
I shew her soon my soul's aboon the warks o' creeping things."

his feckless hairy oubit cam' hirpling by the linn,
A swirl o' wind cam' doun the glen, and blew that oubit in.
Oh, when he took the water, the saumon fry they rose,
And tigg'd him a' to pieces sma', by head and tail and toes.

Tak' warning then, young poets a', by this poor oubit's
    shame;
Though Pegasus may nicher loud, keep Pegasus at hame.
O haud your hands frae inkhorns, though a' the Muses woo;
For critics lie, like saumon fry, to mak' their meals o' you.

Charles Kingsley.

DOUBLE BALLADE OF PRIMITIVE MAN

He lived in a cave by the seas,
    He lived upon oysters and foes,
But his list of forbidden degrees
    An extensive morality shows;
Geological evidence goes
    To prove he had never a pan,
But he shaved with a shell when he chose,—
    'Twas the manner of Primitive Man.

He worshipp'd the rain and the breeze,
    He worshipp'd the river that flows,
And the Dawn, and the Moon, and the trees
    And bogies, and serpents, and crows;
He buried his dead with their toes
    Tucked-up, an original plan,
Till their knees came right under their nose,—
    'Twas the manner of Primitive Man.

His communal wives, at his ease,
    He would curb with occasional blows
Or his State had a queen, like the bees
    (As another philosopher trows):
When he spoke, it was never in prose,
    But he sang in a strain that would scan,
For (to doubt it, perchance, were morose)
    'Twas the manner of Primitive Man!

On the coasts that incessantly freeze,
  With his stones, and his bones, and his bows,
On luxuriant tropical leas,
  Where the summer eternally glows,
He is found, and his habits disclose
  (Let theology say what she can)
That he lived in the long, long agos,
  'Twas the manner of Primitive Man!

From a status like that of the Crees
  Our society's fabric arose,—
Develop'd, evolved, if you please,
  But deluded chronologists chose,
In a fancied accordance with Mos
  es, 4000 B.C. for the span
When he rushed on the world and its woes,—
  'Twas the manner of Primitive Man.

But the mild anthropologist—*he's*
  Not *recent* inclined to suppose
Flints Palæolithic like these,
  Quaternary bones such as those!
In Rhinoceros, Mammoth and Co.'s
  First epoch the Human began
Theologians all to expose,—
  'Tis the *mission* of Primitive Man.

ENVOY

Max, proudly your Aryans pose,
  But their rigs they undoubtedly ran,.
For, as every Darwinian knows,
  'Twas the manner of Primitive Man!'

Andrew Lang:.

PHILLIS'S AGE

How old may Phillis be, you ask,
  Whose beauty thus all hearts engages?.
To answer is no easy task:
  For she has really two ages.

Stiff in brocade, and pinch'd in stays,
  Her patches, paint, and jewels on;
All day let envy view her face,
  And Phillis is but twenty-one.

Paint, patches, jewels laid aside,
  At night astronomers agree,
The evening has the day belied;
  And Phillis is some forty-three.

Matthew Prior.

V

CYNICISM

GOOD AND BAD LUCK

Good Luck is the gayest of all gay girls;
  Long in one place she will not stay:
Back from your brow she strokes the curls,
  Kisses you quick and flies away.

But Madame Bad Luck soberly comes
  And stays—no fancy has she for flitting;
Snatches of true-love songs she hums,
  And sits by your bed, and brings her knitting.

John Hay.

BANGKOLIDYE

" Gimme my scarlet tie,"

Says I.
" Gimme my brownest boots and hat,
Gimme a vest with a pattern fancy,
Gimme a gel with some style, like Nancy,
And then—well, it's gimes as I'll be at,
Seein' as its bangkolidye,"

Says I.

" May miss it, but we'll try,"

Says I.
Nancy ran like a frightened 'en
Hup the steps of the bloomin' styeshun.
Bookin'-orfus at last! Salvyeshun!

334

An' the two returns was five-and-ten.
" An' travellin' mikes your money fly,"
Says I.

" This atmosphere is 'igh,"
Says I.
Twelve in a carriage is pretty thick,
When 'ite of the twelve is a sittin', smokin';
Nancy started 'er lawkin, and jokin',
Syin' she 'oped as we shouldn't be sick;
" Don't go on, or you'll mike me die! "
Says I.

" Three styeshuns we've porst by,"
Says I.
" So hout we get at the next, my gel."
When we got hout, she wer pale and saint-like,
White in the gills, and sorter faint-like,
An' said my cigaw 'ad a powerful smell,
" Well, it's the sime as I always buy,"
Says I.

" 'Ites them clouds in the sky,"
Says I.
" Don't like 'em at all," I says, " that's flat—
Black as your boots and sorter thick'nin'."
" If it's wet," says she, " it *will* be sick'nin'.
I wish as I'd brought my other 'at."
" You thinks too much of your finery,"
Says I.

" Keep them sanwidjus dry,"
Says I,
When the rine came down in a reggiler sheet.
But what can yo do with one umbrella,
And a damp gel strung on the arm of a fella?
" Well, rined-on 'am ain't pleasant to eat,
If yer don't believe it, just go an try,"
Says I.

"There is some gels whort cry,"

> Says I.

"And there is some don't shed a tear,
But just get tempers, and when they has'em
Reaches a pint in their sarcasem,
As on'y a dorg could bear to 'ear."
This unto Nancy by-and-by,

> Says I.

All's hover now. And why,

> Says I.

But why did I wear them boots, that vest?
The bloom is off 'em; they're sad to see;
And hev'rythin's off twixt Nancy and me;
And my trousers is off and gone to be pressed—
And ain't this a blimed bangkolidye?

> Says I.

> *Barry Pain*

PENSÉES DE NOËL

When the landlord wants the rent
Of your humble tenement;
When the Christmas bills begin
Daily, hourly pouring in;
When you pay your gas and poor rate,
Tip the rector, fee the curate,
Let this thought your spirit cheer—
Christmas comes but once a year.

When the man who brings the coal
Claims his customary dole:
When the postman rings and knocks
For his usual Christmas-box:
When you're dunned by half the town
With demands for half-a-crown,—
Think, although they cost you dear,
Christmas comes but once a year.

When you roam ɪrom shop to shop,
Seeking, till you nearly drop,
Christmas cards and small donations
For the maw of your relations,
Questing vainly 'mid the heap
For a thing that's nice, and cheap:
Think, and check the rising tear,
Christmas comes but once a year.

Though for three successive days
Business quits her usual ways;
Though the milkman's voice be dumb;
Though the paper doesn't come;
Though you want tobacco, but
Find that all the shops are shut:
Bravely still your sorrows bear—
Christmas comes but once a year.

When mince-pies you can't digest
Join with waits to break your rest:
When, oh when, to crown your woe,
Persons who might better know
Think it needful that you should
Don a gay convivial mood:—
    Bear with fortitude and patience
    These afflicting dispensations:
    Man was born to suffer here:
    Christmas comes but once a year.

A. D. Godley.

A BALLADE OF AN ANTI-PURITAN

THEY spoke of Progress spiring round,
Of Light and Mrs. Humphry Ward—
It is not true to say I frowned,
Or ran about the room and roared;
I might have simply sat and snored—
I rose politely in the club
And said, " I feel a little bored;
Will someone take me to a pub ? "

The new world's wisest did surround
Me; and it pains me to record
I did not think their views profound,
Or their conclusions well assured;
The simple life I can't afford,
Besides, I do not like the grub—
I want a mash and sausage, " scored "—
Will someone take me to a pub?

I know where Men can still be found,
Anger and clamorous accord,
And virtues growing from the ground,
And fellowship of beer and board,
And song, that is a sturdy cord,
And hope, that is a hardy shrub,
And goodness, that is God's last word—
Will someone take me to a pub?

ENVOI

Prince, Bayard would have smashed his sword
To see the sort of knights you dub—
Is that the last of them—O Lord!
Will someone take me to a pub?

G. K. Chesterton.

PESSIMISM

IN the age that was golden, the halcyon time,
    All the billows were balmy and breezes were bland.
Then the poet was never hard up for a rhyme,
Then the milk and the honey flew free and were prime,
    And the voice of the turtle was heard in the land.

In the times that are guilty the winds are perverse,
    Blowing fair for the sharper and foul for the dupe.
Now the poet's condition could scarcely be worse,
Now the milk and the honey are strained through the purse
    And the voice of the turtle is dead in the soup.

Newton Mackintosh.

CYNICAL ODE TO AN ULTRA-CYNICAL PUBLIC

You prefer a buffoon to a scholar,
A harlequin to a teacher,
A jester to a statesman,
An Anonyma flaring on horseback
To a modest and spotless woman—
                    Brute of a public!

You think that to sneer shows wisdom,
That a gibe outvalues a reason;
That slang, such as thieves delight in,
Is fit for the lips of the gentle,
And rather a grace than a blemish,
                    Thick-headed public!

You think that if merit's exalted
'Tis excellent sport to decry it,
And trail its good name in the gutter;
And that cynics, white-gloved and cravatted,
Are the cream and quintessence of all things,
                    Ass of a public!

You think that success must be merit,
That honour and virtue and courage
Are all very well in their places,
But that money's a thousand times better;
Detestable, stupid, degraded
                    Pig of a public!

Charles Mackay.

YOUTH AND ART

It once might have been, once only:
    We lodged in a street together.
You, a sparrow on the house-top lonely,
    I, a lone she-bird of his feather.

Your trade was with sticks and clay,
   You thumbed, thrust, patted and polished,
Then laughed, " They will see some day
   Smith made, and Gibson demolished."

My business was song, song, song;
   I chirped, cheeped, trilled and twittered,
" Kate Brown's on the boards ere long,
   And Grisi's existence embittered! "

I earned no more by a warble
   Than you by a sketch in plaster;
You wanted a piece of marble,
   I needed a music-master.

We studied hard in our styles,
   Chipped each at a crust like Hindoos,
For air, looked out on the tiles,
   For fun watched each other's windows.

You lounged, like a boy of the South,
   Cap and blouse—nay, a bit of beard too;
Or you got it rubbing your mouth
   With fingers the clay adhered to.

And I—soon managed to find
   Weak points in the flower-fence facing,
Was forced to put up a blind
   And be safe in my corset-lacing.

No harm! It was not my fault
   If you never turned your eyes' tail up,
As I shook upon E *in alt.,*
   Or ran the chromatic scale up:

For spring bade the sparrows pair,
   And the boys and girls gave guesses,
And stalls in our streets looked rare
   With bulrush and watercresses.

Why did not you pinch a flower
   In a pellet of clay and fling it?
Why did I not put a power
   Of thanks in a look, or sing it?

I did look, sharp as a lynx,
   (And yet the memory rankles,)
When models arrived, some minx
   Tripped up-stairs, she and her ankles.

But I think I gave you as good!
   " That foreign fellow—who can know
How she pays, in a playful mood,
   For his tuning her that piano? "

Could you say so, and never say,
   " Suppose we join hands and fortunes,
And I fetch her from over the way,
   Her, piano, and long tunes and short tunes? "

No, no; you would not be rash,
   Nor I rasher and something over:
You've to settle yet Gibson's hash,
   And Grisi yet lives in clover.

But you meet the Prince at the Board,
   I'm queen myself at *bals-paré,*
I've married a rich old lord,
   And you're dubbed knight and an R. A.

Each life's unfulfilled, you see;
   It hangs still, patchy and scrappy:
We have not sighed deep, laughed free,
   Starved, feasted, despaired—been happy.

And nobody calls you a dunce,
   And people suppose me clever:
This could but have happened once,
   And we missed it, lost it forever.

                        Robert Browning.

THE BACHELOR'S DREAM

My pipe is lit, my grog is mixed,
My curtains drawn and all is snug;
Old Puss is in her elbow-chair,
And Tray is sitting on the rug.
Last night I had a curious dream,
Miss Susan Bates was Mistress Mogg—
What d'ye think of that, my cat?
What d'ye think of that, my dog?

She looked so fair, she sang so well,
I could but woo and she was won;
Myself in blue, the bride in white,
The ring was placed, the deed was done!
Away we went in chaise-and-four,
As fast as grinning boys could flog—
What d'ye think of that, my cat?
What d'ye think of that, my dog?

At times we had a spar, and then
Mamma must mingle in the song—
The sister took a sister's part—
The maid declared her master wrong—
The parrot learned to call me "Fool!"
My life was like a London fog—
What d'ye think of that, my cat?
What d'ye think of that, my dog?

My Susan's taste was superfine,
As proved by bills that had no end;
I never had a decent coat—
I never had a coin to spend!
She forced me to resign my club,
Lay down my pipe, retrench my grog—
What d'ye think of that, my cat?
What d'ye think of that, my dog?

Each Sunday night we gave a rout
To fops and flirts, a pretty list;
And when I tried to steal away,
I found my study full of whist!
Then, first to come, and last to go,
There always was a Captain Hogg—
What d'ye think of that, my cat?
What d'ye think of that, my dog?

Now was not that an awful dream
For one who single is and snug—
With Pussy in the elbow chair,
And Tray reposing on the rug?—
If I must totter down the hill,
'Tis safest done without a clog—
What d'ye think of that, my cat?
What d'ye think of that, my dog?

Thomas Hood.

ALL THINGS EXCEPT MYSELF I KNOW

I KNOW when milk does flies contain;
  I know men by their bravery;
I know fair days from storm and rain;
  And what fruit apple-trees supply;
  And from their gums the trees descry;
I know when all things smoothly flow;
  I know who toil or idle lie;
All things except myself I know.

I know the doublet by the grain;
  The monk beneath the hood can spy;
Master from man can ascertain;
  I know the nun's veiled modesty;
  I know when sportsmen fables ply;
Know fools who creams and dainties stow;
  Wine from the butt I certify;
All things except myself I know.

Know horse from mule by tail and mane;
  I know their worth or high or low;
Bell, Beatrice, I know the twain;
  I know each chance of cards and dice;
  I know what visions prophesy,
Bohemian heresies, I trow;
  I know men of each quality;
All things except myself I know.

ENVOY

Prince, I know all things 'neath the sky,
  Pale cheeks from those of rosy glow;
I know death whence can no man fly;
  All things except myself I know.

François Villon.

THE JOYS OF MARRIAGE

How uneasy is his life,
Who is troubled with a wife!
Be she ne'er so fair or comely,
Be she ne'er so foul or homely,
Be she ne'er so young and toward,
Be she ne'er so old and froward,
Be she kind, with arms enfolding,
Be she cross, and always scolding,
Be she blithe or melancholy,
Have she wit, or have she folly,
Be she wary, be she squandering,
Be she staid, or be she wandering,
Be she constant, be she fickle,
Be she fire, or be she ickle;
Be she pious or ungodly,
Be she chaste, or what sounds oddly:
Lastly, be she good or evil,
Be she saint, or be she devil,—
Yet, uneasy is his life
Who is married to a wife.

Charles Cotton.

THE THIRD PROPOSITION

ℐF I were thine, I'd fail not of endeavour
          The loftiest,
᾽o make thy daily life, now and forever,
          Supremely blest—
᾽d watch thy moods, I'd toil and wait, with yearning,
ncessant incense at thy dear shrine burning,
          If I were thine.

f thou wert mine, quite changed would be these features.
          Then, I suspect,
᾽hou wouldst the humblest prove of loving creatures,
          And not object
᾽o do the very things I am declaring
᾽d undertake for *thee,* with selfless daring,
          If thou wert mine.

f we were ours? And now, here comes the riddle!
          How would that work?
᾽m sure *you'd* never stoop to second fiddle,
          And—I might shirk
᾽he part of serf. And, likewise, each might neither
᾽e willing slave or servitor of either,
          If we were ours!

                              Madeline Bridges.

THE BALLAD OF CASSANDRA BROWN

᾽HOUGH I met her in the summer, when one's heart lies
          round at ease,
᾽s it were in tennis costume, and a man's not hard to
          please,
᾽et I think that any season to have met her was to love,
᾽hile her tones, unspoiled, unstudied, had the softness of
          the dove.

᾽t request she read us poems in a nook among the pines,
᾽nd her artless voice lent music to the least melodious
          lines;

Though she lowered her shadowing lashes, in an earnes
 reader's wise,
Yet we caught blue, gracious glimpses of the heavens whic'
 were her eyes.

As in paradise I listened—ah, I did not understand
That a little cloud, no larger than the average huma
 hand,
Might, as stated oft in fiction, spread into a sable pall,
When she said that she should study Elocution in the fall

I admit her earliest efforts were not in the Ercles vein;
She began with "Little Maaybel, with her faayce agains
 the payne
And the beacon-light a-t-r-r-remble"—which, although i
 made me wince,
Is a thing of cheerful nature to the things she's rendere
 since.

Having heard the Soulful Quiver, she acquired the Melt
 ing Mo-o-an,
And the way she gave "Young Grayhead" would hav
 liquefied a stone.
Then the Sanguinary Tragic did her energies employ,
And she tore my taste to tatters when she slew "The Polis
 Boy."

It's not pleasant for a fellow when the jewel of his soul
Wades through slaughter on the carpet, while her orbs i
 frenzy roll;
What was I that I should murmur? Yet it gave me grievou
 pain
That she rose in social gatherings, and Searched among
 the Slain.

I was forced to look upon her in my desperation dumb,
Knowing well that when her awful opportunity was com
She would give us battle, murder, sudden death at ver
 least,
As a skeleton of warning, and a blight upon the feast.

Once, ah! once I fell a-dreaming; some one played a polo-
    naise
I associated strongly with those happier August days;
And I mused, "I'll speak this evening," recent pangs for-
    gotten quite—
Sudden shrilled a scream of anguish: "Curfew shall not
    ring to-night!"

Ah, that sound was as a curfew, quenching rosy, warm
    romance—
Were it safe to wed a woman one so oft would wish in
    France?
Oh, as she "cul-limbed" that ladder, swift my mounting
    hope came down,
I am still a single cynic; she is still Cassandra Brown!

Helen Gray Cone.

WHAT'S IN A NAME?

In letters large upon the frame,
    That visitors might see,
The painter placed his humble name:
    O'Callaghan McGee.

And from Beersheba unto Dan,
    The critics with a nod
Exclaimed: "This painting Irishman
    Adores his native sod.

"His stout heart's patriotic flame
    There's naught on earth can quell;
He takes no wild romantic name
    To make his pictures sell!"

Then poets praise in sonnets neat
    His stroke so bold and free;
No parlour wall was thought complete
    That hadn't a McGee.

All patriots before McGee
    Threw lavishly their gold;
His works in the Academy
    Were very quickly sold.

His "Digging Clams at Barnegat,"
    His "When the Morning smiled,"
His "Seven Miles from Ararat,"
    His "Portrait of a Child,"

Were purchased in a single day
    And lauded as divine.—
    .   .   .   .   .   .
That night as in his *atelier*
    The artist sipped his wine,

And looked upon his gilded frames,
    He grinned from ear to ear:—
"They little think my *real* name's
    V. Stuyvesant De Vere!"

                        R. K. Munkittrick.

TOO LATE

"Ah! si la jeunesse savait,—si la vieillesse pouvait!"

THERE sat an old man on a rock,
    And unceasing bewailed him of Fate,—
That concern where we all must take stock,
    Though our vote has no hearing or weight;
        And the old man sang him an old, old song,—
        Never sang voice so clear and strong
        That it could drown the old man's for long,
            For he sang the song "Too late! too late!"

When we want, we have for our pains
    The promise that if we but wait
Till the want has burned out of our brains,
    Every means shall be present to state;

While we send for the napkin the soup gets cold,
While the bonnet is trimming the face grows old,
When we've matched our buttons the pattern is sold
    And everything comes too late,—too late!

" When strawberries seemed like red heavens,—
  Terrapin stew a wild dream,—
When my brain was at sixes and sevens,
  If my mother had 'folks' and ice cream,
    Then I gazed with a lickerish hunger
    At the restaurant man and fruit-monger,—
    But oh! how I wished I were younger
      When the goodies all came in a stream! in a stream!

" I've a splendid blood horse, and—a liver
  That it jars into torture to trot;
My row-boat's the gem of the river,—
  Gout makes every knuckle a knot!
    I can buy boundless credits on Paris and Rome,
    But no palate for *ménus*,—no eyes for a dome,—
    Those belonged to the youth who must tarry at home,
      When no home but an attic he'd got,—he'd got!

" How I longed, in that lonest of garrets,
  Where the tiles baked my brains all July,
For ground to grow two pecks of carrots,
  Two pigs of my own in a sty,
    A rosebush,—a little thatched cottage,—
    Two spoons—love—a basin of pottage!—
    Now in freestone I sit,—and my dotage,—
      With a woman's chair empty close by, close by!

" Ah! now, though I sit on a rock,
  I have shared one seat with the great;
I have sat—knowing naught of the clock—
  On love's high throne of state;
    But the lips that kissed, and the arms that caressed,
    To a mouth grown stern with delay were pressed,
    And circled a breast that their clasp had blessed,
      Had they only not come too late,—too late! "

                      Fitz Hugh Ludlow.

THE ANNUITY

I GAED to spend a week in Fife—
  An unco week it proved to be—
For there I met a waesome wife
  Lamentin' her viduity.
Her grief brak out sae fierce and fell,
I thought her heart wad burst the shell;
And,—I was sae left to mysel',—
  I sell't her an annuity.

The bargain lookit fair eneugh—
  She just was turned o' saxty-three—
I couldna guessed she'd prove sae teugh,
  By human ingenuity.
But years have come, and years have gane,
And there she's yet as stieve as stane—
The limmer's growin' young again,
  Since she got her annuity.

She's crined' awa' to bane and skin,
  But that, it seems, is nought to me;
She's like to live—although she's in
  The last stage o' tenuity.
She munches wi' her wizen'd gums,
An' stumps about on legs o' thrums;
But comes, as sure as Christmas comes,
  To ca' for her annuity.

I read the tables drawn wi' care
  For an insurance company;
Her chance o' life was stated there,
  Wi' perfect perspicuity.
But tables here or tables there,
She's lived ten years beyond her share,
An' 's like to live a dozen mair,
  To ca' for her annuity.

Last Yule she had a fearfu' host,
    I thought a kink might set me free—
I led her out, 'mang snaw and frost,
    Wi' constant assiduity.
But deil ma' care—the blast gaed by,
And miss'd the auld anatomy—
It just cost me a tooth, for bye
    Discharging her annuity.

If there's a sough o' cholera,
    Or typhus,—wha sae gleg as she?
She buys up baths, an' drugs, an' a',
    In siccan superfluity!
She doesna need—she's fever proof—
The pest walked o'er her very roof—
She tauld me sae—an' then her loof
    Held out for her annuity.

Ae day she fell, her arm she brak—
    A compound fracture as could be—
Nae leech the cure wad undertake,
    Whate'er was the gratuity.
It's cured! She handles 't like a flail—
It does as weel in bits as hale—
But I'm a broken man mysel'
    Wi' her and her annuity.

Her broozled flesh and broken banes
    Are weel as flesh and banes can be.
She beats the taeds that live in stanes,
    An' fatten in vacuity!
They die when they're exposed to air—
They canna thole the atmosphere;
But her!—expose her onywhere—
    She lives for her annuity.

If mortal means could nick her thread,
    Sma' crime it wad appear to me;
Ca't murder, or ca't homicide,
    I'd justify 't—an' do it tae.

But how to fell a withered wife
That's carved out o' the tree o' life—
The timmer limmer daurs the knife
    To settle her annuity.

I'd try a shot: but whar's the mark?—
    Her vital parts are hid frae me;
Her backbane wanders through her sark
    In an unkenn'd corkscrewity.
She's palsified—an shakes her head
Sae fast about, ye scarce can see;
It's past the power o' steel or lead
    To settle her annuity.

She might be drowned—but go she'll not
    Within a mile o' loch or sea;
Or hanged—if cord could grip a throat
    O' siccan exiguity.
It's fitter far to hang the rope—
It draws out like a telescope;
'Twad tak a dreadfu' length o' drop
    To settle her annuity.

Will puzion do't?—It has been tried;
    But, be't in hash or fricassee,
That's just the dish she can't abide,
    Whatever kind o' gout it hae.
It's needless to assail her doubts,
She gangs by instinct, like the brutes,
An' only eats an' drinks what suits
    Hersel' and her annuity.

The Bible says the age o' man
    Threescore and ten, perchance, may be;
She's ninety-four. Let them who can,
    Explain the incongruity.
She should hae lived afore the flood—
She's come o' patriarchal blood,
She's some auld Pagan mummified
    Alive for her annuity.

She's been embalmed inside and oot—
   She's sauted to the last degree—
There's pickle in her very snoot
   Sae caper-like an' cruety.
Lot's wife was fresh compared to her—
They've kyanized the useless knir,
She canna decompose—nae mair
   Than her accursed annuity.

The water-drop wears out the rock,
   As this eternal jaud wears me;
I could withstand the single shock,
   But not the continuity.
It's pay me here, an' pay me there,
An' pay me, pay me, evermair—
I'll gang demented wi' despair—
   I'm charged for her annuity.

George Outram.

K. K.—CAN'T CALCULATE

WHAT poor short-sighted worms we be;
   For we can't calculate,
With any sort of sartintee,
   What is to be our fate.

These words Prissilla's heart did reach,
   And caused her tears to flow,
When first she heard the Elder preach,
   About six months ago.

How true it is what he did state,
   And thus affected her,
That nobody can't calculate
   What is a-gwine to occur.

When we retire, can't calculate
   But what afore the morn
Our housen will conflaggerate,
   And we be left forlorn.

Can't calculate when we come in
From any neighborin' place,
Whether we'll ever go out agin
To look on natur's face.

Can't calculate upon the weather,
It always changes so;
Hain't got no means of telling whether
It's gwine to rain or snow.

Can't calculate with no precision
On naught beneath the sky;
And so I've come to the decision
That 't ain't worth while to try.

Frances M. Whitcher.

NORTHERN FARMER

NEW STYLE

Dosn't thou 'ear my 'erse's legs, as they canters awaäy?
Proputty, proputty, proputty—that's what I 'ears 'em saäy.
Proputty, proputty, proputty—Sam, thou's an ass for thy
  paaïns:
Theer's moor sense i' one o' 'is legs nor in all thy braaïns.

Woä—theer's a craw to pluck wi' tha, Sam: yon's parson's
  'ouse—
Dosn't thou knaw that a man mun be eäther a man or a
  mouse?
Time to think on it, then; for thou'll be twenty to weeäk.
Proputty, proputty—woä then, woä—let ma 'ear mysén
  speäk.

Me an' thy muther, Sammy, 'as beän a-talkin' o' thee;
Thou's been talkin' to muther, an' she beän a-tellin' it me.
Thou'll not marry for munny—thou's sweet upo' parson's
  lass—
Noä—thou'll marry for luvv—an' we boäth of us thinks tha
  an ass.

Seeä'd her to-daäy goä by—Saäint's-daäy—they was ringing
the bells.
She's a beauty, thou thinks—an' soä is scoors o' gells.
Them as 'as munny an' all—wot's a beauty?—the flower as
blaws.
But proputty, proputty sticks, an' proputty, proputty graws.

Do'ant be stunt: taäke time: I knaws what maäkes tha sa
mad.
Warn't I craäzed fur the lasses mysén when I wur a lad?
But I knaw'd a Quaäker feller as often 'as towd ma this:
"Do'ant thou marry for munny, but goä wheer munny is!"

An' I went wheer munny war: an' thy mother coom to 'and,
Wi' lots o' munny laaïd by, an' a nicetish bit o' land.
Maäybe she warn't a beauty: I niver giv it a thowt—
But warn't she as good to cuddle an' kiss as a lass as 'ant
nowt?

Parson's lass 'ant nowt, an' she weänt 'a nowt when 'e's deäd,
Mun be a guvness, lad, or summut, and addle her breäd:
Why? fur 'e's nobbut a curate, an' weänt niver git naw
'igher;
An' 'e's maäde the bed as 'e ligs on afoor 'e coom'd to the
shire.

An' thin 'e coom'd to the parish wi' lots o' 'Varsity debt,
Stook to his taäil they did, an' 'e 'ant got shut on 'em yet.
An' 'e ligs on 'is back i' the grip, wi noän to lend 'im a shove,
Woorse nor a far-welter'd yowe: fur, Sammy, 'e married fur
luvv.

Luvv? what's luvv? thou can luvv thy lass an' 'er munny too,
Maäkin' 'em goä togither, as they've good right to do.
Couldn't I luvv thy muther by cause o' 'er munny laaïd by?
Naäy—for I luvv'd her a vast sight moor fur it: reäson
why.

Ay, an' thy muther says thou wants to marry the lass,
Cooms of a gentleman burn; an' we boäth on us thinks tha
    an ass.
Woä then, proputty, wiltha?—an ass as near as mays nowt—
Woä then, wiltha? dangtha!—the bees is as fell as owt.

Breäk me a bit o' the esh for his 'eäd, lad, out o' the fence!
Gentleman burn! What's gentleman burn? Is it shillins
    an' pence?
Proputty, proputty's ivrything 'ere, an', Sammy, I'm blest
If it isn't the saäme oop yonder, fur them as 'as it's the best.

'Tisn' them as 'as munny as breäks into 'ouses an' steäls,
Them as 'as coöts to their backs an 'taäkes their regular
    meäls.
Noä, but it's them as niver knaws wheer a meäl's to be 'ad.
Taäke my word for it, Sammy, the poor in a loomp is bad.

Them or thir feythers, tha sees, mun 'a beän a laäzy lot.
Fur work mun 'a gone to the gittin' whiniver munny was
    got.
Feyther 'ad ammost nowt; leästways 'is munny was 'id.
But 's tued an' moil'd 'issén deäd, an' 'e died a good un, 'e
    did.

Looök thou theer wheer Wrigglesby beck cooms out by the
    'ill!
Feyther run oop to the farm, an' I runs oop to the mill;
An' I'll run oop to the brig, an' that thou'll live to see;
And if thou marries a good un I'll leäve the land to thee.

Thim's my noätions, Sammy, wheerby I meäns to stick;
But if thou marries a bad un, I'll leäve the land to Dick.—
Coom oop, proputty, proputty—that's what I 'ears 'im saäy—
Proputty, proputty, proputty—canter an' canter awaäy.

                              Lord Tennyson.

FIN DE SIECLE

Life is a gift that most of us hold dear:
　　I never asked the spiteful gods to grant it;
Held it a bore—in short; and now it's here,
　　　　I do not want it.

Thrust into life, I eat, smoke, drink, and sleep,
　　My mind's a blank I seldom care to question;
The only faculty I active keep
　　　　Is my digestion.

Like oyster on his rock, I sit and jest
　　At others' dreams of love or fame or pelf,
Discovering but a languid interest
　　　　Even in myself.

An oyster: ah! beneath the quiet sea
　　To know no care, no change, no joy, no pain,
The warm salt water gurgling into me
　　　　And out again.

While some in life's old roadside inns at ease
　　Sit careless, all unthinking of the score
Mine host chalks up in swift unseen increase
　　　　Behind the door;

Bound like Ixion on life's torture-wheel,
　　I whirl inert in pitiless gyration,
Loathing it all; the one desire I feel,
　　　　Annihilation!

　　　　　　　　　　　　Unknown.

THEN AG'IN

Jim Bowker, he said, ef he'd had a fair show,
And a big enough town for his talents to grow,
And the least bit assistance in hoein' his row,
　　　　Jim Bowker, he said,
He'd filled the world full of the sound of his name,
An' clim the top round in the ladder of fame.

It may have been so;
I dunno;
Jest so, it might been,
Then ag'in—

But he had tarnal luck—everythin' went ag'in him,
The arrers of fortune they allus' 'ud pin him;
So he didn't get no chance to show off what was in him.
Jim Bowker, he said,
Ef he'd had a fair show, you couldn't tell where he'd come,
An' the feats he'd a-done, an' the heights he'd a-clum—
It may have been so;
I dunno;
Jest so, it might been,
Then ag'in—

But we're all like Jim Bowker, thinks I, more or less—
Charge fate for our bad luck, ourselves for success,
An' give fortune the blame for all our distress,
As Jim Bowker, he said,
Ef it hadn't been for luck an' misfortune an' sich,
We might a-been famous, an' might a-been rich.
It might be jest so;
I dunno;
Jest so, it might been,
Then ag'in—

Sam Walter Foss.

THE PESSIMIST

NOTHING to do but work,
  Nothing to eat but food.
Nothing to wear but clothes,
  To keep one from going nude.

Nothing to breathe but air,
  Quick as a flash 't is gone;
Nowhere to fall but off,
  Nowhere to stand but on.

Nothing to comb but hair,
    Nowhere to sleep but in bed,
Nothing to weep but tears,
    Nothing to bury but dead.

Nothing to sing but songs,
    Ah, well, alas! alack!
Nowhere to go but out,
    Nowhere to come but back.

Nothing to see but sights,
    Nothing to quench but thirst,
Nothing to have but what we've got
    Thus through life we are cursed.

Nothing to strike but a gait;
    Everything moves that goes.
Nothing at all but common sense
    Can ever withstand these woes.

                                        Ben King.

WITHOUT AND WITHIN

My coachman, in the moonlight there,
    Looks through the side-light of the door;
I hear him with his brethren swear,
    As I could do,—but only more.

Flattening his nose against the pane,
    He envies me my brilliant lot,
Breathes on his aching fist in vain,
    And dooms me to a place more hot.

He sees me in to supper go,
    A silken wonder by my side,
Bare arms, bare shoulders, and a row
    Of flounces, for the door too wide.

He thinks how happy is my arm,
    'Neath its white-gloved and jewelled load;
And wishes me some dreadful harm,
    Hearing the merry corks explode.

Meanwhile I inly curse the bore
  Of hunting still the same old coon,
And envy him, outside the door,
  The golden quiet of the moon.

The winter wind is not so cold
  As the bright smile he sees me win,
Nor the host's oldest wine so old
  As our poor gabble, sour and thin.

I envy him the rugged prance
  By which his freezing feet he warms,
And drag my lady's chains, and dance,
  The galley-slave of dreary forms.

Oh, could he have my share of din,
  And I his quiet—past a doubt
'Twould still be one man bored within,
  And just another bored without.

James Russell Lowell.

SAME OLD STORY

History, and nature, too, repeat themselves, they say;
Men are only habit's slaves; we see it every day.
Life has done its best for me—I find it tiresome still;
For nothing's everything at all, and everything is nil.
  Same old get-up, dress, and tub;
  Same old breakfast; same old club;
  Same old feeling; same old blue;
  Same old story—nothing new!

Life consists of paying bills as long as you have health;
Woman? She'll be true to you—as long as you have wealth;
Think sometimes of marriage, if the right girl I could strike;
But the more I see of girls, the more they are alike.
  Same old giggles, smiles, and eyes;
  Same old kisses; same old sighs;
  Same old chaff you; same adieu;
  Same old story—nothing new!

Go to theatres sometimes to see the latest plays;
Same old plots I played with in my happy childhood's days;
Hero, same; same villain; and same heroine in tears,
Starving, homeless, in the snow—with diamonds in her ears.
    Same stern father making "bluffs";
    Leading man all teeth and cuffs;
    Same soubrettes, still twenty-two;
    Same old story—nothing new!

Friend of mine got married; in a year or so, a boy!
Father really foolish in his fond paternal joy;
Talked about that "kiddy," and became a dreadful bore—
Just as if a baby never had been born before.
    Same old crying, only more;
    Same old business, walking floor;
    Same old "kitchy—coochy—coo!"
    Same old baby—nothing new!

Harry B. Smith.

VI

EPIGRAMS

WOMAN'S WILL

MEN, dying, make their wills, but wives
　　Escape a work so sad;
Why should they make what all their lives
　　The gentle dames have had?

John G. Saxe.

CYNICUS TO W. SHAKESPEARE

You wrote a line too much, my sage,
　　Of seers the first, and first of sayers;
For only half the world's a stage,
　　And only all the women players.

James Kenneth Stephen.

SENEX TO MATT. PRIOR

AH! Matt, old age has brought to me
Thy wisdom, less thy certainty;
The world's a jest, and joy's a trinket;
I knew that once,—but now I think it.

James Kenneth Stephen.

TO A BLOCKHEAD

You beat your pate, and fancy wit will come:
Knock as you please, there's nobody at home.

Alexander Pope.

THE FOOL AND THE POET

SIR, I admit your general rule,
That every poet is a fool,
But you yourself may serve to show it,
That every fool is not a poet.

Alexander Pope.

A RHYMESTER

JEM writes his verses with more speed
    Than the printer's boy can set 'em;
Quite as fast as we can read,
    And only not so fast as we forget 'em.

Samuel Taylor Coleridge.

GILES'S HOPE

WHAT? rise again with *all* one's bones,
    Quoth Giles, I hope you fib:
I trusted, when I went to Heaven,
    To go without my rib.

Samuel Taylor Coleridge.

COLOGNE

IN Köln, a town of monks and bones,
And pavements fanged with murderous stones,
And rags, and hags, and hideous wenches,
I counted two-and-seventy stenches,
All well defined, and separate stinks!
Ye nymphs that reign o'er sewers and sinks,
The river Rhine, it is well known,
Doth wash your city of Cologne;
But tell me, nymphs, what power divine
Shall henceforth wash the river Rhine?

Samuel Taylor Coleridge.

AN ETERNAL POEM

YOUR poem must *eternal* be,
Dear sir, it can not fail,
For 'tis incomprehensible,
And wants both *head* and *tail*.

Samuel Taylor Coleridge.

ON A BAD SINGER

SWANS sing before they die:—'twere no bad thing,
Should certain persons die before they sing.

Samuel Taylor Coleridge.

JOB

SLY Beelzebub took all occasions
To try Job's constancy and patience.
He took his honor, took his health;
He took his children, took his wealth,
His servants, horses, oxen, cows,—
But cunning Satan did *not* take his spouse.

But Heaven, that brings out good from evil,
And loves to disappoint the devil,
Had predetermined to restore
Twofold all he had before;
His servants, horses, oxen, cows—
Short-sighted devil, *not* to take his spouse!

Samuel Taylor Coleridge.

REASONS FOR DRINKING

IF all be true that I do think,
There are five reasons we should drink;
Good wine—a friend—or being dry—
Or lest we should be by and by—
Or any other reason why.

Dr. Henry Aldrich.

SMATTERERS

ALL smatterers are more brisk and pert
Than those that understand an art;
As little sparkles shine more bright
Than glowing coals, that give them light.

Samuel Butler.

HYPOCRISY

HYPOCRISY will serve as well
To propagate a church, as zeal;
As persecution and promotion
Do equally advance devotion:
So round white stones will serve, they say,
As well as eggs to make hens lay.

Samuel Butler.

TO DOCTOR EMPIRIC

WHEN men a dangerous disease did 'scape,
Of old, they gave a cock to Æsculape;
Let me give two, that doubly am got free;
From my disease's danger, and from thee.

Ben Jonson.

A REMEDY WORSE THAN THE DISEASE

I SENT for Ratcliffe; was so ill,
    That other doctors gave me over:
He felt my pulse, prescribed his pill,
    And I was likely to recover.

But when the wit began to wheeze,
    And wine had warm'd the politician,
Cured yesterday of my disease,
    I died last night of my physician.

Matthew Prior.

A WIFE

LORD ERSKINE, at women presuming to rail,
Calls a wife " a tin canister tied to one's tail";
And fair Lady Anne, while the subject he carries on,
Seems hurt at his Lordship's degrading comparison.
But wherefore degrading? consider'd aright,
A canister's useful, and polish'd, and bright:
And should dirt its original purity hide,
That's the fault of the puppy to whom it is tied.

Richard Brinsley Sheridan.

THE HONEY-MOON

THE honey-moon is very strange.
Unlike all other moons the change
  She regularly undergoes.
She rises at the full; then loses
Much of her brightness; then reposes
  Faintly; and then . . has naught to lose.

Walter Savage Landor.

DIDO

IMPROMPTU EPIGRAM ON THE LATIN GERUNDS

WHEN Dido found Æneas would not come,
She mourn'd in silence, and was *Di-do-dum*(*b*).

Richard Porson.

AN EPITAPH

A LOVELY young lady I mourn in my rhymes:
She was pleasant, good-natured, and civil sometimes.
Her figure was good: she had very fine eyes,
And her talk was a mixture of foolish and wise.
Her adorers were many, and one of them said,
" She waltzed rather well! It's a pity she's dead!"

George John Cayley.

ON TAKING A WIFE

"Come, come," said Tom's father, "at your time of life,
   There's no longer excuse for thus playing the rake.—
It is time you should think, boy, of taking a wife."—
   "Why, so it is, father,—whose wife shall I take?"

Thomas Moore.

UPON BEING OBLIGED TO LEAVE A PLEASANT PARTY

FROM THE WANT OF A PAIR OF BREECHES TO DRESS FOR DINNER IN

Between Adam and me the great difference is,
   Though a paradise each has been forced to resign,
That he never wore breeches till turn'd out of his,
   While, for want of my breeches, I'm banish'd from mine.

Thomas Moore.

SOME LADIES

Some ladies now make pretty songs,
   And some make pretty nurses;
Some men are great at righting wrongs
   And some at writing verses.

Frederick Locker-Lampson.

ON A SENSE OF HUMOUR

He cannot be complete in aught
   Who is not humorously prone;
A man without a merry thought
   Can hardly have a funny-bone.

Frederick Locker-Lampson.

ON HEARING A LADY PRAISE A CERTAIN REV. DOCTOR'S EYES

I CANNOT praise the Doctor's eyes;
I never saw his glance divine;
He always shuts them when he prays,
And when he preaches he shuts mine.

George Outram.

EPITAPH INTENDED FOR HIS WIFE

HERE lies my wife: here let her lie!
Now she's at rest, and so am I.

John Dryden.

TO A CAPRICIOUS FRIEND

IMITATED FROM MARTIAL

IN all thy humors, whether grave or mellow,
Thou 'rt such a touchy, testy, pleasant fellow;
Hast so much wit, and mirth, and spleen about thee,
There is no living with thee, nor without thee.

Joseph Addison.

WHICH IS WHICH

" GOD bless the King! God bless the faith's defender!
God bless—no harm in blessing—the Pretender.
But who pretender is, and who is king,
God bless us all, that's quite another thing."

John Byrom.

ON A FULL-LENGTH PORTRAIT OF BEAU MARSH

PLACED BETWEEN THE BUSTS OF NEWTON AND POPE

" IMMORTAL Newton never spoke
　　More truth than here you'll find;
Nor Pope himself e'er penn'd a joke
　　More cruel on mankind.

" The picture placed the busts between,
　　Gives satire all its strength;
Wisdom and Wit are little seen—
　　But Folly at full length."

Lord Chesterfield.

ON SCOTLAND

" HAD Cain been Scot, God would have changed his doom;
Nor forced him wander, but confined him home."

Cleveland.

MENDAX

SEE yonder goes old Mendax, telling lies
To that good easy man with whom he's walking;
How know I that? you ask, with some surprise;
Why, don't you see, my friend, the fellow's talking.

Lessing.

TO A SLOW WALKER AND QUICK EATER

So slowly you walk, and so quickly you eat,
You should march with your mouth, and devour with your
　feet.

Lessing.

WHAT'S MY THOUGHT LIKE?

Quest.—Why is a Pump like Viscount Castlereagh?
Answ.—Because it is a slender thing of wood,
That up and down its awkward arm doth sway,
And coolly spout, and spout, and spout away,
    In one weak, washy, everlasting flood!

Thomas Moore.

OF ALL THE MEN

Of all the men one meets about,
    There's none like Jack—he's everywhere:
At church—park—auction—dinner—rout—
    Go when and where you will, he's there.
Try the West End, he's at your back—
    Meets you, like Eurus, in the East—
You're call'd upon for " How do, Jack?"
    One hundred times a day, at least.
A friend of his one evening said,
    As home he took his pensive way,
" Upon my soul, I fear Jack's dead—
    I've seen him but three times to-day!"

Thomas Moore.

ON BUTLER'S MONUMENT

While Butler, needy wretch, was yet alive,
No generous patron would a dinner give.
See him, when starved to death and turn'd to dust,
Presented with a monumental bust.
The poet's fate is here in emblem shown—
He ask'd for *bread,* and he received a *stone.*

Rev. Samuel Wesley.

A CONJUGAL CONUNDRUM

WHICH is of greater value, prythee, say,
  The Bride or Bridegroom?—must the truth be told?
Alas, it must! The Bride is given away—
  The Bridegroom's often regularly sold.

Unknown.

VII

BURLESQUE

LOVERS AND A REFLECTION

I<small>N</small> moss-prankt dells which the sunbeams flatter
  (And heaven it knoweth what that may mean;
Meaning, however, is no great matter)
  Where woods are a-tremble with words a-tween;

Thro' God's own heather we wonned together,
  I and my Willie (O love my love):
I need hardly remark it was glorious weather,
  And flitter-bats wavered alow, above:

Boats were curtseying, rising, bowing,
  (Boats in that climate are so polite,)
And sands were a ribbon of green endowing,
  And O the sun-dazzle on bark and bight!

Thro' the rare red heather we danced together
  (O love my Willie,) and smelt for flowers:
I must mention again it was glorious weather,
  Rhymes are so scarce in this world of ours:

By rises that flushed with their purple favors,
  Thro' becks that brattled o'er grasses sheen,
We walked or waded, we two young shavers,
  Thanking our stars we were both so green.

We journeyed in parallels, I and Willie,
  In fortunate parallels! Butterflies,
Hid in weltering shadows of daffodilly
  Or Marjoram, kept making peacock eyes:

Song-birds darted about, some inky
    As coal, some snowy (I ween) as curds;
Or rosy as pinks, or as roses pinky—
    They reck of no eerie To-come, those birds!

But they skim over bents which the mill-stream washes,
    Or hang in the lift 'neath a white cloud's hem;
They need no parasols, no goloshes;
    And good Mrs. Trimmer she feedeth them.

Then we thrid God's cowslips (as erst his heather),
    That endowed the wan grass with their golden blooms;
And snapt—(it was perfectly charming weather)—
    Our fingers at Fate and her goddess-glooms:

And Willie 'gan sing—(Oh, his notes were fluty;
    Wafts fluttered them out to the white-winged sea)—
Something made up of rhymes that have done much duty,
    Rhymes (better to put it) of " ancientry ":

Bowers of flowers encountered showers
    In William's carol—(O love my Willie!)
Then he bade sorrow borrow from blithe to-morrow
    I quite forget what—say a daffodilly.

A nest in a hollow, " with buds to follow,"
    I think occurred next in his nimble strain;
And clay that was " kneaden " of course in Eden—
    A rhyme most novel I do maintain:

Mists, bones, the singer himself, love-stories,
    And all least furlable things got furled;
Not with any design to conceal their glories,
    But simply and solely to rhyme with world.

O if billows and pillows and hours and flowers,
    And all the brave rhymes of an elder day,
Could be furled together, this genial weather,
    And carted or carried on wafts away,
Nor ever again trotted out—ah me!
How much fewer volumes of verse there'd be.

                    Charles Stuart Calverley.

OUR HYMN

At morning's call
The small-voiced pug dog welcomes in the sun,
And flea-bit mongrels wakening one by one,
    Give answer all.

When evening dim
Draws rounds us, then the lovely caterwaul,
Tart solo, sour duet and general squall,
    These are our hymn.

                 Oliver Wendell Holmes.

"SOLDIER, REST!"

A Russian sailed over the blue Black Sea
  Just when the war was growing hot,
And he shouted, " I'm Tjalikavakeree—
Karindabrolikanavandorot—
      Schipkadirova—
      Ivandiszstova—
      Sanilik—
      Danilik—
      Varagobhot!"

A Turk was standing upon the shore
  Right where the terrible Russian crossed;
And he cried, "Bismillah! I'm Abd el Kor—
Bazaroukilgonautoskobrosk—
      Getzinpravadi—
      Kilgekosladji—
      Grivido—
      Blivido—
      Jenikodosk!"

So they stood like brave men, long and well,
  And they called each other their proper names,
Till the lockjaw seized them, and where they fell
  They buried them both by the Irdosholames—
      Kalatalustchuk—
      Mischaribustchup—
        Bulgari—
        Dulgari—
      Sagharimainz.

Robert J. Burdette.

IMITATION

Calm and implacable,
Eying disdainfully the world beneath,
Sat Humpty-Dumpty on his mural eminence
In solemn state:
And I relate his story
In verse unfettered by the bothering restrictions of rhyme
    or metre,
In verse (or " rhythm," as I prefer to call it)
Which, consequently, is far from difficult to write.

He sat. And at his feet
The world passed on—the surging crowd
Of men and women, passionate, turgid, dense,
Keenly alert, lethargic, or obese.
(Those two lines scan!)

Among the rest
He noted Jones; Jones with his Roman nose,
His eyebrows—the left one streaked with a dash of gray—
And yellow boots.
Not that Jones
Has anything in particular to do with the story;
But a descriptive phrase
Like the above shows that the writer is
A Master of Realism.

Let us proceed. Suddenly from his seat
Did Humpty-Dumpty slip. Vainly he clutched
The impalpable air. Down and down,
Right to the foot of the wall,

Right on to the horribly hard pavement that ran beneath it
Humpty-Dumpty, the unfortunate Humpty-Dumpty,
Fell.

And him, alas! no equine agency,
Him no power of regal battalions—
Resourceful, eager, strenuous—
Could ever restore to the lofty eminence
Which once was his.
Still he lies on the very identical
Spot where he fell—lies, as I said on the ground,
Shamefully and conspicuously abased!

Anthony C. Deane.

THE MIGHTY MUST

COME mighty Must!
   Inevitable Shall!
In thee I trust.
   Time weaves my coronal!
Go mocking Is!
   Go disappointing Was!
That I am this
   Ye are the cursed cause!
Yet humble second shall be first,
      I ween;
And dead and buried be the curst
      Has Been!

Oh weak Might Be!
   Oh, May, Might, Could, Would, Should!
How powerless ye
   For evil or for good!
In every sense
   Your moods I cheerless call,
Whate'er your tense
   Ye are imperfect, all!
Ye have deceived the trust I've shown
      In ye!
Away! The Mighty Must alone
      Shall be!

W. S. Gilbert.

MIDSUMMER MADNESS

A SOLILOQUY

I AM a hearthrug—
   Yes, a rug—
Though I cannot describe myself as snug;
Yet I know that for me they paid a price
For a Turkey carpet that would suffice
(But we live in an age of rascal vice).
     Why was I ever woven,
For a clumsy lout, with a wooden leg,
To come with his endless Peg! Peg!
     Peg! Peg!
   With a wooden leg,
Till countless holes I'm drove in.
("Drove," I have said, and it should be "driven";
A hearthrug's blunders should be forgiven,
For wretched scribblers have exercised
    Such endless bosh and clamour,
So improvidently have improvised,
That they've utterly ungrammaticised
    Our ungrammatical grammar).
    And the coals
    Burn holes,
   Or make spots like moles,
And my lily-white tints, as black as your hat turn,
And the housemaid (a matricide, will-forging slattern),
    Rolls
    The rolls
   From the plate, in shoals,
When they're put to warm in front of the coals;
And no one with me condoles,
For the butter stains on my beautiful pattern.
But the coals and rolls, and sometimes soles,
Dropp'd from the frying-pan out of the fire,
Are nothing to raise my indignant ire,
    Like the Peg! Peg!
Of that horrible man with the wooden leg.

This moral spread from me,
Sing it, ring it, yelp it—
Never a hearthrug be,
That is if you can help it.

Unknown.

MAVRONE

ONE OF THOSE SAD IRISH POEMS, WITH NOTES

From Arranmore the weary miles I've come;
    An' all the way I've heard
A Shrawn [1] that's kep' me silent, speechless, dumb,
    Not sayin' any word.
An' was it then the Shrawn of Eire, [2] you'll say,
    For him that died the death on Carrisbool?
It was not that; nor was it, by the way,
    The Sons of Garnim [3] blitherin' their drool;
Nor was it any Crowdie of the Shee, [4]
    Or Itt, or Himm, nor wail of Barryhoo [5]
For Barrywhich that stilled the tongue of me.

[1] A Shrawn is a pure Gaelic noise, something like a groan, more like a shriek, and most like a sigh of longing.

[2] Eire was daughter of Carne, King of Connaught. Her lover, Murdh of the Open Hand, was captured by Greatcoat Mackintosh, King of Ulster, on the plain of Carrisbool, and made into soup. Eire's grief on this sad occasion has become proverbial.

[3] Garnim was second cousin to Manannan MacLir. His sons were always sad about something. There were twenty-two of them, and they were all unfortunate in love at the same time, just like a chorus at the opera. "Blitherin' their drool" is about the same as "dreeing their weird."

[4] The Shee (or "Sidhe," as I should properly spell it if you were not so ignorant) were, as everybody knows, the regular, stand-pat, organization fairies of Erin. The Crowdie was their annual convention, at which they made melancholy sounds. The Itt and Himm were the irregular, or insurgent, fairies. They *never* got any offices or patronage. See MacAlester, *Polity of the Sidhe of West Meath*, page 985.

[5] The Barryhoo is an ancient Celtic bird about the size of a Mavis, with lavender eyes and a black-crape tail. It continually mourns its mate (Barrywhich, feminine form), which has an hereditary predisposition to an early and tragic demise and invariably dies first.

'Twas but my own heart cryin' out for you
Magraw![6] Bulleen, shinnanigan, Boru,
Aroon, Machree, Aboo![7]

Arthur Guiterman.

[6] Magraw, a Gaelic term of endearment, often heard on the
baseball fields of Donnybrook.
[7] These last six words are all that tradition has preserved of
the original incantation by means of which Irish rats were rhymed
to death. Thereby hangs a good Celtic tale, which I should be
glad to tell you in this note; but the publishers say that being
prosed to death is as bad as being rhymed to death, and that
the readers won't stand for any more.

LILIES

LILIES, lilies, white lilies and yellow—
Lilies, lilies, purple lilies and golden—
Calla lilies, tiger lilies, lilies of the valley—
Lilies, lilies, lilies—
Bulb, bud and blossom—
What made them lilies?
If they were not lilies they would have to be something else,
    would they not?
What was it that made them lilies instead of making them
    violets or roses or geraniums or petunias?
What was it that made you yourself and me myself? What?
Alas! I do not know!

Don Marquis.

FOR I AM SAD

No usual words can bear the woe I feel,
No tralatitions trite give me relief!
O Webster! lend me words to voice my grief
Bitter as quassia, quass or kumquat peel!
For I am sad . . . bound on the cosmic wheel,
What mad chthonophagy bids slave and chief
Through endless cycles bite the earth like beef,
By turns each cannibal and each the meal?
Turn we to nature Webster, and we see
Your whidah bird refuse all strobile fruit,

Your tragacanth in tears ooze from the tree . . .
We hear your flammulated owlets hoot!
Turn we to nature, Webster, and we find
Few creatures have a quite contented mind.
Your koulan there, with dyslogistic snort,
Will leave his phacoid food on worts to browse,
While glactophorous Himalayan cows
The knurled kohl-rabi spurn in uncouth sport;
No margay climbs margosa trees; the short
Gray mullet drink no mulse, nor house
In pibcorns when the youth of Wales carouse . . .
No tournure doth the toucan's tail contort . . .
So I am sad! . . . and yet, on Summer eves,
When xebecs search the whishing scree for whelk,
And the sharp sorrel lifts obcordate leaves,
And cryptogamous plants fulfil the elk,
I see the octopus play with his feet,
And find within this sadness something sweet.

The thing we like about that poem is its recognition of all
the sorrow there is in the universe . . . its *unflinching* recogni-
tion, we might say, if we were not afraid of praising our own
work too highly . . . combined with its happy ending.

One feels, upon reading it, that, although everything every-
where is very sad, and all wrong, one has only to have patience
and after a while everything everywhere will be quite right and
very sweet.

No matter how interested one may be in these literary prob-
lems, one must cease discussing them at times or one will be
late to one's meals.

Don Marquis.

A LITTLE SWIRL OF VERS LIBRE

NOT COVERED, STRANGE TO SAY, BY THE PENAL CODE

I AM numb from world-pain—
I sway most violently as the thoughts course through me,
And athwart me,
And up and down me—
Thoughts of cosmic matters,
Of the mergings of worlds within worlds,

And unutterabilities
And room-rent,
And other tremendously alarming phenomena,
Which stab me,
Rip me most outrageously;
(Without a semblance, mind you, of respect for the Hague
        Convention's rules governing soul-slitting.)
Aye, as with the poniard of the Finite pricking the rainbow-
        bubble of the Infinite!
(Some figure, that!)
(Some little rush of syllables, that!)—
And make me—(are you still whirling at my coat-tails,
        reader?)
Make me—ahem, where was I?—oh, yes—make me,
In a sudden, overwhelming gust of soul-shattering rebellion,
Fall flat on my face!

                                        Thomas R. Ybarra.

YOUNG LOCHINVAR

THE TRUE STORY IN BLANK VERSE

OH! young Lochinvar has come out of the West,
Thro' all the wide border his horse has no equal,
Having cost him forty-five dollars at the market,
Where good nags, fresh from the country,
With burrs still in their tails are selling
For a song; and save his good broad sword
He weapon had none, except a seven-shooter
Or two, a pair of brass knuckles, and an Arkansaw

Toothpick in his boot, so, comparatively speaking,
He rode all unarmed, and he rode all alone,
Because there was no one going his way.
He stayed not for brake, and he stopped not for
Toll-gates; he swam the Eske River where ford
There was none, and saved fifteen cents
In ferriage, but lost his pocket-book, containing
Seventeen dollars and a half, by the operation.

Ere he alighted at the Netherby mansion
He stopped to borrow a dry suit of clothes,
And this delayed him considerably, so when
He arrived the bride had consented—the gallant
Came late—for a laggard in love and a dastard in war
Was to wed the fair Ellen, and the guests had assembled.

So, boldly he entered the Netherby Hall
Among bridesmen and kinsmen and brothers and
Brothers-in-law and forty or fifty cousins;
Then spake the bride's father, his hand on his sword
(For the poor craven bridegroom ne'er opened his head)

" Oh, come ye in peace here, or come ye in anger,
Or to dance at our bridal, young Lord Lochinvar? "
" I long wooed your daughter, and she will tell you
I have the inside track in the free-for-all
For her affections! my suit you denied; but let
That pass, while I tell you, old fellow, that love
Swells like the Solway, but ebbs like its tide,
And now I am come with this lost love of mine
To lead but one measure, drink one glass of beer;
There are maidens in Scotland more lovely by far
That would gladly be bride to yours very truly."

The bride kissed the goblet, the knight took it up,
He quaffed off the nectar and threw down the mug,
Smashing it into a million pieces, while
He remarked that he was the son of a gun
From Seven-up and run the Number Nine.
She looked down to blush, but she looked up again
For she well understood the wink in his eye;
He took her soft hand ere her mother could
Interfere, " Now tread we a measure; first four
Half right and left; swing," cried young Lochinvar.

One touch to her hand and one word in her ear,
When they reached the hall door and the charger
Stood near on three legs eating post hay;
So light to the croup the fair lady he swung,
Then leaped to the saddle before her.
" She is won! we are gone! over bank, bush, and spar,
They'll have swift steeds that follow "—but in the

Excitement of the moment he had forgotten
To untie the horse, and the poor brute could
Only gallop in a little circus around the
Hitching-post; so the old gent collared
The youth and gave him the awfullest lambasting
That was ever heard of on Canobie Lee;
So dauntless in war and so daring in love,
Have ye e'er heard of gallant like young Lochinvar?

Unknown.

IMAGISTE LOVE LINES

I LOVE my lady with a deep purple love;
She fascinates me like a fly
Struggling in a pot of glue.
Her eyes are grey, like twin ash-cans,
Just emptied, about which still hovers
A dainty mist.
Her disposition is as bright as a ten-cent shine,
Yet her kisses are tender and goulashy.
I love my lady with a deep purple love.

Unknown.

BYGONES

Or ever a lick of Art was done,
    Or ever a one to care,
I was a Purple Polygon,
    And you were a Sky-Blue Square.

You yearned for me across a void,
　For I lay in a different plane,
I'd set my heart on a Red Rhom*boid*,
　And your sighing was in vain.

You pined for me as well I knew,
　And you faded day by day,
Until the Square that was heavenly Blue,
　Had paled to an ashen grey.

A myriad years or less or more,
　Have softly fluttered by,
Matters are much as they were before,
　Except 'tis I that sigh.

I yearn for you, but I have no chance,
　You lie in a different plane,
I break my heart for a single glance,
　And I break said heart in vain.

And ever I grow more pale and wan,
　And taste your old despair,
When I was a Purple Polygon,
　And you were a Sky-Blue Square.

Bert Leston Taylor.

JUSTICE TO SCOTLAND

AN UNPUBLISHED POEM BY BURNS

O MICKLE yeuks the keckle doup,
　An' a' unsicker girns the graith,
For wae and wae! the crowdies loup
　O'er jouk an' hallan, braw an' baith
Where ance the coggie hirpled fair,
　And blithesome poortith toomed the loof,
There's nae a burnie giglet rare
　But blaws in ilka jinking coof.

The routhie bield that gars the gear
    Is gone where glint the pawky een.
And aye the stound is birkin lear
    Where sconnered yowies wheeped yestreen,
The creeshie rax wi' skelpin' kaes
    Nae mair the howdie bicker whangs,
Nor weanies in their wee bit claes
    Glour light as lammies wi' their sangs.

Yet leeze me on my bonny byke!
    My drappie aiblins blinks the noo,
An' leesome luve has lapt the dyke
    Forgatherin' just a wee bit fou.
And Scotia! while thy rantin' lunt
    Is mirk and moop with gowans fine,
I'll stowlins pit my unco brunt,
    An' cleek my duds for auld lang syne.

Unknown.

LAMENT OF THE SCOTCH-IRISH EXILE

OH, I want to win me hame
    To my ain countrie,
The land frae whence I came
    Far away across the sea;
Bit I canna find it there, on the atlas anywhere,
And I greet and wonder sair
    Where the deil it can be?

I hae never met a man,
    In a' the warld wide,
Who has trod my native lan'
    Or its distant shores espied;
But they tell me there's a place where my hypothetic race
Its dim origin can trace—
    Tipperary-on-the-Clyde.

But anither answers: " Nae,
   Ye are varra far frae richt;
Glasgow town in Dublin Bay
   Is the spot we saw the licht."
But I dinna find the maps bearing out these pawkie chaps,
And I sometimes think perhaps
   It has vanished out o' sight.

Oh, I fain wad win me hame
   To that undiscovered lan'
That has neither place nor name
   Where the Scoto-Irishman
May behold the castles fair by his fathers builded there
Many, many ages ere
   Ancient history began.

James Jeffrey Roche.

A SONG OF SORROW [1]

A LULLABYLET FOR A MAGAZINELET

WAN from the wild and woful West—
   Sleep, little babe, sleep on!
Mother will sing to—you know the rest—
   Sleep, little babe, sleep on!
Softly the sand steals slowly by,
Cursed be the curlew's chittering cry;
By-a-by, oh, by-a-by!
   Sleep, little babe, sleep on!

Rosy and sweet come the hush of night—
   Sleep, little babe, sleep on!
(Twig to the lilt, I have got it all right)
   Sleep, little babe, sleep on!
Dark are the dark and darkling days
Winding the webbed and winsome ways,
Homeward she creeps in dim amaze—
   Sleep, little babe, sleep on!
    (But it waked up, drat it!)

Charles Battell Loomis.

THE REJECTED " NATIONAL HYMNS "

I

BY H - - - Y W. L - NGF - - - - W

BACK in the years when Phlagstaff, the Dane, was monarch
   Over the sea-ribb'd land of the fleet-footed Norsemen,
Once there went forth young Ursa to gaze at the heavens—
   Ursa—the noblest of all the Vikings and horsemen.

Musing, he sat in his stirrups and viewed the horizon,
   Where the Aurora lapt stars in a North-polar manner,
Wildly he started,—for there in the heavens before him
   Flutter'd and flam'd the original Star Spangled Banner.

II

BY J - HN GR - - NL - - F WH - - T - - R

My Native Land, thy Puritanic stock
   Still finds its roots firm-bound in Plymouth Rock,
And all thy sons unite in one grand wish—
   To keep the virtues of Preservèd Fish.

Preservèd Fish, the Deacon stern and true,
   Told our New England what her sons should do,
And if they swerve from loyalty and right,
   Then the whole land is lost indeed in night.

III

BY DR. OL - V - R W - ND - L H - LMES

A DIAGNOSIS of our hist'ry proves
   Our native land a land its native loves;
Its birth a deed obstetric without peer,
   Its growth a source of wonder far and near.

To love it more behold how foreign shores
   Sink into nothingness beside its stores;
Hyde Park at best—though counted ultra-grand—
   The " Boston Common " of Victoria's land.

IV

BY R - LPH W - LDO EM - R - - N

SOURCE immaterial of material naught,
  Focus of light infinitesimal,
Sum of all things by sleepless Nature wrought,
  Of which the normal man is decimal.

Refract, in prism immortal, from thy stars
  To the stars bent incipient on our flag,
The beam translucent, neutrifying death,
  And raise to immortality the rag.

V

BY W - LL - - M C - LL - N B - Y - NT

THE sun sinks softly to his Ev'ning Post,
  The sun swells grandly to his morning crown;
Yet not a star our Flag of Heav'n has lost,
  And not a sunset stripe with him goes down.

So thrones may fall, and from the dust of those
  New thrones may rise, to totter like the last;
But still our Country's nobler planet glows
  While the eternal stars of Heaven are fast.

VI

BY N. P. W - LL - IS

ONE hue of our Flag is taken
  From the cheeks of my blushing Pet,
And its stars beat time and sparkle
  Like the studs on her chemisette.

Its blue is the ocean shadow
  That hides in her dreamy eyes,
It conquers all men, like her,
  And still for a Union flies.

VII

BY TH - M - S B - IL - Y ALD - - CH

The little brown squirred hops in the corn,
　The cricket quaintly sings,
The emerald pigeon nods his head,
　And the shad in the river springs,
The dainty sunflow'r hangs its head
　On the shore of the summer sea;
And better far that I were dead,
　If Maud did not love me.

I love the squirrel that hops in the corn,
　And the cricket that quaintly sings;
And the emerald pigeon that nods his head,
　And the shad that gaily springs.
I love the dainty sunflow'r, too,
　And Maud with her snowy breast;
I love them all;—but I love—I love—
　I love my country best.

Robert H. Newell

THE EDITOR'S WOOING

We love thee, Ann Maria Smith,
　And in thy condescension
We see a future full of joys
　Too numerous to mention.

There's Cupid's arrow in thy glance,
　That by thy love's coercion
Has reached our melting heart of hearts,
　And asked for one insertion.

With joy we feel the blissful smart;
　And ere our passion ranges,
We freely place thy love upon
　The list of our exchanges.

There's music in thy lowest tone,
    And silver in thy laughter:
And truth—but we will give the full
    Particulars hereafter.

Oh, we could tell thee of our plans
    All obstacles to scatter;
But we are full just now, and have
    A press of other matter.

Then let us marry, Queen of Smiths,
    Without more hesitation:
The very thought doth give our blood
    A larger circulation.

Robert H. Newell

THE BABY'S DÉBUT [1]

A BURLESQUE IMITATION OF WORDSWORTH—REJECTED ADDRESSES

[Spoken in the character of Nancy Lake, a girl eight years of age, who is drawn upon the stage in a child's chaise by Samuel Hughes, her uncle's porter.]

My brother Jack was nine in May,
And I was eight on New-year's-day;
    So in Kate Wilson's shop
Papa (he's my papa and Jack's)
Bought me, last week, a doll of wax,
    And brother Jack a top.
Jack's in the pouts, and this it is—
He thinks mine came to more than his;

[1] "The author does not, in this instance, attempt to copy any of the higher attributes of Mr. Wordsworth's poetry; but has succeeded perfectly in the imitation of his mawkish affectations of childish simplicity and nursery stammering. We hope it will make him ashamed of his *Alice Fell*, and the greater part of his last volumes—of which it is by no means a parody, but a very fair, and indeed we think a flattering, imitation."—*Edinburg Review.*

So to my drawer he goes,
Takes out the doll, and, O, my stars!
He pokes her head between the bars,
And melts off half her nose!

Quite cross, a bit of string I beg,
And tie it to his peg-top's peg,
And bang, with might and main,
Its head against the parlor-door:
Off flies the head, and hits the floor,
And breaks a window-pane.

This made him cry with rage and spite:
Well, let him cry, it serves him right.
A pretty thing, forsooth!
If he's to melt, all scalding hot,
Half my doll's nose, and I am not
To draw his peg-top's tooth!

Aunt Hannah heard the window break,
And cried, " O naughty Nancy Lake,
Thus to distress your aunt:
No Drury Lane for you to-day!"
And while papa said, "Pooh, she may!"
Mamma said, "No, she sha'n't!"

Well, after many a sad reproach,
They got into a hackney-coach,
And trotted down the street.
I saw them go: one horse was blind,
The tails of both hung down behind,
Their shoes were on their feet.

The chaise in which poor brother Bill
Used to be drawn to Pentonville,
Stood in the lumber-room:
I wiped the dust from off the top,
While Molly mopped it with a mop,
And brushed it with a broom.

My uncle's porter, Samuel Hughes,
Came in at six to black the shoes,
    (I always talk to Sam:)
So what does he, but takes, and drags
Me in the chaise along the flags,
    And leaves me where I am.

My father's walls are made of brick,
But not so tall and not so thick
    As these; and, goodness me!
My father's beams are made of wood,
But never, never half so good
    As those that now I see.

What a large floor! 'tis like a town!
The carpet, when they lay it down,
    Won't hide it, I'll be bound;
And there's a row of lamps!—my eye!
How they do blaze! I wonder why
    They keep them on the ground.

At first I caught hold of the wing,
And kept away; but Mr. Thing-
    umbob, the prompter man,
Gave with his hand my chaise a shove,
And said, " Go on, my pretty love;
    Speak to 'em little Nan.

" You've only got to curtsy, whisp-
er, hold your chin up, laugh and lisp,
    And then you're sure to take:
I've known the day when brats, not quite
Thirteen, got fifty pounds a night;
    Then why not Nancy Lake?"

But while I'm speaking, where's papa?
And where's my aunt? and where's mamma?
    Where's Jack? O there they sit!
They smile, they nod; I'll go my ways,
And order round poor Billy's chaise,
    To join them in the pit.

And now, good gentlefolks, I go
To join mamma, and see the show;
   So, bidding you adieu,
I curtsy like a pretty miss,
And if you'll blow to me a kiss,
   I'll blow a kiss to you.
            [Blows a kiss, and exit.]
                James Smith.

THE CANTELOPE

Side by side in the crowded streets,
   Amid its ebb and flow,
We walked together one autumn morn;
   ('Twas many years ago!)

The markets blushed with fruits and flowers;
   (Both Memory and Hope!)
You stopped and bought me at the stall,
   A spicy cantelope.

We drained together its honeyed wine,
   We cast the seeds away;
I slipped and fell on the moony rinds,
   And you took me home on a dray!

The honeyed wine of your love is drained;
   I limp from the fall I had;
The snow-flakes muffle the empty stall,
   And everything is sad.

The sky is an inkstand, upside down,
   It splashes the world with gloom;
The earth is full of skeleton bones,
   And the sea is a wobbling tomb!
                Bayard Taylor.

POPULAR BALLAD: "NEVER FORGET YOU PARENTS"

A YOUNG man once was sitting
  Within a swell café,
The music it was playing sweet—
  The people was quite gay.
But he alone was silent,
  A tear was in his eye—
A waitress she stepped up to him, and
  Asked him gently why.

(Change to Minor)

He turned to her in sorrow and
  At first he spoke no word,
But soon he spoke unto her, for
  She was an honest girl.
He rose up from the table
  In that elegant café,
And in a voice replete with tears
  To her he then did say:

CHORUS

Never forget your father,
  Think all he done for you;
A mother is a boy's best friend,
  So loving, kind, and true,
If it were not for them, I'm sure
  I might be quite forlorn;
And if your parents had not have lived
  You would not have been born.

A hush fell on the laughing throng,
  It made them feel quite bad,
For most of them was people, and
  Some parents they had had.
Both men and ladies did shed tears.
  The music it did cease,
For all knew he had spoke the truth
  By looking at his face.

(Change to Minor)

The waitress she wept bitterly
    And others was in tears
It made them think of the old home
    They had not saw in years.
And while their hearts was heavy and
    Their eyes they was quite red.
This brave and honest boy again
    To them these words he said:

CHORUS

Never forget your father,
    Think all he done for you;
A mother is a boy's best friend,
    So loving, kind, and true,
If it were not for them, I'm sure
    I might be quite forlorn;
And if your parents had not have lived
    You would not have been born.

Franklin P. Adams.

HOW A GIRL WAS TOO RECKLESS OF GRAMMAR

Matilda Maud Mackenzie frankly hadn't any chin,
Her hands were rough, her feet she turned invariably in;
    Her general form was German,
        By which I mean that you
    Her waist could not determine
        Within a foot or two.
And not only did she stammer,
But she used the kind of grammar
    That is called, for sake of euphony, askew.

From what I say about her, don't imagine I desire
A prejudice against this worthy creature to inspire.
    She was willing, she was active,
        She was sober, she was kind,
    But she *never* looked attractive
        And she *hadn't* any mind.

I knew her more than slightly,
And I treated her politely
When I met her, but of course I wasn't blind!

Matilda Maud Mackenzie had a habit that was droll,.
She spent her morning seated on a rock or on a knoll,.
And threw with much composure
A smallish rubber ball
At an inoffensive osier
By a little waterfall;
But Matilda's way of throwing
Was like other people's mowing,
And she never hit the willow-tree at all!

One day as Miss Mackenzie with uncommon ardour tried
To hit the mark, the missile flew exceptionally wide.
And, before her eyes astounded,
On a fallen maple's trunk
Ricochetted and rebounded
In the rivulet, and sunk!
Matilda, greatly frightened,
In her grammar unenlightened,
Remarked, "Well now I ast yer, who'd 'er thunk?"

But what a marvel followed! From the pool at once there
rose
A frog, the sphere of rubber balanced deftly on his nose.
He beheld her fright and frenzy
And, her panic to dispel,
On his knee by Miss Mackenzie
He obsequiously fell.
With quite as much decorum
As a speaker in a forum
He started in his history to tell.

"Fair maid," he said, "I beg you do not hesitate or wince,
If you'll promise that you'll wed me, I'll at once become
a prince;
For a fairy, old and vicious,
An enchantment round me spun!"
Then he looked up, unsuspicious,
And he saw what he had won,

And in terms of sad reproach, he
Made some comments, *sotto voce,*
  (Which the publishers have bidden me to shun!)

Matilda Maud Mackenzie said, as if she meant to scold;
" I *never!* Why, you forward thing! Now, ain't you awful
      bold! "
  Just a glance he paused to give her,
    And his head was seen to clutch,
  Then he darted to the river,
    And he dived to beat the Dutch!
While the wrathful maiden panted
" I don't think he was enchanted! "
  (And he really didn't look it overmuch!)

THE MORAL

In one's language one conservative should be;
Speech is silver and it never should be free!

Guy Wetmore Carryl.

BEHOLD THE DEEDS!

CHANT ROYAL

(Being the Plaint of Adolphe Culpepper Ferguson, Salesman
of Fancy Notions, held in durance of his Landlady for a failure
to connect on Saturday night.)

I

I WOULD that all men my hard case might know;
  How grievously I suffer for no sin:
I, Adolphe Culpepper Ferguson, for lo!
  I, of my landlady am lockèd in.
For being short on this sad Saturday,
Nor having shekels of silver wherewith to pay,
She has turned and is departed with my key;
Wherefore, not even as other boarders free,
  I sing (as prisoners to their dungeon stones
When for ten days they expiate a spree):
  Behold the deeds that are done of Mrs. Jones!

II

One night and one day have I wept my woe;
  Nor wot I when the morrow doth begin,
If I shall have to write to Briggs & Co.,
  To pray them to advance the requìsite tin
For ransom of their salesman, that he may
Go forth as other boarders go alway—
As those I hear now flocking from their tea,
Led by the daughter of my landlady
  Pianoward. This day for all my moans,
Dry bread and water have been servèd me.
  Behold the deeds that are done of Mrs. Jones!

III

Miss Amabel Jones is musical, and so
  The heart of the young he-boarder doth win,
Playing " The Maiden's Prayer," adagio—
  That fetcheth him, as fetcheth the banco skin
The innocent rustic. For my part, I pray:
That Badarjewska maid may wait for aye
Ere sits she with a lover, as did we
Once sit together, Amabel! Can it be
  That all of that arduous wooing not atones
For Saturday shortness of trade dollars three?
  Behold the deeds that are done of Mrs. Jones!

IV

Yea! she forgets the arm was wont to go
  Around her waist. She wears a buckle whose pin
Galleth the crook of the young man's elbow;
  I forget not, for I that youth have been.
Smith was aforetime the Lothario gay.
Yet once, I mind me, Smith was forced to stay
Close in his room. Not calm, as I, was he;
But his noise brought no pleasaunce, verily.
  Small ease he gat of playing on the bones,
Or hammering on his stove-pipe, that I see.
  Behold the deeds that are done of Mrs. Jones!

V

hou, for whose fear the figurative crow
I eat, accursed be thou and all thy kin!
hee will I show up—yea, up will I show
   Thy too thick buckwheats, and thy tea too thin.
y! here I dare thee, ready for the fray!
hou dost not keep a first-class house, I say!
 does not with the advertisements agree.
hou lodgest a Briton with a pugaree,
   And thou hast harbored Jacobses and Cohns,
lso a Mulligan. Thus denounce I thee!
   Behold the deeds that are done of Mrs. Jones!

ENVOY

oarders! the worst I have not told to ye:
he hath stole my trousers, that I may not flee
   Privily by the window. Hence these groans,
here is no fleeing in a *robe de nuit*.
   Behold the deeds that are done of Mrs. Jones!

H. C. Bunner.

VILLON'S STRAIGHT TIP TO ALL CROSS COVES

"Tout aux tavernes et aux fiells"

SUPPOSE you screeve? or go cheap-jack?
   Or fake the broads? or fig a nag?
Or thimble-rig? or knap a yack?
   Or pitch a snide? or smash a rag?
Suppose you duff? or nose and lag?
   Or get the straight, and land your pot?
How do you melt the multy swag?
Booze and the blowens cop the lot.

Fiddle, or fence, or mace, or mack;
   Or moskeneer, or flash the drag;
Dead-lurk a crib, or do a crack;
   Pad with a slang, or chuck a fag;

Bonnet, or tout, or mump and gag;
Rattle the tats, or mark the spot;
You cannot bag a single stag;
Booze and the blowens cop the lot.

Suppose you try a different tack,
And on the square you flash your flag?
At penny-a-lining make your whack,
Or with the mummers mug and gag?
For nix, for nix the dibbs you bag!
At any graft, no matter what,
Your merry goblins soon stravag:
Booze and the blowens cop the lot.

THE MORAL

It's up the spout and Charley Wag
With wipes and tickers and what not
Until the squeezer nips your scrag,
Booze and the blowens cop the lot.

William Ernest Henley.

CULTURE IN THE SLUMS

Inscribed to an Intense Poet

RONDEAU

" O CRIKEY, Bill! " she ses to me, she ses.
  " Look sharp," ses she, " with them there sossiges.
Yea! sharp with them there bags of mysteree!
For lo! " she ses, " for lo! old pal," ses she,
  " I'm blooming peckish, neither more nor less."

Was it not prime—I leave you all to guess
How prime!—to have a Jude in love's distress
  Come spooning round, and murmuring balmilee,
                " O crikey, Bill! "

For in such rorty wise doth Love express
His blooming views, and asks for your address,
    And makes it right, and does the gay and free.
    I kissed her—I did so! And her and me
Was pals. And if that ain't good business,
                      " O crikey, Bill!"

II. VILLANELLE

Now ain't they utterly too-too
    (She ses, my Missus mine, ses she),
Them flymy little bits of Blue.

Joe, just you kool 'em—nice and skew
    Upon our old meogginee,
Now ain't they utterly too-too?

They're better than a pot'n' a screw,
    They're equal to a Sunday spree,
Them flymy little bits of Blue!

Suppose I put 'em up the flue,
    And booze the profits, Joe? Not me.
Now ain't they utterly too-too?

I do the 'Igh Art fake, I do.
    Joe, I'm consummate; and I *see*
Them flymy little bits of Blue.

Which Joe, is why I ses ter you—
    Æsthetic-like, and limp, and free—
Now *ain't* they utterly too-too,
Them flymy little bits of Blue?

III. BALLADE

I often does a quiet read
    At Booty Shelly's poetry;
I thinks that Swinburne at a screed
    Is really almost too too fly;

At Signor Vagna's harmony
I likes a merry little flutter;
  I've had at Pater many a shy;
In fact, my form's the Bloomin' Utter.

My mark's a tidy little feed,
  And 'Enery Irving's gallery,
To see old 'Amlick do a bleed,
  And Ellen Terry on the die,
  Or Frankey's ghostes at hi-spy,
And parties carried on a shutter.
  Them vulgar Coupeaus is my eye!
In fact my form's the Bloomin' Utter.

The Grosvenor's nuts—it is, indeed!
  I goes for 'Olman 'Unt like pie.
It's equal to a friendly lead
  To see B. Jones's judes go by.
  Stanhope he make me fit to cry.
Whistler he makes me melt like butter.
  Strudwick he makes me flash my cly—
In fact, my form's the Bloomin' Utter.

ENVOY

I'm on for any Art that's 'Igh;
I talks as quiet as I can splutter;
  I keeps a Dado on the sly;
In fact, my form's the Bloomin' Utter.

William Ernest Henley.

THE LAWYER'S INVOCATION TO SPRING

WHEREAS, on certain boughs and sprays
  Now divers birds are heard to sing,
And sundry flowers their heads upraise,
  Hail to the coming on of Spring!

The songs of those said birds arouse
  The memory of our youthful hours,

As green as those said sprays and boughs,
    As fresh and sweet as those said flowers.

The birds aforesaid—happy pairs—
    Love, 'mid the aforesaid boughs, inshrines
In freehold nests; themselves their heirs,
    Administrators, and assigns.

O busiest term of Cupid's Court,
    Where tender plaintiffs actions bring,—
Season of frolic and of sport,
    Hail, as aforesaid, coming Spring!

                        Henry Howard Brownell.

NORTH, EAST, SOUTH, AND WEST

AFTER R. K.

Oh! I have been North, and I have been South, and the
    East hath seen me pass,
And the West hath cradled me on her breast, that is cir-
    cled round with brass,
And the world hath laugh'd at me, and I have laugh'd at
    the world alone,
With a loud hee-haw till my hard-work'd jaw is stiff as a
    dead man's bone!

Oh! I have been up and I have been down and over the
    sounding sea,
And the sea-birds cried as they dropp'd and died at the ter-
    rible sight of me,
For my head was bound with a star, and crown'd with the
    fire of utmost hell,
And I made this song with a brazen tongue and a more
    than fiendish yell:

"Oh! curse you all, for the sake of men who have liv'd
    and died for spite,
And be doubly curst for the dark ye make where there
    ought to be but light,

And be trebly curst by the deadly spell of a woman's last
    ing hate,—
And drop ye down to the mouth of hell who would climb
    to the Golden Gate!"

Then the world grew green and grim and grey at the hor-
    rible noise I made,
And held up its hands in a pious way when I call'd a spade
    a spade;
But I cared no whit for the blame of it, and nothing at
    all for its praise,
And the whole consign'd with a tranquil mind to a sempi-
    ternal blaze!

All this have I sped, and have brought me back to work
    at the set of sun,
And I set my seal to the thoughts I feel in the twilight
    one by one,
For I speak but sooth in the name of Truth when I write
    such things as these;

   .   .   .   .

And the whole I send to a critical friend who is learnèd in
    Kiplingese!

                                 Unknown.

MARTIN LUTHER AT POTSDAM

What lightning shall light it? What thunder shall tell it?
    In the height of the height, in the depth of the deep?
Shall the sea-storm declare it, or paint it, or smell it?
    Shall the price of a slave be its treasure to keep?
When the night has grown near with the gems on her
    bosom,
    When the white of mine eyes is the whiteness of snow,
When the cabman—in liquor—drives a blue roan, a kicker,
    Into the land of the dear long ago.

Ah!—Ah, again!—You will come to me, fall on me—
    You are *so* heavy, and I am *so* flat.
And I? I shall not be at home when you call on me,
    But stray down the wind like a gentleman's hat:

I shall list to the stars when the music is purple,
    Be drawn through a pipe, and exhaled into rings;
Turn to sparks, and then straightway get stuck in the gate-
      way
    That stands between speech and unspeakable things.

As I mentioned before, by what light is it lighted?
    Oh! Is it fourpence, or piebald, or gray?
Is it a mayor that a mother has knighted
    Or is it a horse of the sun and the day?
Is it a pony? If so, who will change it?
    O golfer, be quiet, and mark where it scuds,
And think of its paces—of owners and races—
    Relinquish the links for the study of studs.

Not understood? Take me hence! Take me yonder!
    Take me away to the land of my rest—
There where the Ganges and other gees wander,
    And uncles and antelopes act for the best,
And all things are mixed and run into each other
    In a violet twilight of virtues and sins,
With the church-spires below you and no one to show you
    Where the curate leaves off and the pew-rent begins!

In the black night through the rank grass the snakes peer—
    The cobs and the cobras are partial to grass—
And a boy wanders out with a knowledge of Shakespeare
    That's not often found in a boy of his class,
And a girl wanders out without any knowledge,
    And a bird wanders out, and a cow wanders out,
Likewise one wether, and they wander together—
    There's a good deal of wandering lying about.

But its all for the best; I've been told by my friends, Sir,
    That in verses I'd written the meaning was slight;
I've tried with no meaning—to make 'em amends, Sir—
    And find that this kind's still more easy to write.
The title has nothing to do with the verses,

But think of the millions—the laborers who
In busy employment find deepest enjoyment,
And yet, like my title, have nothing to do!

Barry Pain.

AN IDYLL OF PHATTE AND LEENE

THE hale John Sprat—oft called for shortness, Jack—
Had married—had, in fact, a wife—and she
Did worship him with wifely reverence.
He, who had loved her when she was a girl,
Compass'd her too, with sweet observances;
E'en at the dinner table did it shine.
For he—liking no fat himself—he never did,
With jealous care piled up her plate with lean,
Not knowing that all lean was hateful to her.
And day by day she thought to tell him o 't,
And watched the fat go out with envious eye,
But could not speak for bashful delicacy.

At last it chanced that on a winter day,
The beef—a prize joint!—little was but fat;
So fat, that John had all his work cut out,
To snip out lean fragments for his wife,
Leaving, in very sooth, none for himself;
Which seeing, she spoke courage to her soul,
Took up her fork, and, pointing to the joint
Where 'twas the fattest, piteously she said;
" Oh, husband! full of love and tenderness!
What is the cause that you so jealously
Pick out the lean for me. I like it not!
Nay, loathe it—'tis on the fat that I would feast;
O me, I fear you do not like my taste! "

Then he, dropping his horny-handled carving knife,
Sprinkling therewith the gravy o'er her gown,
Answer'd, amazed: " What! you like fat, my wife!
And never told me. Oh, this is not kind!
Think what your reticence has wrought for us;
How all the fat sent down unto the maid—

Who likes not fat—for such maids never do—
Has been put in the waste-tub, sold for grease,
And pocketed as servant's perquisite!
Oh, wife! this news is good; for since, perforce,
A joint must be not fat nor lean, but both;
Our different tastes will serve our purpose well;
For, while you eat the fat—the lean to me
Falls as my cherished portion. Lo! 'tis good!"
So henceforth—he that tells the tale relates—
In John Sprat's household waste was quite unknown;
For he the lean did eat, and she the fat,
And thus the dinner-platter was all cleared.

Unknown.

THE HOUSE THAT JACK BUILT

AND this reft house is that the which he built,
Lamented Jack! and here his malt he piled.
Cautious in vain! these rats that squeak so wild,
Squeak not unconscious of their father's guilt.
Did he not see her gleaming through the glade!
Belike 'twas she, the maiden all forlorn.
What though she milked no cow with crumpled horn,
Yet, aye she haunts the dale where erst she strayed:
And aye before her stalks her amorous knight!
Still on his thighs their wonted brogues are worn,
And through those brogues, still tattered and betorn,
His hindward charms gleam an unearthly white.

Samuel Taylor Coleridge.

PALABRAS GRANDIOSAS

AFTER T— B— A—

I LAY i' the bosom of the sun,
Under the roses dappled and dun.
I thought of the Sultan Gingerbeer,
In his palace beside the Bendemeer,
With his Afghan guards and his eunuchs blind,
And the harem that stretched for a league behind.

The tulips bent i' the summer breeze,
Under the broad chrysanthemum-trees,
And the minstrel, playing his culverin,
Made for mine ears a merry din.
If I were the Sultan, and he were I,
Here i' the grass he should loafing lie,
And I should bestride my zebra steed,
And ride to the hunt of the centipede:
While the pet of the harem, Dandeline,
Should fill me a crystal bucket of wine,
And the kislar aga, Up-to-Snuff,
Should wipe my mouth when I sighed, " Enough! "
And the gay court poet, Fearfulbore,
Should sit in the hall when the hunt was o'er,
And chant me songs of silvery tone,
Not from Hafiz, but—mine own!

Ah, wee sweet love, beside me here,
I am not the Sultan Gingerbeer,
Nor you the odalisque Dandeline,
Yet I am yourn, and you are mine!

Bayard Taylor.

A LOVE PLAYNT—1370

To yow, my Purse, and to noon other wighte,
  Complayne I, for ye be my lady dere!
I am so sorry now that ye been lyghte,
  For, certes, yf ye make me hevy chere,
  Me were as leef be layde upon my beere.
For whiche unto your mercie thus I crye,
Beethe hevy ageyne, or elles mote I die!

Now voucheth sauf this day, or hyt be nighte,
  That I of yow the blissful soun may here,
Or see your colour lyke the sunnè brighte,
  That of yellòwnesse haddè never pere.
  Ye be my lyf! ye be myn herty's stere!
Quenè of comfort and good companye!
Beethe hevy ageyne, or elles mote I die!

Now, Purse! that ben to me my lyve's lyghte,
    And surety as doune in this world here,
Out of this toune helpè me through your myghte,
    Syn that you wole not bene my tresorere;
    For I am shave as nigh as is a frere.
But I pray unto your curtesye,
Beethe hevy ageyne, or elles mote I die!

Godfrey Turner.

DARWINITY

Power to thine elbow, thou newest of sciences,
    All the old landmarks are ripe for decay;
Wars are but shadows, and so are alliances,
    Darwin the great is the man of the day.

All other 'ologies want an apology;
    Bread's a mistake—Science offers a stone;
Nothing is true but Anthropobiology—
    Darwin the great understands it alone.

Mighty the great evolutionist teacher is
    Licking Morphology clean into shape;
Lord! what an ape the Professor or Preacher is
    Ever to doubt his descent from an ape.

Man's an Anthropoid—he cannot help that, you know—
    First evoluted from Pongos of old;
He's but a branch of the catarrhine cat, you know—
    Monkey I mean—that's an ape with a cold.

Fast dying out are man's later Appearances,
    Cataclysmitic Geologies gone;
Now of Creation completed the clearance is,
    Darwin alone you must anchor upon.

Primitive Life—Organisms were chemical,
    Busting spontaneous under the sea;
Purely subaqueous, panaquademical,
    Was the original Crystal of Me.

I'm the Apostle of mighty Darwinity,
   Stands for Divinity—sounds much the same—
Apo-theistico-Pan-Asininity
   Only can doubt whence the lot of us came.

Down on your knees, Superstition and Flunkeydom!
   Won't you accept such plain doctrines instead?
What is so simple as primitive Monkeydom
   Born in the sea with a cold in its head?

                      Herman C. Merivale.

SELECT PASSAGES FROM A COMING POET

DISENCHANTMENT

My Love has sicklied unto Loath,
   And foul seems all that fair I fancied—
The lily's sheen's a leprous growth,
   The very buttercups are rancid.

ABASEMENT

With matted head a-dabble in the dust,
   And eyes tear-sealèd in a saline crust
I lie all loathly in my rags and rust—
Yet learn that strange delight may lurk in self-disgust.

STANZA WRITTEN IN DEPRESSION NEAR DULWICH

The lark soars up in the air;
   The toad sits tight in his hole;
And I would I were certain which of the pair
   Were the truer type of my soul!

TO MY LADY

Twine, lanken fingers, lily-lithe,
   Gleam, slanted eyes, all beryl-green,
Pout, blood-red lips that burst a-writhe,
   Then—kiss me, Lady Grisoline!

THE MONSTER

Uprears the monster now his slobberous head,
  Its filamentous chaps her ankles brushing;
Her twice-five roseal toes are cramped in dread,
  Each maidly instep mauven-pink is flushing.

A TRUMPET BLAST

Pale Patricians, sunk in self-indulgence,
  Blink your blearèd eyes. Behold the Sun—
Burst proclaim in purpurate effulgence,
  Demos dawning, and the Darkness done!

F. Anstey.

THE ROMAUNT OF HUMPTY DUMPTY

'Tis midnight, and the moonbeam sleeps
  Upon the garden sward;
My lady in yon turret keeps
  Her tearful watch and ward.
" Beshrew me! " mutters, turning pale,
  The stalwart seneschal;
" What's he, that sitteth, clad in mail
  Upon our castle wall? "

" Arouse thee, friar of orders grey;
  What ho! bring book and bell!
Ban yonder ghastly thing, I say;
  And, look ye, ban it well!
By cock and pye, the Humpty's face! "
  The form turned quickly round;
Then totter'd from its resting-place—

. . . . . .

That night the corse was found.

The king, with hosts of fighting men
  Rode forth at break of day;
Ah! never gleamed the sun till then
  On such a proud array.

But all that army, horse and foot,
  Attempted, quite in vain,
Upon the castle wall to put
  The Humpty up again.

Henry S. Leigh.

THE WEDDING

LADY Clara Vere de Vere!
I hardly know what I must say,
But I'm to be Queen of the May, mother,
I'm to be Queen of the May!
I am half-crazed; I don't feel grave,
    Let me rave!

Whole weeks and months, early and late,
To win his love I lay in wait.
    Oh, the Earl was fair to see,
    As fair as any man could be;—
    The wind is howling in turret and tree!

We two shall be wed tomorrow morn,
  And I shall be the Lady Clare,
And when my marriage morn shall fall,
  I hardly know what I shall wear.
    But I shan't say " my life is dreary,"
    And sadly hang my head,
    With the remark, " I'm very weary,
    And wish that I were dead."

But on my husband's arm I'll lean,
  And roundly waste his plenteous gold,
Passing the honeymoon serene
  In that new world which is the old.
For down we'll go and take the boat
Beside St. Katherine's docks afloat,
Which round about its prow has wrote—
  " The Lady of Shalotter "
(Mondays and Thursdays,—Captain Foat),
  Bound for the Dam of Rotter.

Thomas Hood, Jr.

IN MEMORIAM TECHNICAM

I count it true which sages teach—
  That passion sways not with repose,
  That love, confounding these with those,
Is ever welding each with each.

And so when time has ebbed away,
  Like childish wreaths too lightly held,
  The song of immemorial eld
Shall moan about the belted bay.

Where slant Orion slopes his star,
  To swelter in the rolling seas,
  Till slowly widening by degrees
The grey climbs upward from afar.

And golden youth and passion stray
  Along the ridges of the strand,—
  Not far apart, but hand in hand,—
With all the darkness danced away!

               Thomas Hood, Jr.

"SONGS WITHOUT WORDS"

I cannot sing the old songs,
  Though well I know the tune,
Familiar as a cradle-song
  With sleep-compelling croon;
Yet though I'm filled with music
  As choirs of summer birds
"I cannot sing the old songs"—
  I do not know the words.

I start on "Hail Columbia,"
  And get to "heav'n-born band,"
And there I strike an up-grade
  With neither steam nor sand;

" Star Spangled Banner " downs me
　　Right in my wildest screaming,
I start all right, but dumbly come
　　To voiceless wreck at " streaming."

So, when I sing the old songs,
　　Don't murmur or complain
If " Ti, diddy ah da, tum dum,"
　　Should fill the sweetest strain.
I love " Tolly um dum di do,"
　　And the " trilla-la yeep da " birds,
But " I cannot sing the old songs "—
　　I do not know the words.

Robert J. Burdette.

AT THE SIGN OF THE COCK

FRENCH STYLE, 1898

Being an Ode in further " Contribution to the Song of French
History," dedicated, without malice or permission to Mr. George
Meredith.

I

ROOSTER her sign,
Rooster her pugnant note, she struts
Evocative, amazon spurs aprick at heel;
Nid-nod the authentic stump
Of the once ensanguined comb vermeil as wine;
With conspuent doodle-doo
Hails breach o' the hectic dawn of yon New Year,
Last issue up to date
Of quiverful Fate ·
Evolved spontaneous; hails with tonant trump
The spiriting prime o' the clashed carillon-peal;
Ruffling her caudal plumes derisive of scuts;
Inconscient how she stalks an immarcessibly absurd
Bird.

II

Mark where her Equatorial Pioneer
Delirant on the tramp goes littoralwise.
His Flag at furl, portmanteaued; drains to the dregs
The penultimate brandy-bottle, coal-on-the-head-piece gift
Of who avenged the Old Sea-Rover's smirch.
Marchant he treads the all-along of inarable drift
On dubiously connivent legs,
The facile prey of predatory flies;
Panting for further; sworn to lurch
Empirical on to the Menelik-buffered, enhavened blue,
Rhyming—see Cantique I.—with doodle-doo.

III

Infuriate she kicked against Imperial fact;
Vulnant she felt
What pin-stab should have stained Another's pelt
Puncture her own Colonial lung-balloon,
Volant to nigh meridian. Whence rebuffed,
The perjured Scythian she lacked
At need's pinch, sick with spleen of the rudely cuffed
Below her breath she cursed; she cursed the hour
When on her spring for him the young Tyrannical broke
Amid the unhallowed wedlock's vodka-shower,
She passionate, he dispassionate; tricked
Her wits to eye-blind; borrowed the ready as for dower;
Till from the trance of that Hymettus-moon
She woke,
A nuptial-knotted derelict;
Pensioned with Rescripts other aid declined
By the plumped leech saturate urging Peace
In guise of heavy-armed Gospeller to men,
Tyrannical unto fraternal equal liberal, her. Not she;
Not till Alsace her consanguineous find
What red deteutonising artillery
Shall shatter her beer-reek alien police
The just-now pluripollent; not till then.

IV

More pungent yet the esoteric pain
Squeezing her pliable vitals nourishes feud
Insanely grumous, grumously insane.
For lo!
Past common balmly on the Bordereau,
Churns she the skim o' the gutter's crust
With Anti-Judaic various carmagnole,
Whooped praise of the Anti-just;
Her boulevard brood
Gyratory in convolvements militant-mad;
Theatrical of faith in the Belliform,
Her Og,
Her Monstrous. Fled what force she had
To buckle the jaw-gape, wide agog
For the Preconcerted One,
The Anticipated, ripe to clinch the whole;
Queen-bee to hive the hither and thither volant swarm.

Bides she his coming; adumbrates the new
Expurgatorial Divine,
Her final effulgent Avatar,
Postured outside a trampling mastodon
Black as her Baker's charger; towering; visibly gorged
With blood of traitors. Knee-grip stiff,
Spine straightened, on he rides;
Embossed the Patriot's brow with hieroglyph
Of martial *dossiers,* nothing forged
About him save his armour. So she bides
Voicing his advent indeterminably far,
Rooster her sign,
Rooster her conspuent doodle-doo.

V

Behold her, pranked with spurs for bloody sport,
How she acclaims,
A crapulous chanticleer,
Breach of the hectic dawn of yon New Year.
Not yet her fill of rumours sucked,

Inebriate of honour; blushfully wroth;
Tireless to play her old primeval games;
Her plumage preened the yet unplucked
Liks sails of a galleon, rudder hard amort
With crepitant mast
Fronting the hazard to dare of a dual blast
The intern and the extern, blizzards both.

Owen Seaman.

PRESTO FURIOSO

AFTER WALT WHITMAN

SPONTANEOUS Us!
O my Camarados! I have no delicatesse as a diplomat, but
    I go blind on Libertad!
Give me the flap-flap of the soaring Eagle's pinions!
Give me the tail of the British lion tied in a knot inextrica-
    ble, not to be solved anyhow!
Give me a standing army (I say "give me," because just at
    present we want one badly, armies being often useful
    in time of war).

I see our superb fleet (I take it that we are to have a superb
    fleet built almost immediately);
I observe the crews prospectively; they are constituted of
    various nationalities, not necessarily American;
I see them sling the slug and chew the plug;
I hear the drum begin to hum;

Both the above rhymes are purely accidental, and contrary
    to my principles.
We shall wipe the floor of the mill-pond with the scalps of
    able-bodied British tars!
I see Professor Edison about to arrange for us a torpedo-
    hose on wheels, likewise an infernal electro-semaphore;
I see Henry Irving dead sick and declining to play Corporal
    Brewster;
Cornell, I yell! I yell Cornell!

I note the Manhattan boss leaving his dry-goods store and
    investing in a small Gatling-gun and a ten-cent
    banner;

I further note the Identity evolved out of forty-four spa-
    cious and thoughtful States;

I note Canada as shortly to be merged in that Identity;
    similarly Van Diemen's Land, Gibraltar, and Strat-
    ford-on-Avon;

Briefly, I see creation whipped!

O ye Colonels! I am with you (I too am a Colonel and on
    the pension-list);

I drink to the lot of you; to Colonels Cleveland, Hitt, Van-
    derbilt, Chauncey M. Depew, O'Donovan Rossa, and
    the late Colonel Monroe;

I drink an egg-flip, a morning-caress, an eye-opener, a
    maiden-bosom, a vermuth-cocktail, three sherry-cob-
    blers, and a gin-sling!

Good old Eagle!

Owen Seaman.

TO JULIA IN SHOOTING TOGS

AND A HERRICKOSE VEIN

WHENAS to shoot my Julia goes,
Then, then (methinks), how bravely shows
That rare arrangement of her clothes!

So shod as when the Huntress Maid
With thumping buskin bruised the glade,
She moveth, making earth afraid.

Against the sting of random chaff
Her leathern gaiters circle half
The arduous crescent of her calf.

Unto th' occasion timely fit,
My love's attire doth show her wit,
And of her legs a little bit.

Sorely it sticketh in my throat,
She having nowhere to bestow't,
To name the absent petticoat.

In lieu whereof a wanton pair
Of knickerbockers she doth wear,
Full windy and with space to spare.

Enlargèd by the bellying breeze,
Lord! how they playfully do ease
The urgent knocking of her knees!

Lengthways curtailèd to her taste
A tunic circumvents her waist,
And soothly it is passing chaste.

Upon her head she hath a gear
Even such as wights of ruddy cheer
Do use in stalking of the deer.

Haply her truant tresses mock
Some coronal of shapelier block,
To wit, the bounding billy-cock.

Withal she hath a loaded gun,
Whereat the pheasants, as they run,
Do make a fair diversiòn.

For very awe, if so she shoots,
My hair upriseth from the roots,
And lo! I tremble in my boots!

Owen Seaman.

FAREWELL

PROVOKED BY CALVERLEY'S " FOREVER "

" Farewell! " Another gloomy word
    As ever into language crept.
'Tis often written, never heard,
    Except

In playhouse. Ere the hero flits—
  In handcuffs—from our pitying view.
"Farewell!" he murmurs, then exits
      R. U.

"Farewell" is much too sighful for
  An age that has not time to sigh.
We say, "I'll see you later," or
      "Good by!"

When, warned by chanticleer, you go
  From her to whom you owe devoir,
"Say not 'good by,'" she laughs, "but
      'Au Revoir!'"

Thus from the garden are you sped;
  And Juliet were the first to tell
You, you were silly if you said
      "Farewell!"

"Farewell," meant long ago, before
  It crept, tear-spattered, into song,
"Safe voyage!" "Pleasant journey!" or
      "So long!"

But gone its cheery, old-time ring;
  The poets made it rhyme with knell—
Joined it became a dismal thing—
      "Farewell!"

"Farewell!" into the lover's soul
  You see Fate plunge the fatal iron.
All poets use it. It's the whole
      Of Byron.

"I only feel—farewell!" said he;
  And always fearful was the telling—
Lord Byron was eternally
      Farewelling.

" Farewell! " A dismal word, 'tis true
  (And why not tell the truth about it!);
But what on earth would poets do
  Without it?

         Bert Leston Taylor.

HERE IS THE TALE

AFTER RUDYARD KIPLING

Here is the tale—and you must make the most of it!
  Here is the rhyme—ah, listen and attend!
Backwards—forwards—read it all and boast of it
  If you are anything the wiser at the end!

Now Jack looked up—it was time to sup, and the bucket was
    yet to fill,
And Jack looked round for a space and frowned, then
    beckoned his sister Jill,
And twice he pulled his sister's hair, and thrice he smote her
    side;
" Ha' done, ha' done with your impudent fun—ha' done with
    your games! " she cried;
" You have made mud-pies of a marvellous size—finger and
    face are black,
You have trodden the Way of the Mire and Clay—now up
    and wash you, Jack!
Or else, or ever we reach our home, there waiteth an angry
    dame—
Well you know the weight of her blow—the supperless open
    shame!
Wash, if you will, on yonder hill—wash, if you will, at the
    spring,—
Or keep your dirt, to your certain hurt, and an imminent
    walloping! "

" You must wash—you must scrub—you must scrape! "
    growled Jack, " you must traffic with cans and pails,
Nor keep the spoil of the good brown soil in the rim of your
    finger-nails!

The morning path you must tread to your bath—you must
    wash ere the night descends,
And all for the cause of conventional laws and the soap-
    makers' dividends!
But if 'tis sooth that our meal in truth depends on our
    washing, Jill,
By the sacred right of our appetite—haste—haste to the top
    of the hill!"

They have trodden the Way of the Mire and Clay, they have
    toiled and travelled far,
They have climbed to the brow of the hill-top now, where
    the bubbling fountains are,
They have taken the bucket and filled it up—yea, filled it up
    to the brim;
But Jack he sneered at his sister Jill, and Jill she jeered
    at him:
"What, blown already!" Jack cried out (and his was a
    biting mirth!)
"You boast indeed of your wonderful speed—but what is the
    boasting worth?
Now, if you can run as the antelope runs and if you can
    turn like a hare,
Come, race me, Jill, to the foot of the hill—and prove your
    boasting fair!"
"Race? What is a race" (and a mocking face had Jill as
    she spake the word)
"Unless for a prize the runner tries? The truth indeed ye
    heard,
For I can run as the antelope runs, and I can turn like a
    hare:—
The first one down wins half-a-crown—and I will race you
    there!"
"Yea, if for the lesson that you will learn (the lesson of
    humbled pride)
The price you fix at two-and-six, it shall not be denied;
Come, take your stand at my right hand, for here is the
    mark we toe:
Now, are you ready, and are you steady? Gird up your petti-
    coats! Go!"

And Jill she ran like a winging bolt, a bolt from the bow
  released,
But Jack like a stream of the lightning gleam, with its path-
  way duly greased;
He ran down hill in front of Jill like a summer-lightning
  flash—
Till he suddenly tripped on a stone, or slipped, and fell to
  the earth with a crash.
Then straight did rise on his wondering eyes the constella-
  tions fair,
Arcturus and the Pleiades, the Greater and Lesser Bear,
The swirling rain of a comet's train he saw, as he swiftly
  fell—
And Jill came tumbling after him with a loud triumphant
  yell:
" You have won, you have won, the race is done! And as
  for the wager laid—
You have fallen down with a broken crown—the half-crown
  debt is paid! "

They have taken Jack to the room at the back where the
  family medicines are,
And he lies in bed with a broken head in a halo of vinegar;
While, in that Jill had laughed her fill as her brother fell
  to earth,
She had felt the sting of a walloping—she hath paid the
  price of her mirth!

Here is the tale—and now you have the whole of it,
Here is the story—well and wisely planned,
Beauty—Duty—these make up the soul of it—
But, ah, my little readers, will you mark and understand?
                                        Anthony C. Deane.

THE WILLOWS

THE skies they were ashen and sober,
    The streets they were dirty and drear;
It was night in the month of October,
    Of my most immemorial year;

Like the skies I was perfectly sober,
　　As I stopped at the mansion of Shear,—
At the " Nightingale,"—perfectly sober,
　　And the willowy woodland, down here.

Here once in an alley Titanic
　　Of Ten-pins,—I roamed with my soul,—
　　Of Ten-pins,—with Mary, my soul;
They were days when my heart was volcanic,
　　And impelled me to frequently roll,
　　And made me resistlessly roll,
Till my ten-strikes created a panic
　　In the realms of the Boreal pole,
Till my ten-strikes created a panic
　　With the monkey atop of his pole.

I repeat, I was perfectly sober,
　　But my thoughts they were palsied and sear,—
　　My thoughts were decidedly queer;
For I knew not the month was October,
　　And I marked not the night of the year;
I forgot that sweet *morçeau* of Auber
　　That the band oft performèd down here;
And I mixed the sweet music of Auber
　　With the Nightingale's music by Shear.

And now as the night was senescent',
　　And star-dials pointed to morn,
　　And car-drivers hinted of morn,
At the end of the path a liquescent
　　And bibulous lustre was born:
'Twas made by the bar-keeper present,
　　Who mixèd a duplicate horn,—
His two hands describing a crescent
　　Distinct with a duplicate horn.

And I said: " This looks perfectly regal;
　　For it's warm, and I know I feel dry,—
　　I am confident that I feel dry.
We have come past the emeu and eagle,
　　And watched the gay monkey on high;

Let us drink to the emeu and eagle,—
    To the swan and the monkey on high—
    To the eagle and monkey on high;
For this bar-keeper will not inveigle,—
    Bully boy with the vitreous eye;
He surely would never inveigle,—
    Sweet youth with the crystalline eye."

But Mary, uplifting her finger,
    Said, " Sadly this bar I mistrust,—
    I fear that this bar does not trust.
Oh, hasten! oh, let us not linger!
    Oh, fly!—let us fly—ere we must! "
In terror she cried, letting sink her
    Parasol till it trailed in the dust,—
In agony sobbed, letting sink her
    Parasol till it trailed in the dust,—
    Till it sorrowfully trailed in the dust.

Then I pacified Mary, and kissed her,
    And tempted her into the room,
    And conquer'd her scruples and gloom;
And we passed to the end of the vista,
    But were stopped by the warning of doom—
    By some words that were warning of doom.
And I said, " What is written, sweet sister,
    At the opposite end of the room? "
She sobbed, as she answered, " All liquors
    Must be paid for ere leaving the room."

Then my heart it grew ashen and sober,
    As the streets were deserted and drear—
    For my pockets were empty and drear;
And I cried, " It was surely October,
    On this very night of last year,
    That I journeyed—I journeyed down here—
    That I brought a fair maiden down here,
    On this night of all nights in the year.
    Ah! to me that inscription is clear:

Well I know now I'm perfectly sober,
Why no longer they credit me here,—
Well I know now that music of Auber,
And this Nightingale, kept by one Shear."

Bret Harte.

A BALLAD

IN THE MANNER OF R - DY - RD K - PL - NG

As I was walkin' the jungle round, a-killin' of tigers an' time;
I seed a kind of an author man a writin' a rousin' rhyme;
'E was writin' a mile a minute an' more, an' I sez to 'im,
   " 'Oo are you?"
Sez 'e, " I'm a poet—'er majesty's poet—soldier an' sailor,
   too!"

An 'is poem began in Ispahan an' ended in Kalamazoo,
It 'ad army in it, an' navy in it, an' jungle sprinkled through,
For 'e was a poet—'er majesty's poet—soldier an' sailor, too!

An' after, I met 'im all over the world, a doin' of things a
   host;
'E 'ad one foot planted in Burmah, an' one on the Gloucester
   coast;
'Es 'alf a sailor an' 'alf a whaler, 'e's captain, cook and crew,
But most a poet—'er majesty's poet—soldier an' sailor too!
'E's often Scot an' 'e's often not, but 'is work is never
   through
For 'e laughs at blame, an' 'e writes for fame, an' a bit for
   revenoo,—
Bein' a poet—'er majesty's poet—soldier an' sailor too!

'E'll take you up to the Ar'tic zone, 'e'll take you down to
   the Nile,
'E'll give you a barrack ballad in the Tommy Atkins style,
Or 'e'll sing you a Dipsy Chantey, as the bloomin' bo'suns
   do,
For 'e is a poet—'er majesty's poet—soldier an' sailor too.
An' there isn't no room for others, an' there's nothin' left
   to do;

E 'as sailed the main from the 'Orn to Spain, 'e 'as tramped
    the jungle through,
An' written up all there is to write—soldier an' sailor, too!

There are manners an' manners of writin', but 'is is the
    proper way,
An' it ain't so hard to be a bard if you'll imitate Rudyard K.;
But sea an' shore an' peace an' war, an' everything else in
    view—
E 'as gobbled the lot!—'er majesty's poet—soldier an' sailor,
    too.
E's not content with 'is Indian 'ome, 'e's looking for regions
    new,
In another year 'e'll ave swept 'em clear, an' what'll the
    rest of us do?
E's crowdin' us out!—'er majesty's poet—soldier an' sailor
    too!

Guy Wetmore Carryl.

THE TRANSLATED WAY

Being a lyric translation of Heine's " Du bist wie eine Blume,"
as it is usually done.

THOU art like unto a Flower,
    So pure and clean thou art;
I view thee and much sadness
    Steals to me in the heart.

To me it seems my Hands I
    Should now impose on your
Head, praying God to keep you
    So fine and clean and pure.

Franklin P. Adams.

COMMONPLACES

RAIN on the face of the sea,
    Rain on the sodden land,
And the window-pane is blurred with rain
    As I watch it, pen in hand.

Mist on the face of the sea,
  Mist on the sodden land,
Filling the vales as daylight fails,
  And blotting the desolate sand.

Voices from out of the mist,
  Calling to one another:
" Hath love an end, thou more than friend,
  Thou dearer than ever brother? "

Voices from out of the mist,
  Calling and passing away;
But I cannot speak, for my voice is weak,
  And . . . this is the end of my lay.

Rudyard Kipling

ANGELO ORDERS HIS DINNER

I, ANGELO, obese, black-garmented,
Respectable, much in demand, well fed
With mine own larder's dainties, where, indeed,
Such cakes of myrrh or fine alyssum seed,
Thin as a mallow-leaf, embrowned o' the top.
Which, cracking, lets the ropy, trickling drop
Of sweetness touch your tongue, or potted nests
Which my recondite recipe invests
With cold conglomerate tidbits—ah, the bill!
(You say), but given it were mine to fill
My chests, the case so put were yours, we'll say
(This counter, here, your post, as mine to-day),
And you've an eye to luxuries, what harm
In smoothing down your palate with the charm
Yourself concocted? There we issue take;
And see! as thus across the rim I break
This puffy paunch of glazed embroidered cake,
So breaks, through use, the lust of watering chaps
And craveth plainness: do I so? Perhaps;
But that's my secret. Find me such a man
As Lippo yonder, built upon the plan

Of heavy storage, double-navelled, fat
From his own giblet's oils, an Ararat
Uplift o'er water, sucking rosy draughts
From Noah's vineyard,—crisp, enticing wafts
Yon kitchen now emits, which to your sense
Somewhat abate the fear of old events,
Qualms to the stomach,—I, you see, am slow
Unnecessary duties to forego,—
You understand? A venison haunch, *haut gout.*
Ducks that in Cimbrian olives mildly stew.
And sprigs of anise, might one's teeth provoke
To taste, and so we wear the complex yoke
Just as it suits,—my liking, I confess,
More to receive, and to partake no less,
Still more obese, while through thick adipose
Sensation shoots, from testing tongue to toes
Far off, dim-conscious, at the body's verge,
Where the froth-whispers of its waves emerge
On the untasting sand. Stay, now! a seat
Is bare: I, Angelo, will sit and eat.

Bayard Taylor.

THE PROMISSORY NOTE

In the lonesome latter years
    (Fatal years!)
To the dropping of my tears
Danced the mad and mystic spheres
In a rounded, reeling rune,
    'Neath the moon,
To the dripping and the dropping of my tears.

Ah, my soul is swathed in gloom,
    (Ulalume!)
In a dim Titanic tomb,
For my gaunt and gloomy soul
Ponders o'er the penal scroll,
O'er the parchment (not a rhyme),
Out of place,—out of time,—
I am shredded, shorn, unshifty,
    (Oh, the fifty!)

And the days have passed, the three,
Over me!
And the debit and the credit are as one to him and me!

'Twas the random runes I wrote
At the bottom of the note,
(Wrote and freely
Gave to Greeley)
In the middle of the night,
In the mellow, moonless night,
When the stars were out of sight,
When my pulses, like a knell,
(Israfel!)
Danced with dim and dying fays
O'er the ruins of my days,
O'er the dimeless, timeless days,
When the fifty, drawn at thirty,
Seeming thrifty, yet the dirty
Lucre of the market, was the most that I could raise!

Fiends controlled it,
(Let him hold it!)
Devils held for me the inkstand and the pen;
Now the days of grace are o'er,
(Ah, Lenore!)
I am but as other men;
What is time, time, time,
To my rare and runic rhyme,
To my random, reeling rhyme,
By the sands along the shore,
Where the tempest whispers, "Pay him!" and I answer
"Nevermore!"

Bayard Taylor.

CAMERADOS

EVERYWHERE, everywhere, following me;
Taking me by the buttonhole, pulling off my boots, hustling
me with the elbows;
Sitting down with me to clams and the chowder-kettle;

lunging naked at my side into the sleek, irascible surges;
oothing me with the strain that I neither permit nor pro-
　　hibit;
'locking this way and that, reverent, eager, orotund, irre-
　　pressible;
)enser than sycamore leaves when the north-winds are scour-
　　ing Paumanok;
Vhat can I do to restrain them? Nothing, verily nothing,
:verywhere, everywhere, crying aloud for me;
'rying, I hear; and I satisfy them out of my nature;
ınd he that comes at the end of the feast shall find some-
　　thing over.
Vhatever they want I give; though it be something else, they
　　shall have it.
)runkard, leper, Tammanyite, small-pox and cholera patient,
　　shoddy and codfish millionnaire,
ınd the beautiful young men, and the beautiful young
　　women, all the same,
:rowding, hundreds of thousands, cosmical multitudes,
3uss me and hang on my hips and lean up to my shoulders,
:verywhere listening to my yawp and glad whenever they
　　hear it;
:verywhere saying, say it, Walt, we believe it:
:verywhere, everywhere.

Bayard Taylor.

THE LAST RIDE TOGETHER

FROM HER POINT OF VIEW

When I had firmly answered " No,"
And he allowed that that was so,
I really thought I should be free
For good and all from Mr. B.,
　　And that he would soberly acquiesce.
I said that it would be discreet
That for awhile we should not meet;
I promised that I would always feel
A kindly interest in his weal;
I thanked him for his amorous zeal;
　　In short, I said all I could but " yes."

I said what I'm accustomed to;
I acted as I always do.
I promised he should find in me
A friend,—a sister, if that might be;
    But he was still dissatisfied.
He cerṭainly was most polite;
He said exactly what was right,
He acted very properly,
Except indeed for this, that he
Insisted on inviting me
    To come with him for " one more last ride."

A little while in doubt I stood:
A ride, no doubt, would do me good;
I had a habit and a hat
Extremely well worth looking at;
    The weather was distinctly f̥ne.
My horse, too, wanted exercise,
And time, when one is riding, flies;
Besides, it really seemed, you see,
The only way of ridding me
Of pertinacious Mr. B.;
    So my head I graciously incline.

I won't say much of what happened next;
I own I was extremely vexed.
Indeed I should have been aghast
If any one had seen what passed;
    But nobody need ever know
That, as I leaned forward to stir the fire,
He advanced before I could well retire;
And I suddenly felt, to my great alarm,
The grasp of a warm, unlicensed arm,
An embrace in which I found no charm;
    I was awfully glad when he let me go.

Then we began to ride; my steed
Was rather fresh, too fresh indeed,

And at first I thought of little, save
The way to escape an early grave,
    As the dust rose up on either side.
My stern companion jogged along
On a brown old cob both broad and strong.
He looked as he does when he's writing verse,
Or endeavoring not to swear and curse,
Or wondering where he has left his purse;
    Indeed it was a sombre ride.

I spoke of the weather to Mr. B.,
But he neither listened nor spoke to me.
I praised his horse, and I smiled the smile
Which was wont to move him once in a while.
    I said I was wearing has favorite flowers,
But I wasted my words on the desert air,
For he rode with a fixed and gloomy stare.
I wonder what he was thinking about.
As I don't read verse, I shan't find out.
It was something subtle and deep, no doubt,
    A theme to detain a man for hours.

Ah! there was the corner where Mr. S.
So nearly induced me to whisper " yes ";
And here it was that the next but one
Proposed on horseback, or would have done,
    Had his horse not most opportunely shied;
Which perhaps was due to the unseen flick
He received from my whip; 'twas a scurvy trick,
But I never could do with that young man,—
I hope his present young woman can.
Well, I must say, never, since time began,
    Did I go for a duller or longer ride.

He never smiles and he never speaks;
He might go on like this for weeks;
He rolls a slightly frenzied eye
Towards the blue and burning sky,
    And the cob bounds on with tireless stride.

If we aren't home for lunch at two
I don't know what papa will do;
But I know full well he will say to me,
" I never approved of Mr. B.;
It's the very devil that you and he
    Ride, ride together, forever ride."

James Kenneth Stephen.

IMITATION OF WALT WHITMAN

WHO am I?

I have been reading Walt Whitman, and know not whethe
    he be me, or me he;—

Or otherwise!

Oh, blue skies! oh, rugged mountains! oh, mighty, rollin
    Niagara!

O, chaos and everlasting bosh!

I am a poet; I swear it! If you do not believe it you are
    dolt, a fool, an idiot!

Milton, Shakespere, Dante, Tommy Moore, Pope, never, bu
    Byron, too, perhaps, and last, not least, Me, and th
    Poet Close.

We send our resonance echoing down the adamantine cañon
    of the future!

We live forever! The worms who criticise us (asses!) laugh
    scoff, jeer, and babble—die!

Serve them right.

What is the difference between Judy, the pride of Flee
    Street, the glory of Shoe Lane, and Walt Whitman

Start not! 'Tis no end of a minstrel show who perpend
    this query;

'Tis no brain-racking puzzle from an inner page of th
    Family Herald,

No charade, acrostic (double or single), conundrum, riddle
    rebus, anagram, or other guess-work.

I answer thus: We both write truths—great, stern, solemn
    unquenchable truths—couched in more or less ridicu
    lous language.

as a rule use rhyme, he does not; therefore, I am his
  Superior (which is also a lake in his great and glori-
  ous country).
scorn, with the unutterable scorn of the despiser of petti-
  ness, to take a mean advantage of him.
e writes, he sells, he is read (more or less); why then
  should I rack my brains and my rhyming dictionary?
  I will see the public hanged first!
sing of America, of the United States, of the stars and
  stripes of Oshkosh, of Kalamazoo, and of Salt Lake
  City.
sing of the railroad cars, of the hotels, of the breakfasts,
  the lunches, the dinners, and the suppers;
f the soup, the fish, the entrées, the joints, the game, the
  puddings and the ice-cream.
sing all—I eat all—I sing in turn of Dr. Bluffem's Anti-
  bilious Pills.
o subject is too small, too insignificant, for Nature's poet.
sing of the cocktail, a new song for every cocktail, hundreds
  of songs, hundreds of cocktails.
; is a great and a glorious land! The Mississippi, the Mis-
  souri, and a million other torrents roll their waters to
  the ocean.
; is a great and glorious land! The Alleghanies, the Cats-
  kills, the Rockies (see atlas for other mountain ranges
  too numerous to mention) pierce the clouds!
nd the greatest and most glorious product of this great
  and glorious land is Walt Whitman;
'his must be so, for he says it himself.
'here is but one greater than he between the rising and the
  setting sun.
'here is but one before whom he meekly bows his humbled
  head.
)h, great and glorious land, teeming producer of all things,
  creator of Niagara, and inventor of Walt Whitman,
:rase your national advertisements of liver pads and cures
  for rheumatism from your public monuments, and
  inscribe thereon in letters of gold the name *Judy*.

                                                    Unknown.

SALAD

O cool in the summer is salad,
　　And warm in the winter is love;
And a poet shall sing you a ballad
　　Delicious thereon and thereof.
A singer am I, if no sinner,
　　My muse has a marvellous wing,
And I willingly worship at dinner
　　The Sirens of Spring.

Take endive—like love it is bitter,
　　Take beet—for like love it is red;
Crisp leaf of the lettuce shall glitter,
　　And cress from the rivulet's bed;
Anchovies, foam-born, like the lady
　　Whose beauty has maddened this bard;
And olives, from groves that are shady;
　　And eggs—boil 'em hard.

Mortimer Collins.

IF

If life were never bitter,
　　And love were always sweet,
Then who would care to borrow
A moral from to-morrow—
If Thames would always glitter,
　　And joy would ne'er retreat,
If life were never bitter,
　　And love were always sweet!

If care were not the waiter
　　Behind a fellow's chair,
When easy-going sinners
Sit down to Richmond dinners,
And life's swift stream flows straighter,
　　By Jove, it would be rare,
If care were not the waiter
　　Behind a fellow's chair.

If wit were always radiant,
  And wine were always iced,
And bores were kicked out straightway
Through a convenient gateway;
Then down the year's long gradient
  'Twere sad to be enticed,
If wit were always radiant,
  And wine were always iced.

Mortimer Collins.

THE JABBERWOCKY OF AUTHORS

'Twas gilbert. The kchesterton
  Did locke and bennett in the reed.
All meredith was the nicholson,
  And harrison outqueed.

Beware the see-enn-william, son,
  The londonjack with call that's wild.
Beware the gertroo datherton
  And richardwashburnchild.

He took his brady blade in hand;
  Long time the partridge foe he sought.
Then stood a time by the oppenheim
  In deep mcnaughton thought.

In warwick deeping thought he stood—
  He poised on edithwharton brink;
He cried, " Ohbernardshaw! I could
  If basilking would kink."

Rexbeach! rexbeach!—and each on each
  O. Henry's mantles ferber fell.
It was the same'sif henryjames
  Had wally eaton well.

" And hast thou writ the greatest book?
  Come to thy birmingham, my boy!
Oh, beresford way! Oh, holman day!"
  He kiplinged in his joy.

'Twas gilbert. The kchesterton
  Did locke and bennett in the reed.
All meredith was the nicholson,
  And harrison outqueed.

Harry Persons Taber.

THE TOWN OF NICE

MAY, 1874

THE town of Nice! the town of Nice!
  Where once mosquitoes buzzed and stung,
And never gave me any peace,
    The whole year round when I was young!
      Eternal winter chills it yet,
      It's always cold, and mostly wet.

Lord Brougham sate on the rocky brow,
  Which looks on sea-girt Cannes, I wis,
But wouldn't like to sit there now,
    Unless 'twere warmer than it is;
      I went to Cannes the other day,
      But found it much too damp to stay.

The mountains look on Monaco,
  And Monaco looks on the sea;
And, playing there some hours ago,
    I meant to win enormously;
      But, tho' my need of coin was bad
      I lost the little that I had.

Ye have the southern charges yet—
  Where is the southern climate gone?
Of two such blessings, why forget
    The cheaper and the seemlier one?
      My weekly bill my wrath inspires;
      Think ye I meant to pay for fires?

Why should I stay? No worse art thou,
  My country! on thy genial shore
The local east-winds whistle now,
  The local fogs spread more and more;
    But in the sunny south, the weather
    Beats all you know of put together.

I cannot eat—I cannot sleep—
  The waves are not so blue as I;
Indeed, the waters of the deep
  Are dirty-brown, and so's the sky:
    I get dyspepsia when I dine—
    Oh, dash that pint of country-wine!

                 Herman C. Merivale.

THE WILLOW-TREE

ANOTHER VERSION

Long by the willow-trees
  Vainly they sought her,
Wild rang the mother's screams
  O'er the gray water:
Where is my lovely one?
  Where is my daughter?

"Rouse thee, Sir Constable—
  Rouse thee and look;
Fisherman, bring your net,
  Boatman, your hook.
Beat in the lily-beds,
  Dive in the brook!"

Vainly the constable
  Shouted and called her;
Vainly the fisherman
  Beat the green alder;
Vainly he flung the net,
  Never it hauled her!

Mother beside the fire
　　Sat, her nightcap in;
Father, in easy chair,
　　Gloomily napping,
When at the window-sill
　　Came a light tapping!

And a pale countenance
　　Looked through the casement,
Loud beat the mother's heart,
　　Sick with amazement,
And at the vision which
　　Came to surprise her,
Shrieked in an agony—
　　"Lor'! it's Elizar!"

Yes, 'twas Elizabeth—
　　Yes, 'twas their girl;
Pale was her cheek, and her
　　Hair out of curl.
"Mother," the loving one,
　　Blushing exclaimed,
"Let not your innocent
　　Lizzy be blamed.

"Yesterday, going to Aunt
　　Jones's to tea,
Mother, dear mother, I
　　Forgot the door-key!
And as the night was cold
　　And the way steep,
Mrs. Jones kept me to
　　Breakfast and sleep."

Whether her Pa and Ma
　　Fully believed her,
That we shall never know,
　　Stern they received her;
And for the work of that
　　Cruel, though short, night
Sent her to bed without
　　Tea for a fortnight.

MORAL

Hey diddle diddlety,
Cat and the fiddlety,
Maidens of England, take caution by she!
Let love and suicide
Never tempt you aside,
And always remember to take the door-key.

W. M. Thackeray.

A BALLADE OF BALLADE-MONGERS

AFTER THE MANNER OF MASTER FRANÇOIS VILLON OF PARIS

In Ballades things always contrive to get lost,
    And Echo is constantly asking where
Are last year's roses and last year's frost?
    And where are the fashions we used to wear?
And what is a " gentleman," and what is a " player "?
    Irrelevant questions I like to ask:
Can you reap the tret as well as the tare?
    And who was the Man in the Iron Mask?

What has become of the ring I tossed
    In the lap of my mistress false and fair?
Her grave is green and her tombstone mossed;
    But who is to be the next Lord Mayor?
And where is King William, of Leicester Square?
    And who has emptied my hunting flask?
And who is possessed of Stella's hair?
    And who was the Man in the Iron Mask?

And what became of the knee I crossed,
    And the rod and the child they would not spare?
And what will a dozen herring cost
    When herring are sold at three halfpence a pair?
And what in the world is the Golden Stair?
    Did Diogenes die in a tub or cask,
Like Clarence, for love of liquor there?
    And who was the Man in the Iron Mask?

ENVOY

Poets, your readers have much to bear,
For Ballade-making is no great task,
If you do not remember, I don't much care
Who was the man in the Iron Mask.

Augustus M. Moore.

VIII

BATHOS

THE CONFESSION

There's somewhat on my breast, father,
    There's somewhat on my breast!
The livelong day I sigh, father,
    And at night I cannot rest.
I cannot take my rest, father,
    Though I would fain do so;
A weary weight oppresseth me—
    This weary weight of woe!

'Tis not the lack of gold, father,
    Nor want of worldly gear;
My lands are broad, and fair to see,
    My friends are kind and dear.
My kin are leal and true, father,
    They mourn to see my grief;
But, oh! 'tis not a kinsman's hand
    Can give my heart relief!

'Tis not that Janet's false, father,
    'Tis not that she's unkind;
Though busy flatterers swarm around,
    I know her constant mind.
'Tis not *her* coldness, father,
    That chills my laboring breast;
It's that confounded cucumber
    I ate, and can't digest.

                  Richard Harris Barham.

IF YOU HAVE SEEN

GOOD reader! if you e'er have seen,
   When Phœbus hastens to his pillow,
The mermaids, with their tresses green,
   Dancing upon the western billow:
If you have seen, at twilight dim,
When the lone spirit's vesper hymn
   Floats wild along the winding shore:
If you have seen, through mist of eve,
The fairy train their ringlets weave,
Glancing along the spangled green;—
   If you have seen all this and more,
God bless me! what a deal you've seen!

Thomas Moore.

CIRCUMSTANCE

THE ORANGE

IT ripen'd by the river banks,
   Where, mask and moonlight aiding,
Dons Blas and Juan play their pranks,
   Dark Donnas serenading.

By Moorish damsel it was pluck'd,
   Beneath the golden day there;
By swain 'twas then in London suck'd—
   Who flung the peel away there.

He could not know in Pimlico,
   As little she in Seville,
That *I* should reel upon that peel,
   And—wish them at the devil!

Frederick Locker-Lampson.

ELEGY

The jackals prowl, the serpents hiss
In what was once Persepolis.
Proud Babylon is but a trace
Upon the desert's dusty face.
The topless towers of Ilium
Are ashes. Judah's harp is dumb.
The fleets of Nineveh and Tyre
Are down with Davy Jones, Esquire
And all the oligarchies, kings,
And potentates that ruled these things
Are gone! But cheer up; don't be sad;
Think what a lovely time they had!

Arthur Guiterman.

OUR TRAVELLER

If thou would'st stand on Etna's burning brow,
With smoke above, and roaring flame below;
And gaze adown that molten gulf reveal'd,
Till thy soul shudder'd and thy senses reel'd:
If thou wouldst beard Niag'ra in his pride,
Or stem the billows of Propontic tide;
Scale all alone some dizzy Alpine *haut,*
And shriek "Excelsior!" among the snow:
Would'st tempt all deaths, all dangers that may be—
Perils by land, and perils on the sea;
This vast round world, I say, if thou wouldst view it—
Then, why the dickens don't you go and do it?

Henry Cholmondeley-Pennell.

OPTIMISM

Be brave, faint heart,
The dough shall yet be cake;
Be strong, weak heart,
The butter is to come.
Some cheerful chance will right the apple-cart,

The devious pig will gain the lucky mart,
 Loquacity be dumb,—
  Collapsed the fake.
 Be brave, faint heart!

 Be strong, weak heart,
  The path will be made plain;
 Be brave, faint heart,
  The bore will crawl away.
The upside down will turn to right side up,
The stiffened lip compel that slipping cup,
  The doldrums of the day
  Be not in vain.
 Be strong, weak heart!

 Be brave, faint heart,
  The jelly means to jell;
 Be strong, weak heart,
  The hopes are in the malt.
The wrong side in will yet turn right side out,
The long-time lost come down yon cormorant spout.
  Life still is worth her salt:
  What ends well's well.
 Be brave, faint heart!

      Newton Mackintosh.

THE DECLARATION

'TWAS late, and the gay company was gone,
And light lay soft on the deserted room
From alabaster vases, and a scent
Of orange-leaves, and sweet verbena came
Through the unshutter'd window on the air.
And the rich pictures with their dark old tints
Hung like a twilight landscape, and all things
Seem'd hush'd into a slumber. Isabel,
The dark-eyed, spiritual Isabel
Was leaning on her harp, and I had stay'd
To whisper what I could not when the crowd
Hung on her look like worshipers. I knelt,

And with the fervor of a lip unused
To the cool breath of reason, told my love.
There was no answer, and I took the hand
That rested on the strings, and press'd a kiss
Upon it unforbidden—and again
Besought her, that this silent evidence
That I was not indifferent to her heart,
Might have the seal of one sweet syllable.
I kiss'd the small white fingers as I spoke,
And she withdrew them gently, and upraised
Her forehead from its resting-place, and look'd
Earnestly on me—*She had been asleep!*

N. P. Willis.

HE CAME TO PAY

THE editor sat with his head in his hands
  And his elbows at rest on his knees;
He was tired of the ever-increasing demands
  On his time, and he panted for ease.
The clamor for copy was scorned with a sneer,
  And he sighed in the lowest of tones:
" Won't somebody come with a dollar to cheer
  The heart of Emanuel Jones?"

Just then on the stairway a footstep was heard
  And a rap-a-tap loud at the door,
And the flickering hope that had been long deferred
  Blazed up like a beacon once more;
And there entered a man with a cynical smile
  That was fringed with a stubble of red,
Who remarked, as he tilted a sorry old tile
  To the back of an average head:

" I have come here to pay "—Here the editor cried:
  " You're as welcome as flowers in spring!
Sit down in this easy armchair by my side,
  And excuse me awhile till I bring

A lemonade dashed with a little old wine
   And a dozen cigars of the best . . .
Ah! Here we are! This, I assure you, is fine;
   Help yourself, most desirable guest."

The visitor drank with a relish, and smoked
   Till his face wore a satisfied glow,
And the editor, beaming with merriment, joked
   In a joyous, spontaneous flow;
And then, when the stock of refreshments was gone,
   His guest took occasion to say,
In accents distorted somewhat by a yawn,
   " My errand up here is to pay—"

But the generous scribe, with a wave of his hand,
   Put a stop to the speech of his guest,
And brought in a melon, the finest the land
   Ever bore on its generous breast;
And the visitor, wearing a singular grin,
   Seized the heaviest half of the fruit,
And the juice, as it ran in a stream from his chin,
   Washed the mud of the pike from his boot.

Then, mopping his face on a favorite sheet
   Which the scribe had laid carefully by,
The visitor lazily rose to his feet
   With the dreariest kind of a sigh,
And he said, as the editor sought his address,
   In his books to discover his due:
" I came here to pay—my respects to the press,
   And to borrow a dollar of you! "

Parmenas Mix.

THE FORLORN ONE

Ah! why those piteous sounds of woe,
  Lone wanderer of the dreary night?
Thy gushing tears in torrents flow,
  Thy bosom pants in wild affright!

And thou, within whose iron breast
  Those frowns austere too truly tell,
Mild pity, heaven-descended guest,
  Hath never, never deign'd to dwell.

"That rude, uncivil touch forego,"
  Stern despot of a fleeting hour!
Nor "make the angels weep" to know
  The fond "fantastic tricks" of power!

Know'st thou not "mercy is not strain'd,
  But droppeth as the gentle dew,"
And while it blesseth him who gain'd,
  It blesseth him who gave it, too?

Say, what art thou? and what is he,
  Pale victim of despair and pain,
Whose streaming eyes and bended knee
  Sue to thee thus—and sue in vain?

Cold callous man!—he scorns to yield,
  Or aught relax his felon gripe,
But answers, "I'm Inspector Field
  And this here warment's prigg'd your wipe."

                    Richard Harris Barham.

RURAL RAPTURES

'Tis sweet at dewy eve to rove
   When softly sighs the western breeze,
And wandering 'mid the starlit grove
   To take a pinch of snuff and sneeze.

'Tis sweet to see in daisied field
   The flocks and herds their pleasure take;
But sweeter are the joys they yield
   In tender chop and juicy steak.

'Tis sweet to hear the murmurous sound
   That from the vocal woods doth rise,
To mark the pigeons wheeling round,
   And think how nice they'd be in pies.

When nightingales pour from their throats
   Their gushing melody, 'tis sweet;
Yet sweeter 'tis to catch the notes
   That issue from Threadneedle Street.

Unknown.

A FRAGMENT

His eye was stern and wild—his cheek was pale and cold
   as clay;
Upon his tightened lip a smile of fearful meaning lay.
He mused awhile—but not in doubt—no trace of doubt
   was there;
It was the steady solemn pause of resolute despair.
Once more he looked upon the scroll—once more its words
   he read—
Then calmly, with unflinching hand, its folds before him
   spread.
I saw him bare his throat, and seize the blue-cold gleam-
   ing steel,
And grimly try the tempered edge he was so soon to feel!
A sickness crept upon my heart, and dizzy swam my head—

I could not stir—I could not cry—I felt benumbed and
dead;
Black icy horrors struck me dumb, and froze my senses
o'er;
I closed my eyes in utter fear, and strove to think no
more.

   .   .   .   .

Again I looked: a fearful change across his face had
passed—
He seemed to rave—on cheek and lip a flaky foam was
cast;
He raised on high the glittering blade—then first I found
a tongue—
" Hold, madman! stay thy frantic deed! " I cried, and forth
I sprung;
He heard me, but he heeded not; one glance around he
gave,
And ere I could arrest his hands, he had—begun to *shave!*

Unknown.

THE BITER BIT

THE sun is in the sky, mother, the flowers are springing
fair,
And the melody of woodland birds is stirring in the air;
The river, smiling to the sky, glides onward to the sea,
And happiness is everywhere, oh, mother, but with me!

They are going to the church, mother—I hear the marriage
bell
It booms along the upland—oh! it haunts me like a knell;
He leads her on his arm, mother, he cheers her faltering
step,
And closely to his side she clings—she does, the demirep!

They are crossing by the stile, mother, where we so oft have
stood,
The stile beside the shady thorn, at the corner of the wood;

And the boughs, that wont to murmur back the words that
    won my ear,
Wave their silver branches o'er him, as he leads his bridal
    fere.

He will pass beside the stream, mother, where first my hand
    he pressed,
By the meadow where, with quivering lip, his passion he
    confessed;
And down the hedgerows where we've strayed again and yet
    again;
But he will not think of me, mother, his broken-hearted
    Jane!

He said that I was proud, mother, that I looked for rank
    and gold,
He said I did not love him—he said my words were cold;
He said I kept him off and on, in hopes of higher game—
And it may be that I did, mother; but who hasn't done the
    same.

I did not know my heart, mother—I know it now too late;
I thought that I without a pang could wed some nobler
    mate;
But no nobler suitor sought me—and he has taken wing,
And my heart is gone, and I am left a lone and blighted
    thing.

You may lay me in my bed, mother—my head is throbbing
    sore;
And, mother, prithee, let the sheets be duly aired before;
And, if you'd please, my mother dear, your poor desponding
    child,
Draw me a pot of beer, mother, and, mother, draw it mild!

William E. Aytoun.

COMFORT IN AFFLICTION

" Wherefore starts my bosom's lord?
  Why this anguish in thine eye?
Oh, it seems as thy heart's chord
  Had broken with that sigh!

" Rest thee, my dear lord, I pray,
  Rest thee on my bosom now!
And let me wipe the dews away,
  Are gathering on thy brow.

" There, again! that fevered start!
  What, love! husband! is thy pain?
There is a sorrow in thy heart,
  A weight upon thy brain!

" Nay, nay, that sickly smile can ne'er
  Deceive affection's searching eye;
'Tis a wife's duty, love, to share
  Her husband's agony.

" Since the dawn began to peep,
  Have I lain with stifled breath;
Heard thee moaning in thy sleep,
  As thou wert at grips with death.

" Oh, what joy it was to see
  My gentle lord once more awake!
Tell me, what is amiss with thee?
  Speak, or my heart will break! "

" Mary, thou angel of my life,
  Thou ever good and kind;
'Tis not, believe me, my dear wife,
  The anguish of the mind!

" It is not in my bosom, dear,
  No, nor in my brain, in sooth;
But, Mary, oh, I feel it here,
  Here in my wisdom tooth!

" Then give,—oh, first, best antidote,—
Sweet partner of my bed!
Give me thy flannel petticoat
To wrap around my head!"

William E. Aytoun.

THE HUSBAND'S PETITION

COME hither, my heart's darling,
Come, sit upon my knee,
And listen, while I whisper,
A boon I ask of thee.
You need not pull my whiskers
So amorously, my dove;
'Tis something quite apart from
The gentle cares of love.

I feel a bitter craving—
A dark and deep desire,
That glows beneath my bosom
Like coals of kindled fire.
The passion of the nightingale,
When singing to the rose,
Is feebler than the agony
That murders my repose!

Nay, dearest! do not doubt me,
Though madly thus I speak—
I feel thy arms about me,
Thy tresses on my cheek:
I know the sweet devotion
That links thy heart with mine—
I know my soul's emotion
Is doubly felt by thine:

And deem not that a shadow
  Hath fallen across my love:
No, sweet, my love is shadowless,
  As yonder heaven above.
These little taper fingers—
  Ah! Jane, how white they be!—
Can well supply the cruel want
  That almost maddens me.

Thou wilt not sure deny me
  My first and fond request;
I pray thee, by the memory
  Of all we cherish best—
By all the dear remembrance
  Of those delicious days,
When, hand in hand, we wandered
  Along the summer braes:

By all we felt, unspoken,
  When 'neath the early moon,
We sat beside the rivulet,
  In the leafy month of June;
And by the broken whisper,
  That fell upon my ear,
More sweet than angel-music,
  When first I woo'd thee, dear!

By that great vow which bound thee
  Forever to my side,
And by the ring that made thee
  My darling and my bride!
Thou wilt not fail nor falter,
  But bend thee to the task—
A BOILED SHEEP'S HEAD ON SUNDAY
  Is all the boon I ask.

                    William E. Aytoun.

LINES WRITTEN AFTER A BATTLE

BY AN ASSISTANT SURGEON OF THE NINETEENTH NANKEENS

STIFF are the warrior's muscles,
  Congeal'd, alas! his chyle;
No more in hostile tussles
  Will he excite his bile.
Dry is the epidermis,
  A vein no longer bleeds—
And the communis vermis
  Upon the warrior feeds.

Compress'd, alas! the thorax,
  That throbbed with joy or pain;
Not e'en a dose of borax
  Could make it throb again.
Dried up the warrior's throat is,
  All shatter'd too, his head:
Still is the epiglottis—
  The warrior is dead.

Unknown.

LINES

ADDRESSED TO ** **** ***** ON THE 29TH OF SEPTEMBER,
WHEN WE PARTED FOR THE LAST TIME

I HAVE watch'd thee with rapture, and dwelt on thy charms,
  As link'd in Love's fetters we wander'd each day;
And each night I have sought a new life in thy arms,
  And sigh'd that our union could last not for aye.

But thy life now depends on a frail silken thread,
  Which I even by kindness may cruelly sever,
And I look to the moment of parting with dread,
  For I feel that in parting I lose thee forever.

Sole being that cherish'd my poor troubled heart!
    Thou know'st all its secrets—each joy and each grief;
And in sharing them all thou did'st ever impart
    To its sorrows a gentle and soothing relief.

The last of a long and affectionate race,
    As thy days are declining I love thee the more,
For I feel that thy loss I can never replace—
    That thy death will but leave me to weep and deplore.

Unchanged, thou shalt live in the mem'ry of years,
    I cannot—I will not—forget what thou wert!
While the thoughts of thy love as they call forth my tears,
    In fancy will wash thee once more—MY LAST SHIRT.

Unknown.

THE IMAGINATIVE CRISIS

OH, solitude! thou wonder-working fay,
Come nurse my feeble fancy in your arms,
Though I, and thee, and fancy town-pent lay,
Come, call around, a world of country charms.
Let all this room, these walls dissolve away,
And bring me Surrey's fields to take their place:
This floor be grass, and draughts as breezes play;
Yon curtains trees, to wave in summer's face;
My ceiling, sky; my water-jug a stream;
My bed, a bank, on which to muse and dream.
The spell is wrought: imagination swells
My sleeping-room to hills, and woods, and dells!
I walk abroad, for naught my footsteps hinder,
And fling my arms. Oh! mi! I've broke the *winder!*

Unknown.

IX

PARODY

THE HIGHER PANTHEISM IN A NUTSHELL

ONE, who is not, we see; but one, whom we see not, is;
Surely, this is not that; but that is assuredly this.

What, and wherefore, and whence: for under is over and
   under;
If thunder could be without lightning, lightning could be
   without thunder.

Doubt is faith in the main; but faith, on the whole, is
   doubt;
We cannot believe by proof; but could we believe with-
   out?

Why, and whither, and how? for barley and rye are not
   clover;
Neither are straight lines curves; yet over is under and
   over.

One and two are not one; but one and nothing is two;
Truth can hardly be false, if falsehood cannot be true.

Parallels all things are; yet many of these are askew;
You are certainly I; but certainly I am not you.

One, whom we see not, is; and one, who is not, we see;
Fiddle, we know, is diddle; and diddle, we take it, is dee.

Algernon Charles Swinburne.

NEPHELIDIA

'ROM the depth of the dreamy decline of the dawn through
a notable nimbus of nebulous moonshine,
Pallid and pink as the palm of the flag-flower that flickers
with fear of the flies as they float,
\re they looks of our lovers that lustrously lean from a
marvel of mystic miraculous moonshine,
These that we feel in the blood of our blushes that thicken
and threaten with throbs through the throat?
'hicken and thrill as a theatre thronged at appeal of an
actor's appalled agitation,
Fainter with fear of the fires of the future than pale
with the promise of pride in the past;
'lushed with the famishing fulness of fever that reddens
with radiance of rathe recreation,
Gaunt as the ghastliest of glimpses that gleam through
the gloom of the gloaming when ghosts go aghast?
Nay, for the nick of the tick of the time is a tremulous
touch on the temples of terror,
Strained as the sinews yet strenuous with strife of the
dead who is dumb as the dust-heaps of death;
Surely no soul is it, sweet as the spasm of erotic emotional
exquisite error,
Bathed in the balms of beatified bliss, beatific itself by
beatitude's breath.
Surely no spirit or sense of a soul that was soft to the spirit
and soul of our senses
Sweetens the stress of surprising suspicion that sobs in
the semblance and sound of a sigh;
Only this oracle opens Olympian, in mystical moods and
triangular tenses,—
" Life is the lust of a lamp for the light that is dark
till the dawn of the day when we die."
Mild is the mirk and monotonous music of memory, melod-
iously mute as it may be,
While the hope in the heart of a hero is bruised by the
breach of men's rapiers, resigned to the rod;
Made meek as a mother whose bosom-beats bound with the
bliss-bringing bulk of a balm-breathing baby,

As they grope through the grave-yard of creeds, unde
skies growing green at a groan for the grimness o
God.
Blank is the book of his bounty beholden of old, and it
binding is blacker than bluer:
Out of blue into black is the scheme of the skies, an
their dews are the wine of the bloodshed of things
Till the darkling desire of delight shall be free as a faw
that is freed from the fangs that pursue her,
Till the heart-beats of hell shall be hushed by a hym
from the hunt that has harried the kennel of king

Algernon Charles Swinburne.

UP THE SPOUT

I

Hi! Just you drop that! Stop, I say!
Shirk work, think slink off, twist friend's wrist?
Where that spined sand's lined band's the bay—
Lined blind with true sea's blue, as due—
Promising—not to pay?

II

For the sea's debt leaves wet the sand;
Burst worst fate's weight's in one burst gun?
A man's own yacht, blown—What? off land?
Tack back, or veer round here, then—queer!
Reef points, though—understand?

III

I'm blest if I do. Sigh? be blowed!
Love's doves make break life's ropes, eh? Tropes!
Faith's brig, baulked, sides caulked, rides at road;
Hope's gropes befogged, storm-dogged and bogged—
Clogged, water-logged, her load!

IV

Stowed, by Jove, right and tight, away.
  No show now how best plough sea's brow,
Wrinkling—breeze quick, tease thick, ere day,
  Clear sheer wave's sheen of green, I mean,
With twinkling wrinkles—eh?

V

Sea sprinkles wrinkles, tinkles light
  Shells' bells—boy's joys that hap to snap!
It's just sea's fun, breeze done, to spite
  God's rods that scourge her surge, I'd urge—
Not proper, is it—quite?

VI

See, fore and aft, life's craft undone!
  Crank plank, split spritsail—mark, sea's lark!
That gray cold sea's old sprees, begun
  When men lay dark i' the ark, no spark,
All water—just God's fun!

VII

Not bright, at best, his jest to these
  Seemed—screamed, shrieked, wreaked on kin for sin!
When for mirth's yell earth's knell seemed please
  Some dumb new grim great whim in him
Made Jews take chalk for cheese.

VIII

Could God's rods bruise God's Jews? Their jowls
  Bobbed, sobbed, gaped, aped, the plaice in face!
None heard, 'tis odds, his—God's—folk's howls.
  Now, how must I apply, to try
This hookiest-beaked of owls?

IX

Well, I suppose God knows—I don't.
   Time's crimes mark dark men's types, in stripes
Broad as fen's lands men's hands were wont
   Leave grieve unploughed, though proud and loud
With birds' words—No! he won't!

X

One never should think good impossible.
   Eh? say I'd hide this Jew's oil's cruse—
His shop might hold bright gold, engrossible
   By spy—spring's air takes there no care
To wave the heath-flower's glossy bell!

XI

But gold bells chime in time there, coined—
   Gold! Old Sphinx winks there—"Read my screed!"
Doctrine Jews learn, use, burn for, joined
   (Through new craft's stealth) with health and
      wealth—
At once all three purloined!

XII

I rose with dawn, to pawn, no doubt,
   (Miss this chance, glance untried aside?)
John's shirt, my—no! Ay, so—the lout!
   Let yet the door gape, store on floor
And not a soul about?

XIII

Such men lay traps, perhaps—and I'm
   Weak—meek—mild—child of woe, you know!
But theft, I doubt, my lout calls crime.
   Shrink? Think! Love's dawn in pawn—you spawn
Of Jewry! Just in time!

Algernon Charles Swinburne.

IN IMMEMORIAM

WE seek to know, and knowing seek;
We seek, we know, and every sense
Is trembling with the great Intense
And vibrating to what we speak.

We ask too much, we seek too oft,
We know enough, and should no more;
And yet we skim through Fancy's lore
And look to earth and not aloft.

A something comes from out the gloom;
I know it not, nor seek to know;
I only see it swell and grow,
And more than this world would presume.

Meseems, a circling void I fill,
And I, unchanged where all is changed;
It seems unreal; I own it strange,
Yet nurse the thoughts I cannot kill.

I hear the ocean's surging tide,
Raise quiring on its carol-tune;
I watch the golden-sickled moon,
And clearer voices call beside.

O Sea! whose ancient ripples lie
On red-ribbed sands where seaweeds shone;
O Moon! whose golden sickle's gone;
O Voices all! like ye I die!

Cuthbert Bede.

LUCY LAKE

POOR Lucy Lake was overgrown,
    But somewhat underbrained.
She did not know enough, I own,
    To go in when it rained.

Yet Lucy was constrained to go;
  Green bedding,—you infer.
Few people knew she died, but oh,
  The difference to her!

Newton Mackintosh.

THE COCK AND THE BULL

You see this pebble-stone? It's a thing I bought
Of a bit of a chit of a boy i' the mid o' the day—
I like to dock the smaller parts-o'-speech,
As we curtail the already cur-tailed cur
(You catch the paronomasia, play 'po' words?)
Did, rather, i' the pre-Landseerian days.
Well, to my muttons. I purchased the concern,
And clapt it i' my poke, having given for same
By way o' chop, swop, barter or exchange—
"Chop" was my snickering dandiprat's own term—
One shilling and fourpence, current coin o' the realm.
O-n-e one and f-o-u-r four
Pence, one and fourpence—you are with me, sir?—
What hour it skills not: ten or eleven o' the clock,
One day (and what a roaring day it was
Go shop or sight-see—bar a spit o' rain!)
In February, eighteen sixty nine,
Alexandrina Victoria, Fidei,
Hm—hm—how runs the jargon? being on the throne.

Such, sir, are all the facts, succinctly put,
The basis or substratum—what you will—
Of the impending eighty thousand lines.
"Not much in 'em either," quoth perhaps simple Hodge.
But there's a superstructure. Wait a bit.

Mark first the rationale of the thing:
Hear logic rivel and levigate the deed.
That shilling—and for matter o' that, the pence—
I had o' course upo' me—wi' me say—
(*Mecum*'s the Latin, make a note o' that)
When I popp'd pen i' stand, scratched ear, wiped snout,

Let everybody wipe his own himself)
Sniff'd—tch!—at snuffbox; tumbled up, he-heed,
Haw-haw'd (not he-haw'd, that's another guess thing):
Then fumbled at, and stumbled out of, door,
: shoved the timber ope wi' my omoplat;
And *in vestibulo,* i' the lobby to-wit,
(Iacobi Facciolati's rendering, sir,)
Donned galligaskins, antigropeloes,
And so forth; and, complete with hat and gloves,
One on and one a-dangle i' in my hand,
And ombrifuge (Lord love you!) cas o' rain,
I flopped forth, 'sbuddikins! on my own ten toes,
(I do assure you there be ten of them)
And went clump-clumping up hill and down dale
To find myself o' the sudden i' front o' the boy.
Put case I hadn't 'em on me, could I ha' bought
This sort-o'-kind-o'-what-you-might-call-toy,
This pebble-thing, o' the boy-thing? Q. E. D.
That's proven without aid for mumping Pope,
Sleek porporate or bloated cardinal.
(Isn't it, old Fatchops? You're in Euclid now.)
So, having the shilling—having i' fact a lot—
And pence and halfpence, ever so many o' them,
I purchased, as I think I said before,
The pebble (*lapis, lapidis, di, dem, de*—
What nouns 'crease short i' the genitive, Fatchops, eh?)
O, the boy, a bare-legg'd beggarly son of a gun,
For one-and-fourpence. Here we are again.
Now Law steps in, bewigged, voluminous-jaw'd;
Investigates and re-investigates.
Was the transaction illegal? Law shakes head.
Perpend, sir, all the bearings of the case.

At first the coin was mine, the chattel his.
But now (by virtue of the said exchange
And barter) *vice versa* all the coin,
Rer juris operationem, vests
I' the boy and his assigns till ding o' doom;
In sæcula sæculo-o-orum;
(I think I hear the Abate mouth out that.)
To have and hold the same to him and them . . .

Confer some idiot on Conveyancing.
Whereas the pebble and every part thereof,
And all that appertaineth thereunto,
Quodcunque pertinet ad em rem,
(I fancy, sir, my Latin's rather pat)
Or shall, will, may, might, can, could, would, or should,
Subaudi cætera—clap we to the close—
For what's the good of law in such a case o' the kind
Is mine to all intents and purposes.
This settled, I resume the thread o' the tale.

Now for a touch o' the vendor's quality.
He says a gen'lman bought a pebble of him,
(This pebble i' sooth, sir, which I hold i' my hand)—
And paid for 't, *like* a gen'lman, on the nail.
"Did I o'ercharge him a ha'penny? Devil a bit.
Fiddlepin's end! Get out, you blazing ass!
Gabble o' the goose. Don't bugaboo-baby *me!*
Go double or quits? Yah! tittup! what's the odds?"
—There's the transaction viewed in the vendor's light.

Next ask that dumpled hag, stood snuffling by,
With her three frowsy blowsy brats o' babes,
The scum o' the Kennel, cream o' the filth-heap—Faugh!
Aie, aie, aie, aie! ὀτοτοτοτοτοῖ,
('Stead which we blurt out, Hoighty toighty now)—
And the baker and candlestick maker, and Jack and Gill,
Blear'd Goody this and queasy Gaffer that,
Ask the Schoolmaster, Take Schoolmaster first.
He saw a gentleman purchase of a lad
A stone, and pay for it *rite* on the square,
And carry it off *per saltum,* jauntily
Propria quæ maribus, gentleman's property now
(Agreeable to the law explained above).
In proprium usum, for his private ends,
The boy he chucked a brown i' the air, and bit
I' the face the shilling; heaved a thumping stone
At a lean hen that ran cluck-clucking by,
(And hit her, dead as nail i' post o' door,)
Then *abiit*—What's the Ciceronian phrase?
Excessit, evasit, erupit—off slogs boy;

)ff like bird, *avi similis*—(you observed
'he dative? Pretty i' the Mantuan!)—*Anglice*
)ff in three flea skips. *Hactenus,* so far,
›o good, *tam bene. Bene, satis, male,*—
Vhere was I with my trope 'bout one in a quag?
 did once hitch the Syntax into verse
'erbum personale,* a verb personal,
'oncordat*—ay, " agrees," old Fatchops—*cum
/ominativo,* with its nominative,
'enere,* i' point of gender, *numero,*
›' number, *et persona,* and person. *Ut,*
nstance: *Sol ruit,* down flops sun, *et* and,
/ontes umbrantur,* out flounce mountains. Pah!
 xcuse me, sir, I think I'm going mad.

'ou see the trick on't, though, and can yourself
'ontinue the discourse *ad libitum.*
 ; takes up about eighty thousand lines,
 . thing imagination boggles at;
 nd might, odds-bobs, sir! in judicious hands
 xtend from here to Mesopotamy.

Charles Stuart Calverley.

BALLAD

THE auld wife sat at her ivied door,
    (*Butter and eggs and a pound of cheese*)
A thing she had frequently done before;
    And her spectacles lay on her apron'd knees.

The piper he piped on the hilltop high,
    (*Butter and eggs and a pound of cheese*)
Till the cow said " I die," and the goose asked " Why?"
    And the dog said nothing, but search'd for fleas.

The farmer he strode through the square farmyard;
    (*Butter and eggs and a pound of cheese*)
His last brew of ale was a trifle hard—
    The connection of which the plot one sees.

The farmer's daughter hath frank blue eyes;
  (*Butter and eggs and a pound of cheese*)
She hears the rooks caw in the windy skies,
    As she sits at her lattice and shells her peas.

The farmer's daughter hath ripe red lips;
  (*Butter and eggs and a pound of cheese*)
If you try to approach her, away she skips
    Over tables and chairs with apparent ease.

The farmer's daughter hath soft brown hair;
  (*Butter and eggs and a pound of cheese*)
And I met with a ballad, I can't say where,
    Which wholly consisted of lines like these.

PART II

She sat with her hands 'neath her dimpled cheeks,
  (*Butter and eggs and a pound of cheese*)
And spake not a word. While a lady speaks
    There is hope, but she didn't even sneeze.

She sat, with her hands 'neath her crimson cheeks;
  (*Butter and eggs and a pound of cheese*)
She gave up mending her father's breeks,
    And let the cat roll in her new chemise.

She sat with her hands 'neath her burning cheeks,
  (*Butter and eggs and a pound of cheese*)
And gazed at the piper for thirteen weeks;
    Then she follow'd him o'er the misty leas.

Her sheep follow'd her, as their tails did them,
  (*Butter and eggs and a pound of cheese*)
And this song is consider'd a perfect gem,
    And as to the meaning, it's what you please.

Charles Stuart Calverley.

DISASTER

'TWAS ever thus from childhood's hour!
  My fondest hopes would not decay;
I never loved a tree or flower
  Which was the first to fade away!
The garden, where I used to delve
  Short-frock'd, still yields me pinks in plenty;
The pear-tree that I climbed at twelve
  I see still blossoming, at twenty.

I never nursed a dear gazelle;
  But I was given a parroquet—
(How I did nurse him if unwell!)
  He's imbecile, but lingers yet.
He's green, with an enchanting tuft;
  He melts me with his small black eye;
He'd look inimitable stuffed,
  And knows it—but he will not die!

I had a kitten—I was rich
  In pets—but all too soon my kitten
Became a full-sized cat, by which
  I've more than once been scratched and bitten
And when for sleep her limbs she curl'd
  One day beside her untouch'd plateful,
And glided calmly from the world,
  I freely own that I was grateful.

And then I bought a dog—a queen!
  Ah, Tiny, dear departing pug!
She lives, but she is past sixteen
  And scarce can crawl across the rug.
I loved her beautiful and kind;
  Delighted in her pert bow-wow;
But now she snaps if you don't mind;
  'Twere lunacy to love her now.

I used to think, should e'er mishap
  Betide my crumple-visaged Ti,
In shape of prowling thief, or trap,
  Or coarse bull-terrier—I should die.
But ah! disasters have their use,
  And life might e'en be too sunshiny;
Nor would I make myself a goose,
  If some big dog should swallow Tiny.

Charles Stuart Calverley.

WORDSWORTHIAN REMINISCENCE

I WALKED and came upon a picket fence,
And every picket went straight up and down,
And all at even intervals were placed,
All painted green, all pointed at the top,
And every one inextricably nailed
Unto two several cross-beams, which did go,
Not as the pickets, but quite otherwise,
And they two crossed, but back of all were posts.

O beauteous picket fence, can I not draw
Instruction from thee? Yea, for thou dost teach,
That even as the pickets are made fast
To that which seems all at cross purposes,
So are our human lives, to the Divine,
But, oh! not purposeless, for even as they
Do keep stray cows from trespass, we, no doubt,
Together guard some plan of Deity.

Thus did I moralise. And from the beams
And pickets drew a lesson to myself,—
But where the posts came in, I could not tell.

Unknown.

INSPECT US

Out of the clothes that cover me
  Tight as the skin is on the grape,
I thank whatever gods may be
  For my unconquerable shape.

In the fell clutch of bone and steel
  I have not whined nor cried aloud;
Whatever else I may conceal,
  I show my thoughts unshamed and proud.

The forms of other actorines
  I put away into the shade;
All of them flossy near-blondines
  Find and shall find me unafraid.

It matters not how straight the tape,
  How cold the weather is, or warm—
I am the mistress of my shape—
  I am the captain of my form.

Edith Daniell.

THE MESSED DAMOZEL

AT THE CUBIST EXHIBITION

The Messed Damozel leaned out
  From the gold cube of Heav'n;
There were three cubes within her hands,
  And the cubes in her hair were seven;
I looked, and looked, and looked, and looked—
  I could not see her, even.

Her robe, a cube from clasp to hem,
  Was moderately clear;
Methought I saw two cubic eyes,
  When I had looked a year;
But when I turned to tell the world,
  Those eyes did disappear!

It was the rampart of some house
    That she was standing on;
That much, at least, was plain to me
    As her I gazed upon;
But even as I gazed, alas!
    The rampart, too, was gone!

(I saw her smile!) Oh, no, I didn't,
    Though long mine eyes did stare;
The cubes closed down and shut her out;
    I wept in deep despair;
But this I know, and know full well—
    She simply wasn't there!

Charles Hanson Towne.

A MELTON MOWBRAY PORK-PIE

STRANGE pie that is almost a passion,
    O passion immoral for pie!
Unknown are the ways that they fashion,
    Unknown and unseen of the eye.
The pie that is marbled and mottled,
    The pie that digests with a sigh:
For all is not Bass that is bottled,
    And all is not pork that is pie.

Richard Le Gallienne.

ISRAFIDDLESTRINGS

IN heaven a Spirit doth dwell
    Whose heart strings are a fiddle,
(The reason he sings so well—
This fiddler Israfel),
And the giddy stars (will any one tell
Why giddy?) to attend his spell
    Cease their hymns in the middle.

On the height of her go
  Totters the Moon, and blushes
  As the song of that fiddle rushes
Across her bow.
  The red Lightning stands to listen,
And the eyes of the Pleiads glisten
As each of the seven puts its fist in
  Its eye, for the mist in.

And they say—it's a riddle—
  That all these listening things,
That stop in the middle
For the heart-strung fiddle
  With such the Spirit sings,
Are held as on the griddle
  By these unusual strings.

Wherefore thou art not wrong,
  Israfel! in that thou boastest
Fiddlestrings uncommon strong;
To thee the fiddlestrings belong
  With which thou toastest
Other hearts as on a prong.

Yes! heaven is thine, but this
  Is a world of sours and sweets,
  Where cold meats are cold meats,
And the eater's most perfect bliss
  Is the shadow of him who treats.

If I could griddle
As Israfiddle
  Has griddled—he fiddle as I,—
He might not fiddle so wild a riddle
  As this mad melody,
While the Pleiads all would leave off in the middle
  Hearing my griddle-cry.

                                        Unknown.

AFTER DILETTANTE CONCETTI

" Why do you wear your hair like a man,
            Sister Helen?
This week is the third since you began."
" I'm writing a ballad; be still if you can,
            Little brother.
        (O Mother Carey, mother!
What chickens are these between sea and heaven?)"

" But why does your figure appear so lean,
            Sister Helen?
And why do you dress in sage, sage green?"
" Children should never be heard, if seen,
            Little brother?
        (O Mother Carey, mother!
What fowls are a-wing in the stormy heaven!) "

" But why is your face so yellowy white,
            Sister Helen?
And why are your skirts so funnily tight?"
" Be quiet, you torment, or how can I write,
            Little brother?
        (O Mother Carey, mother!
How gathers thy train to the sea from the heaven!)"

" And who's Mother Carey, and what is her train,
            Sister Helen?
And why do you call her again and again?"
" You troublesome boy, why that's the refrain,
            Little brother.
        (O Mother Carey, mother!
What work is toward in the startled heaven?) "

" And what's a refrain? What a curious word,
            Sister Helen!
Is the ballad you're writing about a sea-bird?"
" Not at all; why should it be? Don't be absurd,
            Little brother.
        (O Mother Carey, mother!
Thy brood flies lower as lowers the heaven.) "

(A big brother speaketh:)
" The refrain you've studied a meaning had,
      Sister Helen!
It gave strange force to a weird ballad.
But refrains have become a ridiculous ' fad,'
      Little brother.
    And Mother Carey, mother,
Has a bearing on nothing in earth or heaven.

" But the finical fashion has had its day,
      Sister Helen.
And let's try in the style of a different lay
To bid it adieu in poetical way,
      Little brother.
    So, Mother Carey, mother!
Collect your chickens and go to—heaven."

(*A pause. Then the big brother singeth, accompany-
ing himself in a plaintive wise on the triangle.*)

" Look in my face. My name is Used-to-was;
   I am also called Played-out, and Done to Death,
   And It-will-wash-no-more. Awakeneth
Slowly but sure awakening it has,
The common-sense of man; and I, alas!
   The ballad-burden trick, now known too well,
   And turned to scorn, and grown contemptible—
A too transparent artifice to pass.

" What a cheap dodge I am! The cats who dart
   Tin-kettled through the streets in wild surprise
   Assail judicious ears not otherwise;
And yet no critics praise the urchin's ' art,'
Who to the wretched creature's caudal part
   Its foolish empty-jingling ' burden ' ties."

                  H. D. Traill.

WHENCENESS OF THE WHICH

SOME DISTANCE AFTER TENNYSON

COME into the Whenceness Which,
  For the fierce Because has flown:
Come into the Whenceness Which,
  I am here by the Where alone;
And the Whereas odors are wafted abroad
  Till I hold my nose and groan.

Queen Which of the Whichbud garden of What's
  Come hither the jig is done.
In gloss of Isness and shimmer of Was,
  Queen Thisness and Which in one;
Shine out, little Which, sunning over the bangs,
  To the Nowness, and be its sun.

There has fallen a splendid tear
  From the Is flower at the fence;
She is coming, my Which, my dear,
  And as she Whistles a song of the Whence,
The Nowness cries, "She is near, she is near."
  And the Thingness howls, "Alas!"
The Whoness murmurs, "Well, I should smile,"
  And the Whatlet sobs, "I pass."

                                        Unknown.

THE LITTLE STAR

SCINTILLATE, scintillate, globule orific,
Fain would I fathom thy nature's specific.
Loftily poised in ether capacious,
Strongly resembling a gem carbonaceous.

When torrid Phœbus refuses his presence
And ceases to lamp with fierce incandescence,
Then you illumine the regions supernal,
Scintillate, scintillate, semper nocturnal.

Then the victim of hospiceless peregrination
Gratefully hails your minute coruscation.
He could not determine his journey's direction
But for your bright scintillating protection.

Unknown.

THE ORIGINAL LAMB

Oh, Mary had a little lamb, regarding whose cuticular
The fluff exterior was white and kinked in each particular.
On each occasion when the lass was seen perambulating,
The little quadruped likewise was there a gallivating.

One day it did accompany her to the knowledge dispensary,
Which to every rule and precedent was recklessly contrary.
Immediately whereupon the pedagogue superior,
Exasperated, did eject the lamb from the interior.

Then Mary, on beholding such performance arbitrary,
Suffused her eyes with saline drops from glands called
    lachrymary,
And all the pupils grew thereat tumultuously hilarious,
And speculated on the case with wild conjectures various.

" What makes the lamb love Mary so? " the scholars asked
    the teacher.
He paused a moment, then he tried to diagnose the creature.
" Oh pecus amorem Mary habit omnia temporum."
" Thanks, teacher dear," the scholars cried, and awe crept
    darkly o'er 'em.

Unknown.

SAINTE MARGÉRIE

Slim feet than lilies tenderer,—
    Margérie!
That scarce upbore the body of her,
Naked upon the stones they were;—
    C'est ça Sainte Margérie!

White as a shroud the silken gown,—
  Margérie!
That flowed from shoulder to ankle down,
With clear blue shadows along it thrown;
  C'est ça Sainte Margérie!

On back and bosom withouten braid,—
  Margérie!
In crispèd glory of darkling red,
Round creamy temples her hair was shed;—
  C'est ça Sainte Margérie!

Eyes, like a dim sea, viewed from far,—
  Margérie!
Lips that no earthly love shall mar,
More sweet that lips of mortals are;—
  C'est ça Sainte Margérie!

The chamber walls are cracked and bare;—
  Margérie!
Without the gossips stood astare
At men her bed away that bare; —
  C'est ça Sainte Margérie!

Five pennies lay her hand within,—
  Margérie!
So she her fair soul's weal might win,
Little she reck'd of dule or teen;—
  C'est ça Sainte Margérie!

Dank straw from dunghill gathered,—
  Margérie!
Where fragrant swine have made their bed,
Thereon her body shall be laid;—
  C'est ça Sainte Margérie!

Three pennies to the poor in dole,—
  Margérie!
One to the clerk her knell shall toll,
And one to masses for her soul;—
  C'est ça Sainte Margérie!

                              Unknown.

ROBERT FROST

RELATES THE DEATH OF THE TIRED MAN

THERE were two of us left in the berry-patch;
Bryan O'Lin and Jack had gone to Norwich.—
They called him Jack a' Nory, half in fun
And half because it seemed to anger him.—
So there we stood and let the berries go,
Talking of men we knew and had forgotten.
A sprawling, humpbacked mountain frowned on us
And blotted out a smouldering sunset cloud
That broke in fiery ashes. " Well," he said,
" Old Adam Brown is dead and gone; you'll never
See him any more. He used to wear
A long, brown coat that buttoned down before.
That's all I ever knew of him; I guess that's all
That anyone remembers. Eh?" he said,
And then, without a pause to let me answer,
He went right on.
      " How about Dr. Foster?"
" Well, how *about* him?" I managed to reply.
He glared at me for having interrupted.
And stopped to pick his words before he spoke;
Like one who turns all personal remarks
Into a general survey of the world.
Choosing his phrases with a finicky care
So they might fit some vague opinions,
Taken, third-hand, from last year's *New York Times*
And jumbled all together into a thing
He thought was his philosophy.
      " Never mind;
There's more in Foster than you'd understand.
But," he continued, darkly as before,
" What do you make of Solomon Grundy's case?
You know the gossip when he first came here.
Folks said he'd gone to smash in Lunenburg,
And four years in the State Asylum here
Had almost finished him. It was Sanders' job
That put new life in him. A clear, cool day;
The second Monday in July it was.

'Born on a Monday,' that is what they said.
Remember the next few days? I guess you don't;
That was before your time. Well, Tuesday night
He said he'd go to church; and just before the prayer
He blurts right out, 'I've come here to get christened.
If I am going to have a brand new life
I'll have a new name, too.' Well, sure enough
They christened him, though I've forgotten what;
And Etta Stark, (you know, the pastor's girl)
Her head upset by what she called romance,
She went and married him on Wednesday noon.
Thursday the sun or something in the air
Got in his blood and right off he took sick.
Friday the thing got worse, and so did he;
And Saturday at four o'clock he died.
Buried on Sunday with the town decked out
As if it was a circus-day. And not a soul
Knew why they went or what he meant to them
Or what he died of. What would be *your* guess?"
"Well," I replied, "it seems to me that he,
Just coming from a sedentary life,
Felt a great wave of energy released,
And tried to crowd too much in one short week.
The laws of physics teach—"
　　　　"No, not at all.
He never knew 'em. He was just tired," he said.

Louis Untermeyer.

OWEN SEAMAN

ESTABLISHES THE "ENTENTE CORDIALE" BY RECITING "THE
SINGULAR STUPIDITY OF J. SPRATT, ESQ.," IN THE MANNER OF
GUY WETMORE CARRYL.

Of all the mismated pairs ever created
　　The worst of the lot were the Spratts.
Their life was a series of quibbles and queries
　　And quarrels and squabbles and spats.
They argued at breakfast, they argued at tea,
And they argued from midnight to quarter past three.

The family Spratt-head was rather a fat-head,
  And a bellicose body to boot.
He was selfish and priggish and worse, he was piggish—
  A regular beast of a brute.
At table his acts were incredibly mean;
He gave his wife fat—and *he* gobbled the lean!

What's more, she was censured whenever she ventured.
  To dare to object to her fare;
He said " It ain't tasteful, but we can't be wasteful;
  And *someone* must eat what is there! "
But his coarseness exceeded all bounds of control
When he laughed at her Art and the State of her Soul.

So what with his jeering and fleering and sneering,
  He plagued her from dawn until dark.
He bellowed " I'll teach ye to read Shaw and Nietzsche "—
  And he was as bad as his bark.
" The place for a woman——" he'd start, very glib. . . .
And so on, for two or three hours *ad lib.*

So very malignant became his indignant
  Remarks about " Culture " and " Cranks,"
That at last she revolted. She up and she bolted
  And entered the militant ranks. . . .
When she died, after breaking nine-tenths of the laws,
She left all her money and jewels to the Cause!

And *THE MORAL* is this (though a bit abstruse):
What's sauce for a more or less proper goose,
When it rouses the violent, feminine dander,
Is apt to be sauce for the propaganda.

                              Louis Untermeyer.

THE MODERN HIAWATHA

HE killed the noble Mudjokivis.
Of the skin he made him mittens,
Made them with the fur side inside
Made them with the skin side outside.
He, to get the warm side inside,
Put the inside skin side outside;
He, to get the cold side outside,
Put the warm side fur side inside.
That's why he put the fur side inside,
Why he put the skin side outside,
Why he turned them inside outside.

Unknown.

SOMEWHERE-IN-EUROPE-WOCKY

'TWAS brussels, and the loos liège
  Did meuse and arras in latour;
All vimy were the metz maubege,
  And the tsing-tau namur.

" Beware the petrograd, my son—
  The jaws that bite, the claws that plough!
Beware the posen, and verdun
  The soldan mons glogau! "

He took his dixmude sword in hand;
  Long time his altkirch foe he sought;
Then rested he 'neath the warsaw tree,
  And stood awhile in thought.

And as in danzig thought he stood
  The petrograd, with eyes of flame,
Came ypring through the cracow wood,
  And longwied as it came.

One two! One two! and through and through
　　The dixmude blade went snicker-snack;
He left it dead, and with its head
　　He gallipolied back.

" And hast thou slain the petrograd?
　　Come to my arms, my krithnia boy!
O chanak day! Artois! Grenay!"
　　He woevred in his joy.

'Twas brussels, and the loos liège
　　Did meuse and arras in latour;
All vimy were the metz maubege,
　　And the tsing-tau namur.

F. G. Hartswick.

RIGID BODY SINGS

Gin a body meet a body
　　Flyin' through the air,
Gin a body hit a body,
　　Will it fly? and where?
Ilka impact has its measure,
　　Ne'er a' ane hae I,
Yet a' the lads they measure me,
　　Or, at least, they try.

Gin a body meet a body
　　Altogether free,
How they travel afterwards
　　We do not always see.
Ilka problem has its method
　　By analytics high;
For me, I ken na ane o' them,
　　But what the waur am I?

J. C. Maxwell.

A BALLAD OF HIGH ENDEAVOR

Ah Night! blind germ of days to be,
　　Ah, me! ah me!
　　(Sweet Venus, mother!)
What wail of smitten strings hear we?
　　(Ah me! ah me!
　　　　　　Hey diddle dee!)

Ravished by clouds our Lady Moon,
　　Ah me! ah me!
　　(Sweet Venus, mother!)
Sinks swooning in a lady-swoon
　　(Ah me! ah me!
　　　　　　Dum diddle dee!)

What profits it to rise i' the dark?
　　Ah me! ah me!
　　(Sweet Venus, mother!)
If love but over-soar its mark
　　(Ah me! ah me!
　　　　　　Hey diddle dee!)

What boots to fall again forlorn?
　　Ah me! ah me!
　　(Sweet Venus, mother!)
Scorned by the grinning hound of scorn,
　　(Ah me! ah me!
　　　　　　Dum diddle dee!)

Art thou not greater who art less?
　　Ah me! ah me!
　　(Sweet Venus, mother!)
Low love fulfilled of low success?
　　(Ah me! ah me!
　　　　　　Hey diddle dee!)

Unknown.

FATHER WILLIAM

" You are old, Father William," the young man said,
  " And your hair has become very white;
And yet you incessantly stand on your head—
  Do you think, at your age, it is right? "

" In my youth," Father William replied to his son,
  " I feared it might injure the brain;
But now that I'm perfectly sure I have none,
  Why, I do it again and again."

" You are old," said the youth, " as I mentioned before,
  And have grown most uncommonly fat;
Yet you turned a back somersault in at the door—
  Pray, what is the reason of that? "

" In my youth," said the sage, as he shook his gray locks,
  " I kept all my limbs very supple
By the use of this ointment—one shilling the box—
  Allow me to sell you a couple."

" You are old," said the youth, " and your jaws are too weak
  For anything tougher than suet;
Yet you finished the goose, with the bones and the beak;
  Pray, how did you manage to do it? "

" In my youth," said his father, " I took to the law,
  And argued each case with my wife;
And the muscular strength which it gave to my jaw,
  Has lasted the rest of my life."

" You are old," said the youth; " one would hardly suppose
  That your eye was as steady as ever;
Yet you balanced an eel on the end of your nose—
  What made you so awfully clever? "

" I have answered three questions, and that is enough,"
  Said his father; " don't give yourself airs!
Do you think I can listen all day to such stuff?
  Be off, or I'll kick you down-stairs! "

                                        Lewis Carroll.

THE POETS AT TEA

1—(*Macaulay, who made it*)

POUR, varlet, pour the water,
  The water steaming hot!
A spoonful for each man of us,
  Another for the pot!
We shall not drink from amber,
  Nor Capuan slave shall mix
For us the snows of Athos
  With port at thirty-six;
Whiter than snow the crystals,
  Grown sweet 'neath tropic fires,
More rich the herbs of China's field,
The pasture-lands more fragrance yield;
For ever let Britannia wield
  The tea-pot of her sires!

2—(*Tennyson, who took it hot*)

I think that I am drawing to an end:
For on a sudden came a gasp for breath,
And stretching of the hands, and blinded eyes,
And a great darkness falling on my soul.
O Hallelujah! . . . Kindly pass the milk.

3—(*Swinburne, who let it get cold*)

As the sin that was sweet in the sinning
  Is foul in the ending thereof,
As the heat of the summer's beginning
  Is past in the winter of love:
O purity, painful and pleading!
  O coldness, ineffably gray!
Oh, hear us, our handmaid unheeding,
  And take it away!

4—(*Cowper, who thoroughly enjoyed it*)

The cosy fire is bright and gay,
The merry kettle boils away
    And hums a cheerful song.
I sing the saucer and the cup;
Pray, Mary, fill the tea-pot up,
    And do not make it strong.

5—(*Browning, who treated it allegorically*)

Tut! Bah! We take as another case—
    Pass the bills on the pills on the window-sill; notice the
    capsule
(A sick man's fancy, no doubt, but I place
    Reliance on trade-marks, Sir)—so perhaps you'll
Excuse the digression—this cup which I hold
    Light-poised—Bah, it's spilt in the bed!—well, let's on go—
Hold Bohea and sugar, Sir; if you were told
    The sugar was salt, would the Bohea be Congo?

6—(*Wordsworth, who gave it away*)

" Come, little cottage girl, you seem
    To want my cup of tea;
And will you take a little cream?
    Now tell the truth to me."

She had a rustic, woodland grin,
    Her cheek was soft as silk,
And she replied, " Sir, please put in
    A little drop of milk."

" Why, what put milk into your head?
    'Tis cream my cows supply; "
And five times to the child I said,
    " Why, pig-head, tell me, why? "

" You call me pig-head," she replied;
    " My proper name is Ruth.
I called that milk "—she blushed with pride—
    " You bade me speak the truth."

7—(*Poe, who got excited over it*)

Here's a mellow cup of tea, golden tea!
What a world of rapturous thought its fragrance brings to
    me!
  Oh, from out the silver cells
  How it wells!
  How it smells!
Keeping tune, tune, tune
To the tintinnabulation of the spoon.
And the kettle on the fire
Boils its spout off with desire,
With a desperate desire
And a crystalline endeavour
Now, now to sit, or never,
On the top of the pale-faced moon,
But he always came home to tea, tea, tea, tea, tea,
    Tea to the n—th.

8—(*Rossetti, who took six cups of it*)

The lilies lie in my lady's bower
(O weary mother, drive the cows to roost),
They faintly droop for a little hour;
My lady's head droops like a flower.

She took the porcelain in her hand
(O weary mother, drive the cows to roost);
She poured; I drank at her command;
Drank deep, and now—you understand!
(O weary mother, drive the cows to roost.)

9—(*Burns, who liked it adulterated*)

Weel, gin ye speir, I'm no inclined,
Whusky or tay—to state my mind,
    Fore ane or ither;
  For, gin I tak the first, I'm fou,
  And gin the next, I'm dull as you,
    Mix a' thegither.

0—(*Walt Whitman, who didn't stay more than a minute*)

)ne cup for myself-hood,
1any for you. Allons, camerados, we will drink together,
) hand-in-hand! That tea-spoon, please, when you've done
        with it.
Vhat butter-colour'd hair you've got. I don't want to be
        personal.
\ll right, then, you needn't. You're a stale-cadaver.
Eighteen-pence if the bottles are returned.
\llons, from all bat-eyed formula.

Barry Pain.

HOW OFTEN

THEY stood on the bridge at midnight,
    In a park not far from the town;
They stood on the bridge at midnight,
    Because they didn't sit down.

The moon rose o'er the city,
    Behind the dark church spire;
The moon rose o'er the city
    And kept on rising higher.

How often, oh, how often!
    They whispered words so soft;
How often, oh, how often;
    How often, oh, how oft!

Ben King.

IF I SHOULD DIE TO-NIGHT

IF I should die to-night
And you should come to my cold corpse and say,
Weeping and heartsick o'er my lifeless clay—
    If I should die to-night,
And you should come in deepest grief and woe—
And say: " Here's that ten dollars that I owe,"
    I might arise in my large white cravat
    And say, " What's that? "

If I should die to-night
And you should come to my cold corpse and kneel,
Clasping my bier to show the grief you feel,
I say, if I should die to-night
And you should come to me, and there and then
Just even hint 'bout paying me that ten,
I might arise the while,
But I'd drop dead again.

Ben King.

"THE DAY IS DONE"

THE day is done, and darkness
From the wing of night is loosed,
As a feather is wafted downward,
From a chicken going to roost.

I see the lights of the baker,
Gleam through the rain and mist,
And a feeling of sadness comes o'er me,
That I cannot well resist.

A feeling of sadness and longing
That is not like being sick,
And resembles sorrow only
As a brickbat resembles a brick.

Come, get for me some supper,—
A good and regular meal—
That shall soothe this restless feeling,
And banish the pain I feel.

Not from the pastry bakers,
Not from the shops for cake;
I wouldn't give a farthing
For all that they can make.

For, like the soup at dinner,
   Such things would but suggest
Some dishes more substantial,
   And to-night I want the best.

Go to some honest butcher,
   Whose beef is fresh and nice,
As any they have in the city
   And get a liberal slice.

Such things through days of labor,
   And nights devoid of ease,
For sad and desperate feelings,
   Are wonderful remedies.

They have an astonishing power
   To aid and reinforce,
And come like the " finally, brethren,"
   That follows a long discourse.

Then get me a tender sirloin
   From off the bench or hook.
And lend to its sterling goodness
   The science of the cook.

And the night shall be filled with comfort,
   And the cares with which it begun
Shall fold up their blankets like Indians,
   And silently cut and run.

Phœbe Cary.

JACOB

HE dwelt among " Apartments let,"
   About five stories high;
A man, I thought, that none would get,
   And very few would try.

A boulder, by a larger stone
Half hidden in the mud,
Fair as a man when only one
Is in the neighborhood.

He lived unknown, and few could tell
When Jacob was not free;
But he has got a wife—and O!
The difference to me!

Phœbe Cary.

BALLAD OF THE CANAL

WE were crowded in the cabin,
Not a soul had room to sleep;
It was midnight on the waters,
And the banks were very steep.

'Tis a fearful thing when sleeping
To be startled by the shock,
And to hear the rattling trumpet
Thunder, " Coming to a lock! "

So we shuddered there in silence,
For the stoutest berth was shook,
While the wooden gates were opened
And the mate talked with the cook.

And as thus we lay in darkness,
Each one wishing we were there,
" We are through! " the captain shouted,
And he sat down on a chair.

And his little daughter whispered,
Thinking that he ought to know,
" Isn't travelling by canal-boats
Just as safe as it is slow? "

Then he kissed the little maiden,
And with better cheer we spoke,
And we trotted into Pittsburg,
When the morn looked through the smoke.

Phœbe Cary.

THERE'S A BOWER OF BEAN-VINES

THERE'S a bower of bean-vines in Benjamin's yard,
  And the cabbages grow round it, planted for greens;
In the time of my childhood 'twas terribly hard
  To bend down the bean-poles, and pick off the beans.

That bower and its products I never forget,
  But oft, when my landlady presses me hard,
I think, are the cabbages growing there yet,
  Are the bean-vines still bearing in Benjamin's yard?

No, the bean-vines soon withered that once used to wave,
  But some beans had been gathered, the last that hung on;
And a soup was distilled in a kettle, that gave
  All the fragrance of summer when summer was gone.

Thus memory draws from delight, ere it dies,
  An essence that breathes of it awfully hard;
As thus good to my taste as 'twas then to my eyes,
  Is that bower of bean-vines in Benjamin's yard.

Phœbe Cary.

REUBEN

THAT very time I saw, (but thou couldst not),
Walking between the garden and the barn,
Reuben, all armed; a certain aim he took
At a young chicken, standing by a post,
And loosed his bullet smartly from his gun,
As he would kill a hundred thousand hens.
But I might see young Reuben's fiery shot
Lodged in the chaste board of the garden fence,
And the domesticated fowl passed on
In henly meditation, bullet free.

Phœbe Cary.

THE WIFE

Her washing ended with the day,
  Yet lived she at its close,
And passed the long, long night away
  In darning ragged hose.

But when the sun in all its state
  Illumed the Eastern skies,
She passed about the kitchen grate
  And went to making pies.

Phœbe Cary.

WHEN LOVELY WOMAN

When lovely woman wants a favor,
  And finds, too late, that man won't bend,
What earthly circumstance can save her
  From disappointment in the end?

The only way to bring him over,
  The last experiment to try,
Whether a husband or a lover,
  If he have feeling is—to cry.

Phœbe Cary.

JOHN THOMPSON'S DAUGHTER

A fellow near Kentucky's clime
  Cries, "Boatman, do not tarry,
And I'll give thee a silver dime
  To row us o'er the ferry."

"Now, who would cross the Ohio,
  This dark and stormy water?"
"O, I am this young lady's beau,
  And she, John Thompson's daughter.

" We've fled before her father's spite
   With great precipitation;
And should he find us here to-night,
   I'd lose my reputation.

" They've missed the girl and purse beside,
   His horsemen hard have pressed me;
And who will cheer my bonny bride,
   If yet they shall arrest me? "

Out spoke the boatman then in time,
   " You shall not fail, don't fear it;
I'll go, not for your silver dime,
   But for your manly spirit.

" And by my word, the bonny bird
   In danger shall not tarry;
For though a storm is coming on,
   I'll row you o'er the ferry."

By this the wind more fiercely rose,
   The boat was at the landing;
And with the drenching rain their clothes
   Grew wet where they were standing.

But still, as wilder rose the wind,
   And as the night grew drearer;
Just back a piece came the police,
   Their tramping sounded nearer.

" Oh, haste thee, haste! " the lady cries,
   " It's anything but funny;
I'll leave the light of loving eyes,
   But not my father's money! "

And still they hurried in the face
   Of wind and rain unsparing;
John Thompson reached the landing place—
   His wrath was turned to swearing.

For by the lightning's angry flash,
   His child he did discover;
One lovely hand held all the cash,
   And one was round her lover!

"Come back, come back!" he cried in woe,
   Across the stormy water;
"But leave the purse, and you may go,
   My daughter, oh, my daughter!"

'Twas vain; they reached the other shore
   (Such doom the Fates assign us);
The gold he piled went with his child,
   And he was left there *minus*.

Phœbe Cary.

A PORTRAIT

HE is to weet a melancholy carle:
Thin in the waist, with bushy head of hair,
As hath the seeded thistle, when a parle
It holds with Zephyr, ere it sendeth fair
Its light balloons into the summer air;
Thereto his beard had not begun to bloom.
No brush had touched his cheek, or razor sheer;
No care had touched his cheek with mortal doom,
But new he was and bright, as scarf from Persian loom.

Ne carèd he for wine, or half and half;
Ne carèd he for fish, or flesh, or fowl;
And sauces held he worthless as the chaff;
He 'sdeigned the swine-head at the wassail-bowl:
Ne with lewd ribbalds sat he cheek by jowl;
Ne with sly lemans in the scorner's chair;
But after water-brooks this pilgrim's soul
Panted and all his food was woodland air;
Though he would oft-times feast on gilliflowers rare.

The slang of cities in no wise he knew,
Tipping the wink to him was heathen Greek;
He sipped no " olden Tom," or " ruin blue,"
Or Nantz, or cherry-brandy, drunk full meek
By many a damsel brave and rouge of cheek;
Nor did he know each aged watchman's beat,
Nor in obscurèd purlieus would be seek
For curlèd Jewesses, with ankles neat,
Who, as they walk abroad, make tinkling with their feet.

John Keats.

ANNABEL LEE

'Twas more than a million years ago,
　　Or so it seems to me,
That I used to prance around and beau
　　The beautiful Annabel Lee.
There were other girls in the neighborhood
　　But none was a patch to she.

And this was the reason that long ago,
　　My love fell out of a tree,
And busted herself on a cruel rock;
　　A solemn sight to see,
For it spoiled the hat and gown and looks
　　Of the beautiful Annabel Lee.

We loved with a love that was lovely love,
　　I and my Annabel Lee,
And we went one day to gather the nuts
　　That men call hickoree.
And I stayed below in the rosy glow
　　While she shinned up the tree,
But no sooner up than down kerslup
　　Came the beautiful Annabel Lee.

And the pallid moon and the hectic noon
　　Bring gleams of dreams for me,
Of the desolate and desperate fate
　　Of the beautiful Annabel Lee.

And I often think as I sink on the brink
Of slumber's sea, of the warm pink link
That bound my soul to Annabel Lee;
And it wasn't just best for her interest
To climb that hickory tree,
For had she stayed below with me,
We'd had no hickory nuts maybe,
But I should have had my Annabel Lee.

Stanley Huntley.

HOME SWEET HOME WITH VARIATIONS

Being suggestions of the various styles in which an old theme
might have been treated by certain metrical composers.

FANTASIA

I

The original theme as John Howard Payne wrote it:

'MID pleasures and palaces though we may roam,
Be it ever so humble, there's no place like home!
A charm from the skies seems to hallow it there,
Which, seek through the world, is not met with elsewhere.

Home, home! Sweet, Sweet Home!
There's no place like Home!

An exile from home, splendor dazzles in vain!
Oh, give me my lowly thatched cottage again!
The birds singing gaily that came at my call!
Give me them! and the peace of mind, dearer than all.

Home, home! Sweet, Sweet Home!
There's no place like Home!

II

As Algernon Charles Swinburne might have wrapped it up
in variations.)

'Mid pleasures and palaces—)

As sea-foam blown of the winds, as blossom of brine that is
    drifted
  Hither and yon on the barren breast of the breeze,
Though we wander on gusts of a god's breath, shaken and
    shifted,
  The salt of us stings and is sore for the sobbing seas.
For home's sake hungry at heart, we sicken in pillared
    porches
  Of bliss made sick for a life that is barren of bliss,
For the place whereon is a light out of heaven that sears
    not nor scorches,
  Nor elsewhere than this.

An exile from home, splendor dazzles in vain—)

For here we know shall no gold thing glisten,
  No bright thing burn, and no sweet thing shine;
Nor love lower never an ear to listen
  To words that work in the heart like wine.
    What time we are set from our land apart,
    For pain of passion and hunger of heart,
Though we walk with exiles fame faints to christen,
  Or sing at the Cytherean's shrine.

Variation: An exile from home—)

Whether with him whose head
Of gods is honored,
With song made splendent in the sight of men—
  Whose heart most sweetly stout,
  From ravishing France cast out,
Being firstly hers, was hers most wholly then—
  Or where on shining seas like wine
  The dove's wings draw the drooping Erycine.

(Give me my lowly thatched cottage—)

For Joy finds Love grow bitter,
And spreads his wings to quit her,
At thought of birds that twitter
　　Beneath the roof-tree's straw—
　　Of birds that come for calling,
　　No fear or fright appalling,
　　When dews of dusk are falling,
Or daylight's draperies draw.

(Give me them, and the peace of mind—)

Give me these things then back, though the giving
　　Be at cost of earth's garner of gold;
There is no life without these worth living,
　　No treasure where these are not told.
For the heart give the hope that it knows not,
　　Give the balm for the burn of the breast—
For the soul and the mind that repose not,
　　Oh, give us a rest!

III

(As Mr. Francis Bret Harte might have woven it into touching tale of a western gentleman in a red shirt.)

　　　Brown o' San Juan,
　　　　Stranger, I'm Brown.
　　Come up this mornin' from 'Frisco—
　　　　Be'n a-saltin' my specie-stacks down.

　　　Be'n a-knockin' around,
　　　　Fer a man from San Juan,
　　Putty consid'able frequent—
　　　　Jes' catch onter that streak o' the dawn!

　　　Right thar lies my home—
　　　　Right thar in the red—
　　I could slop over, stranger, in po'try—
　　　　Would spread out old Shakspoke cold dead.

Stranger, you freeze to this: there ain't no kinder gin-palace,
Nor no variety-show lays over a man's own rancho.
Maybe it hain't no style, but the Queen in the Tower o'
London,
Ain't got naathin' I'd swop for that house over thar on the
hill-side.

Thar is my ole gal, 'n' the kids, 'n' the rest o' my live-stock;
Thar my Remington hangs, and thar there's a griddle-cake
br'ilin'—
For the two of us, pard—and thar, I allow, the heavens
Smile more friendly-like than on any other locality.

Stranger, nowhere else I don't take no satisfaction.
Gimme my ranch, 'n' them friendly old Shanghai chickens—
I brung the original pair f'm the States in eighteen-'n'-
fifty—
Gimme me them and the feelin' of solid domestic comfort.

Yer parding, young man—
But this landscape a kind
Er flickers—I 'low 'twuz the po'try—
I thought that my eyes hed gone blind.

Take that pop from my belt!
Hi, thar!—gimme yer han'—
Or I'll kill myself—Lizzie—she's left me—
Gone off with a purtier man!

Thar, I'll quit—the ole gal
An' the kids—run away!
I be derned! Howsomever, come in, pard—
The griddle-cake's thar, anyway.

IV

*(As Austin Dobson might have translated it from Horace, if
it had ever occurred to Horace to write it.)*

RONDEAU

At home alone, O Nomades,
Although Mæcenas' marble frieze

Stand not between you and the sky,
Nor Persian luxury supply
Its rosy surfeit, find ye ease.

Tempt not the far Ægean breeze;
With home-made wine and books that please,
To duns and bores the door deny,
At home, alone.

Strange joys may lure. Your deities
Smile here alone. Oh, give me these:
Low eaves, where birds familiar fly,
And peace of mind, and, fluttering by,
My Lydia's graceful draperies,
At home, alone.

V

(As it might have been constructed in 1744, Oliver Goldsmith
at 19, writing the first stanza, and Alexander Pope, a
52, the second.)

HOME! at the word, what blissful visions rise,
Lift us from earth, and draw us toward the skies;
'Mid mirag'd towers, or meretricious joys,
Although we roam, one thought the mind employs:
Or lowly hut, good friend, or loftiest dome,
Earth knows no spot so holy as our Home.
There, where affection warms the father's breast,
There is the spot of heav'n most surely blest.
Howe'er we search, though wandering with the wind
Through frigid Zembla, or the heats of Ind,
Not elsewhere may we seek, nor elsewhere know,
The light of heaven upon our dark below.

When from our dearest hope and haven reft,
Delight nor dazzles, nor is luxury left,
We long, obedient to our nature's law,
To see again our hovel thatched with straw:

See birds that know our avenaceous store
Stoop to our hand, and thence repleted soar:
But, of all hopes the wanderer's soul that share,
His pristine peace of mind's his final prayer.

VI

(As Walt Whitman might have written all around it.)

I

ou over there, young man with the guide-book, red-bound,
    covered flexibly with red linen,
Come here, I want to talk with you; I, Walt, the Manhat-
    tanese, citizen of these States, call you.
Yes, and the courier, too, smirking, smug-mouthed, with
    oil'd hair; a garlicky look about him generally; him,
    too, I take in, just as I would a coyote or a king, or
    a toad-stool, or a ham-sandwich, or anything, or any-
    body else in the world.
Where are you going?
You want to see Paris, to eat truffles, to have a good time;
    in Vienna, London, Florence, Monaco, to have a good
    time; you want to see Venice.
Come with me. I will give you a good time; I will give you
    all the Venice you want, and most of the Paris.
I, Walt, I call to you. I am all on deck! Come and loafe
    with me! Let me tote you around by your elbow and
    show you things.
You listen to my ophicleide!
Home!
Home, I celebrate. I elevate my fog-whistle, inspir'd by the
    thought of home.
Come in!—take a front seat; the jostle of the crowd not
    minding; there is room enough for all of you.
This is my exhibition—it is the greatest show on earth—
    there is no charge for admission.
All you have to pay me is to take in my romanza.

II

1. The brown-stone house; the father coming home worri‹
   from a bad day's business; the wife meets him in t‹
   marble pav'd vestibule; she throws her arms abo
   him; she presses him close to her; she looks him f‹
   in the face with affectionate eyes; the frown from ‹
   brow disappearing.

   Darling, she says, Johnny has fallen down and cut ‹
   head; the cook is going away, and the boiler leaks.

2. The mechanic's dark little third-story room, seen in ‹
   flash from the Elevated Railway train; the sewin‹
   machine in a corner; the small cook-stove; the wh‹
   family eating cabbage around a kerosene lamp; of t
   clatter and roar and groaning wail of the Elevat
   train unconscious; of the smell of the cabbage unco‹
   scious.

   Me, passant, in the train, of the cabbage not quite
   unconscious.

3. The French Flat; the small rooms, all right-angles, u‹
   individual; the narrow halls; the gaudy, cheap deco‹
   tions everywhere.

   The janitor and the cook exchanging compliments up a‹
   down the elevator-shaft; the refusal to send up mo‹
   coal, the solid splash of the water upon his head, t
   language he sends up the shaft, the triumphant laug‹
   ter of the cook, to her kitchen retiring.

4. The widow's small house in the suburbs of the city; t‹
   widow's boy coming home from his first day do‹
   town; he is flushed with happiness and pride; he is ‹
   longer a school-boy, he is earning money; he tak‹
   on the airs of a man and talks learnedly of busine‹

5. The room in the third-class boarding-house; the me‹
   little hard-coal fire, the slovenly Irish servant-g‹
   making it, the ashes on the hearth, the faded furn‹
   ture, the private provender hid away in the closet, t
   dreary backyard out the window; the young girl at t
   glass, with her mouth full of hairpins, doing up ‹
   hair to go downstairs and flirt with the young fello‹
   in the parlor.

6. The kitchen of the old farm-house; the young convict just returned from prison—it was his first offense, and the judges were lenient on him.

He is taking his first meal out of prison; he has been received back, kiss'd, encourag'd to start again; his lungs, his nostrils expand with the big breaths of free air; with shame, with wonderment, with a trembling joy, his heart too, expanding.

The old mother busies herself about the table; she has ready for him the dishes he us'd to like; the father sits with his back to them, reading the newspaper, the newspaper shaking and rustling much; the children hang wondering around the prodigal—they have been caution'd: Do not ask where our Jim has been; only say you are glad to see him.

The elder daughter is there, palefac'd, quiet; her young man went back on her four years ago; his folks would not let him marry a convict's sister. She sits by the window, sewing on the children's clothes, the clothes not only patching up; her hunger for children of her own invisibly patching up.

The brother looks up; he catches her eye, he fearful, apologetic; she smiles back at him, not reproachfully smiling, with loving pretence of hope smiling—it is too much for him; he buries his face in the folds of the mother's black gown.

7. The best room of the house, on the Sabbath only open'd; the smell of horse-hair furniture and mahogany varnish; the ornaments on the what-not in the corner; the wax fruit, dusty, sunken, sagged in, consumptive-looking, under a glass globe, the sealing-wax imitation of coral; the cigar boxes with shells plastered over, the perforated card-board motto.

The kitchen; the housewife sprinkling the clothes for the fine ironing to-morrow—it is the Third-day night, and the plain things are ready iron'd, now in cupboards, in drawers stowed away.

The wife waiting for the husband—he is at the tavern, jovial, carousing; she, alone in the kitchen sprinkling clothes —the little red wood clock with peaked top, with pen-

dulum wagging behind a pane of gayly painted glass,
strikes twelve.

The sound of the husband's voice on the still night air—he is
singing: "We won't go home until morning!"—the
wife arising, toward the wood-shed hastily going,
stealthily entering, the voice all the time coming
nearer, inebriate, chantant.

The husband passing the door of the wood-shed; the club
over his head, now with his head in contact; the
sudden cessation of the song; the benediction of peace
over the domestic foyer temporarily resting.

I sing the soothing influences of home.

You, young man, thoughtlessly wandering, with courier, with
guide-book wandering,

You hearken to the melody of my steam-calliope

Yawp!

H. C. Bunner.

AN OLD SONG BY NEW SINGERS

IN THE ORIGINAL

MARY had a little lamb,
  Its fleece was white as snow,—
And everywhere that Mary went
  The lamb was sure to go.

(As Austin Dobson writes it.)

TRIOLET

A little lamb had Mary, sweet,
  With a fleece that shamed the driven snow.
Not alone Mary went when she moved her feet
(For a little lamb had Mary, sweet),
And it tagged her 'round with a pensive bleat,
  And wherever she went it wanted to go;
A little lamb had Mary, sweet,
  With a fleece that shamed the driven snow.

(*As Mr. Browning has it.*)

You knew her?—Mary the small,
How of a summer,—or, no, was it fall?
You'd never have thought it, never believed,
But the girl owned a lamb last fall.

Its wool was subtly, silky white,
Color of lucent obliteration of night,
Like the shimmering snow or—our Clothild's arm!
You've seen her arm—her right, I mean—
The other she scalded a-washing, I ween—
How white it is and soft and warm?

Ah, there was soul's heart-love, deep, true, and tender,
Wherever went Mary, the maiden so slender,
There followed, his all-absorbed passion, inciting,
That passionate lambkin—her soul's heart delighting—
Ay, every place that Mary sought in,
That lamb was sure to soon be caught in.

(*As Longfellow might have done it.*)

Fair the daughter known as Mary,
Fair and full of fun and laughter,
Owned a lamb, a little he-goat,
Owned him all herself and solely.
White the lamb's wool as the Gotchi—
The great Gotchi, driving snowstorm.
Hither Mary went and thither,
But went with her to all places,
Sure as brook to run to river,
Her pet lambkin following with her.

(*How Andrew Lang sings it.*)

RONDEAU

A wonderful lass was Marie, petite,
And she looked full fair and passing sweet—
   And, oh! she owned—but cannot you guess
   What pet can a maiden so love and caress
As a tiny lamb with a plaintive bleat

And mud upon his dainty feet
And a gentle veally odour of meat,
   And a fleece to finger and kiss and press—
      White as snow?

Wherever she wandered, in lane or street,
As she sauntered on, there at her feet
   She would find that lambkin—bless
      The dear!—treading on her dainty dress,
Her dainty dress, fresh and neat—
      White as snow!

(*Mr. Algernon C. Swinburne's idea.*)

VILLANELLE

Dewy-eyed with shimmering hair,
   Maiden and lamb were a sight to see,
For her pet was white as she was fair.

And its lovely fleece was beyond compare,
   And dearly it loved its Mistress Marie,
Dewy-eyed, with shimmering hair.

Its warpéd wool was an inwove snare,
   To tangle her fingers in, where they could be
(For her pet was white as she was fair).

Lost from sight, both so snow-white were,
   And the lambkin adored the maiden wee,
Dewy-eyed with shimmering hair.

Th' impassioned incarnation of rare,
   Of limpid-eyed, luscious-lipped, loved beauty,
And her pet was white as she was fair.

Wherever she wandered, hither and there,
   Wildly that lambkin sought with her to be,
With the dewy-eyed, with shimmering hair,
And a pet as white as its mistress was fair.

A. C. Wilkie.

MORE IMPRESSIONS

LA FUITE DES OIES

To outer senses they are geese,
  Dull drowsing by a weedy pool;
  But try the impression trick. Cool! Cool!
Snow-slumbering sentinels of Peace!

Deep silence on the shadowy flood,
  Save rare sharp stridence (that means " quack "),
  Low amber light in Ariel track
Athwart the dun (that means the mud).

And suddenly subsides the sun,
  Bulks mystic, ghostly, thrid the gloom
  (That means the white geese waddling home),
And darkness reigns! (See how it's done?)
                    Oscuro Wildgoose.

NURSERY RHYMES À LA MODE

*(Our nurseries will soon be too cultured to admit the old
  rhymes in their Philistine and unæsthetic garb. They
  may be redressed somewhat on this model.)*

Oh, but she was dark and shrill,
  (Hey-de-diddle and hey-de-dee!)
  The cat that (on the first April)
  Played the fiddle on the lea.
Oh, and the moon was wan and bright,
  (Hey-de-diddle and hey-de-dee!)
  The Cow she looked nor left nor right,
  But took it straight at a jump, pardie!
The hound did laugh to see this thing,
  (Hey-de-diddle and hey-de-dee!)
As it was parlous wantoning,
  (Ah, good my gentles, laugh not ye,)

And underneath a dreesome moon
　Two lovers fled right piteouslie;
A spooney plate with a plated spoon,
　(Hey-de-diddle and hey-de-dee!)

POSTSCRIPT

Then blame me not, altho' my verse
　Sounds like an echo of C. S. C.
Since still they make ballads that worse and worse
　Savor of diddle and hey-de-dee.

Unknown.

A MAUDLE-IN BALLAD

TO HIS LILY

My lank limp lily, my long lithe lily,
My languid lily-love fragile and thin,
With dank leaves dangling and flower-flap chilly,
That shines like the shin of a Highland gilly!
Mottled and moist as a cold toad's skin!
Lustrous and leper-white, splendid and splay!
Art thou not Utter and wholly akin
To my own wan soul and my own wan chin,
And my own wan nose-tip, tilted to sway
The peacock's feather, *sweeter than sin,*
That I bought for a halfpenny yesterday?

My long lithe lily, my languid lily,
My lank limp lily-love, how shall I win—
Woo thee to wink at me? Silver lily,
How shall I sing to thee, softly or shrilly?
What shall I weave for thee—what shall I spin—
Rondel, or rondeau, or virelai?
Shall I buzz like a bee with my face thrust in
Thy choice, chaste chalice, or choose me a tin
Trumpet, or touchingly, tenderly play
On the weird bird-whistle, *sweeter than sin,*
That I bought for a halfpenny yesterday.

My languid lily, my lank limp lily,
My long lithe lily-love, men may grin—
Say that I'm soft and supremely silly—
What care I while you whisper stilly;
What care I while you smile? Not a pin!
While you smile, you whisper—'Tis sweet to decay?

I have watered with chlorodine, tears of chagrin,
The churchyard mould I have planted thee in,
Upside down in an intense way,
In a rough red flower-pot, *sweeter than sin,*
That I bought for a halfpenny yesterday.

Unknown.

GILLIAN

JACK and Jille
    I have made me an end of the moods of maidens,
      I have loosed me, and leapt from the links of love;
    From the kiss that cloys and desire that deadens,
      The woes that madden, the words that move.
    In the dim last days of a spent September,
      When fruits are fallen, and flies are fain;
    Before you forget, and while I remember,
      I cry as I shall cry never again.

Went up a hylle
    Where the strong fell faints in the lazy levels
      Of misty meadows, and streams that stray;
    We raised us at eve from our rosy revels,
      With the faces aflame for the death of the day;
    With pale lips parted, and sighs that shiver,
      Low lids that cling to the last of love:
    We left the levels, we left the river,
      And turned us and toiled to the air above.

To fetch a paile of water,
    By the sad sweet springs that have salved our sorrow,
    The fates that haunt us, the grief that grips—
    Where we walk not to-day nor shall walk not to-
        morrow—

The wells' of Lethe for wearied lips.
With souls nor shaken with tears nor laughter,
   With limp knees loosed as of priests that pray,
We bowed us and bent to the white well-water,
   We dipped and we drank it and bore away.

Jack felle downe
   The low light trembled on languid lashes,
     The haze of your hair on my mouth was blown,
Our love flashed fierce from its fading ashes,
     As night's dim net on the day was thrown.
What was it meant for, or made for, that minute,
     But that our lives in delight should be dipt?
Was it yours, or my fault, or fate's, that in it
     Our frail feet faltered, our steep steps slipt.

And brake his crowne, and Jille came tumblynge after.
   Our linked hands loosened and lapsed in sunder,
     Love from our limbs as a shift was shed,
But paused a moment, to watch with wonder
     The pale pained body, the bursten head.
While our sad souls still with regrets are riven,
     While the blood burns bright on our bruised brows,
I have set you free, and I stand forgiven—
     And now I had better go call my cows.

                             Unknown.

EXTRACTS FROM THE RUBAIYAT OF OMAR CAYENNE

Wake! for the Hack can scatter into flight
Shakespeare and Dante in a single Night!
   The Penny-a-Liner is Abroad, and strikes
Our Modern Literature with blithering Blight.

Before Historical Romances died,
Methought a Voice from Art's Olympus cried,
   "When all Dumas and Scott is still for Sale,
Why nod o'er drowsy Tales, by Tyros tried?"

A Book of Limericks—Nonsense, anyhow—
Alice in Wonderland, the Purple Cow
   Beside me singing on Fifth Avenue—
Ah, this were Modern Literature enow!

Ah, my Beloved, write the Book that clears
To-Day of dreary Debt and sad Arrears;
   To-morrow!—Why, To-Morrow I may see
My Nonsense popular as Edward Lear's.

And we, that now within the Editor's Room
Make merry while we have our little Boom,
   Ourselves must we give way to next month's Set—
Girls with Three Names, who know not Who from Whom!

As then the Poet for his morning Sup
Fills with a Metaphor his mental Cup,
   Do you devoutly read your Manuscripts
That Someone may, before you burn them up!

And if the Bosh you write, the Trash you read,
End in the Garbage-Barrel—take no Heed;
   Think that you are no worse than other Scribes,
Who scribble Stuff to meet the Public Need.

So, when Who's-Who records your silly Name,
You'll think that you have found the Road to Fame;
   And though ten thousand other Names are there,
You'll fancy you're a Genius, just the Same!

Why, if an Author can fling Art aside,
And in a Book of Balderdash take pride,
   Were't not a Shame—were't not a Shame for him
A Conscientious Novel to have tried?

And fear not, if the Editor refuse
Your work, he has no more from which to choose;
   The Literary Microbe shall bring forth
Millions of Manuscripts too bad to use.

The Woman's Touch runs through our Magazines;
For her the Home, and Mother-Tale, and Scenes
    Of Love-and-Action, Happy at the End—
The same old Plots, the same old Ways and Means.

But if, in spite of this, you build a Plot
Which these immortal Elements has not,
    You gaze To-Day upon a Slip, which reads,
" The Editor Regrets "—and such-like Rot.

Waste not your Ink, and don't attempt to use
That subtle Touch which Editors refuse;
    Better be jocund at two cents a word,
Than, starving, court an ill-requited Muse!

Strange—is it not?—that of the Authors who
Publish in England, such a mighty Few
    Make a Success, though here they score a Hit?
The British Public knows a Thing or Two!

The Scribe no question makes of Verse or Prose,
But what the Editor demands, he shows;
    And he who buys three thousand words of Drool,
He knows what People want—you Bet He knows!

Would but some wingèd Angel bring the News
Of Critic who reads Books that he Reviews,
    And make the stern Reviewer do as well
Himself, before he Meed of Praise refuse!

Ah, Love, could you and I perchance succeed
In boiling down the Million Books we read
    Into One Book, and edit that a Bit—
There'd be a WORLD'S BEST LITERATURE indeed!

                              Gelett Burgess.

DIVERSIONS OF THE RE-ECHO CLUB

It is with pleasure that we announce our ability to offer to the public the papers of the Re-Echo Club. This club, somewhat after the order of the Echo Club, late of Boston, takes pleasure in trying to better what is done. On the occasion of the meeting of which the following gems of poesy are the result, the several members of the club engaged to write up the well-known tradition of the Purple Cow in more elaborate form than the quatrain made famous by Mr. Gelett Burgess:

> " I NEVER saw a Purple Cow,
> I never hope to see one;
> But I can tell you, anyhow,
> I'd rather see than be one."

The first attempt here cited is the production of Mr. John Milton:

> Hence, vain, deluding cows.
> The herd of folly, without colour bright,
> How little you delight,
> Or fill the Poet's mind, or songs arouse!
> But, hail! thou goddess gay of feature!
> Hail, divinest purple creature!
> Oh, Cow, thy visage is too bright
> To hit the sense of human sight.
> And though I'd like, just once, to see thee,
> I never, never, never'd be thee!

MR. P. BYSSHE SHELLEY:

> Hail to thee, blithe spirit!
> Cow thou never wert;
> But in life to cheer it
> Playest thy full part
> In purple lines of unpremeditated art.

> The pale purple colour
> Melts around thy sight
> Like a star, but duller,
> In the broad daylight.
> I'd see thee, but I would not be thee if I might.

We look before and after
At cattle as they browse;
Our most hearty laughter
Something sad must rouse.
Our sweetest songs are those that tell of Purple Cows.

MR. W. WORDSWORTH:

She dwelt among the untrodden ways
Beside the springs of Dee;
A Cow whom there were few to praise
And very few to see.

A violet by a mossy stone
Greeting the smiling East
Is not so purple, I must own,
As that erratic beast.
She lived unknown, that Cow, and so
I never chanced to see;
But if I had to be one, oh,
The difference to me!

MR. T. GRAY:

The curfew tolls the knell of parting day,
The lowing herd winds slowly o'er the lea;
I watched them slowly wend their weary way,
But, ah, a Purple Cow I did not see.
Full many a cow of purplest ray serene
Is haply grazing where I may not see;
Full many a donkey writes of her, I ween,
But neither of these creatures would I be.

MR. J. W. RILEY:

There, little Cow, don't cry!
You are brindle and brown, I know.
And with wild, glad hues
Of reds and blues,
You never will gleam and glow.
But though not pleasing to the eye,
There, little Cow, don't cry, don't cry.

LORD A. TENNYSON:

Ask me no more. A cow I fain would see
   Of purple tint, like to a sun-soaked grape—
   Of purple tint, like royal velvet cape—
But such a creature I would never be—
      Ask me no more.

MR. R. BROWNING:

All that I know
   Of a certain Cow
Is it can throw,
   Somewhere, somehow,
Now a dart of red,
   Now a dart of blue
(That makes purple, 'tis said).
   I would fain see, too.
This Cow that darkles the red and the blue!

MR. J. KEATS:

A cow of purple is a joy forever.
Its loveliness increases. I have never
Seen this phenomenon. Yet ever keep
A brave lookout; lest I should be asleep
When she comes by. For, though I would not be one,
I've oft imagined 'twould be joy to see one.

MR. D. G. ROSSETTI:

The Purple Cow strayed in the glade;
   (Oh, my soul! but the milk is blue!)
She strayed and strayed and strayed and strayed
   (And I wail and I cry Wa-hoo!)

I've never seen her—nay, not I;
   (Oh, my soul! but the milk is blue!)
Yet were I that Cow I should want to die.
   (And I wail and I cry Wa-hoo!)
But in vain my tears I strew.

MR. T. ALDRICH:

Somewhere in some faked nature place,
  In Wonderland, in Nonsense Land,
Two darkling shapes met face to face,
  And bade each other stand.

"And who are you?" said each to each;
  "Tell me your title, anyhow."
One said, "I am the Papal Bull,"
  "And I the Purple Cow."

MR. E. ALLAN POE:

Open then I flung a shutter,
And, with many a flirt and flutter,
In there stepped a Purple Cow which gayly tripped around
    my floor.
Not the least obeisance made she,
Not a moment stopped or stayed she,
But with mien of chorus lady perched herself above my
    door.
On a dusty bust of Dante perched and sat above my door.

And that Purple Cow unflitting
Still is sitting—still is sitting
On that dusty bust of Dante just above my chamber door,
And her horns have all the seeming
Of a demon's that is screaming,
And the arc-light o'er her streaming
Casts her shadow on the floor.
And my soul from out that pool of Purple shadow on the
    floor,
Shall be lifted Nevermore!

MR. H. LONGFELLOW:

The day is done, and the darkness
  Falls from the wing of night
As ballast is wafted downward
  From an air-ship in its flight.

I dream of a purple creature
  Which is not as kine are now;
And resembles cattle only
  As Cowper resembles a cow.

Such cows have power to quiet
  Our restless thoughts and rude;
They come like the Benedictine
  That follows after food.

MR. A. SWINBURNE:

Oh, Cow of rare rapturous vision,
  Oh, purple, impalpable Cow,
Do you browse in a Dream Field Elysian,
  Are you purpling pleasantly now?
By the side of wan waves do you languish?
  Or in the lithe lush of the grove?
While vainly I search in my anguish,
  O Bovine of mauve!

Despair in my bosom is sighing,
  Hope's star has sunk sadly to rest;
Though cows of rare sorts I am buying,
  Not one breathes a balm to my breast.
Oh, rapturous rose-crowned occasion,
  When I such a glory might see!
But a cow of a purple persuasion
  I never would be.

MR. A. DOBSON:

I'd love to see
  A Purple Cow,
Oh, Goodness me!
I'd love to see
But not to be
  One.   Anyhow,
I'd love to see
  A Purple Cow.

MR. O. HERFORD:

Children, observe the Purple Cow,
You cannot see her, anyhow;
And, little ones, you need not hope
Your eyes will e'er attain such scope.
But if you ever have a choice
To be, or see, lift up your voice
And choose to see. For surely you
Don't want to browse around and moo.

MR. H. C. BUNNER:

Oh, what's the way to Arcady,
  Where all the cows are purple?
Ah, woe is me! I never hope
On such a sight my eyes to ope;
But as I sing in merry glee
Along the road to Arcady,
Perchance full soon I may espy
A Purple Cow come dancing by.
  Heigho! I then shall see one.
Her horns bedecked with ribbons gay,
And garlanded with rosy may,—
  A tricksy sight. Still I must say
  I'd rather see than be one.

MR. A. SWINBURNE:

(Who was so enthused that he made a second attempt.)

Only in dim, drowsy depths of a dream do I dare to de-
  light in deliciously dreaming
Cows there may be of a passionate purple,—cows of a vio-
  lent violet hue;

Ne'er have I seen such a sight, I am certain it is but a
  demi-delirious dreaming—
Ne'er may I happily harbour a hesitant hope in my heart
  that my dream may come true.

Sad is my soul, and my senses are sobbing so strong is
    my strenuous spirit to see one.
Dolefully, drearily doomed to despair as warily wearily
    watching I wait;

Thoughts thickly thronging are thrilling and throbbing;
    to *see* is a glorious gain—but to *be* one!
That were a darker and direfuller destiny, that were a fear-
    fuller, frightfuller fate!

MR. R. KIPLING:

In the old ten-acre pasture,
    Lookin' eastward toward a tree,
There's a Purple Cow a-settin'
    And I know she thinks of me.
For the wind is in the gum-tree,
    And the hay is in the mow,
And the cow-bells are a-calling
    " Come and see a Purple Cow! "

But I am not going now,
    Not at present, anyhow,
For I am not fond of purple, and
    I can't abide a cow;
No, I shall not go to-day,
    Where the Purple Cattle play.
But I think I'd rather see one,
    Than to be one, anyhow.

                                    Carolyn Wells.

STYX RIVER ANTHOLOGY

ALICE BEN BOLT

I COULDN'T help weeping with delight
When the boys kissed me and called me sweet.
It was foolish, I know,
To weep when I was glad;
But I was young and I wasn't very well.
I was nervous, weak, anemic,

A sort of human mimosa; and I hadn't much brains,
And my mind wouldn't jell, anyhow.
That's why I trembled with fear when they frowned.
But they didn't frown often,
For I was sweetly pretty and most pliable.
But, oh, the grim joke of asking Ben Bolt if he remembered me!
Me!
Why, it was Ben Bolt who—
Well, never mind. He paid for this granite slab,
And it's as stylish as any in the church yard.
But I wish I had a more becoming shroud.

THE BLESSED DAMOZEL

I was one of those long, lanky, loose-jointed girls
Who fool people into believing
They are willowy and psychic and mysterious.
I was always hungry; I never ate enough to satisfy me,
For fear I'd get fat.
Oh, how little the world knows of the bitterness of life
To a woman who tries to keep thin!
Many thought I died of a broken heart,
But it was an empty stomach.
Then Mr. Rossetti wrote about me.
He described me all dolled up in some ladies' wearing
   apparel
That I wore at a fancy ball.
I had fasted all day, and had had my hair marcelled
And my face corrected.
And I *was* a dream.
But he seemed to think he really saw me,
Seemed to think I appeared to him after my death.
Oh, fudge!
Those spiritualists are always seeing things!

ENOCH ARDEN

Yes, it was the eternal triangle,
Only they didn't call it that then.
Of course everybody thought I was all broken up

When I found Annie wed to Philip,
But, as a matter of fact,
  didn't care so much;
For she was one of those self-starting weepers,
And a man can't stand blubbering all the time.
And, then, of course,
When I was off on that long sea trip—
Oh, well, you know what sailors are.

LITTLE EVA

To be honest,
  didn't mind dying,
For I had
One of these here now
Dressy deaths.
It was staged, you know,
And, like Samson,
My death brought down the house.
I was a smarty kid,
And they were less frequent then than later.
Oh, I was the Mary Pickford of my time,
And I rest content
With my notoriety.

LUCY

Yes, I am in my grave,
And you bet it makes a difference to him!
For we were to be married,—at least, I think we were,
And he'd made me promise to deed him the house.
But I had to go and get appendicitis,
And they took me to the hospital.
It was a nice hospital, clean,
And Tables Reserved For Ladies.
Well, my heart gave out.
He came and stood over my grave,
And registered deep concern.
And now, he's going round with that
Hen-minded Hetty What's-her-name!
Her with her Whistler's Mother and her Baby Stuart

On her best-room wall!
And I hate her, and I'm glad she squints.
Well, I suppose I lived my life,
But it was Life in name only.
And I'm mad at the whole world!

OPHELIA

No, it wasn't suicide,
But I had heard so much of those mud baths,
I thought I'd try one.
Ugh! it was a mess!
Weeds, slime, and tangled vines! Oh, me!
Had I been Annette Kellerman
Or even a real mermaid,
I had lived to tell the tale.
But I slid down and under,
And so Will Shaxpur told it for me.
Just as well.
But I think my death scene is unexcelled
By any in cold print.
It beats that scrawny, red-headed old thing of Tom Hood's
All hollow!

CASABIANCA

I played to the Grand Stand!
Sure I did,
And I made good.
Ain't I in McGuffey's Third Reader?
Don't they speak pieces about me Friday afternoons?
Don't everybody know the first two lines of my story,—
And no more?
Say, I was there with the goods,
Wasn't I?
And it paid.
But I wish Movin' Pitchers had been invented then!

ANNABEL LEE

They may say all they like
About germs and micro-crocuses,—
Or whatever they are!
But my set opinion is,—
If you want to get a good, old-fashioned chills and fever,
Just poke around
In a damp, messy place by the sea,
Without rubbers on.
A good cold wind,
Blowing out of a cloud, by night,
Will give you a harder shaking ague
Than all the bacilli in the Basilica.
It did me.

ANGUS MC PHAIRSON

Oh, of course,
It's always some dratted petticoat!
Just because that little flibbertigibbet, Annie Laurie
Had a white throat and a blue e'e,
She played the very devil with my peace of mind.
She'd dimple at me
Till I was aboot crazy;
And then laugh at me through her dimples!
She was my bespoke.
And I'd beg her to have the banns called,—
But there was no pinning her down.
Well, she was so bonny
That like a fool, I said I'd lay me doon
And dee for her.
And,—like a fool,—
I did.

Carolyn Wells.

ANSWER TO MASTER WITHER'S SONG, "SHALL I, WASTING IN DESPAIR?"

Shall I, mine affections slack,
'Cause I see a woman's black?
Or myself, with care cast down,
'Cause I see a woman brown?
Be she blacker than the night,
Or the blackest jet in sight!
  If she be not so to me,
    What care I how black she be?

Shall my foolish heart be burst,
'Cause I see a woman's curst?
Or a thwarting hoggish nature
Joinèd in as bad a feature?
Be she curst or fiercer than
Brutish beast, or savage man!
  If she be not so to me,
    What care I how curst she be?

Shall a woman's vices make
Me her vices quite forsake?
Or her faults to me made known,
Make me think that I have none?
Be she of the most accurst,
And deserve the name of worst!
  If she be not so to me,
    What care I how bad she be?

'Cause her fortunes seem too low,
Shall I therefore let her go?
He that bears an humble mind
And with riches can be kind,
Think how kind a heart he'd have,
If he were some servile slave!
  And if that same mind I see
    What care I how poor she be?

Poor, or bad, or curst, or black,
I will ne'er the more be slack!
If she hate me (then believe!)
She shall die ere I will grieve!
If she like me when I woo
I can like and love her too!
   If that she be fit for me!
   What care I what others be?

Ben Jonson.

SONG OF THE SPRINGTIDE

O Season supposed of all free flowers,
   Made lovely by light of the sun,
Of garden, of field, and of tree-flowers,
   Thy singers are surely in fun!
Or what is it wholly unsettles
   Thy sequence of shower and shine,
And maketh thy pushings and petals
   To shrivel and pine?

Why is it that o'er the wild waters
   That beastly North-Easter still blows,
Dust-dimming the eyes of our daughters,
   Blue-nipping each nice little nose?
Why is it these sea-skirted islands
   Are plagued with perpetual chills,
Driving men to Italian or Nile-lands
   From Albion's ills?

Happy he, O Springtide, who hath found thee,
   All sunlit, in luckier lands,
With thy garment of greenery round thee,
   And belted with blossomy bands.
From us by the blast thou art drifted,
   All brag of thy beauties is bosh;
When the songs of thy singers are sifted,
   They simply won't wash.

What lunatic lune, what vain vision,
   Thy laureate, Springtide, may move
To sing thee,—oh, bitter derision!
   A season of laughter and love?
You make a man mad beyond measure,
   O Spring, and thy lauders like thee:
Thy flowers, thy pastimes and pleasures,
     Are fiddlededee!

Unknown.

THE VILLAGE CHOIR

HALF a bar, half a bar,
Half a bar onward!
Into an awful ditch
Choir and precentor hitch,
Into a mess of pitch,
   They led the Old Hundred.
Trebles to right of them,
Tenors to left of them,
Basses in front of them,
   Bellowed and thundered.
Oh, that precentor's look,
When the sopranos took
Their own time and hook
   From the Old Hundred!
Screeched all the trebles here,
Boggled the tenors there,
Raising the parson's hair,
   While his mind wandered;
Theirs not to reason why
This psalm was pitched too high:
Theirs but to gasp and cry
   Out the Old Hundred.
Trebles to right of them,
Tenors to left of them,
Basses in front of them,
   Bellowed and thundered.

Stormed they with shout and yell,
Not wise they sang nor well,
Drowning the sexton's bell,
  While all the church wondered.

Dire the percentor's glare,
Flashed his pitchfork in air
Sounding fresh keys to bear
  Out the Old Hundred.
Swiftly he turned his back,
Reached he his hat from rack,
Then from the screaming pack,
  Himself he sundered.
Tenors to right of him,
Tenors to left of him,
Discords behind him,
  Bellowed and thundered.
Oh, the wild howls they wrought:
Right to the end they fought!
Some tune they sang, but not,
  Not the Old Hundred.

Unknown.

MY FOE

JOHN ALCOHOL, my foe, John,
  When we were first acquaint,
I'd siller in my pockets, John,
  Which noo, ye ken, I want;
I spent it all in treating, John,
  Because I loved you so;
But mark ye, how you've treated me,
  John Alcohol, my foe.

John Alcohol, my foe, John,
  We've been ower lang together,
Sae ye maun tak' ae road, John,
  And I will take anither;
For we maun tumble down, John,
  If hand in hand we go;
And I shall hae the bill to pay,
  John Alcohol, my foe.

John Alcohol, my foe, John,
  Ye've blear'd out a' my een,
And lighted up my nose, John,
  A fiery sign atween!
My hands wi' palsy shake, John,
  My locks are like the snow;
Ye'll surely be the death of me,
  John Alcohol, my foe.

John Alcohol, my foe, John,
  'Twas love to you, I ween,
That gart me rise sae ear', John,
  And sit sae late at e'en;
The best o' friens maun part, John,
  It grieves me sair, ye know;
But "we'll nae mair to yon town,"
  John Alcohol, my foe.

John Alcohol, my foe, John,
  Ye've wrought me muckle skaith;
And yet to part wi' you, John,
  I own I'm unko' laith;
But I'll join the temperance ranks, John,
  Ye needna say me no;
It's better late than ne'er do weel,
  John Alcohol, my foe.

Unknown.

NURSERY SONG IN PIDGIN ENGLISH

Singee a songee sick a pence,
  Pockee muchee lye;
Dozen two time blackee bird
  Cookee in e pie.
When him cutee topside
  Birdee bobbery sing;
Himee tinkee nicey dish
  Setee foree King!

Kingee in a talkee loom
    Countee muchee money;
Queeny in e kitchee,
    Chew-chee breadee honey.
Servant galo shakee,
    Hangee washee clothes;
Cho-chop comee blackie bird,
    Nipee off her nose!

Unknown.

FATHER WILLIAM

'You are old, Father William," the young man said,
    " And your nose has a look of surprise;
Your eyes have turned round to the back of your head,
    And you live upon cucumber pies."
" I know it, I know it," the old man replied,
    " And it comes from employing a quack,
Who said if I laughed when the crocodile died
    I should never have pains in my back."

'You are old, Father William," the young man said,
    " And your legs always get in your way;
You use too much mortar in mixing your bread,
    And you try to drink timothy hay."
" Very true, very true," said the wretched old man,
    " Every word that you tell me is true;
And it's caused by my having my kerosene can
    Painted red where it ought to be blue."

" You are old, Father William," the young man said,
    " And your teeth are beginning to freeze,
Your favorite daughter has wheels in her head,
    And the chickens are eating your knees."
" You are right," said the old man, " I cannot deny,
    That my troubles are many and great,
But I'll butter my ears on the Fourth of July,
    And then I'll be able to skate."

Unknown.

A POE-'EM OF PASSION

It was many and many a year ago,
　　On an island near the sea,
That a maiden lived whom you mightn't know
　　By the name of Cannibalee;
And this maiden she lived with no other thought
　　Than a passionate fondness for me.

I was a child, and she was a child—
　　Tho' her tastes were adult Feejee—
But she loved with a love that was more than love,
　　My yearning Cannibalee;
With a love that could take me roast or fried
　　Or raw, as the case might be.

And that is the reason that long ago,
　　In that island near the sea,
I had to turn the tables and eat
　　My ardent Cannibalee—
Not really because I was fond of her,
　　But to check her fondness for me.

But the stars never rise but I think of the size
　　Of my hot-potted Cannibalee,
And the moon never stares but it brings me night
　　mares
　　Of my spare-rib Cannibalee;
And all the night-tide she is restless inside,
Is my still indigestible dinner-belle bride,
In her pallid tomb, which is Me,
In her solemn sepulcher, Me.

　　　　　　　　　　　C. F. Lummis.

IOW THE DAUGHTERS COME DOWN AT DUNOON

How do the daughters
Come down at Dunoon?
Daintily,
Tenderly,
Fairily,
Gingerly,
Glidingly,
Slidingly,
Slippingly,
Skippingly,
Trippingly,
Clippingly,
Bumpingly,
Thumpingly,
Stumpingly,
Clumpingly,
Starting and bolting,
And darting and jolting,
And tottering and staggering,
And lumbering and slithering,
And hurrying and scurrying,
And worrying and flurrying,
And rushing and leaping and crushing and creeping;
Feathers a-flying all—bonnets untying all—
Petticoats rapping and flapping and slapping all,
Crinolines flowing and blowing and showing all
Balmorals, dancing and glancing, entrancing all;
Feats of activity—
Nymphs on declivity—
Mothers in extacies—
Fathers in vextacies—
,ady-loves whisking and frisking and clinging on
'rue-lovers puffing and blowing and springing on,
)ashing and clashing and shying and flying on,
3lushing and flushing and wriggling and giggling on,
'easing and pleasing and squeezing and wheezing on,
:verlastingly falling and bawling and sprawling on,
'umbling and rumbling and grumbling and stumbling on,

Any fine afternoon,
About July or June—
That's just how the Daughters
Come down at Dunoon!

H. Cholmondeley Pennell.

TO AN IMPORTUNATE HOST

DURING DINNER AND AFTER TENNYSON

Ask me no more: I've had enough Chablis;
    The wine may come again, and take the shape,
    From glass to glass, of " Mountain " or of " Cape; "
But, my dear boy, when I have answered thee,
                    Ask me no more.

Ask me no more: what answer should I give,
    I love not pickled pork nor partridge pie;
    I feel if I took whisky I should die!
Ask me no more—for I prefer to live:
                    Ask me no more.

Ask me no more: unless my fate is sealed,
    And I have striven against you all in vain.
    Let your good butler bring me Hock again:
Then rest, dear boy. If for this once I yield,
                    Ask me no more!

Unknown.

CREMATION

BY A BURNING ADMIRER OF SIR HENRY THOMPSON

To Urn, or not to Urn? that is the question:
Whether 'tis nobler for our frames to suffer
The shows and follies of outrageous custom,
Or to take fire—against a sea of zealots—

And by consuming, end them? To Urn—to keep—
No more: and while we keep, to say we end
Contagion and the thousand graveyard ills
That flesh is heir to—'tis a consume-ation
Devoutly to be wished! To burn—to keep—
To keep! Perchance to lose—aye, there's the rub:
For in the course of things what duns may come,
Or who may shuffle off our Dresden urn,
Must give us pause. There's the respect
That makes inter-i-ment of so long use.
For who would have the pall and plumes of hire,
The tradesman's prize—a proud man's obsequies,
The chaffering for graves, the legal fee,
The cemetery beadle and the rest,
When he himself might his few ashes make
With a mere furnace? Who would tombstones bear,
And lie beneath a lying epitaph,
But that the dread of simmering after death—
That uncongenial furnace from whose burn
No incremate returns—weakens the will,
And makes us rather bear the graves we have
Than fly to ovens that we know not of?
This, Thompson, does make cowards of us all.
And thus the wisdom of incineration
Is thick-laid o'er with the pale ghost of nought,
And incremators of great pith and courage
With this regard their faces turn awry,
And shudder at cremation.

William Sawyer.

AN IMITATION OF WORDSWORTH

THERE is a river clear and fair,
'Tis neither broad nor narrow;
  It winds a little here and there—
  It winds about like any hare;
And then it takes as straight a course
As on the turnpike road a horse,
  Or through the air an arrow.

The trees that grow upon the shore,
Have grown a hundred years or more;
  So long there is no knowing.
Old Daniel Dobson does not know
When first these trees began to grow;
But still they grew, and grew, and grew,
As if they'd nothing else to do,
  But ever to be growing.

The impulses of air and sky
Have rear'd their stately heads so high,
  And clothed their boughs with green;
Their leaves the dews of evening quaff,—
  And when the wind blows loud and keen,
I've seen the jolly timbers laugh,
  And shake their sides with merry glee—
Wagging their heads in mockery.

Fix'd are their feet in solid earth,
  Where winds can never blow;
But visitings of deeper birth
  Have reach'd their roots below.
For they have gain'd the river's brink,
And of the living waters drink.

There's little Will, a five years child—
  He is my youngest boy:
To look on eyes so fair and wild,
  It is a very joy:—
He hath conversed with sun and shower
And dwelt with every idle flower,
  As fresh and gay as them.
He loiters with the briar rose,—
The blue-belles are his play-fellows,
  That dance upon their slender stem.

And I have said, my little Will,
Why should not he continue still
  A thing of Nature's rearing?

A thing beyond the world's control—
A living vegetable soul,—
  No human sorrow fearing.

It were a blessed sight to see
That child become a Willow-tree,
  His brother trees among.
He'd be four times as tall as me,
  And live three times as long.

Catharine M. Fanshawe.

THE LAY OF THE LOVE-LORN

PARODY ON TENNYSON'S "LOCKSLEY HALL"

COMRADES, you may pass the rosy. With permission of the
  chair,
I shall leave you for a little, for I'd like to take the air.

Whether 'twas the sauce at dinner, or that glass of ginger-
  beer,
Or these strong cheroots, I know not, but I feel a little queer.

Let me go. Now, Chuckster, blow me, 'pon my soul, this
  is too bad!
When you want me, ask the waiter, he knows where I'm
  to be had!

Whew! This is a great relief now! Let me but undo my
  stock;
Resting here beneath the porch, my nerves will steady like
  a rock.

In my ears I hear the singing of a lot of favourite tunes—
Bless my heart, how very odd! Why, surely, there's a brace
  of moons!

See—the stars! How bright they twinkle, winking with a
frosty glare,
Like my faithless cousin Amy when she drove me to despair.

Oh, my cousin, spider-hearted! Oh, my Amy! No, con-
found it!
I must wear the mournful willow—all around my hat I've
bound it.

Falser than the Bank of Fancy, frailer than a shilling
glove,
Puppet to a father's anger, minion to a nabob's love!

Is it well to wish thee happy? Having known me, could
you ever
Stoop to marry half a heart, and little more than half a
liver?

Happy! Damme! Thou shalt lower to his level day by
day,
Changing from the best of china to the commonest of clay.

As the husband is, the wife is. He is stomach-plagued and
old,
And his curry soups will make thy cheek the colour of his
gold.

When his feeble love is sated, he will hold thee surely then
Something lower than his hookah, something less than his
cayenne.

What is this? His eyes are pinky. Was't the claret? Oh,
no, no—
Bless your soul, it was the salmon—salmon always makes
him so.

Take him to thy dainty chamber, soothe him with thy
lightest fancies,
He will understand thee, won't he—pay thee with a lover's
glances?

Louder than the loudest trumpet, harsh as harshest ophi-
        cleide,
Nasal respirations answer the endearments of his bride.

Sweet response, delightful music! Gaze upon thy noble
        charge
Till the spirit fill thy bosom that inspired the meek Lafarge.

Better thou wert dead before me, better, better that I stood
Looking on thy murdered body, like the injured Daniel
        Good!

Better thou and I were lying, cold and limber-stiff and
        dead,
With a pan of burning charcoal underneath our nuptial
        bed!

Cursed be the Bank of England's notes, that tempt the soul
        to sin!
Cursed be the want of acres—doubly cursed the want of
        tin!

Cursed be the marriage contract, that enslaved thy soul to
        greed!
Cursed be the sallow lawyer, that prepared and drew the
        deed!

Cursed be his foul apprentice, who the loathsome fees did
        earn!
Cursed be the clerk and parson—cursed be the whole con-
        cern!

Oh, 'tis well that I should bluster; much I'm like to make
        of that.
Better comfort have I found in singing " All Around My
        Hat."

But that song, so wildly plaintive, palls upon my British
        ears.
'Twill not do to pine for ever: I am getting up in years.

Can't I turn the honest penny, scribbling for the weekly
press,
And in writing Sunday libels drown my private wretched-
ness?

Oh, to feel the wild pulsation that in manhood's dawn I
knew,
When my days were all before me, and my years were
twenty-two;

When I smoked my independent pipe along the Quadrant
wide,
With the many larks of London flaring up on every side;

When I went the pace so wildly, caring little what might
come,
Coffee-milling care and sorrow, with a nose-adapted thumb;

Felt the exquisite enjoyment, tossing nightly off, oh, heavens!
Brandy at the Cider Cellars, kidneys smoking-hot at Evans';

Or in the Adelphi sitting, half in rapture, half in tears,
Saw the glorious melodrama conjure up the shades of years—

Saw Jack Sheppard, noble stripling, act his wondrous feats
again,
Snapping Newgate's bars of iron, like an infant's daisy
chain;

Might was right, and all the terrors which had held the
world in awe
Were despised and prigging prospered, spite of Laurie, spite
of law.

In such scenes as these I triumphed, ere my passion's edge
was rusted,
And my cousin's cold refusal left me very much disgusted!

Since, my heart is sore and withered, and I do not care a
curse
Whether worse shall be the better, or the better be the worse.

Hark! my merry comrades call me, bawling for another
jorum;
They would mock me in derision, should I thus appear before
'em.

Womankind no more shall vex me, such, at least, as go
arrayed
In the most expensive satins, and the newest silk brocade.

I'll to Afric, lion-haunted, where the giant forest yields
Rarer robes and finer tissue than are sold at Spitalfields.

Or to burst all chains of habit, flinging habit's self aside,
I shall walk the tangled jungle in mankind's primeval pride;

Feeding on the luscious berries and the rich casava root,
Lots of dates and lots of guavas, clusters of forbidden fruit.

Never comes the trader thither, never o'er the purple main
Sounds the oath of British commerce, or the accents of
Cockaigne.

There, methinks, would be enjoyment, where no envious rule
prevents;
Sink the steamboats! Cuss the railways! Rot, oh, rot the
Three per Cents!

There the passions, cramped no longer, shall have space to
breathe, my cousin!
I will take some savage woman—nay, I'll take at least a
dozen.

There I'll rear my young mulattoes, as no Bond Street brats
are reared:
They shall dive for alligators, catch the wild goats by the
beard,

Whistle to the cockatoos, and mock the hairy-faced baboon,
Worship mighty Mumbo Jumbo, in the mountains of the
Moon.

I, myself, in far Timbuctoo, leopard's blood will daily quaff,
Ride a-tiger-hunting, mounted on a thorough-bred giraffe.

Fiercely shall I shout the war-whoop, as some sullen stream
he crosses,
Startling from their noon-day slumbers iron-bound rhinoc-
eroses.

Fool! Again, the dream, the fancy! But I know my words
are mad,
For I hold the gray barbarian lower than the Christian cad.

I, the swell, the city dandy! I to seek such horrid places,
I to haunt with squalid Negroes, blubber-lips, and monkey
faces!

I to wed with Coromantees! I, who managed—very near—
To secure the heart and fortune of the widow Shillibeer!

Stuff and nonsense! Let me never fling a single chance
away.
Maids ere now, I know, have loved me, and another maiden
may.

Morning Post (*The Times* won't trust me), help me, as I
know you can;
I will pen an advertisement—that's a never-failing plan:

"WANTED—By a bard in wedlock, some young interesting
woman.
Looks are not so much an object, if the shiners be forth-
coming!

"Hymen's chains, the advertiser vows, shall be but silken
fetters.
Please address to A. T., Chelsea. N.B.—You must pay the
letters."

That's the sort of thing to do it. Now I'll go and taste the
balmy.
Rest thee with thy yellow nabob, spider-hearted cousin Amy!

Aytoun and *Martin*.

ONLY SEVEN

A PASTORAL STORY AFTER WORDSWORTH

I MARVELL'D why a simple child,
  That lightly draws its breath,
Should utter groans so very wild,
  And look as pale as Death.

Adopting a parental tone,
  I ask'd her why she cried;
The damsel answered with a groan,
  " I've got a pain inside!

" I thought it would have sent me mad
  Last night about eleven."
Said I, " What is it makes you bad?"
How many apples have you had?"
  She answered, " Only seven!"

" And are you sure you took no more,
  My little maid?" quoth I;
" Oh, please, sir, mother gave me four,
  But *they* were in a pie!"

" If that's the case," I stammer'd out,
  " Of course you've had eleven."
The maiden answer'd with a pout,
  " I ain't had more nor seven!"

I wonder'd hugely what she meant,
  And said, " I'm bad at riddles;
But I know where little girls are sent
  For telling taradiddles.

" Now, if you won't reform," said I,
  " You'll never go to Heaven."
But all in vain; each time I try,
That little idiot makes reply,
  " I ain't had more nor seven!"

POSTSCRIPT

To borrow Wordsworth's name was wrong,
    Or slightly misapplied;
And so I'd better call my song,
    " Lines after Ache-Inside."

Henry S. Leigh.

'TWAS EVER THUS

I NEVER rear'd a young gazelle,
    (Because, you see, I never tried);
But had it known and loved me well,
    No doubt the creature would have died.
My rich and aged Uncle John
    Has known me long and loves me well
But still persists in living on—
    I would he were a young gazelle.

I never loved a tree or flower;
    But, if I had, I beg to say
The blight, the wind, the sun, or shower
    Would soon have withered it away.
I've dearly loved my Uncle John,
    From childhood to the present hour,
And yet he will go living on—
    I would he were a tree or flower!

Henry S. Leigh.

FOAM AND FANGS

O NYMPH with the nicest of noses;
    And finest and fairest of forms;
Lips ruddy and ripe as the roses
    That sway and that surge in the storms;
O buoyant and blooming Bacchante,
    Of fairer than feminine face,
Rush, raging as demon of Dante—
    To this, my embrace!

The foam and the fangs and the flowers,
  The raving and ravenous rage
Of a poet as pinion'd in powers
  As a condor confined in a cage!
My heart in a haystack I've hidden,
  As loving and longing I lie,
Kiss open thine eyelids unbidden—
  I gaze and I die!

I've wander'd the wild waste of slaughter,
  I've sniffed up the sepulchre's scent,
I've doated on devilry's daughter,
  And murmur'd much more than I meant;
I've paused at Penelope's portal,
  So strange are the sights that I've seen,
And mighty's the mind of the mortal
  Who knows what I mean.

Walter Parke.

X

NARRATIVE

LITTLE BILLEE

THERE were three sailors of Bristol City
 Who took a boat and went to sea,
But first with beef and captain's biscuits,
 And pickled pork they loaded she.

There was gorging Jack, and guzzling Jimmy,
 And the youngest he was little Billee.
Now when they'd got as far as the Equator
 They'd nothing left but one split pea.

Says gorging Jack to guzzling Jimmy,
 " I am extremely hungaree."
To gorging Jack says guzzling Jimmy,
 " We've nothing left, us must eat we."

Says gorging Jack to guzzling Jimmy,
 " With one another we shouldn't agree!
There's little Bill, he's young and tender,
 " We're old and tough, so let's eat he."

" O Billy! we're going to kill and eat you,
 So undo the button of your chemie."
When Bill received this information,
 He used his pocket-handkerchie.

" First let me say my catechism,
 Which my poor mother taught to me."
" Make haste! make haste! " says guzzling Jimmy,
 While Jack pulled out his snicker-snee.

Then Bill went up to the main-top-gallant-mast,
    And down he fell on his bended knee,
He scarce had come to the Twelfth Commandment
    When up he jumps—"There's land I see!"

"Jerusalem and Madagascar,
    And North and South Amerikee,
There's the British flag a-riding at anchor,
    With Sir Admiral Napier, K.C.B."

So when they got aboard of the Admiral's,
    He hanged fat Jack and flogged Jimmee,
But as for little Bill, he made him
    The captain of a Seventy-three.

                W. M. Thackeray.

THE CRYSTAL PALACE

WITH ganial foire
  Thransfuse me loyre,
Ye sacred nymphs of Pindus,
    The whoile I sing
    That wondthrous thing,
The Palace made o' windows!

  Say, Paxton, truth,
  Thou wondthrous youth,
What sthroke of art celistial,
    What power was lint
    You to invint
This combineetion cristial.

  O would before
  That Thomas Moore,
Likewoise the late Lord Boyron,
    Thim aigles sthrong
    Of godlike song,
Cast oi on that cast oiron!

And saw thim walls,
And glittering halls,
Thim rising slendther columns,
Which I, poor pote,
Could not denote,
No, not in twinty vollums.

My Muse's words
Is like the bird's
That roosts beneath the panes there;
Her wings she spoils
'Gainst them bright toiles,
And cracks her silly brains there.

This Palace tall,
This Cristial Hall,
Which Imperors might covet,
Stands in High Park
Like Noah's Ark,
A rainbow bint above it.

The towers and fanes,
In other scaynes,
The fame of this will undo,
Saint Paul's big doom,
Saint Payther's, Room.
And Dublin's proud Rotundo.

'Tis here that roams,
As well becomes
Her dignitee and stations,
Victoria Great,
And houlds in state
The Congress of the Nations.

Her subjects pours
From distant shores,
Her Injians and Canajians,
And also we,
Her kingdoms three,
Attind with our allagiance.

Here come likewise
Her bould allies,
Both Asian and Europian;
From East and West
They send their best
To fill her Coornucopean.

I seen (thank Grace!)
This wondthrous place
(His Noble Honour Misther
H. Cole it was
That gave the pass,
And let me see what is there).

With conscious proide
I stud insoide
And look'd the World's Great Fair in,
Until me sight
Was dazzled quite,
And couldn't see for staring.

There's holy saints
And window paints,
By maydiayval Pugin;
Alhamborough Jones
Did paint the tones,
Of yellow and gambouge in.

There's fountains there
And crosses fair;
There's water-gods with urrns;
There's organs three,
To play, d'ye see,
" God save the Queen," by turrns.

There's statues bright   -
Of marble white,
Of silver, and of copper;
And some in zinc,
And some, I think,
That isn't over proper.

There's staym injynes,
That stands in lines,
Enormous and amazing,
That squeal and snort
Like whales in sport,
Or elephants a-grazing.

There's carts and gigs,
And pins for pigs,
There's dibblers and there's harrows,
And ploughs like toys
For little boys,
And illigant wheelbarrows.

For thim genteels
Who ride on wheels,
There's plenty to indulge 'em:
There's droskys snug
From Paytersbug,
And vayhycles from Bulgium.

There's cabs on stands
And shandthrydanns;
There's wagons from New York here;
There's Lapland sleighs
Have cross'd the seas,
And jaunting cyars from Cork here.

Amazed I pass
From glass to glass,
Deloighted I survey 'em;
Fresh wondthers grows
Before me nose
In this sublime Musayum!

Look, here's a fan
From far Japan,
A sabre from Damasco:
There's shawls ye get
From far Thibet,
And cotton prints from Glasgow.

There's German flutes,
Marocky boots,
And Naples macaronies;
Bohaymia
Has sent Behay;
Polonia her polonies.

There's granite flints
That's quite imminse,
There's sacks of coals and fuels,
There's swords and guns,
And soap in tuns,
And gingerbread and jewels.

There's taypots there,
And cannons rare;
There's coffins fill'd with roses;
There's canvas tints,
Teeth insthrumints,
And shuits of clothes by Moses.

There's lashins more
Of things in store,
But thim I don't remimber;
Nor could disclose
Did I compose
From May time to Novimber!

Ah, Judy thru!
With eyes so blue,
That you were here to view it!
And could I screw
But tu pound tu,
'Tis I would thrait you to it!

So let us raise
Victoria's praise,
And Albert's proud condition
That takes his ayse
As he surveys
This Cristial Exhibition.

W. M. Thackeray.

THE WOFLE NEW BALLAD OF JANE RONEY AND MARY BROWN

An igstrawnary tail I vill tell you this veek—
I stood in the Court of A'Beckett the Beak,
Vere Mrs. Jane Roney, a vidow, I see,
Who charged Mary Brown with a robbin' of she.

This Mary was pore and in misery once,
And she came to Mrs. Roney it's more than twelve monce
She adn't got no bed, nor no dinner, nor no tea,
And kind Mrs. Roney gave Mary all three.

Mrs. Roney kep Mary for ever so many veeks
(Her conduct disgusted the best of all Beax),
She kept her for nothink, as kind as could be,
Never thinking that this Mary was a traitor to she.

"Mrs. Roney, O Mrs. Roney, I feel very ill;
Will you jest step to the doctor's for to fetch me a pill?"
"That I will, my pore Mary," Mrs. Roney says she:
And she goes off to the doctor's as quickly as may be.

No sooner on this message Mrs. Roney was sped,
Than hup gits vicked Mary, and jumps out a bed;
She hopens all the trunks without never a key—
She bustes all the boxes, and vith them makes free.

Mrs. Roney's best linning gownds, petticoats, and close,
Her children's little coats and things, her boots and her hose,
She packed them, and she stole 'em, and avay vith them did
    flee
Mrs. Roney's situation—you may think vat it vould be!

Of Mary, ungrateful, who had served her this vay,
Mrs. Roney heard nothink for a long year and a day,
Till last Thursday, in Lambeth, ven whom should she see?
But this Mary, as had acted so ungrateful to she.

She was leaning on the helbo of a worthy young man;
They were going to be married, and were walkin hand in
       hand;
And the church-bells was a ringing for Mary and he,
And the parson was ready, and a waitin' for his fee.

When up comes Mrs. Roney, and faces Mary Brown,
Who trembles, and castes her eyes upon the ground.
She calls a jolly pleaseman, it happens to be me;
I charge this young woman, Mr. Pleaseman, says she.

Mrs. Roney, o, Mrs. Roney, o, do let me go,
I acted most ungrateful I own, and I know,
But the marriage bell is ringin, and the ring you may see,
And this young man is a waitin, says Mary, says she.

I don't care three fardens for the parson and clark,
And the bell may keep ringing from noon day to dark.
Mary Brown, Mary Brown, you must come along with me.
And I think this young man is lucky to be free.

So, in spite of the tears which bejewed Mary's cheek,
I took that young gurl to A'Beckett the Beak;
That exlent justice demanded her plea—
But never a sullable said Mary said she.

On account of her conduck so base and so vile,
That wicked young gurl is committed for trile,
And if she's transpawted beyond the salt sea,
It's a proper reward for such willians as she.

Now, you young gurls of Southwark for Mary who veep,
From pickin and stealin your ands you must keep,
Or it may be my dooty, as it was Thursday veek
To pull you all hup to A'Beckett the Beak.

                W. M. Thackeray.

KING JOHN AND THE ABBOT

An ancient story Ile tell you anon
Of a notable prince, that was called King John;
And he ruled England with maine and with might,
For he did great wrong, and maintein'd little right.

And Ile tell you a story, a story so merrye,
Concerning the Abbot of Canterbùrye;
How for his house-keeping, and high renowne,
They rode poste for him to fair London towne.

An hundred men, the king did heare say,
The abbot kept in his house every day;
And fifty golde chaynes, without any doubt,
In velvet coates waited the abbot about.

How now, father abbot, I heare it of thee,
Thou keepest a farre better house than mee,
And for thy house-keeping and high renowne,
I feare thou work'st treason against my crown.

My liege, quo' the abbot, I would it were knowne,
I never spend nothing but what is my owne;
And I trust your grace will doe me no deere
For spending of my owne true-gotten geere.

Yes, yes, father abbot, thy fault it is highe,
And now for the same thou needest must dye;
For except thou canst answer me questions three,
Thy head shall be smitten from thy bodie.

And first, quo' the king, when I'm in this stead,
With my crowne of golde so faire on my head,
Among all my liege-men, so noble of birthe,
Thou must tell me to one penny what I am worthe.

Secondlye, tell me, without any doubt,
How soone I may ride the whole world about,
And at the third question thou must not shrink,
But tell me here truly what I do think.

O, these are hard questions for my shallow witt,
Nor I cannot answer your grace as yet;
But if you will give me but three weekes space,
Ile do my endeavour to answer your grace.

Now three weeks space to thee will I give.
And that is the longest time thou hast to live;
For if thou dost not answer my questions three,
Thy lands and thy livings are forfeit to mee.

Away rode the abbot, all sad at that word,
And he rode to Cambridge and Oxenford;
But never a doctor there was so wise,
That could with his learning an answer devise.

Then home rode the abbot, of comfort so cold,
And he mett his shepheard agoing to fold:
How now, my lord abbot, you are welcome home
What newes do you bring us from good King John?

Sad newes, sad newes, shepheard, I must give:
That I have but three days more to live;
For if I do not answer him questions three,
My head will be smitten from my bodìe.

The first is to tell him there in that stead,
With his crowne of golde so fair on his head
Among all his liege-men so noble of birth,
To within one penny of what he is worth.

The seconde, to tell him, without any doubt,
How soone he may ride this whole world about:
And at the third question I must not shrinke,
But tell him there truly what he does thinke.

Now cheare up, sire abbot, did you never hear yet,
That a fool he may learne a wise man witt?
Lend me horse, and serving-men, and your apparel,
And I'll ride to London to answere your quarrel.

Nay frowne not, if it hath bin told unto mee,
I am like your lordship, as ever may bee:
And if you will but lend me your gowne,
There is none shall knowe us in fair London towne.

Now horses and serving-men thou shalt have,
With sumptuous array most gallant and brave;
With crozier, and miter, and rochet, and cope,
Fit to appeare 'fore our fader the pope.

Now welcome, sire abbot, the king he did say,
'Tis well thou'rt come back to keepe thy day;
For and if thou canst answer my questions three,
Thy life and thy living both saved shall bee.

And first, when thou seest me here in this stead,
With my crown of golde so fair on my head,
Among all my liege-men so noble of birthe,
Tell me to one penny what I am worth.

For thirty pence our Saviour was sold
Among the false Jewes, as I have bin told:
And twenty-nine is the worth of thee,
For I thinke, thou art one penny worser than hee.

The king he laughed, and swore by St. Bittel,
I did not think I had been worth so littel!
—Now secondly tell me, without any doubt,
How soone I may ride this whole world about.

You must rise with the sun, and ride with the same,
Until the next morning he riseth againe;
And then your grace need not make any doubt
But in twenty-four hours you'll ride it about.

The king he laughed, and swore by St. Jone,
I did not think it could be gone so soone!
—Now from the third question thou must not shrinke,
But tell me here truly what I do thinke.

Yea, that shall I do, and make your grace merry:
You thinke I'm the abbot of Canterbùry;

But I'm his poor shepheard, as plain you may see,
That am come to beg pardon for him and for mee.

The king he laughed, and swore by the masse,
Ile make thee lord abbot this day in his place!
Now naye, my liege, be not in such specde,
For alacke I can neither write, ne reade.

Four nobles a week, then, I will give thee,
For this merry jest thou hast showne unto mee:
And tell the old abbot, when thou comest home,
Thou hast brought him a pardon from good King John.

From *Percy's Reliques.*

ON THE DEATH OF A FAVORITE CAT,

DROWNED IN A TUB OF GOLDFISHES

'Twas on a lofty vase's side,
Where China's gayest art had dyed
   The azure flowers that blow,
Demurest of the tabby kind,
The pensive Selima, reclined,
   Gazed on the lake below.

Her conscious tail her joy declared;
The fair round face, the snowy beard,
   The velvet of her paws,
Her coat that with the tortoise vies,
Her ears of jet, and emerald eyes,
   She saw, and purred applause.

Still had she gaz'd, but, 'midst the tide,
Two angel forms were seen to glide,
   The Genii of the stream:
Their scaly armor's Tyrian hue,
Through richest purple, to the view
   Betrayed a golden gleam.

The hapless nymph with wonder saw:
A whisker first, and then a claw,
  With many an ardent wish,
She stretched in vain to reach the prize:
What female heart can gold despise?
  What Cat's averse to fish?

Presumptuous maid! with looks intent,
Again she stretched, again she bent,
  Nor knew the gulf between:
(Malignant Fate sat by and smiled)
The slippery verge her feet beguiled;
  She tumbled headlong in.

Eight times emerging from the flood,
She mewed to every watery god
  Some speedy aid to send.
No Dolphin came, no Nereid stirred,
Nor cruel Tom or Susan heard:
  A fav'rite has no friend!

From hence, ye Beauties! undeceived,
Know one false step is ne'er retrieved,
  And be with caution bold:
Not all that tempts your wandering eyes,
And heedless hearts, is lawful prize,
  Nor all that glistens gold.

Thomas Gray.

MISADVENTURES AT MARGATE

A LEGEND OF JARVIS'S JETTY

MR. SIMPKINSON (*loquitur*)

I was in Margate last July, I walk'd upon the pier,
I saw a little vulgar Boy—I said "What make you here?—
The gloom upon your youthful cheek speaks any thing but
    joy;
Again I said, "What make you here, you little vulgar Boy?"

He frown'd, that little vulgar Boy—he deem'd I meant to
    scoff:
And when the little heart is big, a little " sets it off ";
He put his finger in his mouth, his little bosom rose,—
He had no little handkerchief to wipe his little nose!

" Hark! don't you hear, my little man?—it's striking nine," I
    said,
" An hour when all good little boys and girls should be in bed.
Run home and get your supper, else your Ma' will scold—Oh!.
    fie!—
It's very wrong indeed for little boys to stand and cry!"

The tear-drop in his little eye again began to spring,
His bosom throbb'd with agony—he cried like any thing!
I stoop'd, and thus amidst his sobs I heard him murmur—
    " Ah
I haven't got no supper! and I haven't got no Ma'!!—

' My father, he is on the seas,—my mother's dead and gone!'
And I am here, on this here pier, to roam the world alone;
I have not had, this live-long day, one drop to cheer my heart,
Nor ' brown' to buy a bit of bread with,—let alone a tart.

" If there's a soul will give me food, or find me in employ,
By day or night, then blow me tight!" (he was a vulgar
    Boy);
' And now I'm here, from this here pier it is my fixed intent
To jump, as Mr. Levi did from off the Monu-ment!"

" Cheer up! cheer up! my little man—cheer up!" I kindly
    said.
You are a naughty boy to take such things into your head:
If you should jump from off the pier, you'd surely break
    your legs,
Perhaps your neck—then Bogey'd have you, sure as eggs are
    eggs!

" Come home with me, my little man, come home with me
    and sup;
My landlady is Mrs. Jones—we must not keep her up—

There's roast potatoes on the fire,—enough for me and you—
Come home,—you little vulgar Boy—I lodge at Number 2."

I took him home to Number 2, the house beside "The Foy,"
I bade him wipe his dirty shoes,—that little vulgar Boy,—
And then I said to Mistress Jones, the kindest of her sex,
"Pray be so good as go and fetch a pint of double X!"

But Mrs. Jones was rather cross, she made a little noise,
She said she "did not like to wait on little vulgar Boys."
She with her apron wiped the plates, and, as she rubb'd the
    delf,
Said I might "go to Jericho, and fetch my beer myself!"

I did not go to Jericho—I went to Mr. Cobb—
I changed a shilling—(which in town the people call "a
    Bob")—
It was not so much for myself as for that vulgar child—
And I said, "A pint of double X, and please to draw it
    mild!"

When I came back I gazed about—I gazed on stool and
    chair—
I could not see my little friend—because he was not there!
I peep'd beneath the table-cloth—beneath the sofa too—
I said "You little vulgar Boy! why what's become of you?"

I could not see my table-spoons—I look'd, but could not see
The little fiddle-pattern'd ones I use when I'm at tea;
—I could not see my sugar-tongs—my silver watch—oh,
    dear!
I know 'twas on the mantle-piece when I went out for beer.

I could not see my Mackintosh!—it was not to be seen!
Nor yet my best white beaver hat, broad-brimm'd and lined
    with green;
My carpet-bag—my cruet-stand, that holds my sauce and
    soy,—
My roast potatoes!—all are gone!—and so's that vulgar Boy!

rang the bell for Mrs. Jones, for she was down below,
—Oh, Mrs. Jones! what *do* you think?—ain't this a pretty
    go?
—That horrid little vulgar Boy whom I brought here to-
    night,
—He's stolen my things and run away!!"—Says she, "And
    sarve you right!!"

.   .   .   .

Next morning I was up betimes—I sent the Crier round,
All with his bell and gold-laced hat, to say I'd give a pound
To find that little vulgar Boy, who'd gone and used me so;
But when the Crier cried "O Yes!" the people cried, "O
    No!"

I went to "Jarvis' Landing-place," the glory of the town,
There was a common sailor-man a-walking up and down;
I told my tale—he seem'd to think I'd not been treated well,
And called me "Poor old Buffer!" what that means I cannot
    tell.

That sailor-man, he said he'd seen that morning on the
    shore,
A son of—something—'twas a name I'd never heard before,
A little "gallows-looking chap"—dear me; what could he
    mean?
With a "carpet-swab" and "muckingtogs," and a hat turned
    up with green.

He spoke about his "precious eyes," and said he'd seen him
    "sheer,"
—It's very odd that sailor-men should talk so very queer—
And then he hitch'd his trowsers up, as is, I'm told, their
    use,
—It's very odd that sailor-men should wear those things so
    loose.

I did not understand him well, but think he meant to say
He'd seen that little vulgar Boy, that morning swim away

In Captain Large's Royal George about an hour before,
And they were now, as he supposed, "some*wheres*" about t
Nore.

A landsman said, "I *twig* the chap—he's been upon the Mill-
And 'cause he *gammons* so the *flats*, ve calls him Veepin
Bill!"
He said "he'd done me wery brown," and "nicely *stow'd* th
swag."
—That's French, I fancy, for a hat—or else a carpet-bag.

I went and told the constable my property to track;
He asked me if "I did not wish that I might get it back?"
I answered, "To be sure I do!—it's what I come about."
He smiled and said, "Sir, does your mother know that yo
are out?"

Not knowing what to do, I thought I'd hasten back to towr
And beg our own Lord Mayor to catch the Boy who'd "don
me brown."
His Lordship very kindly said he'd try and find him out,
But he "rather thought that there were several vulgar boy
about."

He sent for Mr. Whithair then, and I described "the swag,"
My Mackintosh, my sugar-tongs, my spoons, and carpet-bag
He promised that the New Police should all their power
employ;
But never to this hour have I beheld that vulgar Boy!

MORAL

Remember, then, what when a boy I've heard my Grandma
tell,
"BE WARN'D IN TIME BY OTHERS' HARM, AND YOU SHALL DO FULL
WELL!"
Don't link yourself with vulgar folks, who've got no fix'd
abode,
Tell lies, use naughty words, and say they "wish they may
be blow'd!"

)on't take too much of double X!—and don't at night go out
'o fetch your beer yourself, but make the pot-boy bring your
    stout!
\nd when you go to Margate next, just stop and ring the
    bell,
;ive my respects to Mrs. Jones, and say I'm pretty well!

Richard Harris Barham.

THE GOUTY MERCHANT AND THE STRANGER.

In Broad Street Buildings on a winter night,
Snug by his parlor-fire a gouty wight
Sat all alone, with one hand rubbing
His feet, rolled up in fleecy hose:
While t'other held beneath his nose
The *Public Ledger,* in whose columns grubbing,
    He noted all the sales of hops,
    Ships, shops, and slops;
Gum, galls, and groceries; ginger, gin,
Tar, tallow, turmeric, turpentine, and tin;
When lo! a decent personage in black
Entered and most politely said:
" Your footman, sir, has gone his nightly track
    To the King's Head,
And left your door ajar; which I
Observed in passing by,
    And thought it neighborly to give you notice.'"
" Ten thousand thanks; how very few get,
In time of danger,
Such kind attentions from a stranger!
Assuredly, that fellow's throat is
Doomed to a final drop at Newgate:
He knows, too (the unconscionable elf!),
That there's no soul at home except myself."
" Indeed," replied the stranger (looking grave),
" Then he's a double knave;
He knows that rogues and thieves by scores
Nightly beset unguarded doors:
And see, how easily might one
    Of these domestic foes,
    Even beneath your very nose,

Perform his knavish tricks;
Enter your room, as I have done,
Blow out your candles—*thus*—and *thus*—
Pocket your silver candlesticks,
And—walk off—*thus!* "—
So said, so done; he made no more remark
Nor waited for replies,
But marched off with his prize,
Leaving the gouty merchant in the dark.

Horace Smith.

THE DIVERTING HISTORY OF JOHN GILPIN

SHOWING HOW HE WENT FARTHER THAN HE INTENDED AND CAME SAFE HOME AGAIN

JOHN GILPIN was a citizen of credit and renown;
A train-band captain eke was he, of famous London town.

John Gilpin's spouse said to her dear—" Though wedded
    we have been
These twice ten tedious years, yet we no holiday have seen.

" To-morrow is our wedding-day, and we will then repair
Unto the Bell at Edmonton all in a chaise and pair.

" My sister, and my sister's child, myself, and children
    three,
Will fill the chaise; so you must ride on horseback after
    we."

He soon replied, " I do admire of womankind but one,
And you are she, my dearest dear; therefore it shall be
    done.

" I am a linendraper bold, as all the world doth know;
And my good friend, the calender, will lend his horse to
    go."

Quoth Mrs. Gilpin, "That's well said; and, for that wine
    is dear,
We will be furnished with our own, which is both bright
    and clear."

John Gilpin kissed his loving wife; o'erjoyed was he to
    find
That, though on pleasure she was bent, she had a frugal
    mind.

The morning came, the chaise was brought, but yet was not
    allowed
To drive up to the door, lest all should say that she was
    proud.

So three doors off the chaise was stayed, where they did
    all get in—
Six precious souls, and all agog to dash through thick and
    thin.

Smack went the whip, round went the wheels—were never
    folks so glad;
The stones did rattle underneath, as if Cheapside were mad.

John Gilpin at his horse's side seized fast the flowing
    mane,
And up he got, in haste to ride—but soon came down
    again:

For saddletree scarce reached had he, his journey to begin,
When, turning round his head, he saw three customers
    come in.

So down he came: for loss of time, although it grieved
    him sore,
Yet loss of pence, full well he knew, would trouble him
    much more.

'Twas long before the customers were suited to their mind;
When Betty, screaming, came down-stairs—"The wine is
    left behind!"

"'Good lack!" quoth he—"yet bring it me, my leathern
    belt likewise,
In which I wear my trusty sword when I do exercise."

Now Mistress Gilpin (careful soul!) had two stone bottles
    found,
To hold the liquor that she loved, and keep it safe and
    sound.

Each bottle had a curling ear, through which the belt he
    drew,
And hung a bottle on each side to make his balance true.

Then over all, that he might be equipped from top to toe,
His long red cloak, well brushed and neat, he manfully did
    throw.

Now see him mounted once again upon his nimble steed,
Full slowly pacing o'er the stones, with caution and good
    heed.

But finding soon a smoother road beneath his well-shod
    feet,
The snorting beast began to trot, which galled him in his
    seat.

So, "Fair and softly," John he cried, but John he cried in
    vain;
That trot became a gallop soon, in spite of curb and rein.

So stooping down, as needs he must who cannot sit up-
    right,
He grasped the mane with both his hands, and eke with all
    his might.

His horse, who never in that sort had handled been before,
What thing upon his back had got did wonder more and
    more.

Away went Gilpin, neck or nought; away went hat and
    wig;
He little dreamt, when he set out, of running such a rig.

The wind did blow—the cloak did fly, like streamer long
    and gay;
Till, loop and button failing both, at last it flew away.

Then might all people well discern the bottles he had
    slung—
A bottle swinging at each side, as hath been said or sung.

The dogs did bark, the children screamed, up flew the win-
    dows all;
And every soul cried out, "Well done!" as loud as he
    could bawl.

Away went Gilpin—who but he?   His fame soon spread
    around—
"He carries weight! he rides a race!   'Tis for a thousand
    pound!"

And still as fast as he drew near, 'twas wonderful to view
How in a trice the turnpike men their gates wide open
    threw.

And now, as he went bowing down his reeking head full
    low,
The bottles twain behind his back were shattered at a blow.

Down ran the wine into the road, most piteous to be seen,
Which made his horse's flanks to smoke as they had basted
    been.

But still he seemed to carry weight, with leathern girdle
    braced;
For all might see the bottle necks still dangling at his
    waist.

Thus all through merry Islington these gambols did he
    play,
Until he came unto the Wash of Edmonton so gay;

And there he threw the wash about on both sides of th
    way,
Just like unto a trundling mop, or a wild goose at play.

At Edmonton his loving wife from the balcony spied
Her tender husband, wondering much to see how he di
    ride.

" Stop, stop, John Gilpin! here's the house," they all a
    once did cry;
" The dinner waits, and we are tired." Said Gilpin—" S
    am I! "

But yet his horse was not a whit inclined to tarry there
For why?—his owner had a house full ten miles off, a
    Ware.

So like an arrow swift he flew, shot by an archer strong:
So did he fly—which brings me to the middle of my song

Away went Gilpin out of breath, and sore against his will
Till at his friend the calender's his horse at last stood still

The calender, amazed to see his neighbor in such trim,
Laid down his pipe, flew to the gate, and thus accoste
    him:

" What news? what news? your tidings tell; tell me you
    must and shall—
Say why bareheaded you are come, or why you come a
    all ? "

Now Gilpin had a pleasant wit, and loved a timely joke
And thus unto the calender in merry guise he spoke:

" I came because your horse would come; and, if I well
    forebode,
My hat and wig will soon be here, they are upon the road."

The calender, right glad to find his friend in merry pin,
Returned him not a single word, but to the house went in;

Whence straight he came with hat and wig: a wig that
   flowed behind,
A hat not much the worse for wear—each comedy in its
   kind.

He held them up, and in his turn thus showed his ready
   wit—
"My head is twice as big as yours, they therefore needs
   must fit.

"But let me scrape the dirt away that hangs upon your
   face,
And stop and eat, for well you may be in a hungry case."

Said John, "It is my wedding-day, and all the world would
   stare,
If wife should dine at Edmonton, and I should dine at
   Ware."

So, turning to his horse, he said, "I am in haste to dine;
'Twas for your pleasure you came here—you shall go back
   for mine."

Ah, luckless speech, and bootless boast, for which he paid
   full dear!
For, while he spake, a braying ass did sing most loud and
   clear;

Whereat his horse did snort, as he had heard a lion roar,
And galloped off with all his might, as he had done before.

Away went Gilpin, and away went Gilpin's hat and wig:
He lost them sooner than at first, for why?—they were too
   big.

Now Mistress Gilpin, when she saw her husband posting
   down
Into the country far away, she pulled out half a crown;

And thus unto the youth she said, that drove them to the
  Bell,
"This shall be yours when you bring back my husband safe
  and well."

The youth did ride, and soon did meet John coming back
  amain—
Whom in a trice he tried to stop, by catching at his rein;

But not performing what he meant, and gladly would have
  done,
The frighted steed he frighted more, and made him faster
  run.

Away went Gilpin, and away went post-boy at his heels,
The post-boy's horse right glad to miss the lumbering of
  the wheels.

Six gentlemen upon the road, thus seeing Gilpin fly,
With post-boy scampering in the rear, they raised the hue
  and cry:

"Stop thief! stop thief!—a highwayman!" Not one of
  them was mute;
And all and each that passed that way did join in the pur-
  suit.

And now the turnpike gates again flew open in short space;
The tollmen thinking, as before, that Gilpin rode a race.

And so he did, and won it, too, for he got first to town;
Nor stopped till where he had got up he did again get
  down.

Now let us sing, long live the king! and Gilpin, long live
  he;
And when he next doth ride abroad, may I be there to see!

William Cowper.

PADDY O'RAFTHER

Paddy, in want of a dinner one day,
Credit all gone, and no money to pay,
Stole from a priest a fat pullet, they say,
    And went to confession just afther;
" Your riv'rince," says Paddy, " I stole this fat hen."
" What, what ! " says the priest, " at your ould thricks again ?
Faith, you'd rather be staalin' than sayin' *amen,*
                    Paddy O'Rafther ! "

" Sure, you wouldn't be angry," says Pat, " if you knew
That the best of intintions I had in my view—
For I stole it to make it a present to you,
    And you can absolve me afther."
" Do you think," says the priest, " I'd partake of your theft ?
Of your seven small senses you must be bereft—
You're the biggest blackguard that I know, right and left,
                    Paddy O'Rafther."

" Then what shall I do with the pullet," says Pat,
" If your riv'rince won't take it ? By this and by that
I don't know no more than a dog or a cat
    What your riv'rince would have me be afther."
" Why, then," says his rev'rence, " you sin-blinded owl,
Give back to the man that you stole from his fowl:
For if you do not, 'twill be worse for your sowl,
                    Paddy O'Rafther."

Says Paddy, " I ask'd him to take it—'tis thrue
As this minit I'm talkin', your riv'rince, to you;
But he wouldn't resaive it—so what can I do ? "
    Says Paddy, nigh choken with laughter.
" By my throth," says the priest, " but the case is absthruse;
If he won't take his hen, why the man is a goose:
'Tis not the first time my advice was no use,
                    Paddy O'Rafther."

" But, for sake of your sowl, I would sthrongly advise
To some one in want you would give your supplies—
Some widow, or orphan, with tears in their eyes;
　　And *then* you may come to *me* afther."
So Paddy went off to the brisk Widow Hoy,
And the pullet between them was eaten with joy,
And, says she, " 'Pon my word you're the cleverest boy,
　　　　　　　　　　Paddy O'Rafther."

Then Paddy went back to the priest the next day,
And told him the fowl he had given away
To a poor lonely widow, in want and dismay,
　　The loss of her spouse weeping afther.
" Well, now," says the priest, " I'll absolve you, my lad,
For repentantly making the best of the bad,
In feeding the hungry and cheering the sad,
　　　　　　　　　　Paddy O'Rafther! "

Samuel Lover.

HERE SHE GOES, AND THERE SHE GOES

Two Yankee wags, one summer day,
Stopped at a tavern on their way,
Supped, frolicked, late retired to rest,
And woke to breakfast on the best.
The breakfast over, Tom and Will
Sent for the landlord and the bill;
Will looked it over:—" Very right—
But hold! what wonder meets my sight?
Tom, the surprise is quite a shock! "
" What wonder? where? "　" The clock, the clock! "

Tom and the landlord in amaze
Stared at the clock with stupid gaze,
And for a moment neither spoke;
At last the landlord silence broke,—

" You mean the clock that's ticking there?
I see no wonder, I declare!
Though maybe, if the truth were told,
'Tis rather ugly, somewhat old;
Yet time it keeps to half a minute;
But, if you please, what wonder's in it? "

" Tom, don't you recollect," said Will,
" The clock at Jersey, near the mill,
The very image of this p.esent,
With which I won the wager pleasant? "
Will ended with a knowing wink;
Tom scratched his head and tried to think.
" Sir, begging pardon for inquiring,"
The landlord said, with grin admiring,
" What wager was it? "

         " You remember
It happened, Tom, in last December:
In sport I bet a Jersey Blue
That it was more than he could do
To make his finger go and come
In keeping with the pendulum,
Repeating, till the hour should close,
Still,—' *Here she goes, and there she goes.*'
He lost the bet in half a minute."

" Well, if I would, the deuce is in it! "
Exclaimed the landlord; " try me yet,
And fifty dollars be the bet."
" Agreed, but we will play some trick,
To make you of the bargain sick! "
" I'm up to that! "

         " Don't make us wait,—
Begin,—the clock is striking eight."
He seats himself, and left and right
His finger wags with all its might,
And hoarse his voice and hoarser grows,
With—" *Here she goes, and there she goes!* "

" Hold!" said the Yankee, "Plank the ready!"
The landlord wagged his finger steady,
While his left hand, as well as able,
Conveyed a purse upon the table.
" Tom! with the money let's be off!"
This made the landlord only scoff.

He heard them running down the stair,
But was not tempted from his chair;
Thought he, " The fools! I'll bite them yet!
So poor a trick sha'n't win the bet."
And loud and long the chorus rose
Of—" *Here she goes, and there she goes!*"
While right and left his finger swung,
In keeping to his clock and tongue.

His mother happened in to see
Her daughter: " Where is Mrs. B——?"
" When will she come, do you suppose?
Son!"—
         " *Here she goes, and there she goes!*"
" Here!—where?"—the lady in surprise
His finger followed with her eyes:
" Son! why that steady gaze and sad?
Those words,—that motion,—are you mad?
But here's your wife, perhaps she knows,
And—"
         " *Here she goes, and there she goes!*"

His wife surveyed him with alarm,
And rushed to him, and seized his arm;
He shook her off, and to and fro
His finger persevered to go;
While curled his very nose with ire
That *she* against him should conspire;
And with more furious tone arose
The—" *Here she goes, and there she goes!*"

" Lawks!" screamed the wife, " I'm in a whirl!
Run down and bring the little girl;

She is his darling, and who knows
But—"
   " Here she goes, and there she goes!"

"Lawks! he is mad! What made him thus?
Good Lord! what will become of us?
Run for a doctor,—run, run, run,—
For Doctor Brown and Doctor Dun,
And Doctor Black and Doctor White,
And Doctor Gray, with all your might!"

The doctors came, and looked, and wondered,
And shook their heads, and paused and pondered.
Then one proposed he should be bled,—
"No, leeched you mean," the other said,
"Clap on a blister!" roared another,—
"No! cup him,"—"No, trepan him, brother."
A sixth would recommend a purge,
The next would an emetic urge;
The last produced a box of pills,
A certain cure for earthly ills:
"I had a patient yesternight,"
Quoth he, "and wretched was her plight,
And as the only means to save her,
Three dozen patent pills I gave her;
And by to-morrow I suppose
That—"
   "Here she goes, and there she goes!"

"You are all fools!" the lady said,—
"The way is just to shave his head.
Run! bid the barber come anon."
"Thanks, mother!" thought her clever son;
"You help the knaves that would have bit me,
But all creation sha'n't outwit me!"
Thus to himself while to and fro
His finger perseveres to go,
And from his lips no accent flows
But,—*"Here she goes, and there she goes!"*
The barber came—"Lord help him! what
A queerish customer I've got;

But we must do our best to save him,—
So hold him, gemmen, while I shave him!"
But here the doctors interpose,—
"A woman never—"

           "There she goes!"

"A woman is no judge of physic,
Not even when her baby is sick.
He must be bled,"—"No, cup him,"—"Pills!"
And all the house the uproar fills.

What means that smile? what means that shiver?
The landlord's limbs with rapture quiver,
And triumph brightens up his face,
His finger yet will win the race;
The clock is on the stroke of nine,
And up he starts,—"'Tis mine! 'tis mine!"
"What do you mean?"

        "I mean the fifty;
I never spent an hour so thrifty.
But you who tried to make me lose,
Go, burst with envy, if you choose!
But how is this? where are they?"

           "Who?"

"The gentlemen,—I mean the two
Came yesterday,—are they below?"
"They galloped off an hour ago."
"Oh, dose me! blister! shave and bleed!
For, hang the knaves, I'm mad indeed!"

          James Nack.

THE QUAKER'S MEETING

A TRAVELLER wended the wilds among,
With a purse of gold and a silver tongue;
His hat it was broad, and all drab were his clothes,
For he hated high colors—except on his nose,
And he met with a lady, the story goes.
    Heigho! *yea* thee and *nay* thee.

The damsel she cast him a merry blink,
And the traveller nothing was loth, I think,
Her merry black eye beamed her bonnet beneath,
And the Quaker, he grinned, for he'd very good teeth,
And he asked, " Art thee going to ride on the heath?"

" I hope you'll protect me, kind sir," said the maid,
" As to ride this heath over, I'm sadly afraid;
For robbers, they say, here in numbers abound,
And I wouldn't for anything I should be found,
For, between you and me, I have five hundred pound."

" If that is thee own, dear," the Quaker, he said,
" I ne'er saw a maiden I sooner would wed;
And I have another five hundred just now,
In the padding that's under my saddle-bow,
And I'll settle it all upon thee, I vow!"

The maiden she smil'd, and her rein she drew,
" Your offer I'll take, but I'll not take you,"
A pistol she held at the Quaker's head—
" Now give me your gold, or I'll give you my lead,
'Tis under the saddle, I think you said."

The damsel she ripped up the saddle-bow,
And the Quaker was never a quaker till now!
And he saw, by the fair one he wished for a bride,
His purse borne away with a swaggering stride,
And the eye that shamm'd tender, now only defied.

" The spirit doth move me, friend Broadbrim," quoth she,
" To take all this filthy temptation from thee,
For Mammon deceiveth, and beauty is fleeting,
Accept from thy maiden this right-loving greeting,
For much doth she profit by this Quaker's meeting!

" And hark! jolly Quaker, so rosy and sly,
Have righteousness, more than a wench, in thine eye;
Don't go again peeping girls' bonnets beneath,
Remember the one that you met on the heath,
Her name's Jimmy Barlow, I tell to your teeth."

"Friend James," quoth the Quaker, "pray listen to me,
For thou canst confer a great favor, d'ye see;
The gold thou hast taken is not mine, my friend,
But my master's; and truly on thee I depend,
To make it appear I my trust did defend.

"So fire a few shots thro' my clothes, here and there,
To make it appear 'twas a desp'rate affair."
So Jim he popp'd first through the skirt of his coat,
And then through his collar—quite close to his throat;
"Now one thro' my broadbrim," quoth Ephraim, "I vote."

"I have but a brace," said bold Jim, "and they're spent,
And I won't load again for a make-believe rent."—
"Then!"—said Ephraim, producing his pistols, "just give
My five hundred pounds back, or, as sure as you live,
I'll make of your body a riddle or sieve."

Jim Barlow was diddled—and, tho' he was game,
He saw Ephraim's pistol so deadly in aim,
That he gave up the gold, and he took to his scrapers,
And when the whole story got into the papers,
They said that "*the thieves were no match for the Quakers.*"
　　Heigho! *yea* thee and *nay* thee.

Samuel Lover.

THE JESTER CONDEMNED TO DEATH

One of the Kings of Scanderoon,
　　A royal jester
Had in his train, a gross buffoon,
　　Who used to pester
The court with tricks inopportune,
Venting on the highest folks his
Scurvy pleasantries and hoaxes.

It needs some sense to play the fool,
Which wholesome rule
  Occurred not to our jackanapes,
Who consequently found his freaks
  Lead to innumerable scrapes,
And quite as many tricks and tweaks,
    Which only seemed to make him faster
    Try the patience of his master.

Some sin, at last, beyond all measure
Incurred the desperate displeasure
  Of his Serene and raging Highness:
Whether he twitched his most revered
And sacred beard,
    Or had intruded on the shyness
    Of the seraglio, or let fly
    An epigram at royalty,
None knows: his sin was an occult one,
But records tell us that the Sultan,
Meaning to terrify the knave,
    Exclaimed, " 'Tis time to stop that breath;
Thy doom is sealed, presumptuous slave!
    Thou stand'st condemned to certain death:

" Silence, base rebel! no replying!
    But such is my indulgence still,
    That, of my own free grace and will,
I leave to thee the mode of dying."
" Thy royal will be done—'tis just,"
Replied the wretch, and kissed the dust.
    " Since my last moment to assuage,
Your majesty's humane decree
Has deigned to leave the choice to me,
    I'll die, so please you, of old age! "

Horace Smith.

THE DEACON'S MASTERPIECE;

OR, THE WONDERFUL "ONE-HOSS SHAY"

A Logical Story

Have you hèard of the wonderful one-hoss shay,
That was built in such a logical way,
It ran a hundred years to a day,
And then, of a sudden, it—ah, but stay,
I'll tell you what happened without delay,—
Scaring the parson into fits,
Frightening the people out of their wits—
Have you ever heard of that, I say?

Seventeen hundred and fifty-five,
Georgius Secundus was then alive—
Stuffy old drone from the German hive.
That was the year when Lisbon-town
Saw the earth open and gulp her down,
And Braddock's army was done so brown,
Left without a scalp to its crown.
It was on the terrible earthquake-day
That the Deacon finished his one-hoss shay.

Now in building of chaises, I'll tell you what,
There is always *somewhere* a weakest spot—
In hub, tire, or felloe, in spring or thill,
In panel, or crossbar, or floor, or sill,
In screw, bolt, thorough brace—lurking still,
Find it somewhere you must and will—
Above or below, or within or without—
And that's the reason, beyond a doubt,
A chaise *breaks down,* but doesn't *wear out.*

But the Deacon swore (as Deacons do,
With an "I dew vam" or an "I tell *yeou*"),
He would build one shay to beat the taown
'n' the keounty 'n' all the kentry raoun';
It should be so built that it *couldna'* break daown;

—" Fur," said the Deacon, " 't's mighty plain
That the weakes' place mus' stan' the strain;
'n' the way t' fix it, uz I maintain,
    Is only jest
T' make that place uz strong uz the rest."

So the deacon inquired of the village folk
Where he could find the strongest oak,
That couldn't be split nor bent nor broke—
That was for spokes and floor and sills;
He sent for lancewood to make the thills;
The cross-bars were ash, from the straightest trees;
The panels of white-wood, that cuts like cheese,
But lasts like iron for things like these;
The hubs of logs from the " Settler's ellum "—
Last of its timber—they couldn't sell 'em,

Never an axe had seen their chips,
And the wedges flew from between their lips;
Their blunt ends frizzled like celery-tips;
Step and prop-iron, bolt and screw,
Spring, tire, axle, and linch-pin too,
Steel of the finest, bright and blue;
Thorough-broke bison-skin, thick and wide;
Boot, top, dasher, from tough old hide
Found in the pit when the tanner died.
That was the way he " put her through "—
" There! " said the deacon, " naow she'll dew! "

Do! I tell you, I rather guess
She was a wonder, and nothing less.
Colts grew horses, beards turned gray,
Deacon and deaconess dropped away,
Children and grandchildren—where were they?
But there stood the stout old one-hoss shay
As fresh as on Lisbon earthquake-day!

Eighteen hundred;—it came and found
The deacon's masterpiece strong and sound.
Eighteen hundred increased by ten;—
" Hahnsum kerridge " they called it then.

Eighteen hundred and twenty came;—
Running as usual; much the same.
Thirty and forty at last arrive,
And then came fifty and FIFTY-FIVE.

Little of all we value here
Wakes on the morn of its hundredth year
Without both feeling and looking queer.
In fact, there's nothing that keeps its youth,
So far as I know but a tree and truth.
(That is a moral that runs at large;
Take it—you're welcome.—No extra charge.)

FIRST OF NOVEMBER—The Earthquake-day—
There are traces of age in the one-hoss shay,
A general flavour of mild decay,
But nothing local, as one may say.
There couldn't be—for the deacon's art
Had made it so like in every part
That there wasn't a chance for one to start.
For the wheels were just as strong as the thills,
And the floor was just as strong as the sills,
And the panels just as strong as the floor,
And the whippletree neither less nor more,
And the back-crossbar as strong as the fore,
And spring and axle and hub *encore*.
And yet, *as a whole* it is past a doubt
In another hour it will be *worn out!*

First of November, 'Fifty-five!
This morning the parson takes a drive.
Now, small boys, get out of the way!
Here comes the wonderful one-hoss shay,
Drawn by a rat-tailed, ewe-necked bay,
" Huddup! " said the parson.—Off went they.

The parson was working his Sunday's text—
Had got to *fifthly*, and stopped perplexed
At what the—Moses—was coming next.
All at once the horse stood still,
Close by the meet'n'-house on the hill.

—First a shiver, and then a thrill,
Then something decidedly like a spill—
And the parson was sitting upon a rock
At half-past nine by the meet'n'-house clock—
Just the hour of the earthquake shock!
—What do you think the parson found,
When he got up and stared around?
The poor old chaise in a heap or mound,
As if it had been to the mill and ground!
You see, of course, if you're not a dunce,
How it went to pieces all at once,—
All at once and nothing first—
Just as bubbles do when they burst.

End of the wonderful one-hoss shay.
Logic is logic. That's all I say.

Oliver Wendell Holmes.

THE BALLAD OF THE OYSTERMAN

It was a tall young oysterman lived by the river-side;
His shop was just upon the bank, his boat was on the tide.
The daughter of a fisherman, that was so straight and slim,
Lived over on the other bank, right opposite to him.

It was the pensive oysterman that saw a lovely maid,
Upon a moonlight evening, a-sitting in the shade;
He saw her wave her handkerchief, as much as if to say,
" I'm wide awake, young oysterman, and all the folks away."

Then up arose the oysterman, and to himself said he,
" I guess I'll leave the skiff at home, for fear that folks
        should see;
I read it in the story-book, that, for to kiss his dear,
Leander swam the Hellespont—and I will swim this here."

And he has leaped into the waves, and crossed the shining
        stream,
And he has clambered up the bank, all in the moonlight
        gleam;

O there were kisses sweet as dew, and words as soft as rain—
But they have heard her father's step, and in he leaps again!

Out spoke the ancient fisherman—" O what was that, my
    daughter? "
" 'Twas nothing but a pebble, sir, I threw into the water."
" And what is that, pray tell me, love, that paddles off so
    fast? "
" It's nothing but a porpoise, sir, that's been a-swimming
    past."

Out spoke the ancient fisherman—" Now bring me my har-
    poon!
I'll get into my fishing-boat, and fix the fellow soon."
Down fell that pretty innocent, as falls a snow-white lamb;
Her hair drooped round her pallid cheeks, like sea-weed on
    a clam.

Alas for those two loving ones! she waked not from her
    swound,
And he was taken with the cramp, and in the waves was
    drowned;
But Fate has metamorphosed them, in pity of their wo,
And now they keep an oyster-shop for mermaids down below.

Oliver Wendell Holmes.

THE WELL OF ST. KEYNE

A WELL there is in the west country,
    And a clearer one never was seen;
There is not a wife in the west country
    But has heard of the Well of St. Keyne.

An oak and an elm-tree stand beside,
    And behind doth an ash-tree grow,
And a willow from the bank above
    Droops to the water below.

A traveller came to the Well of St. Keyne,
    Joyfully he drew nigh,

For from cock-crow he had been travelling,
And there was not a cloud in the sky.

He drank of the water so cool and clear,
For thirsty and hot was he;
And he sat down upon the bank
Under the willow-tree.

There came a man from the house hard by
At the well to fill his pail;
On the well-side he rested it,
And he bade the stranger hail.

"Now art thou a bachelor, stranger?" quoth he,
"For an if thou hast a wife,
The happiest draught thou hast drank this day
That ever thou didst in thy life.

"Or hast thy good woman, if one thou hast,
Ever here in Cornwall been?
For an if she have, I'll venture my life
She has drank of the Well of St. Keyne."

"I have left a good woman who never was here,"
The stranger he made reply;
"But that my draught should be the better for that,
I pray you answer me why?"

"St. Keyne," quoth the Cornishman, "many a time
Drank of this crystal well,
And before the angels summon'd her,
She laid on the water a spell.

"If the husband of this gifted well
Shall drink before his wife,
A happy man thenceforth is he,
For he shall be master for life.

"But if the wife should drink of it first,
God help the husband then!"

The stranger stooped to the Well of St. Keyne,
And drank of the water again.

"You drank of the well, I warrant, betimes?"
He to the Cornishman said:
But the Cornishman smiled as the stranger spake,
And sheepishly shook his head.

"I hasten'd as soon as the wedding was done,
And left my wife in the porch;
But i' faith she had been wiser than me,
For she took a bottle to church."

Robert Southey.

THE JACKDAW OF RHEIMS

THE Jackdaw sat on the Cardinal's chair!
Bishop, and Abbot, and Prior were there;
　　Many a monk, and many a friar,
　　Many a knight and many a squire,
With a great many more of lesser degree—
In sooth, a goodly company;
And they served the Lord Primate on bended knee.
　　Never, I ween,
　　Was a prouder seen,
Read of in books, or dreamt of in dreams,
Than the Cardinal Lord Archbishop of Rheims!

　　In and out
　　Through the motley rout,
That little Jackdaw kept hopping about;
　　Here and there,
　　Like a dog in a fair,
　　Over comfits and cates,
　　And dishes and plates,
Cowl and cope, and rochet and pall,
Mitre and crosier, he hopped upon all!
　　With saucy air,
　　He perched on the chair
Where, in state, the great Lord Cardinal sat
In the great Lord Cardinal's great red hat;

And he peered in the face
Of his Lordship's grace,
With a satisfied look, as if he would say,
" We two are the greatest folks here to-day! "
And the priests, with awe,
As such freaks they saw,
Said, " The devil must be in that little Jackdaw! "

The feast was over, the board was cleared,
The flawns and the custards had all disappeared,
And six little singing-boys—dear little souls!
In nice clean faces, and nice white stoles,
Came, in order due,
Two by two,
Marching that grand refectory through!

A nice little boy held a golden ewer,
Embossed and filled with water, as pure
As any that flows between Rheims and Namur,
Which a nice little boy stood ready to catch
In a fine golden hand-basin made to match.
Two nice little boys, rather more grown,
Carried lavender-water and eau-de-Cologne;
And a nice little boy had a nice cake of soap,
Worthy of washing the hands of the Pope.
One little boy more
A napkin bore,
Of the best white diaper, fringed with pink,
And a cardinal's hat marked in " permanent ink."

The great Lord Cardinal turns at the sight
Of these nice little boys dressed all in white:
From his finger he draws
His costly turquoise,
And, not thinking at all about little Jackdaws,
Deposits it straight
By the side of his plate,
While the nice little boys on his Eminence wait;
Till, when nobody's dreaming of any such thing,
That little Jackdaw hops off with the ring!

There's a cry and a shout,
    And a deuce of a rout,
And nobody seems to know what they're about,
But the monks have their pockets all turned inside out;
    The friars are kneeling,
    And hunting and feeling
The carpet, the floor, and the walls, and the ceiling.
    The Cardinal drew
    Off each plum-coloured shoe,
And left his red stockings exposed to the view;
    He peeps and he feels,
    In the toes and the heels;
They turn up the dishes, they turn up the plates,
They take up the poker and poke out the grates,
    They turn up the rugs,
    They examine the mugs—
    But no! no such thing;
    They can't find THE RING!
And the Abbot declared that " when nobody twigged it,
Some rascal or other had popped in and prigged it."

The Cardinal rose with a dignified look,
He called for his candle, his bell, and his book!
    In holy anger and pious grief,
    He solemnly cursed that rascally thief!
    He cursed him at board, he cursed him in bed;
    From the sole of his foot to the crown of his head;
    He cursed him in sleeping, that every night
    He should dream of the devil, and wake in a fright;
    He cursed him in eating, he cursed him in drinking.
    He cursed him in coughing, in sneezing, in winking;
    He cursed him in sitting, in standing, in lying;
    He cursed him in walking, in riding, in flying;
    He cursed him in living, he cursed him in dying!—
Never was heard such a terrible curse!
    But, what gave rise
    To no little surprise,
Nobody seemed one penny the worse!

The day was gone,
The night came on,
The monks and the friars they searched till dawn;
When the Sacristan saw,
On crumpled claw,
Come limping a poor little lame Jackdaw;
No longer gay,
As on yesterday;
His feathers all seemed to be turned the wrong way;
His pinions drooped, he could hardly stand,
His head was as bald as the palm of your hand;
His eye so dim,
So wasted each limb,
That, heedless of grammar, they all cried " THAT's HIM!
That's the scamp that has done this scandalous thing!
That's the thief that has got my Lord Cardinal's ring!"

The poor little Jackdaw,
When the monks he saw,
Feebly gave vent to the ghost of a caw,
And turned his bald head, as much as to say,
" Pray be so good as to walk this way!"
Slower and slower
He limped on before,
Till they came to the back of the belfry door,
Where the first thing they saw,
Midst the sticks and the straw,
Was the RING in the nest of that little Jackdaw!

Then the great Lord Cardinal called for his book,
And off that terrible curse he took;
The mute expression
Served in lieu of confession,
And, being thus coupled with full restitution,
The Jackdaw got plenary absolution!
When these words were heard,
That poor little bird
Was so changed in a moment, 'twas really absurd;
He grew sleek and fat;
In addition to that,
A fresh crop of feathers came thick as a mat!

His tail waggled more
Even than before;
But no longer it wagged with an impudent air,
No longer he perched on the Cardinal's chair,
He hopped now about
With a gait devout;
At matins, at vespers, he never was out;
And, so far from any more pilfering deeds,
He always seemed telling the Confessor's beads.

If any one lied, or if any one swore,
Or slumbered in prayer-time and happened to snore,
That good Jackdaw
Would give a great "Caw!"
As much as to say, "Don't do so any more!"
While many remarked, as his manners they saw,
That they "never had known such a pious Jackdaw!"
He long lived the pride
Of that country side,
And at last in the odour of sanctity died;
When, as words were too faint
His merits to paint,
The Conclave determined to make him a Saint;
And on newly-made Saints and Popes, as you know,
It's the custom, at Rome, new names to bestow,
So they canonised him by the name of Jim Crow!

Richard Harris Barham.

THE KNIGHT AND THE LADY

The Lady Jane was tall and slim,
The Lady Jane was fair
And Sir Thomas, her lord, was stout of limb,
And his cough was short, and his eyes were dim,
And he wore green "specs" with a tortoise shell rim,
And his hat was remarkably broad in the brim,
And she was uncommonly fond of him—
And they were a loving pair!
And wherever they went, or wherever they came,
Every one hailed them with loudest acclaim;

Far and wide,
The people cried,
All sorts of pleasure, and no sort of pain,
To Sir Thomas the good, and the fair Lady Jane!

Now Sir Thomas the good, be it well understood,
Was a man of very contemplative mood—
He would pour by the hour, o'er a weed or a flower,
Or the slugs, that came crawling out after a shower;
Black beetles, bumble-bees, blue-bottle flies,
And moths, were of no small account in his eyes;
An "industrious flea," he'd by no means despise,
While an "old daddy long-legs," whose long legs and thighs
Passed the common in shape, or in color, or size,
He was wont to consider an absolute prize.
Giving up, in short, both business and sport, he
Abandoned himself, *tout entier,* to philosophy.

Now as Lady Jane was tall and slim,
And Lady Jane was fair.
And a good many years the junior of him,
There are some might be found entertaining a notion,
That such an entire, and exclusive devotion,
To that part of science, folks style entomology,
Was a positive shame,
And, to such a fair dame,
Really demanded some sort of apology;
Ever poking his nose into this, and to that—
At a gnat, or a bat, or a cat, or a rat,
At great ugly things, all legs and wings,
With nasty long tails, armed with nasty long stings
And eternally thinking, and blinking, and winking,
At grubs—when he ought of *her* to be thinking.
But no! ah no! 'twas by no means so
With the fair Lady Jane,
Tout au contraire, no lady so fair,
Was e'er known to wear more contented an air;
And—let who would call—every day she was there
Propounding receipts for some delicate fare,
Some toothsome conserve, of quince, apple or pear
Or distilling strong waters—or potting a hare--

Or counting her spoons, and her crockery ware;
Enough to make less gifted visitors stare.

Nay more; don't suppose
With such doings as those
This account of her merits must come to a close;
No!—examine her conduct more closely, you'll find
She by no means neglected improving her mind;
For there all the while, with an air quite bewitching
She sat herring-boning, tambouring, or stitching,
Or having an eye to affairs of the kitchen.
Close by her side,
Sat her kinsman, MacBride—
Captain Dugald MacBride, Royal Scots Fusiliers;—
And I doubt if you'd find, in the whole of his clan,
A more highly intelligent, worthy young man;
And there he'd be sitting,
While she was a-knitting,
Reading aloud, with a very grave look,
Some very " wise saw," from some very good book—
No matter who came,
It was always the same,
The Captain was reading aloud to the dame,
Till, from having gone through half the books on the shelf,
They were *almost* as wise as Sir Thomas himself.

Well it happened one day—
I really can't say
The particular month;—but I *think* 'twas in May,
'Twas I *know* in the spring-time, when " nature looks gay,"
As the poet observes—and on tree-top and spray,
The dear little dickey birds carol away,
That the whole of the house was thrown into affright,
For no soul could conceive what was gone with the Knight.

It seems he had taken
A light breakfast—bacon,
An egg, a little broiled haddock—at most
A round and a half of some hot buttered toast,
With a slice of cold sirloin from yesterday's roast.

And then, let me see,—
He had two,—perhaps three
ups, with sugar and cream, of strong gunpowder tea,—
But no matter for that—
He had called for his hat,
'ith the brim that I've said was so broad and so flat,
nd his "specs" with the tortoise-shell rim, and his cane.
'ith the crutch-handled top, which he used to sustain
is steps in his walk, or to poke in the shrubs
r the grass, when unearthing his worms or his grubs;
hus armed he set out on a ramble—a-lack!
e *set out,* poor dear soul!—but he never came back!
    "First dinner bell" rang
    Out its euphonous clang
t five—folks kept early hours then—and the "last"
ing-donged, as it ever was wont, at half-past.
ill the master was absent—the cook came and said, he
eared dinner would spoil, having been so long ready,
hat the puddings her ladyship thought such a treat
Ie was morally sure, would be scarce fit to eat!
aid the lady, "Dish up! Let the meal be served straight,
nd let two or three slices be put on a plate,
nd kept hot for Sir Thomas."—Captain Dugald said grace,
hen set himself down in Sir Thomas' place.

Vearily, wearily, all that night,
    That live-long night did the hours go by;
        And the Lady Jane,
        In grief and pain,
    She sat herself down to cry!
        And Captain MacBride,
        Who sat by her side,
hough I really can't say that he actually cried,
    At least had a tear in his eye!
s much as can well be expected, perhaps,
rom "very young fellows," for very "old chaps."
        And if he had said
        What he'd got in his head,
Twould have been, "Poor old Duffer, he's certainly dead!"

The morning dawned—and the next—and the next
And all in the mansion were still perplexed;
    No knocker fell,
    His approach to tell;
Not so much as a runaway ring at the bell.

Yet the sun shone bright upon tower and tree,
And the meads smiled green as green may be,
And the dear little dickey birds caroled with glee,
And the lambs in the park skipped merry and free.—
Without, all was joy and harmony!

And thus 'twill be—nor long the day—
Ere we, like him, shall pass away!
Yon sun that now our bosoms warms,
Shall shine—but shine on other forms;
Yon grove, whose choir so sweetly cheers
Us now, shall sound on other ears;
The joyous lambs, as now, shall play,
But other eyes its sports survey;
The stream we loved shall roll as fair,
The flowery sweets, the trim parterre,
Shall scent, as now, the ambient air;
The tree whose bending branches bear
The one loved name—shall yet be there—
But where the hand that carved it? Where?

        These were hinted to me as the very ideas
Which passed through the mind of the fair Lady Jane,
As she walked on the esplanade to and again,
    With Captain MacBride,
    Of course at her side,
Who could not look *quite* so forlorn—though he tried,
An " idea " in fact, had got into *his* head,
That if " poor dear Sir Thomas " should really be dead,
It might be no bad " spec " to be there in his stead,
And by simply contriving, in due time, to wed
    A lady who was young and fair,
    A lady slim and tall,
To set himself down in comfort there,
    The lord of Tapton Hall.

Thinks he, " We have sent
Half over Kent,
nd nobody knows how much money's been spent,
et no one's been found to say which way he went!
ere's a fortnight and more has gone by, and we've tried
very plan we could hit on—and had him well cried

  ' MISSING!! *Stolen or Strayed,*
   Lost or Mislaid,
 GENTLEMAN;—middle-aged, sober and staid;
toops slightly;—and when he left home was arrayed
 a sad-colored suit, somewhat dingy and frayed;
 ad spectacles on with a tortoise-shell rim,
nd a hat rather low crowned, and broad in the brim.

  Whoe'er shall bear,
  Or send him with care,
Right side uppermost) home; or shall give notice where
aid middle-aged GENTLEMAN is; or shall state
ny fact, that may tend to throw light on his fate,
o the man at the turnpike, called *Tappington Gate,*
hall receive a reward of *Five Pounds* for his trouble.
.B. If defunct, the *Reward* will be double!! '

  " Had he been above ground,
  He *must* have been found.
o; doubtless he's shot—or he's hanged—or he's drowned!
  Then his widow—ay! ay!
  But what will folks say?—
o address her at once, at so early a day.
ell—what then—who cares!—let 'em say what they may."

  When a man has decided
  As Captain MacBride did,
nd once fully made up his mind on the matter, he
an't be too prompt in unmasking his battery.
Ie began on the instant, and vowed that her eyes
ar exceeded in brilliance the stars in the skies;
hat her lips were like roses, her cheeks were like lilies;
Ier breath had the odor of daffadowndillies!—
ith a thousand more compliments, equally true,
xpressed in similitudes equally new!

  Then his left arm he placed
  Round her jimp, taper waist—

Ere she fixed to repulse or return his embrace,
Up came running a man at a deuce of a pace,
With that very peculiar expression of face
Which always betokens dismay or disaster,
Crying out—'twas the gard'ner—" Oh, ma'am! we've foun
   master!! "
" Where! where? " screamed the lady; and echo screamed
   " Where? "
      The man couldn't say " there! "
      He had no breath to spare,
But gasping for breath he could only respond
By pointing—he pointed, alas! TO THE POND.
'Twas e'en so; poor dear Knight, with his " specs " and h
   hat,
He'd gone poking his nose into this and to that;
When close to the side of the bank, he espied
An uncommon fine tadpole, remarkably fat!
     He stooped;—and he thought her
     His own;—he had caught her!
Got hold of her tail—and to land almost brought her,
When—he plumped head and heels into fifteen feet water

   The Lady Jane was tall and slim,
      The Lady Jane was fair,
Alas! for Sir Thomas!—she grieved for him,
As she saw two serving men sturdy of limb,
      His body between them bear;
She sobbed and she sighed, she lamented and cried,
   For of sorrow brimful was her cup;
She swooned, and I think she'd have fallen down and died
     If Captain MacBride
     Hadn't been by her side
With the gardener;—they both their assistance supplied,
   And managed to hold her up.
     But when she " comes to,"
     Oh! 'tis shocking to view
   The sight which the corpse reveals!
     Sir Thomas' body,
     It looked so odd—he
   Was half eaten up by the eels!

His waistcoat and hose,
And the rest of his clothes,
ere all gnawed through and through;
And out of each shoe,
An eel they drew;
nd from each of his pockets they pulled out two!
nd the gardener himself had secreted a few,
As well might be supposed he'd do,
or, when he came running to give the alarm,
e had six in the basket that hung on his arm.

ood Father John was summoned anon;
oly water was sprinkled and little bells tinkled,
And tapers were lighted,
And incense ignited,
nd masses were sung, and masses were said,
ll day, for the quiet repose of the dead,
nd all night no one thought about going to bed.

ut Lady Jane was tall and slim,
And Lady Jane was fair,
nd ere morning came, that winsome dame
ad made up her mind, or—what's much the same—
ad *thought about,* once more " changing her name,"
And she said with a pensive air,
'o Thompson the valet, while taking away,
Vhen supper was over, the cloth and the tray,
Eels a many I've ate; but any
So good ne'er tasted before!—
hey're a fish too, of which I'm remarkably fond—
o—pop Sir Thomas again in the pond—
Poor dear!—*he'll catch us some more.*"

MORAL

ll middle-aged gentlemen let me advise,
f you're married, and hav'n't got very good eyes,
on't go poking about after blue-bottle flies.
f you've spectacles, don't have a tortoise-shell rim,
nd don't go near the water—unless you can swim.

Married ladies, especially such as are fair,
Tall and slim, I would next recommend to beware,
How, on losing one spouse, they give way to despair,
But let them reflect, there are fish, and no doubt on't,
As good *in* the river, as ever came *out* on't.

Richard Harris Barham.

AN EASTERN QUESTION

My William was a soldier, and he says to me, says he,
" My Susan, I must sail across the South Pacific sea;
For we've got to go to Egypt for to fight the old Khedive
But when he's dead I'll marry you, as sure as I'm alive! "

'Twere hard for me to part with him; he couldn't read no
     write,
So I never had love letters for to keep my memory bright;
But Jim, who is our footman, took the *Daily Telegraph,*
And told me William's reg-i-ment mowed down the foe lik
     chaff.

So every day Jim come to me to read the Eastern news,
And used to bring me bouquets, which I scarcely coul
     refuse;
Till one fine day it happened—*how* it happened, goodnes
     knows,—
He put his arm around me and he started to propose.

I put his hand from off me, and I said in thrilling tones,
" I like you, Jim, but *never* will I give up William Jones;
It ain't no good your talking, for my heart is firm and fixed
For William is engaged to me, and naught shall come be-
     twixt."

So Jim he turned a ghastly pale to find there was no hope;
And made remarks about a pond, and razors, and a rope;
The other servants pitied him, and Rosie said as much;
But Rosie was too flighty, and he didn't care for such.

he weeks and months passed slowly, till I heard the Eastern war
'as over, and my William would soon be home once more;
nd I was proud and happy for I knew that I could say
d been true to my sweet William all the years he'd been away.

ays Jim to me, " I love you, Sue, you know full well I do,
nd evermore whilst I draw breath I vow I will be true;
ut my feelings are too sensitive, I really couldn't stand
-seeing of that soldier taking hold your little hand.

So I've made my mind up finally to throw myself away;
here's Rosie loves me truly, and no more I'll say her nay;
ve bought a hat on purpose, and I'm going to hire a ring,
nd I've borrowed father's wedding suit that looks the very thing."

o Jim he married Rosie, just the very day before
Iy William's reg-i-ment was due to reach their native shore;
was there to see him landed and to give him welcome home,
And take him to my arms from which he never more should roam.

But I couldn't see my William, for the men were all alike,
With their red coats and their rifles, and their helmets with a spike;
So I curtseys to a sergeant who was smiling very kind,
"Where's William Jones?" I asks him, "if so be you wouldn't mind?"

Then he calls a gawky, red-haired chap, that stood good six-feet two:
" Here, Jones," he cries, "this lady here's enquiring after you."
"Not me!" I says, "I want a man who 'listed from our Square;
With a small moustache, but growing fast, and bright brown curly hair."

The sergeant wiped his eye, and took his helmet from **|**
    head,
" I'm very sorry, ma'am," he said, " *that* William Jones
    dead;
He died from getting sunstroke, and we envied him his l**|**
For we were melted to our bones, the climate was that hot

So that's how 'tis that I'm condemned to lead a single life,
For the sergeant, who was struck with me, already had a wif**|**
And Jim is tied to Rosie, and can't get himself untied,
Whilst the man that I was faithful to has been and go**|**
    and died!

H. M. Paull.

MY AUNT'S SPECTRE

They tell me (but I really can't
    Imagine such a rum thing),
It is the phantom of my Aunt,
    Who ran away—or something.

It is the very worst of bores:
    (My Aunt was most delightful).
It prowls about the corridors,
    And utters noises frightful.

At midnight through the rooms It glides,
    Behaving very coolly,
Our hearts all throb against our sides—
    The lights are burning bluely.

The lady, in her living hours,
    Was the most charming vixen
That ever this poor sex of ours
    Delighted to play tricks on.

Yes, that's her portrait on the wall,
    In quaint old-fangled bodice:
Her eyes are blue—her waist is small—
    A ghost! Pooh, pooh,—a goddess!

A fine patrician shape, to suit
    My dear old father's sister—
Lips softly curved, a dainty foot:
    Happy the man that kissed her!

Light hair of crisp irregular curl
    Over fair shoulders scattered—
Egad, she was a pretty girl,
    Unless Sir Thomas flattered!

And who the deuce, in these bright days,
    Could possibly expect her
To take to dissipated ways,
    And plague us as a spectre?

Mortimer Collins.

CASEY AT THE BAT

It looked extremely rocky for the Mudville nine that day,
The score stood four to six with but an inning left to play.
And so, when Cooney died at first, and Burrows did the
        same,
A pallor wreathed the features of the patrons of the game.
A straggling few got up to go, leaving there the rest,
With that hope which springs eternal within the human
        breast.
For they thought if only Casey could get a whack at that,
They'd put up even money with Casey at the bat.
But Flynn preceded Casey, and likewise so did Blake,
And the former was a pudding and the latter was a fake;
So on that stricken multitude a death-like silence sat,
For there seemed but little chance of Casey's getting to the
        bat.
But Flynn let drive a single to the wonderment of all,
And the much despisèd Blakey tore the cover off the ball,
And when the dust had lifted and they saw what had
        occurred,
There was Blakey safe on second, and Flynn a-hugging
        third.

Then from the gladdened multitude went up a joyous yell,
It bounded from the mountain top and rattled in the dell,
It struck upon the hillside, and rebounded on the flat,
For Casey, mighty Casey, was advancing to the bat.

There was ease in Casey's manner as he stepped into his
    place,
There was pride in Casey's bearing and a smile on Casey's
    face,
And when responding to the cheers he lightly doffed his hat,
No stranger in the crowd could doubt, 'twas Casey at the
    bat.

Ten thousand eyes were on him as he rubbed his hands with
    dirt,
Five thousand tongues applauded as he wiped them on his
    shirt;
And while the writhing pitcher ground the ball into his
    hip—
Defiance gleamed from Casey's eye—a sneer curled Casey's
    lip.

And now the leather-covered sphere came hurtling through
    the air,
And Casey stood a-watching it in haughty grandeur there;
Close by the sturdy batsman the ball unheeded sped—
"That hain't my style," said Casey—"Strike one," the Um-
    pire said.

From the bleachers black with people there rose a sullen roar,
Like the beating of the storm waves on a stern and distant
    shore,
"Kill him! kill the Umpire!" shouted some one from the
    stand—
And it's likely they'd have done it had not Casey raised his
    hand.

With a smile of Christian charity great Casey's visage shone,
He stilled the rising tumult and he bade the game go on;
He signalled to the pitcher and again the spheroid flew,
But Casey still ignored it and the Umpire said "Strike
    two."

"Fraud!" yelled the maddened thousands, and the echo an-
    swered "Fraud."
But one scornful look from Casey and the audience was
    awed;

They saw his face grow stern and cold; they saw his muscles
strain,
And they knew that Casey would not let that ball go by
again.
The sneer is gone from Casey's lip; his teeth are clenched
with hate,
He pounds with cruel violence his bat upon the plate;
And now the pitcher holds the ball, and now he lets it go,
And now the air is shattered by the force of Casey's blow.
Oh! somewhere in this favored land the sun is shining
bright,
The band is playing somewhere, and somewhere hearts are
light,
And somewhere men are laughing, and somewhere children
shout;
But there is no joy in Mudville—mighty Casey has " Struck
Out."

Ernest Lawrence Thayer.

THE PIED PIPER OF HAMELIN

HAMELIN Town's in Brunswick,
By famous Hanover City;
  The river Weser, deep and wide,
  Washes its wall on the southern side;
  A pleasanter spot you never spied;
But, when begins my ditty,
  Almost five hundred years ago,
  To see the townsfolk suffer so
    From vermin was a pity.

  Rats!
They fought the dogs, and killed the cats,
  And bit the babies in the cradles,
And ate the cheeses out of the vats,
  And licked the soup from the cook's own ladles,
  Split open the kegs of salted sprats,
  Made nests inside men's Sunday hats,
  And even spoiled the women's chats,

By drowning their speaking
With shrieking and squeaking
In fifty different sharps and flats.

At last the people in a body
    To the Town Hall came flocking:
" Tis clear," cried they, " our Mayor's a noddy;
    And as for our Corporation—shocking
To think we buy gowns lined with ermine
For dolts that can't or won't determine
What's best to rid us of our vermin!
You hope, because you're old and obese,
To find in the furry civic robe ease?
Rouse up, Sirs! Give your brains a racking
To find the remedy we're lacking,
Or, sure as fate, we'll send you packing! "
At this the Mayor and Corporation
Quaked with a mighty consternation.

An hour they sate in council,
    At length the Mayor broke silence:
" For a guilder I'd my ermine gown sell!
    I wish I were a mile hence!
It's easy to bid one rack one's brain—
I'm sure my poor head aches again
I've scratched it so, and all in vain.
Oh, for a trap, a trap, a trap! "

Just as he said this, what should hap
At the chamber door but a gentle tap?
" Bless us," cried the Mayor, " what's that? "
(With the Corporation as he sat,
Looking little though wondrous fat;
Nor brighter was his eye, nor moister,
Than a too-long-opened oyster,
Save when at noon his paunch grew mutinous
For a plate of turtle green and glutinous),
" Only a scraping of shoes on the mat?
Anything like the sound of a rat
Makes my heart go pit-a-pat! "

" Come in ! "—the Mayor cried, looking bigger:
And in did come the strangest figure.
His queer long coat from heel to head
Was half of yellow and half of red;
And he himself was tall and thin,
With sharp blue eyes, each like a pin,
And light loose hair, yet swarthy skin,
No tuft on cheek nor beard on chin,
But lips where smiles went out and in;
There was no guessing his kith and kin:
And nobody could enough admire
The tall man and his quaint attire.
Quoth one: " It's as my great grandsire,
Starting up at the Trump of Doom's tone,
Had walked this way from his painted tombstone! "

He advanced to the council-table;
And, " Please your honours," said he, " I'm able,
By means of a secret charm, to draw
All creatures living beneath the sun,
That creep or swim or fly or run,
After me so as you never saw!
And I chiefly use my charm
On creatures that do people harm,
The mole and toad and newt and viper;
And people call me the Pied Piper."
(And here they noticed round his neck
A scarf of red and yellow stripe,
To match with his coat of the selfsame cheque;
And at the scarf's end hung a pipe;
And his fingers, they noticed, were ever straying
As if impatient to be playing
Upon this pipe, as low it dangled
Over his vesture so old-fangled.)
" Yet," said he, " poor piper as I am,
In Tartary I freed the Cham,
Last June, from his huge swarms of gnats;
I eased in Asia the Nizam
Of a monstrous brood of vampyre bats:
And as for what your brain bewilders,
If I can rid your town of rats,

Will you give me a thousand guilders?"
"One? fifty thousand!" was the exclamation
Of the astonished Mayor and Corporation.

Into the street the Piper stept,
    Smiling first a little smile,
As if he knew what magic slept
    In his quiet pipe the while;
Then, like a musical adept,
To blow the pipe his lips he wrinkled,
And green and blue his sharp eyes twinkled
Like a candle flame where salt is sprinkled;
And ere three shrill notes the pipe uttered,
You heard as if an army muttered;
And the muttering grew to a grumbling;
And the grumbling grew to a mighty rumbling;
And out of the house the rats came tumbling.
Great rats, small rats, lean rats, brawny rats,
Brown rats, black rats, grey rats, tawny rats,
Grave old plodders, gay young friskers,
    Fathers, mothers, uncles, cousins,
Cocking tails and pricking whiskers,
    Families by tens and dozens,
Brothers, sisters, husbands, wives—
Followed the Piper for their lives.
From street to street he piped advancing,
And step by step they followed dancing,
Until they came to the river Weser
Wherein all plunged and perished
—Save one, who, stout as Julius Cæsar,
Swam across and lived to carry
(As he the manuscript he cherished)
To Rat-land home his commentary,
Which was, " At the first shrill notes of the pipe,
I heard a sound as of scraping tripe,
And putting apples wondrous ripe,
Into a cider-press's gripe:
And a moving away of pickle-tub boards.
And a leaving ajar of conserve cupboards,
And a drawing the corks of train-oil-flasks.
And a breaking the hoops of butter-casks:

And it seemed as if a voice
(Sweeter far than by harp or by psaltery
Is breathed) called out, Oh rats, rejoice!
The world is grown to one vast drysaltery!
So munch on, crunch on, take your nuncheon,
Breakfast, supper, dinner, luncheon!
And just as a bulky sugar puncheon,
All ready staved, like a great sun shone
Glorious scarce an inch before me,
Just as methought it said, Come, bore me!
—I found the Weser rolling o'er me."

You should have heard the Hamelin people
Ringing the bells till they rocked the steeple.
" Go," cried the Mayor, " and get long poles!
Poke out the nests and block up the holes!
Consult with carpenters and builders,
And leave in our town not even a trace
Of the rats! "—when suddenly, up the face
Of the piper perked in the market-place,
With a " First, if you please, my thousand guilders! "

A thousand guilders! The Mayor looked blue;
So did the Corporation too.
For council dinners made rare havock
With Claret, Moselle, Vin-de-Grave, Hock;
And half the money would replenish
Their cellar's biggest butt with Rhenish.
To pay this sum to a wandering fellow
With a gipsy coat of red and yellow!
" Beside," quoth the Mayor with a knowing wink,
" Our business was done at the river's brink;
We saw with our eyes the vermin sink,
And what's dead can't come to life, I think.
So, friend, we're not the folks to shrink
From the duty of giving you something to drink,
And a matter of money to put in your poke;
But as for the guilders, what we spoke
Of them, as you very well know, was in joke;
Beside, our losses have made us thrifty:
A thousand guilders! Come, take fifty! "

The Piper's face fell, and he cried,
"No trifling! I can't wait, beside!
I've promised to visit by dinner time
Bagdad, and accept the prime
Of the Head Cook's pottage, all he's rich in,
For having left in the Caliph's kitchen,
Of a nest of scorpions no survivor:
With him I proved no bargain-driver,
With you, don't think I'll bate a stiver!
And folks who put me in a passion
May find me pipe after another fashion."

"How?" cried the Mayor, "d'ye think I'll brook
Being worse treated than a Cook?
Insulted by a lazy ribald
With idle pipe and vesture piebald?
You threaten us, fellow? Do your worst,
Blow your pipe there till you burst!"

Once more he stept into the street;
And to his lips again
Laid his long pipe of smooth straight cane;
And ere he blew three notes (such sweet
Soft notes as yet musician's cunning
    Never gave the enraptured air),
There was a rustling, that seemed like a bustling
Of merry crowds justling at pitching and hustling,
Small feet were pattering, wooden shoes clattering,
Little hands clapping and little tongues chattering,
And, like fowls in a farmyard when barley is scattering,
Out came the children running.
All the little boys and girls,
With rosy cheeks and flaxen curls
And sparkling eyes and teeth like pearls,
Tripping and skipping, ran merrily after
The wonderful music with shouting and laughter.

The Mayor was dumb, and the Council stood
As if they were changed into blocks of wood,
Unable to move a step, or cry
To the children merrily skipping by,
And could only follow with the eye

That joyous crowd at the Piper's back.
But how the Mayor was on the rack,
And the wretched Council's bosoms beat,
As the Piper turned from the High Street
To where the Weser rolled its waters
Right in the way of their sons and daughters!
However he turned from South to West,
And to Koppelberg Hill his steps addressed,
And after him the children pressed;
Great was the joy in every breast.
" He never can cross that mighty top!
  He's forced to let the piping drop,
And we shall see our children stop! "
When, lo, as they reached the mountain's side,
A wondrous portal opened wide,
As if a cavern were suddenly hollowed;
And the Piper advanced and the children followed,
And when all were in to the very last,
The door in the mountain-side shut fast.
Did I say—all? No! one was lame,
And could not dance the whole of the way;
And in after years, if you would blame
His sadness, he was used to say,—
" It's dull in our town since my playmates left;
I can't forget that I'm bereft
Of all the pleasant sights they see,
Which the Piper also promised me;
For he led us, he said, to a joyous land,
Joining the town and just at hand,
Where waters gushed and fruit-trees grew,
And flowers put forth a fairer hue,
And everything was strange and new;
The sparrows were brighter than peacocks here,
And their dogs outran our fallow deer,
And honey-bees had lost their stings;
And horses were born with eagle's wings;
And just as I became assured
My lame foot would be speedily cured,
The music stopped, and I stood still,
And found myself outside the Hill,
Left alone against my will,

To go now limping as before,
And never hear of that country more!"

Alas, alas, for Hamelin!
  There came into many a burgher's pate
  A text which says, that Heaven's Gate
  Opes to the Rich at as easy rate
As the needle's eye takes a camel in!
The Mayor sent East, West, North, and South,
To offer the Piper by word of mouth,
  Wherever it was men's lot to find him,
Silver and gold to his heart's content,
If he'd only return the way he went,
  And bring the children all behind him.
But when they saw 'twas a lost endeavour,
And Piper and dancers were gone for ever,
They made a decree that lawyers never
  Should think their records dated duly
If, after the day of the month and year,
These words did not as well appear,
  " And so long after what happened here
  On the twenty-second of July,
Thirteen hundred and seventy-six:"
And the better in memory to fix
The place of the Children's last retreat,
They called it the Pied Piper's Street—
Where any one playing on pipe or tabor
Was sure for the future to lose his labour.
Nor suffered they hostelry or tavern
  To shock with mirth a street so solemn;
But opposite the place of the cavern
  They wrote the story on a column,
And on the great Church Window painted
The same, to make the world acquainted
How their children were stolen away,
And there it stands to this very day.
And I must not omit to say
That in Transylvania there's a tribe
Of alien people that ascribe
The outlandish ways and dress,
On which their neighbours lay such stress,

To their fathers and mothers having risen
Out of some subterraneous prison,
Into which they were trepanned
Long time ago in a mighty band
Out of Hamelin town in Brunswick Land,
But how or why, they don't understand.

So, Willy, let me and you be wipers
Of scores out with all men—especially pipers;
And, whether they pipe us free from rats or from mice,
If we've promised them aught, let us keep our promise.

Robert Browning.

THE GOOSE

I KNEW an old wife lean and poor,
    Her rags scarce held together;
There strode a stranger to the door,
    And it was windy weather.

He held a goose upon his arm,
    He utter'd rhyme and reason,
" Here, take the goose, and keep you warm,
    It is a stormy season."

She caught the white goose by the leg,
    A goose—'twas no great matter.
The goose let fall a golden egg
    With cackle and with clatter.

She dropt the goose, and caught the pelf,
    And ran to tell her neighbours;
And bless'd herself, and cursed herself,
    And rested from her labours.

And feeding high, and living soft,
    Grew plump and able-bodied;
Until the grave churchwarden doff'd,
    The parson smirk'd and nodded.

So sitting, served by man and maid,
   She felt her heart grow prouder:
But, ah! the more the white goose laid
   It clack'd and cackled louder.

It clutter'd here, it chuckled there;
   It stirr'd the old wife's mettle:
She shifted in her elbow-chair,
   And hurl'd the pan and kettle.

" A quinsy choke thy cursed note! "
   Then wax'd her anger stronger.
" Go, take the goose, and wring her throat,
   I will not bear it longer."

Then yelp'd the cur, and yawl'd the cat;
   Ran Gaffer, stumbled Gammer.
The goose flew this way and flew that,
   And fill'd the house with clamour.

As head and heels upon the floor
   They flounder'd all together,
There strode a stranger to the door,
   And it was windy weather:

He took the goose upon his arm,
   He utter'd words of scorning;
" So keep you cold, or keep you warm,
   It is a stormy morning."

The wild wind rang from park and plain,
   And round the attics rumbled,
Till all the tables danced again,
   And half the chimneys tumbled.

The glass blew in, the fire blew out,
   The blast was hard and harder.
Her cap blew off, her gown blew up,
   And a whirlwind clear'd the larder:

And while on all sides breaking loose
   Her household fled the danger,
Quoth she, " The Devil take the goose,
   And God forget the stranger! "

Lord Tennyson.

THE BALLAD OF CHARITY

It was in a pleasant deepô, sequestered from the rain,
That many weary passengers were waitin' for the train;
Piles of quite expensive baggage, many a gorgeous portmantó,
Ivory-handled umberellas made a most touristic show.

Whereunto there came a person, very humble was his mien,
Who took an observation of the interestin' scene;
Closely scanned the umberellas, watched with joy the mighty
   trunks,
And observed that all the people were securin' Pullman
   bunks:

Who was followed shortly after by a most unhappy tramp,
Upon whose features poverty had jounced her iron stamp;
And to make a clear impression as bees sting you while they
   buzz,
She had hit him rather harder than she generally does.

For he was so awful ragged, and in parts so awful bare,
That the folks were quite repulsioned to behold him begging
   there;
And instead of drawing currency from out their pocket-books,
They drew themselves asunder with aversionary looks.

Sternly gazed the first newcomer on the unindulgent crowd,
Then in tones which pierced the deepô he solilicussed
   aloud:—
" I hev trevelled o'er this cont'nent from Quebec to Bogotáw,
But sech a set of scallawags as these I never saw.

" Ye are wealthy, ye are gifted, ye have house and lands and
   rent,
Yet unto a suff'rin' mortal ye will not donate a cent;

Ye expend your missionaries to the heathen and the Jew,
But there isn't any heathen that is half as small as you.

"Ye are lucky—ye hev cheque-books and deeposits in the
    bank,
And ye squanderate your money on the titled folks of rank;
The onyx and the sardonyx upon your garments shine,
An' ye drink at every dinner p'r'aps a dollar's wuth of wine.

"Ye are goin' for the summer to the islands by the sea,
Where it costs four dollars daily—setch is not for setch as
    me;
Iv'ry-handled umberellas do not come into my plan,
But I kin give a dollar to this suff'rin' fellow-man.

"Hand-bags made of Rooshy leather are not truly at my
    call,
Yet in the eyes of Mussy I am richer 'en you all,
For I kin give a dollar wher' you dare not stand a dime,
And never miss it nother, nor regret it ary time."

Sayin' this he drew a wallet from the inner of his vest,
And gave the tramp a daddy, which it was his level best;
Other people havin' heard him soon to charity inclined—
One giver soon makes twenty if you only get their wind.

The first who gave the dollar led the other one about,
And at every contribution he a-raised a joyful shout,
Exclaimin' how 'twas noble to relieviate distress,
And remarkin' that our duty is our present happiness.

Thirty dollars altogether were collected by the tramp,
When he bid 'em all good evenin' and went out into the
    damp,
And was followed briefly after by the one who made the
    speech,
And who showed by good example how to practise as to
    preach.

Which soon around the corner the couple quickly met,
And the tramp produced the specie for to liquidate his debt;

And the man who did the preachin' took his twenty of the
    sum,
Which you see that out of thirty left a tenner for the bum.

And the couple passed the summer at Bar Harbor with the
    rest,
Greatly changed in their appearance and most elegently
    dressed.
Any fowl with change of feathers may a brilliant bird be-
    come:
Oh, how hard is life for many! oh, how sweet it is for
    some!

Charles Godfrey Leland.

THE POST CAPTAIN

When they heard the Captain humming and beheld the
    dancing crew,
On the " Royal Biddy " frigate was Sir Peter Bombazoo;
His mind was full of music and his head was full of tunes,
And he cheerfully exhibited on pleasant afternoons.

He could whistle, on his fingers, an invigorating reel,
And could imitate a piper on the handles of the wheel;
He could play in double octaves, too, all up and down the
    rail,
Or rattle off a rondo on the bottom of a pail.

Then porters with their packages and bakers with their buns,
And countesses in carriages and grenadiers with guns,
And admirals and commodores arrived from near and far,
To listen to the music of this entertaining tar.

When they heard the Captain humming and beheld the
    dancing crew,
The commodores severely said, "Why, this will never do!"
And the admirals all hurried home, remarking, "This is
    most
Extraordinary conduct for a captain at his post."

Then they sent some sailing-orders to Sir Peter, in a boat,
And he did a little fifing on the edges of the note;
But he read the sailing orders, as of course he had to do,
And removed the " Royal Biddy " to the Bay of Boohgabooh.

Now, Sir Peter took it kindly, but it's proper to explain
He was sent to catch a pirate out upon the Spanish Main.
And he played, with variations, an imaginary tune
On the buttons of his waistcoat, like a jocular bassoon.

Then a topman saw the pirate come a-sailing in the bay,
And reported to the Captain in the ordinary way.
" I'll receive him," said Sir Peter, " with a musical salute,"
And he gave some imitations of a double-jointed flute.

Then the Pirate cried derisively, " I've heard it done before! "
And he hoisted up a banner emblematical of gore.
But Sir Peter said serenely, " You may double-shot the guns
While I sing my little ballad of ' The Butter on the Buns.' "

Then the Pirate banged Sir Peter and Sir Peter banged him
    back,
And they banged away together as they took another tack.
Then Sir Peter said, politely, " You may board him, if you
    like,"
And he played a little dirge upon the handle of a pike.

Then the " Biddies " poured like hornets down upon the
    Pirate's deck
And Sir Peter caught the Pirate and he took him by the
    neck,
And remarked, " You must excuse me, but you acted like a
    brute
When I gave my imitation of that double-jointed flute."

So they took that wicked Pirate and they took his wicked
    crew,
And tied them up with double knots in packages of two.
And left them lying on their backs in rows upon the beach
With a little bread and water within comfortable reach.

Now the Pirate had a treasure (mostly silverware and gold),
And Sir Peter took and stowed it in the bottom of his hold;
And said, " I will retire on this cargo of doubloons,
And each of you, my gallant crew, may have some silver
    spoons."

Now commodores in coach-and-fours and corporals in cabs,
And men with carts of pies and tarts and fishermen with
    crabs,
And barristers with wigs, in gigs, still gather on the strand,
But there isn't any music save a little German band.

                        Charles E. Carryl.

ROBINSON CRUSOE'S STORY

THE night was thick and hazy
  When the *Piccadilly Daisy*
Carried down the crew and captain in the sea;
  And I think the water drowned 'em,
  For they never, never found 'em,
And I know they didn't come ashore with me.

Oh! 'twas very sad and lonely
  When I found myself the only
Population on this cultivated shore;
  But I've made a little tavern
  In a rocky little cavern,
And I sit and watch for people at the door.

I spent no time in looking
  For a girl to do my cooking,
As I'm quite a clever hand at making stews;
  But I had that fellow Friday
  Just to keep the tavern tidy,
And to put a Sunday polish on my shoes.

I have a little garden
  That I'm cultivating lard in,
As the things I eat are rather tough and dry;

For I live on toasted lizards,
Prickly pears and parrot gizzards,
And I'm really very fond of beetle pie.

The clothes I had were furry,
And it made me fret and worry
When I found the moths were eating off the hair;
And I had to scrape and sand 'em,
And I boiled 'em and I tanned 'em,
Till I got the fine morocco suit I wear.

I sometimes seek diversion
In a family excursion,
With the few domestic animals you see;
And we take along a carrot
As refreshment for the parrot,
And a little can of jungleberry tea.

Then we gather as we travel
Bits of moss and dirty gravel,
And we chip off little specimens of stone;
And we carry home as prizes
Funny bugs of handy sizes,
Just to give the day a scientific tone.

If the roads are wet and muddy
We remain at home and study,—
For the Goat is very clever at a sum,—
And the Dog, instead of fighting
Studies ornamental writing,
While the Cat is taking lessons on the drum.

We retire at eleven,
And we rise again at seven;
And I wish to call attention, as I close,
To the fact that all the scholars
Are correct about their collars,
And particular in turning out their toes.

Charles E. Carryl.

BEN BLUFF

BEN BLUFF was a whaler, and many a day
Had chased the huge fish about Baffin's old Bay;
But time brought a change his diversion to spoil,
And that was when Gas took the shine out of Oil.

He turned up his nose at the fumes of the coke,
And swore the whole scheme was a bottle of smoke;
As to London, he briefly delivered his mind,
" Sparma-city," said he,—but the city declined.

So Ben cut his line in a sort of a huff,
As soon as his whales had brought profits enough,
And hard by the Docks settled down for his life,
But, true to his text, went to Wales for a wife.

A big one she was, without figure or waist,
More bulky than lovely, but that was his taste;
In fat she was lapped from her sole to her crown,
And, turned into oil, would have lighted a town.

But Ben, like a whaler, was charmed with the match,
And thought, very truly, his spouse a great catch;
A flesh-and-blood emblem of Plenty and Peace,
And would not have changed her for Helen of Greece!

For Greenland was green in his memory still;
He'd quitted his trade, but retained the good-will;
And often when softened by bumbo and flip,
Would cry till he blubbered about his old ship.

No craft like the *Grampus* could work through a floe,
What knots she could run, and what tons she could stow!
And then that rich smell he preferred to the rose,
By just nosing the hold without holding his nose.

Now Ben he resolved, one fine Saturday night,
A snug arctic circle of friends to invite;

Old tars in the trade, who related old tales,
And drank, and blew clouds that were " very like whales."

Of course with their grog there was plenty of chat,
Of canting, and flenching, and cutting up fat;
And how gun-harpoons into fashion had got,
And if they were meant for the gun-whale or not?

At last they retired, and left Ben to his rest,
By fancies cetaceous and drink well possessed,
When, lo! as he lay by his partner in bed,
He heard something blow through two holes in its head!

" A start! " muttered Ben, in the *Grampus* afloat,
And made but one jump from the deck to the boat!
" Huzza! pull away for the blubber and bone,—
I look on that whale as already my own! "

Then groping about by the light of the moon,
He soon laid his hand on his trusty harpoon;
A moment he poised it, to send_it more pat,
And then made a plunge to imbed it in fat!

" Starn all! " he sang out, " as you care for your lives,—
Starn all! as you hope to return to your wives,—
Stand by for the flurry! she throws up the foam!
Well done, my old iron; I've sent you right home! "

And scarce had he spoken, when lo! bolt upright
The leviathan rose in a great sheet of white,
And swiftly advanced for a fathom or two,
As only a fish out of water could do.

" Starn all! " echoed Ben, with a movement aback,
But too slow to escape from the creature's attack;
If flippers it had, they were furnished with nails,—
" You willin, I'll teach you that women ain't whales! "

" Avast! " shouted Ben, with a sort of a screech,
" I've heard a whale spouting, but here is a speech! "

" A-spouting, indeed!—very pretty," said she;
" But it's you I'll blow up, not the froth of the sea!

" To go to pretend to take *me* for a fish!
You great polar bear—but I know what you wish;
You're sick of a wife that your hankering balks,
You want to go back to some young Esquimaux!"

" O dearest," cried Ben, frightened out of his life,
" Don't think I would go for to murder a wife
I must long have bewailed!" But she only cried, " Stuff!"
Don't name it, you brute, you've *be-whaled* me enough!"

" Lord, Polly!" said Ben, "such a deed could I do?
I'd rather have murdered all Wapping than you!
Come, forgive what is past." " O you monster!" she cried,
" It was none of your fault that it passed off one side!"

However, at last she inclined to forgive;
" But, Ben, take this warning as long as you live,—
If the love of harpooning so strong must prevail,
Take a whale for a wife,—not a wife for a whale!"

Thomas Hood.

THE PILGRIMS AND THE PEAS

A BRACE of sinners, for no good,
    Were order'd to the Virgin Mary's shrine,
Who at Loretto dwelt, in wax, stone, wood,
    And in a fair white wig look'd wondrous fine.

Fifty long miles had those sad rogues to travel,
With something in their shoes much worse than gravel;
In short, their toes so gentle to amuse,
The priest had order'd peas into their shoes:

A nostrum, famous in old popish times,
For purifying souls that stunk with crimes;
    A sort of apostolic salt,
    Which popish parsons for its powers exalt,

For keeping souls of sinners sweet,
Just as our kitchen salt keeps meat.

The knaves set off on the same day,
Peas in their shoes, to go and pray:
  But very different was their speed, I wot:
One of the sinners gallop'd on,
Swift as a bullet from a gun;
  The other limp'd, as if he had been shot.

One saw the Virgin soon—*peccavi* cried—
  Had his soul whitewash'd all so clever;
Then home again he nimbly hied,
  Made fit with saints above to live forever.

In coming back, however, let me say,
He met his brother rogue about half-way,
Hobbling, with outstretch'd arms and bended knees,
Damning the souls and bodies of the peas;
His eyes in tears, his cheeks and brow in sweat,
Deep sympathizing with his groaning feet.

"How now," the light-toed, white-wash'd pilgrim broke,
  "You lazy lubber!"
"Odds curse it!" cried the other, "'tis no joke;
My feet, once hard as any rock,
  Are now as soft as blubber.

"Excuse me, Virgin Mary, that I swear:
As for Loretto, I shall not go there;
No! to the Devil my sinful soul must go,
For damme if I ha'n't lost every toe.
But, brother sinner, pray explain
How 'tis that you are not in pain?
What power hath work'd a wonder for your toes?
Whilst I, just like a snail, am crawling,
Now swearing, now on saints devoutly bawling,
  Whilst not a rascal comes to ease my woes?

"How is't that *you* can like a greyhound go,
  Merry as if that naught had happen'd, burn ye!"
"Why," cried the other, grinning, "you must know,

That, just before I ventured on my journey,
   To walk a little more at ease,
  I took the liberty to boil *my* peas."

John Wolcot.

TAM O'SHANTER

When chapman billies leave the street,
And drouthy neibors neibors meet,
As market days are wearin' late,
And folk begin to tak the gate:

While we sit bousing at the nappy,
And gettin' fou and unco happy,
We thinkna on the lang Scots miles,
The mosses, waters, slaps, and stiles,
That lie between us and our hame,
Whare sits our sulky sullen dame,
Gathering her brows like gathering storm,
Nursing her wrath to keep it warm.

This truth fand honest Tam o'Shanter,
As he frae Ayr ae night did canter
(Auld Ayr, wham ne'er a town surpasses
For honest men and bonny lasses).

O Tam! hadst thou but been sae wise
As ta'en thy ain wife Kate's advice!
She tauld thee weel thou wast a skellum,
A blethering, blustering, drunken blellum;
That frae Nevember till October,
Ae market day thou wasna sober;
That ilka melder, wi' the miller
Thou sat as lang as thou hadst siller;
That every naig was ca'd a shoe on,
The smith and thee gat roaring fou on;
That at the Lord's house, even on Sunday,
Thou drank wi' Kirkton Jean till Monday.
She prophesied, that, late or soon,
Thou wouldst be found deep drown'd in Doon!

Or catch'd wi' warlocks i' the mirk,
By Alloway's auld haunted kirk.

Ah, gentle dames! it gars me greet
To think how mony counsels sweet,
How mony lengthen'd, sage advices,
The husband frae the wife despises!

But to our tale:—Ae market night,
Tam had got planted unco right,
Fast by an ingle, bleezing finely,
Wi' reaming swats, that drank divinely;
And at his elbow, Souter Johnny,
His ancient, trusty, drouthy crony;
Tam lo'ed him like a very brither—
They had been fou for weeks thegither!
The night drave on wi' sangs and clatter,
And aye the ale was growing better:
The landlady and Tam grew gracious,
Wi' favours secret, sweet, and precious
The Souter tauld his queerest stories,
The landlord's laugh was ready chorus:
The storm without might rair and rustle—
Tam didna mind the storm a whistle.

Care, mad to see a man sae happy,
E'en drown'd himsel' amang the nappy!
As bees flee hame wi' lades o' treasure,
The minutes wing'd their way wi' pleasure;
Kings may be blest, but Tam was glorious,
O'er a' the ills o' life victorious!

But pleasures are like poppies spread,
You seize the flower, its bloom is shed!
Or like the snowfall in the river,
A moment white—then melts for ever;
Or like the borealis race,
That flit ere you can point their place
Or like the rainbow's lovely form,
Evanishing amid the storm.
Nae man can tether time or tide;
The hour approaches Tam maun ride;

That hour, o' night's black arch the keystane,
That dreary hour he mounts his beast in;
And sic a night he taks the road in
As ne'er poor sinner was abroad in.

The wind blew as 'twad blawn its last;
The rattling showers rose on the blast;
The speedy gleams the darkness swallow'd;
Loud, deep, and lang, the thunder bellow'd:
That night, a child might understand
The deil had business on his hand.

Weel mounted on his grey mare Meg,
A better never lifted leg,
Tam skelpit on through dub and mire,
Despising wind, and rain, and fire;
Whiles holding fast his guid blue bonnet,
Whiles crooning o'er some auld Scots sonnet;
Whiles glowering round wi' prudent cares,
Lest bogles catch him unawares:
Kirk-Alloway was drawing nigh,
Whare ghaists and houlets nightly cry.
By this time he was 'cross the foord,
Whare in the snaw the chapman smoor'd;
And past the birks and meikle stane
Whare drunken Charlie brak's neck-bane:
And through the whins, and by the cairn
Whare hunters fand the murder'd bairn;
And near the thorn, aboon the well,
Whare Mungo's mither hang'd hersel'.
Before him Doon pours a' his floods;
The doubling storm roars through the woods;
The lightnings flash frae pole to pole;
Near and more near the thunders roll;
When, glimmering through the groaning trees,
Kirk-Alloway seem'd in a bleeze;
Through ilka bore the beams were glancing,
And loud resounded mirth and dancing.

Inspiring bold John Barleycorn!
What dangers thou canst mak us scorn!
Wi' tippenny, we fear nae evil;
Wi' usquebae, we'll face the devil!—
The swats sae ream'd in Tammie's noddle,
Fair play, he cared na deils a boddle.
But Maggie stood right sair astonish'd,
Till, by the heel and hand admonish'd,
She ventured forward on the light;
And, wow! Tam saw an unco sight!
Warlocks and witches in a dance;
Nae cotillon brent-new frae France,
But hornpipes, jigs, strathspeys, and reels,
Put life and mettle i' their heels:
At winnock-bunker, i' the east,
There sat auld Nick, in shape o' beast;
A towzie tyke, black, grim, and large,
To gie them music was his charge;
He screw'd the pipes, and gart them skirl,
Till roof and rafters a' did dirl.
Coffins stood round, like open presses,
That shaw'd the dead in their last dresses;
And by some devilish cantrip slight
Each in its cauld hand held a light,—
By which heroic Tam was able
To note upon the haly table,
A murderer's banes in gibbet airns;
Twa span-lang, wee, unchristian bairns;
A thief, new-cutted frae a rape,
Wi' his last gasp his gab did gape;
Five tomahawks, wi' bluid red-rusted;
Five scimitars, wi' murder crusted;
A garter, which a babe had strangled;
A knife, a father's throat had mangled,
Whom his ain son o' life bereft,
The grey hairs yet stack to the heft:
Wi' mair o' horrible and awfu',
Which even to name wad be unlawfu'.

As Tammie glower'd, amazed and curious
The mirth and fun grew fast and furious

The piper loud and louder blew,
The dancers quick and quicker flew;
They reel'd, they set, they cross'd, they cleekit,
Till ilka carlin swat and reekit,
And coost her duddies to the wark,
And linket at it in her sark.
Now Tam! O Tam! had thae been queans,
A' plump and strappin' in their teens,
Their sarks, instead o' creeshie flannen,
Been snaw-white seventeen-hunder linen!
Thir breeks o' mine, my only pair,
That ance were plush, o' guid blue hair,
I wad hae gien them aff my hurdies,
For ae blink o' the bonny burdies!

But wither'd beldams, auld and droll,
Rigwoodie hags, wad spean a foal,
Lowpin' and flingin' on a cummock,
I wonder didna turn thy stomach.

But Tam kenn'd what was what fu' brawlie,
"There was ae winsome wench and walie,"
That night enlisted in the core
(Lang after kenn'd on Carrick shore;
For mony a beast to dead she shot,
And perish'd money a bonny boat,
And shook baith meikle corn and bear,
And kept the country-side in fear).
Her cutty sark, o' Paisley harn,
That, while a lassie, she had worn,
In longitude though sorely scanty,
It was her best, and she was vauntie.

Ah! little kenn'd thy reverend grannie,
That sark she coft for her wee Nannie,
Wi' twa pund Scots ('twas a' her riches),
Wad ever graced a dance o' witches!

But here my Muse her wing maun core,
Sic flights are far beyond her power;
To sing how Nannie lap and flang
(A souple jade she was, and strang),
And how Tam stood, like ane bewitch'd,
And thought his very een enriched.
Even Satan glower'd, and fidged fu' fain,
And hotch'd and blew wi' might and main;
Till first ae caper, syne anither,
Tam tint his reason a' thegither,
And roars out, "Weel done, Cutty-sark!"
And in an instant a' was dark:
And scarcely had he Maggie rallied,
When out the hellish legion sallied.
As bees bizz out wi' angry fyke,
When plundering herds assail their byke,
As open pussie's mortal foes,
When, pop! she starts before their nose;
As eager runs the market-crowd,
When "Catch the thief!" resounds aloud;
So Maggie runs, the witches follow,
Wi' mony an eldritch screech and hollow.

Ah, Tam! ah, Tam! thou'lt get thy fairin'!
In hell they'll roast thee like a herrin'!
In vain thy Kate awaits thy comin'!
Kate soon will be a woefu' woman!
Now, do thy speedy utmost, Meg,
And win the keystane of the brig;
There at them thou thy tail may toss,
A running stream they darena cross;
But ere the keystane she could make,
The fient a tail she had to shake!
For Nannie, far before the rest,
Hard upon noble Maggie prest,
And flew at Tam wi' furious ettle;
But little wist she Maggie's mettle—
Ae spring brought off her master hale,
But left behind her ain grey tail:
The carlin caught her by the rump,
And left poor Maggie scarce a stump.

Now, wha this tale o' truth shall read,
Ilk man and mother's son, take heed:
Whane'er to drink you are inclined,
Or cutty-sarks run in your mind,
Think! ye may buy the joys ower dear—
Remember Tam o' Shanter's mare.

Robert Burns.

THAT GENTLE MAN FROM BOSTON TOWN

AN IDYL OF OREGON

Two webfoot brothers loved a fair
  Young lady, rich and good to see;
And oh, her black abundant hair!
  And oh, her wondrous witchery!
Her father kept a cattle farm,
These brothers kept her safe from harm:

From harm of cattle on the hill;
  From thick-necked bulls loud bellowing
The livelong morning, loud and shrill,
  And lashing sides like anything;
From roaring bulls that tossed the sand
And pawed the lilies from the land.

There came a third young man. He came
  From far and famous Boston town.
He was not handsome, was not "game,"
  But he could "cook a goose" as brown
As any man that set foot on
The sunlit shores of Oregon.

This Boston man he taught the school,
  Taught gentleness and love alway,
Said love and kindness, as a rule,
  Would ultimately "make it pay."
He was so gentle, kind, that he
Could make a noun and verb agree.

So when one day the brothers grew
    All jealous and did strip to fight,
He gently stood between the two,
    And meekly told them 'twas not right.
"I have a higher, better plan,"
Outspake this gentle Boston man.

"My plan is this: Forget this fray
    About that lily hand of hers;
Go take your guns and hunt all day
    High up yon lofty hill of firs,
And while you hunt, my loving doves,
Why, I will learn which one she loves."

The brothers sat the windy hill,
    Their hair shone yellow, like spun gold,
Their rifles crossed their laps, but still
    They sat and sighed and shook with cold.
Their hearts lay bleeding far below;
Above them gleamed white peaks of snow.

Their hounds lay couching, slim and neat;
    A spotted circle in the grass.
The valley lay beneath their feet;
    They heard the wide-winged eagles pass.
The eagles cleft the clouds above;
Yet what could they but sigh and love?

"If I could die," the elder sighed,
    "My dear young brother here might wed."
"Oh, would to Heaven I had died!"
    The younger sighed, with bended head.
Then each looked each full in the face
And each sprang up and stood in place.

"If I could die,"—the elder spake,—
    "Die by your hand, the world would say
'Twas accident;—and for her sake,
    Dear brother, be it so, I pray."
"Not that!" the younger nobly said;
Then tossed his gun and turned his head.

And fifty paces back he paced!
  And as he paced he drew the ball;
Then sudden stopped and wheeled and faced
  His brother to the death and fall!
Two shots rang wild upon the air!
But lo! the two stood harmless there!

An eagle poised high in the air;
  Far, far below the bellowing
Of bullocks ceased, and everywhere
  Vast silence sat all questioning.
The spotted hounds ran circling round
Their red, wet noses to the ground.

And now each brother came to know
  That each had drawn the deadly ball;
And for that fair girl far below
  Had sought in vain to silent fall.
And then the two did gladly " shake,"
And thus the elder bravely spake:

" Now let us run right hastily
  And tell the kind schoolmaster all!
Yea! yea! and if she choose not me,
  But all on you her favors fall,
This valiant scene, till all life ends,
Dear brother, binds us best of friends."

The hounds sped down, a spotted line,
  The bulls in tall, abundant grass,
Shook back their horns from bloom and vine,
  And trumpeted to see them pass—
They loved so good, they loved so true,
These brothers scarce knew what to do.

They sought the kind schoolmaster out
  As swift as sweeps the light of morn;
They could but love, they could not doubt
  This man so gentle, " in a horn,"
They cried, " Now whose the lily hand—
That lady's of this webfoot land?"

They bowed before that big-nosed man,
  That long-nosed man from Boston town;
They talked as only lovers can,
  They talked, but he could only frown;
And still they talked, and still they plead;
It was as pleading with the dead.

At last this Boston man did speak—
  " Her father has a thousand ceows,
An hundred bulls, all fat and sleek;
  He also had this ample heouse."
The brothers' eyes stuck out thereat,
So far you might have hung your hat.

" I liked the looks of this big heouse—
  My lovely boys, won't you come in?
Her father has a thousand ceows,
  He also had a heap of tin.
The guirl? Oh yes, the guirl, you see—
The guirl, just neow she married me."

Joaquin Miller.

THE YARN OF THE "NANCY BELL"

'Twas on the shores that round our coast
  From Deal to Ramsgate span,
That I found alone on a piece of stone
  An elderly naval man.

His hair was weedy, his beard was long,
  And weedy and long was he,
And I heard this wight on the shore recite,
  In a singular minor key:

" Oh, I am a cook and the captain bold,
  And the mate of the *Nancy* brig,
And a bo'sun tight, and a midshipmite,
  And the crew of the captain's gig."

And he shook his fists and he tore his hair,
  Till I really felt afraid,
For I couldn't help thinking the man had been drinking,
  And so I simply said:

' Oh, elderly man, it's little I know
  Of the duties of men of the sea,
And I'll eat my hand if I understand
  How you can possibly be

" At once a cook, and a captain bold,
  And the mate of the *Nancy* brig,
And a bo'sun tight, and a midshipmite,
  And the crew of the captain's gig."

Then he gave a hitch to his trousers, which
  Is a trick all seamen larn,
And having got rid of a thumping quid,
  He spun this painful yarn:

" 'Twas in the good ship *Nancy Bell*
  That we sailed to the Indian Sea,
And there on a reef we come to grief,
  Which has often occurred to me.

" And pretty nigh all the crew was drowned
  (There was seventy-seven o' soul),
And only ten of the *Nancy's* men
  Said ' here' to the muster-roll.

" There was me and the cook and the captain bold,
  And the mate of the *Nancy* brig,
And the bo'sun tight, and a midshipmite,
  And the crew of the captain's gig.

" For a month we'd neither wittles nor drink,
  Till a-hungry we did feel,
So we drawed a lot, and accordin' shot
  The captain for our meal.

"The next lot fell to the *Nancy's* mate,
    And a delicate dish he made;
Then our appetite with the midshipmite
    We seven survivors stayed.

"And then we murdered the bos'un tight,
    And he much resembled pig;
Then we wittled free, did the cook and me,
    On the crew of the captain's gig.

"Then only the cook and me was left,
    And the delicate question, 'Which
Of us two goes to the kettle?' arose,
    And we argued it out as sich.

"For I loved that cook as a brother, I did,
    And the cook he worshipped me;
But we'd both be blowed if we'd either be stowed
    In the other chap's hold, you see.

"'I'll be eat if you dines off me,' says Tom.
    'Yes, that,' says I, 'you'll be,—
I'm boiled if I die, my friend,' quoth I.
    And 'Exactly so,' quoth he.

"Says he, 'Dear James, to murder me
    Were a foolish thing to do,
For don't you see that you can't cook *me*,
    While I can—and will—cook *you!*'

"So he boils the water, and takes the salt
    And the pepper in portions true
(Which he never forgot), and some chopped shalot,
    And some sage and parsley too.

"'Come here,' says he, with a proper pride,
    Which his smiling features tell,
''Twill soothing be if I let you see
    How extremely nice you'll smell.'

" And he stirred it round and round and round,
  And he sniffed at the foaming froth;
When I ups with his heels, and smothers his squeals
  In the scum of the boiling broth.

" And I eat that cook in a week or less,
  And—as I eating be
The last of his chops, why, I almost drops,
  For a vessel in sight I see.

. . . . . .

" And I never larf, and I never smile,
  And I never lark or play,
But sit and croak, and a single joke
  I have,—which is to say:

" Oh, I am a cook and a captain bold,
  And the mate of the *Nancy* brig,
And a bos'un tight, and a midshipmite,
  And the crew of the captain's gig."

W. S. Gilbert.

FERDINANDO AND ELVIRA

OR, THE GENTLE PIEMAN

PART I

AT a pleasant evening party I had taken down to supper
One whom I will call Elvira, and we talked of love and
  Tupper.

Mr. Tupper and the Poets, very lightly with them dealing,
For I've always been distinguished for a strong poetic
  feeling.

Then we let off paper crackers, each of which contained a
  motto,
And she listened while I read them, till her mother told
  her not to.

Then she whispered, " To the ballroom we had better, dear
     be walking;
If we stop down here much longer, really people will be
     talking."

There were noblemen in coronets, and military cousins,
There were captains by the hundred, there were baronets by
     dozens.

Yet she heeded not their offers, but dismissed them with a
     blessing;
Then she let down all her back hair, which had taken long
     in dressing.

Then she had convulsive sobbings in her agitated throttle
Then she wiped her pretty eyes and smelt her pretty smell-
     ing bottle.

So I whispered, " Dear Elvira, say,—what can the matter
     be with you?
Does anything you've eaten, darling Popsy, disagree with
     you? "

But spite of all I said, her sobs grew more and more dis-
     tressing,
And she tore her pretty back hair, which had taken long
     in dressing.

Then she gazed upon the carpet, at the ceiling, then above
     me,
And she whispered, " Ferdinando, do you really, *really* love
     me? "

" Love you? " said I, then I sighed, and then I gazed upon
     her sweetly—
For I think I do this sort of thing particularly neatly.

" Send me to the Arctic regions, or illimitable azure,
On a scientific goose-chase, with my Coxwell or my Glaisher!

"Tell me whither I may hie me—tell me, dear one, that I
 may know—
Is it up the highest Andes? down a horrible volcano?"

But she said, "It isn't polar bears, or hot volcanic grottoes;
Only find out who it is that writes those lovely cracker
 mottoes!"

PART II

"Tell me, Henry Wadsworth, Alfred, Poet Close, or Mister
 Tupper,
Do you write the bon-ton mottoes my Elvira pulls at sup-
 per?"

But Henry Wadsworth smiled, and said he had not had
 that honor;
And Alfred, too, disclaimed the words that told so much
 upon her.

"Mister Martin Tupper, Poet Close, I beg of you inform
 us;"
But my question seemed to throw them both into a rage
 enormous.

Mister Close expressed a wish that he could only get anigh
 to me;
And Mister Martin Tupper sent the following reply to me:

"A fool is bent upon a twig, but wise men dread a ban-
 dit,"—
Which I know was very clever; but I didn't understand it.

Seven weary years I wandered—Patagonia, China, Nor-
 way,
Till at last I sank exhausted at a pastrycook his doorway.

There were fuchsias and geraniums, and daffodils and myr-
 tle;
So I entered, and I ordered half a basin of mock turtle.

He was plump and he was chubby, he was smooth and he
  was rosy,
And his little wife was pretty and particularly cosy.

And he chirped and sang, and skipped about, and laughed
  with laughter hearty—
He was wonderfully active for so very stout a party.

And I said, " O gentle pieman, why so very, very merry?
Is it purity of conscience, or your one-and-seven sherry? "

But he answered, " I'm so happy—no profession could be
  dearer—
If I am not humming ' Tra la la ' I'm singing ' Tirer, lirer! '

" First I go and make the patties, and the puddings, and
  the jellies,
Then I make a sugar bird-cage, which upon a table swell is:

" Then I polish all the silver, which a supper-table lacquers:
Then I write the pretty mottoes which you find inside the
  crackers—"

" Found at last! " I madly shouted. " Gentle pieman, you
  astound me! "
Then I waved the turtle soup enthusiastically round me.

And I shouted and I danced until he'd quite a crowd around
  him,
And I rushed away, exclaiming, " I have found him! I
  have found him! "

And I heard the gentle pieman in the road behind me trill-
  ing,
" ' Tira! lira! ' stop him, stop him! ' Tra! la! la! ' the soup's
  a shilling! "

But until I reached Elvira's home, I never, never waited,
And Elvira to her Ferdinand's irrevocably mated!

W. S. Gilbert.

GENTLE ALICE BROWN

IT was a robber's daughter, and her name was Alice Brown.
Her father was the terror of a small Italian town;
Her mother was a foolish, weak, but amiable old thing;
But it isn't of her parents that I'm going for to sing.

As Alice was a-sitting at her window-sill one day,
A beautiful young gentleman he chanced to pass that way;
She cast her eyes upon him, and he looked so good and
true,
That she thought, " I could be happy with a gentleman like
you! "

And every morning passed her house that cream of gentle-
men,
She knew she might expect him at a quarter unto ten,
A sorter in the Custom-house, it was his daily road
(The Custom-house was fifteen minutes' walk from her
abode.)

But Alice was a pious girl, who knew it wasn't wise
To look at strange young sorters with expressive purple
eyes;
So she sought the village priest to whom her family con-
fessed,
The priest by whom their little sins were carefully assessed.

" Oh, holy father," Alice said, " 'twould grieve you, would
it not?
To discover that I was a most disreputable lot!
Of all unhappy sinners I'm the most unhappy one! "
The padre said, " Whatever have you been and gone and
done? "

" I have helped mamma to steal a little kiddy from its dad,
I've assisted dear papa in cutting up a little lad.
I've planned a little burglary and forged a little cheque,
And slain a little baby for the coral on its neck! "

The worthy pastor heaved a sigh, and dropped a silent tear—
And said, "You mustn't judge yourself too heavily, my
dear—
It's wrong to murder babies, little corals for to fleece;
But sins like these one expiates at half-a-crown apiece.

"Girls will be girls—you're very young, and flighty in your
mind;
Old heads upon young shoulders we must not expect to find:
We mustn't be too hard upon these little girlish tricks—
Let's see—five crimes at half-a-crown—exactly twelve-and-
six."

"Oh, father," little Alice cried, "your kindness makes me
weep,
You do these little things for me so singularly cheap—
Your thoughtful liberality I never can forget;
But oh, there is another crime I haven't mentioned yet!

"A pleasant-looking gentleman, with pretty purple eyes,
I've noticed at my window, as I've sat a-catching flies;
He passes by it every day as certain as can be—
I blush to say I've winked at him and he has winked at
me!"

"For shame," said Father Paul, "my erring daughter! On
my word
This is the most distressing news that I have ever heard.
Why, naughty girl, your excellent papa has pledged your
hand
To a promising young robber, the lieutenant of his band!

"This dreadful piece of news will pain your worthy par-
ents so!
They are the most remunerative customers I know;
For many many years they've kept starvation from my
doors,
I never knew so criminal a family as yours!

"The common country folk in this insipid neighborhood
Have nothing to confess, they're so ridiculously good;
And if you marry any one respectable at all,
Why, you'll reform, and what will then become of Father
Paul?"

The worthy priest, he up and drew his cowl upon his crown,
And started off in haste to tell the news to Robber Brown;
To tell him how his daughter, who was now for marriage fit,
Had winked upon a sorter, who reciprocated it.

Good Robber Brown, he muffled up his anger pretty well,
He said, " I have a notion, and that notion I will tell;
I will nab this gay young sorter, terrify him into fits,
And get my gentle wife to chop him into little bits.

" I've studied human nature, and I know a thing or two,
Though a girl may fondly love a living gent, as many do—
A feeling of disgust upon her senses there will fall
When she looks upon his body chopped particularly small."

He traced that gallant sorter to a still suburban square;
He watched his opportunity and seized him unaware;
He took a life-preserver and he hit him on the head,
And Mrs. Brown dissected him before she went to bed.

And pretty little Alice grew more settled in her mind,
She nevermore was guilty of a weakness of the kind,
Until at length good Robber Brown bestowed her pretty hand
On the promising young robber, the lieutenant of his band.

W. S. Gilbert.

THE STORY OF PRINCE AGIB

STRIKE the concertina's melancholy string!
Blow the spirit-stirring harp like anything!
    Let the piano's martial blast
    Rouse the Echoes of the Past,
For of Agib, Prince of Tartary, I sing!

Of Agib, who, amid Tartaric scenes,
Wrote a lot of ballet music in his teens:
    His gentle spirit rolls
    In the melody of souls—
Which is pretty, but I don't know what it means.

Of Agib, who could readily, at sight,
Strum a march upon the loud Theodolite.
  He would diligently play
  On the Zoetrope all day,
And blow the gay Pantechnicon all night.

One winter—I am shaky in my dates—
Came two starving Tartar minstrels to his gates;
  Oh, Allah be obeyed,
  How infernally they played!
I remember that they called themselves the " Oüaits."

Oh! that day of sorrow, misery, and rage
I shall carry to the Catacombs of Age,
  Photographically lined
  On the tablet of my mind,
When a yesterday has faded from its page!

Alas! Prince Agib went and asked them in;
Gave them beer, and eggs, and sweets, and scent, and tin.
  And when (as snobs would say)
  They had "put it all away,"
He requested them to tune up and begin.

Though its icy horror chill you to the core,
I will tell you what I never told before,—
  The consequences true
  Of that awful interview,
For I listened at the keyhole in the door!

They played him a sonata—let me see!
" Medulla oblongata"—key of G.
  Then they began to sing
  That extremely lovely thing,
" Scherzando! ma non troppo, ppp."

He gave them money, more than they could count,
Scent from a most ingenious little fount,
  More beer, in little kegs,
  Many dozen hard-boiled eggs,
And goodies to a fabulous amount.

Now follows the dim horror of my tale
And I feel I'm growing gradually pale,
    For, even at this day,
    Though its sting has passed away,
When I venture to remember it, I quail!

The elder of the brothers gave a squeal,
All-overish it made me for to feel;
    " Oh, Prince," he says, says he,
    " If a Prince indeed you be,
I've a mystery I'm going to reveal!

" Oh, listen, if you'd shun a horrid death,
To what the gent who's speaking to you saith:
    No ' Oüaits ' in truth are we,
    As you fancy that we be;
For (ter-remble!) I am Aleck—this is Beth!"

Said Agib, " Oh! accursed of your kind,
I have heard that ye are men of evil mind!"
    Beth gave a fearful shriek—
    But before he'd time to speak
I was mercilessly collared from behind.

In number ten or twelve, or even more,
They fastened me full length upon the floor.
    On my face extended flat,
    I was walloped with a cat
For listening at the keyhole of a door.

Oh! the horror of that agonizing thrill!
(I can feel the place in frosty weather still).
    For a week from ten to four
    I was fastened to the floor,
While a mercenary wopped me with a will.

They branded me and broke me on a wheel,
And they left me in an hospital to heal;
    And, upon my solemn word,
    I have never never heard
What those Tartars had determined to reveal.

But that day of sorrow, misery, and rage,
I shall carry to the Catacombs of Age,
    Photographically lined
    On the tablet of my mind,
When a yesterday has faded from its page.

               W. S. Gilbert.

SIR GUY THE CRUSADER

Sir Guy was a doughty crusader,
    A muscular knight,
    Ever ready to fight,
A very determined invader,
    And Dickey de Lion's delight.

Lenore was a Saracen maiden,
    Brunette, statuesque,
    The reverse of grotesque;
Her pa was a bagman from Aden,
    Her mother she played in burlesque.

A *coryphée,* pretty and loyal,
    In amber and red,
    The ballet she led;
Her mother performed at the Royal,
    Lenore at the Saracen's Head.

Of face and of figure majestic,
    She dazzled the cits—
    Ecstaticised pits;—
Her troubles were only domestic,
    But drove her half out of her wits.

Her father incessantly lashed her,
    On water and bread
    She was grudgingly fed;
Whenever her father he thrashed her,
    Her mother sat down on her head.

Guy saw her, and loved her, with reason,
 For beauty so bright
 Sent him mad with delight;
He purchased a stall for the season
 And sat in it every night.

His views were exceedingly proper,
 He wanted to wed,
 So he called at her shed
And saw her progenitor whop her—
 Her mother sit down on her head.

" So pretty," said he, " and so trusting!
 You brute of a dad,
 You unprincipled cad,
Your conduct is really disgusting,
 Come, come, now admit it's too bad!

" You're a turbaned old Turk, and malignant—
 Your daughter Lenore
 I intensely adore,
And I cannot help feeling indignant,
 A fact that I hinted before;

To see a fond father employing
 A deuce of a knout
 For to bang her about,
To a sensitive lover's annoying."
 Said the bagman, " Crusader, get out."

Says Guy, " Shall a warrior laden
 With a big spiky knob
 Sit in peace on his cob,
While a beautiful Saracen maiden
 Is whipped by a Saracen snob?

" To London I'll go from my charmer."
 Which he did, with his loot
 (Seven hats and a flute),
And was nabbed for his Sydenham armour
 At Mr. Ben-Samuel's suit.

Sir Guy he was lodged in the Compter;
    Her pa, in a rage,
    Died (don't know his age);
His daughter she married the prompter,
    Grew bulky and quitted the stage.

W. S. Gilbert.

KITTY WANTS TO WRITE

KITTY wants to write! Kitty intellectual!
    What has been effectual to turn her stockings blue?
Kitty's seventh season has brought sufficient reason,
    She has done 'most everything that there is left to do!
    Half of them to laugh about and half of them to rue,—
Now we wait in terror for Kitty's wildest error.
    What has she to write about? Wheeeeeeeeew!

Kitty wants to write! Débutante was Kitty,
    Frivolous and witty as ever bud that blew.
Kitty lacked sobriety, yet she ran society,
    A leader whom the chaperons indulged a year or two;
    Corner-men, eligibles, dancing-dolls she knew,—
Kitty then was slighted, ne'er again invited;
    What has she to write about? Wheeeeeeeeew!

Kitty wants to write! At the Social Settlement
    Girls of Kitty's mettle meant a mission for a few;
Men to teach the classes, men to mould the masses,
    Men to follow Kitty to adventures strange and new.
    Some of her benevolence was hidden out of view!—
A patroness offended, Kitty's slumming ended.
    What is there to write about? Wheeeeeeeeew!

Kitty wants to write! Kitty was a mystic,
    Deep from cabalistic lore many hints she drew!
Freaks of all description, Hindoo and Egyptian,
    Prattled in her parlor—such a wild and hairy crew!
    Many came for money, and one or two to woo—
Kitty's pet astrologer wanted to acknowledge her!
    What has she to write about? Wheeeeeeeeew!

Kitty wants to write! Kitty was a doctor;
Nothing ever shocked her, though they hazed a little, too!
Kitty learned of medicos how a heart unsteady goes,
Besides a score of secrets that are secrets still to you.
Kitty's course in medicine gave her many a clue—
Much of modern history now is less a mystery.
What has she to write about? Wheeeeeeeew!

Kitty wants to write! Everybody's writing!
Won't it be exciting, the panic to ensue?
We who all have known her, think what we have shown her!
Read it in the magazines! Which half of *this* is true?
Where did she get *that* idea? Is it him, or who?—
Kitty's wretched enemies now will learn what venom is!
What has she to write about? Wheeeeeeeew!

Gelett Burgess.

DIGHTON IS ENGAGED!

Dighton is engaged! Think of it and tremble!
Two-and-twenty ladies who have known him must dissemble;
Two-and-twenty ladies in a panic must repeat,
"Dighton is a gentleman; will Dighton be discreet?"
All the merry maidens who have known him at his best
Wonder what the girl is like, and if he has confessed.
Dighton the philanderer, will he prove a slanderer?
A man gets confidential ere the honeymoon has sped—
Dighton was a rover then, Dighton lived in clover then;
Dighton is a gentleman—but Dighton is to wed!

Dighton is engaged! Think of it, Corinna!
Watch and see his fiancée smile on you at dinner!
Watch and hear his fiancée whisper, "*That's* the one?"
Try and raise a blush for what you said was "only fun."
Long have you been wedded; have you then forgot?
If you have, I'll venture that a certain man has not!
Dighton had a way with him; did you ever play with him?
Now that dream is over and the episode is dead.
Dighton never harried you after Charlie married you;
Dighton is a gentleman—but Dighton is to wed!

Dighton is engaged! Think of it, Bettina!
Did you ever love him when the sport was rather keener?
Did you ever kiss him as you sat upon the stairs?
Did you ever tell him of your former love affairs?
Think of it uneasily and wonder if his wife
Soon will know the amatory secrets of your life!
    Dighton was impressible, you were quite accessible—
The bachelor who marries late is apt to lose his head.
    Dighton wouldn't hurt you; does it disconcert you?
Dighton. is a gentleman—but Dighton is to wed!

Dighton is engaged! Tremble, Mrs. Alice!
When he comes no longer will you bear the lady malice?
Now he comes to dinner, and he smokes cigars with Clint,
But he never makes a blunder and he never drops a hint;
He's a universal uncle, with a welcome everywhere,
He adopts his sweetheart's children and he lets 'em pull his
    hair.
    Dighton has a memory bright and sharp as emery,
He *could* tell them fairy stories that would make you rather
    red!
    Dighton can be trusted, though; Dighton's readjusted,
    though!
Dighton is a gentleman—but Dighton is to wed!

Gelett Burgess.

PLAIN LANGUAGE FROM TRUTHFUL JAMES

TABLE MOUNTAIN, 1870

WHICH I wish to remark—
    And my language is plain—
That for ways that are dark,
    And for tricks that are vain,
The heathen Chinee is peculiar,
    Which the same I would rise to explain.

Ah Sin was his name;
  And I will not deny
In regard to the same
  What that name might imply;
But his smile it was pensive and childlike,
  As I frequent remarked to Bill Nye.

It was August the third;
  And quite soft was the skies:
Which it might be inferred
  That Ah Sin was likewise;
Yet he played it that day upon William
  And me in a way I despise.

Which we had a small game,
  And Ah Sin took a hand.
It was Euchre. The same
  He did not understand;
But he smiled as he sat by the table,
  With a smile that was childlike and bland.

Yet the cards they were stocked
  In a way that I grieve,
And my feelings were shocked
  At the state of Nye's sleeve:
Which was stuffed full of aces and bowers,
  And the same with intent to deceive.

But the hands that were played
  By that heathen Chinee,
And the points that he made,
  Were quite frightful to see—
Till at last he put down a right bower,
  Which the same Nye had dealt unto me.

Then I looked up at Nye,
  And he gazed upon me;
And he rose with a sigh,
  And said, " Can this be?
We are ruined by Chinese cheap labour—"
  And he went for that heathen Chinee.

In the scene that ensued
  I did not take a hand;
But the floor it was strewed
  Like the leaves on the strand
With the cards that Ah Sin had been hiding,
  In the game " he did not understand."

In his sleeves, which were long,
  He had twenty-four packs—
Which was coming it strong,
  Yet I state but the facts;
And we found on his nails, which were taper,
  What is frequent in tapers—that's wax.

Which is why I remark,
  And my language is plain,
That for ways that are dark,
  And for tricks that are vain,
The heathen Chinee is peculiar—
  Which the same I am free to maintain.

Bret Harte.

THE SOCIETY UPON THE STANISLAUS

I RESIDE at Table Mountain, and my name is Truthful James;
I am not up to small deceit, or any sinful games;
And I'll tell in simple language what I know about the row
That broke up our society upon the Stanislow.

But first I would remark, that it is not a proper plan
For any scientific man to whale his fellow-man,
And, if a member don't agree with his peculiar whim,
To lay for that same member for to " put a head " on him.

Now, nothing could be finer or more beautiful to see
Than the first six months' proceedings of that same society,
Till Brown of Calaveras brought a lot of fossil bones
That he found within a tunnel near the tenement of Jones.

Then Brown he read a paper, and he reconstructed there,
From those same bones, an animal that was extremely rare;
And Jones then asked the Chair for a suspension of the
      rules,
Till he could prove that those same bones was one of his lost
      mules.

Then Brown he smiled a bitter smile and said he was at
      fault,
It seemed he had been trespassing on Jones's family vault;
He was a most sarcastic man, this quiet Mr. Brown,
And on several occasions he had cleaned out the town.

Now, I hold it is not decent for a scientific gent
To say another is an ass—at least, to all intent;
Nor should the individual who happens to be meant
Reply by heaving rocks at him to any great extent.

Then Abner Dean of Angel's raised a point of order, when
A chunk of old red sandstone took him in the abdomen,
And he smiled a kind of sickly smile, and curled up on the
      floor,
And the subsequent proceedings interested him no more.

For, in less time than I write it, every member did engage
In a warfare with the remnants of a palæozoic age;
And the way they heaved those fossils in their anger was a
      sin,
Till the skull of an old mammoth caved the head of Thomp-
      son in.

And this is all I have to say of these improper games
For I live at Table Mountain, and my name is Truthful
      James;
And I've told, in simple language, what I know about the
      row
That broke up our society upon the Stanislow.

                                        Bret Harte.

" JIM "

Say there! P'r'aps
Some on you chaps
    Might know Jim Wild?
Well,—no offence:
Thar ain't no sense
    In gittin' riled!

Jim was my chum
    Up on the Bar:
That's why I come
    Down from up yar,
Lookin' for Jim.
Thank ye, sir! *you*
Ain't of that crew,—
    Blest if you are!

Money?—Not much;
    That ain't my kind:
I ain't no such.
    Rum?—I don't mind,
Seein' it's you.

Well, this yer Jim,
Did you know him?—
Jess 'bout your size;
Same kind of eyes;—

Well, that is strange:
    Why, it's two year
    Since he came here,
Sick, for a change.
Well, here's to us:
    Eh?
The h—, you say!
    Dead?
That little cuss?

What makes you star,—
You over thar?
Can't a man drop
's glass 'n yer shop
But you must rar'?
    It wouldn't take
    D— much to break
You and your bar.

    Dead!
Poor—little—Jim!
—Why, thar was me,
Jones, and Bob Lee,
Harry and Ben,—
No—account men:
Then to take *him!*

Well, thar—Good-bye—
No more, sir,—I—
    Eh?
What's that you say?—
Why, dern it!—sho!—
No? Yes! By Jo!

    Sold!
Sold! Why, you limb!
You ornery,
    Derned old
Long-legged Jim!

Bret Harte.

WILLIAM BROWN OF OREGON

They called him Bill, the hired man,
  But she, her name was Mary Jane,
  The Squire's daughter; and to reign
The belle from Ber-she-be to Dan
Her little game. How lovers rash
  Got mittens at the spelling school!
  How many a mute, inglorious fool
Wrote rhymes and sighed and died—mustache!

This hired man had loved her long,
    Had loved her best and first and last,
    Her very garments as she passed
For him had symphony and song.
So when one day with sudden frown
    She called him "Bill," he raised his head,
    He caught her eye and, faltering, said,
"I love you; and my name is Brown."

She fairly waltzed with rage; she wept;
    You would have thought the house on fire.
    She told her sire, the portly squire,
Then smelt her smelling-salts, and slept.
Poor William did what could be done;
    He swung a pistol on each hip,
    He gathered up a great ox-whip,
And drove toward the setting sun.

He crossed the great back-bone of earth,
    He saw the snowy mountains rolled
    Like mighty billows; saw the gold
Of awful sunsets; felt the birth
Of sudden dawn that burst the night
    Like resurrection; saw the face
    Of God and named it boundless space
Ringed round with room and shoreless light.

Her lovers passed. Wolves hunt in packs,
    They sought for bigger game; somehow
    They seemed to see above her brow
The forky sign of turkey tracks.
The teter-board of life goes up,
    The teter-board of life goes down,
    The sweetest face must learn to frown;
The biggest dog has been a pup.

O maidens! pluck not at the air;
    The sweetest flowers I have found
    Grow rather close unto the ground,
And highest places are most bare.

Why, you had better win the grace
  Of our poor cussed Af-ri-can,
  Than win the eyes of every man
In love alone with his own face.

At last she nursed her true desire.
  She sighed, she wept for William Brown,
  She watched the splendid sun go down
Like some great sailing ship on fire,
Then rose and checked her trunk right on;
  And in the cars she lunched and lunched,
  And had her ticket punched and punched,
Until she came to Oregon.

She reached the limit of the lines,
  She wore blue specs upon her nose,
  Wore rather short and manly clothes,
And so set out to reach the mines.
Her pocket held a parasol
  Her right hand held a Testament,
  And thus equipped right on she went,
Went water-proof and water-fall.

She saw a miner gazing down,
  Slow stirring something with a spoon;
  " O, tell me true and tell me soon,
What has become of William Brown? "
He looked askance beneath her specs,
  Then stirred his cocktail round and round,
  Then raised his head and sighed profound,
And said, " He's handed in his checks."

Then care fed on her damaged cheek,
  And she grew faint, did Mary Jane,
  And smelt her smelling-salts in vain,
She wandered, weary, worn, and weak.
At last, upon a hill alone,
  She came, and there she sat her down;
  For on that hill there stood a stone.
And, lo! that stone read, " William Brown."

"O William Brown! O William Brown!
 And here you rest at last," she said,
 "With this lone stone above your head,
And forty miles from any town!
I will plant cypress trees, I will,
 And I will build a fence around,
 And I will fertilise the ground
With tears enough to turn a mill."

She went and got a hired man,
 She brought him forty miles from town,
 And in the tall grass squatted down
And bade him build as she should plan.
But cruel cow-boys with their bands
 They saw, and hurriedly they ran
 And told a bearded cattle man
Somebody builded on his lands.

He took his rifle from the rack,
 He girt himself in battle pelt,
 He stuck two pistols in his belt,
And, mounting on his horse's back,
He plunged ahead. But when they showed
 A woman fair, about his eyes
 He pulled his hat, and he likewise
Pulled at his beard, and chewed and chewed.

At last he gat him down and spake:
 "O lady dear, what do you here?"
 "I build a tomb unto my dear,
I plant sweet flowers for his sake."
The bearded man threw his two hands
 Above his head, then brought them down
 And cried, "Oh, I am William Brown,
And this the corner-stone of my lands!"

Joaquin Miller.

LITTLE BREECHES

I DON'T go much on religion,
   I never ain't had no show;
But I've got a middlin' tight grip, sir,
   On a handful o' things I know.
I don't pan out on the prophets
   And free-will and that sort of thing—
But I be'lieve in God and the angels,
   Ever sence one night last spring.

I come into town with some turnips,
   And my little Gabe come along—
No four-year-old in the county
   Could beat him for pretty and strong—
Peart and chipper and sassy,
   Always ready to swear and fight—
And I'd larnt him to chaw terbacker
   Jest to keep his milk-teeth white.

The snow come down like a blanket
   As I passed by Taggart's store;
I went in for a jug of molasses
   And left the team at the door.
They scared at something and started—
   I heard one little squall,
And hell-to-split over the prairie!
   Went team, Little Breeches, and all.

Hell-to-split over the prairie!
   I was almost froze with skeer;
But we rousted up some torches,
   And sarched for 'em far and near.
At last we struck hosses and wagon,
   Snowed under a soft white mound,
Upsot, dead beat, but of little Gabe
   No hide nor hair was found.

And here all hope soured on me
　　Of my fellow-critter's aid;
I jest flopped down on my marrow-bones,
　　Crotch-deep in the snow, and prayed.

　　　．　　　．　　　．　　　．　　　．

By this, the torches was played out,
　　And me and Isrul Parr
Went off for some wood to a sheepfold
　　That he said was somewhar thar.

We found it at last, and a little shed
　　Where they shut up the lambs at night;
We looked in and seen them huddled thar,
　　So warm and sleepy and white;
And thar sot Little Breeches and chirped,
　　As peart as ever you see,
" I want a chaw of terbacker,
　　And that's what's the matter of me."

How did he git thar? Angels.
　　He could never have walked in that storm:
They jest scooped down and toted him
　　To whar it was safe and warm.
And I think that saving a little child,
　　And fotching him to his own,
Is a derned sight better business
　　Than loafing around the Throne.

John Hay.

THE ENCHANTED SHIRT

THE King was sick. His cheek was red,
　　And his eye was clear and bright;
He ate and drank with a kingly zest,
　　And peacefully snored at night.

But he said he was sick, and a king should know,
　　And doctors came by the score.
They did not cure him. He cut off their heads,
　　And sent to the schools for more.

At last two famous doctors came,
  And one was as poor as a rat,—
He had passed his life in studious toil,
  And never found time to grow fat.

The other had never looked in a book;
  His patients gave him no trouble:
If they recovered, they paid him well;
  If they died, their heirs paid double.

Together they looked at the royal tongue,
  As the King on his couch reclined;
In succession they thumped his august chest,
  But no trace of disease could find.

The old sage said, "You're as sound as a nut."
  "Hang him up," roared the King in a gale—
In a ten-knot gale of royal rage;
  The other leech grew a shade pale;

But he pensively rubbed his sagacious nose,
  And thus his prescription ran—
*The King will be well, if he sleeps one night
  In the Shirt of a Happy Man.*

.   .   .   .   .

Wide o'er the realm the couriers rode,
  And fast their horses ran,
And many they saw, and to many they spoke,
  But they found no Happy Man.

They found poor men who would fain be rich,
  And rich who thought they were poor;
And men who twisted their waist in stays,
  And women that shorthose wore.

They saw two men by the roadside sit,
  And both bemoaned their lot;
For one had buried his wife, he said,
  And the other one had not.

At last they came to a village gate,
    A beggar lay whistling there;
He whistled, and sang, and laughed, and rolled
    On the grass in the soft June air.

The weary courtiers paused and looked
    At the scamp so blithe and gay;
And one of them said, " Heaven save you, friend!
    You seem to be happy to-day."

" O yes, fair sirs," the rascal laughed,
    And his voice rang free and glad;
" An idle man has so much to do
    That he never has time to be sad."

" This is our man," the courier said;
    " Our luck has lead us aright.
I will give you a hundred ducats, friend,
    For the loan of your shirt to-night."

The merry blackguard lay back on the grass,
    And laughed till his face was black;
" I would do it, God wot," and he roared with the fun,
    " But I haven't a shirt to my back."

    .   .   .   .   .

Each day to the King the reports came in
    Of his unsuccessful spies,
And the sad panorama of human woes
    Passed daily under his eyes.

And he grew ashamed of his useless life,
    And his maladies hatched in gloom;
He opened his windows and let the air
    Of the free heaven into his room.

And out he went in the world, and toiled
    In his own appointed way;
And the people blessed him, the land was glad,
    And the King was well and gay.

John Hay.

JIM BLUDSO

Wal, no! I can't tell whar he lives,
  Because he don't live, you see;
Leastways, he's got out of the habit
  Of livin' like you and me.
Whar have you been for the last three years
  That you haven't heard folks tell
How Jemmy Bludso passed-in his checks,
  The night of the Prairie Belle?

He weren't no saint—them engineers
  Is all pretty much alike—
One wife in Natchez-under-the-Hill,
  And another one here in Pike.
A keerless man in his talk was Jim,
  And an awkward man in a row—
But he never flunked, and he never lied;
  I reckon he never knowed how.

And this was all the religion he had—
  To treat his engines well;
Never be passed on the river;
  To mind the pilot's bell;
And if ever the Prairie Belle took fire,
  A thousand times he swore,
He'd hold her nozzle agin the bank
  Till the last soul got ashore.

All boats have their day on the Mississip,
  And her day come at last.
The Movastar was a better boat,
  But the Belle she wouldn't be passed;
And so come tearin' along that night,—
  The oldest craft on the line,
With a nigger squat on her safety valve,
  And her furnace crammed, rosin and pine.

The fire bust out as she clared the bar,
    And burnt a hole in the night,
And quick as a flash she turned, and made
    To that willer-bank on the right.
There was runnin' and cursin', but Jim yelled out
    Over all the infernal roar,
" I'll hold her nozzle agin the bank
    Till the last galoot's ashore."

Through the hot black breath of the burnin' boat
    Jim Bludso's voice was heard,
And they all had trust in his cussedness,
    And know he would keep his word.
And, sure's you're born, they all got off
    Afore the smokestacks fell,—
And Bludso's ghost went up alone
    In the smoke of the Prairie Belle.

He weren't no saint—but at jedgment
    I'd run my chance with Jim,
'Longside of some pious gentlemen
    That wouldn't shook hands with him.
He'd seen his duty, a dead-sure thing—
    And went for it thar and then:
And Christ ain't a going to be too hard
    On a man that died for men.

John Hay.

WRECK OF THE "JULIE PLANTE"

On wan dark night on Lac St. Pierre,
    De win' she blow, blow, blow,
An' de crew of de wood scow " Julie Plante "
    Got scar't an' run below;
For de win' she blow lak hurricane,
    Bimeby she blow some more,
An' de scow bus' up on Lac St. Pierre,
    Wan arpent from de shore.

De Captinne walk on de fronte deck,
  An' walk de hin' deck, too—
He call de crew from up de hole
  He call de cook also.
De cook she's name was Rosie,
  She come from Montreal,
Was chambre maid on lumber barge,
  On de Grande Lachine Canal.

De win' she blow from nor'—eas'—wes'—
  De sout' win' she blow, too,
W'en Rosie cry " Mon cher Captinne,
  Mon cher, w'at I shall do? "
Den de Captinne t'row de big ankerre,
  But still de scow she dreef,
De crew he can't pass on de shore,
  Becos' he los' hees skeef.

De night was dark, lak' one black cat,
  De wave run high an' fas',
W'en de Captinne tak' de Rosie girl
  An' tie her to de mas'.
Den he also tak' de life preserve,
  An' jomp off on de lak',
An' say, " Good by, ma Rosie dear,
  I go drown for your sak'."

Nex' morning very early,
  'Bout ha'f-pas' two—t'ree—four—
De Captinne, scow, an' de poor Rosie
  Was corpses on de shore;
For he win' she blow lak' hurricane
  Bimeby she blow some more,
An' de scow bus' up on Lac St. Pierre,
  Wan arpent from de shore.

MORAL

Now, all good wood scow sailor man
  Tak' warning by dat storm,
An' go an' marry some nice French girl
  An' leev on wan beeg farm;

De win' can blow lak' hurricane,
An' s'pose she blow some more,
You can't get drown on Lac St. Pierre,
So long you stay on shore.

William Henry Drummond.

THE ALARMED SKIPPER

"IT WAS AN ANCIENT MARINER"

MANY a long, long year ago,
Nantucket skippers had a plan
Of finding out, though "lying low,"
How near New York their schooners ran.

They greased the lead before it fell,
And then, by sounding through the night,
Knowing the soil that stuck, so well,
They always guessed their reckoning right.

A skipper gray, whose eyes were dim,
Could tell, by *tasting*, just the spot,
And so below he'd "dowse the glim"—
After, of course, his "something hot."

Snug in his berth, at eight o'clock,
This ancient skipper might be found;
No matter how his craft would rock,
He slept—for skippers' naps are sound!

The watch on deck would now and then
Run down and wake him, with the lead;
He'd up, and taste, and tell the men
How many miles they went ahead.

One night, 'twas Jotham Marden's watch,
A curious wag—the peddler's son—
And so he mused (the wanton wretch),
"To-night I'll have a grain of fun.

" We're all a set of stupid fools
To think the skipper knows by *tasting*
What ground he's on—Nantucket schools
Don't teach such stuff, with all their basting!"

And so he took the well-greased lead
And rubbed it o'er a box of earth
That stood on deck—a parsnip-bed—
And then he sought the skipper's berth.

" Where are we now, sir? Please to taste."
The skipper yawned, put out his tongue,
Then ope'd his eyes in wondrous haste,
And then upon the floor he sprung!

The skipper stormed and tore his hair,
Thrust on his boots, and roared to Marden,
" *Nantucket's sunk, and here we are*
Right over old Marm Hackett's garden!"

James Thomas Fields.

THE ELDERLY GENTLEMAN

By the side of a murmuring stream an elderly gentleman sat.
On the top of his head was a wig, and a-top of his wig was
his hat.

The wind it blew high and blew strong, as the elderly gentle-
man sat;
And bore from his head in a trice, and plunged in the river
his hat.

The gentleman then took his cane which lay by his side
as he sat;
And he dropped in the river his wig, in attempting to get
out his hat.

His breast it grew cold with despair, and full in his eye
madness sat;
So he flung in the river his cane to swim with his wig, and
his hat.

Cool reflection at last came across while this elderly gentle-
man sat;
So he thought he would follow the stream and look for his
cane, wig, and hat.

His head being thicker than common, o'er-balanced the rest
of his fat;
And in plumped this son of a woman to follow his wig,
cane, and hat.

George Canning.

SAYING NOT MEANING

Two gentlemen their appetite had fed,
When opening his toothpick-case, one said,
" It was not until lately that I knew
That *anchovies* on *terrâ firmâ* grew.
" Grow! " cried the other, " yes, they *grow,* indeed,
Like other fish, but not upon the land;
You might as well say grapes grow on a reed,
Or in the Strand! "

" Why, sir," returned the irritated other,
" My brother,
When at Calcutta
Beheld them *bonâ fide* growing;
He wouldn't utter
A lie for love or money, sir; so in
This matter you are thoroughly mistaken."
" Nonsense, sir! nonsense! I can give no credit
To the assertion—none e'er saw or read it;
Your brother, like his evidence, should be shaken."

" Be shaken, sir! let me observe, you are
Perverse—in short—"
" Sir," said the other, sucking his cigar,
And then his port—
" If you will say impossibles are true,
You may affirm just anything you please—
That swans are quadrupeds, and lions blue,
And elephants inhabit Stilton cheese!

Only you must not *force* me to believe
What's propagated merely to deceive."

" Then you force me to say, sir, you're a fool,"
    Return'd the bragger.
Language like this no man can suffer cool:
    It made the listener stagger;
    So, thunder-stricken, he at once replied,
    " The traveler *lied*
Who had the impudence to tell it you; "
" Zounds! then d'ye mean to swear before my face
That anchovies *don't* grow like cloves and mace? "
    " I *do!* "

Disputants often after hot debates
    Leave the contention as they found it—bone,
And take to duelling or thumping *têtes;*
    Thinking by strength of artery to atone
For strength of argument; and he who winces
From force of words, with force of arms convinces!

With pistols, powder, bullets, surgeons, lint,
    Seconds, and smelling-bottles, and foreboding,
    Our friends advanced; and now portentous loading
(Their hearts already loaded) serv'd to show
It might be better they shook hands—but no;
    When each opines himself, though frighten'd, right,
    Each is, in courtesy, oblig'd to fight!
And they *did* fight: from six full measured paces
    The unbeliever pulled his trigger first;
And fearing, from the braggart's ugly faces,
    The whizzing lead had whizz'd its very worst,
Ran up, and with a *duelistic* fear
    (His ire evanishing like morning vapors),
Found him possess'd of one remaining ear,
    Who in a manner sudden and uncouth,
    Had given, not lent, the other ear to truth;
For while the surgeon was applying lint,
He, wriggling, cried—" The deuce is in't—
    " Sir, I *meant*—CAPERS! "

William Basil Wake.

HANS BREITMANN'S PARTY

Hans Breitmann gife a barty;
   Dey had biano-blayin':
I felled in lofe mit a Merican frau,
   Her name was Madilda Yane.
She hat haar as prown ash a pretzel,
   Her eyes vas himmel-plue,
Und ven dey looket indo mine,
   Dey shplit mine heart in two.

Hans Breitmann gife a barty:
   I vent dere, you'll pe pound.
I valtzet mit Madilda Yane
   Und vent shpinnen round und round.
De pootiest Fräulein in de house,
   She vayed 'pout dwo hoondred pound,
Und efery dime she gife a shoomp
   She make de vindows sound.

Hans Breitmann gife a barty:
   I dells you it cost him dear.
Dey rolled in more ash sefen kecks
   Of foost-rate Lager Beer,
Und venefer dey knocks de shpicket in
   De Deutschers gifes a cheer.
I dinks dat so vine a barty
   Nefer coom to a het dis year.

Hans Breitmann gife a barty:
   Dere all vas Souse und Brouse;
Ven de sooper comed in, de gompany
   Did make demselfs to house.
Dey ate das Brot und Gensy broost,
   De Bratwurst und Braten fine,
Und vash der Abendessen down
   Mit four parrels of Neckarwein.

Hans Breitmann gife a barty.
   We all cot troonk ash bigs.
I poot mine mout to a parrel of bier,
   Und emptied it oop mit a schwigs.
Und denn I gissed Madilda Yane
   Und she shlog me on de kop,
Und de gompany fited mit daple-lecks
   Dill be coonshtable made oos shtop.

Hans Breitmann gife a barty—
   Where ish dat barty now!
Where ish de lofely golden cloud
   Dat float on de moundain's prow?
Where ish de himmelstrahlende Stern—
   De shtar of de shpirit's light?
All goned afay mit de Lager Beer—
   Afay in de Ewigkeit!

Charles Godfrey Leland.

BALLAD BY HANS BREITMANN

Der noble Ritter Hugo
   Von Schwillensaufenstein
Rode out mit shpeer and helmet,
   Und he coom to de panks of de Rhine.

Und oop dere rose a meermaid,
   Fot hadn't got nodings on,
Und she say, " Oh, Ritter Hugo,
   Vhere you goes mit yourself alone? "

And he says, " I ride in de creenwood,
   Mit helmet und mit shpeer,
Till I cooms into em Gasthaus,
   Und dere I trinks some beer."

Und den outshpoke the maiden
   Vot hadn't got nodings on:
" I ton't tink mooch of beoplesh
   Dat goes mit demselfs alone.

" You'd petter coom down in de wasser,
　　Vhere deres heaps of dings to see,
Und hafe a shplendid tinner
　　Und drafel along mit me.

" Dere you sees de fisch a schwimmin',
　　Und you catches dem efery von: "—
So sang dis wasser maiden,
　　Vot hadn't got nodings on.

" Dere ish drunks all full mit money
　　In ships dat vent down of old;
Und you helpsh yourself, by dunder!
　　To shimmerin' crowns of gold.

" Shoost look at these shpoons and vatches!
　　Shoost see dese diamant rings!
Coom down and fill your pockets,
　　And I'll giss you like efery dings.

" Vot you vanst mit your schnapps and lager?
　　Come down into der Rhine!
Der ish pottles de Kaiser Charlemagne
　　Vonce filled mit gold-red wine! "

Dat fetched him—she shtood all shpell-pound;
　　She pooled his coat-tails down;
She drawed him oonder der wasser,
　　De maiden mit nodings on.

　　　　　　　　　　　　Charles Godfrey Leland.

GRAMPY SINGS A SONG

Row-diddy, dow de, my little sis,
Hush up your teasin' and listen to this:
'Tain't much of a jingle, 'tain't much of a tune,
But it's spang-fired truth about Chester Cahoon.
The thund'rinest fireman Lord ever made
Was Chester Cahoon of the Tuttsville Brigade.
He was boss of the tub and the foreman of hose;
When the 'larm rung he'd start, sis, a-sheddin' his clothes,

—Slung cote and slung wes'cote and kicked off his shoes,
A-runnin' like fun, for he'd no time to lose.
And he'd howl down the ro'd in a big cloud of dust,
For he made it his brag he was allus there fust.
—Allus there fust, with a whoop and a shout,
And he never shut up till the fire was out.
And he'd knock out the winders and save all the doors,
And tear off the clapboards, and rip up the floors,
For he allus allowed 'twas a tarnation sin
To 'low 'em to burn, for you'd want 'em agin.
He gen'rally stirred up the most of his touse
In hustling to save the outside of the house.
And after he'd wrassled and hollered and pried,
He'd let up and tackle the stuff 'twas inside.
To see him you'd think he was daft as a loon,
But that was jest habit with Chester Cahoon.

Row diddy-iddy, my little sis,
Now see what ye think of a doin' like this:
The time of the fire at Jenkins' old place
It got a big start—was a desprit case;
The fambly they didn't know which way to turn.
And by gracious, it looked like it all was to burn.
But Chester Cahoon—oh, that Chester Cahoon,
He sailed to the roof like a reg'lar balloon;
Donno how he done it, but done it he did,
—Went down through the scuttle and shet down the lid.
And five minutes later that critter he came
To the second floor winder surrounded by flame.
He lugged in his arms, sis, a stove and a bed,
And balanced a bureau right square on his head.
His hands they was loaded with crockery stuff,
China and glass; as if that warn't enough,
He'd rolls of big quilts round his neck like a wreath,
And carried Mis' Jenkins' old aunt with his teeth.
You're right—gospel right, little sis,—didn't seem
The critter'd git down, but he called for the stream,
And when it come strong and big round as my wrist,
He stuck out his legs, sis, and give 'em a twist;
And he hooked round the water jes' if 'twas a rope,
And down he come easin' himself on the slope,

—So almighty spry that he made that 'ere stream
As fit for his pupp'us' as if 'twas a beam.
Oh, the thund'rinest fireman Lord ever made
Was Chester Cahoon of the Tuttsville Brigade.

Holman F. Day.

THE FIRST BANJO

Go 'way, fiddle; folks is tired o' hearin' you a-squawkin'—
Keep silence fur yo' betters!—don't you heah de banjo
    talkin'?
About de 'possum's tail she's gwine to lecter—ladies, listen!—
About de ha'r whut isn't dar, an' why de ha'r is missin':

" Dar's gwine to be a' oberflow," said Noah, lookin' solemn—
Fur Noah tuk the " *Herald*," an' he read de ribber column—
An' so he sot his hands to wuk a-cl'arin' timber-patches,
An' 'lowed he's gwine to build a boat to beat de steamah
    Natchez.

Ol' Noah kep' a-nailin' an' a-chippin' an' a-sawin';
An' all de wicked neighbours kep' a-laughin' an' a-pshawin';
But Noah didn't min' 'em, knowin' whut wuz gwine to
    happen:
An' forty days an' forty nights de rain it kep' a-drappin'.

Now, Noah had done cotched a lot ob ebry sort o' beas'es—
Ob all de shows a-trabbelin', it beat 'em all to pieces!
He had a Morgan colt an' sebral head o' Jarsey cattle—
An' druv 'em 'board de Ark as soon 's he heered de thunder
    rattle.

Den sech anoder fall ob rain!—it come so awful hebby,
De ribber riz immejitly, an' busted troo de lebbee;
De people all wuz drownded out—'cep' Noah an' de critters,
An' men he'd hired to work de boat—an' one to mix de bitters.

De Ark she kep' a-sailin' an' a-sailin', *an'* a-sailin';
De lion got his dander up, an' like to bruk de palin';

De sarpints hissed; de painters yelled; tell, whut wid all de
    fussin',
You c'u'dn't hardly heah de mate a-bossin' round' an'
    cussin'.

Now, Ham, he only nigger whut wuz runnin' on de packet,
Got lonesome in de barber-shop, and c'u'dn't stan' de racket;
An' so, fur to amuse he-se'f, he steamed some wood an'
    bent it,
An' soon he had a banjo made—de fust dat wuz invented.

He wet de ledder, stretched it on; made bridge an' screws
    an aprin;
An' fitted in a proper neck—'twas berry long and tap'rin';
He tuk some tin, an' twisted him a thimble fur to ring it;
An' den de mighty question riz: how wuz he gwine to
    string it?

De 'possum had as fine a tail as dis dat I's a-singin';
De ha'r's so long an' thick an' strong,—des fit fur banjo-
    stringin';
Dat nigger shaved 'em off as short as wash-day-dinner
    graces;
An' sorted ob 'em by de size, f'om little E's to basses.

He strung her, tuned her, struck a jig,—'twus " Nebber
    min' de wedder,"—
She soun' like forty-lebben bands a-playin' all togedder;
Some went to pattin'; some to dancin': Noah called de
    figgers;
An' Ham he sot an' knocked de tune, de happiest ob niggers!

Now, sence dat time—it's mighty strange—dere's not de
    slightes' showin'
Ob any ha'r at all upon de 'possum's tail a-growin';
An' curi's, too, dat nigger's ways: his people nebber los'
    'em—
Fur whar you finds de nigger—dar's de banjo an' de 'possum!

                         Irwin Russell.

THE ROMANCE OF THE CARPET

Basking in peace in the warm spring sun,
South Hill smiled upon Burlington.

The breath of May! and the day was fair,
And the bright motes danced in the balmy air.

And the sunlight gleamed where the restless breeze
Kissed the fragrant blooms on the apple-trees.

His beardless cheek with a smile was spanned,
As he stood with a carriage whip in his hand.

And he laughed as he doffed his bobtail coat,
And the echoing folds of the carpet smote.

And she smiled as she leaned on her busy mop,
And said she'd tell him when to stop.

So he pounded away till the dinner-bell
Gave him a little breathing spell.

But he sighed when the kitchen clock struck one,
And she said the carpet wasn't done.

But he lovingly put in his biggest licks,
And he pounded like mad till the clock struck six.

And she said, in a dubious sort of way,
That she guessed he could finish it up next day.

Then all that day, and the next day, too,
That fuzz from the dirtless carpet flew.

And she'd give it a look at eventide,
And say, " Now beat on the other side."

And the new days came as the old days went,
And the landlord came for his regular rent.

And the neighbors laughed at the tireless broom,
And his face was shadowed with clouds of gloom.

Till at last, one cheerless winter day,
He kicked at the carpet and slid away.

Over the fence and down the street,
Speeding away with footsteps fleet.

And never again the morning sun
Smiled on him beating his carpet-drum.

And South Hill often said with a yawn,
" Where's the carpet-martyr gone? "

Years twice twenty had come and passed
And the carpet swayed in the autumn blast.

For never yet, since that bright spring-time,
Had it ever been taken down from the line.

Over the fence a gray-haired man
Cautiously clim, clome, clem, clum, clamb.

He found him a stick in the old woodpile,
And he gathered it up with a sad, grim smile.

A flush passed over his face forlorn
As he gazed at the carpet, tattered and torn.

And he hit it a most resounding thwack,
Till the startled air gave his echoes back.

And out of the window a white face leaned,
And a palsied hand the pale face screened.

She knew his face; she gasped, and sighed,
" A little more on the other side."

Right down on the ground his stick he throwed,
And he shivered and said, " Well, I am blowed! "

And he turned away, with a heart full sore,
And he never was seen not more, not more.

Robert J. Burdette.

THE HUNTING OF THE SNARK

" Come, listen, my men, while I tell you again
　　The five unmistakable marks
By which you may know, wheresoever you go,
　　The warranted genuine Snarks.

" Let us take them in order. The first is the taste,
　　Which is meagre and hollow, but crisp:
Like a coat that is rather too tight in the waist,
　　With a flavor of Will-o'-the-wisp.

" Its habit of getting up late you'll agree
　　That it carries too far when I say
That it frequently breakfasts at five-o'clock tea,
　　And dines on the following day.

．　　．　　．　　．　　．　　．　　．

" The fourth is its fondness for bathing-machines,
　　Which it constantly carries about,
And believes that they add to the beauty of scenes—
　　A sentiment open to doubt.

" The fifth is ambition. It next will be right
　　To describe each particular batch;
Distinguishing those that have feathers, and bite,
　　From those that have whiskers, and scratch.

" For, although common Snarks do no manner of harm,
　　Yet I feel it my duty to say
Some are Boojums—" The Bellman broke off in alarm,
　　For the Baker had fainted away.

They roused him with muffins—they roused him with ice—
　　They roused him with mustard and cress—
They roused him with jam and judicious advice—
　　They set him conundrums to guess.

When at length he sat up and was able to speak,
   His sad story he offered to tell;
And the Bellman cried "Silence! Not even a shriek!"
   And excitedly tingled his bell.

There was silence supreme! Not a shriek, not a scream,
   Scarcely even a howl or a groan,
As the man they called "Ho!" told his story of woe
   In an antediluvian tone.

"My father and mother were honest, though poor—"
   "Skip all that!" cried the Bellman in haste,
"If it once becomes dark, there's no chance of a Snark,
   We have hardly a minute to waste!"

"I skip forty years," said the Baker, in tears,
   "And proceed without further remark
To the day when you took me aboard of your ship
   To help you in hunting the Snark.

"A dear uncle of mine (after whom I was named)
   Remarked, when I bade him farewell—"
"Oh, skip your dear uncle," the Bellman exclaimed,
   As he angrily tingled his bell.

"He remarked to me then," said that mildest of men,
   "'If your Snark be a Snark, that is right;
Fetch it home by all means—you may serve it with greens
   And it's handy for striking a light.

"'You may seek it with thimbles—and seek it with care;
   You may hunt it with forks and hope;
You may threaten its life with a railway-share;
   You may charm it with smiles and soap—

"'But oh, beamish nephew, beware of the day,
   If your Snark be a Boojum! For then
You will softly and suddenly vanish away
   And never be met with again!'

"It is this, it is this that oppresses my soul,
  When I think of my uncle's last words:
And my heart is like nothing so much as a bowl
  Brimming over with quivering curds!

"I engage with the Snark—every night after dark—
  In a dreamy delirious fight:
I serve it with greens in those shadowy scenes,
  And I use it for striking a light:

"But if ever I meet with a Boojum, that day,
  In a moment (of this I am sure),
I shall softly and suddenly vanish away—
  And the notion I cannot endure!"

Lewis Carroll.

THE OLD MAN AND JIM

OLD man never had much to say—
    'Ceptin' to Jim,—
And Jim was the wildest boy he had—
    And the Old man jes' wrapped up in him!
Never heerd him speak but once
Er twice in my life,—and first time was
When the army broke out, and Jim he went,
The Old man backin' him, fer three months.—
And all 'at I heerd the Old man say
Was, jes' as we turned to start away,—
    "Well; good-bye, Jim:
        Take keer of yourse'f!"

'Peard-like, he was more satisfied
    Jes' *lookin'* at Jim,
And likin' him all to hisse'f-like, see?—
    'Cause he was jes' wrapped up in him!
And over and over I mind the day
The Old man come and stood round in the way
While we was drillin', a-watchin' Jim—
And down at the deepot a-heerin' him say,—
    "Well; good-bye, Jim:
        Take keer of yourse'f!"

Never was nothin' about the farm
    Disting'ished Jim;—
Neighbours all ust to wonder why
    The Old man 'peared wrapped up in him:
But when Cap. Biggler, he writ back,
'At Jim was the bravest boy we had
In the whole dern rigiment, white er black,
And his fightin' good as his farmin' bad—
'At he had led, with a bullet clean
Bored through his thigh, and carried the flag
Through the bloodiest battle you ever seen,—
The Old man wound up a letter to him
'At Cap. read to us, 'at said,—" Tell Jim
    Good-bye;
        And take keer of hisse'f."

Jim come back jes' long enough
    To take the whim
'At he'd like to go back in the cavelry—
    And the Old man jes' wrapped up in him!—
Jim 'lowed 'at he'd had sich luck afore,
Guessed he'd tackle her three years more.
And the Old man give him a colt he'd raised
And follered him over to Camp Ben Wade,
And laid around fer a week er so,
Watchin' Jim on dress-parade—
Tel finally he rid away,
And last he heerd was the Old man say,—
    " Well; good-bye, Jim:
        Take keer of yourse'f! "

Tuk the papers, the Old man did,
    A-watchin' fer Jim—
Fully believin' he'd make his mark
    Some way—jes' wrapped up in him!—
And many a time the word 'u'd come
'At stirred him up like the tap of a drum—
At Petersburg, fer instance, where
Jim rid right into their cannons there,
And tuk 'em, and p'inted 'em t'other way,
And socked it home to the boys in grey,

As they skooted fer timber, and on and on—
Jim a lieutenant and one arm gone,
And the Old man's words in his mind all day,—
        " Well; good-bye, Jim:
                Take keer of yourse'f! "

Think of a private, now, perhaps,
        We'll say like Jim,
'At's clumb clean up to the shoulder-straps—
        And the Old man jes' wrapped up in him!
Think of him—with the war plum' through,
And the glorious old Red-White-and-Blue
A-laughin' the news down over Jim,
And the Old man, bendin' over him—
The surgeon turnin' away with tears
'At hadn't leaked fer years and years—
As the hand of the dyin' boy clung to
His father's, the old voice in his ears,—
        " Well; good-bye, Jim:
                Take keer of yourse'f! "

James Whitcomb Riley.

A SAILOR'S YARN

This is the tale that was told to me,
By a battered and shattered son of the sea—
To me and my messmate, Silas Green,
When I was a guileless young marine.

" 'Twas the good ship *Gyascutus,*
        All in the China seas,
With the wind a-lee and the capstan free
        To catch the summer breeze.

" 'Twas Captain Porgie on the deck,
        To his mate in the mizzen hatch,
While the boatswain bold, in the forward hold,
        Was winding the larboard watch.

"'Oh, how does our good ship head to-night?
 How heads our gallant craft?'
'Oh, she heads to the E. S. W. by N.,
 And the binnacle lies abaft!'

"'Oh, what does the quadrant indicate,
 And how does the sextant stand?'
'Oh, the sextant's down to the freezing point,
 And the quadrant's lost a hand!'

"'Oh, and if the quadrant has lost a hand,
 And the sextant falls so low,
It's our bodies and bones to Davy Jones
 This night are bound to go!

"'Oh, fly aloft to the garboard strake!
 And reef the spanker boom;
Bend a studding sail on the martingale,
 To give her weather room.

"'Oh, boatswain, down in the for'ard hold
 What water do you find?'
'Four foot and a half by the royal gaff
 And rather more behind!'

"'Oh, sailors, collar your marline spikes
 And each belaying pin;
Come stir your stumps, and spike the pumps,
 Or more will be coming in!'

"They stirred their stumps, they spiked the pumps,
 They spliced the mizzen brace;
Aloft and alow they worked, but oh!
 The water gained apace.

"They bored a hole above the keel
 To let the water out;
But, strange to say, to their dismay,
 The water in did spout.

" Then up spoke the Cook of our gallant ship,
  And he was a lubber brave:
' I have several wives in various ports,
  And my life I'd orter save.'

" Then up spoke the Captain of Marines,
  Who dearly loved his prog:
' It's awful to die, and it's worse to be dry,
  And I move we pipe to grog.'

" Oh, then 'twas the noble second mate
  What filled them all with awe;
The second mate, as bad men hate,
  And cruel skipper's jaw.

" He took the anchor on his back,
  And leaped into the main;
Through foam and spray he clove his way,
  And sunk and rose again!

" Through foam and spray, a league away
  The anchor stout he bore;
Till, safe at last, he made it fast
  And warped the ship ashore!

" 'Taint much of a job to talk about,
  But a ticklish thing to see,
And suth'in to do, if I say it, too,
  For that second mate was me! "

Such was the tale that was told to me
By that modest and truthful son of the sea,
And I envy the life of a second mate,
Though captains curse him and sailors hate,
For he ain't like some of the swabs I've seen,
As would go and lie to a poor marine.

James Jeffrey Roche.

THE CONVERTED CANNIBALS

Upon an island, all alone,
   They lived, in the Pacific;
Somewhere within the Torrid Zone,
   Where heat is quite terrific.
'Twould shock you were I to declare
The many things they did not wear,
     Altho' no doubt
     One's best without
Such things in heat terrific.

Though cannibals by birth were they,
   Yet, since they'd first existed,
Their simple menu day by day
   Of such-like things consisted:
Omelets of turtle's eggs, and yams,
And stews from freshly-gathered clams,
     Such things as these
     Were,—if you please,—
Of what their fare consisted.

But after dinner they'd converse,
   Nor did their topic vary;
Wild tales of gore they would rehearse,
   And talk of *missionary.*
They'd gaze upon each other's joints,
And indicate the tender points.
     Said one: "For us
     'Tis dangerous
To *think* of *missionary.*"

Well, on a day, upon the shore,
   As flotsam, or as jetsam,
Some wooden cases,—ten, or more,—
   Were cast up. "Let us get some,
And see, my friend, what they contain;
The chance may not occur again,"
     Said good Who-zoo.
     Said Tum-tum, "Do;
We'll both wade out and get some."

The cases held,—what do you think?—
"PRIME MISSIONARY—TINNED."
Nay! gentle reader, do not shrink—
　The man who made it sinned:
He thus had labelled bloater-paste
To captivate the native taste.
　　　He hoped, of course,
　　　This fraud to force
　On them. In this he sinned.

Our simple friends knew naught of sin;
　They thought that this confection
Was missionary in a tin
　According to direction.
For very joy they shed salt tears.
" 'Tis what we've waited for, for years,"
　　　Said they.　" Hooray!
　　　We'll feast to-day
　According to direction."

" 'Tis very tough," said one, for he
　The tin and all had eaten.
" Too salt," the other said, " for me;
　The flavour might be beaten."
It was enough.　Soon each one swore
He'd missionary eat no more:
　　　Their tastes were cured,
　　　They felt assured
　This flavour might be beaten.

And, should a missionary call
　To-day, he'd find them gentle,
With no perverted tastes at all,
　And manners ornamental;
He'd be received, I'm bound to say,
In courteous and proper way;
　　　Nor need he fear
　　　To taste their cheer
　However ornamental.

G. E. Farrow.

THE RETIRED PORK-BUTCHER AND THE SPOOK

I MAY as well
Proceed to tell
About a Mister Higgs,
Who grew quite rich
In trade—the which
Was selling pork and pigs.

From trade retired,
He much desired
To rank with gentlefolk,
So bought a place
He called " The Chase,"
And furnished it—old oak.

Ancestors got
(Twelve pounds the lot,
In Tottenham Court Road);
A pedigree—
For nine pounds three,—
The Heralds' Court bestowed.

Within the hall,
And on the wall,
Hung armour bright and strong.
" To Ethelbred "—
The label read—
" De Higgs, this did belong."

'Twas *quite* complete,
This country seat,
Yet neighbours stayed away.
Nobody called,—
Higgs was blackballed,—
Which caused him great dismay.

"Why *can* it be?"
One night said he
When thinking of it o'er.
There came a knock
('Twas twelve o'clock)
Upon his chamber door.

Higgs cried, "Come in!"
A vapour thin
The keyhole wandered through.
Higgs rubbed his eyes
In mild surprise:
A ghost appeared in view.

"I beg," said he,
"You'll pardon me,
In calling rather late.
A family ghost,
I seek a post,
With wage commensurate.

"I'll serve you well;
My 'fiendish yell'
Is certain sure to please.
'Sepulchral tones,'
And 'rattling bones,'
I'm *very* good at these.

"Five bob I charge
To roam at large,
With 'clanking chains' *ad lib.;*
I do such things
As 'gibberings'
At one-and-three per gib.

"Or, by the week,
I merely seek
Two pounds—which is not dear;
Because I need,
Of course, *no* feed,
No washing, and *no* beer."

Higgs thought it o'er
A bit, before
He hired the family ghost,
But, finally,
He did agree
To give to him the post.

It got about—
You know, no doubt,
How quickly such news flies—
Throughout the place,
From " Higgses Chase "
Proceeded ghostly cries.

The rumour spread,
Folks shook their head,
But dropped in one by one.
A bishop came
(Forget his name),
And then the thing was done.

For afterwards
All left their cards,
" Because," said they, " you see,
One who can boast
A family ghost
Respectable *must* be."

When it was due,
The " ghostes's " screw
Higgs raised—as was but right—
They often play,
In friendly way,
A game of cards at night.

G. E. Farrow.

SKIPPER IRESON'S RIDE

Of all the rides since the birth of time,
Told in story or sung in rhyme,—
On Apuleius's Golden Ass,
Or one-eyed Calendar's horse of brass,
Witch astride of a human back,
Islam's prophet on Al-Borak,—
The strangest ride that ever was sped
Was Ireson's, out from Marblehead!
  Old Floyd Ireson, for his hard heart,
    Tarred and feathered and carried in a cart
      By the women of Marblehead!

Body of turkey, head of owl,
Wings a-droop like a rained-on fowl,
Feathered and ruffled in every part,
Skipper Ireson stood in the cart.
Scores of women, old and young,
Strong of muscle, and glib of tongue,
Pushed and pulled up the rocky lane,
Shouting and singing the shrill refrain:
  "Here's Flud Oirson, fur his horrd horrt,
    Torr'd an' futherr'd an' corr'd in a corrt
      By the women o' Morble'ead!"

Wrinkled scolds with hands on hips,
Girls in bloom of cheek and lips,
Wild-eyed, free-limbed, such as chase
Bacchus round some antique vase,
Brief of skirt, with ankles bare,
Loose of kerchief and loose of hair,
With conch-shells blowing and fish-horns' twang,
Over and over the Mænads sang:
  "Here's Flud Oirson, fur his horrd horrt,
    Torr'd an' futherr'd an' corr'd in a corrt
      By the women o' Morble'ead!"

Small pity for him!—He sailed away
From a leaking ship, in Chaleur Bay,—
Sailed away from a sinking wreck,
With his own town's-people on her deck!
"Lay by! lay by!" they called to him.
Back he answered, "Sink or swim!
Brag of your catch of fish again!"
And off he sailed through the fog and rain!
  Old Floyd Ireson, for his hard heart,
  Tarred and feathered and carried in a cart
    By the women of Marblehead!

Fathoms deep in dark Chaleur
That wreck shall lie forevermore.
Mother and sister, wife and maid,
Looked from the rocks of Marblehead
Over the moaning and rainy sea,—
Looked for the coming that might not be!
What did the winds and the sea-birds say
Of the cruel captain who sailed away?—
  Old Floyd Ireson, for his hard heart,
  Tarred and feathered and carried in a cart
    By the women of Marblehead!

Through the street, on either side,
Up flew windows, doors swung wide;
Sharp-tongued spinsters, old wives gray,
Treble lent the fish-horn's bray.
Sea-worn grandsires, cripple-bound,
Hulks of old sailors run aground,
Shook head, and fist, and hat, and cane,
And cracked with curses the hoarse refrain:
  "Here's Flud Oirson, fur his horrd horrt,
  Torr'd an' futherr'd an' corr'd in a corrt
    By the women o' Morble'ead!"

Sweetly along the Salem road
Bloom of orchard and lilac showed.
Little the wicked skipper knew
Of the fields so green and the sky so blue.

Riding there in his sorry trim,
Like an Indian idol glum and grim,
Scarcely he seemed the sound to hear
Of voices shouting, far and near:
   "Here's Flud Oirson, fur his horrd horrt,
   Torr'd an' futherr'd an' corr'd in a corrt
     By the women o' Morble'ead!"

"Hear me, neighbors!" at last he cried,—
"What to me is this noisy ride?
What is the shame that clothes the skin
To the nameless horror that lives within?
Waking or sleeping, I see a wreck,
And hear a cry from a reeling deck!
Hate me and curse me,—I only dread
The hand of God and the face of the dead!"
   Said old Floyd Ireson, for his hard heart,
   Tarred and feathered and carried in a cart
     By the women of Marblehead!

Then the wife of the skipper lost at sea
Said, "God has touched him! Why should we?"
Said an old wife, mourning her only son:
"Cut the rogue's tether and let him run!"
So with soft relentings and rude excuse,
Half scorn, half pity, they cut him loose,
And gave him a cloak to hide him in,
And left him alone with his shame and sin.
   Poor Floyd Ireson, for his hard heart,
   Tarred and feathered and carried in a cart
     By the women of Marblehead!

J. G. Whittier.

DARIUS GREEN AND HIS FLYING-MACHINE

If ever there lived a Yankee lad,
Wise or otherwise, good or bad,
Who, seeing the birds fly, didn't jump
With flapping arms from stake or stump,
    Or, spreading the tail
    Of his coat for a sail,

Take a soaring leap from post or rail,
And wonder why
He couldn't fly,
And flap and flutter and wish and try—
If ever you knew a country dunce
Who didn't try that as often as once,
All I can say is, that's a sign
He never would do for a hero of mine.

An aspiring genius was D. Green:
The son of a farmer, age fourteen;
His body was long and lank and lean—
Just right for flying, as will be seen;
He had two eyes as bright as a bean,
And a freckled nose that grew between,
A little awry—for I must mention
That he had riveted his attention
Upon his wonderful invention,
Twisting his tongue as he twisted the strings,
And working his face as he worked the wings,
And with every turn of gimlet and screw
Turning and screwing his mouth round too,
Till his nose seemed bent
To catch the scent,
Around some corner, of new-baked pies,
And his wrinkled cheeks and his squinting eyes
Grew puckered into a queer grimace,
That made him look very droll in the face,
And also very wise.
And wise he must have been, to do more
Than ever a genius did before,
Excepting Dædalus of yore
And his son Icarus, who wore
Upon their backs
Those wings of wax
He had read of in the old almanacs.
Darius was clearly of the opinion
That the air is also man's dominion,
And that, with paddle or fin or pinion,
We soon or late shall navigate
The azure as now we sail the sea.

The thing looks simple enough to me;
        And if you doubt it,
Hear how Darius reasoned about it.
          " The birds can fly an' why can't I?
          Must we give in," says he with a grin.
          " That the bluebird an' phœbe
          Are smarter'n we be?
Jest fold our hands an' see the swaller
An' blackbird an' catbird beat us holler?
Doos the little chatterin', sassy wren,
No bigger'n my thumb, know more than men?
          Just show me that!
          Ur prove 't the bat
Hez got more brains than's in my hat.
An' I'll back down, an' not till then!"
He argued further: " Nur I can't see
What's th' use o' wings to a bumble-bee,
Fur to git a livin' with, more'n to me;—
          Ain't my business
          Important's his'n is?
          That Icarus
          Made a perty muss—
Him an' his daddy Dædalus
They might 'a' knowed wings made o' wax
Wouldn't stand sun-heat an' hard whacks.
          I'll make mine o' luther,
          Ur suthin' ur other."

And he said to himself, as he tinkered and planned:
" But I ain't goin' to show my hand
To mummies that never can understand
The fust idee that's big an' grand."
So he kept his secret from all the rest,
Safely buttoned within his vest;
And in the loft above the shed
Himself he locks, with thimble and thread
And wax and hammer and buckles and screws
And all such things as geniuses use;—
Two bats for patterns, curious fellows!
A charcoal-pot and a pair of bellows;
Some wire, and several old umbrellas;

A carriage-cover, for tail and wings;
A piece of harness; and straps and strings;
   And a big strong box,
   In which he locks
These and a hundred other things.
His grinning brothers, Reuben and Burke
And Nathan and Jotham and Solomon, lurk
Around the corner to see him work—
Sitting cross-legged, like a Turk,
Drawing the waxed-end through with a jerk,
And boring the holes with a comical quirk
Of his wise old head, and a knowing smirk.
But vainly they mounted each other's backs,
And poked through knot-holes and pried through cracks;
With wood from the pile and straw from the stacks
He plugged the knot-holes and caulked the cracks;
And a dipper of water, which one would think
He had brought up into the loft to drink
   When he chanced to be dry,
   Stood always nigh,
   For Darius was sly!
And whenever at work he happened to spy
At chink or crevice a blinking eye,
He let the dipper of water fly.
"Take that! an' ef ever ye git a peep,
Guess ye'll ketch a weasel asleep!"
   And he sings as he locks
   His big strong box:—

  "The weasel's head is small an' trim,
  An' he is little an' long an' slim,
  An' quick of motion an' nimble of limb,
    An' ef you'll be
    Advised by me,
  Keep wide awake when ye're ketchin' him!"

   So day after day
He stitched and tinkered and hammered away,
   Till at last 'twas done—
The greatest invention under the sun!
"An' now," says Darius, "hooray fur some fun!"

'Twas the Fourth of July,
And the weather was dry,
And not a cloud was on all the sky,
Save a few light fleeces, which here and there,
Half mist, half air,
Like foam on the ocean went floating by—
Just as lovely a morning as ever was seen
For a nice little trip in a flying-machine.
Thought cunning Darius: "Now I shan't go
Along 'ith the fellers to see the show.
I'll say I've got sich a terrible cough!
An' then, when the folks 'ave all gone off,
I'll hev full swing fur to try the thing,
An' practise a little on the wing."
"Ain't goin' to see the celebration?"
Says brother Nate. "No; botheration!
I've got sich a cold—a toothache—I—
My gracious!—feel's though I should fly!"
Said Jotham, "Sho!
Guess ye better go."
But Darius said, "No!
Shouldn't wonder 'f you might see me, though,
'Long 'bout noon, ef I git red
O' this jumpin', thumpin' pain 'n my head."
For all the while to himself he said:—

"I tell ye what!
I'll fly a few times around the lot,
To see how 't seems, then soon's I've got
The hang o' the thing, ez likely's not,
I'll astonish the nation,
An' all creation,
By flyin' over the celebration!
Over their heads I'll sail like an eagle;
I'll balance myself on my wings like a sea-gull:
I'll dance on the chimbleys; I'll stand on the steeple;
I'll flop up to winders an' scare the people!
I'll light on the liberty-pole, an' crow;
An' I'll say to the gawpin' fools below,
'What world's this 'ere
That I've come near?'

Fur I'll make 'em b'lieve I'm a chap f'm the moon;
An' I'll try to race 'ith their ol' balloon!'"
     He crept from his bed;
And, seeing the others were gone, he said,
" I'm gittin' over the cold 'n my head."
     And away he sped,
To open the wonderful box in the shed.

His brothers had walked but a little way,
When Jotham to Nathan chanced to say,
" What is the feller up to, hey!"
" Don'o'—the 's suthin' ur other to pay,
Ur he wouldn't 'a' stayed tu hum to-day."
Says Burke, " His toothache's all 'n his eye!
He never 'd missed a Fo'th-o'-July,
Ef he hedn't got some machine to try."
Then Sol, the little one, spoke: " By darn!
Le's hurry back an' hide 'n the barn,
An' pay him fur tellin' us that yarn!"
" Agreed!" Through the orchard they creep back
Along by the fences, behind the stack,
And one by one, through a hole in the wall,
In under the dusty barn they crawl,
Dressed in their Sunday garments all;
And a very astonishing sight was that,
When each in his cobwebbed coat and hat
Came up through the floor like an ancient rat
     And there they hid;
     And Reuben slid
The fastenings back, and the door undid.
     " Keep dark!" said he,
" While I squint an' see what the' is to see."

As knights of old put on their mail—
     From head to foot an iron suit,
Iron jacket and iron boot,
Iron breeches, and on the head
No hat, but an iron pot instead,
     And under the chin the bail,
(I believe they called the thing a helm,)
Then sallied forth to overwhelm

The dragons and pagans that plagued the earth
     So this *modern* knight
     Prepared for flight,
Put on his wings and strapped them tight
Jointed and jaunty, strong and light—
Buckled them fast to shoulder and hip;
Ten feet they measured from tip to tip
And a helm had he, but that he wore,
Not on his head, like those of yore,
     But more like the helm of a ship.

     " Hush! " Reuben said,
     " He's up in the shed!
He's opened the winder—I see his head!
He stretches it out, an' pokes it about,
Lookin' to see 'f the coast is clear,
     An' nobody near;—
Guess he don' o' who's hid in here!
He's riggin' a spring-board over the sill!
Stop laffin', Solomon! Burke, keep still!
He's a climbin' out now—Of all the things!
What's he got on? I vum, it's wings!
An' that 'tother thing? I vum, it's a tail!
An' there he sits like a hawk on a rail!
Steppin' careful, he travels the length
Of his spring-board, and teeters to try its strength.
Now he stretches his wings, like a monstrous bat;
Peeks over his shoulder; this way an' that,
Fur to see 'f the' 's any one passin' by;
But the' 's on'y a caf an' goslin nigh.
They turn up at him a wonderin' eye,
To see— The dragon! he's goin' to fly!
Away he goes! Jimminy! what a jump!
     Flop—flop—an' plump
     To the ground with a thump!
Flutt'rin' an' flound'rin' all 'n a lump! "

As a demon is hurled by an angel's spear,
Heels over head, to his proper sphere—
Heels over head, and head over heels,
Dizzily down the abyss he wheels—

So fell Darius. Upon his crown,
In the midst of the barn-yard, he came down,
In a wonderful whirl of tangled strings,
Broken braces and broken springs,
Broken tail and broken wings,
Shooting-stars, and various things;
Barn-yard litter of straw and chaff,
And much that wasn't so sweet by half.
Away with a bellow fled the calf,
And what was that? Did the gosling laugh?
'Tis a merry roar from the old barn-door,
And he hears the voice of Jotham crying,
" Say, D'rius! how do you like flyin'? "
Slowly, ruefully, where he lay,
Darius just turned and looked that way,
As he stanched his sorrowful nose with his cuff.
" Wal, I like flyin' well enough,"
He said; " but the' ain't such a thunderin' sight
O' fun in 't when ye come to light."

I just have room for the MORAL here:
And this is the moral—Stick to your sphere.
Or if you insist, as you have the right,
On spreading your wings for a loftier flight,
The moral is—Take care how you light.

John Townsend Trowbridge.

A GREAT FIGHT

" THERE was a man in Arkansaw
    As let his passions rise,
And not unfrequently picked out
    Some other varmint's eyes.

" His name was Tuscaloosa Sam
    And often he would say,
' There's not a cuss in Arkansaw
    I can't whip any day.'

" One morn, a stranger passin' by,
　　Heard Sammy talkin' so,
And down he scrambled from his hoss,
　　And off his coat did go.

" He sorter kinder shut one eye,
　　And spit into his hand,
And put his ugly head one side,
　　And twitched his trowsers' band.

" ' My boy,' says he, ' it's my belief,
　　Whomever you may be,
That I kin make you screech, and smell
　　Pertiklor agony.'

" ' I'm thar,' said Tuscaloosa Sam,
　　And chucked his hat away;
' I'm thar,' says he, and buttoned up
　　As far as buttons may.

" He thundered on the stranger's mug,
　　The stranger pounded he;
And oh! the way them critters fit
　　Was beautiful to see.

" They clinched like two rampageous bears,
　　And then went down a bit;
They swore a stream of six-inch oaths
　　And fit, and fit, and fit.

" When Sam would try to work away,
　　And on his pegs to git,
The stranger'd pull him back; and so,
　　They fit, and fit, and fit!

" Then like a pair of lobsters, both
　　Upon the ground were knit,
And yet the varmints used their teeth,
　　And fit, and fit, and fit! !

" The sun of noon was high above,
   And hot enough to split,
But only riled the fellers more,
   That fit, and fit, and fit! ! !

" The stranger snapped at Samy's nose,
   And shortened it a bit;
And then they both swore awful hard,
   And fit, and fit, and fit! ! ! !

" The mud it flew, the sky grew dark,
   And all the litenins lit;
But still them critters rolled about,
   And fit, and fit, and fit! ! ! ! !

" First Sam on top, then t'other chap;
   When one would make a hit,
The other'd smell the grass; and so
   They fit, and fit, and fit! ! ! ! ! !

" The night came on, the stars shone out
   As bright as wimmen's wit;
And still them fellers swore and gouged,
   And fit, and fit, and fit! ! ! ! ! ! !

" The neighbours heard the noise they made,
   And thought an earthquake lit;
Yet all the while 'twas him and Sam
   As fit, and fit, and fit! ! ! ! ! ! ! !

" For miles around the noise was heard;
   Folks couldn't sleep a bit,
Because them two rantankerous chaps
   Still fit, and fit, and fit! ! ! ! ! ! ! ! !

" But jist at cock-crow, suddenly,
   There came an awful pause,
And I and my old man run out
   To ascertain the cause.

" The sun was rising in the yeast,
  And lit the hull concern;
But not a sign of either chap
  Was found at any turn.

" Yet, in the region where they fit,
  We found, to our surprise,
One pint of buttons, two big knives,
  Some whiskers, and four eyes! "

Robert Henry Newell.

THE DONNYBROOK JIG

OH! 'twas Dermot O'Nolan M'Figg,
That could properly handle a twig,
  He wint to the fair, and kicked up a dust there,
In dancing a Donnybrook jig—with his twig.
Oh! my blessing to Dermot M'Figg.

Whin he came to the midst of the fair,
He was all in a paugh for fresh air,
  For the fair very soon, was as full—as the moon,
Such mobs upon mobs as were there, oh rare!
So more luck to sweet Donnybrook Fair.

But Dermot, his mind on love bent,
In search of his sweetheart he went,
  Peep'd in here and there, as he walked through the fair,
And took a small drop in each tent—as he went,—
Oh! on whisky and love he was bent.

And who should he spy in a jig,
With a meal-man so tall and so big,
  But his own darling Kate, so gay and so nate?
Faith! her partner he hit him a dig—the pig,
He beat the meal out of his wig.

The piper, to keep him in tune,
Struck up a gay lilt very soon;
  Until an arch wag cut a hole in the bag,

And at once put an end to the tune—too soon—
Och! the music flew up to the moon.

The meal-man he looked very shy,
While a great big tear stood in his eye,
   He cried, " Lord, how I'm kilt, all alone for that jilt;
With her may the devil fly high in the sky,
For I'm murdered, and don't know for why."

" Oh! " says Dermot, and he in the dance,
Whilst a step to'ards his foe did advance,
   " By the Father of Men, say but that word again,
And I'll soon knock you back in a trance—to your dance,
For with me you'd have but small chance."

" But," says Kitty, the darlint, says she,
" If you'll only just listen to me,
   It's myself that will show that he can't be your foe,
Though he fought for his cousin—that's me," says she,
" For sure Billy's related to me.

" For my own cousin-jarmin, Anne Wild,
Stood for Biddy Mulroony's first child;
   And Biddy's step-son, sure he married Bess Dunn,
Who was gossip to Jenny, as mild a child
As ever at mother's breast smiled.

" And may be you don't know Jane Brown,
Who served goat's-whey in Dundrum's sweet town?
   'Twas her uncle's half-brother, who married my mother,
And bought me this new yellow gown, to go down
When the marriage was held in Milltown."

" By the powers, then," says Dermot, " 'tis plain,
Like the son of that rapscallion Cain,
   My best friend I have kilt, though no blood is spilt,
But the devil a harm did I mane—that's plain;
And by me he'll be ne'er kilt again."

Viscount Dillon.

UNFORTUNATE MISS BAILEY

A CAPTAIN bold from Halifax who dwelt in country quarters,
Betrayed a maid who hanged herself one morning in her
Garters.
His wicked conscience smited him, he lost his Stomach
daily,
And took to drinking Ratafia while thinking of Miss Bailey.

One night betimes he went to bed, for he had caught a
Fever;
Says he, " I am a handsome man, but I'm a gay Deceiver."
His candle just at twelve o'clock began to burn quite palely,
A Ghost stepped up to his bedside and said " Behold Miss
Bailey! "

" Avaunt, Miss Bailey! " then he cries, " your Face looks
white and mealy."
" Dear Captain Smith," the ghost replied, " you've used me
ungenteelly;
The Crowner's 'Quest goes hard with me because I've acted
frailly,
And Parson Biggs won't bury me though I am dead Miss
Bailey."

" Dear Corpse! " said he, " since you and I accounts must
once for all close,
There really is a one pound note in my regimental Small-
clothes;
I'll bribe the sexton for your grave." The ghost then van-
ished gaily
Crying " Bless you, Wicked Captain Smith, Remember poor
Miss Bailey."

Unknown.

THE LAIRD O' COCKPEN

The last two stanzas were added by Miss Ferrier.

THE Laird o' Cockpen, he's proud and he's great;
His mind is ta'en up wi' the things o' the state;
He wanted a wife his braw house to keep;
But favour wi' wooin' was fashious to seek.

Doun by the dyke-side a lady did dwell,
At his table-head he thought she'd look well
M'Clish's ae daughter o' Claverse-ha' Lee—
A pennyless lass wi' a lang pedigree.

His wig was well-pouther'd, as guid as when new,
His waistcoat was white, his coat it was blue:
He put on a ring, a sword, and cock'd hat—
And wha could refuse the Laird wi' a' that?

He took the grey mare, and rade cannilie—
And rapped at the yett o' Claverse-ha' Lee;
" Gae tell mistress Jean to come speedily ben:
She's wanted to speak wi' the Laird o' Cockpen."

Mistress Jean she was makin' the elder-flower wine;
" And what brings the Laird at sic a like time? "
She put off her apron, and on her silk gown,
Her mutch wi' red ribbons, and gaed awa' down.

And when she cam' ben, he boued fu' low;
And what was his errand he soon let her know,
Amazed was the Laird when the lady said, Na,
And wi' a laigh curtsie she turned awa'.

Dumfounder'd he was, but nae sigh did he gi'e;
He mounted his mare, and rade cannilie;
And aften he thought, as he gaed through the **glen**,
" She's daft to refuse the Laird o' Cockpen."

And now that the Laird his exit had made,
Mistress Jean she reflected on what she had said;
" Oh! for ane I'll get better, it's waur I'll get ten—
I was daft to refuse the Laird o' Cockpen."

Neist time that the Laird and the Lady were seen,
They were gaun arm and arm to the kirk on the green;
Now she sits in the ha' like a weel-tappit hen,
But as yet there's nae chickens appeared at Cockpen.

Lady Nairne.

A WEDDING

I TELL thee, Dick, where I have been;
Where I the rarest things have seen;
　　Oh, things without compare!
Such sights again can not be found
　In any place on English ground,
　　Be it at wake or fair.

At Charing Cross, hard by the way
Where we (thou know'st) do sell our hay,
　　There is a house with stairs;
And there did I see coming down
Such folks as are not in our town;
　　Vorty at least, in pairs.

Amongst the rest one pest'lent fine
(His beard no bigger tho' than thine)
　　Walk'd on before the rest;
Our landlord looks like nothing to him;
The King (God bless him!) 'twould undo him
　　Should he go still so drest.

At Course-a-park, without all doubt,
He should have first been taken out
　　By all the maids i' th' town:
Though lusty Roger there had been,
Or little George upon the green,
　　Or Vincent of the crown.

But wot you what? The youth was going
To make an end of all his woing;
   The parson for him staid:
Yet by his leave, for all his haste,
He did not so much wish all past,
   Perchance as did the maid.

The maid (and thereby hangs a tale)
For such a maid no Whitson-ale
   Could ever yet produce;
No grape that's kindly ripe, could be
So round, so plump, so soft, as she
   Nor half so full of juyce.

Her finger was so small, the ring
Would not stay on which they did bring;
   It was too wide a peck:
And, to say truth (for out it must),
It look'd like the great collar (just)
   About our young colt's neck.

Her feet beneath her petticoat,
Like little mice, stole in and out,
   As if they fear'd the light:
But oh! she dances such a way;
No sun upon an Easter day
   Is half so fine a sight.

Her cheeks so rare a white was on,
No daisie makes comparison
   (Who sees them is undone);
For streaks of red were mingled there,
Such as are on a Cath'rine pear,
   The side that's next the Sun.

Her lips were red; and one was thin,
Compared to that was next her chin
   (Some bee had stung it newly);
But, Dick, her eyes so guard her face,
I durst no more upon them gaze,
   Than on a Sun in July.

Her mouth so small, when she does speak,
Thou'dst swear her teeth her words did break,
    That they might passage get;
But she so handled still the matter,
They came as good as ours, or better,
    And are not spent a whit.

Passion, oh me! how I run on!
There's that that would be thought upon,
    I trow, besides the bride.
The business of the kitchen's great;
For it is fit that men should eat,
    Nor was it there denied.

Just in the nick the Cook knock'd thrice,
And all the waiters in a trice
    His summons did obey;
Each serving man, with dish in hand,
March'd boldly up like our train'd band,
    Presented, and away.

When all the meat was on the table,
What man of knife, or teeth, was able
    To stay to be entreated?
And this the very reason was,
Before the parson could say grace
    The company was seated.

Now hats fly off, and youths carouse;
Healths first go round, and then the house,
    The bride's came thick and thick;
And when 'twas named another's health,
Perhaps he made it hers by stealth,
    (And who could help it, Dick?)

O' th' sudden, up they rise and dance;
Then sit again, and sigh, and glance:
    Then dance again, and kiss:
Thus sev'ral ways the time did pass,
Till ev'ry woman wish'd her place,
    And ev'ry man wish'd his.

By this time all were stol'n aside
To counsel and undress the bride;
  But that he must not know:
But yet 'twas thought he guest her mind,
And did not mean to stay behind
  Above an hour or so.

Sir John Suckling.

XI

TRIBUTE

THE AHKOND OF SWAT

Who, or why, or which, or *what,*
        Is the Ahkond of Swat?

Is he tall or short, or dark or fair?
Does he sit on a stool or sofa or chair,   or Squat,
        The Ahkond of Swat?

Is he wise or foolish, young or old?
Does he drink his soup and his coffee cold,   or Hot,
        The Ahkond of Swat?

Does he sing or whistle, jabber or talk,
And when riding abroad does he gallop or walk,
            or Trot,
        The Ahkond of Swat?

Does he wear a turban, a fez, or a hat?
Does he sleep on a mattress, a bed or a mat,   or a Cot,
        The Ahkond of Swat?

When he writes a copy in round-hand size,
Does he cross his t's and finish his i's   with a Dot,
        The Ahkond of Swat?

Can he write a letter concisely clear,
Without a speck or a smudge or smear   or a Blot,
        The Ahkond of Swat?

Do his people like him extremely well?
Or do they, whenever they can, rebel,   or Plot,
         At the Ahkond of Swat?

If he catches them then, either old or young,
Does he have them chopped in pieces or hung,
           or Shot,
        The Ahkond of Swat?

Do his people prig in the lanes or park?
Or even at times, when days are dark,   Garotte?
        Oh, the Ahkond of Swat?

Does he study the wants of his own dominion?
Or doesn't he care for public opinion   a Jot,
        The Ahkond of Swat?·

To amuse his mind do his people show him
Pictures, or any one's last new poem,   or What,
        For the Ahkond of Swat?

At night if he suddenly screams and wakes,
Do they bring him only a few small cakes,   or a Lot,
        For the Ahkond of Swat?

Does he live on turnips, tea or tripe,
Does he like his shawl to be marked with a stripe
          or a Dot,
        The Ahkond of Swat?

Does he like to lie on his back in a boat
Like the lady who lived in that isle remote,   Shalott.
        The Ahkond of Swat?

Is he quiet, or always making a fuss?
Is his steward a Swiss or a Swede or a Russ,
          or a Scot,
        The Ahkond of Swat?

Does he like to sit by the calm blue wave?
Or to sleep and snore in a dark green cave,   or a Grott,
      The Ahkond of Swat?

Does he drink small beer from a silver jug?
Or a bowl? or a glass? or a cup? or a mug?
             or a Pot,
      The Ahkond of Swat?

Does he beat his wife with a gold-topped pipe,
When she lets the gooseberries grow too ripe,   or Rot,
      The Ahkond of Swat?

Does he wear a white tie when he dines with his friends,
And tie it neat in a bow with ends,   or a Knot,
      The Ahkond of Swat?

Does he like new cream, and hate mince-pies?
When he looks at the sun does he wink his eyes,
            or Not,
      The Ahkond of Swat?

Does he teach his subjects to roast and bake?
Does he sail about on an inland lake,   in a Yacht,
      The Ahkond of Swat?

Some one, or nobody knows I wot
Who or which or why or what
      Is the Ahkond of Swat!
         Edward Lear.

THE AHKOOND OF SWAT

"The Ahkoond of Swat is dead."—London Papers of
Jan. 22, 1878.

    WHAT, what, what,
        What's the news from Swat?
      Sad news,
      Bad news,
    Comes by the cable led

Through the Indian Ocean's bed,
Through the Persian Gulf, the Red
Sea and the Med-
Iterranean—he's dead;
The Ahkoond is dead!

For the Ahkoond I mourn,
    Who wouldn't?
He strove to disregard the message stern,
    But he Ahkoodn't.
Dead, dead, dead:
    (Sorrow, Swats!)
Swats wha hae wi' Ahkoond bled,
Swats whom he hath often led
Onward to a gory bed,
    Or to victory,
      As the case might be.
        Sorrow, Swats!
Tears shed,
    Shed tears like water.
Your great Ahkoond is dead!
    That Swats the matter!

Mourn, city of Swat,
Your great Ahkoond is not,
But laid 'mid worms to rot.
His mortal part alone, his soul was caught
    (Because he was a good Ahkoond)
    Up to the bosom of Mahound.
Though earthly walls his frame surround
(Forever hallowed by the ground!)

And skeptics mock the lowly mound
And say " He's now of no Ahkoond! "
    His soul is in the skies—
The azure skies that bend above his loved
    Metropolis of Swat.
  He sees with larger, other eyes,
  Athwart all earthly mysteries—
    He knows what's Swat.

Let Swat bury the great Ahkoond
　　With a noise of mourning and of lamentation!
Let Swat bury the great Ahkoond
　　With the noise of the mourning of the Swattish nation!
　　Fallen is at length
　　Its tower of strength;
　　Its sun is dimmed ere it had nooned;
　　Dead lies the great Ahkoond,
　　The great Ahkoond of Swat
　　Is not!

George Thomas Lanigan.

DIRGE OF THE MOOLLA OF KOTAL,

RIVAL OF THE AKHOOND OF SWAT

I

ALAS, unhappy land; ill-fated spot
Kotal—though where or what
On earth Kotal is, the bard has forgot;
Further than this indeed he knoweth not—
It borders upon Swat!

II

When sorrows come, they come not single spies,
　　But in battal-
Ions: the gloom that lay on Swat now lies
　　Upon Kotal,
On sad Kotal whose people ululate
For their loved Moolla late.
Put away his little turban,
And his narghileh embrowned,
The lord of Kotal—rural urban—
'S gone unto his last Akhoond,
'S gone to meet his rival Swattan,
'S gone, indeed, but not forgotten.

III

His rival, but in what?
Wherein did the deceased Akhoond of Swat
Kotal's lamented Moolla late,
As it were, emulate?
Was it in the tented field
With crash of sword on shield,
While backward meaner champions reeled
And loud the tom-tom pealed?
Did they barter gash for scar
With the Persian scimetar
Or the Afghanistee tulwar,
While loud the tom-tom pealed—
While loud the tom-tom pealed,
And the jim-jam squealed,
And champions less well heeled
Their war-horses wheeled
And fled the presence of these mortal big bugs o' the field?
Was Kotal's proud citadel—
Bastioned, walled, and demi-luned,
Beaten down with shot and shell
By the guns of the Akhoond?
Or were wails despairing caught, as
The burghers pale of Swat
Cried in panic, " Moolla ad Portas? "
    —Or what?
Or made each in the cabinet his mark
Kotalese Gortschakoff, Swattish Bismarck?
Did they explain and render hazier
The policies of Central Asia?
Did they with speeches from the throne,
    Wars dynastic,
Entents cordiales,
Between Swat and Kotal;
Holy alliances,
And other appliances
Of statesmen with morals and consciences plastic
Come by much more than their own?
Made they mots, as " There to-day is
No more Himalayehs,"

Or, if you prefer it, " There to-day are
No more Himalaya?"
Or, said the Akhoond, " Sah,
L'Etat de Swat c'est moi?"
Khabu, did there come great fear
On thy Khabuldozed Ameer
 Ali Shere?
Or did the Khan of far
 Kashgar
Tremble at the menace hot
Of the Moolla of Kotal,
" I will extirpate thee, pal
Of my foe the Akhoond of Swat?"
 Who knows
Of Moolla and Akhoond aught more than I did?
Namely, in life they rivals were, or foes,
And in their deaths not very much divided?
If any one knows it,
Let him disclose it!

George Thomas Lanigan.

THE BALLAD OF BOUILLABAISSE

A STREET there is in Paris famous,
 For which no rhyme our language yields,
Rue Neuve des Petits Champs its name is—
 The New Street of the Little Fields.
And here's an inn, not rich and splendid,
 But still in comfortable case;
The which in youth I oft attended,
 To eat a bowl of Bouillabaisse.

This Bouillabaisse a noble dish is—
 A sort of soup, or broth, or brew,
Or hotchpotch of all sorts of fishes,
 That Greenwich never could outdo:
Green herbs, red peppers, mussels, saffron,
 Soles, onions, garlic, roach, and dace:
All these you eat at Terré's tavern
 In that one dish of Bouillabaisse.

Indeed, a rich and savoury stew 'tis;
  And true philosophers, methinks,
Who love all sorts of natural beauties,
  Should love good victuals and good drinks.
And Cordelier or Benedictine
  Might gladly, sure, his lot embrace,
Nor find a fast-day too afflicting,
  Which served him up a Bouillabaisse.

I wonder if the house still there is?
  Yes, here the lamp is, as before;
The smiling red-cheeked *écaillère* is
  Still opening oysters at the door.
Is Terré still alive and able?
  I recollect his droll grimace:
He'd come and smile before your table,
  And hope you liked your Bouillabaisse.

We enter—nothing's changed or older.
  " How's Monsieur Terré, waiter, pray? "
The waiter stares, and shrugs his shoulder—
  " Monsieur is dead this many a day."
" It is the lot of saint and sinner,
  So honest Terré's run his race."
" What will Monsieur require for dinner? "
  " Say, do you still cook Bouillabaisse? "

" Oh, oui, Monsieur," 's the waiter's answer;
  " Quel vin Monsieur désire-t-il? "
" Tell me a good one."—" That I can, Sir:
  The Chambertin with yellow seal."
" So Terré's gone," I say, and sink in
  My old accustom'd corner-place;
" He's done with feasting and with drinking,
  With Burgundy and with Bouillabaisse."

My old accustom'd corner here is,
  The table still is in the nook;
Ah! vanished many a busy year is
  This well-known chair since last I took.

When first I saw ye, *cari luoghi,*
   I'd scarce a beard upon my face,
And now a grizzled, grim old fogy,
   I sit and wait for Bouillabaisse.

Where are you, old companions trusty
   Of early days here met to dine?
Come, waiter! quick, a flagon crusty—
   I'll pledge them in the good old wine.
The kind old voices and old faces
   My memory can quick retrace;
Around the board they take their places,
   And share the wine and Bouillabaisse.

There's Jack has made a wondrous marriage;
   There's laughing Tom is laughing yet;
There's brave Augustus drives his carriage;
   There's poor old Fred in the *Gazette;*
On James's head the grass is growing:
   Good Lord! the world has wagged apace
Since here we set the claret flowing,
   And drank, and ate the Bouillabaisse.

Ah me! how quick the days are flitting!
   I mind me of a time that's gone,
When here I'd sit, as now I'm sitting,
   In this same place—but not alone.
A fair young form was nestled near me,
   A dear dear face looked fondly up,
And sweetly spoke and smiled to cheer me
   —There's no one now to share my cup.
   .   .   .   .   .   .

I drink it as the Fates ordain it.
   Come, fill it, and have done with rhymes:
Fill up the lonely glass, and drain it
   In memory of dear old times.
Welcome the wine, whate'er the seal is;
   And sit you down and say your grace
With thankful heart, whate'er the meal is.
   —Here comes the smoking Bouillabaisse!

                                 W. M. Thackeray.

OULD DOCTOR MACK

YE may tramp the world over
From Delhi to Dover,
And sail the salt say from Archangel to Arragon,
Circumvint back
Through the whole Zodiack,
But to ould Docther Mack ye can't furnish a paragon.
Have ye the dropsy,
The gout, the autopsy?
Fresh livers and limbs instantaneous he'll shape yez,
No ways infarior
In skill, but suparior,
And lineal postarior to Ould Aysculapius.

Chorus
He and his wig wid the curls so carroty,
Aigle eye, and complexion clarety:
Here's to his health,
Honor and wealth,
The king of his kind and the crame of all charity!

How the rich and the poor,
To consult for a cure,
Crowd on to his doore in their carts and their carriages,
Showin' their tongues
Or unlacin' their lungs,
For divle one symptom the docther disparages.
Troth, an' he'll tumble,
For high or for humble,
From his warm feather-bed wid no cross contrariety;
Makin' as light
Of nursin' all night
The beggar in rags as the belle of society.

Chorus—He and his wig, etc.

And as if by a meracle,
Ailments hysterical,
Dad, wid one dose of bread-pills he can smother,

And quench the love-sickness
Wid wonderful quickness,
By prescribin' the right boys and girls to aich other.
And the sufferin' childer—
Your eyes 'twould bewilder
To see the wee craythurs his coat-tails unravellin',
And aich of them fast
On some treasure at last,
Well knowin' ould Mack's just a toy-shop out travellin'.

Chorus—He and his wig, etc.

Thin, his doctherin' done,
In a rollickin' run
Wid the rod or the gun, he's the foremost to figure.
By Jupiter Ammon,
What jack-snipe or salmon
E'er rose to backgammon his tail-fly or trigger!
And hark! the view-hollo!
'Tis Mack in full follow
On black " Faugh-a-ballagh " the country-side sailin'.
Och, but you'd think
'Twas old Nimrod in pink,
Wid his spurs cryin' chink over park-wall and palin'.

Chorus

He and his wig wid the curls so carroty,
Aigle eye, and complexion clarety:
Here's to his health,
Honor and wealth!
Hip, hip, hooray! wid all hilarity,
Hip, hip, hooray! That's the way,
All at once, widout disparity!
One more cheer
For our docther dear,
The king of his kind and the crame of all charity.
Hip, hip, hooray!

Alfred Perceval Graves.

FATHER O'FLYNN

Of priests we can offer a charmin' variety,
Far renowned for larnin' and piety;
Still, I'd advance ye, widout impropriety,
  Father O'Flynn as the flower of them all.

CHORUS
Here's a health to you, Father O'Flynn,
Slainté, and slainté, and slainté agin;
  Powerfulest preacher, and
  Tenderest teacher, and
Kindliest creature in ould Donegal.

Don't talk of your Provost and Fellows of Trinity,
Famous for ever at Greek and Latinity,
Dad and the divels and all at Divinity,
  Father O'Flynn 'd make hares of them all!
  Come, I venture to give you my word,
  Never the likes of his logic was heard,
    Down from Mythology
    Into Thayology,
  Troth! and Conchology if he'd the call.
      Chorus.

Och! Father O'Flynn, you've the wonderful way wid you,
All ould sinners are wishful to pray wid you,
All the young childer are wild for to play wid you,
  You've such a way wid you, Father avick!
  Still for all you've so gentle a soul,
  Gad, you've your flock in the grandest control;
    Checking the crazy ones,
    Coaxin' onaisy ones,
  Liftin' the lazy ones on wid the stick.
      Chorus.

And though quite avoidin' all foolish frivolity,
Still at all seasons of innocent jollity,
Where was the play-boy could claim an equality
  At comicality, Father, wid you?

Once the Bishop looked grave at your jest,
Till this remark set him off wid the rest:
    "Is it lave gaiety
    All to the laity?
Cannot the clargy be Irishmen too?"
        Chorus.

        Alfred Perceval Graves.

THE BALD-HEADED TYRANT

O THE quietest home in earth had I,
    No thought of trouble, no hint of care;
Like a dream of pleasure the days fled by,
    And Peace had folded her pinions there.
But one day there joined in our household band
A bald-headed tyrant from No-man's-land.

Oh, the despot came in the dead of night,
    And no one ventured to ask him why;
Like slaves we trembled before his might,
    Our hearts stood still when we heard him cry;
For never a soul could his power withstand,
That bald-headed tyrant from No-man's-land.

He ordered us here, and he sent us there—
    Though never a word could his small lips speak—
With his toothless gums and his vacant stare,
    And his helpless limbs so frail and weak,
Till I cried, in a voice of stern command,
"Go up, thou bald-head from No-man's-land!"

But his abject slaves they turned on me;
    Like the bears in Scripture, they'd rend me there,
The while they worshiped with bended knee
    This ruthless wretch with the missing hair;
For he rules them all with relentless hand,
This bald-headed tyrant from No-man's-land.

Then I searched for help in every clime,
   For peace had fled from my dwelling now,
Till I finally thought of old Father Time,
   And low before him I made my bow.
"Wilt thou deliver me out of his hand,
This bald-headed tyrant from No-man's-land?"

Old Time he looked with a puzzled stare,
   And a smile came over his features grim.
"I'll take the tyrant under my care:
   Watch what my hour-glass does to him.
The veriest humbug that ever was planned
Is this same bald-head from No-man's-land."

Old Time is doing his work full well—
   Much less of might does the tyrant wield;
But, ah! with sorrow my heart will swell,
   And sad tears fall as I see him yield.
Could I stay the touch of that shriveled hand,
I would keep the bald-head from No-man's-land.

For the loss of peace I have ceased to care;
   Like other vassals, I've learned, forsooth,
To love the wretch who forgot his hair
   And hurried along without a tooth,
And he rules me too with his tiny hand,
This bald-headed tyrant from No-man's-land.

                  Mary E. Vandyne.

BARNEY McGEE

BARNEY McGEE, there's no end of good luck in you,
Will-o'-the-wisp, with a flicker of Puck in you,
Wild as a bull-pup, and all of his pluck in you—
Let a man tread on your coat and he'll see!
Eyes like the lakes of Killarney for clarity,
Nose that turns up without any vulgarity,

Smile like a cherub, and hair that is carroty—
Whoop, you're a rarity, Barney McGee!
Mellow as Tarragon,
Prouder than Aragon—
Hardly a paragon,
You will agree—
Here's all that's fine to you!
Books and old wine to you!
Girls be divine to you,
Barney McGee!

Lucky the day when I met you unwittingly,
Dining where vagabonds came and went flittingly.
Here's some *Barbera* to drink it befittingly.
That day at Silvio's, Barney McGee!
Many's the time we have quaffed our Chianti there,
Listened to Silvio quoting us Dante there—
Once more to drink Nebiolo Spumante there,
How we'd pitch Pommery into the sea!
There where the gang of us
Met ere Rome rang of us,
They had the hang of us
To a degree.
How they would trust to you!
That was but just to you.
Here's o'er their dust to you,
Barney McGee!

Barney McGee, when you're sober you scintillate,
But when you're in drink you're the pride of the intellect;
Divil a one of us ever came in till late,
Once at the bar where you happened to be—
Every eye there like a spoke in you centering,
You with your eloquence, blarney, and bantering—
All Vagabondia shouts at your entering,
King of the Tenderloin, Barney McGee!
There's no satiety
In your society
With the variety
Of your *esprit*.

Here's a long purse to you,
And a great thirst to you!
Fate be no worse to you,
Barney McGee!

Och, and the girls whose poor hearts you deracinate,
Whirl and bewilder and flutter and fascinate!
Faith, it's so killing you are, you assassinate—
Murder's the word for you, Barney McGee!
Bold when they're sunny, and smooth when they're showery—
Oh, but the style of you, fluent and flowery!
Chesterfield's way, with a touch of the Bowery!
How would they silence you, Barney machree?
Naught can your gab allay,
Learned as Rabelais
(You in his abbey lay
Once on the spree).
Here's to the smile of you,
(Oh, but the guile of you!)
And a long while of you,
Barney McGee!

Facile with phrases of length and Latinity,
Like honorificabilitudinity,
Where is the maid could resist your vicinity,
Wiled by the impudent grace of your plea?
Then your vivacity and pertinacity
Carry the day with the divil's audacity;
No mere veracity robs your sagacity
Of perspicacity, Barney McGee.
When all is new to them,
What will you do to them?
Will you be true to them?
Who shall decree?
Here's a fair strife to you!
Health and long life to you!
And a great wife to you, Barney McGee!

Barney McGee, you're the pick of gentility;
Nothing can phase you, you've such a facility;
Nobody ever yet found your utility—

There is the charm of you, Barney McGee;
Under conditions that others would stammer in,
Still unperturbed as a cat or a Cameron,
Polished as somebody in the Decameron,
Putting the glamour on price or Pawnee.
In your meanderin',
Love and philanderin',
Calm as a mandarin
Sipping his tea!
Under the art of you,
Parcel and part of you,
Here's to the heart of you,
Barney McGee!

You who were ever alert to befriend a man,
You who were ever the first to defend a man,
You who had always the money to lend a man,
Down on his luck and hard up for a V!
Sure, you'll be playing a harp in beatitude
(And a quare sight you will be in that attitude)—
Some day, where gratitude seems but a platitude,
You'll find your latitude, Barney McGee.
That's no flim-flam at all,
Frivol or sham at all,
Just the plain—Damn it all,
Have one with me!
Here's one and more to you!
Friends by the score to you,
True to the core to you,
Barney McGee!

Richard Hovey.

ADDRESS TO THE TOOTHACHE

My curse upon your venom'd stang,
That shoots my tortur'd gooms alang;
An' thro' my lug gies monie a twang,
         Wi' gnawing vengeance,
Tearing my nerves wi' bitter pang,
         Like racking engines!

A' down my beard the slavers trickle!
I throw the wee stools o'er the mickle,
While round the fire the giglets keckle
        To see me loup;
An', raving mad, I wish a heckle
        Were i' their doup!

When fevers burn, or ague freezes,
Rheumatics gnaw, or colic squeezes,
Our neebors sympathize to ease us
        Wi' pitying moan;
But thee!—thou hell o' a' diseases,
        They mock our groan!

Of a' the num'rous human dools,
Ill-hairsts, daft bargains, cutty-stools,
Or worthy frien's laid i' the mools,
        Sad sight to see!
The tricks o' knaves, or fash o' fools,
        Thou bear'st the gree!

Whare'er that place be priests ca' hell,
Whare a' the tones o' misery yell,
An' rankèd plagues their numbers tell
        In dreadfu' raw,
Thou, Toothache, surely bear'st the bell
        Amang them a'!

O thou grim, mischief-making chiel,
That gars the notes o' discord squeel,
'Till humankind aft dance a reel
        In gore a shoe-thick;—
Gie a' the faes o' Scotland's weal
        A towmond's toothache!

Robert Burns.

A FAREWELL TO TOBACCO

MAY the Babylonish curse
Straight confound my stammering verse,
If I can a passage see
In this word-perplexity,
Or a fit expression find,
Or a language to my mind,
(Still the phrase is wide or scant)
To take leave of thee, *great plant!*

Or in any terms relate
Half my love, or half my hate:
For I hate, yet love thee so,
That, whichever thing I show,
The plain truth will seem to be
A contrain'd hyperbole,
And the passion to proceed
More from a mistress than a weed.

Sooty retainer to the vine,
Bacchus' black servant, negro fine;
Sorcerer, that mak'st us dote upon
Thy begrimed complexion,
And, for thy pernicious sake,
More and greater oaths to break
Than reclaimèd lovers take
'Gainst women: thou thy siege dost lay
Much too in the female way,
While thou suck'st the laboring breath
Faster than kisses or than death.

Thou in such a cloud dost bind us
That our worst foes cannot find us,
And ill-fortune, that would thwart us,
Shoots at rovers, shooting at us;
While each man, through thy height'ning steam,
Does like a smoking Etna seem,
And all about us does express
(Fancy and wit in richest dress)
A Sicilian fruitfulness.

Thou through such a mist dost show us
That our best friends do not know us,
And, for those allowèd features,
Due to reasonable creatures,
Liken'st us to fell Chimeras,
Monsters,—that who see us, fear us;
Worse than Cerberus or Geryon,
Or, who first loved a cloud, Ixion.

Bacchus we know, and we allow
His tipsy rites. But what art thou
That but by reflex canst show
What his deity can do,
As the false Egyptian spell
Aped the true Hebrew miracle?
Some few vapors thou may'st raise,
The weak brain may serve to amaze,
But to the reins and nobler heart
Canst nor life nor heat impart.

Brother of Bacchus, later born,
The old world was sure forlorn
Wanting thee, that aidest more
The god's victories than, before,
All his panthers, and the brawls
Of his piping Bacchanals.
These, as stale, we disallow,
Or judge of *thee* meant: only thou
His true Indian conquest art;
And, for ivy round his dart,
The reformèd god now weaves
A finer thyrsus of thy leaves.

Scent to match thy rich perfume
Chemic art did ne'er presume
Through her quaint alembic strain,
None so sov'reign to the brain;
Nature, that did in thee excel,
Framed again no second smell,

Roses, violets, but toys
For the smaller sort of boys,
Or for greener damsels meant;
Thou art the only manly scent.

   Stinkingest of the stinking kind!
Filth of the mouth and fog of the mind!
Africa, that brags her foison,
Breeds no such prodigious poison!
Henbane, nightshade, both together,
Hemlock, aconite—

                       Nay, rather,
Plant divine, of rarest virtue;
Blisters on the tongue would hurt you!
'Twas but in a sort I blamed thee;
None e'er prosper'd who defamed thee;
Irony all, and feign'd abuse,
Such as perplex'd lovers use,
At a need, when, in despair
To paint forth their fairest fair,
Or in part but to express
That exceeding comeliness
Which their fancies doth so strike,
They borrow language of dislike;
And, instead of Dearest Miss,
Jewel, Honey, Sweetheart, Bliss,
And those forms of old admiring,
Call her Cockatrice and Siren,
Basilisk, and all that's evil,
Witch, Hyena, Mermaid, Devil,
Ethiop, Wench, and Blackamoor,
Monkey, Ape, and twenty more;
Friendly Trait'ress, loving Foe—
Not that she is truly so,
But no other way they know
A contentment to express,
Borders so upon excess,
That they do not rightly wot
Whether it be from pain or not.

Or, as men constrain'd to part
With what's nearest to their heart,
While their sorrow's at the height,
Lose discrimination quite,
And their hasty wrath let fall,
To appease their frantic gall,
On the darling thing whatever,
Whence they feel it death to sever
Though it be, as they, perforce,
Guiltless of the sad divorce.

For I must (nor let it grieve thee,
Friendliest of plants, that I must) leave thee.
For thy sake, TOBACCO, I
Would do anything but die,
And but seek to extend my days
Long enough to sing thy praise.
But, as she who once hath been
A king's consort is a queen
Ever after, nor will bate
Any tittle of her state
Though a widow, or divorced,
So I, from thy converse forced,
The old name and style retain,
A right Katherine of Spain;
And a seat, too, 'mongst the joys
Of the blest Tobacco Boys;
Where, though I, by sour physician,
Am debarr'd the full fruition
Of thy favors, I may catch
Some collateral sweets, and snatch
Sidelong odors, that give life
Like glances from a neighbor's wife;
And still live in the by-places
And the suburbs of thy graces;
And in thy borders take delight,
An unconquer'd Canaanite.

Charles Lamb.

JOHN BARLEYCORN

THERE were three kings into the east,
  Three kings both great and high;
And they hae sworn a solemn oath
  John Barleycorn should die.

They took a plough and plough'd him down,
  Put clods upon his head;
And they hae sworn a solemn oath
  John Barleycorn was dead.

But the cheerful spring came kindly on,
  And showers began to fall:
John Barleycorn got up again,
  And sore surprised them all.

The sultry suns of summer came,
  And he grew thick and strong;
His head weel arm'd wi' pointed spears,
  That no one should him wrong.

The sober autumn enter'd mild,
  When he grew wan and pale;
His bending joints and drooping head
  Show'd he began to fail.

His colour sicken'd more and more,
  He faded into age;
And then his enemies began
  To show their deadly rage.

They've ta'en a weapon, long and sharp,
  And cut him by the knee;
Then tied him fast upon a cart,
  Like a rogue for forgerie.

They laid him down upon his back,
    And cudgell'd him full sore;
They hung him up before the storm,
    And turn'd him o'er and o'er.

They fillèd up a darksome pit
    With water to the brim:
They heavèd in John Barleycorn,
    There let him sink or swim.

They laid him out upon the floor,
    To work him further woe:
And still, as signs of life appear'd,
    They toss'd him to and fro.

They wasted o'er a scorching flame
    The marrow of his bones;
But a miller used him worst of all—
    He crush'd him 'tween two stones.

And they hae ta'en his very heart's blood,
    And drank it round and round,
And still the more and more they drank,
    Their joy did more abound.

John Barleycorn was a hero bold,
    Of noble enterprise;
For if you do but taste his blood,
    'Twill make your courage rise.

'Twill make a man forget his woe;
    'Twill heighten all his joy:
'Twill make the widow's heart to sing,
    Though the tear were in her eye.

Then let us toast John Barleycorn,
    Each man a glass in hand;
And may his great posterity
    Ne'er fail in old Scotland!

Robert Burns.

STANZAS TO PALE ALE

Oh! I have loved thee fondly, ever
  Preferr'd thee to the choicest wine;
From thee my lips they could not sever
  By saying thou contain'dst strychnine.
Did I believe the slander? Never!
  I held thee still to be divine.

For me thy color hath a charm,
  Although 'tis true they call thee Pale;
And be thou cold when I am warm,
  As late I've been—so high the scale
Of FAHRENHEIT—and febrile harm
  Allay, refrigerating Ale!

How sweet thou art!—yet bitter, too
  And sparkling, like satiric fun;
But how much better thee to brew,
  Than a conundrum or a pun,
It is, in every point of view,
  Must be allow'd by every one.

Refresh my heart and cool my throat,
  Light, airy child of malt and hops!
That dost not stuff, engross, and bloat
  The skin, the sides, the chin, the chops,
And burst the buttons off the coat,
  Like stout and porter—fattening slops!

Unknown.

ODE TO TOBACCO

Thou who, when fears attack,
Bidst them avaunt, and Black
Care, at the horseman's back
  Perching, unseatest;
Sweet, when the morn is gray;
Sweet, when they've cleared away
Lunch; and at close of day
  Possibly sweetest:

I have a liking old
For thee, though manifold
Stories, I know, are told,
    Not to thy credit;
How one (or two at most)
Drops make a cat a ghost—
Useless, except to roast—
    Doctors have said it:

How they who use fusees
All grow by slow degrees
Brainless as chimpanzees,
    Meagre as lizards;
Go mad, and beat their wives;
Plunge (after shocking lives)
Razors and carving knives
    Into their gizzards.

Confound such knavish tricks!
Yet know I five or six
Smokers who freely mix
    Still with their neighbors;
Jones—(who, I'm glad to say,
Asked leave of Mrs. J.)—
Daily absorbs a clay
    After his labors.

Cats may have had their goose
Cooked by tobacco-juice;
Still why deny its use
    Thoughtfully taken?
We're not as tabbies are:
Smith, take a fresh cigar!
Jones, the tobacco-jar!
    Here's to thee, Bacon!

Charles Stuart Calverley.

SONNET TO A CLAM

DUM TACENT CLAIMANT

INGLORIOUS friend! most confident I am
  Thy life is one of very little ease;
    Albeit men mock thee with their similes
And prate of being " happy as a clam! "
What though thy shell protects thy fragile head
  From the sharp bailiffs of the briny sea?
    Thy valves are, sure, no safety-valves to thee,
While rakes are free to desecrate thy bed,
And bear thee off—as foemen take their spoil—
  Far from thy friends and family to roam;
    Forced, like a Hessian, from thy native home,
To meet destruction in a foreign broil!
  Though thou art tender yet thy humble bard
  Declares, O clam! thy case is shocking hard!

                    John G. Saxe.

TO A FLY

TAKEN OUT OF A BOWL OF PUNCH

AH! poor intoxicated little knave,
Now senseless, floating on the fragrant wave;
  Why not content the cakes alone to munch?
Dearly thou pay'st for buzzing round the bowl;
Lost to the world, thou busy sweet-lipped soul—
  Thus Death, as well as Pleasure, dwells with Punch.

Now let me take thee out, and moralize—
Thus 'tis with mortals, as it is with flies,
  Forever hankering after Pleasure's cup:
Though Fate, with all his legions, be at hand,
The beasts, the draught of Circe can't withstand,
  But in goes every nose—they must, will sup.

Mad are the passions, as a colt untamed!
  When Prudence mounts their backs to ride them mild,
They fling, they snort, they foam, they rise inflamed,
  Insisting on their own sole will so wild.

Gadsbud! my buzzing friend, thou art not dead;
The Fates, so kind, have not yet snapped thy thread;
By heavens, thou mov'st a leg, and now its brother.
And kicking, lo, again, thou mov'st another!

And now thy little drunken eyes unclose,
And now thou feelest for thy little nose,
  And, finding it, thou rubbest thy two hands
Much as to say, " I'm glad I'm here again."
And well mayest thou rejoice—'tis very plain,
  That near wert thou to Death's unsocial lands.

And now thou rollest on thy back about,
Happy to find thyself alive, no doubt—
  Now turnest—on the table making rings,
Now crawling, forming a wet track,
Now shaking the rich liquor from thy back,
  Now fluttering nectar from thy silken wings.

Now standing on thy head, thy strength to find,
And poking out thy small, long legs behind;
And now thy pinions dost thou briskly ply;
Preparing now to leave me—farewell, fly!

Go, join thy brothers on yon sunny board,
And rapture to thy family afford—
  There wilt thou meet a mistress, or a wife,
That saw thee drunk, drop senseless in the stream.
Who gave, perhaps, the wide-resounding scream,
  And now sits groaning for thy precious life.

Yes, go and carry comfort to thy friends,
And wisely tell them thy imprudence ends.
Let buns and sugar for the future charm;
These will delight, and feed, and work no harm—

While Punch, the grinning, merry imp of sin,
Invites th' unwary wanderer to a kiss,
Smiles in his face, as though he meant him bliss,
Then, like an alligator, drags him in.

John Wolcot.

ODE TO A BOBTAILED CAT

FELIS INFELIX! Cat unfortunate,
  With nary narrative!
Canst thou no tail relate
    Of how
    (Miaow!)
Thy tail end came to terminate so bluntly
Didst wear it off by
    Sedentary habits
    As do the rabbits?

Didst go a
    Fishing with it,
    Wishing with it
    To "bob" for catfish,
And get bobbed thyself?
    Curses on that fish!

Didst lose it in kittenhood,
    Hungrily chawing it?
Or, gaily pursuing it,
    Did it make tangent
From thy swift circuit?

Did some brother Greyback—
    Yowling
    And howling
In nocturnal strife,
    Spitting and staring
    Cursing and swearing,
    Ripping and tearing,
    Calling thee "Sausagetail,"
Abbreviate thy suffix?

Or did thy jealous wife
    Detect yer
In some sly flirtation,
    And, after caudal lecture,
Bite off thy termination?
And sarve yer right!

Did some mischievous boy,
    Some barbarous boy,
    Eliminate thy finis?
    (Probably!)
    The wretch!
    The villain!
    Cruelly spillin'
    Thy innocent blood!

    Furiously scratch him
Where'er yer may catch him!

Well, Bob, this course now is left,
Since thus of your tail you're bereft:
    Tell your friend that by letter
    From Paris
You have learned the style there is
    To wear the tail short,
    And the briefer the better;
    Such is the passion,
That every Grimalkin will
    Follow your fashion.

Unknown.

A DIRGE

CONCERNING THE LATE LAMENTED KING OF THE CANNIBAL ISLANDS

And so our royal relative is dead!
    And so he rests from gustatory labors!
The white man was his choice, but when he fed
    He'd sometimes entertain his tawny neighbors.
He worshipped, as he said, his " Fe-fo-fum,"
The goddess of the epigastrium.

And missionaries graced his festive board,
 Solemn and succulent, in twos and dozens,
And smoked before their hospitable lord,
 Welcome as if they'd been his second cousins.
When cold, he warmed them as he would his kin—
They came as strangers, and he took them in.

And generous!—oh, wasn't he? I have known him
 Exhibit a celestial amiability:—
He'd eat an enemy, and then would own him
 Of flavor excellent, despite hostility.
The cruelest captain of the Turkish navy
He buried in an honorable grave—y.

He had a hundred wives. To make things pleasant
 They found it quite judicious to adore him;—
And when he dined, the nymphs were always present—
 Sometimes beside him and sometimes—before him.
When he was tired of one, he called her " sweet,"
And told her she was " good enough to eat."

He was a man of taste—and justice, too;
 He opened his mouth for e'en the humblest sinner,
And three weeks stall-fed an emaciate Jew
 Before they brought him to the royal dinner.
With preacher-men he shared his board and wallet
And let them nightly occupy his palate!

We grow like what we eat. Bad food depresses;
 Good food exalts us like an inspiration,
And missionary on the *menu* blesses
 And elevates the Feejee population.
A people who for years, saints, bairns, and women ate
Must soon their vilest qualities eliminate.

But the deceased could never hold a candle
 To those prim, pale-faced people of propriety
Who gloat o'er gossip and get fat on scandal—
 The cannibals of civilized society;
They drink the blood of brothers with their rations,
And crunch the bones of living reputations.

They kill the soul; he only claimed the dwelling.
   They take the sharpened scalpel of surmises
And cleave the sinews when the heart is swelling,
   And slaughter Fame and Honor for their prizes.
They make the spirit in the body quiver;
They quench the Light! He only took the—Liver!

I've known some hardened customers, I wot,
   A few tough fellows—pagans beyond question—
I wish had got into his dinner-pot;
   Although I'm certain they'd defy digestion,
And break his jaw, and ruin his esophagus,
Were he the chief of beings anthropophagous!

How fond he was of children! To his breast
   The tenderest nurslings gained a free admission.
Rank he despised, nor, if they came well dressed,
   Cared if they were plebeian or patrician.
Shade of Leigh Hunt! Oh, guide this laggard pen
To write of one who loved his fellow men!

                William Augustus Croffut.

XII

WHIMSEY

AN ELEGY

ON THE GLORY OF HER SEX, MRS. MARY BLAIZE

GOOD people all, with one accord,
    Lament for Madam Blaize,
Who never wanted a good word—
    From those who spoke her praise.

The needy seldom pass'd her door,
    And always found her kind;
She freely lent to all the poor—
    Who left a pledge behind.

She strove the neighborhood to please
    With manners wondrous winning;
And never follow'd wicked ways—
    Unless when she was sinning.

At church, in silks and satins new,
    With hoop of monstrous size,
She never slumber'd in her pew—
    But when she shut her eyes.

Her love was sought, I do aver,
    By twenty beaux and more;
The King himself has follow'd her—
    When she has walk'd before.

But now, her wealth and finery fled,
    Her hangers-on cut short all;

The doctors found, when she was dead—
 Her last disorder mortal.

Let us lament, in sorrow sore,
 For Kent Street well may say,
That had she lived a twelvemonth more
 She had not died to-day.

      Oliver Goldsmith.

PARSON GRAY

A QUIET home had Parson Gray,
 Secluded in a vale;
His daughters all were feminine,
 And all his sons were male.

How faithfully did Parson Gray
 The bread of life dispense—
Well " posted " in theology,
 And post and rail his fence.

'Gainst all the vices of the age
 He manfully did battle;
His chickens were a biped breed,
 And quadruped his cattle.

No clock more punctually went,
 He ne'er delayed a minute—
Nor ever empty was his purse,
 When he had money in it.

His piety was ne'er denied;
 His truths hit saint and sinner;
At morn he always breakfasted;
 He always dined at dinner.

He ne'er by any luck was grieved,
 By any care perplexed—
No filcher he, though when he preached,
 He always " took " a text.

As faithful characters he drew
    As mortal ever saw;
But ah! poor parson! when he died,
    His breath he could not draw!

Oliver Goldsmith.

THE IRISHMAN AND THE LADY

There was a lady liv'd at Leith,
    A lady very stylish, man;
And yet, in spite of all her teeth,
    She fell in love with an Irishman—
        A nasty, ugly Irishman,
        A wild, tremendous Irishman,
A tearing, swearing, thumping, bumping, ranting, roaring
    Irishman.

His face was no ways beautiful,
    For with small-pox 'twas scarr'd across;
And the shoulders of the ugly dog
    Were almost double a yard across.
        Oh, the lump of an Irishman,
        The whiskey-devouring Irishman,
The great he-rogue with his wonderful brogue—the fighting,
    rioting Irishman!

One of his eyes was bottle-green,
    And the other eye was out, my dear;
And the calves of his wicked-looking legs
    Were more than two feet about, my dear.
        Oh, the great big Irishman,
        The rattling, battling Irishman—
The stamping, ramping, swaggering, staggering, leathering
    swash of an Irishman!

He took so much of Lundy-foot
    That he used to snort and snuffle—O!
And in shape and size the fellow's neck
    Was as bad as the neck of a buffalo.

Oh, the horrible Irishman,
   The thundering, blundering Irishman—
The slashing, dashing, smashing, lashing, thrashing, hash-
   ing Irishman!

   His name was a terrible name, indeed,
      Being Timothy Thady Mulligan;
   And whenever he emptied his tumbler of punch
      He'd not rest till he fill'd it full again.
      The boosing, bruising Irishman,
      The 'toxicated Irishman—
The whiskey, frisky, rummy, gummy, brandy, no **dandy**
   Irishman!

   This was the lad the lady lov'd,
      Like all the girls of quality;
   And he broke the skulls of the men of Leith,
      Just by the way of jollity.
      Oh, the leathering Irishman,
      The barbarous, savage Irishman—
The hearts of the maids, and the gentlemen's heads, were
   bothered, I'm sure, by this Irishman!

                William Maginn.

THE CATARACT OF LODORE

" How does the water
   Come down at Lodore? "
   My little boy asked me
   Thus, once on a time;
And moreover he tasked me
   To tell him in rhyme.
   Anon at the word,
There first came one daughter,
   And then came another,
   To second and third
   The request of their brother,
And to hear how the water
   Comes down at Lodore,
   With its rush and its roar,

As many a time
They had seen it before.
So I told them in rhyme,
For of rhymes I had store;
And 'twas in my vocation
For their recreation
That so I should sing;
Because I was Laureate
To them and the King.

From its sources which well
In the tarn on the fell;
From its fountains
In the mountains,
Its rills and its gills;
Through moss and through brake,
It runs and it creeps
For a while till it sleeps
In its own little lake.
And thence at departing,
Awakening and starting,
It runs through the reeds,
And away it proceeds,
Through meadow and glade,
In sun and in shade,
And through the wood-shelter,
Among crags in its flurry,
Helter-skelter,
Hurry-skurry,
Here it comes sparkling,
And there it lies darkling;
Now smoking and frothing
Its tumult and wrath in,
Till, in this rapid race
On which it is bent,
It reaches the place
Of its steep descent.

The cataract strong
Then plunges along,
Striking and raging

As if a war waging
Its caverns and rocks among;
Rising and leaping,
Sinking and creeping,
Swelling and sweeping,
Showering and springing,
Flying and flinging,
Writhing and wringing,
Eddying and whisking,
Spouting and frisking,
Turning and twisting
Around and around
With endless rebound:
Smiting and fighting,
A sight to delight in;
Confounding, astounding,
Dizzying and deafening the ear with its sound.

Collecting, projecting,
Receding and speeding,
And shocking and rocking,
And darting and parting,
And threading and spreading,
And whizzing and hissing,
And dripping and skipping,
And hitting and splitting,
And shining and twining,
And rattling and battling,
And shaking and quaking,
And pouring and roaring,
And waving and raving,
And tossing and crossing,
And flowing and going,
And running and stunning,
And foaming and roaming,
And dinning and spinning,
And dropping and hopping,
And working and jerking,
And guggling and struggling,
And heaving and cleaving,
And moaning and groaning;

And glittering and frittering,
And gathering and feathering,
And whitening and brightening,
And quivering and shivering,
And hurrying and skurrying,
And thundering and floundering;

Dividing and gliding and sliding,
And falling and brawling and sprawling,
And driving and riving and striving,
And sprinkling and twinkling and wrinkling,
And sounding and bounding and rounding,
And bubbling and troubling and doubling,
And grumbling and rumbling and tumbling,
And clattering and battering and shattering;

Retreating and beating and meeting and sheeting,
Delaying and straying and playing and spraying,
Advancing and prancing and glancing and dancing,
Recoiling, turmoiling and toiling and boiling,
And gleaming and streaming and steaming and beaming,
And rushing and flushing and brushing and gushing,
And flapping and rapping and clapping and slapping,
And curling and whirling and purling and twirling,
And thumping and plumping and bumping and jumping,
And dashing and flashing and splashing and clashing;
And so never ending, but always descending,
Sounds and motions forever and ever are blending,
All at once and all o'er, with a mighty uproar,—
And this way the water comes down at Lodore.

Robert Southey.

LAY OF THE DESERTED INFLUENZAED

Doe, doe!
I shall dever see her bore!
Dever bore our feet shall rove
The beadows as of yore!
Dever bore with byrtle boughs

Her tresses shall I twide—
Dever bore her bellow voice
Bake bellody with bide!
Dever shall we lidger bore,
 Abid the flow'rs at dood,
Dever shall we gaze at dight
 Upon the tedtder bood!
   Ho, doe, doe!
Those berry tibes have flowd,
Ad I shall dever see her bore,
 By beautiful! by owd!
   Ho, doe, doe!

I shall dever see her bore,
She will forget be id a bonth,
 (Bost probably before)—
She will forget the byrtle boughs,
 The flow'rs we plucked at dood,
Our beetigs by the tedtder stars.
 Our gazigs at the bood.

Ad I shall dever see agaid
 The Lily and the Rose;
The dabask cheek! the sdowy brow!
 The perfect bouth ad dose!
   Ho, doe, doe!
Those berry tibes have flowd—
Ad I shall dever see her bore,
 By beautiful! by owd!!

H. Cholmondeley-Pennell.

BELAGCHOLLY DAYS

CHILLY DOVEBBER with his boadigg blast
 Dow cubs add strips the beddow add the lawd,
Eved October's suddy days are past—
 Add Subber's gawd!

I kdow dot what it is to which I cligg
 That stirs to sogg add sorrow, yet I trust
That still I sigg, but as the liddets sigg—
 Because I bust.

Add dow, farewell to roses add to birds,
  To larded fields and tigkligg streablets eke;
Farewell to all articulated words
  I faid would speak.

Farewell, by cherished strolliggs od the sward,
  Greed glades add forest shades, farewell to you;
With sorrowing heart I, wretched add forlord,
  Bid you—achew! ! !

Unknown.

RHYME OF THE RAIL

Singing through the forests,
  Rattling over ridges,
Shooting under arches,
  Rumbling over bridges,
Whizzing through the mountains,
  Buzzing o'er the vale—
Bless me! this is pleasant,
  Riding on the Rail!

Men of different "stations"
  In the eye of Fame
Here are very quickly
  Coming to the same.
High and lowly people,
  Birds of every feather,
On a common level
  Travelling together.

Gentleman in shorts,
  Looming very tall;
Gentleman at large,
  Talking very small;
Gentleman in tights,
  With a loose-ish mien;
Gentleman in grey,
  Looking rather green;

Gentleman quite old,
   Asking for the news;
Gentleman in black,
   In a fit of blues;
Gentleman in claret,
   Sober as a vicar;
Gentleman in tweed,
   Dreadfully in liquor!

Stranger on the right,
   Looking very sunny,
Obviously reading
   Something very funny.
Now the smiles are thicker,
   Wonder what they mean?
Faith, he's got the KNICKER-
BOCKER Magazine!

Stranger on the left,
   Closing up his peepers;
Now he snores again,
   Like the Seven Sleepers;
At his feet a volume
   Gives the explanation,
How the man grew stupid
   From " Association."

Ancient maiden lady
   Anxiously remarks,
That there must be peril
   'Mong so many sparks;
Roguish-looking fellow,
   Turning to the stranger,
Says it's his opinion
   She is out of danger!

Woman with her baby,
   Sitting *vis-à-vis,*
Baby keeps a-squalling,
   Woman looks at me;

Asks about the distance,
  Says it's tiresome talking,
Noises of the cars
  Are so very shocking!

Market-woman, careful
  Of the precious casket,
Knowing eggs are eggs,
  Tightly holds her basket;
Feeling that a smash,
  If it came, would surely
Send her eggs to pot
  Rather prematurely.

Singing through the forests,
  Rattling over ridges,
Shooting under arches,
  Rumbling over bridges,
Whizzing through the mountains,
  Buzzing o'er the vale;
Bless me! this is pleasant,
  Riding on the Rail!

John G. Saxe.

ECHO

I ASKED of Echo, t'other day
  (Whose words are often few and funny),
What to a novice she could say
  Of courtship, love, and matrimony.
  Quoth Echo plainly,—" Matter-o'-money!"

Whom should I marry? Should it be
  A dashing damsel, gay and pert,
A pattern of inconstancy;
  Or selfish, mercenary flirt?
  Quoth Echo, sharply,—" Nary flirt!"

What if, aweary of the strife
  That long has lured the dear deceiver,
She promise to amend her life,
  And sin no more; can I believe her?
  Quoth Echo, very promptly,—"Leave her!"

But if some maiden with a heart
  On me should venture to bestow it,
Pray, should I act the wiser part
  To take the treasure or forego it?
  Quoth Echo, with decision,—"Go it!"

But what if, seemingly afraid
  To bind her fate in Hymen's fetter,
She vow she means to die a maid,
  In answer to my loving letter?
  Quoth Echo, rather coolly,—"Let her!"

What if, in spite of her disdain,
  I find my heart intwined about
With Cupid's dear delicious chain
  So closely that I can't get out?
  Quoth Echo, laughingly,—"Get out!"

But if some maid with beauty blest,
  As pure and fair as Heaven can make her,
Will share my labor and my rest
  Till envious Death shall overtake her?
  Quoth Echo (sotto voce),—"Take her!"

John G. Saxe.

SONG

Echo, tell me, while I wander
  O'er this fairy plain to prove him,
If my shepherd still grows fonder,
  Ought I in return to love him?
  Echo: Love him, love him!

If he loves, as is the fashion,
    Should I churlishly forsake him?
Or in pity to his passion,
    Fondly to my bosom take him?
      Echo: Take him, take him!

Thy advice then, I'll adhere to,
    Since in Cupid's chains I've led him;
And with Henry shall not fear to
    Marry, if you answer, "Wed him!"
      Echo: Wed him, wed him!

Joseph Addison.

A GENTLE ECHO ON WOMAN

IN THE DORIC MANNER

Shepherd.	ECHO, I ween, will in the woods reply,
	And quaintly answer questions: shall I try?
Echo.	Try.
Shepherd.	What must we do our passion to express?
Echo.	Press.
Shepherd.	How shall I please her, who ne'er loved before?
Echo.	Before.
Shepherd.	What most moves women when we them address?
Echo.	A dress.
Shepherd.	Say, what can keep her chaste whom I adore?
Echo.	A door.
Shepherd.	If music softens rocks, love tunes my lyre.
Echo.	Liar.
Shepherd.	Then teach me, Echo, how shall I come by her?
Echo.	Buy her.
Shepherd.	When bought, no question I shall be her dear?
Echo.	Her deer.
Shepherd.	But deer have horns: how must I keep her under?
Echo.	Keep her under.
Shepherd.	But what can glad me when she's laid on bier?
Echo.	Beer.
Shepherd.	What must I do so women will be kind?
Echo.	Be kind.

Shepherd.	What must I do when women will be cross?
Echo.	Be cross.
Shepherd.	Lord, what is she that can so turn and wind?
Echo.	Wind.
Shepherd.	If she be wind, what stills her when she blows?
Echo.	Blows.
Shepherd.	But if she bang again, still should I bang her?
Echo.	Bang her.
Shepherd.	Is there no way to moderate her anger?
Echo.	Hang her.
Shepherd.	Thanks, gentle Echo! right thy answers tell
	What woman is and how to guard her well.
Echo.	Guard her well.

Dean Swift.

LAY OF ANCIENT ROME

OH, the Roman was a rogue,
   He erat was, you bettum;
He ran his automobilus
   And smoked his cigarettum.
He wore a diamond studibus
   And elegant cravattum,
A maxima cum laude shirt
   And such a stylish hattum!

He loved the luscious hic-haec-hoc,
   And bet on games and equi;
At times he won at others though,
   He got it in the nequi;
He winked, (quo usque tandem?) at
   Puellas on the Forum,
And sometimes, too, he even made
   Those goo-goo oculorum!

He frequently was seen
   At combats gladiatorial
And ate enough to feed
   Ten boarders at Memorial;

He often went on sprees
  And said, on starting homus,
" Hic labour—opus est,
  Oh, where's my hic—hic—domus? "

Although he lived in Rome,—
  Of all the arts the middle—
He was, (excuse the phrase,)
  A horrid individ'l;
Ah, what a different thing
  Was the homo (dative, hominy)
Of far away B. C.
  From us of Anno Domini.

              Thomas R. Ybarra.

A NEW SONG

OF NEW SIMILES

My passion is as mustard strong;
  I sit all sober sad;
Drunk as a piper all day long,
  Or like a March-hare mad.

Round as a hoop the bumpers flow;
  I drink, yet can't forget her;
For though as drunk as David's sow
  I love her still the better.

Pert as a pear-monger I'd be,
  If Molly were but kind;
Cool as a cucumber could see
  The rest of womankind.

Like a stuck pig I gaping stare,
  And eye her o'er and o'er;
Lean as a rake, with sighs and care,
  Sleek as a mouse before.

Plump as a partridge was I known,
    And soft as silk my skin;
My cheeks as fat as butter grown,
    But as a goat now thin!

I melancholy as a cat,
    Am kept awake to weep;
But she, insensible of that,
    Sound as a top can sleep.

Hard is her heart as flint or stone,
    She laughs to see me pale;
And merry as a grig is grown,
    And brisk as bottled ale.

The god of Love at her approach
    Is busy as a bee;
Hearts sound as any bell or roach,
    Are smit and sigh like me.

Ah me! as thick as hops or hail
    The fine men crowd about her;
But soon as dead as a door-nail
    Shall I be, if without her.

Straight as my leg her shape appears,
    O were we join'd together!
My heart would be scot-free from cares,
    And lighter than a feather.

As fine as five-pence is her mien,
    No drum was ever tighter;
Her glance is as the razor keen,
    And not the sun is brighter.

As soft as pap her kisses are,
    Methinks I taste them yet;
Brown as a berry is her hair,
    Her eyes as black as jet.

As smooth as glass, as white as curds
  Her pretty hand invites;
Sharp as her needle are her words,
  Her wit like pepper bites.

Brisk as a body-louse she trips,
  Clean as a penny drest;
Sweet as a rose her breath and lips,
  Round as the globe her breast.

Full as an egg was I with glee,
  And happy as a king:
Good Lord! how all men envied me!
  She loved like any thing.

But false as hell, she, like the wind,
  Chang'd, as her sex must do;
Though seeming as the turtle kind,
  And like the gospel true.

If I and Molly could agree,
  Let who would take Peru!
Great as an Emperor should I be,
  And richer than a Jew.

Till you grow tender as a chick,
  I'm dull as any post;
Let us like burs together stick,
  And warm as any toast.

You'll know me truer than a die,
  And wish me better sped;
Flat as a flounder when I lie,
  And as a herring dead.

Sure as a gun she'll drop a tear
  And sigh, perhaps, and wish,
When I am rotten as a pear,
  And mute as any fish.

John Gay.

THE AMERICAN TRAVELLER

To Lake Aghmoogenegamook
    All in the State of Maine,
A man from Wittequergaugaum came
    One evening in the rain.

" I am a traveller," said he,
    " Just started on a tour,
And go to Nomjamskillicook
    To-morrow morn at four."

He took a tavern-bed that night,
    And, with the morrow's sun,
By way of Sekledobskus went,
    With carpet-bag and gun.

A week passed on, and next we find
    Our native tourist come
To that sequestered village called
    Genasagarnagum.

From thence he went to Absequoit,
    And there—quite tired of Maine—
He sought the mountains of Vermont,
    Upon a railroad train.

Dog Hollow, in the Green Mount State,
    Was his first stopping-place;
And then Skunk's Misery displayed
    Its sweetness and its grace.

By easy stages then he went
    To visit Devil's Den;
And Scrabble Hollow, by the way,
    Did come within his ken.

Then *via* Nine Holes and Goose Green
    He travelled through the State;
And to Virginia, finally,
    Was guided by his fate.

Within the Old Dominion's bounds,
　　He wandered up and down;
To-day at Buzzard's Roost ensconced,
　　To-morrow, at Hell Town.

At Pole Cat, too, he spent a week,
　　Till friends from Bull Ring came,
And made him spend a day with them
　　In hunting forest-game.

Then, with his carpet-bag in hand,
　　To Dog Town next he went;
Though stopping at Free Negro Town,
　　Where half a day he spent.

From thence, into Negationburg
　　His route of travel lay;
Which having gained, he left the State,
　　And took a southward way.

North Carolina's friendly soil
　　He trod at fall of night,
And, on a bed of softest down,
　　He slept at Hell's Delight.

Morn found him on the road again,
　　To Lousy Level bound;
At Bull's Tail, and Lick Lizard, too,
　　Good provender he found.

The country all about Pinch Gut
　　So beautiful did seem
That the beholder thought it like
　　A picture in a dream.

But the plantations near Burnt Coat
　　Were even finer still,
And made the wondering tourist feel
　　A soft, delicious thrill.

At Tear Shirt, too, the scenery
  Most charming did appear,
With Snatch It in the distance far,
  And Purgatory near.

But, spite of all these pleasant scenes,
  The tourist stoutly swore
That home is brightest, after all,
  And travel is a bore.

So back he went to Maine, straightway;
  A little wife he took;
And now is making nutmegs at
  Moosehicmagunticook.

Robert H. Newell.

THE ZEALLESS XYLOGRAPHER

DEDICATED TO THE END OF THE DICTIONARY

A xylographer started to cross the sea
  By means of a Xanthic Xebec;
But, alas! he sighed for the Zuyder Zee,
  And feared he was in for a wreck.
He tried to smile, but all in vain,
  Because of a Zygomatic pain;
And as for singing, his cheeriest tone
  Reminded him of a Xylophone—
Or else, when the pain would sharper grow,
  His notes were as keen as a Zuffolo.
And so it is likely he did not find
  On board Xenodochy to his mind.
The fare was poor, and he was sure
  Xerofphagy he could not endure;
Zoöphagous surely he was, I aver,
  This dainty and starving Xylographer.
Xylophagous truly he could not be—
  No sickly vegetarian he!
He'd have blubbered like any old Zeuglodon
  Had Xerophthalmia not come on.
And the end of it was he never again
  In a Xanthic Xebec went sailing the main.

Mary Mapes Dodge.

THE OLD LINE FENCE

ZIG-ZAGGING it went
On the line of the farm,
And the trouble it caused
Was often quite warm,
THE OLD LINE FENCE.
It was changed every year
By decree of the court,
To which, when worn out,
Our sires would resort
WITH THE OLD LINE FENCE.
In hoeing their corn,
When the sun, too, was hot,
They surely would jaw,
Punch or claw, when they got
TO THE OLD LINE FENCE.
In dividing the lands
It fulfilled no desires,
But answered quite well
In " dividing " our sires,
THIS OLD LINE FENCE.
Though sometimes in this
It would happen to fail,
When, with top rail in hand,
One would flare up and scale
THE OLD LINE FENCE!
Then the conflict was sharp
On debatable ground,
And the fertile soil there
Would be mussed far around
THE OLD LINE FENCE.
It was shifted so oft
That no flowers there grew.
What frownings and clods,
And what words were shot through
THE OLD LINE FENCE!
Our sires through the day
There would quarrel or fight,
With a vigour and vim,
But 'twas different at night

By the old line fence.
    The fairest maid there
    You would have descried
        That ever leaned soft
        On the opposite side
          Of an old line fence.
    Where our fathers built hate
    There we builded our love,
    Breathed our vows to be true
    With our hands raised above
The old line fence.
    Its place might be changed,
    But there we would meet,
        With our heads through the rails,
        And with kisses most sweet,
        At the old line fence.
    It was love made the change,
    And the clasping of hands
    Ending ages of hate,
    And between us now stands
Not a sign of line fence.
    No debatable ground
    Now enkindles alarms.
        I've the girl I met there,
        And, well, both of the farms,
        And no line fence.

              A. W. Bellaw.

O-U-G-H

A FRESH HACK AT AN OLD KNOT

I'm taught p-l-o-u-g-h
    S'all be pronouncé " plow."
" Zat's easy w'en you know," I say,
    " Mon Anglais, I'll get through! "

My teacher say zat in zat case,
    O-u-g-h is " oo."
And zen I laugh and say to him,
    " Zees Anglais make me cough."

He say " Not ' coo,' but in zat word,
    O-u-g-h is ' off,' "
Oh, Sacre bleu! such varied sounds
    Of words makes me hiccough!

He say, " Again mon frien' ees wrong;
    O-u-g-h is ' up "
In hiccough." Zen I cry, " No more,
    You make my t'roat feel rough."

" Non, non! " he cry, " you are not right;
    O-u-g-h is ' uff.' "
I say, " I try to spik your words,
    I cannot spik zem though! "

" In time you'll learn, but now you're wrong!
    O-u-g-h is ' owe.' "
" I'll try no more, I s'all go mad,
    I'll drown me in ze lough! "

" But ere you drown yourself," said he,
    " O-u-g-h is ' ock.' "
He taught no more, I held him fast,
    And killed him wiz a rough.

                  Charles Battell Loomis.

ENIGMA ON THE LETTER H

'Twas whispered in heaven, 'twas muttered in hell,
And echo caught faintly the sound as it fell;
On the confines of earth 'twas permitted to rest,
And the depths of the ocean its presence confessed;
'Twill be found in the sphere when 'tis riven asunder,
Be seen in the lightning, and heard in the thunder.
'Twas allotted to man with his earliest breath,
It assists at his birth and attends him in death,
Presides o'er his happiness, honor, and health,
Is the prop of his house and the end of his wealth,

In the heaps of the miser is hoarded with care,
But is sure to be lost in his prodigal heir.
It begins every hope, every wish it must bound,
It prays with the hermit, with monarchs is crowned;
Without it the soldier, the sailor, may roam,
But woe to the wretch who expels it from home.
In the whisper of conscience 'tis sure to be found,
Nor e'en in the whirlwind of passion is drowned;
'Twill soften the heart, but, though deaf to the ear,
It will make it acutely and instantly hear;
But, in short, let it rest like a delicate flower;
Oh, breathe on it softly, it dies in an hour.

Catherine Fanshawe.

TRAVESTY OF MISS FANSHAWE'S ENIGMA

I DWELLS in the Hearth, and I breathes in the Hair;
If you searches the Hocean, you'll find that I'm there.
The first of all Hangels in Holympus am Hi,
Yet I'm banished from 'Eaven, expelled from on 'igh.
But, though on this Horb I'm destined to grovel,
I'm ne'er seen in an 'Ouse, in an 'Ut, nor an 'Ovel.
Not an 'Orse, not an 'Unter e'er bears me, alas!
But often I'm found on the top of a Hass.
I resides in a Hattic, and loves not to roam,
And yet I'm invariably absent from 'Ome.
Though 'Ushed in the 'Urricane, of the Hatmosphere part,
I enters no 'Ed, I creeps into no 'Art.
Only look, and you'll see in the Heye Hi appear;
Only 'Ark, and you'll 'Ear me just breathe in the Hear.
Though in sex not an 'E, I am (strange paradox)
Not a bit of an 'Effer, but partly a Hox.
Of Heternity I'm the beginning! and, mark,
Though I goes not with Noar, I'm first in the Hark.
I'm never in 'Ealth, have with Fysic no power,
I dies in a month, but comes back in a Hour.

Horace Mayhew.

AN ELEGY ON THE DEATH OF A MAD DOG

Good people all, of every sort,
  Give ear unto my song;
And if you find it wondrous short,—
  It cannot hold you long.

In Islington there was a man,
  Of whom the world might say
That still a godly race he ran,—
  Whene'er he went to pray.

A kind and gentle heart he had,
  To comfort friends and foes;
The naked every day he clad,—
  When he put on his clothes.

And in that town a dog was found,
  As many dogs there be,
Both mongrel, puppy, whelp, and hound,
  And curs of low degree.

The dog and man at first were friends;
  But when a pique began,
The dog, to gain some private ends,
  Went mad, and bit the man.

Around from all the neighboring streets,
  The wondering neighbors ran,
And swore the dog had lost his wits
  To bite so good a man.

The wound it seemed both sore and sad
  To every Christian eye;
And while they swore the dog was mad
  They swore the man would die.

But soon a wonder came to light,
  That showed the rogues they lied;
The man recovered of the bite,
  The dog it was that died.

                                    Oliver Goldsmith.

AN EPITAPH

Interred beneath this marble stone
Lie sauntering Jack and idle Joan.
While rolling threescore years and one
Did round this globe their courses run.
If human things went ill or well,
If changing empires rose or fell,
The morning past, the evening came,
And found this couple just the same.
They walked and ate, good folks. What then?
Why, then they walked and ate again;
They soundly slept the night away;
They did just nothing all the day,
Nor sister either had, nor brother;
They seemed just tallied for each other.
Their moral and economy
Most perfectly they made agree;
Each virtue kept its proper bound,
Nor trespassed on the other's ground.
Nor fame nor censure they regarded;
They neither punished nor rewarded.
He cared not what the footman did;
Her maids she neither praised nor chid;
So every servant took his course,
And, bad at first, they all grew worse;
Slothful disorder filled his stable,
And sluttish plenty decked her table.
Their beer was strong, their wine was port;
Their meal was large, their grace was short.
They gave the poor the remnant meat,
Just when it grew not fit to eat.
They paid the church and parish rate,
And took, but read not, the receipt;
For which they claimed their Sunday's due
Of slumbering in an upper pew.
No man's defects sought they to know,
So never made themselves a foe.
No man's good deeds did they commend,
So never raised themselves a friend.

Nor cherished they relations poor,
That might decrease their present store;
Nor barn nor house did they repair,
That might oblige their future heir.
They neither added nor confounded;
They neither wanted nor abounded.
Nor tear nor smile did they employ
At news of grief or public joy
When bells were rung and bonfires made,
If asked, they ne'er denied their aid;
Their jug was to the ringers carried,
Whoever either died or married.
Their billet at the fire was found,
Whoever was deposed or crowned.
Nor good, nor bad, nor fools, nor wise;
They would not learn, nor could advise;
Without love, hatred, joy, or fear,
They led—a kind of—as it were;
Nor wished, nor cared, nor laughed, nor cried.
And so they lived, and so they died.

Matthew Prior.

OLD GRIMES

OLD Grimes is dead; that good old man
  We never shall see more:
He used to wear a long, black coat,
  All button'd down before.

His heart was open as the day,
  His feelings all were true;
His hair was some inclined to gray—
  He wore it in a queue.

Whene'er he heard the voice of pain,
  His breast with pity burn'd;
The large, round head upon his cane
  From ivory was turn'd.

Kind words he ever had for all;
  He knew no base design:
His eyes were dark and rather small,
  His nose was aquiline.

He lived at peace with all mankind,
  In friendship he was true:
His coat had pocket-holes behind,
  His pantaloons were blue.

Unharm'd, the sin which earth pollutes
  He pass'd securely o'er,
And never wore a pair of boots
  For thirty years or more.

But good old Grimes is now at rest,
  Nor fears misfortune's frown:
He wore a double-breasted vest—
  The stripes ran up and down.

He modest merit sought to find,
  Any pay it its desert:
He had no malice in his mind,
  No ruffles on his shirt.

His neighbors he did not abuse—
  Was sociable and gay:
He wore large buckles on his shoes,
  And changed them every day.

His knowledge, hid from public gaze,
  He did not bring to view,
Nor made a noise, town-meeting days,
  As many people do.

His worldly goods he never threw
  In trust to fortune's chances,
But lived (as all his brothers do)
  In easy circumstances.

Thus undisturb'd by anxious cares,
   His peaceful moments ran;
And everybody said he was
   A fine old gentleman.

Albert Gorton Greene.

THE ENDLESS SONG

Oh, I used to sing a song,
An' dey said it was too long,
So I cut it off de en'
To accommodate a frien'
       Nex' do', nex' do'—
To accommodate a frien' nex' do'.

But it made de matter wuss
Dan it had been at de fus,
'Ca'ze de en' was gone, an' den
Co'se it didn't have no en'
       Any mo', any mo'—
Oh, it didn't have no en' any mo'!

So, to save my frien' from sinnin',
I cut off de song's beginnin';
Still he cusses right along
Whilst I sings *about* my song
       Jes so, jes so—
Whilst I sings *about* my song *jes so.*

How to please 'im is my riddle,
So I'll fall back on my fiddle;
For I'd stan' myself on en'
To accommodate a frien'
       Nex' do', nex' do'—
To accommodate a frien' nex' do'.

Ruth McEnery Stuart.

THE HUNDRED BEST BOOKS

FIRST there's the Bible,
   And then the Koran,
Odgers on Libel,
   Pope's Essay on Man,
Confessions of Rousseau,
   The Essays of Lamb,
Robinson Crusoe
   And Omar Khayyam,
Volumes of Shelley
   And Venerable Bede,
Machiavelli
   And Captain Mayne Reid,
Fox upon Martyrs
   And Liddell and Scott,
Stubbs on the Charters,
   The works of La Motte,
The Seasons by Thomson,
   And Paul de Verlaine,
Theodore Mommsen
   And Clemens (Mark Twain),
The Rocks of Hugh Miller,
   The Mill on the Floss,
The Poems of Schiller,
   The Iliados,
Don Quixote (Cervantes),
   La Pucelle by Voltaire,
Inferno (that's Dante's),
   And Vanity Fair,
Conybeare-Howson,
   Brillat-Savarin,
And Baron Munchausen,
   Mademoiselle De Maupin,
The Dramas of Marlowe,
   The Three Musketeers,
Clarissa Harlowe,
   And the Pioneers,
Sterne's Tristram Shandy,
   The Ring and the Book,

And Handy Andy,
   And Captain Cook,
The Plato of Jowett,
   And Mill's Pol. Econ.,
The Haunts of Howitt,
   The Encheiridion,
Lothair by Disraeli,
   And Boccaccio,
The Student's Paley,
   And Westward Ho!
The Pharmacopœia,
   Macaulay's Lays,
Of course The Medea,
   And Sheridan's Plays,
The Odes of Horace,
   And Verdant Green,
The Poems of Morris,
   The Faery Queen,
The Stones of Venice,
   Natural History (White's),
And then Pendennis,
   The Arabian Nights,
Cicero's Orations,
   Plain Tales from the Hills,
The Wealth of Nations,
   And Byles on Bills,
As in a Glass Darkly,
   Demosthenes' Crown,
The Treatise of Berkeley,
   Tom Hughes's Tom Brown,
The Mahabharata,
   The Humour of Hook,
The Kreutzer Sonata,
   And Lalla Rookh,
Great Battles by Creasy,
   And Hudibras,
And Midshipman Easy,
   And Rasselas,
Shakespeare *in extenso*
   And the Æneid,
And Euclid (Colenso),

The Woman who Did,
Poe's Tales of Mystery,
    Then Rabelais,
Guizot's French History,
    And Men of the Day,
Rienzi, by Lytton,
    The Poems of Burns,
The Story of Britain,
    The Journey (that's Sterne's),
The House of Seven Gables,
    Carroll's Looking-glass,
Æsop his Fables,
    And Leaves of Grass,
Departmental Ditties,
    The Woman in White,
The Tale of Two Cities,
    Ships that Pass in the Night,
Meredith's Feverel,
    Gibbon's Decline,
Walter Scott's Peveril,
    And—some verses of mine.

                                Mostyn T. Pigott.

THE COSMIC EGG

Upon a rock, yet uncreate,
Amid a chaos inchoate,
An uncreated being sate;
Beneath him, rock,
Above him, cloud.
And the cloud was rock,
And the rock was cloud.
The rock then growing soft and warm,
The cloud began to take a form,
A form chaotic, vast and vague,
Which issued in the cosmic egg.
Then the Being uncreate
On the egg did incubate,
And thus became the incubator;

And of the egg did allegate,
And thus became the alligator;
And the incubator was potentate,
But the alligator was potentator.

Unknown.

FIVE WINES

BRISK methinks I am, and fine
When I drink my cap'ring wine;
Then to love I do incline,
When I drink my wanton wine;
And I wish all maidens mine,
When I drink my sprightly wine;
Well I sup and well I dine,
When I drink my frolic wine;
But I languish, lower, and pine,
When I want my fragrant wine.

Robert Herrick.

A RHYME FOR MUSICIANS

HÄNDEL, Bendel, Mendelssohn,
Brendel, Wendel, Jadassohn,
Müller, Hiller, Heller, Franz,
Plothow, Flotow, Burto, Ganz.

Meyer, Geyer, Meyerbeer,
Heyer, Weyer, Beyer, Beer,
Lichner, Lachner, Schachner, Dietz,
Hill, Will, Brüll, Grill, Drill, Reiss, Rietz.

Hansen, Jansen, Jensen, Kiehl,
Siade, Gade, Laade, Stiehl,
Naumann, Riemann, Diener, Wurst,
Niemann, Kiemann, Diener, Furst.

Kochler, Dochler, Rubinstein,
Himmel, Hummel, Rosenhain,
Lauer, Bauer, Kleinecke,
Homberg, Plomberg, Reinecke.

E. Lemke.

MY MADELINE

SERENADE IN M FLAT

SUNG BY MAJOR MARMADUKE MUTTONHEAD TO
MADEMOISELLE MADELINE MENDOZA

My Madeline! my Madeline!
Mark my melodious midnight moans;
Much may my melting music mean,
My modulated monotones.

My mandolin's mild minstrelsy,
My mental music magazine,
My mouth, my mind, my memory,
Must mingling murmur "Madeline!"

Muster 'mid midnight masquerades,
Mark Moorish maidens, matrons' mien;
'Mongst Murcia's most majestic maids,
Match me my matchless Madeline.

Mankind's malevolence may make
Much melancholy musing mine;
Many my motives may mistake,
My modest merits much malign.

My Madeline's most mirthful mood
Much mollifies my mind's machine,
My mournfulness's magnitude
Melts—make me merry, Madeline!

Match-making mas may machinate,
Manœuvring misses me mis-ween;
Mere money may make many mate,
My magic motto's "Madeline!"

Melt, most mellifluous melody,
   'Midst Murcia's misty mounts marine;
Meet me 'mid moonlight; marry me,
   Madonna mia! my Madeline!

Walter Parke.

SUSAN SIMPSON

Sudden swallows swiftly skimming,
   Sunset's slowly spreading shade,
Silvery songsters sweetly singing,
   Summer's soothing serenade.

Susan Simpson strolled sedately,
   Stifling sobs, suppressing sighs.
Seeing Stephen Slocum, stately
   She stopped, showing some surprise.

" Say," said Stephen, " sweetest sigher;
   Say, shall Stephen spouseless stay? "
Susan, seeming somewhat shyer,
   Showed submissiveness straightway.

Summer's season slowly stretches,
   Susan Simpson Slocum she—
So she signed some simple sketches—
   Soul sought soul successfully.

   ·   ·   ·   ·   ·   ·

Six Septembers Susan swelters;
   Six sharp seasons snow supplies;
Susan's satin sofa shelters
   Six small Slocums side by side.

Unknown.

THE MARCH TO MOSCOW

THE Emperor Nap he would set off
On a summer excursion to Moscow;
The fields were green and the sky was blue,
Morbleu! Parbleu!
What a splendid excursion to Moscow!

Four hundred thousand men and more
Must go with him to Moscow:
There were Marshals by the dozen,
And Dukes by the score;
Princes a few, and Kings one or two;
While the fields are so green, and the sky so blue,
Morbleu! Parbleu!
What a pleasant excursion to Moscow!

There was Junot and Augereau,
Heigh-ho for Moscow!
Dombrowsky and Poniatowsky,
Marshall Ney, lack-a-day!
General Rapp, and the Emperor Nap;
Nothing would do,
While the fields were so green, and the sky so blue,
Morbleu! Parbleu!
Nothing would do
For the whole of his crew,
But they must be marching to Moscow.

The Emperor Nap he talk'd so big
That he frighten'd Mr. Roscoe.
John Bull, he cries, if you'll be wise,
Ask the Emperor Nap if he will please
To grant you peace upon your knees,
Because he is going to Moscow!
He'll make all the Poles come out of their holes,
And beat the Russians, and eat the Prussians;
For the fields are green, and the sky is blue,
Morbleu! Parbleu!
And he'll certainly march to Moscow!

And Counsellor Brougham was all in a fume
At the thought of the march to Moscow:
The Russians, he said, they were undone,
   And the great Fee-Faw-Fum
    Would presently come,
With a hop, step, and jump, unto London,
   For, as for his conquering Russia,
   However some persons might scoff it,
   Do it he could, do it he would,
And from doing it nothing would come but good,
   And nothing could call him off it.
Mr. Jeffrey said so, who must certainly know,
   For he was the Edinburgh Prophet.
They all of them knew Mr. Jeffrey's Review,
Which with Holy Writ ought to be reckon'd:
It was, through thick and thin, to its party true,
   Its back was buff, and its sides were blue,
     Morbleu! Parbleu!
It served them for law and for gospel too.

But the Russians stoutly they turned to
    Upon the road to Moscow.
Nap had to fight his way all through;
They could fight, though they could not parlez-vous;
But the fields were green, and the sky was blue,
     Morbleu! Parbleu!
   And so he got to Moscow.

He found the place too warm for him,
   For they set fire to Moscow.
To get there had cost him much ado,
And then no better course he knew
While the fields were green, and the sky was blue,
     Morbleu! Parbleu!
But to march back again from Moscow.

The Russians they stuck close to him
   All on the road from Moscow.
There was Tormazow and Jemalow,
And all the others that end in ow;
Milarodovitch and Jaladovitch,

And Karatschkowitch,
And all the others that end in itch;
Schamscheff, Souchosaneff,
And Schepaleff,
And all the others that end in eff:
Wasiltschikoff, Kotsomaroff,
And Tchoglokoff,
And all the others that end in off;
Rajeffsky, and Novereffsky,
And Rieffsky,
And all the others that end in effsky;
Oscharoffsky and Rostoffsky,
And all the others that end in offsky;
And Platoff he play'd them off,
And Shouvaloff he shovell'd them off,
And Markoff he mark'd them off,
And Krosnoff he cross'd them off,
And Touchkoff he touch'd them off,
And Boroskoff he bored them off,
And Kutousoff he cut them off,
And Parenzoff he pared them off,
And Worronzoff he worried them off,
And Doctoroff he doctor'd them off,
And Rodinoff he flogg'd them off.
And, last of all, an Admiral came,
A terrible man with a terrible name,
A name which you all know by sight very well,
But which no one can speak, and no one can spell.
They stuck close to Nap with all their might;
They were on the left and on the right
Behind and before, and by day and by night;
He would rather parlez-vous than fight;
But he look'd white, and he look'd blue.
Morbleu! Parbleu!
When parlez-vous no more would do.
For they remember'd Moscow.

And then came on the frost and snow
All on the road from Moscow.
The wind and the weather he found, in that hour,
Cared nothing for him, nor for all his power;

For him who, while Europe crouch'd under his **rod**,
Put his trust in his Fortune, and not in his God.
Worse and worse every day the elements grew,
The fields were so white and the sky was so blue,
   Sacrebleu!   Ventrebleu!
  What a horrible journey from Moscow!

  What then thought the Emperor Nap
   Upon the road from Moscow?
Why, I ween he thought it small delight
To fight all day, and to freeze all night;
And he was besides in a very great fright,
  For a whole skin he liked to be in;
  And so not knowing what else to do,
When the fields were so white, and the sky so blue,
   Morbleu! Parbleu!
  He stole away,—I tell you true,—
   Upon the road from Moscow.
'Tis myself, quoth he, I must mind most;
So the devil may take the hindmost.

  Too cold upon the road was he;
  Too hot had he been at Moscow;
  But colder and hotter he may be,
  For the grave is colder than Moscovy;
And a place there is to be kept in view,
Where the fire is red, and the brimstone blue,
   Morbleu! Parbleu!
   Which he must go to,
   If the Pope say true,
If he does not in time look about him;
  Where his namesake almost
  He may have for his Host;
He has reckon'd too long without him;
If that Host get him in Purgatory,
He won't leave him there alone with his glory;
  But there he must stay for a very long day,
  For from thence there is no stealing away,
  As there was on the road from Moscow.

      Robert Southey.

HALF HOURS WITH THE CLASSICS

Ah, those hours when by-gone sages
  Led our thoughts through Learning's ways,
When the wit of sunnier ages,
  Called once more to Earth the days
When rang through Athens' vine-hung lanes
Thy wild, wild laugh, Aristophanes!

Pensive through the land of Lotus,
  Sauntered we by Nilus' side;
Garrulous old Herodotus
  Still our mentor, still our guide,
Prating of the mystic bliss
Of Isis and of Osiris.

All the learn'd ones trooped before us,
  All the wise of Hellas' land,
Down from mythic Pythagoras,
  To the hemlock drinker grand.
Dark the hour that closed the gates
Of gloomy Dis on thee, Socrates.

Ah, those hours of tend'rest study,
  When Electra's poet told
Of Love's cheek once warm and ruddy,
  Pale with grief, with death chill cold!
Sobbing low like summer tides
Flow thy verses, Euripides!

High our hearts beat when Cicero
  Shook the Capitolian dome;
How we shuddered, watching Nero
  'Mid the glare of blazing Rome!
How those records still affright us
On thy gloomy page, Tacitus!

Back to youth I seem to glide, as
  I recall those by-gone scenes,

When we conned o'er Thucydides,
Or recited Demosthenes.

L'ENVOI

Ancient sages, pardon these
Somewhat doubtful quantities.

H. J. DeBurgh.

ON THE OXFORD CARRIER

HERE lieth one, who did most truly prove
That he could never die while he could move;
So hung his destiny never to rot
While he might still jog on and keep his trot;
Made of sphere metal, never to decay
Until his revolution was at stay.
Time numbers motion, yet (without a crime
'Gainst old truth) motion number'd out his time
And like an engine moved with wheel and weight,
His principles being ceased, he ended straight.
Rest, that gives all men life, gave him his death,
And too much breathing put him out of breath;
Nor were it contradiction to affirm,
Too long vacation hasten'd on his term.
Merely to drive the time away he sicken'd,
Fainted, and died, nor would with ale be quicken'd;
"Nay," quoth he, on his swooning bed outstretch'd,
"If I mayn't carry, sure I'll ne'er be fetch'd,
But vow, though the cross doctors all stood hearers,
For one carrier put down to make six bearers."
Ease was his chief disease; and to judge right,
He died for heaviness that his cart went light:
His leisure told him that his time was come.
And lack of load made his life burdensome.
That even to his last breath (there be that say't),
As he were press'd to death, he cried, "More weight;"
But, had his doings lasted as they were,
He had been an immortal carrier.
Obedient to the moon he spent his date
In course reciprocal, and had his fate

Link'd to the mutual flowing of the seas,
Yet (strange to think) his wane was his increase:
His letters are deliver'd all, and gone,
Only remains the superscription.

John Milton.

NINETY-NINE IN THE SHADE

O FOR a lodge in a garden of cucumbers!
    O for an iceberg or two at control!
O for a vale which at mid-day the dew cumbers!
    O for a pleasure-trip up to the pole!

O for a little one-story thermometer,
    With nothing but zeroes all ranged in a row!
O for a big double-barreled hygrometer,
    To measure this moisture that rolls from my brow!

O that this cold world were twenty times colder!
    (That's irony red-hot it seemeth to me);
O for a turn of its dreaded cold shoulder!
    O what a comfort an ague would be!

O for a grotto frost-lined and rill-riven,
    Scooped in the rock under cataract vast!
O for a winter of discontent even!
    O for wet blankets judiciously cast!

O for a soda-fount spouting up boldly
    From every hot lamp-post against the hot sky!
O for proud maiden to look on me coldly,
    Freezing my soul with a glance of her eye!

Then O for a draught from a cup of cold pizen,
    And O for a resting-place in the cold grave!
With a bath in the Styx where the thick shadow lies on
    And deepens the chill of its dark-running wave.

Rossiter Johnson.

THE TRIOLET

Easy is the triolet,
　If you really learn to make it!
Once a neat refrain you get,
Easy is the triolet.
As you see!—I pay my debt
　With another rhyme. Deuce take it,
Easy is the triolet,
　If you really learn to make it!

William Ernest Henley.

THE RONDEAU

You bid me try, Blue-eyes, to write
A Rondeau. What! forthwith?—to-night?
　Reflect? Some skill I have, 'tis true;
　But thirteen lines!—and rhymed on two!—
"Refrain," as well. Ah, hapless plight!

Still there are five lines—ranged aright.
These Gallic bonds, I feared, would fright
　My easy Muse. They did, till you—
　　　　　You bid me try!

That makes them eight.—The port's in sight;
'Tis all because your eyes are bright!
　Now just a pair to end in " oo,"—
　When maids command, what can't we do?
Behold! The Rondeau—tasteful, light—
　　　　　You bid me try!

Austin Dobson.

LIFE [1]

1. WHY all this toil for triumphs of an hour?
2. Life's a short summer, man a flower.
3. By turns we catch the vital breath and die—
4. The cradle and the tomb, alas! so nigh.
5. To be, is better far than not to be.
6. Though all man's life may seem a tragedy;
7. But light cares speak when mighty griefs are dumb,
8. The bottom is but shallow whence they come.
9. Your fate is but the common lot of all:
10. Unmingled joys here to no man befall,
11. Nature to each allots his proper sphere;
12. Fortune makes folly her peculiar care;
13. Custom does often reason overrule,
14. And throw a cruel sunshine on a fool.
15. Live well; how long or short, permit to Heaven;
16. They who forgive most, shall be most forgiven.
17. Sin may be clasped so close we cannot see its face—
18. Vile intercourse where virtue has no place.
19. Then keep each passion down, however dear;
20. Thou pendulum betwixt a smile and tear.
21. Her sensual snares, let faithless pleasure lay,
22. With craft and skill, to ruin and betray;
23. Soar not too high to fall, but stoop to rise.
24. We masters grow of all that we despise.
25. Oh, then, renounce that impious self-esteem;
26. Riches have wings, and grandeur is a dream.
27. Think not ambition wise because 'tis brave,
28. The paths of glory lead but to the grave.
29. What is ambition?—'tis a glorious cheat!—
30. Only destructive to the brave and great.

[1] 1. Young; 2. Dr. Johnson; 3. Pope; 4. Prior; 5. Sewell; 6. Spenser; 7. Daniell; 8. Sir Walter Raleigh; 9. Longfellow; 10. Southwell; 11. Congreve; 12. Churchill; 13. Rochester; 14. Armstrong; 15. Milton; 16. Bailey; 17. Trench; 18. Somerville; 19. Thomson; 20. Byron; 21. Smollett; 22. Crabbe; 23. Massinger; 24. Cowley; 25. Beattie; 26. Cowper; 27. Sir Walter Davenant; 28. Gray; 29. Willis; 30. Addison; 31. Dryden; 32. Francis Quarles; 33. Watkins; 34. Herrick; 35. William Mason; 36. Hill; 37. Dana; 38. Shakespeare.

31. What's all the gaudy glitter of a crown?
32. The way to bliss lies not on beds of down.
33. How long we live, not years but actions tell;
34. That man lives twice who lives the first life well.
35. Make, then, while yet ye may, your God your friend,
36. Whom Christians worship yet not comprehend.
37. The trust that's given guard, and to yourself be just;
38. For, live we how we can, yet die we must.

Unknown.

ODE TO THE HUMAN HEART

BLIND Thamyris, and blind Mæonides,
   Pursue the triumph and partake the gale!
Drop tears as fast as the Arabian trees,
   To point a moral or adorn a tale.

Full many a gem of purest ray serene,
   Thoughts that do often lie too deep for tears,
Like angels' visits, few and far between,
   Deck the long vista of departed years.

Man never is, but always to be bless'd;
   The tenth transmitter of a foolish face,
Like Aaron's serpent, swallows up the rest,
   And makes a sunshine in the shady place.

For man the hermit sigh'd, till woman smiled,
   To waft a feather or to drown a fly,
(In wit a man, simplicity a child,)
   With silent finger pointing to the sky.

But fools rush in where angels fear to tread
   Far out amid the melancholy main;
As when a vulture on Imaus bred,
   Dies of a rose in aromatic pain.

Laman Blanchard

A STRIKE AMONG THE POETS

In his chamber, weak and dying,
  While the Norman Baron lay,
Loud, without, his men were crying,
  " Shorter hours and better pay."

Know you why the ploughman, fretting,
  Homeward plods his weary way
Ere his time? He's after getting
  Shorter hours and better pay.

See! the *Hesperus* is swinging
  Idle in the wintry bay,
And the skipper's daughter's singing,
  " Shorter hours and better pay."

Where's the minstrel boy? I've found him
  Joining in the labour fray
With his placards slung around him,
  " Shorter hours and better pay."

Oh, young Lochinvar is coming;
  Though his hair is getting grey,
Yet I'm glad to hear him humming,
  " Shorter hours and better pay."

E'en the boy upon the burning
  Deck has got a word to say,
Something rather cross concerning
  Shorter hours and better pay.

Lives of great men all remind us
  We can make as much as they,
Work no more, until they find us
  Shorter hours and better pay.

Hail to thee, blithe spirit! (Shelley)
  Wilt thou be a blackleg? Nay.
Soaring, sing above the mêlée,
  " Shorter hours and better pay."

Unknown.

WHATEVER IS, IS RIGHT

Lives there a man with soul so dead
Who never to himself has said,
    " Shoot folly as it flies " ?
Oh! more than tears of blood can tell,
Are in that word, farewell, farewell!
    'Tis folly to be wise.

And what is friendship but a name,
That boils on Etna's breast of flame?
    Thus runs the world away.
Sweet is the ship that's under sail
To where yon taper cheers the vale,
    With hospitable ray!

Drink to me only with thine eyes
Through cloudless climes and starry skies!
    My native land, good night!
Adieu, adieu, my native shore;
'Tis Greece, but living Greece no more—
    Whatever is, is right!

       Laman Blanchard.

NOTHING

Mysterious Nothing! how shall I define
Thy shapeless, baseless, placeless emptiness?
Nor form, nor colour, sound, nor size is thine,
Nor words nor fingers can thy voice express;
But though we cannot thee to aught compare,
A thousand things to thee may likened be,
And though thou art with nobody nowhere,
Yet half mankind devote themselves to thee.
How many books thy history contain;
How many heads thy mighty plans pursue;
What labouring hands thy portion only gain;
What busy bodies thy doings only do!
To thee the great, the proud, the giddy bend,
And—like my sonnet—all in nothing end.

       Richard Porson.

DIRGE

To the memory of Miss Ellen Gee, of Kew, who died in consequence of being stung in the eye.

PEERLESS yet hapless maid of Q!
　Accomplish'd LN G!
Never again shall I and U
　Together sip our T.

For, ah! the Fates I know not Y,
　Sent 'midst the flowers a B,
Which ven'mous stung her in the I,
　So that she could not C.

LN exclaim'd, "Vile spiteful B!
　If ever I catch U
On jess'mine, rosebud, or sweet P,
　I'll change your singing Q.

"I'll send you like a lamb or U
　Across th' Atlantic C.
From our delightful village Q
　To distant O Y E.

"A stream runs from my wounded I,
　Salt as the briny C
As rapid as the X or Y,
　The OIO or D.

"Then fare thee ill, insensate B!
　Who stung, nor yet knew Y,
Since not for wealthy Durham's C
　Would I have lost my I."

They bear with tears fair LN G
　In funeral R A,
A clay-cold corse now doom'd to B
　Whilst I mourn her DK.

Ye nymphs of Q, then shun each B,
 List to the reason Y;
For should A B C U at T,
 He'll surely sting your I.

Now in a grave L deep in Q,
 She's cold as cold can B,
Whilst robins sing upon A U
 Her dirge and LEG.

Unknown.

O D V

CQNTAINING A FULL, TRUE, AND PARTICULAR ACCOUNT OF THE
TERRIBLE FATE OF ABRAHAM ISAACS, OF IVY LANE

"True 'tis P T, and P T 'tis, 'tis true."

IN I V Lane, of C T fame,
 There lived a man D C,
And A B I 6 was his name,
 Now mark his history.

Long time his conduct free from blame
 Did merit L O G,
Until an evil spirit came
 In the shape of O D V.

"O! that a man into his mouth
 Should put an N M E
To steal away his brains"—no drouth
 Such course from sin may free.

Well, A B drank, the O T loon!
 And learned to swear, sans ruth;
And then he gamed, and U Z soon
 To D V 8 from truth.

An hourly glass with him was play,
  He'd swallow that with phlegm;
Judge what he'd M T in a day,
  "X P D *Herculem.*"

Of virtue none to sots, I trow,
  With F E K C prate;
And 0 of N R G could now
  From A B M N 8.

Who on strong liquor badly dote,
  Soon poverty must know;
Thus A B in a C D coat
  Was shortly forced to go.

From poverty D C T he caught,
  And cheated not A F U,
For what he purchased paying 0,
  Or but an "I O U."

Or else when he had tried B 4,
  To shirk a debt, his wits,
He'd cry, "You shan't wait N E more,
  I'll W or quits.

So lost did I 6 now A P R,
  That said his wife, said she,
"F U act so, your fate quite clear
  Is for 1 2 4 C."

His inside soon was out and out
  More fiery than K N;
And while his state was thereabout
  A cough C V R came.

He I P K Q N A tried,
  And linseed T and rue;
But 0 could save him, so he died
  As every 1 must 2.

Poor wight! till black in' the face he raved,
'Twas P T S 2 C
His latest spirit "spirit" craved—
His last words, "O D V."

MORAL

I'll not S A to preach and prate,
    But tell U if U do
Drink O D V at such R 8,
    Death will 4 stall U 2.

O U then who A Y Z have,
    Shun O D V as a wraith,
For 'tis a bonus to the grave,
    An S A unto death.

Unknown.

A MAN OF WORDS

A MAN of words and not of deeds,
Is like a garden full of weeds;
And when the weeds begin to grow,
It's like a garden full of snow;
And when the snow begins to fall,
It's like a bird upon the wall;
And when the bird away does fly,
It's like an eagle in the sky;
And when the sky begins to roar,
It's like a lion at the door;
And when the door begins to crack,
It's like a stick across your back;
And when your back begins to smart,
It's like a penknife in your heart;
And when your heart begins to bleed,
You're dead, and dead, and dead indeed.

Unknown.

SIMILES

As wet as a fish—as dry as a bone;
As live as a bird—as dead as a stone;
As plump as a partridge—as poor as a rat;
As strong as a horse—as weak as a cat;
As hard as a flint—as soft as a mole;
As white as a lily—as black as a coal;
As plain as a pike-staff—as rough as a bear;
As light as a drum—as free as the air;
As heavy as lead—as light as a feather;
As steady as time—uncertain as weather;
As hot as an oven—as cold as a frog;
As gay as a lark—as sick as a dog;
As slow as the tortoise—as swift as the wind;
As true as the Gospel—as false as mankind;
As thin as a herring—as fat as a pig;
As proud as a peacock—as blithe as a grig;
As savage as tigers—as mild as a dove;
As stiff as a poker—as limp as a glove;
As blind as a bat—as deaf as a post;
As cool as a cucumber—as warm as a toast;
As flat as a flounder—as round as a ball;
As blunt as a hammer—as sharp as an awl;
As red as a ferret—as safe as the stocks;
As bold as a thief—as sly as a fox;
As straight as an arrow—as crook'd as a bow;
As yellow as saffron—as black as a sloe;
As brittle as glass—as tough as gristle;
As neat as my nail—as clean as a whistle;
As good as a feast—as bad as a witch;
As light as is day—as dark as is pitch;
As brisk as a bee—as dull as an ass;
As full as a tick—as solid as brass.

Unknown.

NO!

No sun—no moon!
No morn—no noon—
No dawn—no dusk—no proper time of day—
No sky—no earthly view—
No distance looking blue—
No road—no street—no " t'other side the way "—
No end to any Row—
No indications where the Crescents go—
No top to any steeple—
No recognitions of familiar people—
No courtesies for showing 'em—
No knowing 'em!
No travelling at all—no locomotion,
No inkling of the way—no notion—
" No go "—by land or ocean—
No mail—no post—
No news from any foreign coast—
No park—no ring—no afternoon gentility—
No company—no nobility—
No warmth, no cheerfulness, no healthful ease,
No comfortable feel in any member—
No shade, no shine, no butterflies, no bees,
No fruits, no flowers, no leaves, no birds,
November!

Thomas Hood.

FAITHLESS SALLY BROWN

Young Ben he was a nice young man,
  A carpenter by trade;
And he fell in love with Sally Brown,
  That was a lady's maid.

But as they fetched a walk one day,
  They met a press-gang crew;
And Sally she did faint away,
  Whilst Ben he was brought to.

The boatswain swore with wicked words,
    Enough to shock a saint,
That though she did seem in a fit,
    'Twas nothing but a feint.

" Come, girl," said he, " hold up your head,
    He'll be as good as me;
For when your swain is in our boat,
    A boatswain he will be."

So when they'd made their game of her,
    And taken off her elf,
She roused, and found she only was
    A coming to herself.

" And is he gone, and is he gone?"
    She cried, and wept outright:
" Then I will to the water side,
    And see him out of sight."

A waterman came up to her,—
    " Now, young woman," said he,
" If you weep on so, you will make
    Eye-water in the sea."

" Alas! they've taken my beau, Ben,
    To sail with old Benbow; "
And her woe began to run afresh,
    As if she'd said, " Gee woe! "

Says he, " They've only taken him
    To the Tender-ship, you see; "
" The Tender-ship," cried Sally Brown,
    " What a hard-ship that must be!

" O! would I were a mermaid now,
    For then I'd follow him;
But, O!—I'm not a fish-woman,
    And so I cannot swim.

"Alas! I was not born beneath
    The virgin and the scales,
So I must curse my cruel stars,
    And walk about in Wales."

Now Ben had sailed to many a place
    That's underneath the world;
But in two years the ship came home,
    And all her sails were furled.

But when he called on Sally Brown,
    To see how she got on,
He found she'd got another Ben,
    Whose Christian name was John.

"O, Sally Brown, O, Sally Brown,
    How could you serve me so?
I've met with many a breeze before,
    But never such a blow!"

Then reading on his 'bacco-box,
    He heaved a heavy sigh,
And then began to eye his pipe,
    And then to pipe his eye.

And then he tried to sing "All's Well,"
    But could not, though he tried;
His head was turned, and so he chewed
    His pigtail till he died.

His death, which happened in his berth,
    At forty-odd befell:
They went and told the sexton, and
    The sexton tolled the bell.

Thomas Hood.

TIM TURPIN

Tim Turpin he was gravel blind,
　And ne'er had seen the skies:
For Nature, when his head was made,
　Forgot to dot his eyes.

So, like a Christmas pedagogue,
　Poor Tim was forced to do,—
Look out for pupils, for he had
　A vacancy for two.

There's some have specs to help their sight
　Of objects dim and small;
But Tim had *specks* within his eyes,
　And could not see at all.

Now Tim he wooed a servant maid,
　And took her to his arms;
For he, like Pyramus, had cast
　A wall-eye on her charms.

By day she led him up and down
　Where'er he wished to jog,
A happy wife, although she led
　The life of any dog.

But just when Tim had lived a month
　In honey with his wife,
A surgeon oped his Milton eyes,
　Like oysters, with a knife.

But when his eyes were opened thus,
　He wished them dark again;
For when he looked upon his wife,
　He saw her very plain.

Her face was bad, her figure worse,
　He couldn't bear to eat;
For she was anything but like
　A Grace before his meat.

Now Tim he was a feeling man:
　For when his sight was thick,
It made him feel for everything,—
　But that was with a stick.

So, with a cudgel in his hand,—
　It was not light or slim,—
He knocked at his wife's head until
　It opened unto him.

And when the corpse was stiff and cold,
　He took his slaughtered spouse,
And laid her in a heap with all
　The ashes of her house.

But, like a wicked murderer,
　He lived in constant fear
From day to day, and so he cut
　His throat from ear to ear.

The neighbors fetched a doctor in:
　Said he, " This wound I dread
Can hardly be sewed up,—his life
　Is hanging on a thread."

But when another week was gone,
　He gave him stronger hope,—
Instead of hanging on a thread,
　Of hanging on a rope.

Ah! when he hid his bloody work,
　In ashes round about,
How little he supposed the truth
　Would soon be sifted out!

But when the parish dustman came,
　His rubbish to withdraw,
He found more dust within the heap
　Than he contracted for!

A dozen men to try the fact,
    Were sworn that very day;
But though they all were jurors, yet
    No conjurors were they.

Said Tim unto those jurymen,
    "You need not waste your breath,
For I confess myself, at once,
    The author of her death.

"And O, when I reflect upon
    The blood that I have spilt,
Just like a button is my soul,
    Inscribed with double *guilt!*"

Then turning round his head again
    He saw before his eyes
A great judge, and a little judge,
    The judges of a-size!

The great judge took his judgment-cap,
    And put it on his head,
And sentenced Tim by law to hang
    Till he was three times dead.

So he was tried, and he was hung
    (Fit punishment for such)
On Horsham drop, and none can say
    It was a drop too much.

                        Thomas Hood.

FAITHLESS NELLY GRAY

BEN BATTLE was a soldier bold,
    And used to war's alarms:
But a cannon-ball took off his legs,
    So he laid down his arms!

Now, as they bore him off the field,
　Said he, " Let others shoot,
For here I leave my second leg,
　And the Forty-second Foot! "

The army surgeons made him limbs:
　Said he, " They're only pegs;
But there's as wooden members quite,
　As represent my legs! "

Now Ben he loved a pretty maid,
　Her name was Nelly Gray;
So he went to pay her his devours
　When he'd devoured his pay!

But when he called on Nelly Gray,
　She made him quite a scoff;
And when she saw his wooden legs,
　Began to take them off!

" O Nelly Gray! O Nelly Gray!
　Is this your love so warm?
The love that loves a scarlet coat,
　Should be more uniform! "

Said she, " I loved a soldier once,
　For he was blithe and brave;
But I will never have a man
　With both legs in the grave!

" Before you had those timber toes,
　Your love I did allow,
But then you know, you stand upon
　Another footing now! "

" O Nelly Gray! O Nelly Gray!
　For all your jeering speeches,
At duty's call I left my legs
　In Badajos's breaches! "

" Why, then," said she, " you've lost the feet
Of legs in war's alarms,
And now you cannot wear your shoes
Upon your feats of arms! "

" Oh, false and fickle Nelly Gray;
I know why you refuse:
Though I've no feet—some other man
Is standing in my shoes!

" I wish I ne'er had seen your face;
But now a long farewell!
For you will be my death—alas!
You will not be my Nell! "

Now, when he went from Nelly Gray,
His heart so heavy got—
And life was such a burden grown,
It made him take a knot!

So round his melancholy neck
A rope he did entwine,
And, for his second time in life
Enlisted in the Line!

One end he tied around a beam,
And then removed his pegs,
And as his legs were off,—of course,
He soon was off his legs!

And there he hung till he was dead
As any nail in town,—
For though distress had cut him up,
It could not cut him down!

A dozen men sat on his corpse,
To find out why he died—
And they buried Ben in four cross-roads,
With a stake in his inside!

Thomas Hood.

SALLY SIMPKIN'S LAMENT

" Oh! what is that comes gliding in,
    And quite in middling haste?
It is the picture of my Jones,
    And painted to the waist.

" It is not painted to the life,
    For where's the trousers blue?
O Jones, my dear!—Oh, dear! my Jones,
    What is become of you?"

" O Sally, dear, it is too true,—
    The half that you remark
Is come to say my other half
    Is bit off by a shark!

" O Sally, sharks do things by halves,
    Yet most completely do!
A bite in one place seems enough,
    But I've been bit in two.

" You know I once was all your own,
    But now a shark must share!
But let that pass—for now to you
    I'm neither here nor there.

" Alas! death has a strange divorce
    Effected in the sea,
It has divided me from you,
    And even me from me!

" Don't fear my ghost will walk o' nights
    To haunt, as people say;
My ghost *can't* walk, for, oh! my legs
    Are many leagues away!

" Lord! think when I am swimming round,
    And looking where the boat is,
A shark just snaps away a *half*,
    Without ' a *quarter's notice.*'

" One half is here, the other half
    Is near Columbia placed;
O Sally, I have got the whole
    Atlantic for my waist.

" But now, adieu—a long adieu!
    I've solved death's awful riddle,
And would say more, but I am doomed
    To break off in the middle! "

           Thomas Hood.

DEATH'S RAMBLE

ONE day the dreary old King of Death
    Inclined for some sport with the carnal,
So he tied a pack of darts on his back,
    And quietly stole from his charnel.

His head was bald of flesh and of hair,
    His body was lean and lank;
His joints at each stir made a crack, and the cur
    Took a gnaw, by the way, at his shank.

And what did he do with his deadly darts,
    This goblin of grisly bone?
He dabbled and spilled man's blood, and he killed
    Like a butcher that kills his own.

The first he slaughtered it made him laugh
    (For the man was a coffin-maker),
To think how the mutes, and men in black suits,
    Would mourn for an undertaker.

Death saw two Quakers sitting at church;
    Quoth he, " We shall not differ."
And he let them alone, like figures of stone,
    For he could not make them stiffer.

He saw two duellists going to fight,
  In fear they could not smother;
And he shot one through at once—for he knew
  They never would shoot each other.

He saw a watchman fast in his box,
  And he gave a snore infernal;
Said Death, " He may keep his breath, for his sleep
  Can never be more eternal."

He met a coachman driving a coach
  So slow that his fare grew sick;
But he let him stray on his tedious way,
  For Death only wars on the *quick*.

Death saw a tollman taking a toll,
  In the spirit of his fraternity;
But he knew that sort of man would extort.
  Though summoned to all eternity.

He found an author writing his life,
  But he let him write no further;
For Death, who strikes whenever he likes,
  Is jealous of all self-murther!

Death saw a patient that pulled out his purse,
  And a doctor that took the sum;
But he let them be—for he knew that the " fee "
  Was a prelude to " faw " and " fum."

He met a dustman ringing a bell,
  And he gave him a mortal thrust;
For himself, by law, since Adam's flaw,
  Is contractor for all our dust.

He saw a sailor mixing his grog,
  And he marked him out for slaughter;
For on water he scarcely had cared for death,
  And never on rum-and-water.

Death saw two players playing at cards,
  But the game wasn't worth a dump,
For he quickly laid them flat with a spade,
  To wait for the final trump!

Thomas Hood.

PANEGYRIC ON THE LADIES

READ ALTERNATE LINES

THAT man must lead a happy life
  Who's free from matrimonial chains,
Who is directed by a wife
  Is sure to suffer for his pains.

Adam could find no solid peace
  When Eve was given for a mate;
Until he saw a woman's face
  Adam was in a happy state.

In all the female race appear
  Hypocrisy, deceit, and pride;
Truth, darling of a heart sincere,
  In woman never did reside.

What tongue is able to unfold
  The failings that in woman dwell?
The worth in woman we behold
  Is almost imperceptible.

Confusion take the man, I say,
  Who changes from his singleness,
Who will not yield to woman's sway
  Is sure of earthly blessedness.

Unknown.

AMBIGUOUS LINES

READ WITH A COMMA AFTER THE FIRST NOUN IN EACH LINE

I saw a peacock with a fiery tail
I saw a blazing comet pour down hail
I saw a cloud all wrapt with ivy round
I saw a lofty oak creep on the ground
I saw a beetle swallow up a whale
I saw a foaming sea brimful of ale
I saw a pewter cup sixteen feet deep
I saw a well full of men's tears that weep
I saw wet eyes in flames of living fire
I saw a house as high as the moon and higher
I saw the glorious sun at deep midnight
I saw the man who saw this wondrous sight.

I saw a pack of cards gnawing a bone
I saw a dog seated on Britain's throne
I saw King George shut up within a box
I saw an orange driving a fat ox
I saw a butcher not a twelvemonth old
I saw a great-coat all of solid gold
I saw two buttons telling of their dreams
I saw my friends who wished I'd quit these themes.

Unknown.

SURNAMES

Men once were surnamed for their shape or estate
    (You all may from history worm it),
There was Louis the bulky, and Henry the Great,
    John Lackland, and Peter the Hermit:
But now, when the doorplates of misters and dames
    Are read, each so constantly varies;
From the owner's trade, figure, and calling, surnames
    Seem given by the rule of contraries.

Mr. Wise is a dunce, Mr. King is a whig,
  Mr. Coffin's uncommonly sprightly,
And huge Mr. Little broke down in a gig
  While driving fat Mrs. Golightly.
At Bath, where the feeble go more than the stout
  (A conduct well worthy of Nero),
Over poor Mr. Lightfoot, confined with the gout,
  Mr. Heavyside danced a bolero.

Miss Joy, wretched maid, when she chose Mr. Love,
  Found nothing but sorrow await her;
She now holds in wedlock, as true as a dove,
  That fondest of mates, Mr. Hayter.
Mr. Oldcastle dwells in a modern-built hut;
  Miss Sage is of madcaps the archest;
Of all the queer bachelors Cupid e'er cut,
  Old Mr. Younghusband's the starchest.

Mr. Child, in a passion, knock'd down Mr. Rock;
  Mr. Stone like an aspen-leaf shivers;
Miss Pool used to dance, but she stands like a stock
  Ever since she became Mrs. Rivers.
Mr. Swift hobbles onward, no mortal knows how,
  He moves as though cords had entwined him;
Mr. Metcalf ran off upon meeting a cow,
  With pale Mr. Turnbull behind him.

Mr. Barker's as mute as a fish in the sea,
  Mr. Miles never moves on a journey,
Mr. Gotobed sits up till half after three,
  Mr. Makepeace was bred an attorney.
Mr. Gardener can't tell a flower from a root,
  Mr. Wild with timidity draws back,
Mr. Ryder performs all his journeys on foot,
  Mr. Foot all his journeys on horseback.

Mr. Penny, whose father was rolling in wealth,
  Consumed all the fortune his dad won;
Large Mr. Le Fever's the picture of health;
  Mr. Goodenough is but a bad one;

Mr. Cruikshank stept into three thousand a year
By showing his leg to an heiress:
Now I hope you'll acknowledge I've made it quite clear
Surnames ever go by contraries.

James Smith.

A TERNARY OF LITTLES, UPON A PIPKIN OF JELLY SENT TO A LADY

A LITTLE saint best fits a little shrine,
A little prop best fits a little vine;
As my small cruse best fits my little wine.

A little seed best fits a little soil,
A little trade best fits a little toil;
As my small jar best fits my little oil.

A little bin best fits a little bread,
A little garland fits a little head;
As my small stuff best fits my little shed.

A little hearth best fits a little fire,
A little chapel fits a little choir;
As my small bell best fits my little spire.

A little stream best fits a little boat,
A little lead best fits a little float;
As my small pipe best fits my little note.

A little meat best fits a little belly,
As sweetly, lady, give me leave to tell ye,
This little pipkin fits this little jelly.

Robert Herrick.

A CARMAN'S ACCOUNT OF A LAW-SUIT

MARRY, I lent my gossip my mare, to fetch home coals,
And he her drownéd into the quarry holes;
And I ran to the Consistory, for to 'plain,
And there I happened among a greedy meine.
They gave me first a thing they call Citandum;
Within eight days, I got but Libellandum;
Within a month, I got Ad oppenendum;
In half a year, I got Interloquendum;
And then I got—how call ye it?—Ad replicandum.
But I could never one word yet understand them;
And then, they caused me cast out many placks,
And made me pay for four-and-twenty acts.
But, ere they came half gait to Concludendum,
The fiend one plack was left for to defend him.
Thus they postponed me two years, with their train,
Then, hodie ad octo, bade me come again,
And then, these rooks, they roupit wonder fast,
For sentence silver, they criéd at the last.
Of Pronunciandum they made me wonder fain;
But I got never my good grey mare again.

Sir David Lindesay.

OUT OF SIGHT, OUT OF MIND

THE oft'ner seen, the more I lust,
The more I lust, the more I smart,
The more I smart, the more I trust,
The more I trust, the heavier heart,
The heavy heart breeds mine unrest,
Thy absence therefore I like best.

The rarer seen, the less in mind,
The less in mind, the lesser pain,
The lesser pain, less grief I find,
The lesser grief, the greater gain,
The greater gain, the merrier I,
Therefore I wish thy sight to fly.

The further off, the more I joy,
The more I joy, the happier life,
The happier life, less hurts annoy,
The lesser hurts, pleasure most rife,
Such pleasures rife shall I obtain
When distance doth depart us train.

Barnaby Googe.

NONGTONGPAW

JOHN BULL for pastime took a prance,
Some time ago, to peep at France;
To talk of sciences and arts,
And knowledge gain'd in foreign parts.
Monsieur, obsequious, heard him speak,
And answer'd John in heathen Greek:
To all he ask'd, 'bout all he saw,
'Twas, *Monsieur, je vous n'entends pas.*

John, to the Palais-Royal come,
Its splendor almost struck him dumb.
" I say, whose house is that there here? "
" House! *Je vous n'entends pas, Monsieur.*"
" What, Nongtongpaw again! " cries John;
" This fellow is some mighty Don:
No doubt he's plenty for the maw,
I'll breakfast with this Nongtongpaw."

John saw Versailles from Marli's height,
And cried, astonish'd at the sight,
" Whose fine estate is that there here? "
" State! *Je vous n'entends pas, Monsieur.*"
" His? what! the land and houses, too?
The fellow's richer than a Jew:
On *everything* he lays his claw!
I'd like to dine with Nongtongpaw."

Next tripping came a courtly fair,
John cried, enchanted with her air,
" What lovely wench is that there here? "

"Ventch! *Je vous n'entends pas, Monsieur.*"
"What, he again? Upon my life!
A palace, lands, and then a wife
Sir Joshua might delight to draw!
I'd like to sup with Nongtongpaw."

"But hold! whose funeral's that?" cries John.
"*Je vous n'entends pas.*"—"What! is he gone?
Wealth, fame, and beauty could not save
Poor Nongtongpaw then from the grave!
His race is run, his game is up,—
I'd with him breakfast, dine, and sup;
But since he chooses to withdraw,
Good night t'ye, Mounseer Nongtongpaw!"

Charles Dibdin.

LOGICAL ENGLISH

I said, "This horse, sir, will you shoe?"
  And soon the horse was shod.
I said, "This deed, sir, will you do?"
  And soon the deed was dod!

I said, "This stick, sir, will you break?"
  At once the stick he broke.
I said, "This coat, sir, will you make?"
  And soon the coat he moke!

Unknown.

LOGIC

I have a copper penny and another copper penny,
  Well, then, of course, I have two copper pence;
I have a cousin Jenny and another cousin Jenny,
  Well, pray, then, do I have two cousin Jence?

Unknown.

THE CAREFUL PENMAN

A Persian penman named Aziz,
  Remarked, " I think I know my biz.
For when I write my name as is,
  It is Aziz as is Aziz."

Unknown.

QUESTIONS WITH ANSWERS

What is earth, sexton?—A place to dig graves;
What is earth, rich men?—A place to work slaves,
What is earth, grey-beard?—A place to grow old;
What is earth, miser?—A place to dig gold;
What is earth, school-boy?—A place for my play;
What is earth, maiden?—A place to be gay;
What is earth, seamstress?—A place where I weep;
What is earth, sluggard?—A good place to sleep;
What is earth, soldier?—A place for a battle;
What is earth, herdsman?—A place to raise cattle;
What is earth, widow?—A place of true sorrow;
What is earth, tradesman?—I'll tell you to-morrow;
What is earth, sick man?—'Tis nothing to me;
What is earth, sailor?—My home is the sea;
What is earth, statesman?—A place to win fame;
What is earth, author?—I'll write there my name;
What is earth, monarch?—For my realm 'tis given;
What is earth, Christian?—The gateway of heaven.

Unknown.

CONJUGAL CONJUGATIONS

Dear maid, let me speak
  What I never yet spoke:
You have made my heart squeak
  As it never yet squoke,
And for sight of you, both my eyes ache as they ne'er before
oak.

With your voice my ears ring,
    And a sweeter ne'er rung,
Like a bird's on the wing
    When at morn it has wung.
And gladness to me it doth bring, such as never voice brung.

My feelings I'd write,
    But they cannot be wrote,
And who can indite
    What was never indote!
And my love I hasten to plight—the first that I plote.

Yes, you would I choose,
    Whom I long ago chose,
And my fond spirit sues
    As it never yet sose,
And ever on you do I muse, as never man mose.

The house where you bide
    Is a blessed abode;
Sure, my hopes I can't hide,
    For they will not be hode,
And no person living has sighed, as, darling, I've sode.

Your glances they shine
    As no others have shone,
And all else I'd resign
    That a man could resone,
And surely no other could pine as I lately have pone.

And don't you forget
    You will ne'er be forgot,
You never should fret
    As at times you have frot,
I would chase all the cares that beset, if they ever besot.

For you I would weave
    Songs that never were wove,
And deeds I'd achieve
    Which no man yet achove,
And for me you never should grieve, as for you I have grove.

I'm as worthy a catch
As ever was caught.
O, your answer I watch
As a man never waught,
And we'd make the most elegant match as ever was maught.

Let my longings not sink;
I would die if they sunk.
O, I ask you to think
As you never have thunk,
And our fortunes and lives let us link, as no lives could be
    lunk.

A. W. Bellaw.

LOVE'S MOODS AND SENSES

Sally Salter, she was a young lady who taught,
And her friend Charley Church was a preacher who praught!
Though his enemies called him a screecher who scraught.

His heart when he saw her kept sinking and sunk,
And his eye, meeting hers, began winking and wunk;
While she in her turn fell to thinking, and thunk.

He hastened to woo her, and sweetly he wooed,
For his love grew until to a mountain it grewed,
And what he was longing to do then he doed.

In secret he wanted to speak, and he spoke,
To seek with his lips what his heart long had soke;
So he managed to let the truth leak, and it loke.

He asked her to ride to the church, and they rode,
They so sweetly did glide, that they both thought they glode,
And they came to the place to be tied, and were tode.

Then, "homeward" he said, "let us drive" and they drove,
And soon as they wished to arrive, they arrove;
For whatever he couldn't contrive she controve.

The kiss he was dying to steal, then he stole:
At the feet where he wanted to kneel, then he knole,
And said, "I feel better than ever I fole."

So they to each other kept clinging, and clung;
While time his swift circuit was winging, and wung;
And this was the thing he was bringing, and brung:

The man Sally wanted to catch, and had caught—
That she wanted from others to snatch, and had snaught—
Was the one that she now liked to scratch and she scraught.

And Charley's warm love began freezing and froze,
While he took to teasing, and cruelly toze
The girl he had wished to be squeezing and squoze.

"Wretch!" he cried, when she threatened to leave him, and
left,
"How could you deceive me, as you have deceft?"
And she answered, "I promised to cleave, and I've cleft!"

Unknown.

THE SIEGE OF BELGRADE

An Austrian army, awfully array'd,
Boldly by battery besiege Belgrade;
Cossack commanders cannonading come,
Deal devastation's dire destructive doom;
Ev'ry endeavour engineers essay,
For fame, for freedom, fight, fierce furious fray.
Gen'rals 'gainst gen'rals grapple,—gracious God!
How honors Heav'n heroic hardihood!
Infuriate, indiscriminate in ill,
Just Jesus, instant innocence instill!
Kinsmen kill kinsmen, kindred kindred kill.
Labour low levels longest, loftiest lines;
Men march 'midst mounds, motes, mountains,
murd'rous mines.
Now noisy, noxious numbers notice nought,
Of outward obstacles o'ercoming ought;

Poor patriots perish, persecution's pest!
Quite quiet Quakers " Quarter, quarter," quest;
Reason returns, religion, right, redounds,
Suwarow stop such sanguinary sounds!
Truce to thee, Turkey, terror to thy train!
Unwise, unjust, unmerciful Ukraine!
Vanish vile vengeance, vanish victory vain!
Why wish we warfare? wherefore welcome won
Xerxes, Xantippus, Xavier, Xenophon?
Yield, ye young Yaghier yeomen, yield your yell!
Zimmerman's, Zoroaster's, Zeno's zeal
Again attract; arts against arms appeal.
All, all ambitious aims, avaunt, away!
Et cetera, et cetera, et ceterae.

Unknown.

THE HAPPY MAN

LA GALISSE now I wish to touch;
   Droll air! if I can strike it,
I'm sure the song will please you much;
   That is, if you should like it.

La Galisse was, indeed, I grant,
   Not used to any dainty,
When he was born; but could not want
   As long as he had plenty.

Instructed with the greatest care,
   He always was well bred,
And never used a hat to wear
   But when 'twas on his head.

His temper was exceeding good,
   Just of his father's fashion;
And never quarrels boiled his blood
   Except when in a passion.

His mind was on devotion bent;
   He kept with care each high day,
And Holy Thursday always spent
   The day before Good Friday.

He liked good claret very well,
   I just presume to think it;
For ere its flavour he could tell
   He thought it best to drink it.

Than doctors more he loved the cook,
   Though food would make him gross,
And never any physic took
   But when he took a dose.

Oh, happy, happy is the swain
   The ladies so adore;
For many followed in his train
   Whene'er he walked before.

Bright as the sun his flowing hair
   In golden ringlets shone;
And no one could with him compare,
   If he had been alone.

His talents I cannot rehearse,
   But every one allows
That whatsoe'er he wrote in verse,
   No one could call it prose.

He argued with precision nice,
   The learnèd all declare;
And it was his decision wise,
   No horse could be a mare.

His powerful logic would surprise,
   Amaze, and much delight:
He proved that dimness of the eyes
   Was hurtful to the sight.

They liked him much—so it appears
Most plainly—who preferred him;
And those did never want their ears
Who any time had heard him.

He was not always right, 'tis true,
And then he must be wrong;
But none had found it out, he knew,
If he had held his tongue.

Whene'er a tender tear he shed,
'Twas certain that he wept;
And he would lie awake in bed,
Unless, indeed, he slept.

In tilting everybody knew
His very high renown;
Yet no opponents he o'erthrew
But those that he knocked down.

At last they smote him in the head,—
What hero ever fought all?
And when they saw that he was dead,
They knew the wound was mortal.

And when at last he lost his breath,
It closed his every strife;
For that sad day that sealed his death
Deprived him of his life.

Gilles Ménage.

THE BELLS

Oh, it's H-A-P-P-Y I am, and it's F-R-double-E,
And it's G-L-O-R-Y to know that I'm S-A-V-E-D.
Once I was B-O-U-N-D by the chains of S-I-N
And it's L-U-C-K-Y I am that all is well again.

Oh, the bells of Hell go ting-a-ling-a-ling
   For you, but not for me.
The bells of Heaven go sing-a-ling-a-ling
   For there I soon shall be.
Oh, Death, where is thy sting-a-ling-a-ling
   Oh, Grave, thy victorie-e.
No Ting-a-ling-a-ling, no sting-a-ling-a-ling
   But sing-a-ling-a-ling for me.

Unknown.

TAKINGS

He took her fancy when he came,
   He took her hand, he took a kiss,
He took no notice of the shame
   That glowed her happy cheek at this.

He took to come of afternoons,
   He took an oath he'd ne'er deceive,
He took her master's silver spoons,
   And after that he took his leave.

Thomas Hood, Jr.

A BACHELOR'S MONO-RHYME

Do you think I'd marry a woman
   That can neither cook nor sew,
Nor mend a rent in her gloves
   Or a tuck in her furbelow;
Who spends her time in reading
   The novels that come and go;
Who tortures heavenly music,
   And makes it a thing of woe;
Who deems three-fourths of my income
   Too little, by half, to show
What a figure she'd make, if I'd let her,
   'Mid the belles of Rotten Row;
Who has not a thought in her head
   Where thoughts are expected to grow,
Except of trumpery scandals
   Too small for a man to know?

Do you think I'd wed with *that,*
  Because both high and low
Are charmed by her youthful graces
  And her shoulders white as snow?
Ah no! I've a wish to be happy,
  I've a thousand a year or so,
'Tis all I can expect
  That fortune will bestow!
So, pretty one, idle one, stupid one!
  You're not for me, I trow,
To-day, nor yet to-morrow,
  No, no! decidedly no!

Charles Mackay.

THE ART OF BOOK-KEEPING

How hard, when those who do not wish
  To lend, that's lose, their books,
Are snared by anglers—folks that fish
  With literary hooks;

Who call and take some favourite tome,
  But never read it through;
They thus complete their set at home,
  By making one at you.

Behold the bookshelf of a dunce
  Who borrows—never lends;
Yon work, in twenty volumes, once
  Belonged to twenty friends.

New tales and novels you may shut
  From view—'tis all in vain;
They're gone—and though the leaves are " cut "
  They never " come again."

For pamphlets lent I look around,
  For tracts my tears are spilt;
But when they take a book that's bound,
  'Tis surely extra guilt.

A circulating library
　　Is mine—my birds are flown;
There's one odd volume left, to be
　　Like all the rest, a-lone.

I, of my " Spenser " quite bereft,
　　Last winter sore was shaken;
Of " Lamb " I've but a quarter left,
　　Nor could I save my " Bacon."

My " Hall " and " Hill " were levelled flat,
　　But " Moore " was still the cry;
And then, although I threw them " Sprat,"
　　They swallowed up my " Pye."

O'er everything, however slight,
　　They seized some airy trammel;
They snatched my " Hogg " and " Fox " one night,
　　And pocketed my " Campbell."

And then I saw my " Crabbe " at last,
　　Like Hamlet's, backward go;
And as my tide was ebbing fast,
　　Of course I lost my " Rowe."

I wondered into what balloon
　　My books their course had bent;
And yet, with all my marvelling, soon
　　I found my " Marvell " went.

My " Mallet " served to knock me down,
　　Which makes me thus a talker;
And once, while I was out of town,
　　My " Johnson " proved a " Walker."

While studying o'er the fire one day
　　My " Hobbes " amidst the smoke;
They bore my " Colman " clean away,
　　And carried off my " Coke."

They picked my " Locke," to me far more
    Than Bramah's patent's worth;
And now my losses I deplore,
    Without a " Home " on earth.

If once a book you let them lift,
    Another they conceal,
For though I caught them stealing " Swift,"
    As swiftly went my " Steele."

" Hope " is not now upon my shelf,
    Where late he stood elated;
But, what is strange, my " Pope " himself
    Is excommunicated.

My little " Suckling " in the grave
    Is sunk, to swell the ravage;
And what 'twas Crusoe's fate to save
    'Twas mine to lose—a " Savage."

Even " Glover's " works I cannot put
    My frozen hands upon ;
Though ever since I lost my " Foote,"
    My " Bunyan " has been gone

My " Hoyle " with " Cotton " went; oppressed,
    My " Taylor " too must fail;
To save my " Goldsmith " from arrest,
    In vain I offered " Bayle."

I " Prior," sought, but could not see
    The " Hood " so late in front;
And when I turned to hunt for " Lee,"
    Oh! where was my " Leigh Hunt! "

I tried to laugh, old care to tickle,
    Yet could not " Tickell " touch;
And then, alas! I missed my " Mickle,"
    And surely mickle's much.

'Tis quite enough my griefs to feed,
　My sorrows to excuse,
To think I cannot read my " Reid,"
　Nor even use my " Hughes."

To " West," to " South," I turn my head,
　Exposed alike to odd jeers;
For since my " Roger Ascham's " fled,
　I ask 'em for my " Rogers."

They took my " Horne "—and " Horne Tooke " too,
　And thus my treasures flit;
I feel when I would " Hazlitt " view,
　The flames that it has lit.

My word's worth little, " Wordsworth " gone,
　If I survive its doom;
How many a bard I doted on
　Was swept off—with my " Broome."

My classics would not quiet lie,
　A thing so fondly hoped;
Like Dr. Primrose, I may cry,
　" My ' Livy ' has eloped! "

My life is wasting fast away—
　I suffer from these shocks;
And though I fixed a lock on " Grey,"
　There's grey upon my locks.

I'm far from young—am growing pale—
　I see my " Butter " fly;
And when they ask about my *ail,*
　'Tis " Burton " I reply.

They still have made me slight returns,
　And thus my griefs divide;
For oh! they've cured me of my " Burns,"
　And eased my " Akenside."

But all I think I shall not say,
　　Nor let my anger burn;
For as they never found me " Gay,"
　　They have not left me " Sterne."

Laman Blanchard.

AN INVITATION TO THE ZOOLOGICAL GARDENS

BY A STUTTERING LOVER

I have found out a gig-gig-gift for my fuf-fuf-fair,
　　I have found where the rattlesnakes bub-bub-breed;
Will you co-co-come, and I'll show you the bub-bub-bear,
　　And the lions and tit-tit-tigers at fuf-fuf-feed.

I know where the co-co-cockatoo's song
　　Makes mum-mum-melody through the sweet vale;
Where the mum-monkeys gig-gig-grin all the day long,
　　Or gracefully swing by the tit-tit-tit-tail.

You shall pip-play, dear, some did-did-delicate joke
　　With the bub-bub-bear on the tit-tit-top of his pip-pip-pip
　　pole;
But observe, 'tis forbidden to pip-pip-poke
　　At the bub-bub-bear with your pip-pip-pink pip-pip-pip
　　pip-parasol!

You shall see the huge elephant pip-pip-play,
　　You shall gig-gig-gaze on the stit-stit-stately raccoon;
And then, did-did-dear, together we'll stray
　　To the cage of the bub-bub-blue-faced bab-bab-boon.

You wished (I r-r-remember it well,
　　And I lul-lul-loved you the m-m-more for the wish)
To witness the bub-bub-beautiful pip-pip-pel-
　　ican swallow the l-l-live little fuf-fuf-fish!

Unknown.

A NOCTURNAL SKETCH

EVEN is come; and from the dark Park, hark,
The signal of the setting sun—one gun!
And six is sounding from the chime, prime time
To go and see the Drury-Lane, Dane slain,—
Or hear Othello's jealous doubt spout out,—
Or Macbeth raving at that shade-made blade,
Denying to his frantic clutch much touch;—
Or else to see Ducrow with wide stride ride
Four horses as no other man can span;
Or in the small Olympic Pit, sit split
Laughing at Liston, while you quiz his phiz.
Anon Night comes, and with her wings brings things
Such as, with his poetic tongue, Young sung;
The gas up-blazes with its bright white light,
And paralytic watchmen prowl, howl, growl,
About the streets and take up Pall-Mall Sal,
Who, hasting to her nightly jobs, robs fobs.

Now thieves to enter for your cash, smash, crash,
Past drowsy Charley, in a deep sleep, creep,
But frightened by Policeman B 3, flee,
And while they're going, whisper low, " No go! "
Now puss, while folks are in their beds, treads leads.
And sleepers waking, grumble—" Drat that cat! "
Who in the gutter caterwauls, squalls, mauls
Some feline foe, and screams in shrill ill-will.

Now Bulls of Bashan, of a prize size, rise
In childish dreams, and with a roar gore poor
Georgy, or Charley, or Billy, willy-nilly;—
But Nursemaid, in a nightmare rest, chest-pressed,
Dreameth of one of her old flames, James Games.
And that she hears—what faith is man's!—Ann's banns
And his, from Reverend Mr. Rice, twice, thrice:
White ribbons flourish, and a stout shout out,
That upward goes, shows Rose knows those bows' woes!

Thomas Hood.

LOVELILTS

THINE eyes, dear one, dot dot, are like, dash, what?
They, pure as sacred oils, bless and anoint
My sin-swamped soul which at thy feet sobs out,
O exclamation point, O point, O point!

Ah, had I words, blank blank, which, dot, I've not,
I'd swoon in songs which should'st illume the dark
With light of thee. Ah, God (it's *strong* to swear)
Why, why, interrogation mark, why, mark?

Dot dot dot dot. And so, dash, yet, but nay!
My tongue takes pause; some words must not be said,
For fear the world, cold hyphen-eyed, austere,
Should'st shake thee by the throat till reason fled.

One hour of love we've had. Dost thou recall
Dot dot dash blank interrogation mark?
The night was ours, blue heaven over all
Dash, God! dot stars, keep thou our secret dark!

Marion Hill.

JOCOSA LYRA

IN our hearts is the Great One of Avon
　　　　Engraven,
And we climb the cold summits once built on
　　　　By Milton.

But at times not the air that is rarest
　　　　Is fairest,
And we long in the valley to follow
　　　　Apollo.

Then we drop from the heights atmospheric
　　　　To Herrick,
Or we pour the Greek honey, grown blander,
　　　　Of Landor;

Or our cosiest nook in the shade is
      Where Praed is,
Or we toss the light bells of the mocker
      With Locker.

Oh, the song where not one of the Graces
      Tight-laces,—
Where we woo the sweet Muses not starchly
      But archly,—

Where the verse, like a piper a-Maying,
      Comes playing,—
And the rhyme is as gay as a dancer
      In answer,—

It will last till men weary of pleasure
      In measure!
It will last till men weary of laughter . . .
      And after!

                 Austin Dobson.

TO A THESAURUS

O PRECIOUS code, volume, tome,
  Book, writing, compilation, work
Attend the while I pen a pome,
  A jest, a jape, a quip, a quirk.

For I would pen, engross, indite,
  Transcribe, set forth, compose, address,
Record, submit—yea, even write
  An ode, an elegy to bless—

To bless, set store by, celebrate,
  Approve, esteem, endow with soul,
Commend, acclaim, appreciate,
  Immortalize, laud, praise, extol.

Thy merit, goodness, value, worth,
　　Experience, utility—
O manna, honey, salt of earth,
　　I sing, I chant, I worship thee!

How could I manage, live, exist,
　　Obtain, produce, be real, prevail,
Be present in the flesh, subsist,
　　Have place, become, breathe or inhale.

Without thy help, recruit, support,
　　Opitulation, furtherance,
Assistance, rescue, aid, resort,
　　Favour, sustention and advance?

Alack! Alack! and well-a-day!
　　My case would then be dour and sad,
Likewise distressing, dismal, gray,
　　Pathetic, mournful, dreary, bad.

　　·　　·　　·　　·　　·　　·　　·

Though I could keep this up all day,
　　This lyric, elegiac, song,
Meseems hath come the time to say
　　Farewell! Adieu! Good-by! So long!

　　　　　　　　　　Franklin P. Adams.

THE FUTURE OF THE CLASSICS

No longer, O scholars, shall Plautus
　　Be taught us.
No more shall professors be partial
　　To Martial.
　　No ninny
Will stop playing " shinney "
　　For Pliny.
Not even the veriest Mexican Greaser
　　Will stop to read Cæsar.
No true son of Erin will leave his potato
To list to the love-lore of Ovid or Plato.

Old Homer,
That hapless old roamer,
Will ne'er find a rest 'neath collegiate dome or
Anywhere else. As to Seneca,
Any cur
Safely may snub him, or urge ill
Effects from the reading of Virgil.
Cornelius Nepos
Wont keep us
Much longer from pleasure's light errands—
Nor Terence.
The irreverent now may all scoff in ease
At the shade of poor old Aristophanes.
And moderns it now doth behoove in all
Ways to despise poor old Juvenal;
And to chivvy
Livy.
The class-room hereafter will miss a row
Of eager young students of Cicero.
The 'longshoreman—yes, and the dock-rat, he's
Down upon Socrates.
And what'll
Induce us to read Aristotle?
We shall fail in
Our duty to Galen.
No tutor henceforward shall rack us
To construe old Horatius Flaccus.
We have but a wretched opinion
Of Mr. Justinian.
In our classical pabulum mix we've no wee sop
Of Æsop.
Our balance of intellect asks for no ballast
From Sallust.
With feminine scorn no fair Vassar-bred lass at us
Shall smile if we own that we cannot read Tacitus.
No admirer shall ever now wreathe with begonias
The bust of Suetonius.
And so, if you follow me,
We'll have to cut Ptolemy.
Besides, it would just be considered facetious
To look at Lucretius.

And you can
Not go in Society if you read Lucan,
And we cannot have any fun
Out of Xenophon.

Unknown.

CAUTIONARY VERSES

My little dears, who learn to read, pray early, learn to shun
That very silly thing indeed which people call a pun;
Read Entick's rules, and 'twill be found how simple an
offence
It is to make the selfsame sound afford a double sense.

For instance, ale may make you ail, your aunt an ant may
kill,
You in a vale may buy a veil and Bill may pay the bill.
Or if to France your bark you steer, at Dover it may be
A peer appears upon the pier, who blind, still goes to sea.

Thus, one might say, when, to a treat, good friends accept our
greeting,
'Tis meet that men who meet to eat should eat their meat
when meeting;
Brawn on the board's no bore indeed, although from boar
prepared;
Nor can the fowl on which we feed, foul feeding be declared.

Thus one ripe fruit may be a pear, and yet be pared again,
And still be one, which seemeth rare until we do explain.
It therefore should be all your aim to speak with ample care,
For who, however fond of game, would choose to swallow
hair?

A fat man's gait may make us smile, who have no gate to
close;
The farmer sitting on his stile no stylish person knows.
Perfumers men of scents must be; some Scilly men are
bright;
A brown man oft deep read we see, a black a wicked wight.

Most wealthy men good manors have, however vulgar they;
And actors still the harder slave the oftener they play;
So poets can't the baize obtain, unless their tailors choose;
While grooms and coachmen, not in vain, each evening seek
    the Mews.

The dyer, who by dyeing lives, a dire life maintains;
The glazier, it is known, receives his profits for his panes;
By gardeners thyme is tied, 'tis true, when spring is in its
    prime,
But time or tide won't wait for you if you are tied for time.

Then now you see, my little dears, the way to make a pun;
A trick which you, through coming years, should sedulously
    shun;
The fault admits of no defence; for wheresoe'er 'tis found,
You sacrifice for sound the sense; the sense is never sound.

So let your words and actions too, one single meaning prove,
And, just in all you say or do, you'll gain esteem and love;
In mirth and play no harm you'll know when duty's task is
    done,
But parents ne'er should let you go unpunished for a pun!

                      Theodore Hook.

THE WAR: A—Z

An Austrian Archduke, assaulted and assailed,
Broke Belgium's barriers, by Britain bewailed,
Causing consternation, confused chaotic crises;
Diffusing destructive, death dealing devices.
England engaged earnestly, eager every ear,
France fought furiously, forsaking foolish fear,
Great German garrisons grappled Gallic guard,
Hohenzollern Hussars hammered, heavy, hard.
Infantry, Imperial, Indian, Irish, intermingling,
Jackets jaunty, joking, jesting, jostling, jingling.
Kinetic, Kruppised Kaiser, kingdom's killing knight,
Laid Louvain lamenting, London lacking light,

Mobilising millions, marvellous mobility,
Numberless nonentities, numerous nobility.
Oligarchies olden opposed olive offering,
Prussia pressed Paris, Polish protection proffering,
Quaint Quebec quickly quartered quotidian quota,
Renascent Russia, resonant, reported regal rota.
Scotch soldiers, sterling, songs stalwart sung,
" Tipperary " thundered through titanic tongue.
United States urging unarmament, unwanted,
Visualised victory vociferously vaunted,
Wilson's warnings wasted, world war wild,
Xenian Xanthochroi Xantippically X-iled.
Yorkshire's young yeomen yelling youthfully,
" Zigzag Zeppelins, Zuyder Zee."

John R. Edwards.

LINES TO MISS FLORENCE HUNTINGDON

Sweet maiden of Passamaquoddy
    Shall we seek for communion of souls
Where the deep Mississippi meanders
    Or the distant Saskatchewan rolls?

Ah, no!—for in Maine I will find thee
    A sweetly sequestrated nook,
Where the far-winding Skoodoowabskooksis
    Conjoins with the Skoodoowabskook.

There wander two beautiful rivers,
    With many a winding and crook:
The one is the Skoodoowabskooksis;
    The other, the Skoodoowabskook.

Ah, sweetest of haunts! though unmentioned
    In geography, atlas, or book,
How fair is the Skoodoowabskooksis,
    When joining the Skoodoowabskook!

Our cot shall be close by the waters,
　　Within that sequestrated nook,
Reflected by Skoodoowabskooksis,
　　And mirrored in Skoodoowabskook.

You shall sleep to the music of leaflets,
　　By zephyrs in wantonness shook,
To dream of the Skoodoowabskooksis,
　　And, perhaps, of the Skoodoowabskook.

Your food shall be fish from the waters,
　　Drawn forth on the point of a hook,
From murmuring Skoodoowabskooksis,
　　Or meandering Skoodoowabskook.

You shall quaff the most sparkling of waters,
　　Drawn forth from a silvery brook,
Which flows to the Skoodoowabskooksis,
　　And so to the Skoodoowabskook.

And you shall preside at the banquet,
　　And I shall wait on you as cook;
And we'll talk of the Skoodoowabskooksis,
　　And sing of the Skoodoowabskook.

Let others sing loudly of Saco,
　　Of Quoddy and Tattamagouche,
Of Kenebeccasis and Quaco,
　　Of Merigoniche and Buctouche,

Of Nashwaak and Magaguadavique,
　　Or Memmerimammericook:—
There's none like the Skoodoowabskooksis,
　　Excepting the Skoodoowabskook!

Unknown.

TO MY NOSE

Knows he that never took a pinch,
Nosey, the pleasure thence which flows,
Knows he the titillating joys
    Which my nose knows?
O Nose, I am as proud of thee
As any mountain of its snows,
I gaze on thee, and feel that pride
    A Roman knows!

Albert A. Forrester (*Alfred Crowquill*).

A POLKA LYRIC

Qui nunc dancere vult modo,
Wants to dance in the fashion, oh!
Discere debet—ought to know,
Kickere floor cum heel and toe,
    One, two, three,
    Hop with me,
Whirligig, twirligig, rapide.

Polkam jungere, Virgo, vis,
Will you join the polka, miss?
Liberius—most willingly,
Sic agimus—then let us try:
    Nunc vide,
    Skip with me,
Whirlabout, roundabout, celere.

Tum læva cito, tum dextra,
First to the left, and then t'other way;
Aspice retro in vultu,
You look at her, and she looks at you.
    Das palmam
    Change hands, ma'am;
Celere—run away, just in sham.

Barclay Philips.

A *CAT*ALECTIC MONODY!

A CAT I sing, of famous memory,
Though *cat*achrestical my song may be;
In a small garden *cat*acomb she lies,
And *cat*aclysms fill her comrades' eyes;
Borne on the air, the *cat*acoustic song
Swells with her virtues' *cat*alogue along,
No *cat*aplasm could lengthen out her years,
Though mourning friends shed *cat*aracts of tears.
Once loud and strong her *cat*echist-like voice
It dwindled to a *cat*call's squeaking noise;
Most *cat*egorical her virtues shone,
By *cat*enation join'd each one to one;—
But a vile *cat*chpoll dog, with cruel bite,
Like *cat*ling's cut, her strength disabled quite;
Her *cat*erwauling pierced the heavy air,
As *cat*aphracts their arms through legions bear;
'Tis vain! as *cat*erpillars drag away
Their lengths, like *cat*tle after busy day,
She ling'ring died, nor left in kit *kat* the
Embodyment of this *cat*astrophe.

Cruikshank's Omnibus.

ODE FOR A SOCIAL MEETING

WITH SLIGHT ALTERATIONS BY A TEETOTALER

Come! fill a fresh bumper,—for why should we go
      logwood
While the ~~nectar~~ still reddens our cups as they flow?
    decoction
Pour out the ~~rich juices~~ still bright with the sun,
         dye-stuff
Till o'er the brimmed crystal the ~~rubies~~ shall run.
  half-ripened apples
The ~~purple-globed clusters~~ their life-dews have bled;
     taste   sugar of lead
How sweet is the ~~breath~~ of the ~~fragrance they shed!~~
    rank poisons   *wines!!!*
For Summer's ~~last roses~~ lie hid in the ~~wines~~
        stable-boys smoking long-nines
That were garnered by ~~maidens who laughed through the vines,~~

scowl   howl   scoff   sneer
Then a smile, and a glass, and a toast, and a cheer,
strychnine and whiskey, and ratsbane and beer
For all the good wine, and we've some of it here!
In cellar, in pantry, in attic, in hall,
Down, down with the tyrant that masters us all!
Long live the gay servant that laughs for us all!

Oliver Wendell Holmes.

THE JOVIAL PRIEST'S CONFESSION

TRANSLATED FROM THE LATIN OF WALTER DE MAPES,
TIME OF HENRY II

I devise to end my days—in a tavern drinking,
May some Christian hold for me—the glass when I am
    shrinking,
That the cherubim may cry—when they see me sinking,
God be merciful to a soul—of this gentleman's way of
    thinking.

A glass of wine amazingly—enlighteneth one's internals;
'Tis wings bedewed with nectar—that fly up to supernals;
Bottles cracked in taverns—have much the sweeter kernels,
Than the sups allowed to us—in the college journals.

Every one by nature hath—a mold which he was cast in;
I happen to be one of those—who never could write fasting;
By a single little boy—I should be surpass'd in
Writing so: I'd just as lief—be buried; tomb'd and grass'd
    in.

Every one by nature hath—a gift too, a dotation:
I, when I make verses—do get the inspiration
Of the very best of wine—that comes into the nation:
It maketh sermons to astound—for edification.

Just as liquor floweth good—floweth forth my lay so;
But I must moreover eat—or I could not say so;
Naught it availeth inwardly—should I write all day so;
But with God's grace after meat—I beat Ovidius Naso.

Neither is there given to me—prophetic animation,
Unless when I have eat and drank—yea, ev'n to saturation,
Then in my upper story—hath Bacchus domination,
And Phœbus rushes into me, and beggareth all relation.

Leigh Hunt.

LIMERICKS

THERE was an old man of Tobago,
Who lived upon rice, gruel and sago;
   Till, much to his bliss,
   His physician said this:
" To a leg, sir, of mutton, you may go."

There was an old soldier of Bister,
Went walking one day with his sister;
   When a cow, at one poke,
   Tossed her into an oak,
Before the old gentleman missed her.

There was a young man of St. Kitts
Who was very much troubled with fits;
   The eclipse of the moon
   Threw him into a swoon,
When he tumbled and broke into bits.

There was an old man who said, " Gee!
I can't multiply seven by three!
   Though fourteen seems plenty,
   It *might* come to twenty,—
I haven't the slightest idee! "

There was an old man in a pie,
Who said, " I must fly! I must fly!"
    When they said, " You can't do it!"
    He replied that he knew it,
But he *had* to get out of that pie!

A Tutor who tooted the flute
Tried to teach two young tooters to toot;
    Said the two to the Tutor,
    " Is it harder to toot, or
To tutor two tooters to toot?"

                    Carolyn Wells.

RECITED BY A CHINESE INFANT

If-itty-teshi-mow Jays
Haddee ny up-plo-now-shi-buh nays;
    ha! ha!
    He lote im aw dow,
    Witty motti-fy flow;
A-flew-ty ho-lot-itty flays! Hee!

Translation

Infinitesimal James
Had nine unpronounceable names;
    He wrote them all down,
    With a mortified frown,
And threw the whole lot in the flames.

For beauty I am not a star,
There are others more handsome by far;
    But my face I don't mind it,
    For I am behind it,
It's the people in front that I jar.

There was a young lady of Oakham,
Who would steal your cigars and then soak 'em

In treacle and rum,
And then smear them with gum,
So it wasn't a pleasure to smoke 'em.

There was an Old Man in a tree
Who was horribly bored by a bee;
    When they said, "Does it buzz?"
    He replied, "Yes, it does!
It's a regular brute of a bee."

Edward Lear.

There was an Old Man of St. Bees
Who was stung in the arm by a wasp.
    When asked, "Does it hurt?"
    He replied, "No, it doesn't,
But I thought all the while 'twas a hornet."

W. S. Gilbert.

There was an old man of the Rhine,
When asked at what hour he would dine,
    Replied, "At eleven,
    Four, six, three and seven,
And eight and a quarter of nine."

There was a young man of Laconia,
Whose mother-in-law had pneumonia;
    He hoped for the worst,
    And after March first
They buried her 'neath a begonia.

There was a young man of the cape
Who always wore trousers of crêpe;
    When asked, "Don't they tear?"
    He replied, "Here and there;
But they keep such a beautiful shape."

There once were some learned M.D.'s,
Who captured some germs of disease,

And infected a train,
Which without causing pain,
Allowed one to catch it with ease.

Oliver Herford.

There was a young lady of Lynn,
Who was deep in original sin;
     When they said, " Do be good,"
     She said, " Would if I could! "
And straightway went at it ag'in.

I'd rather have fingers than toes;
I'd rather have ears than a nose;
     And as for my hair
     I'm glad it's all there,
I'll be awfully sad when it goes.

Gelett Burgess.

There was a young fellow named Clyde;
Who was once at a funeral spied.
     When asked who was dead,
     He smilingly said,
" *I* don't know,—*I* just came for the ride! "

There was a young lady of Truro,
Who wished a mahogany bureau;
     But her father said, " Dod!
     All the men on Cape Cod
Couldn't buy a mahogany bureau! "

There was a young man of Ostend
Who vowed he'd hold out to the end,
     But when halfway over
     From Calais to Dover,
He done what he didn't intend—

There was a young man of Cohoes,
Wore tar on the end of his nose;

When asked why he done it,
He said for the fun it
Afforded the men of Cohoes.

Robert J. Burdette.

There is a young artist called Whistler,
Who in every respect is a bristler;
    A tube of white lead,
    Or a punch on the head,
Come equally handy to Whistler.

Dante Gabriel Rossetti.

There is a creator named God,
Whose doings are sometimes quite odd;
    He made a painter named Val,
    And I say and I shall,
That he does no great credit to God.

J. M. Whistler.

There was a young lady of station,
" I love man! " was her sole exclamation;
    But when men cried, " You flatter! "
    She replied, " Oh, no matter!
Isle of Man, is the true explanation."

Lewis Carroll.

There was a young lady of Twickenham,
Whose shoes were too tight to walk quick in 'em;
    She came back from her walk,
    Looking white as a chalk,
And took 'em both off and was sick in 'em.

Oliver Herford.

" It's a very warm day," observed Billy.
" I hope that you won't think it silly
    If I say that this heat
    Makes me think 'twould be sweet
If one were a coolie in Chile! "

Tudor Jenks.

There was a young man from Cornell,
Who said, " I'm aware of a smell,
　　But whether it's drains
　　Or human remains,
I'm really unable to tell."

There was a young lady from Joppa,
Whose friends all decided to drop her;
　　She went with a friend
　　On a trip to Ostend,—
And the rest of the story's improper.

There once was a sculptor named Phidias,
Whose statues by some were thought hideous;
　　He made Aphrodite
　　Without any nighty,
Which shocked all the ultra-fastidious.

John woke on Jan. first and felt queer;
Said, " Crackers I'll swear off this year!
　　For the lobster and wine
　　And the rabbit were fine,—
And it certainly wasn't the beer."

There was a young lady of Venice
Who used hard-boiled eggs to play tennis;
　　When they said, " You are wrong,"
　　She replied, " Go along!
You don't know how prolific my hen is! "

There was a young man of Fort Blainey,
Who proposed to his typist named Janey;
　　When his friends said, " Oh, dear!
　　She's so old and so queer! "
He replied, " But the day was so rainy! "

XIII

NONSENSE

LUNAR STANZAS

Night saw the crew like pedlers with their packs
    Altho' it were too dear to pay for eggs;
Walk crank along with coffin on their backs
    While in their arms they bow their weary legs.

And yet 'twas strange, and scarce can one suppose
    That a brown buzzard-fly should steal and wear
His white jean breeches and black woollen hose,
    But thence that flies have souls is very clear.

But, Holy Father! what shall save the soul,
    When cobblers ask three dollars for their shoes?
When cooks their biscuits with a shot-tower roll,
    And farmers rake their hay-cocks with their hoes.

Yet, 'twere profuse to see for pendant light,
    A tea-pot dangle in a lady's ear;
And 'twere indelicate, although she might
    Swallow two whales and yet the moon shine clear.

But what to me are woven clouds, or what,
    If dames from spiders learn to warp their looms?
If coal-black ghosts turn soldiers for the State,
    With wooden eyes, and lightning-rods for plumes?

Oh! too, too shocking! barbarous, savage taste!
    To eat one's mother ere itself was born!
To gripe the tall town-steeple by the waste,
    And scoop it out to be his drinking-horn.

No more: no more! I'm sick and dead and gone;
　　Boxed in a coffin, stifled six feet deep;
Thorns, fat and fearless, prick my skin and bone,
　　And revel o'er me, like a soulless sheep.

Henry Coggswell Knight.

THE WHANGO TREE

THE woggly bird sat on the whango tree,
　　Nooping the rinkum corn,
And graper and graper, alas! grew he,
　　And cursed the day he was born.
His crute was clum and his voice was rum,
　　As curiously thus sang he,
" Oh, would I'd been rammed and eternally clammed
　　Ere I perched on this whango tree."

Now the whango tree had a bubbly thorn,
　　As sharp as a nootie's bill,
And it stuck in the woggly bird's umptum lorn
　　And weepadge, the smart did thrill.
He fumbled and cursed, but that wasn't the worst,
　　For he couldn't at all get free,
And he cried, " I am gammed, and injustibly nammed
　　On the luggardly whango tree."

And there he sits still, with no worm in his bill,
　　Nor no guggledom in his nest;
He is hungry and bare, and gobliddered with care,
　　And his grabbles give him no rest;
He is weary and sore and his tugmut is soar,
　　And nothing to nob has he,
As he chirps, " I am blammed and corruptibly jammed,
　　In this cuggerdom whango tree."

Unknown.

THREE CHILDREN

THREE children sliding on the ice
Upon a summer's day,
As it fell out they all fell in,
The rest they ran away.

Now, had these children been at home,
Or sliding on dry ground,
Ten thousand pounds to one penny
They had not all been drowned.

You parents all that children have,
And you too that have none,
If you would have them safe abroad
Pray keep them safe at home.

Unknown.

'TIS MIDNIGHT

'TIS midnight, and the setting sun
Is slowly rising in the west;
The rapid rivers slowly run,
The frog is on his downy nest.
The pensive goat and sportive cow,
Hilarious, leap from bough to bough.

Unknown.

COSSIMBAZAR

COME fleetly, come fleetly, my hookabadar,
For the sound of the tam-tam is heard from afar.
"Banoolah! Banoolah!" The Brahmins are nigh,
And the depths of the jungle re-echo their cry.
        Pestonjee Bomanjee!
        Smite the guitar;
Join in the chorus, my hookabadar.

Heed not the blast of the deadly monsoon,
Nor the blue Brahmaputra that gleams in the moon.
Stick to thy music, and oh, let the sound
Be heard with distinctness a mile or two round.
　　Jamsetjee, Jeejeebhoy!
　　Sweep the guitar.
Join in the chorus, my hookabadar.

Art thou a Buddhist, or dost thou indeed
Put faith in the monstrous Mohammedan creed?
Art thou a Ghebir—a blinded Parsee?
Not that it matters an atom to me.
　　Cursetjee Bomanjee!
　　Twang the guitar
Join in the chorus, my hookabadar.

Henry S. Leigh.

AN UNSUSPECTED FACT

If down his throat a man should choose
In fun, to jump or slide,
He'd scrape his shoes against his teeth,
Nor dirt his own inside.
But if his teeth were lost and gone,
And not a stump to scrape upon,
He'd see at once how very pat
His tongue lay there by way of mat,
And he would wipe his feet on *that!*

Edward Cannon.

THE CUMBERBUNCE

I strolled beside the shining sea,
I was as lonely as could be;
No one to cheer me in my walk
But stones and sand, which cannot talk—
Sand and stones and bits of shell,
Which never have a thing to tell.

But as I sauntered by the tide
I saw a something at my side,
A something green, and blue, and pink,
And brown, and purple, too, I think.
I would not say how large it was;
I would not venture that, because
It took me rather by surprise,
And I have not the best of eyes.

Should you compare it to a cat,
I'd say it was as large as that;
Or should you ask me if the thing
Was smaller than a sparrow's wing,
I should be apt to think you knew,
And simply answer, " Very true! "

Well, as I looked upon the thing,
It murmured, " Please, sir, can I sing? "
And then I knew its name at once—
It plainly was a Cumberbunce.

You are amazed that I could tell
The creature's name so quickly? Well,
I knew it was not a paper-doll,
A pencil or a parasol,
A tennis-racket or a cheese,
And, as it was not one of these,
And I am not a perfect dunce—
It had to be a Cumberbunce!

With pleading voice and tearful eye
It seemed as though about to cry.
It looked so pitiful and sad
It made me feel extremely bad.
My heart was softened to the thing
That asked me if it, please, could sing.
Its little hand I longed to shake,
But, oh, it had no hand to take!
I bent and drew the creature near,
And whispered in its pale blue ear,
" What! Sing, my Cumberbunce? You can!
Sing on, sing loudly, little man! "

The Cumberbunce, without ado,
Gazed sadly on the ocean blue,
And, lifting up its little head,
In tones of awful longing, said:

" Oh, I would sing of mackerel skies,
    And why the sea is wet,
Of jelly-fish and conger-eels,
    And things that I forget.
And I would hum a plaintive tune
    Of why the waves are hot
As water boiling on a stove,
    Excepting that they're not!

" And I would sing of hooks and eyes,
    And why the sea is slant,
And gayly tips the little ships,
    Excepting that I can't!
I never sang a single song,
    I never hummed a note.
There is in me no melody,
    No music in my throat.

" So that is why I do not sing
Of sharks, or whales, or anything!"

I looked in innocent surprise,
My wonder showing in my eyes.
" Then why, O, Cumberbunce," I cried,
" Did you come walking at my side
And ask me if you, please, might sing,
When you could not warble anything?"

" I did not ask permission, sir,
I really did not, I aver.
You, sir, misunderstood me, quite.
I did not ask you if I *might*.
Had you correctly understood,
You'd know I asked you if I *could*.

So, as I cannot sing a song,
Your answer, it is plain, was wrong.
The fact I could not sing I knew,
But wanted your opinion, too."

A voice came softly o'er the lea.
"Farewell! my mate is calling me!"

I saw the creature disappear,
Its voice, in parting, smote my ear—
"I thought all people understood
The difference 'twixt 'might' and 'could'!"

Paul West.

MR. FINNEY'S TURNIP

MR. FINNEY had a turnip
   And it grew and it grew;
And it grew behind the barn,
   And that turnip did no harm.

There it grew and it grew
   Till it could grow no longer;
Then his daughter Lizzie picked it
   And put it in the cellar.

There it lay and it lay
   Till it began to rot;
And his daughter Susie took it
   And put it in the pot.

And they boiled it and boiled it
   As long as they were able,
And then his daughters took it
   And put it on the table.

Mr. Finney and his wife
   They sat down to sup;
And they ate and they ate
   And they ate that turnip up.

Unknown.

NONSENSE VERSES

Lazy-bones, lazy-bones, wake up and peep!
The cat's in the cupboard, your mother's asleep.
There you sit snoring, forgetting her ills;
Who is to give her her Bolus and Pills?
Twenty fine Angels must come into town,
All for to help you to make your new gown:
Dainty aerial Spinsters and Singers;
Aren't you ashamed to employ such white fingers?
Delicate hands, unaccustom'd to reels,
To set 'em working a poor body's wheels?
Why they came down is to me all a riddle,
And left Hallelujah broke off in the middle:
Jove's Court, and the Presence angelical, cut—
To eke out the work of a lazy young slut.
Angel-duck, Angel-duck, winged and silly,
Pouring a watering-pot over a lily,
Gardener gratuitous, careless of pelf,
Leave her to water her lily herself,
Or to neglect it to death if she chuse it:
Remember the loss is her own if she lose it.

Charles Lamb.

LIKE TO THE THUNDERING TONE

Like to the thundering tone of unspoke speeches,
Or like a lobster clad in logic breeches,
Or like the gray fur of a crimson cat,
Or like the mooncalf in a slipshod hat;
E'en such is he who never was begotten
Until his children were both dead and rotten.

Like to the fiery tombstone of a cabbage,
Or like a crab-louse with its bag and baggage,
Or like the four square circle of a ring,
Or like to hey ding, ding-a, ding-a, ding;
E'en such is he who spake, and yet, no doubt,
Spake to small purpose, when his tongue was out.

Like to a fair, fresh, fading, wither'd rose,
Or like to rhyming verse that runs in prose,
Or like the stumbles of a tinder-box,
Or like a man that's sound yet sickness mocks;
E'en such is he who died and yet did laugh
To see these lines writ for his epitaph.

Bishop Corbet in 17th century.

ÆSTIVATION

In candent ire the solar splendour flames;
The foles, languescent, pend from arid rames;
His humid front the cive, anheling, wipes,
And dreams of erring on ventiferous ripes.

How dolce to vive occult to mortal eyes,
Dorm on the herb with none to supervise,
Carp the suave berries from the crescent vine,
And bibe the flow from longicaudate kine!

To me, alas! no verdurous visions come,
Save yon exiguous pool's conferva-scum—
No concave vast repeats the tender hue
That laves my milk-jug with celestial blue.

Me wretched! let me curr to quercine shades!
Effund your albid hausts, lactiferous maids!
Oh, might I vole to some umbrageous clump,—
Depart—be off,—excede,—evade,—crump!

Oliver Wendell Holmes.

UNCLE SIMON AND UNCLE JIM

Uncle Simon he
Clumb up a tree
To see
What he could see,
When presentlee

Uncle Jim
Clumb up beside of him
And squatted down by he.

Charles Farrar Browne (Artemus Ward).

A TRAGIC STORY

THERE lived a sage in days of yore,
And he a handsome pigtail wore;
But wondered much and sorrowed more,
    Because it hung behind him.

He mused upon this curious case,
And swore he'd change the pigtail's place,
And have it hanging at his face,
    Not dangling there behind him.

Says he, " The mystery I've found,—
I'll turn me round,"—he turned him round;
    But still it hung behind him.

Then round and round, and out and in,
All day the puzzled sage did spin;
In vain—it mattered not a pin,—
    The pigtail hung behind him.

And right and left, and round about,
And up and down, and in and out,
He turned; but still the pigtail stout
    Hung steadily behind him.

And though his efforts never slack,
And though he twist and twirl and tack,
Alas! still faithful to his back,
    The pigtail hangs behind him.

W. M. Thackeray.

SONNET FOUND IN A DESERTED MAD HOUSE

OH that my soul a marrow-bone might seize!
For the old egg of my desire is broken,
Spilled is the pearly white and spilled the yolk, and
As the mild melancholy contents grease
My path the shorn lamb baas like bumblebees.
Time's trashy purse is as a taken token
Or like a thrilling recitation, spoken
By mournful mouths filled full of mirth and cheese.

And yet, why should I clasp the earthful urn?
Or find the frittered fig that felt the fast?
Or choose to chase the cheese around the churn?
Or swallow any pill from out the past?
Ah, no Love, not while your hot kisses burn
Like a potato riding on the blast.

Unknown.

THE JIM-JAM KING OF THE JOU-JOUS

AN ARABIAN LEGEND

Translated from the Arabic

FAR off in the waste of desert sand,
The Jim-jam rules in the Jou-jou land:
He sits on a throne of red-hot rocks,
And moccasin snakes are his curling locks;
And the Jou-jous have the conniption fits
In the far-off land where the Jim-jam sits—
If things are now as things were then.
Allah il Allah! Oo-aye! Amen!

The country's so dry in Jou-jou land
You could wet it down with Sahara sand,
And over its boundaries the air
Is hotter than 'tis—no matter where:
A camel drops down completely tanned
When he crosses the line in Jou-jou land—

If things are now as things were then.
Allah il Allah! Oo-aye! Amen!

A traveller once got stuck in the sand
On the fiery edge of Jou-jou land;
The Jou-jous they confiscated him,
And the Jim-jam tore him limb from limb;
But, dying, he said: "If eaten I am,
I'll disagree with this Dam-jim-jam!
He'll think his stomach's a Hoodoo's den!"
Allah il Allah! Oo-aye! Amen!

Then the Jim-jam felt so bad inside,
It just about humbled his royal pride.
He decided to physic himself with sand,
And throw up his job in the Jou-jou land.
He descended his throne of red-hot rocks,
And hired a barber to cut his locks:
The barber died of the got-'em-again.
Allah il Allah! Oo-aye! Amen!

And now let every good Mussulman
Get all the good from this tale he can.
If you wander off on a Jamboree,
Across the stretch of the desert sea,
Look out that right at the height of your booze
You don't get caught by the Jou-jou-jous!
You may, for the Jim-jam's at it again.
Allah il Allah! Oo-aye! Amen!

Alaric Bertrand Stuart.

TO MARIE

When the breeze from the bluebottle's blustering blim
    Twirls the toads in a tooroomaloo,
And the whiskery whine of the wheedlesome whim
    Drowns the roll of the rattatattoo,
Then I dream in the shade of the shally-go-shee,
    And the voice of the bally-molay
Brings the smell of stale poppy-cods blummered in blee
    From the willy-wad over the way.

Ah, the shuddering shoo and the blinketty-blanks
  When the yungalung falls from the bough
In the blast of a hurricane's hicketty-hanks
  On the hills of the hocketty-how!
Give the rigamarole to the clangery-whang,
  If they care for such fiddlededee;
But the thingumbob kiss of the whangery-bang
  Keeps the higgledy-piggle for me.

L'ENVOI

It is pilly-po-doddle and aligobung
  When the lollypop covers the ground,
Yet the poldiddle perishes punketty-pung
  When the heart jimmy-coggles around.
If the soul cannot snoop at the giggle-some cart,
  Seeking surcease in gluggety-glug,
It is useless to say to the pulsating heart,
  "Panky-doodle ker-chuggetty-chug!"

John Bennett.

MY DREAM

I DREAMED a dream next Tuesday week,
  Beneath the apple-trees;
I thought my eyes were big pork-pies,
  And my nose was Stilton cheese.
The clock struck twenty minutes to six,
  When a frog sat on my knee;
I asked him to lend me eighteenpence,
  But he borrowed a shilling of me.

Unknown.

THE ROLLICKING MASTODON

A ROLLICKING Mastodon lived in Spain,
  In the trunk of a Tranquil Tree.
His face was plain, but his jocular vein
  Was a burst of the wildest glee.
His voice was strong and his laugh so long

That people came many a mile,
And offered to pay a guinea a day
    For the fractional part of a smile.

The Rollicking Mastodon's laugh was wide—
    Indeed, 'twas a matter of family pride;
And oh! so proud of his jocular vein
    Was the Rollicking Mastodon over in Spain.

The Rollicking Mastodon said one day,
    "I feel that I need some air,
For a little ozone's a tonic for bones,
    As well as a gloss for the hair."
So he skipped along and warbled a song
    In his own triumphulant way.
His smile was bright and his skip was light
    As he chirruped his roundelay.

The Rollicking Mastodon tripped along,
    And sang what Mastodons call a song;
But every note of it seemed to pain
    The Rollicking Mastodon over in Spain.

A Little Peetookle came over the hill,
    Dressed up in a bollitant coat;
And he said, "You need some harroway seed,
    And a little advice for your throat."
The Mastodon smiled and said, "My child,
    There's a chance for your taste to grow.
If you polish your mind, you'll certainly find
    How little, how little you know."

The Little Peetookle, his teeth he ground
    At the Mastodon's singular sense of sound;
For he felt it a sort of a musical stain
    On the Rollicking Mastodon over in Spain.

Alas! and alas! has it come to this pass?"
    Said the Little Peetookle. "Dear me!
It certainly seems your horrible screams
    Intended for music must be!"

The Mastodon stopped, his ditty he dropped,
    And murmured, " Good morning, my dear!
I never will sing to a sensitive thing
    That shatters a song with a sneer! "

The Rollicking Mastodon bade him " adieu."
    Of course 'twas a sensible thing to do;
For Little Peetookle is spared the strain
    Of the Rollicking Mastodon over in Spain.

Arthur Macy.

NONSENSE VERSES

THE INVISIBLE BRIDGE

I'D Never Dare to Walk across
    A Bridge I Could Not See;
For Quite afraid of Falling off,
    I fear that I Should Be!

THE LAZY ROOF

THE Roof it has a Lazy Time
    A-lying in the Sun;
The Walls they have to Hold Him Up;
    They do Not Have Much Fun!

MY FEET

MY feet, they haul me Round the House,
    They Hoist me up the Stairs;
I only have to Steer them and
    They Ride me Everywheres.

Gelett Burgess.

SPIRK TROLL-DERISIVE

THE Crankadox leaned o'er the edge of the moon,
    And wistfully gazed on the sea
Where the Gryxabodill madly whistled a tune
    To the air of " Ti-fol-de-ding-dee."

The quavering shriek of the Fliupthecreek
  Was fitfully wafted afar
To the Queen of the Wunks as she powdered her cheek
  With the pulverized rays of a star.

The Gool closed his ear on the voice of the Grig,
  And his heart it grew heavy as lead
As he marked the Baldekin adjusting his wig
  On the opposite side of his head;
And the air it grew chill as the Gryxabodill
  Raised his dank, dripping fins to the skies
To plead with the Plunk for the use of her bill
  To pick the tears out of his eyes.

The ghost of the Zhack flitted by in a trance;
  And the Squidjum hid under a tub
As he heard the loud hooves of the Hooken advance
  With a rub-a-dub-dub-a-dub dub!
And the Crankadox cried as he laid down and died,
  " My fate there is none to bewail! "
While the Queen of the Wunks drifted over the tide
  With a long piece of crape to her tail.

James Whitcomb Riley.

THE MAN IN THE MOON

S<small>AID</small> the Raggedy Man on a hot afternoon,
  " My !
    Sakes !
      What a lot o' mistakes
Some little folks makes on the Man in the Moon
But people that's been up to see him like Me,
And calls on him frequent and intimutly,

Might drop a few hints that would interest you
    Clean!
        Through!
           If you wanted 'em to—
Some actual facts that might interest you!

" O the Man in the Moon has a crick in his back
    Whee!
        Whimm!
           Ain't you sorry for him?
And a mole on his nose that is purple and black;
And his eyes are so weak that they water and run
If he dares to *dream* even he looks at the sun,—
So he jes' dreams of stars, as the doctor's advise—
    My!
        Eyes!
           But isn't he wise—
To jes' dream of stars, as the doctors advise?

" And the Man in the Moon has a boil on his ear—
    Whee!
        Whing!
           What a singular thing!
I know! but these facts are authentic, my dear,—
There's a boil on his ear; and a corn on his chin,—
He calls it a dimple,—but dimples stick in,—
Yet it might be a dimple turned over, you know!
    Whang!
        Ho!
           Why certainly so!—
It might be a dimple turned over, you know!

" And the Man in the Moon has a rheumatic knee,
    Gee!
        Whizz!
           What a pity that is!
And his toes have worked round where his heels ought to be.
So whenever he wants to go North he goes South,
And comes back with porridge crumbs all round his mouth,

And he brushes them off with a Japanese fan,
 Whing!
  Whann!
   What a marvellous man!
What a very remarkably marvellous man!

" And the Man in the Moon," sighed the Raggedy Man,
 " Gits!
  So!
   Sullonesome, you know!
Up there by himself since creation began!—
That when I call on him and then come away,
He grabs me and holds me and begs me to stay,—
Till—well, if it wasn't for *Jimmy-cum-Jim,*
 Dadd!
  Limb!
   I'd go pardners with him!
Jes' jump my bob here and be pardners with him!"

       James Whitcomb Riley.

THE LUGUBRIOUS WHING-WHANG

Out on the margin of moonshine land,
 Tickle me, love, in these lonesome ribs,
Out where the whing-whang loves to stand
Writing his name with his tail on the sand,
And wiping it out with his oogerish hand;
 Tickle me, love, in these lonesome ribs.

Is it the gibber of gungs and keeks?
 Tickle me, love, in these lonesome ribs,
Or what *is* the sound the whing-whang seeks,
Crouching low by the winding creeks,
And holding his breath for weeks and weeks?
 Tickle me, love, in these lonesome ribs.

Aroint him the wraithest of wraithly things!
   Tickle me, love, in these lonesome ribs,
'Tis a fair whing-whangess with phosphor rings,
And bridal jewels of fangs and stings,
And she sits and as sadly and softly sings
As the mildewed whir of her own dead wings;
    Tickle me, dear; tickle me here;
    Tickle me, love, in these lonesome ribs.

James Whitcomb Riley.

THE YONGHY-BONGHY-BO

I

ON the Coast of Coromandel
   Where the early pumpkins blow,
    In the middle of the woods
   Lived the Yonghy-Bonghy-Bo.
Two old chairs, and half a candle,
One old jug without a handle,—
    These were all his worldly goods:
    In the middle of the woods,
    These were all the worldly goods
   Of the Yonghy-Bonghy-Bo,
   Of the Yonghy-Bonghy-Bo.

II

Once, among the Bong-trees walking
   Where the early pumpkins blow,
    To a little heap of stones
   Came the Yonghy-Bonghy-Bo.
There he heard a Lady talking,
To some milk-white Hens of Dorking,
    " 'Tis the Lady Jingly Jones!
    On that little heap of stones
    Sits the Lady Jingly Jones!"
   Said the Yonghy-Bonghy-Bo,
   Said the Yonghy-Bonghy-Bo.

III

"Lady Jingly! Lady Jingly!
　　Sitting where the pumpkins blow,
　　　　Will you come and be my wife?"
　　Said the Yonghy-Bonghy-Bo,
"I am tired of living singly,—
On this coast so wild and shingly,—
　　　　I'm a-weary of my life;
　　　　If you'll come and be my wife,
　　　　Quite serene would be my life!"
　　Said the Yonghy-Bonghy-Bo,
　　Said the Yonghy-Bonghy-Bo.

IV

"On this Coast of Coromandel
　　Shrimps and watercresses grow,
　　　　Prawns are plentiful and cheap,"
　　Said the Yonghy-Bonghy-Bo.
"You shall have my chairs and candle,
And my jug without a handle!
　　　　Gaze upon the rolling deep
　　　　(Fish is plentiful and cheap):
　　　　As the sea, my love is deep!"
　　Said the Yonghy-Bonghy-Bo,
　　Said the Yonghy-Bonghy-Bo.

V

Lady Jingly answered sadly,
　　And her tears began to flow,—
　　　　"Your proposal comes too late,
　　Mr. Yonghy-Bonghy-Bo!
I would be your wife most gladly!"
(Here she twirled her fingers madly,)
　　　　"But in England I've a mate!
　　　　Yes! you've asked me far too late,
　　　　For in England I've a mate,
　　Mr. Yonghy-Bonghy-Bo!
　　Mr. Yonghy-Bonghy-Bo!

VI

" Mr. Jones (his name is Handel,—
  Handel Jones, Esquire & Co.)
    Dorking fowls delights to send,
  Mr. Yonghy-Bonghy-Bo!
Keep, oh, keep your chairs and candle,
And your jug without a handle,—
    I can merely be your friend!
    Should my Jones more Dorkings send,
    I will give you three, my friend!
  Mr. Yonghy-Bonghy-Bo!
  Mr. Yonghy-Bonghy-Bo!

VII

" Though you've such a tiny body,
  And your head so large doth grow,—
    Though your hat may blow away,
  Mr. Yonghy-Bonghy-Bo!
Though you're such a Hoddy Doddy,
Yet I wish that I could modi-
    fy the words I needs must say!
    Will you please to go away?
    That is all I have to say,
  Mr. Yonghy-Bonghy-Bo!
  Mr. Yonghy-Bonghy-Bo! "

VIII

Down the slippery slopes of Myrtle,
  Where the early pumpkins blow,
    To the calm and silent sea
  Fled the Yonghy-Bonghy-Bo.
There, beyond the Bay of Gurtle,
Lay a large and lively Turtle.
    " You're the Cove," he said, " for me:
    On your back beyond the sea,
    Turtle, you shall carry me! "
  Said the Yonghy-Bonghy-Bo,
  Said the Yonghy-Bonghy-Bo.

IX

Through the silent roaring ocean
  Did the Turtle swiftly go;
    Holding fast upon his shell
    Rode the Yonghy-Bonghy-Bo.
With a sad primæval motion
Toward the sunset isles of Boshen
    Still the Turtle bore him well,
    Holding fast upon his shell.
      "Lady Jingly Jones, farewell!"
    Sang the Yonghy-Bonghy-Bo,
    Sang the Yonghy-Bonghy-Bo.

X

From the Coast of Coromandel
  Did that Lady never go,
    On that heap of stones she mourns
    For the Yonghy-Bonghy-Bo.
On that Coast of Coromandel,
In his jug without a handle
    Still she weeps, and daily moans;
    On the little heap of stones
    To her Dorking Hens she moans,
  For the Yonghy-Bonghy-Bo,
  For the Yonghy-Bonghy-Bo.

Edward Lear.

THE JUMBLIES

I

THEY went to sea in a sieve, they did;
  In a sieve they went to sea:
In spite of all their freinds could say,
On a winter's morn, on a stormy day,
  In a sieve they went to sea.
And when the sieve turned round and round,
And every one cried, "You'll all be drowned!"
They called aloud, "Our sieve ain't big;
But we don't care a button, we don't care a fig:
  In a sieve we'll go to sea!"

Far and few, far and few,
　Are the lands where the Jumblies live;
Their heads are green, and their hands are blue;
　And they went to sea in a sieve.

II

They sailed away in a sieve, they did,
　In a sieve they sailed so fast,
With only a beautiful pea-green veil
Tied with a ribbon by way of a sail,
　To a small tobacco-pipe mast.
And every one said who saw them go,
" Oh! won't they soon be upset, you know?
For the sky is dark and the voyage is long,
And, happen what may, it's extremely wrong
　In a sieve to sail so fast."
　　Far and few, far and few,
　　　Are the lands where the Jumblies live;
　　Their heads are green and their hands are blue;
　　　And they went to sea in a sieve.

III

The water it soon came in, it did;
　The water it soon came in:
So, to keep them dry, they wrapped their feet
In a pinky paper all folded neat;
　And they fastened it down with a pin.
And they passed the night in a crockery-jar;
And each of them said, " How wise we are!
Though the sky be dark, and the voyage be long,
Yet we never can think we were rash or wrong,
　While round in our sieve we spin."
　　Far and few, far and few,
　　　Are the lands where the Jumblies live;
　　Their heads are green and their hands are blue;
　　　And they went to sea in a sieve.

IV

And all night long they sailed away;
   And when the sun went down,
They whistled and warbled a moony song
To the echoing sound of a coppery gong,
   In the shade of the mountains brown.
" O Timballoo! How happy we are
When we live in a sieve and a crockery-jar!
And all night long, in the moonlight pale,
We sail away with a pea-green sail
   In the shade of the mountains brown."
     Far and few, far and few,
       Are the lands where the Jumblies live;
       Their heads are green, and their hands are blue;
       And they went to sea in a sieve.

V

They sailed to the Western Sea, they did,—
   To a land all covered with trees;
And they bought an owl and a useful cart,
And a pound of rice, and a cranberry-tart,
   And a hive of silvery bees;
And they bought a pig, and some green jackdaws,
And a lovely monkey with lollipop paws,
And forty bottles of ring-bo-ree,
   And no end of Stilton cheese.
     Far and few, far and few,
       Are the lands where the Jumblies live;
       Their heads are green, and their hands are blue;
       And they went to sea in a sieve.

VI

And in twenty years they all came back,—
   In twenty years or more;
And every one said, " How tall they've grown!
For they've been to the Lakes, and the Torrible Zone,
   And the hills of the Chankly Bore."
And they drank their health, and gave them a feast
Of dumplings made of beautiful yeast;
And every one said, " If we only live,
We, too, will go to sea in a sieve,

To the hills of the Chankly Bore."
  Far and few, far and few,
    Are the lands where the Jumblies live;
    Their heads are green, and their hands are blue;
      And they went to sea in a sieve.

Edward Lear.

THE POBBLE WHO HAS NO TOES

THE Pobble who has no toes
  Had once as many as we;
When they said, " Some day you may lose them all,"
  He replied, " Fish fiddle de-dee! "
And his Aunt Jobiska made him drink
Lavender water tinged with pink;
For she said, " The World in general knows
There's nothing so good for a Pobble's toes! "

The Pobble who has no toes
  Swam across the Bristol Channel;
But before he set out he wrapped his nose
  In a piece of scarlet flannel.
For his Aunt Jobiska said, " No harm
Can came to his toes if his nose is warm;
And it's perfectly known that a Pobble's toes
Are safe—provided he minds his nose."

The Pobble swam fast and well,
  And when boats or ships came near him,
He tinkledy-binkledy-winkled a bell
  So that all the world could hear him.
And all the Sailors and Admirals cried,
When they saw him nearing the farther side,
" He has gone to fish for his Aunt Jobiska's
Runcible Cat with crimson whiskers! "

But before he touched the shore—
  The shore of the Bristol Channel,
A sea-green Porpoise carried away
  His wrapper of scarlet flannel.

And when he came to observe his feet,
Formerly garnished with toes so neat,
His face at once became forlorn
On perceiving that all his toes were gone!

And nobody ever knew,
　From that dark day to the present,
Whoso had taken the Pobble's toes,
　In a manner so far from pleasant.
Whether the shrimps or crawfish gray,
Or crafty mermaids stole them away,
Nobody knew; and nobody knows
How the Pobble was robbed of his twice five toes!

The Pobble who has no toes
　Was placed in a friendly Bark,
And they rowed him back and carried him up
　To his Aunt Jobiska's Park.
And she made him a feast at his earnest wish,
Of eggs and buttercups fried with fish;
And she said, " It's a fact the whole world knows,
That Pobbles are happier without their toes."

Edward Lear.

THE NEW VESTMENTS

There lived an old man in the kingdom of Tess,
Who invented a purely original dress;
And when it was perfectly made and complete,
He opened the door and walked into the street.

By way of a hat he'd a loaf of Brown Bread,
In the middle of which he inserted his head;
His Shirt was made up of no end of dead Mice,
The warmth of whose skins was quite fluffy and nice;
His Drawers were of Rabbit-skins, so were his Shoes,
His Stockings were skins, but it is not known whose;
His Waistcoat and Trowsers were made of Pork Chops;
His Buttons were Jujubes and Chocolate Drops.

His Coat was all Pancakes with Jam for a border,
And a girdle of Biscuits to keep it in order.
And he wore over all, as a screen from bad weather,
A Cloak of green Cabbage leaves, stitched all together.

He had walked a short way, when he heard a great noise
Of all sorts of Beasticles, Birdlings and Boys;
And from every long street and dark lane in the town
Beasts, Birdles and Boys in a tumult rushed down.
Two Cows and a Calf ate his Cabbage leaf Cloak;
Four Apes seized his girdle which vanished like smoke;
Three Kids ate up half of his Pancaky Coat,
And the tails were devoured by an ancient He Goat.
An army of Dogs in a twinkling tore *up* his
Pork Waistcoat and Trowsers to give to their Puppies;
And while they were growling and mumbling the Chops
Ten Boys prigged the Jujubes and Chocolate Drops.
He tried to run back to his house, but in vain,
For scores of fat Pigs came again and again;
They rushed out of stables and hovels and doors,
They tore off his Stockings, his Shoes and his Drawers.
And now from the housetops with screechings descend
Striped, spotted, white, black and grey Cats without end;
They jumped on his shoulders and knocked off his hat,
When Crows, Ducks and Hens made a mincemeat of that.
They speedily flew at his sleeves in a trice
And utterly tore up his Shirt of dead Mice;
They swallowed the last of his Shirt with a squall,—
Whereon he ran home with no clothes on at all.
And he said to himself as he bolted the door,
" I will not wear a similar dress any more,
Any more, any more, any more, nevermore! "

Edward Lear.

THE TWO OLD BACHELORS

Two old Bachelors were living in one house;
One caught a Muffin, the other caught a Mouse.
Said he who caught the Muffin to him who caught the Mouse,
" This happens just in time, for we've nothing in the house,
Save a tiny slice of lemon and a teaspoonful of honey,
And what to do for dinner,—since we haven't any money?
And what can we expect if we haven't any dinner
But to lose our teeth and eyelashes and keep on growing
    thinner ? "

Said he who caught the Mouse to him who caught the Muffin,
" We might cook this little Mouse if we only had some
    Stuffin' !
If we had but Sage and Onions we could do extremely well,
But how to get that Stuffin' it is difficult to tell ! "

And then those two old Bachelors ran quickly to the town
And asked for Sage and Onions as they wandered up and
    down ;
They borrowed two large Onions, but no Sage was to be
    found
In the Shops or in the Market or in all the Gardens round.

But some one said, " A hill there is, a little to the north,
And to its purpledicular top a narrow way leads forth ;
And there among the rugged rocks abides an ancient Sage,—
An earnest Man, who reads all day a most perplexing page.
Climb up and seize him by the toes,—all studious as he sits,—
And pull him down, and chop him into endless little bits !
Then mix him with your Onion (cut up likewise into scraps),
And your Stuffin' will be ready, and very good—perhaps."

And then those two old Bachelors, without loss of time,
The nearly purpledicular crags at once began to climb ;
And at the top among the rocks, all seated in a nook,
They saw that Sage a-reading of a most enormous book.

"You earnest Sage!" aloud they cried, "your book you've
  read enough in!
We wish to chop you into bits and mix you into Stuffin'!"

But that old Sage looked calmly up, and with his awful book
At those two Bachelors' bald heads a certain aim he took;
And over crag and precipice they rolled promiscuous down,—
At once they rolled, and never stopped in lane or field or
  town;
And when they reached their house, they found (besides their
  want of Stuffin')
The Mouse had fled—and previously had eaten up the Muffin.

They left their home in silence by the once convivial door;
And from that hour those Bachelors were never heard of
  more.

Edward Lear.

JABBERWOCKY

'Twas brillig, and the slithy toves
  Did gyre and gimble in the wabe;
All mimsy were the borogoves,
  And the mome raths outgrabe.

"Beware the Jabberwock, my son!
  The jaws that bite, the claws that catch!
Beware the Jubjub bird, and shun
  The frumious Bandersnatch!"

He took his vorpal sword in hand:
  Long time the manxome foe he sought.
So rested he by the Tumtum tree,
  And stood awhile in thought.

And as in uffish thought he stood,
  The Jabberwock with eyes of flame,
Came whiffling through the tulgey wood,
  And burbled as it came!

One, two! One, two! And through, and through
  The vorpal blade went snicker-snack!
He left it dead, and with its head
  He went galumphing back.

" And hast thou slain the Jabberwock?
  Come to my arms, my beamish boy!
Oh, frabjous day! Callooh! callay!"
  He chortled in his joy.

'Twas brillig, and the slithy toves
  Did gyre and gimble in the wabe;
All mimsy were the borogoves
  And the mome raths outgrabe.

Lewis Carroll.

WAYS AND MEANS

I'LL tell thee everything I can;
  There's little to relate.
I saw an aged aged man,
  A-sitting on a gate.
" Who are you, aged man?" I said,
  " And how is it you live?"
His answer trickled through my head
  Like water through a sieve.

He said, " I look for butterflies
  That sleep among the wheat:
I make them into mutton-pies,
  And sell them in the street.
I sell them unto men," he said,
  " Who sail on stormy seas;
And that's the way I get my bread—
  A trifle, if you please."

But I was thinking of a plan
  To dye one's whiskers green,
And always use so large a fan
  That they could not be seen.

So, having no reply to give
  To what the old man said,
I cried, " Come, tell me how you live! "
  And thumped him on the head.

His accents mild took up the tale;
  He said, " I go my ways
And when I find a mountain-rill
  I set it in a blaze;
And thence they make a stuff they call
  Rowland's Macassar Oil—
Yet twopence-halfpenny is all
  They give me for my toil."

But I was thinking of a way
  To feed oneself on batter,
And so go on from day to day
  Getting a little fatter.
I shook him well from side to side,
  Until his face was blue;
" Come, tell me how you live," I cried,
  " And what it is you do! "

He said, " I hunt for haddock's eyes
  Among the heather bright,
And work them into waistcoat-buttons
  In the silent night.
And these I do not sell for gold
  Or coin of silvery shine,
But for a copper halfpenny
  And that will purchase nine.

" I sometimes dig for buttered rolls,
  Or set limed twigs for crabs;
I sometimes search the grassy knolls
  For wheels of Hansom cabs.
And that's the way " (he gave a wink)
  " By which I get my wealth—
And very gladly will I drink
  Your Honor's noble health."

I heard him then, for I had just
   Completed my design
To keep the Menai Bridge from rust
   By boiling it in wine.
I thanked him much for telling me
   The way he got his wealth,
But chiefly for his wish that he
   Might drink my noble health.

And now if e'er by chance I put
   My fingers into glue,
Or madly squeeze a right-hand foot
   Into a left-hand shoe,
Or if I drop upon my toe
   A very heavy weight,
I weep, for it reminds me so
Of that old man I used to know—
Whose look was mild, whose speech was slow,
Whose hair was whiter than the snow,
Whose face was very like a crow,
With eyes, like cinders, all aglow,
Who seemed distracted with his woe,
Who rocked his body to and fro,
And muttered mumblingly, and low,
As if his mouth were full of dough,
Who snorted like a buffalo—
That summer evening, long ago,
   A-sitting on a gate.

Lewis Carroll.

HUMPTY DUMPTY'S RECITATION

" In winter, when the fields are white,
I sing this song for your delight——

" In spring, when woods are getting green,
I'll try and tell you what I mean: "

" In summer, when the days are long,
Perhaps you'll understand the song:

In autumn, when the leaves are brown,
Take pen and ink, and write it down."

" I sent a message to the fish:
I told them ' This is what I wish.'

The little fishes of the sea,
They sent an answer back to me.

The little fishes' answer was,
' We cannot do it, Sir, because——' "

" I sent to them again to say
' It will be better to obey.'

The fishes answered, with a grin,
' Why, what a temper you are in!'

I told them once, I told them twice:
They would not listen to advice.

I took a kettle large and new,
Fit for the deed I had to do.

My heart went hop, my heart went thump:
I filled the kettle at the pump.

Then some one came to me and said,
' The little fishes are in bed.'

I said to him, I said it plain,
' Then you must wake them up again.'

I said it very loud and clear:
I went and shouted in his ear.

But he was very stiff and proud:
He said, ' You needn't shout so loud!'

And he was very proud and stiff:
He said, ' I'd go and wake them, if——'

I took a corkscrew from the shelf:
I went to wake them up myself.

And when I found the door was locked,
I pulled and pushed and kicked and knocked.

And when I found the door was shut,
I tried to turn the handle, but——"

Lewis Carroll.

SOME HALLUCINATIONS

He thought he saw an Elephant,
   That practised on a fife:
He looked again, and found it was
   A letter from his wife.
" At length I realise," he said,
   " The bitterness of Life!"

He thought he saw a Buffalo
   Upon the chimney-piece:
He looked again, and found it was
   His Sister's Husband's Niece.
" Unless you leave this house," he said,
   " I'll send for the Police!"

He thought he saw a Rattlesnake
   That questioned him in Greek:
He looked again, and found it was
   The Middle of Next Week.
" The one thing I regret," he said,
   " Is that it cannot speak!"

He thought he saw a Banker's Clerk
   Descending from the 'bus:
He looked again, and found it was
   A Hippopotamus:
" If this should stay to dine," he said,
   " There won't be much for us!"

He thought he saw an Albatross
  That fluttered round the lamp:
He looked again, and found it was
  A Penny-Postage-Stamp.
" You'd best be getting home," he said;
  " The nights are very damp! "

He thought he saw a Coach-and-Four
  That stood beside his bed:
He looked again, and found it was
  A Bear without a Head.
"Poor thing," he said, " poor silly thing!
  It's waiting to be fed! "

He thought he saw a Kangaroo
  That worked a coffee-mill:
He looked again, and found it was
  A Vegetable-Pill.
" Were I to swallow this," he said,
  " I should be very ill! "

                              Lewis Carroll.

SING FOR THE GARISH EYE

SING for the garish eye,
  When moonless brandlings cling!
Let the froddering crooner cry,
  And the braddled sapster sing.
For never, and never again,
  Will the tottering beechlings play,
For bratticed wrackers are singing aloud,
  And the throngers croon in May!

The wracking globe unstrung,
  Unstrung in the frittering light
Of a moon that knows no day,
  Of a day that knows no night!
Diving away in the crowd
  Of sparkling frets in spray,
The bratticed wrackers are singing aloud,
  And the throngers croon in May!

Hasten, O hapful blue,
　Blue, of the shimmering brow,
Hasten the deed to do
That shall roddle the welkin now!
For never again shall a cloud
　Out-thribble the babbling day,
When bratticed wrackers are singing aloud,
　And the throngers croon in May!

W. S. Gilbert.

THE SHIPWRECK

Upon the poop the captain stands,
　As starboard as may be;
And pipes on deck the topsail hands
To reef the topsail-gallant strands
　Across the briny sea.

" Ho! splice the anchor under-weigh! "
　The captain loudly cried;
" Ho! lubbers brave, belay! belay!
For we must luff for Falmouth Bay
　Before to-morrow's tide."

The good ship was a racing yawl,
　A spare-rigged schooner sloop,
Athwart the bows the taffrails all
In grummets gay appeared to fall,
　To deck the mainsaïl poop.

But ere they made the Foreland Light,
　And Deal was left behind,
The wind it blew great gales that night,
And blew the doughty captain tight,
　Full three sheets in the wind.

And right across the tiller head
　The horse it ran apace,
Whereon a traveller hitched and sped
Along the jib and vanished
　To heave the trysail brace.

What ship could live in such a sea?
  What vessel bear the shock?
" Ho! starboard port your helm-a-lee!
Ho! reef the maintop-gallant-tree,
  With many a running block!"

And right upon the Scilly Isles
  The ship had run aground;
When lo! the stalwart Captain Giles
Mounts up upon the gaff and smiles,
  And slews the compass round.

" Saved! saved!" with joy the sailors cry,
  And scandalize the skiff;
As taut and hoisted high and dry
They see the ship unstoppered lie
  Upon the sea-girt cliff.

And since that day in Falmouth Bay,
  As herring-fishers trawl,
The younkers hear the boatswains say
How Captain Giles that awful day
  Preserved the sinking yawl.

                              E. H. Palmer.

UFFIA

WHEN sporgles spanned the floreate mead
  And cogwogs gleet upon the lea,
Uffia gopped to meet her love
  Who smeeged upon the equat sea.

Dately she walked aglost the sand;
  The boreal wind seet in her face;
The moggling waves yalped at her feet;
  Pangwangling was her pace.

                              Harriet R. White.

'TIS SWEET TO ROAM

'TIS sweet to roam when morning's light
   Resounds across the deep;
And the crystal song of the woodbine bright
   Hushes the rocks to sleep,
And the blood-red moon in the blaze of noon
   Is bathed in a crumbling dew,
And the wolf rings out with a glittering shout,
   To-whit, to-whit, to-whoo!

Unknown.

THREE JOVIAL HUNTSMEN

THERE were three jovial huntsmen,
   As I have heard them say,
And they would go a-hunting
   All on a summer's day.

All the day they hunted,
   And nothing could they find
But a ship a-sailing,
   A-sailing with the wind.

One said it was a ship,
   The other said Nay;
The third said it was a house
   With the chimney blown away.

And all the night they hunted,
   And nothing could they find;
But the moon a-gliding,
   A-gliding with the wind.

One said it was the moon,
   The other said Nay;
The third said it was a cheese,
   And half o't cut away.

Unknown.

KING ARTHUR

WHEN good King Arthur ruled the land,
    He was a goodly king:
He stole three pecks of barley meal,
    To make a bag-pudding.

A bag-pudding the king did make,
    And stuffed it well with plums;
And in it put great lumps of fat,
    As big as my two thumbs.

The king and queen did eat thereof,
    And noblemen beside;
And what they could not eat that night,
    The queen next morning fried.

Unknown.

HYDER IDDLE

HYDER iddle diddle dell,
A yard of pudding is not an ell;
Not forgetting tweedle-dye,
A tailor's goose will never fly.

Unknown.

THE OCEAN WANDERER

BRIGHT breaks the warrior o'er the ocean wave
Through realms that rove not, clouds that cannot save,
Sinks in the sunshine; dazzles o'er the tomb
And mocks the mutiny of Memory's gloom.
Oh! who can feel the crimson ecstasy
That soothes with bickering jar the Glorious Tree?
O'er the high rock the foam of gladness throws,
While star-beams lull Vesuvius to repose:
Girds the white spray, and in the blue lagoon,
Weeps like a walrus o'er the waning moon?

Who can declare?—not thou, pervading boy
Whom pibrochs pierce not, crystals cannot cloy;—
Not thou soft Architect of silvery gleams,
Whose soul would simmer in Hesperian streams,
Th' exhaustless fire—the bosom's azure bliss,
That hurtles, life-like, o'er a scene like this;—
Defies the distant agony of Day—
And sweeps o'er hecatombs—away! away!
Say shall Destruction's lava load the gale,
The furnace quiver and the mountain quail?
Say shall the son of Sympathy pretend
His cedar fragrance with our Chief's to blend?
There, where the gnarled monuments of sand
Howl their dark whirlwinds to the levin brand;
Conclusive tenderness; fraternal grog,
Tidy conjunction; adamantine bog,
Impetuous arrant toadstool; Thundering quince,
Repentant dog-star, inessential Prince,
Expound. Pre-Adamite eventful gun,
Crush retribution, currant-jelly, pun,
Oh! eligible Darkness, fender, sting,
Heav'n-born Insanity, courageous thing.
Intending, bending, scouring, piercing all,
Death like pomatum, tea, and crabs must fall.

Unknown.

SCIENTIFIC PROOF

If we square a lump of pemmican
    And cube a pot of tea,
Divide a musk ox by the span
    From noon to half-past three;
If we calculate the Eskimo
    By solar parallax,
Divide the sextant by a floe
    And multiply the cracks
By nth-powered igloos, we may prove
    All correlated facts.

If we prolongate the parallel
 Indefinitely forth,
And cube a sledge till we can tell
 The real square root of North;
Bisect a seal and bifurcate
 The tangent with a pack
Of Polar ice, we get the rate
 Along the Polar track,
And proof of corollary things
 Which otherwise we lack.

If we multiply the Arctic night
 By X times ox times moose,
And build an igloo on the site
 Of its hypotenuse;
If we circumscribe an arc about
 An Arctic dog and weigh
A segment of it, every doubt
 Is made as clear as day.
We also get the price of ice
 F. O. B. Baffin's Bay.

If we amplify the Arctic breeze
 By logarithmic signs,·
And run through the isosceles
 Imaginary lines,
We find that twice the half of one
 Is equal to the whole.
Which, when the calculus is done,
 Quite demonstrates the Pole.
It also gives its length and breadth
 And what's the price of coal.

J. W. Foley.

THE THINGUMBOB

A PASTEL

The Thingumbob sat at eventide,
  On the shore of a shoreless sea,
Expecting an unexpected attack
  From something it could not foresee.

A still calm rests on the angry waves,
  The low wind whistles a mournful tune,
And the Thingumbob sighs to himself, " Alas,
  I've had no supper now since noon."

Unknown.

WONDERS OF NATURE

Ah! who has seen the mailèd lobster rise,
Clap her broad wings, and, soaring, claim the skies?
When did the owl, descending from her bower,
Crop, 'midst the fleecy flocks, the tender flower;
Or the young heifer plunge, with pliant limb,
In the salt wave, and, fish-like, try to swim?
The same with plants, potatoes 'tatoes breed,
The costly cabbage springs from cabbage-seed;
Lettuce to lettuce, leeks to leeks succeed;
Nor e'er did cooling cucumbers presume
To flower like myrtle, or like violets bloom.

The Anti-Jacobin.

LINES BY AN OLD FOGY

I'm thankful that the sun and moon
  Are both hung up so high,
That no presumptuous hand can stretch
  And pull them from the sky.

If they were not, I have no doubt
But some reforming ass
Would recommend to take them down
And light the world with gas.

Unknown.

A COUNTRY SUMMER PASTORAL

As written by a learned scholar of the city from knowledge
derived from etymological deductions rather than from
actual experience.

I WOULD flee from the city's rule and law,
    From its fashion and form cut loose,
And go where the strawberry grows on its straw,
    And the gooseberry on its goose;
Where the catnip tree is climbed by the cat
    As she crouches for her prey—
The guileless and unsuspecting rat
    On the rattan bush at play.

I will watch at ease for the saffron cow
    And the cowlet in their glee,
As they leap in joy from bough to bough
    On the top of the cowslip tree;
Where the musical partridge drums on his drum,
And the dog devours the dogwood plum
    And the wood chuck chucks his wood,
    In the primitive solitude.

And then to the whitewashed dairy I'll turn,
    Where the dairymaid hastening hies,
Her ruddy and golden-haired butter to churn
    From the milk of her butterflies;
And I'll rise at morn with the early bird,
    To the fragrant farm-yard pass,
When the farmer turns his beautiful herd
    Of grasshoppers out to grass.

Unknown.

TURVEY TOP

'Twas after a supper of Norfolk brawn
    That into a doze I chanced to drop,
And thence awoke in the grey of dawn,
    In the wonder-land of Turvey Top.

A land so strange I never had seen,
    And could not choose but look and laugh—
A land where the small the great includes,
    And the whole is less than the half!

A land where the circles were not lines
    Round central points, as schoolmen show,
And the parallels met whenever they chose,
    And went playing at touch-and-go!

There—except that every round was square,
    And save that all the squares were rounds—
No surface had limits anywhere,
    So they never could beat the bounds.

In their gardens, fruit before blossom came,
    And the trees diminished as they grew;
And you never went out to walk a mile,
    It was the mile that walked to you.

The people there are not tall or short,
    Heavy or light, or stout or thin,
And their lives begin where they should leave off,
    Or leave off where they should begin.

There childhood, with naught of childish glee,
    Looks on the world with thoughtful brow;
'Tis only the aged who laugh and crow,
    And cry " We have done with it now!"

A singular race! what lives they spent!
    Got up before they went to bed!

And never a man said what he meant,
  Or a woman meant what she said.

They blended colours that will not blend,
  All hideous contrasts voted sweet;
In yellow and red their Quakers dress'd,
  And considered it rather neat.

They didn't believe in the wise and good,
  Said the best were worst, the wisest fools;
And 'twas only to have their teachers taught
  That they founded national schools.

They read in "books that are no books,"
  Their classics—chess-boards neatly bound;
Those their greatest authors who never wrote,
  And their deepest the least profound.

Now, such were the folks of that wonder-land,
  A curious people, as you will own;
But are there none of the race abroad,
  Are no specimens elsewhere known?

Well, I think that he whose views of life
  Are crooked, wrong, perverse, and odd,
Who looks upon all with jaundiced eyes—
  Sees himself and believes it God,

Who sneers at the good, and makes the ill,
  Curses a world he cannot mend;
Who measures life by the rule of wrong
  And abuses its aim and end,

The man who stays when he ought to move,
  And only goes when he ought to stop—
Is strangely like the folk in my dream,
  And would flourish in Turvey Top.

William Sawyer.

A BALLAD OF BEDLAM

O LADY wake!—the azure moon
　Is rippling in the verdant skies,
The owl is warbling his soft tune,
　Awaiting but thy snowy eyes.
The joys of future years are past,
　To-morrow's hopes have fled away;
Still let us love, and e'en at last,
　We shall be happy yesterday.

The early beam of rosy night
　Drives off the ebon morn afar,
While through the murmur of the light
　The huntsman winds his mad guitar.
Then, lady, wake! my brigantine
　Pants, neighs, and prances to be free;
Till the creation I am thine.
　To some rich desert fly with me.

Unknown.

XIV

NATURAL HISTORY

THE FASTIDIOUS SERPENT

THERE was a snake that dwelt in Skye,
  Over the misty sea, oh;
He lived upon nothing but gooseberry pie
  For breakfast, dinner and tea, oh.

Now gooseberry pie—as is very well known,—
  Over the misty sea, oh,
Is not to be found under every stone,
  Nor yet upon every tree, oh.

And being so ill to please with his meat,
  Over the misty sea, oh;
The snake had sometimes nothing to eat,
  And an angry snake was he, oh.

Then he'd flick his tongue and his head he'd shake,
  Over the misty sea, oh,
Crying, "Gooseberry pie! For goodness' sake,
  Some gooseberry pie for me, oh."

And if gooseberry pie was not to be had,
  Over the misty sea, oh,
He'd twine and twist like an eel gone mad,
  Or a worm just stung by a bee, oh.

But though he might shout and wriggle about,
  Over the misty sea, oh,
The snake had often to go without
  His breakfast, dinner and tea, oh.

Henry Johnstone.

THE LEGEND OF THE FIRST CAM-U-EL

AN ARABIAN APOLOGUE

Across the sands of Syria,
Or, possibly, Algeria,
Or some benighted neighbourhood of barrenness and drouth,
There came the Prophet Sam-u-el
Upon the Only Cam-u-el—
A bumpy, grumpy Quadruped of discontented mouth.

The atmosphere was glutinous;
The Cam-u-el was mutinous;
He dumped the pack from off his back; with horrid grunts
and squeals
He made the desert hideous;
With strategy perfidious
He tied his neck in curlicues, he kicked his paddy heels.

Then quoth the gentle Sam-u-el,
" You rogue, I ought to lam you well!
Though zealously I've shielded you from every grief and
woe,
It seems, to voice a platitude,
You haven't any gratitude.
I'd like to hear what cause you have for doing thus and so! "

To him replied the Cam-u-el,
" I beg your pardon, Sam-u-el.
I know that I'm a Reprobate, I know that I'm a Freak;
But, oh! this utter loneliness!
My too-distinguished Onliness!
Were there but other Cam-u-els I wouldn't be Unique."

The Prophet beamed beguilingly.
" Aha," he answered, smilingly,
" You feel the need of company? I clearly understand.
We'll speedily create for you
The corresponding mate for you—
Ho! presto, change-o, dinglebat! "—he waved a potent hand,

And, lo! from out Vacuity
    A second Incongruity,
To wit, a Lady Cam-u-el was born through magic art.
    Her structure anatomical,
    Her form and face were comical;
She was, in short, a Cam-u-el, the other's counterpart.

    As Spaniards gaze on Aragon,
    Upon that Female Paragon
So gazed the Prophet's Cam-u-el, that primal Desert Ship.
    A connoisseur meticulous,
    He found her that ridiculous
He grinned from ear to auricle *until he split his lip!*

    Because of his temerity
    That Cam-u-el's posterity
Must wear divided upper lips through all their solemn lives!
    A prodigy astonishing
    Reproachfully admonishing
Those, wicked, heartless married men who ridicule their
    wives.

Arthur Guiterman.

UNSATISFIED YEARNING

    Down in the silent hallway
      Scampers the dog about,
    And whines, and barks, and scratches,
      In order to get out.

    Once in the glittering starlight,
      He straightway doth begin
    To set up a doleful howling
      In order to get in.

R. K. Munkittrick.

KINDLY ADVICE

BE kind to the panther! for when thou wert young,
    In thy country far over the sea,
'Twas a panther ate up thy papa and mama,
    And had several mouthfuls of thee!

Be kind to the badger! for who shall decide
    The depth of his badgery soul?
And think of the tapir, when flashes the lamp
    O'er the fast and the free flowing bowl.

Be kind to the camel! nor let word of thine
    Ever put up his bactrian back;
And cherish the she-kangaroo with her bag,
    Nor venture to give her the sack.

Be kind to the ostrich! for how canst thou hope
    To have such a stomach as it?
And when the proud day of your "bridal" shall come,
    Do give the poor birdie a "bit."

Be kind to the walrus! nor ever forget
    To have it on Tuesday to tea;
But butter the crumpets on only one side,
    Save such as are eaten by thee.

Be kind to the bison! and let the jackal
    In the light of thy love have a share;
And coax the ichneumon to grow a new tail,
    And have lots of larks in its lair!

Be kind to the bustard, that genial bird,
    And humour its wishes and ways;
And when the poor elephant suffers from bile,
    Then tenderly lace up his stays!

Unknown.

KINDNESS TO ANIMALS

SPEAK gently to the herring and kindly to the calf,
Be blithesome with the bunny, at barnacles don't laugh!
Give nuts unto the monkey, and buns unto the bear,
Ne'er hint at currant jelly if you chance to see a hare!
Oh, little girls, pray hide your combs when tortoises draw
    nigh,
And never in the hearing of a pigeon whisper Pie!
But give the stranded jelly-fish a shove into the sea,—
Be always kind to animals wherever you may be!

Oh, make not game of sparrows, nor faces at the ram,
And ne'er allude to mint sauce when calling on a lamb.
Don't beard the thoughtful oyster, don't dare the cod to
    crimp,
Don't cheat the pike, or ever try to pot the playful shrimp.
Tread lightly on the turning worm, don't bruise the butter-
    fly,
Don't ridicule the wry-neck, nor sneer at salmon-fry;
Oh, ne'er delight to make dogs fight, nor bantams disagree,—
Be always kind to animals wherever you may be!

Be lenient with lobsters, and ever kind to crabs,
And be not disrespectful to cuttle-fish or dabs;
Chase not the Cochin-China, chaff not the ox obese,
And babble not of feather-beds in company with geese.
Be tender with the tadpole, and let the limpet thrive,
Be merciful to mussels, don't skin your eels alive;
When talking to a turtle don't mention calipee—
Be always kind to animals wherever you may be.

                                        J. Ashby-Sterry.

TO BE OR NOT TO BE

I

I SOMETIMES think I'd rather crow
And be a rooster than to roost
And be a crow. But I dunno.

II

A rooster he can roost also,
Which don't seem fair when crows can't crow.
Which may help some. Still I dunno.

III

Crows should be glad of one thing, though;
Nobody thinks of eating crow,
While roosters they are good enough
For anyone unless they're tough.

IV

There are lots of tough old roosters, though,
And anyway a crow can't crow,
So mebby roosters stand more show.
It looks that way. But I dunno.

Unknown.

THE HEN

Was once a hen of wit not small
   (In fact, 'twas not amazing),
And apt at laying eggs withal,
Who, when she'd done, would scream and bawl,
   As if the house were blazing.
A turkey-cock, of age mature,
   Felt thereat indignation;
'Twas quite improper, he was sure—
He would no more the thing endure;
   So, after cogitation,
He to the lady straight repaired,
And thus his business he declared:
   "Madam, pray, what's the matter,
That always, when you've laid an egg,
   You make so great a clatter?
I wish you'd do the thing in quiet.
Do be advised by me, and try it."

"Advised by you!" the lady cried,
And tossed her head with proper pride;
"And what do you know, now I pray,
Of the fashion of the present day,
You creature ignorant and low?
However, if you want to know,
This is the reason why I do it:
I lay my egg, and then review it!"

Matthew Claudius.

OF BAITING THE LION

REMEMBERING his taste for blood
  You'd better bait him with a cow;
Persuade the brute to chew the cud
  Her tail suspended from a bough;
It thrills the lion through and through
  To hear the milky creature moo.

Having arranged this simple ruse,
  Yourself you climb a neighboring tree;
See to it that the spot you choose
  Commands the coming tragedy;
Take up a smallish Maxim gun,
  A search-light, whisky, and a bun.

It's safer, too, to have your bike
  Standing immediately below,
In case your piece should fail to strike,
  Or deal an ineffective blow;
The Lion moves with perfect grace,
  But cannot go the scorcher's pace.

Keep open ear for subtle signs;
  Thus, when the cow profusely moans,
That means to say, the Lion dines.
  The crunching sound, of course, is bones;
Silence resumes her ancient reign—
  This shows the cow is out of pain.

But when a fat and torpid hum
    Escapes the eater's unctuous nose,
Turn up the light and let it come
    Full on his innocent repose;
Then pour your shot between his eyes,
    And go on pouring till he dies.

Play, even so, discretion's part;
    Descend with stealth; bring on your gun;
Then lay your hand above his heart
    To see if he is really done;
Don't skin him till you know he's dead
    Or you may perish in his stead!

Years hence, at home, when talk is tall,
    You'll set the gun-room wide agape,
Describing how with just a small
    Pea-rifle, going after ape
You met a Lion unaware,
    And felled him flying through the air.

Owen Seaman.

THE FLAMINGO

Inspired by reading a chorus of spirits in a German play

FIRST VOICE

Oh! tell me have you ever seen a red, long-leg'd Flamingo?
Oh! tell me have you ever yet seen him the water in go?

SECOND VOICE

Oh! yes at Bowling-Green I've seen a red long-leg'd Flamingo,
Oh! yes at Bowling-Green I've there seen him the water in go.

FIRST VOICE

Oh! tell me did you ever see a bird so funny stand-o
When forth he from the water comes and gets upon the land-o?

SECOND VOICE

No! in my life I ne'er did see a bird so funny stand-o
When forth he from the water comes and gets upon the
land-o.

FIRST VOICE

He has a leg some three feet long, or near it, so they say,
Sir.
Stiff upon one alone he stands, t'other he stows away, Sir.

SECOND VOICE

And what an ugly head he's got! I wonder that he'd
wear it.
But rather *more* I wonder that his long, thin neck can
bear it.

FIRST VOICE

And think, this length of neck and legs (no doubt they
have their uses)
Are members of a little frame, much smaller than a goose's!

BOTH

Oh! isn't he a curious bird, that red, long-leg'd Flamingo?
A water bird, a gawky bird, a sing'lar bird, by jingo!

Lewis Gaylord Clark.

WHY DOTH A PUSSY CAT?

Why doth a pussy cat prefer,
  When dozing, drowsy, on the sill,
To purr and purr and purr and purr
  Instead of merely keeping still?
With nodding head and folded paws,
She keeps it up without a cause.

Why doth she flaunt her lofty tail
   In such a stiff right-angled pose?
If lax and limp she let it trail
   'Twould seem more restful, Goodness knows!
When strolling 'neath the chairs or bed,
She lets it bump above her head.

Why doth she suddenly refrain
   From anything she's busied in
And start to wash, with might and main,
   Most any place upon her skin?
Why doth she pick that special spot,
Not seeing if it's soiled or not?

Why doth she never seem to care
   To come directly when you call,
But makes approach from here and there,
   Or sidles half around the wall?
Though doors are opened at her mew,
You often have to push her through.

Why doth she this? Why doth she that?
   I seek for cause—I yearn for clews;
The subject of the pussy cat
   Doth endlessly inspire the mews.
Why doth a pussy cat? Ah, me,
I haven't got the least idee.

Burges Johnson.

THE WALRUS AND THE CARPENTER

THE sun was shining on the sea,
   Shining with all his might:
He did his very best to make
   The billows smooth and bright—
And this was odd, because it was
   The middle of the night.

The moon was shining sulkily,
  Because she thought the sun
Had got no business to be there
  After the day was done—
" It's very rude of him," she said,
  " To come and spoil the fun! "

The sea was wet as wet could be,
  The sands were dry as dry.
You could not see a cloud, because
  No cloud was in the sky:
No birds were flying overhead—
  There were no birds to fly.

The Walrus and the Carpenter
  Were walking close at hand;
They wept like anything to see
  Such quantities of sand:
" If this were only cleared away,"
  They said, " it would be grand! "

" If seven maids with seven mops
  Swept it for half a year,
Do you suppose," the Walrus said,
  " That they could get it clear? "
" I doubt it," said the Carpenter,
  And shed a bitter tear.

" O Oysters come and walk with us! "
  The Walrus did beseech.
" A pleasant walk, a pleasant talk,
  Along the briny beach:
We cannot do with more than four,
  To give a hand to each."

The eldest Oyster looked at him,
  But not a word he said:
The eldest Oyster winked his eye,
  And shook his heavy head—
Meaning to say he did not choose
  To leave the oyster-bed.

But four young Oysters hurried up,
  All eager for the treat:
Their coats were brushed, their faces washed,
  Their shoes were clean and neat—
And this was odd, because, you know,
  They hadn't any feet.

Four other Oysters followed them,
  And yet another four;
And thick and fast they came at last,
  And more, and more, and more—
All hopping through the frothy waves,
  And scrambling to the shore.

The Walrus and the Carpenter
  Walked on a mile or so,
And then they rested on a rock
  Conveniently low:
And all the little Oysters stood
  And waited in a row.

"The time has come," the Walrus said,
  "To talk of many things:
Of shoes—and ships—and sealing-wax—
  Of cabbages—and kings—
And why the sea is boiling hot—
  And whether pigs have wings."

"But wait a bit," the Oysters cried,
  "Before we have our chat;
For some of us are out of breath,
  And all of us are fat!"
"No hurry!" said the Carpenter.
  They thanked him much for that.

"A loaf of bread," the Walrus said,
  "Is what we chiefly need;
Pepper and vinegar besides
  Are very good indeed—
Now, if you're ready, Oysters dear,
  We can begin to feed."

"But not on us," the Oysters cried,
  Turning a little blue.
"After such kindness that would be
  A dismal thing to do!"
"The night is fine," the Walrus said,
  "Do you admire the view?"

"It was so kind of you to come,
  And you are very nice!"
The Carpenter said nothing but,
  "Cut us another slice.
I wish you were not quite so deaf—
  I've had to ask you twice!"

"It seems a shame," the Walrus said,
  "To play them such a trick.
After we've brought them out so far
  And made them trot so quick!"
The Carpenter said nothing but,
  "The butter's spread too thick!"

"I weep for you," the Walrus said,
  "I deeply sympathize."
With sobs and tears he sorted out
  Those of the largest size,
Holding his pocket-handkerchief
  Before his streaming eyes.

"O Oysters," said the Carpenter,
  "You've had a pleasant run!
Shall we be trotting home again?"
  But answer came there none—
And this was scarcely odd, because
  They'd eaten every one.

                              Lewis Carroll.

NIRVANA

I AM
 A Clam!
Come learn of me
Unclouded peace and calm content,
 Serene, supreme tranquillity,
Where thoughtless dreams and dreamless thoughts are
   blent.

When the salt tide is rising to the flood,
 In billows blue my placid pulp I lave;
And when it ebbs I slumber in the mud,
 Content alike with ooze or crystal wave.

I do not shudder when in chowder stewed,
 Nor when the Coney Islander engulfs me raw.
When in the church soup's dreary solitude
 Alone I wander, do I shudder? Naw!

If jarring tempests beat upon my bed,
 Or summer peace there be,
I do not care: as I have said,
 All's one to me;
  A Clam
  I am.

         Unknown.

THE CATFISH

The saddest fish that swims the briny ocean,
 The Catfish I bewail.
I cannot even think without emotion
 Of his distressful tail.
When with my pencil once I tried to draw one,
 (I dare not show it here)
Mayhap it is because I never saw one,
 The picture looked so queer.

I vision him half feline and half fishy,
　A paradox in twins,
Unmixable as vitriol and vichy—
　A thing of fur and fins.
A feline Tantalus, forever chasing
　His fishy self to rend;
His finny self forever self-effacing
　In circles without end.
This tale may have a Moral running through it
　As Æsop had in his;
If so, dear reader, you are welcome to it,
　If you know what it is!

Oliver Herford.

WAR RELIEF

" Can you spare a Threepenny bit,
　Dear Miss Turkey," said Sir Mouse,
" For Job's Turkey's benefit?
　I've engaged the Opera House! "

" Alas! I've naught to spare! "
　Said Miss Turkey, " save advice,
I am getting up a Fair,
　To relieve the Poor Church Mice."

Oliver Herford.

THE OWL AND THE PUSSY-CAT

The Owl and the Pussy-Cat went to sea
　In a beautiful pea-green boat:
They took some honey, and plenty of money
　Wrapped up in a five-pound note.
The Owl looked up to the stars above,
　And sang to a small guitar,
" Oh, lovely Pussy, oh, Pussy, my love,
　What a beautiful Pussy you are,
　　　　You are,
　　　　You are!
What a beautiful Pussy you are! "

Pussy said to the Owl, "You elegant fowl,
　How charmingly sweet you sing!
Oh, let us be married; too long we have tarried:
　But what shall we do for a ring?"
They sailed away for a year and a day,
　To the land where the bong-tree grows;
And there in the wood a Piggy-wig stood,
　　With a ring at the end of his nose,
　　　　His nose,
　　　　His nose,
　　With a ring at the end of his nose.

"Dear Pig, are you willing to sell for one shilling
　Your ring?" Said the Piggy, "I will."
So they took it away and were married next day
　By the Turkey who lives on the hill.
They dined on mince and slices of quince,
　Which they ate with a runcible spoon;
And hand in hand, on the edge of the sand,
　　They danced by the light of the moon,
　　　　The moon,
　　　　The moon,
　　They danced by the light of the moon.

Edward Lear.

MEXICAN SERENADE

When the little armadillo
With his head upon his pillow
　　Sweetly rests,
And the parrakeet and lindo
Flitting past my cabin window
　　Seek their nests,—

When the mists of even settle
Over Popocatapetl,
　　Dropping dew,—
Like the condor, over yonder,
Still I ponder, ever fonder,
　　Dear, of You!

May no revolution shock you,
May the earthquake gently rock you
    To repose,
While the sentimental panthers
Sniff the pollen-laden anthers
    Of the rose!

While the pelican is pining,
While the moon is softly shining
    On the stream,
May the song that I am singing
Send a tender cadence winging
    Through your dream!

I have just one wish to utter—
That you twinkle through your shutter
    Like a star,
While, according to convention,
I shall cas-u-ally mention
    My guitar.

Señorita Maraquita,
Muy bonita, pobracita!—
    Hear me weep!—
But the night is growing wetter,
So I guess that you had better
    Go to sleep.

          Arthur Guiterman.

ORPHAN BORN

I AM a lone, unfathered chick,
    Of artificial hatching,
A pilgrim in a desert wild,
By happier, mothered chicks reviled,
From all relationships exiled,
    To do my own lone scratching.

Fair science smiled upon my birth
One raw and gusty morning;
But ah, the sounds of barnyard mirth
To lonely me have little worth;
Alone am I in all the earth—
An orphan without borning.

Seek I my mother? I would find
A heartless personator;
A thing brass-feathered, man-designed,
With steam-pipe arteries intermined,
And pulseless cotton-batting lined—
A patent incubator.

It wearies me to think, you see—
Death would be better, rather—
Should downy chicks be hatched of me,
By fate's most pitiless decree,
My piping pullets still would be
With never a grandfather.

And when to earth I bid adieu
To seek a planet greater,
I will not do as others do,
Who fly to join the ancestral crew,
For I will just be gathered to
My incubator.

Robert J. Burdette.

DIVIDED DESTINIES

It was an artless Bandar, and he danced upon a pine,
And much I wondered how he lived, and where the beast
might dine,
And many, many other things, till, o'er my morning smoke,
I slept the sleep of idleness and dreamed that Bandar spoke.

He said: "Oh, man of many clothes! sad crawler on the
    Hills!
Observe, I know not Ranken's shop, nor Ranken's monthly
    bills!
I take no heed to trousers or the coats that you call dress;
Nor am I plagued with little cards for little drinks at Mess.

"I steal the bunnia's grain at morn, at noon and eventide
(For he is fat and I am spare), I roam the mountainside,
I follow no man's carriage, and no, never in my life
Have I flirted at Peliti's with another Bandar's wife.

"Oh, man of futile fopperies—unnecessary wraps;
I own no ponies in the Hills, I drive no tall-wheeled traps;
I buy me not twelve-button gloves, 'short-sixes' eke, or
    rings,
Nor do I waste at Hamilton's my wealth on pretty things.

"I quarrel with my wife at home, we never fight abroad;
But Mrs. B. has grasped the fact I am her only lord.
I never heard of fever—dumps nor debts depress my soul;
And I pity and despise you!" Here he pouched my break-
    fast-roll.

His hide was very mangy and his face was very red,
And undisguisedly he scratched with energy his head.
His manners were not always nice, but how my spirit cried
To be an artless Bandar loose upon the mountainside!

So I answered: "Gentle Bandar, an inscrutable Decree
Makes thee a gleesome, fleasome Thou, and me a wretched
    Me.
Go! Depart in peace, my brother, to thy home amid the
    pine;
Yet forget not once a mortal wished to change his lot with
    thine."

Rudyard Kipling.

THE VIPER

YET another great truth I record in my verse,
That some Vipers are venomous, some the reverse;
    A fact you may prove if you try,
By procuring two Vipers and letting them bite;
With the first you are only the worse for a fright,
    But after the second you die.

Hilaire Belloc.

THE LLAMA

THE Llama is a woolly sort of fleecy, hairy goat,
With an indolent expression and an undulating throat,
    Like an unsuccessful literary man.
And I know the place he lives in (or at least I think I do)
It is Ecuador, Brazil or Chile—possibly Peru;
    You must find it in the Atlas if you can.

The Llama of the Pampases you never should confound
(In spite of a deceptive similarity of sound),
    With the Lhama who is Lord of Turkestan.
For the former is a beautiful and valuable beast,
But the latter is not lovable nor useful in the least;
And the Ruminant is preferable surely to the Priest
Who battens on the woful superstitions of the East,
    The Mongol of the Monastery of Shan.

Hilaire Belloc.

THE YAK

As a friend to the children commend me the yak,
    You will find it exactly the thing:
It will carry and fetch, you can ride on its back,
    Or lead it about with a string.

A Tartar who dwells on the plains of Thibet
  (A desolate region of snow)
Has for centuries made it a nursery pet,
  And surely the Tartar should know!

Then tell your papa where the Yak can be got,
  And if he is awfully rich,
He will buy you the creature—or else he will not,
  (I cannot be positive which).

THE FROG

Be kind and tender to the Frog,
  And do not call him names,
As " Slimy-Skin," or " Polly-wog,"
  Or likewise, " Uncle James,"
Or " Gape-a-grin," or " Toad-gone-wrong,"
  Or " Billy-Bandy-knees; "
The Frog is justly sensitive
  To epithets like these.

No animal will more repay
  A treatment kind and fair,
At least, so lonely people say
Who keep a frog (and, by the way,
  They are extremely rare).

Hilaire Belloc.

THE MICROBE

The Microbe is so very small
You cannot make him out at all,
But many sanguine people hope
To see him through a microscope.
His jointed tongue that lies beneath
A hundred curious rows of teeth;
His seven tufted tails with lots
Of lovely pink and purple spots

On each of which a pattern stands,
Composed of forty separate bands;
His eyebrows of a tender green;
All these have never yet been seen—
But Scientists, who ought to know,
Assure us that they must be so. . . .
Oh! let us never, never doubt
What nobody is sure about!

Hilaire Belloc.

THE GREAT BLACK CROW

THE crow—the crow! the great black crow!
He cares not to meet us wherever we go;
He cares not for man, beast, friend, nor foe,
For nothing will eat him he well doth know.
  Know—know! you great black crow!
It's a comfort to feel like a great black crow!

The crow—the crow! the great black crow!
He loves the fat meadow—his taste is low;
He loves the fat worms, and he dines in a row
With fifty fine cousins all black as a sloe.
  Sloe—sloe! you great black crow!
But it's jolly to fare like a great black crow!

The crow—the crow! the great black crow!
He never gets drunk on the rain or snow;
He never gets drunk, but he never says no!
If you press him to tipple ever so.
  So—so! you great black crow!
It's an honour to soak like a great black crow!

The crow—the crow! the great black crow!
He lives for a hundred year and mo';
He lives till he dies, and he dies as slow
As the morning mists down the hill that go.
  Go—go! you great black crow!
But it's fine to live and die like a great black crow!

Philip James Bailey.

THE COLUBRIAD

CLOSE by the threshold of a door nailed fast,
Three kittens sat; each kitten looked aghast.
I, passing swift and inattentive by,
At the three kittens cast a careless eye;
Not much concerned to know what they did there;
Not deeming kittens worth a poet's care.
But presently, a loud and furious hiss
Caused me to stop, and to exclaim, " What's this
When lo! upon the threshold met my view,
With head erect, and eyes of fiery hue,
A viper long as Count de Grasse's queue.
Forth from his head his forked tongue he throws,
Darting it full against a kitten's nose;
Who, having never seen, in field or house,
The like, sat still and silent as a mouse;
Only projecting, with attention due,
Her whiskered face, she asked him, " Who are you? "
On to the hall went I, with pace not slow,
But swift as lightning, for a long Dutch hoe:
With which well armed, I hastened to the spot
To find the viper—but I found him not.
And, turning up the leaves and shrubs around,
Found only that he was not to be found;
But still the kittens, sitting as before,
Sat watching close the bottom of the door.
" I hope," said I, " the villain I would kill
Has slipped between the door and the door-sill;
And if I make despatch, and follow hard,
No doubt but I shall find him in the yard: "
(For long ere now it should have been rehearsed,
'Twas in the garden that I found him first.)
E'en there I found him: there the full-grown cat
His head, with velvet paw, did gently pat;
As curious as the kittens erst had been
To learn what this phenomenon might mean.
Filled with heroic ardour at the sight,
And fearing every moment he would bite,

And rob our household of our only cat
That was of age to combat with a rat;
With outstretched hoe I slew him at the door,
And taught him never to come there no more!

William Cowper.

THE RETIRED CAT

A Poet's Cat, sedate and grave
As poet well could wish to have,
Was much addicted to inquire
For nooks to which she might retire,
And where, secure as mouse in chink,
She might repose, or sit and think.
I know not where she caught the trick;
Nature perhaps herself had cast her
In such a mold PHILOSOPHIQUE,
Or else she learned it of her master.
Sometimes ascending, debonair,
An apple-tree, or lofty pear,
Lodged with convenience in the fork,
She watched the gardener at his work;
Sometimes her ease and solace sought
In an old empty watering-pot,
There wanting nothing, save a fan,
To seem some nymph in her sedan,
Appareled in exactest sort,
And ready to be borne to court.

But love of change it seems has place
Not only in our wiser race;
Cats also feel, as well as we,
That passion's force, and so did she.
Her climbing, she began to find,
Exposed her too much to the wind,
And the old utensil of tin
Was cold and comfortless within:
She therefore wished, instead of those,
Some place of more serene repose,

Where neither cold might come, nor air
Too rudely wanton in her hair,
And sought it in the likeliest mode
Within her master's snug abode.

A drawer, it chanced, at bottom lined
With linen of the softest kind,
With such as merchants introduce
From India, for the ladies' use;
A drawer, impending o'er the rest,
Half open, in the topmost chest,
Of depth enough, and none to spare,
Invited her to slumber there;
Puss with delight beyond expression,
Surveyed the scene and took possession.
Recumbent at her ease, ere long,
And lulled by her own humdrum song,
She left the cares of life behind,
And slept as she would sleep her last,
When in came, housewifely inclined,
The chambermaid, and shut it fast,
By no malignity impelled,
But all unconscious whom it held.

Awakened by the shock (cried puss)
" Was ever cat attended thus!
The open drawer was left, I see,
Merely to prove a nest for me,
For soon as I was well composed,
Then came the maid, and it was closed.
How smooth those 'kerchiefs, and how sweet
Oh what a delicate retreat!
I will resign myself to rest
Till Sol declining in the west,
Shall call to supper, when, no doubt,
Susan will come, and let me out."

The evening came, the sun descended,
And puss remained still unattended.
The night rolled tardily away
(With her indeed 'twas never day),

The sprightly morn her course renewed,
The evening gray again ensued,
And puss came into mind no more
Than if entombed the day before;
With hunger pinched, and pinched for room,
She now presaged approaching doom.
Nor slept a single wink, nor purred,
Conscious of jeopardy incurred.

That night, by chance, the poet, watching,
Heard an inexplicable scratching;
His noble heart went pit-a-pat,
And to himself he said—"What's that?"
He drew the curtain at his side,
And forth he peeped, but nothing spied.
Yet, by his ear directed, guessed
Something imprisoned in the chest;
And, doubtful what, with prudent care
Resolved it should continue there.
At length a voice which well he knew,
A long and melancholy mew,
Saluting his poetic ears,
Consoled him, and dispelled his fears;
He left his bed, he trod the floor,
He 'gan in haste the drawers explore,
The lowest first, and without stop
The next in order to the top.
For 'tis a truth well known to most,
That whatsoever thing is lost,
We seek it, ere it come to light,
In every cranny but the right.
Forth skipped the cat, not now replete
As erst with airy self-conceit,
Nor in her own fond comprehension,
A theme for all the world's attention,
But modest, sober, cured of all
Her notions hyperbolical,
And wishing for a place of rest,
Any thing rather than a chest.
Then stepped the poet into bed
With this reflection in his head:

MORAL

Beware of too sublime a sense
Of your own worth and consequence.
The man who dreams himself so great,
And his importance of such weight,
That all around in all that's done
Must move and act for him alone,
Will learn in school of tribulation
The folly of his expectation.

William Cowper.

A DARWINIAN BALLAD

Oh, many have told of the monkeys of old,
   What a pleasant race they were,
And it seems most true that I and you
   Are derived from an apish pair.
They all had nails, and some had tails,
   And some—no " accounts in arrear";
They climbed up the trees, and they scratched out the—these
   Of course I will not mention here.

They slept in a wood, or wherever they could,
   For they didn't know how to make beds;
They hadn't got huts; they dined upon nuts,
   Which they cracked upon each other's heads.
They hadn't much scope, for a comb, brush or soap,
   Or towels, or kettle or fire.
They had no coats nor capes, for ne'er did these apes
   Invent what they didn't require.

The sharpest baboon never used fork or spoon,
   Nor made any boots for his toes,
Nor could any thief steal a silk handker-chief,
   For no ape thought much of his nose;

They had cold collations; they ate poor relations:
   Provided for thus, by-the-bye.
No Ou-rang-ou-tang a song ever sang—
   He couldn't, and so didn't try.

From these though descended our manners are mended,
   Though still we can grin and backbite!
We cut up each other, be he friend or brother,
   And tales are the fashion—at night.
This origination is all speculation—
   We gamble in various shapes;
So Mr. Darwin may speculate in
   Our ancestors having been apes.

Unknown.

THE PIG

A COLLOQUIAL POEM

Jacob! I do not like to see thy nose
Turn'd up in scornful curve at yonder pig,
It would be well, my friend, if we. like him,
Were perfect in our kind! . . And why despise
The sow-born grunter? . . He is obstinate,
Thou answerest; ugly, and the filthiest beast
That banquets upon offal. . . . Now I pray you
Hear the pig's counsel.

                    Is he obstinate?
We must not, Jacob, be deceived by words;
We must not take them as unheeding hands
Receive base money at the current worth
But with a just suspicion try their sound,
And in the even balance weight them well
See now to what this obstinacy comes:
A poor, mistreated, democratic beast,
He knows that his unmerciful drivers seek
Their profit, and not his. He hath not learned
That pigs were made for man, . . born to be brawn'd
And baconized: that he must please to give
Just what his gracious masters please to take;
Perhaps his tusks, the weapons Nature gave

For self-defense, the general privilege;
Perhaps, . . hark, Jacob! dost thou hear that horn?
Woe to the young posterity of Pork!
Their enemy is at hand.

                              Again. Thou say'st
The pig is ugly. Jacob, look at him!
Those eyes have taught the lover flattery.
His face, . . nay, Jacob! Jacob! were it fair
To judge a lady in her dishabille?
Fancy it dressed, and with saltpeter rouged.
Behold his tail, my friend; with curls like that
The wanton hop marries her stately spouse:
So crisp in beauty Amoretta's hair
Rings round her lover's soul the chains of love.
And what is beauty, but the aptitude
Of parts harmonious? Give thy fancy scope,
And thou wilt find that no imagined change
Can beautify this beast. Place at his end
The starry glories of the peacock's pride,
Give him the swan's white breast; for his horn-hoofs
Shape such a foot and ankle as the waves
Crowded in eager rivalry to kiss
When Venus from the enamor'd sea arose; . .
Jacob, thou canst but make a monster of him!
An alteration man could think, would mar
His pig-perfection.

                              The last charge, . . he lives
A dirty life. Here I could shelter him
With noble and right-reverend precedents.
And show by sanction of authority
That 'tis a very honorable thing
To thrive by dirty ways. But let me rest
On better ground the unanswerable defense.
The pig is a philosopher, who knows
No prejudice. Dirt? . . Jacob, what is dirt?
If matter, . . why the delicate dish that tempts
An o'ergorged epicure to the last morsel
That stuffs him to the throat-gates, is no more.
If matter be not, but as sages say,
Spirit is all, and all things visible
Are one, the infinitely modified,

Think, Jacob, what that pig is, and the mire
Wherein he stands knee-deep!
             And there! the breeze
Pleads with me, and has won thee to a smile
That speaks conviction. O'er yon blossom'd field
Of beans it came, and thoughts of bacon rise.

                    Robert Southey.

A FISH STORY

A WHALE of great porosity
   And small specific gravity,
Dived down with much velocity
   Beneath the sea's concavity.

But soon the weight of water
   Squeezed in his fat immensity,
Which varied—as it ought to—
   Inversely as his density.

It would have moved to pity
   An Ogre or a Hessian,
To see poor Spermaceti
   Thus suffering compression.

The while he lay a-roaring
   In agonies gigantic,
The lamp-oil out came pouring,
   And greased the wide Atlantic.

(Would we'd been in the Navy,
   And cruising there! Imagine us
All in a sea of gravy,
   With billow oleaginous!)

At length old million-pounder,
   Low on a bed of coral,
Gave his last dying flounder,
   Whereto I pen this moral.

MORAL

O, let this tale dramatic,
    Anent the whale Norwegian
And pressure hydrostatic,
    Warn you, my young collegian,

That down-compelling forces
    Increase as you get deeper;
The lower down your course is,
    The upward path's the steeper.

Henry A. Beers.

THE CAMERONIAN CAT

THERE was a Cameronian cat
    Was hunting for a prey,
And in the house she catched a mouse
    Upon the Sabbath-day.

The Whig, being offended
    At such an act profane,
Laid by his book, the cat he took,
    And bound her in a chain.

"Thou damned, thou cursed creature!
    This deed so dark with thee!
Think'st thou to bring to hell below
    My holy wife and me?

"Assure thyself that for the deed
    Thou blood for blood shalt pay,
For killing of the Lord's own mouse
    Upon the Sabbath-day."

The presbyter laid by the book,
    And earnestly he prayed
That the great sin the cat had done
    Might not on him be laid.

And straight to execution
   Poor pussy she was drawn,
And high hanged up upon a tree—
   The preacher sung a psalm.

And, when the work was ended,
   They thought the cat near dead;
She gave a paw, and then a mew,
   And stretchèd out her head.

" Thy name," said he, " shall certainly
   A beacon still remain,
A terror unto evil ones
   For evermore, Amen."

                           Unknown.

THE YOUNG GAZELLE

A MOORE-ISH TALE

IN early youth, as you may guess,
   I revelled in poetic lore,
And while my schoolmates studied less,
   I resolutely studied *Moore*.

Those touching lines from " Lalla Rookh,"—
   " Ah, ever thus—" you know them well,
Such root within my bosom took,
   I wished *I* had a young Gazelle.

Oh, yes! a sweet, a sweet Gazelle,
   " To charm me with its soft black eye,"
So soft, so liquid, that a spell
   Seems in that gem-like orb to lie.

Years, childhood passed, youth fled away,
   My vain desire I'd learned to quell,
Till came that most auspicious day
   When *some one gave me a Gazelle.*

With care, and trouble, and expense,
    'Twas brought from Afric's northern cape;
It seemed of great intelligence,
    And oh! so beautiful a shape.

Its lustrous, liquid eye was bent
    With special lovingness on me;
No gift that mortal could present
    More welcome to my heart could be.

I brought him food with fond caress,
    Built him a hut, snug, neat, and warm;
I called him "Selim," to express
    The marked *s(e)lim*ness of his form.

The little creature grew so tame,
    He "learned to know (the neighbors) well;"
And then the ladies, when they came,
    Oh! how they "nursed that dear Gazelle."

But, woe is me! on earthly ground
    Some ill with every blessing dwells;
And soon to my dismay I found
    That this applies to young Gazelles.

When free allowed to roam indoors,
    The mischief that he did was great;
The walls, the furniture, the floors,
    He made in a terrific state.

He nibbled at the table-cloth,
    And trod the carpet into holes,
And in his gambols, nothing loth,
    Kicked over scuttles full of coals.

To view his image in the glass,
    He reared upon his hinder legs;
And thus one morn I found, alas!
    Two porcelain vases smashed like eggs.

Whatever did his fancy catch
　　By way of food, he would not wait
To be invited, but would snatch
　　It from one's table, hand, or plate.

He riled the dog, annoyed the cat,
　　And scared the goldfish into fits;
He butted through my newest hat,
　　And tore my manuscript to bits.

'Twas strange, so light his hooflets weighed,
　　His limbs as slender as a hare's,
The noise my little Selim made
　　In trotting up and down the stairs.

To tie him up I thought was wise,
　　But loss of freedom gave him pain;
I could not stand those pleading eyes,
　　And so I let him go again.

How sweet to see him skip and prance
　　Upon the gravel or the lawn;
More light in step than fairies' dance,
　　More graceful than an English fawn.

But then he spoilt the garden so,
　　Trod down the beds, raked up the seeds,
And ate the plants—nor did he show
　　The least compunction for his deeds.

He trespassed on the neighbors' ground,
　　And broke two costly melon frames,
With other damages—a pound
　　To pay, resulted from his games.

In short, the mischief was immense
　　That from his gamesome pranks befel,
And, truly, in a double sense,
　　He proved a *very* " dear Gazelle."

At length I sighed—" Ah, ever thus
  Doth disappointment mock each hope;
But 'tis in vain to make a fuss;
  You'll have to go, my antelope."

The chance I wished for did occur;
  A lady going to the East
Was willing; so I gave to her
  That little antelopian beast.

I said, " This antler'd desert child
  In Turkish palaces may roam,
But he is much too free and wild
  To keep in any English home."

Yes, tho' I gave him up with tears,
  Experience had broke the spell,
And if I live a thousand years,
  I'll never have a young Gazelle.

                              Walter Parke.

THE BALLAD OF THE EMEU

O SAY, have you seen at the Willows so green—
  So charming and rurally true—
A Singular bird, with a manner absurd,
  Which they call the Australian Emeu?
            Have you?
  Ever seen this Australian Emeu?

It trots all around with its head on the ground,
  Or erects it quite out of your view;
And the ladies all cry, when its figure they spy,
  " O, what a sweet pretty Emeu!
            Oh! do
  Just look at that lovely Emeu! "

One day to this spot, when the weather was hot,
  Came Matilda Hortense Fortescue;
And beside her there came a youth of high name—

Augustus Florell Montague:
        The two
Both loved that wild foreign Emeu.

With two loaves of bread then they fed it, instead
    Of the flesh of the white cockatoo,
Which once was its food in that wild neighbourhood
    Where ranges the sweet kangaroo
        That, too,
Is game for the famous Emeu!

Old saws and gimlets but its appetite whet
    Like the world famous bark of Peru;
There's nothing so hard that the bird will discard,
    And nothing its taste will eschew,
        That you
Can give that long-legged Emeu!

The time slipped away in this innocent play,
    When up jumped the bold Montague:
" Where's that specimen pin that I gaily did win
    In raffle, and gave unto you,
        Fortescue? "
No word spoke the guilty Emeu!

" Quick! tell me his name whom thou gavest that same,
    Ere these hands in thy blood I imbrue!"
" Nay, dearest," she cried as she clung to his side,
    " I'm innocent as that Emeu!"
        " Adieu!"
He replied, " Miss M. H. Fortescue!"

Down she dropped at his feet, all as white as a sheet,
    As wildly he fled from her view;
He thought 'twas her sin—for he knew not the pin
    Had been gobbled up by the Emeu;
        All through
" I'm innocent as that Emeu!"

Bret Harte.

THE TURTLE AND FLAMINGO

A LIVELY young turtle lived down by the banks
Of a dark rolling stream called the Jingo;
And one summer day, as he went out to play,
Fell in love with a charming flamingo—
An enormously genteel flamingo!
An expansively crimson flamingo!
A beautiful, bouncing flamingo!

Spake the turtle, in tones like a delicate wheeze:
" To the water I've oft seen you in go,
And your form has impressed itself deep on my shell,
You perfectly modelled flamingo!
You tremendously A-1 flamingo!
You in-ex-press-*i*-ble flamingo!

" To be sure, I'm a turtle, and you are a belle,
And my language is not your fine lingo;
But smile on me, tall one, and be my bright flame,
You miraculous, wondrous flamingo!
You blazingly beauteous flamingo!
You turtle-absorbing flamingo!
You inflammably gorgeous flamingo! "

Then the proud bird blushed redder than ever before,
And that was quite un-nec-es-*sa*-ry,
And she stood on one leg and looked out of one eye,
The position of things for to vary,—
This aquatical, musing flamingo!
This dreamy, uncertain flamingo!
This embarrasing, harassing flamingo!

Then she cried to the quadruped, greatly amazed:
" Why your passion toward *me* do you hurtle?
I'm an ornithological wonder of grace,
And you're an illogical turtle,—
A waddling, impossible turtle!
A low-minded, grass-eating turtle!
A highly improbable turtle! "

Then the turtle sneaked off with his nose to the ground
And never more looked at the lasses;
And falling asleep, while indulging his grief,
Was gobbled up whole by Agassiz,—
The peripatetic Agassiz!
The turtle-dissecting Agassiz!
The illustrious, industrious Agassiz!

Go with me to Cambridge some cool, pleasant day,
And the skeleton lover I'll show you;
He's in a hard case, but he'll look in your face,
Pretending (the rogue!) he don't know you!
Oh, the deeply deceptive young turtle!
The double-faced, glassy-cased turtle!
The *green* but a very *mock* turtle!

James Thomas Fields.

XV

JUNIORS

PRIOR TO MISS BELLE'S APPEARANCE

WHAT makes you come *here* fer, Mister,
　　So much to *our* house?—*Say?*
Come to see our big sister!—
An' Charley he says 'at you kissed her
　　An' he ketched you, thuther day!—
Didn' you, Charley?—But we p'omised Belle
And crossed our heart to never to tell—
'Cause *she* gived us some o' them-er
Chawk'lut-drops 'at you bringed to her!

Charley he's my little b'uther—
　　An' we has a-mostest fun,
Don't we, Charley?—Our Muther,
Whenever we whips one-anuther,
　　Tries to whip *us*—an' we *run*—
Don't we, Charley?—An' nen, bime-by,
Nen she gives us cake—an' pie—
Don't she, Charley?—when we come in
An' p'omise never to do it agin!

He's named Charley.—I'm *Willie*—
　　An' I'm got the purtiest name!
But Uncle Bob *he* calls me " Billy "—
Don't he, Charley?—'Nour filly
　　We named " Billy," the same
Ist like me!　An' our Ma said
'At " Bob put foolishnuss into our head! "—
Didn' she, Charley?—An' *she* don't know
Much about *boys!*—'Cause Bob said so!

Baby's a funniest feller!
  Naint no hair on his head—
Is they, Charley? It's meller
Wite up there! An' ef Belle er
  Us ask wuz *we* that way, Ma said,—
" Yes; an' yer *Pa's* head wuz soft as that,
An' it's that way yet! "—An' Pa grabs his hat
An' says, " Yes, childern, she's right about Pa—
'Cause that's the reason he married yer Ma! "

An' our Ma says 'at " Belle couldn'
  Ketch nothin 'at all but ist ' *bows!* ' "
An' *Pa* says 'at " you're soft as puddun! "—
An *Uncle Bob* says " you're a good-un—
  'Cause he can tell by yer nose! "—
Didn' he, Charley? And when Belle'll play
In the poller on th' pianer, some day,
Bob makes up funny songs about you,
Till she gits mad—like he wants her to!

Our sister *Fanny*, she's *'leven*
  Years old. 'At's mucher 'an *I*—
Ain't it, Charley? . . . I'm seven!—
But our sister Fanny's in *Heaven!*
  Nere's where you go ef you die!—
Don't you, Charley? Nen you has *wings*—
Ist like Fanny!—an' *purtiest things!*—
Don't you, Charley? An' nen you can *fly*—
Ist fly—an' *ever'*thing! . . . Wisht *I'd* die!

James Whitcomb Riley.

THERE WAS A LITTLE GIRL

THERE was a little girl,
And she had a little curl
  Right in the middle of her forehead.
When she was good
She was very, very good,
  And when she was bad she was horrid.

One day she went upstairs,
When her parents, unawares,
  In the kitchen were occupied with meals
And she stood upon her head
In her little trundle-bed,
  And then began hooraying with her heels.

Her mother heard the noise,
And she thought it was the boys
  A-playing at a combat in the attic;
But when she climbed the stair,
And found Jemima there,
  She took and she did spank her most emphatic.

                                        Unknown.

THE NAUGHTY DARKEY BOY

THERE was a cruel darkey boy,
  Who sat upon the shore,
A catching little fishes by
  The dozen and the score.

And as they squirmed and wriggled there,
  He shouted loud with glee,
" You surely cannot want to live,
  You're little-er dan me."

Just then with a malicious leer,
  And a capacious smile,
Before him from the water deep
  There rose a crocodile.

He eyed the little darkey boy,
  Then heaved a blubbering sigh,
And said, " You cannot want to live,
  You're little-er than I."

The fishes squirm and wriggle still,
Beside that sandy shore,
The cruel little darkey boy,
Was never heard of more.

Unknown.

DUTCH LULLABY

Wynken, Blynken, and Nod one night
Sailed off in a wooden shoe,—
Sailed on a river of misty light
Into a sea of dew.
"Where are you going, and what do you wish?"
The old moon asked the three.
"We have come to fish for the herring-fish
That live in this beautiful sea;
Nets of silver and gold have we,"
Said Wynken,
Blynken,
And Nod.

The old moon laughed and sung a song,
As they rocked in the wooden shoe;
And the wind that sped them all night long
Ruffled the waves of dew;
The little stars were the herring-fish
That lived in the beautiful sea.
"Now cast your nets wherever you wish,
But never afeard are we!"
So cried the stars to the fishermen three,
Wynken,
Blynken,
And Nod.

All night long their nets they threw
For the fish in the twinkling foam,
Then down from the sky came the wooden shoe,
Bringing the fishermen home:

'Twas all so pretty a sail, it seemed
    As if it could not be;
And some folk thought 'twas a dream they'd dreamed
    Of sailing that beautiful sea;
    But I shall name you the fishermen three:
        Wynken,
        Blynken,
        And Nod.

Wynken and Blynken are two little eyes,
    And Nod is a little head,
And the wooden shoe that sailed the skies
    Is a wee one's trundle-bed;
So shut your eyes while Mother sings
    Of wonderful sights that be,
And you shall see the beautiful things
    As you rock on the misty sea
    Where the old shoe rocked the fishermen three,
        Wynken,
        Blynken,
        And Nod.

                    Eugene Field.

THE DINKEY-BIRD

In an ocean, 'way out yonder
    (As all sapient people know),
Is the land of Wonder-Wander,
    Whither children love to go;
It's their playing, romping, swinging,
    That give great joy to me
While the Dinkey-Bird goes singing
    In the Amfalula-tree!

There the gum-drops grow like cherries,
    And taffy's thick as peas,—
Caramels you pick like berries
    When, and where, and how you please

Big red sugar-plums are clinging
　　To the cliffs beside that sea
Where the Dinkey-Bird is singing
　　In the Amfalula-tree.

So when children shout and scamper
　　And make merry all the day,
When there's naught to put a damper
　　To the ardor of their play;
When I hear their laughter ringing,
　　Then I'm sure as sure can be
That the Dinkey-Bird is singing
　　In the Amfalula-tree.

For the Dinkey-Bird's bravuras
　　And staccatos are so sweet—
His roulades, appogiaturas,
　　And robustos so complete,
That the youth of every nation—
　　Be they near or far away—
Have especial delectation
　　In that gladsome roundelay.

Their eyes grow bright and brighter,
　　Their lungs begin to crow,
Their hearts get light and lighter,
　　And their cheeks are all aglow;
For an echo cometh bringing
　　The news to all and me.
That the Dinkey-Bird is singing
　　In the Amfalula-tree.

I'm sure you'd like to go there
　　To see your feathered friend—
And so many goodies grow there
　　You would like to comprehend!
Speed, little dreams, your winging
　　To that land across the sea
Where the Dinkey-Bird is singing
　　In the Amfalula-Tree!

Eugene Field.

THE LITTLE PEACH

A LITTLE peach in the orchard grew,
A little peach of emerald hue:
Warmed by the sun, and wet by the dew,
      It grew.

One day, walking the orchard through,
That little peach dawned on the view
Of Johnny Jones and his sister Sue—
      Those two.

Up at the peach a club they threw:
Down from the limb on which it grew,
Fell the little peach of emerald hue—
      Too true!

John took a bite, and Sue took a chew,
And then the trouble began to brew,—
Trouble the doctor couldn't subdue,—
      Paregoric too.

Under the turf where the daisies grew,
They planted John and his sister Sue;
And their little souls to the angels flew—
      Boo-hoo!

But what of the peach of emerald hue,
Warmed by the sun, and wet by the dew?
Ah, well! its mission on earth is through—
      Adieu!

            Eugene Field.

COUNSEL TO THOSE THAT EAT

WITH chocolate-cream that you buy in the cake
Large mouthfuls and hurry are quite a mistake.

Wise persons prolong it as long as they can
But putting in practice this excellent plan.

The cream from the chocolate lining they dig
With a Runaway match or a clean little twig.

Many hundreds,—nay, thousands—of scoopings they make
Before they've exhausted a twopenny cake.

With ices 'tis equally wrongful to haste;
You ought to go slowly and dwell on each taste.

Large mouthfuls are painful, as well as unwise,
For they lead to an ache at the back of the eyes.

And the delicate sip is e'en better, one finds,
If the ice is a mixture of different kinds.

Unknown.

HOME AND MOTHER

SLEEP, my own darling,
  By, baby, by;
  Mother is with thee,
  By, baby, by.
There, baby. (Oh, how the wild winds wail!)
Hush, baby. (Turning to sleet and hail;
Ah, how the pine-tree moans and mutters!—
I wonder if Ellen will think of the shutters?)

  Sleep, my own darling.
    By, baby, by;
    Mother is with thee,
    By, baby, by.

Rest thee. (She couldn't have left the blower
Down in the parlor? There's so much to show her!)
By-by, my sweetest. (Now the rain's pouring!
Is it wind or the dining-room fire that's roaring?)

Sleep, my own darling,
By, baby, by;
Mother is with thee,
By, baby, by.

How lovely his forehead!—my own blessed pet!
He's nearly asleep. (Now I mustn't forget
That pork in the brine, and the stair-rods to-morrow.)
Heaven shield him forever from trouble and sorrow!

Sleep, my own darling,
By, baby, by;
Mother is with thee,
By, baby, by.

Those dear little ringlets, so silky and bright!
(I do hope the muffins will be nice and light.)
How lovely he is! (Yes, she said she could fry.)
Oh, what would I do if my baby should die!

Sleep, my own darling,
By, baby, by;
Mother is with thee,
By, baby, by.

That sweet little hand, and the soft, dimpled cheek!
Sleep, darling. (I'll have his clothes shortened this week.
How tightly he's holding my dress; I'm afraid
He'll wake when I move. There! his bed isn't made!)

Sleep, my own darling,
By, baby, by;
In thy soft cradle
Peacefully lie.

(He's settled at last. But I can't leave him so,
Though I ought to be going this instant, I know.
There's everything standing and waiting down-stairs.
Ah me, but a mother is cumbered with cares!)

Mary Mapes Dodge.

LITTLE ORPHANT ANNIE

LITTLE Orphant Annie's come to our house to stay,
An' wash the cups and saucers up, an' brush the crumbs away,
An' shoo the chickens off the porch, an' dust the hearth, an'
　　sweep,
An' make the fire, an' bake the bread, an' earn her board-
　　an'-keep;
An' all us other children, when the supper things is done,
We set around the kitchen fire an' has the mostest fun
A-list'nin' to the witch-tales 'at Annie tells about,
An' the Gobble-uns 'at gits you
　　　　Ef you
　　　　　Don't
　　　　　　Watch
　　　　　　　Out!

Onc't there was a little boy wouldn't say his pray'rs—
An' when he went to bed at night, away up stairs,
His mammy heerd him holler, an' his daddy heerd him bawl,
An' when they turn't the kivvers down, he wasn't there at all!
An' they seeked him in the rafter-room, an' cubby-hole, an'
　　press,
An' seeked him up the chimbly-flue, an' ever'wheres, I guess;
But all they ever found was thist his pants an' roundabout!
An' the Gobble-uns'll git you
　　　　Ef you
　　　　　Don't
　　　　　　Watch
　　　　　　　Out!

An' one time a little girl 'ud allus laugh an' grin,
An' make fun of ever' one, an' all her blood-an'-kin;
An' onc't when they was " company," an' ole folks was there,
She mocked 'em an' shocked 'em, an' said she didn't care!
An' thist as she kicked her heels, an' turn't to run an' hide,
They was two great big Black Things a-standin' by her side,

An' they snatched her through the ceilin' 'fore she knowed
    what she 's about!
An' the Gobble-uns'll git you
      Ef you
        Don't
          Watch
            Out!

An' little Orphant Annie says, when the blaze is blue,
An' the lampwick sputters, an' the wind goes woo-oo!
An' you hear the crickets quit, an' the moon is gray,
An' the lightnin'-bugs in dew is all squenched away,—
You better mind yer parents, and yer teachers fond and dear,
An' churish them 'at loves you, an' dry the orphant's tear,
An' he'p the pore an' needy ones 'at clusters all about,
Er the Gobble-uns'll git you
      Ef you
        Don't
          Watch
            Out!

James Whitcomb Riley.

A VISIT FROM ST. NICHOLAS

'Twas the night before Christmas, when all through the house
Not a creature was stirring, not even a mouse;
The stockings were hung by the chimney with care,
In hopes that St. Nicholas soon would be there;
The children were nestled all snug in their beds,
While visions of sugar-plums danced in their heads;
And mamma in her kerchief, and I in my cap,
Had just settled our brains for a long winter's nap,
When out on the lawn there arose such a clatter,
I sprang from the bed to see what was the matter.

Away to the window I flew like a flash,
Tore open the shutters, and threw up the sash.
The moon on the breast of the new-fallen snow
Gave a luster of mid-day to objects below,
When, what to my wondering eyes should appear,
But a miniature sleigh, and eight tiny reindeer,
With a little old driver, so lively and quick,
I knew in a moment it must be St. Nick.
More rapid than eagles his coursers they came,
And he whistled, and shouted, and called them by name;
" Now, *Dasher!* now, *Dancer!* now, *Prancer* and *Vixen!*
On, *Comet!* on, *Cupid!* on, *Dunder* and *Blitzen!*
To the top of the porch! To the top of the wall!
Now, dash away! Dash away! Dash away all!"
As dry leaves that before the wild hurricane fly,
When they meet with an obstacle, mount to the sky;
So up to the housetop the coursers they flew,
With the sleigh full of toys, and St. Nicholas, too.
And then in a twinkling, I heard on the roof
The prancing and pawing of each little hoof.
As I drew in my head, and was turning around,
Down the chimney St. Nicholas came with a bound.
He was dressed all in fur, from his head to his foot,
And his clothes were all tarnished with ashes and soot;
A bundle of toys he had flung on his back,
And he looked like a peddler just opening his pack.
His eyes—how they twinkled!—his dimples how merry!
His cheeks were like roses, his nose like a cherry!
His droll little mouth was drawn up like a bow,
And the beard of his chin was as white as the snow;
The stump of a pipe he held tight in his teeth,
And the smoke it encircled his head like a wreath;
He had a broad face and a round little belly,
That shook when he laughed like a bowlful of jelly.
He was chubby and plump, a right jolly old elf,
And I laughed when I saw him, in spite of myself;
A wink of his eye and a twist of his head,
Soon gave me to know I had nothing to dread;
He spoke not a word, but went straight to his work,
And filled all the stockings; then turned with a jerk,

And laying his finger aside of his nose,
And giving a nod, up the chimney he rose;
He sprang to his sleigh, to his team gave a whistle,
And away they all flew like the down of a thistle;
But I heard him exclaim, ere he drove out of sight,
" *Happy Christmas to all, and to all a good night!* "

Clement Clarke Moore.

A NURSERY LEGEND

OH! listen, little children, to a proper little song
Of a naughty little urchin who was always doing wrong:
He disobey'd his mammy, and he disobey'd his dad,
And he disobey'd his uncle, which was very near as bad.
He wouldn't learn to cipher, and he wouldn't learn to write,
But he *would* tear up his copy-books to fabricate a kite;
And he used his slate and pencil in so barbarous a way,
That the grinders of his governess got looser ev'ry day.

At last he grew so obstinate that no one could contrive
To cure him of a theory that two and two made five
And, when they taught him how to spell, he show'd his wicked
    whims
By mutilating Pinnock and mislaying Watts's Hymns.
Instead of all such pretty books, (which *must* improve the
    mind,)
He cultivated volumes of a most improper kind;
Directories and almanacks he studied on the sly,
And gloated over Bradshaw's Guide when nobody was by.

From such a course of reading you can easily divine
The condition of his morals at the age of eight or nine.
His tone of conversation kept becoming worse and worse,
Till it scandalised his governess and horrified his nurse.
He quoted bits of Bradshaw that were quite unfit to hear,
And recited from the Almanack, no matter who was near:

He talked of Reigate Junction and of trains both up and
    down,
And referr'd to men who call'd themselves Jones, Robinson,
    and Brown.

But when this naughty boy grew up he found the proverb
    true,
That Fate one day makes people pay for all the wrong they
    do.
He was cheated out of money by a man whose name was
    Brown,
And got crippled in a railway smash while coming up to
    town.
So, little boys and little girls, take warning while you can,
And profit by the history of this unhappy man.
Read Dr. Watts and Pinnock, dears; and when you learn to
    spell,
Shun Railway Guides, Directories, and Almanacks as well!

Henry S. Leigh.

A LITTLE GOOSE

THE chill November day was done,
    The working world home faring;
The wind came roaring through the streets
    And set the gas-lights flaring;
And hopelessly and aimlessly
    The scared old leaves were flying;
When, mingled with the sighing wind,
    I heard a small voice crying.

And shivering on the corner stood
    A child of four, or over;
No cloak or hat her small, soft arms,
    And wind blown curls to cover.
Her dimpled face was stained with tears;
    Her round blue eyes ran over;
She cherished in her wee, cold hand,
    A bunch of faded clover.

And one hand round her treasure while
  She slipped in mine the other:
Half scared, half confidential, said,
  " Oh! please, I want my mother!"
" Tell me your street and number, pet:
  Don't cry, I'll take you to it."
Sobbing she answered, "I forget:
  The organ made me do it.

" He came and played at Milly's steps,
  The monkey took the money;
And so I followed down the street,
  The monkey was so funny.
I've walked about a hundred hours,
  From one street to another:
The monkey's gone, I've spoiled my flowers,
  Oh! please, I want my mother."

" But what's your mother's name? and what
  The street? Now think a minute."
" My mother's name is mamma dear—
  The street—I can't begin it."
" But what is strange about the house,
  Or new—not like the others?"
" I guess you mean my trundle-bed,
  Mine and my little brother's.

" Oh dear! I ought to be at home
  To help him say his prayers,—
He's such a baby he forgets;
  And we are both such players;—
And there's a bar to keep us both
  From pitching on each other,
For Harry rolls when he's asleep:
  Oh dear! I want my mother."

The sky grew stormy; people passed
  All muffled, homeward faring:
You'll have to spend the night with me,"
  I said at last, despairing.

I tied a kerchief round her neck—
  " What ribbon's this, my blossom?"
" Why don't you know?" she smiling, said,
  And drew it from her bosom.

A card with number, street, and name;
  My eyes astonished met it;
" For," said the little one, " you see
  I might sometimes forget it:
And so I wear a little thing
  That tells you all about it;
For mother says she's very sure
  I should get lost without it."

Eliza Sproat Turner.

LEEDLE YAWCOB STRAUSS

I HAF von funny leedle poy,
  Vot comes schust to mine knee;
Der queerest schap, der createst rogue,
  As efer you dit see.
He runs, und schumps, und schmashes dings
  In all barts off der house:
But vot off dot? He vas mine son,
  Mine leedle Yawcob Strauss.

He get der measles und der mumbs
  Und eferyding dot's oudt;
He sbills mine glass off lager bier,
  Poots schnuff indo mine kraut.
He fills mine pipe mit Limburg cheese—
  Dot vas der roughest chouse;
I'd dake dot vrom no oder poy
  But leedle Yawcob Strauss.

He dakes der milk-ban for a dhrum,
  Und cuts mine cane in dwo,
To make der schticks to beat it mit—
  Mine cracious, dot vas drue!

I dinks mine hed vas schplit abart,
   He kicks oup sooch a touse:
But nefer mind; der poys vas few
   Like dot young Yawcob Strauss.

He asks me questions sooch as dese:
   Who baints mine nose so red?
Who vas it cuts dot schmoodth blace oudt
   Vrom der hair ubon mine hed?
Und vere dere plaze goes vrom her lamp
   Vene'er der glim I douse.
How gan I all dose dings eggsblain
   To dot schmall Yawcob Strauss?

I somedimes dink I schall go vild
   Mit sooch a grazy poy,
Und vish vonce more I gould haf rest,
   Und beaceful dimes enshoy;
But ven he vas aschleep in ped
   So guiet as a mouse,
I prays der Lord, "Dake anyding,
   But leaf dot Yawcob Strauss."

              Charles Follen Adams.

A PARENTAL ODE TO MY SON, AGED THREE YEARS AND FIVE MONTHS

Thou happy, happy elf!
(But stop,—first let me kiss away that tear)—
   Thou tiny image of myself!
(My love, he's poking peas into his ear!)
   Thou merry, laughing sprite!
   With spirits feather-light,
Untouched by sorrow, and unsoiled by sin—
(Good Heavens! the child is swallowing a pin!)

   Thou little tricksy Puck!
With antic toys so funnily bestuck,
Light as the singing bird that wings the air—
(The door! the door! he'll tumble down the stair!)

Thou darling of thy sire!
(Why, Jane, he'll set his pinafore afire!)
Thou imp of mirth and joy!
In love's dear chain, so strong and bright a link,
Thou idol of thy parents—(Drat the boy!
There goes my ink!)

Thou cherub—but of earth;
Fit playfellow for Fays, by moonlight pale,
In harmless sport and mirth,
(That dog will bite him if he pulls its tail!)
Thou human humming-bee, extracting honey
From every blossom in the world that blows,
Singing in youth's elysium ever sunny,
(Another tumble!—that's his precious nose!)

Thy father's pride and hope!
(He'll break the mirror with that skipping-rope!)
With pure heart newly stamped from Nature's mint—
(Where *did* he learn that squint?)
Thou young domestic dove!
(He'll have that jug off with another shove!)
Dear nursling of the Hymeneal nest!
(Are those torn clothes his best?)
Little epitome of man!
(He'll climb upon the table, that's his plan!)
Touched with the beauteous tints of dawning life
(He's got a knife!)

Thou enviable being!
No storms, no clouds, in thy blue sky foreseeing,
Play on, play on,
My elfin John!
Toss the light ball—bestride the stick—
(I knew so many cakes would make him sick!)
With fancies, buoyant as the thistle-down,
Prompting the face grotesque, and antic brisk,
With many a lamb-like frisk,
(He's got the scissors, snipping at your gown!)

Thou pretty opening rose!
(Go to your mother, child, and wipe your nose!)
Balmy and breathing music like the South,
(He really brings my heart into my mouth!)
Fresh as the morn, and brilliant as its star,—
(I wish that window had an iron bar!)
Bold as the hawk, yet gentle as the dove,—
    (I'll tell you what, my love,
I cannot write unless he's sent above!)

                    Thomas Hood.

LITTLE MAMMA

WHY is it the children don't love me
    As they do Mamma?
That they put her ever above me—
    " Little Mamma? "
I'm sure I do all that I can do,
What more can a rather big man do,
    Who can't be Mamma—
        Little Mamma?

Any game that the tyrants suggest,
" Logomachy,"—which I detest,—
Doll-babies, hop-scotch, or baseball,
I'm always on hand at the call.
When Noah and the others embark,
I'm the elephant saved in the ark.
I creep, and I climb, and I crawl—
By turns am the animals all.
    For the show on the stair
    I'm always the bear,
Chimpanzee, camel, or kangaroo.
    It is never, " Mamma,—
        Little Mamma,—
        Won't *you?* "

My umbrella's the pony, if any—
None ride on Mamma's parasol:
I'm supposed to have always the penny
For bonbons, and beggars, and all.
My room is the one where they clatter—
Am I reading, or writing, what matter!
My knee is the one for a trot,
My foot is the stirrup for Dot.
If his fractions get into a snarl
Who straightens the tangles for Karl?
Who bounds Massachusetts and Maine,
And tries to bound flimsy old Spain?
     Why,
   It is *I,*
    Papa,—
  Not Little Mamma!

That the youngsters are ingrates don't say.
I think they love me—in a way—
As one does the old clock on the stair,—
Any curious, cumbrous affair
That one's used to having about,
And would feel rather lonely without.
I think that they love me, I say,
In a sort of a tolerant way;
   But it's plain that Papa
  Isn't Little Mamma.

Thus when twilight comes stealing anear,
When things in the firelight look queer;
And shadows the playroom enwrap,
They never climb into my lap
And toy with *my* head, smooth and bare,
As they do with Mamma's shining hair;
Nor feel round my throat and my chin
For dimples to put fingers in;
Nor lock my neck in a loving vise,
And say they're "mousies"—that's mice—
   And will nibble my ears,
    Will nibble and bite
With their little mice-teeth, so sharp and so white,

If I do not kiss them this very minute—
Don't-wait-a-bit-but-at-once-begin-it—
    Dear little Papa!
That's what they say and do to Mamma.

If, mildly hinting, I quietly say that
Kissing's a game that more can play at,
They turn up at once those innocent eyes,
And I suddenly learn to my great surprise
    That my face has " prickles "—
    My moustache tickles.
If, storming their camp, I seize a pert shaver,
And take as a right what was asked as a favor,
    It is, " Oh, Papa,
    How horrid you are—
You taste exactly like a cigar! "

But though the rebels protest and pout,
And make a pretence of driving me out,
I hold, after all, the main redoubt,—
Not by force of arms nor the force of will,
But the power of love, which is mightier still.
And very deep in their hearts, I know,
Under the saucy and petulant " Oh,"
The doubtful " Yes," or the naughty " No,"
    They love Papa.

And down in the heart that no one sees,
Where I hold my feasts and my jubilees,
I know that I would not abate one jot
Of the love that is held by my little Dot
Or my great big boy for their little Mamma,
Though out in the cold it crowded Papa.
I would not abate it the tiniest whit,
And I am not jealous the least little bit;
For I'll tell you a secret: Come, my dears,
And I'll whisper it—right-into-your-ears—
    I, too, love Mamma,
    Little Mamma!

                                    Charles Henry Webb.

THE COMICAL GIRL

THERE was a child, as I have been told,
Who when she was young didn't look very old.
Another thing, too, some people have said,
At the top of her body there grew out a head;
And what perhaps might make some people stare
Her little bald pate was all covered with hair.
Another strange thing which made gossipers talk,
Was that she often attempted to walk.
And then, do you know, she occasioned much fun
By moving so fast as sometimes to run.
Nay, indeed, I have heard that some people say
She often would smile and often would play.
And what is a fact, though it seems very odd,
She had monstrous dislike to the feel of a rod.
This strange little child sometimes hungry would be
And then she delighted her victuals to see.
Even drink she would swallow, and though strangs it appears
Whenever she listened it was with her ears.
With her eyes she could see, and strange to relate
Her peepers were placed in front of her pate.
There, too, was her mouth and also her nose,
And on her two feet were placed her ten toes.
Her teeth, I've been told, were fixed in her gums,
And beside having fingers she also had thumbs.
A droll child she therefore most surely must be,
For not being blind she was able to see.
One circumstance more had slipped from my mind
Which is when not cross she always was kind.
And, strangest of any that yet I have said,
She every night went to sleep on her bed.
And, what may occasion you no small surprise,
When napping, she always shut close up her eyes.

M. Pelham.

BUNCHES OF GRAPES

"Bunches of grapes," says Timothy,
  "Pomegrantes pink," says Elaine;
"A junket of cream and a cranberry tart
  "For me," says Jane.

"Love-in-a-mist," says Timothy,
  "Primroses pale," says Elaine;
"A nosegay of pinks and mignonette
  For me," says Jane.

"Chariots of gold," says Timothy,
  "Silvery wings," says Elaine;
"A bumpety ride in a waggon of hay
  For me," says Jane.

Walter Ramal.

XVI

IMMORTAL STANZAS

THE PURPLE COW

I NEVER saw a Purple Cow,
I never hope to see one;
But I can tell you, anyhow,
I'd rather see than be one.

Gelett Burgess.

THE YOUNG LADY OF NIGER

THERE was a young lady of Niger
Who smiled as she rode on a Tiger;
They came back from the ride
With the lady inside,
And the smile on the face of the Tiger.

Unknown.

THE LAUGHING WILLOW

To see the Kaiser's epitaph
Would make a weeping willow laugh.

Oliver Herford.

SAID OPIE READ

SAID Opie Read to E. P. Roe,
" How do you like Gaboriau? "
" I like him very much indeed! "
Said E. P. Roe to Opie Read.

Julian Street and *James Montgomery Flagg.*

MANILA

OH, dewy was the morning, upon the first of May,
And Dewey was the admiral, down in Manila Bay;
And dewy were the Regent's eyes, them royal orbs of blue,
And do we feel discouraged? We do not think we do!

Eugene F. Ware.

ON THE ARISTOCRACY OF HARVARD

I COME from good old Boston,
  The home of the bean and the cod;
Where the Cabots speak only to Lowells,
  And the Lowells speak only to God!

Dr. Samuel G. Bushnell.

ON THE DEMOCRACY OF YALE

HERE'S to the town of New Haven,
  The home of the truth and the light;
Where God speaks to Jones in the very same tones,
  That he uses with Hadley and Dwight!

Dean Jones.

THE HERRING

" THE Herring he loves the merry moonlight
  And the Mackerel loves the wind,
But the Oyster loves the dredging song
  For he comes of a gentler kind."

Sir Walter Scott.

IF THE MAN

IF the man who turnips cries,
Cry not when his father dies,
'Tis a proof that he had rather
Have a turnip than his father.

Samuel Johnson.

THE KILKENNY CATS

THERE wanst was two cats of Kilkenny,
Each thought there was one cat too many,
   So they quarrell'd and fit,
   They scratch'd and they bit,
   Till, barrin' their nails,
   And the tips of their tails,
Instead of two cats, there warnt any.

Unknown.

POOR DEAR GRANDPAPA

WHAT is the matter with Grandpapa?
   What can the matter be?
He's broken his leg in trying to spell
   Tommy without a T.

D'Arcy W. Thompson.

MORE WALKS

WHENE'ER I take my walks abroad,
   How many rich I see;
There's A. and B. and C. and D.
   All better off than me!

Richard Harris Barham.

INDIFFERENCE

THE cat is in the parlour,
   The dog is in the lake;
The cow is in the hammock,—
   What difference does it make?

MADAME SANS SOUCI

"BON jour, Madame Sans Souci;
Combien coûtent ces soucis ci?"
"Six sous." "Six sous ces soucis ci!
C'est trop cher, Madame Sans Souci!"

A RIDDLE

THE man in the wilderness asked of me
How many strawberries grew in the sea.
I answered him as I thought good,
As many as red herrings grow in the wood.

IF

IF all the land were apple-pie,
   And all the sea were ink;
And all the trees were bread and cheese,
   What should we do for drink?

THE STEIN FAMILY

THERE's a wonderful family, called Stein,
There's Gert and there's Epp and there's Ein;
   Gert's poems are bunk,
   Epp's statues are junk,
And no one can understand Ein.

LIZZIE BORDEN

LIZZIE BORDEN with an ax
Hit her father forty whacks;
When she saw what she had done,
She hit her mother forty-one.

CONTEMPORARY VERSE

THAIS

ONE time in Alexandria, in wicked Alexandria,
Where nights were wild with revelry and life was but a game,
There lived, so the report is, an adventuress and courtesan,
The pride of Alexandria, and Thais was her name.

Nearby, in peace and piety, avoiding all society,
There dwelt a band of holy men who'd built a refuge there;
And in the desert's solitude they spurned all earthly folly to
Devote their days to holy works, to fasting and to prayer.

Now one monk whom I solely mention of this group of holy men
Was known as Athanael; he was famous near and far.
At fasting bouts or prayer with him no other could compare with
  him;
At ground and lofty praying he could do the course in par.

One night while sleeping heavily (from fighting with the devil he
Had gone to bed exhausted while the sun was shining still),
He had a vision Freudian, and though he was annoyed he an-
Alyzed it in the well-known style of Doctors Jung and Brill.

He dreamed of Alexandria, of wicked Alexandria:
A crowd of men were cheering in a manner rather rude
At Thais, who was dancing there, and Athanael, glancing there,
Observed her do the shimmy in what artists call The Nude.

Said he, "This dream fantastical disturbs my thoughts monastical;
Some unsuppressed desire, I fear, has found my monkish cell.
I blushed up to the hat o' me to view that girl's anatomy.
I'll go to Alexandria and save her soul from Hell."

So, pausing not to wonder where he'd put his summer underwear,
He quickly packed his evening clothes, his toothbrush and a vest.
To guard against exposure he threw in some woolen hosiery,
And bidding all the boys goodby, he started on his quest.

The monk, though warned and fortified, was deeply shocked and
mortified
To find, on his arrival, wild debauchery in sway.
While some lay in a stupor, sent by booze of more than two per
cent.,
    The others were behaving in a most immoral way.

Said he to Thais, "Pardon me.   Although this job is hard on me,
I gotta put you wise to what I came down here to tell.
What's all this sousin' gettin' you?   Cut out this pie eyed retinue;
Let's hit the trail together, kid, and save yourself from Hell."

Although this bold admonishment caused Thais some astonish-
ment,
She coyly answered, "Say, you said a heaping mouthful, bo,
This burg's a frost, I'm telling you.   The brand of hooch they're
selling you
Ain't like the stuff we used to get, so let's pack up and go."

So forth from Alexandria, from wicked Alexandria,
Across the desert sands they go beneath the blazing sun;
Till Thais, parched and sweltering, finds refuge in the sheltering
Seclusion of a convent, and the habit of a nun.

But now the monk is terrified to find his fears are verified:
His holy vows of chastity have cracked beneath the strain.
Like one who has a jag on he cries out in grief and agony,
"I'd sell my soul to see her do the shimmy once again."

Alas! his pleadings clamorous, the passionate and amorous,
Have come too late; the courtesan has danced her final dance.
The monk says, "That's a joke on me, for that there dame to croak
on me.
I hadn't oughter passed her up the time I had the chance."

                                                 Newman Levy

RAIN

On the isle of Pago Pago, land of palm trees, rice and sago,
Where the Chinaman and Dago dwell with natives dusky hued,
Lived a dissolute and shady, bold adventuress named Sadie,
Sadie Thompson was the lady, and the life she lived was lewd.

She had practised her profession in our insular possession,
Which, to make a frank confession, people call the Philippines.
There she'd made a tidy profit till the clergy, hearing of it,
Made her life as hot as Tophet, driving her to other scenes.

So this impudent virago hied herself to Pago Pago
Where the Chinaman and Dago to her cottage often came.
Trade was lucrative and merry, till one day the local ferry
Brought a noble missionary, Rev'rend Davidson by name.

Stern, austere and apostolic, life was no amusing frolic.
Braving fevers, colds and colic, he had come with prayers and
    hymns,
Most intolerant of wowsers, to those primitive carousers
Bearing chaste and moral trousers to encase their nether limbs.

In her quaint exotic bower, 'mid a never-ending shower,
Sadie Thompson, by the hour, entertained the local trade.
Every night brought more and more men, soldiers, natives, clerks
    and store-men,
Sailors, gallant man-of-war men, while her gay victrola played.

"Ha!" exclaimed the irate pastor, "straight you're headed for dis-
    aster.
I'll convince you who's the master, shameless woman of the street!"
"Listen, Rev.," said Sadie tartly, (pardon me for punning smartly),
"Though I get your meaning—partly—still, alas, a girl must eat."

"Girl," he cried in indignation, "choose at once between salvation
And immediate deportation from this charming tropic glade.
Like a devastating plague, O Scarlet Dame of Pago Pago,
You're as welcome as lumbago, plying here your brazen trade."

Sadie said, "Though I'm no scoffer, that's a lousy choice you
    proffer,
Still I must accept your offer though my pride has been attacked.
Come on, Rev., and let us kill a flask or two of sarsap'rilla
Here in my delightful villa while I watch you do your act."

Let us veil the tragic sequel, for a pious man but weak will
Find, alas, that he's unequal to a lady's potent charms.
So his long suppressed libido, sharp as steel of famed Toledo,
Spurning prayers and hymns and credo, found surcease in Sadie's
    arms.

There beside the waters tidal, urged by impulse suicidal,
Lay, next day, the shattered idol, cleansed at last of sin and taint.
Here's the moral: Though a preacher fail to make a fallen creature
Pure and saintly as her teacher, she, perhaps, can make a saint.

                              Newman Levy

THE CLEAN PLATTER

    Some painters paint the sapphire sea,
    And some the gathering storm.
    Others portray young lambs at play,
    But most, the female form.
    'Twas trite in that primeval dawn
    When painting got its start,
    That a lady with her garments on
    Is Life, but is she Art?
    By undraped nymphs
    I am not wooed;
    I'd rather painters painted food.

    Food,
    Yes, food,
    Just any old kind of food.
    Pooh for the cook,
    And pooh for the price!
    Some of it's nicer but all of it's nice.
    Pheasant is pleasant, of course,

And terrapin, too, is tasty,
Lobster I freely endorse,
In pate or patty or pasty.
But there's nothing the matter with butter,
And nothing the matter with jam,
And the warmest of greetings I utter
To the ham and yam and clam.
For they're food,
All food
And I think very highly of food.
Though I am broody at times
When bothered by rhymes,
I brood
On food.

Food,
Just food,
Just any old kind of food.
Let it be sour
Or let it be sweet,
As long as you're sure it is something to eat.
Go purloin a sirloin, my pet,
If you'd win a devotion incredible;
And asparagus tips vinaigrette,
Or anything else that is edible.
Bring salad or sausage or scrapple,
A berry or even a beet,
Bring an oyster, an egg, or an apple,
As long as it's something to eat.
For it's food,
It's food;
Never mind what kind of food.
Through thick and through thin
I am constantly in
The mood
For food.

Some singers sing of ladies' eyes,
And some of ladies' lips,
Refined ones praise their ladylike ways,
And coarse ones hymn their hips.

The Oxford Book of English Verse
Is lush with lyrics tender;
A poet, I guess, is more or less,
Preoccupied with gender.
Yet I, though custom call me crude,
Prefer to sing in praise of food.

Ogden Nash

I WANT TO SIT NEXT TO EMILY

I KNOW a girl who for present purposes let us call by the name of
    Emily,
And let me state at once that she is not a member of my immediate
    or unimmediate family;
Neither is her habitat
The city or state where I keep my bed and board and faithful dog
    and talkative parrot and celibate white rabbit at;
I simply say that she lives not as near as the next street and not
    as far away as Samoa,
And I knoa.
I am told that her conversation doesn't appeal to the intellectual
    or arty,
But I must confess that I enjoy sitting next to Emily at a party.
She always refers to Colonel Charles A. Lindbergh as Lucky Lindy
    and to his flight as a hop,
And she says that once she starts eating pretzels and potato chips
    she can never stop;
She is quick to size up a situation, for I have often heard her aver
That she likes lobster but lobster doesn't like her.
She believes that every boy should go to college not so much for
    the sake of learning higher mathematics and physics and
    beautiful poems like Hiawatha and The Last Ride from Ghent
    to Aix,
But particularly because of the useful social contacts that he makes.
She calls the Notre Dames the Fighting Irish despite their indi-
    vidual rather un-Hibernian nomenclature,
And believes that football is an invaluable character-builder and
    war is certainly hell all right but what's the use of trying to
    do anything about it because you can't abolish war until you
    abolish human nature.

She says she is broadminded enough to admire Mencken's jokes and witticisms,

But she wishes he would realize that what this country needs is fewer DEstructive and more CONstructive criticisms.

She says she has her own opinions about Eugene O'Neill but she doesn't want necessarily to fight about them,

But at the same time real life is so full of unpleasant things that she doesn't see why people have to go and write about them.

She likes to visit New York but how New Yorkers live the life they live day in and day out she doesn't know, she is sure,

And she rather sadly says that after all the French are the only people who know anything about l'amour.

She admits that she has often been covered with confusion and shame

Because though she can never forget a face she can never remember a name.

She has a new bon mot of which she is very proud;

She wants to know if you have heard that NRA means No Republicans Allowed.

She says she hasn't told it very well but when George told it to her it was exquisite,

Because George has a gift that way and when all is said and done it's not so much what you say as how you say it, is it?

Dear Emily, let others make horrid remarks about your conversation;

To me in an unrelaxed world it is a haven of relaxation.

Seated beside you, my dear my darling Emily, I can be perfectly polite murmuring yes yes and no no and don't have to fret myself thinking up brilliant and penetrating retorts,

But can wander lonely as a cloud among my own beautiful thorts.

Ogden Nash

POEMS IN PRAISE OF PRACTICALLY NOTHING

I

You buy some flowers for your table;
You tend them tenderly as you're able;
You fetch them water from hither and thither—
What thanks do you get for it all? They wither.

II

Only the wholesomest foods you eat;
You lave and you lave from your head to your feet;
The earth is not steadier on its axis
Than you in the matter of prophylaxis;
You go to bed early, and early you rise;
You scrub your teeth and you scour your eyes—
What thanks do you get for it all?   Nephritis,
Pneumonia, appendicitis,
Renal calculus and gastritis.

III

You get a girl; and you say you love her;
You pan the comparative stars above her;
You roast the comparative roses below her;
You throw the bull that you'll never throw her—
What thanks do you get?   The very first whozis
Who tips his mitt, with him she vamooses.

IV

You buy yourself a new suit of clothes;
The care you give it, God only knows;
The material, of course, is the very best yet;
You get it pressed and pressed and pressed yet;
You keep it free from specks so tiny—
What thanks do you get?   The pants get shiny.

V

You practise every possible virtue;
You hurt not a soul, while others hurt you;
You fetch and carry like a market basket;
What thanks do you get for it?   Me don't ask it!

VI

You leap out of bed; you start to get ready;
You dress and you dress till you feel unsteady;
Hours go by, and you're still busy

Putting on clothes, till your brain is dizzy.
Do you flinch, do you quit, do you go out naked?—
The least little button, you don't forsake it.
What thanks do you get?   Well, for all this mess, yet
When night comes around you've got to undress yet.

Samuel Hoffenstein

A POEM INTENDED TO INCITE THE UTMOST DEPRESSION

CERVANTES, Dostoievsky, Poe,
Drained the dregs and lees of woe;
Gogol, Beethoven and Keats
Got but meager share of sweets.
Milton, Homer, Dante had
Reason to be more than sad;
Caesar and Napoleon
Saw the blood upon their sun;
Martyr, hermit, saint and priest
Lingered long at Sorrow's feast:
Paid with pyre and perishing
For every feather in each wing;—
Well, if such as these could be
So foredoomed to misery,
And Fate despise her own elect—
What the deuce do you expect?

Samuel Hoffenstein

PRIMER

THE camel has a funny hump—
    Well, what of it?
The desert is an awful dump—
    Well, what of it?

The sun it rises every day—
    What about it?
Roosters crow and asses bray—
    What about it?

The stars shine nearly every night—
  Don't bother me with it!
Grass is green and snow is white—
  Get out o' here!

Samuel Hoffenstein

THE PENITENT

I HAD a little Sorrow,
Born of a little Sin,
I found a room all damp with gloom
And shut us all within;
And "Little Sorrow, weep," said I
"And, Little Sin, pray God to die,
And I upon the floor will lie
  And think how bad I've been!"

Alas for pious planning—
  It mattered not a whit!
As far as gloom went in that room,
  The lamp might have been lit!
My Little Sorrow would not weep,
My Little Sin would go to sleep—
To save my soul I could not keep
  My graceless mind on it!

So up I got in anger,
  And took a book I had,
And put a ribbon on my hair
  To please a passing lad.
And, "One thing there's no getting by—
I've been a wicked girl," said I;
"But if I can't be sorry, why,
  I might as well be glad!"

Edna St. Vincent Millay

ON BEING A WOMAN

Why is it, when I am in Rome
I'd give an eye to be at home,
But when on native earth I be,
My soul is sick for Italy?

And why with you, my love, my lord,
Am I spectacularly bored,
Yet do you up and leave me—then
I scream to have you back again?

Dorothy Parker

THEORY

Into love and out again,
　　Thus I went, and thus I go.
Spare your voice, and hold your pen—
　　Well and bitterly I know
All the songs were ever sung,
　　All the words were ever said;
Could it be, when I was young,
　　Some one dropped me on my head?

Dorothy Parker

BALLADE OF UNFORTUNATE MAMMALS

Love is sharper than stones or sticks;
　　Lone as the sea, and a deeper blue;
Loud in the night as a clock that ticks;
　　Longer lived than the Wandering Jew.
　　Show me a love that was done and through,
Tell me a kiss escaped its debt!
　　Son, to your death you'll pay your due—
Women and elephants never forget.

Ever a man, alas, would mix,
   Ever a man, heigh-ho, must woo;
So he's left in the world-old fix,
   Thus is furthered the sale of rue.
   Son, your chances are thin and few—
Won't you ponder before you're set?
   Shoot if you must, but hold in view
Women and elephants never forget.

Down from Caesar past Joynson-Hicks
   Echoes the warning, ever new;
Though they're trained to amusing tricks,
   Gentler, they, than the pigeon's coo,
   Careful, son, of the cursed two—
Either one is a dangerous pet;
   Natural history proves it true—
Women and elephants never forget.

L'ENVOI:

Prince, a precept I'd leave for you,
Coined in Eden, existing yet;
   Skirt the parlor and shun the zoo—
Women and elephants never forget.

Dorothy Parker

SOCIAL NOTE

LADY, lady, should you meet
One whose ways are all discreet,
One who murmurs that his wife
Is the lodestar of his life,
One who keeps assuring you
That he never was untrue,
Never loved another one—
Lady, lady, better run!

Dorothy Parker

CODA

THERE'S little in taking or giving,
　　There's little in water or wine;
This living, this living, this living
　　Was never a project of mine.
Oh, hard is the struggle, and sparse is
　　The gain of the one at the top,
For art is a form of catharsis,
　　And love is a permanent flop,
And work is the province of cattle,
　　And rest's for a clam in a shell,
So I'm thinking of throwing the battle—
　　Would you kindly direct me to hell?

Dorothy Parker

SPRIG FEVER

PARSLEY, parsley, everywhere,
On my daily bill of fare.

See that kippered herring staring
At the silly sprig he's wearing.

Be it steak or creamed potatoes,
Oyster plant or grilled tomatoes,

Squash or scrambled eggs or scrod—
Each must wear its little wad;

Each must huddle underneath
Its accursed parsley wreath.

Parsley, parsley, everywhere.
Damn! I want my victuals bare.

Margaret Fishback

A STRANGE INTERLUDE

I WENT to tea at Elizabeth's house,
   And what did she serve but tea!
I sat as still as a well-bred mouse
When I went to tea at Elizabeth's house;
I didn't snarl and I didn't grouse
   Though I was distressed to see
That tea at my friend Elizabeth's house
   Meant absolutely tea.

Margaret Fishback

COMMUTERS

COMMUTER—one who spends his life
In riding to and from his wife;
A man who shaves and takes a train
And then rides back to shave again.

E. B. W.

NUGATORY

THE little roads I travel
   In this my to-and-froing
Have only served to ravel
   The thread of where I'm going

The thoughts that spin and caper
   Through my attempts at thinking
Convey, when brought to paper,
   Nothing worth pen-and-inking.

And there are days so futile,
   So neither here nor there-ish,
I scarce know what to do till
   It's time to up and perish.

E. B. W.

PUBLISHER'S NOTE:
At the time of this publication of the first edition of THE BOOK OF
HUMOROUS VERSE in 1920, there was no poem by T. A. Daly
included. This omission caused comment and Miss Wells herself
acknowledged it by the clever ballade which Franklin P. Adams re-
produced for her in "The Conning Tower" of the New York Tribune
on December 15th, 1920. Two days later appeared Mr. Daly's reply.

BALLADE OF A CONSPICUOUS OMISSION FROM "THE BOOK OF HUMOROUS VERSE"

YES, I admit I've made a book,
A book of many humorous lays;
I put in stuff by Hood and Hook,
I put in bits of Knight's and Day's.
And gems of Guiterman's and Gay's;
And lines by Cary, Carryl, Cayley;
Yet critics all this question raise,
Why did I leave out T. A. Daly?

Over my Indices I look
(They are enough my brain to faze),
When critics' heads at me are shook,
I feel that I must mend my ways.
This Parthian shaft of F. P. A.'s
I read—no longer laughing gayly—
For, though he favors, he inveighs—
Why did I leave out T. A. Daly?

Christopher Morley then partook
In the discriminating praise;
He said, omit Eliza Cook,
Or leave out Rabelais or Blaize;
Cut out that elegy of Gray's
Or evidences of old Paley;
But—he inquired—in caustic phrase,
Why did I leave out T. A. Daly?

L'ENVOI:

Colyumists, thanks for your bouquets;
And yet I'm sad. Oh, willow waly,
When I crowned many bards with bays,
Why *did* I leave out T. A. Daly?

C. W.

TO TH' MINSTREL GIRL

(Meanin' Carolyn Wells, no less—these soft sounds from "th' wild Harp, flung behind her" whin she came to make up her grand work, "Th' Book of Humorous Verse.")

Th' CRITIC's heel is on ye, sure,
    Carolyn;
There's two o' thim beyant th' dure,
    Carolyn.
But, lookut! Now they're on th' flure!
'Tis you've th' sootherin' talk, to cure
Th' wildest rage av anny boor,
    Carolyn, my Carolyn.

Meself, that deems meself a larp,*
    Carolyn,
Wid manny a "woof," assailed your warp,
    Carolyn:
But, even I have ceased to carp;
Th' rage o' me's no longer sharp,
So soft ye've played upon this Harp,
    Carolyn, my Carolyn.

This insthrumint on which I play,
    Carolyn,
Is savage, whiles, an', whiles, 'tis gay,
    Carolyn—
A uke (shill) lele, ye might say—
But, och! th' fine amends ye pay
Has charmed its rancor all away,
    Carolyn, my Carolyn.

Let F. P. A. an' Morley bleed,
    Carolyn.
Their suff'rin's let ye little heed,
    Carolyn.
There's so much better stuff to read,
An', faith, your book's so grand, indeed,
Sure, bless your heart! ye didn't need,
    Carolyn, *my* carolin'.

                     T. A. Daly

---

*An almost extinct singing bird of the Phillyloo family; appearing now only when a Celtic bard, hunting for rhymes, calls to him from the bogs.

BETWEEN TWO LOVES

I GOTTA lov' for Angela,
    I lov' Carlotta, too.
I no can marry both o' dem,
    So w'at I gona do?

O! Angela ees pretta girl,
She gotta hair so black, so curl,
An' teeth so white as anytheeng.
An' O! she gotta voice to seeng,
Dat mak' your hearta feel eet must
Jump up an' dance or eet weell bust.
An' alla time she seeng, her eyes
Dey smila like Italia's skies,
An' makin' flirtin' looks at you—
But dat ees all w'at she can do.

Carlotta ees no gotta song,
But she ees twice so big an' strong
As Angela, an' she no look
So beautiful—but she can cook.
You oughta see her carry wood!
I tal you w'at, eet do you good.
When she ees be som'body's wife
She worka hard, you bat my life!
She never gattin' tired, too—
But dat ees all w'at she can do.

O! my! I weesh dat Angela
    Was strong for carry wood,
Or else Carlotta gotta song
    An' looka pretta good.
I gotta lov' for Angela.
    I lov' Carlotta, too.
I no can marry both o' dem,
    So w'at I gona do?

                                        T. A. Daly

THE OWL

THE owl is very very wise,
You see his wisdom in his eyes.
He sleeps all day
He hunts all night.
To wit to woo,
He woos all right.

Roland Young

THE JUNGLE PEST

THIS cheerful picture shows the fate
Deserved by William Smith—the late—

When he had killed two lions, he
Was killed, in turn, by number three.

The lion's notable behavior
Was printed in the roto-gravure.

Roland Young

THE MISCEGENEOUS ZEBRA

THE Zebra, born both black and white,
Is just the jungle clown.
The lionesses hunt him up,
The lions hunt him down.
His life, in consequence, is brief
And seems inclined to end in grief.
And so you see, between the two,
He's more contented in the zoo.

Roland Young

THE TRYST

ACCORDING to tradition
    The place where sweethearts meet
Is meadowland and hillside
    And not the city street.

Love lingers when you say it
    By·lake and moonlight glow;
The poets all O. K. it—
    It may be better so!

And yet I keep my trysting
    In the department stores;
I always wait for Emma
    At the revolving doors.
It might dismay the poets,
    And yet it's wholly true—
My heart leaps when I know it's
    My Emma pushing through!

It may be more romantic
    By brook or waterfall,
Yet better meet on pavements
    Than never meet at all;
I want no moon beguiling,
    No dark and bouldered shore,
When I see Emma smiling
    And twirling through the door!

                                    Christopher Morley

THE SHAKESPEREAN BEAR

(The Winter's Tale.   Act III, Scene 3)

WHEN, on our casual way,
    Troubles and dangers accrue
Till there's the devil to pay,
    How shall we carry it through?
    Shakespeare, that oracle true,
Teacher in doubt and despair,
    Told us the best that he knew:
"Exit, pursued by a bear."

That is the line of a play
    Dear to the cognizant few;
Hark to its lilt, and obey!

Constantly keep it in view.
　Fate, the malevolent shrew,
Weaves her implacable snare;
　What is a fellow to do?
"Exit, pursued by a bear."

Take to your heels while you may!
　Sinister tabby-cats mew,
Witches that scheme to betray
　Mingle their horrible brew,
　Thunderclouds darken the blue,
Beelzebub growls from his lair;
　Maybe he's hunting for *you!*—
"Exit, pursued by a bear."

ENVOI

Bores of the dreariest hue,
　Bringers of worry and care,
Watch us respond to our cue,—
　"Exit, pursued by a bear."

Arthur Guiterman

OUR FRIEND THE EGG

OH who that ever lived and loved
Can look upon an egg unmoved?
The egg it is the source of all.
'Tis everyone's ancestral hall.
The bravest chief that ever fought,
The lowest thief that e'er was caught,
The maiden's lips, the harlot's leg,
They one and all came from an egg.

The rocks that once by ocean's surge
Beheld the first of eggs emerge—
Obscure, defenseless, small and cold—
They little knew what eggs could hold.
The gifts the reverent Magi gave,

Pandora's box, Aladdin's cave,
Wars, loves and kingdoms, heaven and hell,
All lay within that tiny shell.

Then join me, gentlemen, I beg,
In honoring our friend the egg.

Clarence Day

MARCO POLO

Marco Polo travelled far,
Went through perils worse than war,
Saw great marvels, distant lands,
Unicorns, and sarabands.

Why and wherefore?   So that when
He had toiled back home again,
He could chant an endless solo
On the deeds of Marco Polo.

Clarence Day

MENELAUS

Menelaus, Menelaus,
    How we feel for you,
We, who fear lest wives betray us
    Even when we're true.
Husbands daily die of bile,
    But oh, despite their sobbing,
Paris wears a hateful smile
    And Helen's heart is throbbing.

Clarence Day

IF I EVER HAVE TIME FOR THINGS THAT MATTER

If I ever have time for things that matter,
    If ever I have the smallest chance,
I'm going to live in
    Little Broom Gardens,
        Moat-by-the-Castle,
            Nettlecombe, Hants.

I'll take my ease and never, never hurry,
    And sit for hours on the top of a stile,
With a friend from
  Wookey, Cress-on-the-Water,
   Spennithorne-Baggot,
    Bury Saint Gile.

Anything can happen, anything at all,
With faith and a moat and a castle wall.

With good Friar Tuck I'll roam through the heather,
    Or shiver for a while by Windrush Rill,
With a headless knight from
  Hangman's Hollow,
   Or a jolly old ghost from
    Traitor's Hill.

Then home at dusk through cowslip meadows,
    And a seat on the settle when day is done,
A dish of tea and a
  Pennyworth of cockles,
   A muffin and a crumpet and a
    Big Bath bun.

Why go to Liverpool, why go to Leeds,
Where nothing *could* happen that any one needs?
                Vilda Sauvage Owens

TO THE CROCUS—WITH MY LOVE

    THE crocus grows in any spot,
    And multiplies an awful lot.

    It doesn't pout, and fail to bloom,
    Because of soil, or lack of room.

    No books are written on the crocus;
    It grows without such hocus-pocus.
              Marion Sturges-Jones

BACKSTAIR BALLAD

IT'S Tuesday morning, Cook, my dear,
And do you know what's to happen?
My head is funny and light and queer,
For I'm asking a lovely chap in.
He isn't the butcher or peddling wax,
Or the man from Stern's or the one from Saks;
He has lovely eyes and he isn't old:
When he says "Sign here!" I can hardly hold
The pencil, Cook,
Or his little blue book!
Come have a look and heart attacks,
For his name is Douglas Dappin.
He came one day when you were out—
The way those things will happen—
And I hardly knew what I *was* about
When I let that lovely chap in.
His braid and brawn and Barrymore legs!
So help me, Cook! I dropped the eggs.
And he says to me with a wonderful smile:
"A package, miss"—you know, with style.
It sounds so tame!
But all the same
I asked his name, and it wasn't Beggs,
And it really was Douglas Dappin.
He works for Marie Blanche & Fee,
And lots of things can happen—
As maybe this afternoon for tea,
When I've asked the lovely chap in.
He hasn't yet, and I haven't said,
And I doubt if I would, but my face gets red
When I have to sign for a skirt or a blouse,
And my heart goes hammering through the house.
For he looks so fine
At a quarter of nine!
Well, he may be mine, and I may be wed—
If his name *is* Douglas Dappin.

David McCord

SIR CHRISTOPHER WREN

Sir Christopher Wren
Said, "I am going to dine with some men.
If anybody calls
Say I am designing St. Paul's."

J. S. MILL

John Stuart Mill
By a mighty effort of will,
Overcame his natural bonhomie
And wrote "Principles of Political Economy."

LORD CLIVE

What I like about Clive
Is that he is no longer alive.
There is a great deal to be said
For being dead.

E. C. Bentley

INDICES

INDEX OF AUTHORS

INDEX OF FIRST LINES

Index of First Lines

INDEX OF TITLES

Index of Titles 1003